Monastic Economies in Late Antique Egypt and Palestine

This book situates discussions of Christian monasticism in Egypt and Palestine within the socio-economic world of the long Late Antiquity, from the golden age of monasticism into and well beyond the Arab conquest (fifth to tenth centuries). Its thirteen chapters present new research into the rich corpus of textual sources and archaeological remains and move beyond traditional studies that have treated monastic communities as religious entities in physical seclusion from society. The volume brings together scholars working across traditional boundaries of subject and geography and explores a diverse range of topics from the production of food and wine to networks of scribes, patronage, and monastic visitation. As such, it paints a vivid picture of busy monastic lives dependent on and led in tandem with the non-monastic world.

LOUISE BLANKE is Lecturer in Late Antique Archaeology at the University of Edinburgh. She has authored *An Archaeology of Egyptian Monasticism: Settlement, Economy, and Daily Life at the White Monastery Federation* (2019) and has directed archaeological projects and participated in fieldwork at sites in Egypt, Denmark, Jordan, and Qatar.

JENNIFER CROMWELL is Senior Lecturer in Ancient History at Manchester Metropolitan University. Her research interests lie in the study of village and monastic life in late antique and early Islamic Egypt. She is the author of *Recording Village Life: A Coptic Scribe in Early Islamic Egypt* (2017).

Monastic Economies in Late Antique Egypt and Palestine

Edited by

LOUISE BLANKE
University of Edinburgh

JENNIFER CROMWELL
Manchester Metropolitan University

Shaftesbury Road, Cambridge CB2 8EA, United Kingdom

One Liberty Plaza, 20th Floor, New York, NY 10006, USA

477 Williamstown Road, Port Melbourne, VIC 3207, Australia

314–321, 3rd Floor, Plot 3, Splendor Forum, Jasola District Centre, New Delhi – 110025, India

103 Penang Road, #05–06/07, Visioncrest Commercial, Singapore 238467

Cambridge University Press is part of Cambridge University Press & Assessment, a department of the University of Cambridge.

We share the University's mission to contribute to society through the pursuit of education, learning and research at the highest international levels of excellence.

www.cambridge.org
Information on this title: www.cambridge.org/9781009278942

DOI: 10.1017/9781009278959

© Cambridge University Press & Assessment 2023

This publication is in copyright. Subject to statutory exception and to the provisions of relevant collective licensing agreements, no reproduction of any part may take place without the written permission of Cambridge University Press & Assessment.

First published 2023
First paperback edition 2025

A catalogue record for this publication is available from the British Library

ISBN   978-1-009-27897-3   Hardback
ISBN   978-1-009-27894-2   Paperback

Cambridge University Press & Assessment has no responsibility for the persistence or accuracy of URLs for external or third-party internet websites referred to in this publication and does not guarantee that any content on such websites is, or will remain, accurate or appropriate.

Contents

List of Figures [*page* vii]
List of Tables [x]
List of Contributors [xi]
Preface [xv]

1 The Monastic Economies in Late Antique Egypt
 and Palestine: Past, Present, and Future [1]
 LOUISE BLANKE AND JENNIFER CROMWELL

   I. THE MONASTIC ESTATE [39]

2 Monastic Estates in Byzantine *Arabia* and *Palaestina*
 (Fourth–Ninth Centuries) [41]
 BASEMA HAMARNEH

3 Monastic Estates in Transition from Byzantine to Islamic
 Egypt: Evidence from Aphrodito [76]
 ISABELLE MARTHOT-SANTANIELLO

4 The Naqlun Fathers and Their Business Affairs: Private
 Assets and Activities of the Monks in a Semi-Anchoritic
 Community in the Late Antique Fayum [99]
 TOMASZ DERDA AND JOANNA WEGNER

   II. PRODUCTION AND CONSUMPTION OF FOOD
       AND MATERIAL GOODS [127]

5 Monastic Vintages: The Economic Role of Wine
 in Egyptian Monasteries in the Sixth to Eighth
 Centuries [129]
 DOROTA DZIERZBICKA

6 Cooking, Baking, and Serving: A Window into the Kitchen
 of Egyptian Monastic Households and the Archaeology
 of Cooking [152]
 DARLENE L. BROOKS HEDSTROM

7 The Refectory and the Kitchen in the Early Byzantine Monastery of Tell Bi'a (Syria): The Egyptian and Palestinian Connections [181]
GÁBOR KALLA

8 It's a Dung Job: Exploring Fuel Disc Production in Egyptian Monasteries [212]
MENNAT-ALLAH EL DORRY

9 Illuminating the Scriptoria: Monastic Book Production at the Medieval Monastery of St Michael [233]
ANDREA MYERS ACHI

III. MONASTIC ENCOUNTERS: TRAVEL, PILGRIMAGE, AND DONATIONS [269]

10 Distinguishing Offerings from Blessings in Early Byzantine Monasticism: The Significance of *P.Ness.* III 79 (ca. 600 AD) [271]
DANIEL F. CANER

11 Staple for Body and Soul: Working at and Visiting the Upper Egyptian Monastery Deir Anba Hadra [298]
LENA SOPHIE KRASTEL, SEBASTIAN OLSCHOK, AND TONIO SEBASTIAN RICHTER

12 The Monastic Landscape of Mount Nebo: An Economic Pattern in the Province of *Arabia* [334]
DAVIDE BIANCHI

13 Travel in the Texts: Monastic Journeys in Late Antique Egypt [359]
PAULA TUTTY

Glossary [387]
Index [390]

Figures

1.1 The solitary hermit has been a common theme in artistic portrayals of monastic life from Late Antiquity until the present day. This sketch shows an early modern imagination of a desert hermit: Hermann Weyer, *Desert Landscape with a Hermit (verso)*, 1615/1620, National Gallery of Art, Washington, DC (this image is in the public domain). [*page 2*]

1.2 Map of Egypt with key sites that are mentioned in the book. Drawn by Louise Blanke. [5]

1.3 Map of Palestine and surrounding area with key sites that are mentioned in the book. Drawn by Louise Blanke. [6]

2.1 Main coenobitic monasteries east of the River Jordan (by M. Ben Jeddou). [44]

2.2 The monastic complex near the stylite tower of Umm er-Rasas (courtesy APAAME, photograph by D. L. Kennedy). [58]

2.3 Valley of Uyun Mousa (photograph by D. Bianchi). [59]

2.4 Aerial view of the monastery of Aaron near Petra (courtesy APAAME, photograph by R. Bewley). [60]

4.1 Map of the Fayum. [102]

4.2 The Naqlun monastery. © Wiesław Małkowski and PCMA Archives. [104]

4.3 The ceramic assemblage from hermitage 89. Drawn by Jarosław Dobrowolski. © PCMA Archives. [114]

4.4 Plan of hermitages 25 and 89. Drawn by Jarosław Dobrowolski. [120]

6.1 Preparing bread at St Antony's Monastery, 1930–1. The Red Sea Monasteries, Egypt. Dumbarton Oaks, Image Collections and Fieldwork Archives. Washington, DC, Trustees for Harvard University. ICFA.BI_DO.REDSEA. [155]

6.2 Monastic kitchen at St Antony's Monastery, 1930–1. The Red Sea Monasteries, Egypt. Dumbarton Oaks, Image Collections

and Fieldwork Archives. Washington, DC, Trustees for Harvard University. ICFA.BI_DO.REDSEA.0016. [160]
6.3 Sixth-century Byzantine illuminated manuscript illustrating Pharaoh's banquet from the *Vienna Genesis*. Wiener Genesis, fol. 17^v. Österreichische Nationalbibliothek, Wien. [161]
6.4 Room 10 in Hermitage 87 at the monastic site of Naqlun in the Fayum Oasis; Godlewski, 'Naqlun 2007', p. 238, fig. 9. Photo courtesy of W. Godlewski, archive PCMA. [167]
6.5 Kitchen with stove and oven in Hermitage 18 at 'Adaima in Upper Egypt; Sauneron, 'The Work of the French Institute of Oriental Archaeology in 1973–1974', pl. XXXI. Photograph of the kitchen in Hermitage 18. Photograph by J.-F. Gout. Courtesy of IFAO. [168]
6.6 'Fireplace in Room 50i' from R. Campbell Thompson's 1913/14 excavation of the monastery of Apa Thomas in Wadi Sarga. AESAR.719. Courtesy of the Trustees of the British Museum. [170]
6.7 Kitchen from Building 48 from John the Little in Wadi Natrun. The kitchen includes a circular oven and a stove with a triple-*kanun* built above a niche for holding fuel. Photo: D. Brooks Hedstrom. [171]
7.1 Ground plan of the excavated area of the Tell Bi'a monastery. [182]
7.2 Monastery of Martyrius (Khirbet el-Murassas, after Hirschfeld, *The Judean Desert Monasteries*, p. 43). [188]
7.3 3D model of the Tell Bi'a monastery (drawing: Lőrinc Tímár). [189]
7.4 The refectory and the kitchen from the north. [191]
7.5 The refectory and the kitchen. [192]
7.6 Building phases of the refectory and its installations (Drawing: Fruzsina Németh). [194]
7.7 The kitchen from the north. [200]
7.8 Aqueduct of the northern court and the cistern under the tower. [202]
7.9 The refectories with circular benches. 1. Tell Bi'a; 2. Apa Jeremiah/Saqqara; 3. Deir el-Bakhit; 4. Apa Shenute/Sohag; 5. Qasr el-Wizz; 6. Deir Anba Hadra (Drawing: Fruzsina Németh). [206]
9.1 Information from the colophons about relationships between patrons and monasteries in the Fayum Oasis. [260]

List of Figures

9.2 Relationships between patrons and manuscripts. [261]
9.3 Network of book producers in the Fayum Oasis. [262]
11.1 The upper and the lower terrace of Deir Anba Hadra (after Monneret de Villard, *Il monastero di S. Simeone*, vol. 1, figs. 39 and 87). [301]
11.2 Schematic floor plan of the economic area (drawing: Sebastian Olschok). [307]
11.3 Mill platforms in OT_74 (photo: Sebastian Olschok). [308]
11.4 Rectangular installation in OT_87 (photo: Sebastian Olschok). [310]
11.5 Rectangular basin in OT_92 (photo: Sebastian Olschok). [311]
11.6 Funerary stela of the priest Mena (photo: Kathryn E. Piquette; drawing: Isa Böhme; © Coptic Museum, Cairo/German Archaeological Institute, Cairo). [316]
11.7 *Dipinto* of Petros, processed with DStretch (photo: Kathryn E. Piquette, © DAH Project). [320]
11.8 Cursive graffito on the north wall of the northern aisle of the church (K_4_003) (photo: Lena S. Krastel, © DAH Project). [322]
12.1 Topographic map of the Nebo region (after Saller, Memorial of Moses, figs 1–2). [335]
12.2 General map of the monastic complex of Siyagha (after Saller, *Memorial of Moses*, pl. 161). [337]
12.3 First architectural phase of the basilica of the Memorial of Moses according to the new hypothesis, second half of fifth century AD (digital drawing by the author). [339]
12.4 Map of the north-western spur of Siyagha (after Saller, *Memorial of Moses*, fig. 3). [343]
12.5 Map of the ecclesiastical building in the Nebo region (after Piccirillo and Alliata, *Mount Nebo*, pl. 1). [344]
12.6 Wine press from the Siyagha monastic complex (photo by M. Piccirillo © SBF Archive, Jerusalem). [346]
12.7 The oven found in room 103 (photo by M. Piccirillo © SBF Archive, Jerusalem). [347]
12.8 The mosaic of the northern *diakonikon*-baptistery (photo by M. Piccirillo © SBF Archive, Jerusalem). [350]

Tables

3.1 Monastic holdings according to the Aphrodito Cadastre. [*page* 80]
3.2 Amounts required by the central administration for the fiscal year 709/10. [91]
7.1 Circular benches in refectories and estimations of their users. [199]
9.1 Touton manuscript information. [253]
9.2 Criteria for attributions of book production centres. [254]
9.3 Manuscripts that were not donated to a monastery of St Michael. [256]
11.1 Reference to the deceased in the funerary stelae (standard formulary) of Deir Anba Hadra (seventh–ninth centuries). [315]
11.2 Standard formulary of visitors' inscriptions (tenth–fourteenth centuries). [318]
11.3 Self-identification of the beneficiary in secondary inscriptions (eleventh–fourteenth centuries). [319]

Contributors

Editors

Louise Blanke is Lecturer in Late Antique Archaeology at the University of Edinburgh and previously a postdoctoral research associate at the University of Cambridge, the University of Oxford (sponsored by the Danish Carlsberg Foundation), and the University of Aarhus. She is the author of *An Archaeology of Egyptian Monasticism: Settlement, Economy, and Daily Life at the White Monastery Federation* (2019), and co-editor of *Cities as Palimpsests: Responses to Antiquity in Eastern Mediterranean Urbanism* (2022). She has directed archaeological projects and participated in fieldwork at sites in Egypt, Denmark, Jordan, and Qatar. She currently directs the ongoing *Late Antique Jerash Project*.

Jennifer Cromwell is Senior Lecturer in Ancient History at Manchester Metropolitan University. Previously, she held research fellowships at the University of Oxford, Macquarie University (Sydney), and the University of Copenhagen. Her research interests lie largely in the social and economic history of late antique and early Islamic Egypt (fourth to ninth centuries AD), especially at a village and monastic level. Her current projects include the edition and publication of Coptic texts from the monastic complex at Wadi Sarga. She is the author of *Recording Village Life: A Coptic Scribe in Early Islamic Egypt* (2017), and co-editor of several volumes, including, most recently, *Observing the Scribe at Work: Scribal Practice in the Ancient World* (2021).

Contributors

Andrea Myers Achi specialises in the art and archaeology of Late Antiquity, with a particular interest in manuscripts and archaeological objects from Christian Egypt and Nubia. Trained as a Byzantinist, Achi's scholarship focuses on late antique and Byzantine art of the Mediterranean Basin and Northeast Africa. She has brought this expertise to bear on exhibitions such as *Art and Peoples of the Kharga Oasis* (2017), *Crossroads: Power and Piety* (2020), and *The Good Life* (2021) at The Metropolitan Museum of Art, and in presentations and publications. She holds a BA from Barnard College and a PhD from New York University.

Davide Bianchi studied Classical and Christian Archaeology in Milan and Jerusalem. After his Master's degree, he worked as an archaeologist in the excavation of the Memorial of Moses on Mount Nebo, and in the Terra Sancta Museum in Jerusalem, where he actively collaborated on preparing the permanent exhibition dedicated to Byzantine monasticism. Since 2017, after his doctorate, he has been Universitätsassistent (Assistant Professor) at the Institute of Classical Archaeology at the University of Vienna. His research interests include the archaeology of Late Antiquity and of early Christianity of the Near East; religious and cultural interactions between Rome and Jerusalem in the Byzantine period; monasticism in the Holy Land; epigraphy; cult of relics; and burial practices in sacred spaces.

Darlene L. Brooks Hedstrom is the Myra and Robert Kraft and Jacob Hiatt Associate Professor in Christian Studies at Brandeis University. She is Chair of Classical Studies and holds a joint appointment in Near Eastern and Judaic Studies. Brooks Hedstrom is an archaeologist and historian of ancient and early Byzantine Christianity with a specialisation in the archaeology and history of monasticism. Her book, *The Monastic Landscape of Late Antique Egypt: An Archaeological Reconstruction* (2017), won the Biblical Archaeology Society's Best Popular Book in Archaeology award in 2019. She serves as Senior Archaeological Consultant for the Yale Monastic Archaeology Project.

Daniel F. Caner is Professor in the Department of Middle Eastern Languages and Cultures at Indiana University, Bloomington. He is author of *Wandering Begging Monks: Spiritual Authority and the Promotion of Monasticism in Late Antiquity* (2002), *History and Hagiography from the Late Antique Sinai* (2010), and *The Rich and the Pure: Philanthropy and the Making of Christian Society in Early Byzantium* (2021).

Tomasz Derda is Professor of Papyrology at the University of Warsaw and member of the editorial board for the *Journal of Juristic Papyrology* and its *Supplements* series. His main publications include: Ἀρσινοΐτης νομός. *Administration of the Fayum under Roman Rule* (2006) and two volumes of Greek papyri from Deir el-Naqlun (1995 and 2008). Since 2018, he has been the director of the Polish Archaeological Mission at Marea in the region of Mareotis (Egypt).

Dorota Dzierzbicka is an archaeologist and Assistant Professor at the Polish Centre of Mediterranean Archaeology, University of Warsaw. Her research interests revolve around the social and economic history of the Nile Valley, from household management to long-distance trade. In her work, she draws on the methodologies of papyrology, archaeology, and historical studies. Her research on wine expands the scope of her doctoral dissertation, which focused on the production and import of wine in Egypt and was published as *ΟΙΝΟΣ: Production and Import of Wine in Graeco-Roman Egypt* (2018).

Mennat-Allah El Dorry is an Egyptologist specialising in archaeobotany. She has worked extensively in the field, particularly on monastic sites, where she has studied monastic foodways and agricultural practices. She worked for over a decade at the Ministry of Antiquities, where she last served as head of the Minister's Scientific Office. El Dorry also served as a postdoctoral research fellow at the Institut français d'archéologie orientale in Cairo and the Polish Centre for Mediterranean Archaeology in Cairo, as well as with the ERC Desert Networks Project (HiSOMA) at the University of Lyon 2. She is a lecturer of archaeobotany at the Faculty of Archaeology, Ain Shams University.

Basema Hamarneh is Professor of Late Antique and Early Christian Archaeology at the Department of Classical Archaeology, University of Vienna. Her research interests and publications focus on urban and rural settlements in the late antique and early Christian periods; Christianisation of Roman Castra; archaeology and artistic expression of the early Christian/Byzantine and early Islamic Near East; monastic and religious identities; and hagiography applied to topographic studies. She is co-editor of the *Mitteilungen zur Christlichen Archäologie* and directs an archaeological excavation in central Jordan.

Gábor Kalla is Docent at the Institute of Archaeological Sciences of Eötvös Loránd University (Budapest). His main research interests are Near Eastern Archaeology and Assyriology, especially Old Babylonian households. His other field of research is Byzantine archaeology. Between 1990 and 1996, he worked for the Deutsche Orient-Gesellschaft on the excavation of the site of Tall Bi'a, where he was responsible for directing the research of the early Byzantine monastery. He is currently preparing the final publication of the excavation results, with a particular focus on the architectural remains and architectural ornaments of the monastery.

Lena Sophie Krastel studied Egyptology at Heidelberg University and is completing her PhD on the Coptic epigraphic evidence from Deir Anba Hadra at Freie Universität Berlin. She has been a member of the Deir Anba Hadra Project since 2013.

Isabelle Marthot-Santaniello is a research assistant at the University of Basel (Switzerland). She holds a PhD in papyrology from École Pratique des Hautes Études (Paris) and is one of the editors of the Basel Papyrus collection (*P.Bas.* II). Her research interests are on the village of Aphrodito, the society of late antique Egypt, and, more recently, the digital palaeography of Greek and Coptic papyri.

Sebastian Olschok studied Medieval Archaeology, Prehistory and Heritage at the University of Bamberg. He wrote his PhD thesis at Freie Universität Berlin about his architectural and archaeological research at the workshop complex at Deir Anba Hadra.

Tonio Sebastian Richter is Professor for Coptology at Freie Universität Berlin. His fields of research include Coptic linguistics, papyrology, and epigraphy; he has published about legal practice, economy, religion, magic, medicine, and sciences in Byzantine and early Islamic Egypt. From 2014 to 2019, he directed the project 'Deir Anba Hadra. Epigraphy, Art, and Architecture of the Monastery on the West Bank of Assuan' of the German Archaeological Institute.

Paula Tutty is a guest researcher at the Theology Faculty of the University of Oslo where she works in collaboration with the ERC-financed project *Storyworlds in Transition: Coptic Apocrypha in Changing Contexts in the Byzantine and Early Islamic Periods*. Working with Greek and Coptic documentary papyri, her present research focuses on fourth-century Egyptian monastic letter collections and the insights they can give us into the social and economic life of the embryonic monastic movement as it evolved in late antique Egypt. Paula's other research interests include the study of Coptic apocryphal writings and their interconnections.

Joanna Wegner is a papyrologist at the University of Warsaw. She is interested in the social and economic context of the development of ecclesiastical and monastic institutions, and the influence of individual networking on community processes. Her main publication is *Monastic Communities in Context. Monasteries, Society, and Economy in Late Antique Egypt* (2021).

Preface

This volume is the result of a conference organised by the editors and held on 16 and 17 March 2016 in Ertegun House, Oxford. Eighteen papers were presented at the conference, most of which have been included in the present volume. We are grateful to Alain Delattre, Arietta Papaconstantinou, Gesa Schenke, Jacob Ashkenazi and Mordechai Aviam, Karel Innemée, and Orit Shamir for their contributions to the meeting. An additional chapter was included in the volume after the conference, and we are grateful to Basema Hamarneh for adding her perspective on monastic economies in Jordan to the book.

The conference was made possible due to the generous support offered by Danmarks Frie Forskningsfond (via Troels Myrup Kristensen's project on the *Emergence of Sacred Travel: Experience, Economy, and Connectivity in Ancient Mediterranean Pilgrimage*) and a Danmarks Frie Forskningsfond–Mobilex grant (as part of Jennifer Cromwell's project *Monasteries as Institutional Powers in Late Byzantine and Early Islamic Egypt: Evidence from Neglected Coptic Sources*). We would also like to thank Bryan Ward-Perkins and Ertegun House for hosting our conference in Oxford. Finally, we are grateful to Michael Sharp for his support throughout the publication process and to Cambridge University Press's two anonymous reviewers for their helpful comments and suggestions.

Some practical notes on the volume. We have made an editorial decision not to use diacritical marks in the transliteration of Arabic. This decision was made from the conviction that those familiar with Arabic will not need them as well as a pragmatic response to the different systems employed within individual chapters. The exception to this practice is in titles and direct quotations from other scholarly works. We have aimed at standardising transliterations throughout chapters, but we have maintained regional differences, which would otherwise confuse the reading of place names (e.g., gebel for mountain in the Egyptian dialect, commonly transliterated jebel in the Syrian dialect).

Several sites discussed within the book are commonly referred to by more than one name. This is particularly relevant for sites with long histories that span multiple periods and languages. We are using the names by which the sites are best known. In some cases, this is the English version of the modern name, in other cases it is the Arabic transliteration.

As a result of the diverse nature of the contributions, we have foregone a list of abbreviation of works cited for the volume. Instead, for papyrological material, all references conform with the *Checklist of Editions of Greek, Latin, Demotic, and Coptic Papyri, Ostraca, and Tablets* (founded by John F. Oates and William H. Willis, and updated now at papyri.info/docs/checklist). For literary sources, texts are referred to in full throughout, rather than by their abbreviation (for the benefit of those not familiar with the various sources in question), and references to principal editions and translations are included where relevant.

1 | The Monastic Economies in Late Antique Egypt and Palestine: Past, Present, and Future

LOUISE BLANKE AND JENNIFER CROMWELL

Introduction

In the late 1970s, the American artist, Stanley Roseman, undertook a project entitled *The Monastic Life*, during which he visited sixty monasteries located throughout Europe. He participated in their daily life and 'made drawings of monks and nuns at prayer, work, and study. He drew them at the communal worship in church and in meditation in the quietude of their cells.'[1] Roseman's 1979 chalk on paper drawing of Benedictine monks at the Abbaye de Solesmes in France depicts two men with shaven heads who are dressed in long hooded robes. They are bent forward with their faces anchored towards the ground. Their eyes are closed, and their hands are carefully placed on their thighs. The men stand alone: they are the focus of the artist's composition; they exist in isolation from their background; they are still, serene, frozen in perpetual worship and detached from their contemporary world. This is the essence of monastic life – the ideal – but it is not the full story.[2]

A decade prior to Roseman's study, Michel Foucault published a short piece outlining his ideas on heterotopies, which he described as 'a kind of effectively enacted utopia'.[3] According to Foucault, heterotopias operate outside of society with a timeframe that is entirely their own. They assume a system of entry and closure that both set them apart and make them accessible. 'Their role is to create a space that is other, another real space, as perfect, as meticulous, as well arranged as ours is messy, ill constructed, and jumbled.'[4]

Roseman's quietude and the otherness afforded by Foucault's heterotopias capture an ideal of the monastic life that was carefully constructed in Late Antiquity and has dominated our perception of monasticism to the present day (Fig. 1.1). It was St Athanasius' hugely influential fourth-century

---

[1] www.stanleyroseman-monasticlife.com.
[2] Roseman's *Two Monks Bowing in Prayer* can be viewed on Washington, DC's National Gallery of Art's website www.nga.gov/collection/art-object-page.60782.html.
[3] Foucault and Miskowiec, 'Of Other Spaces', p. 24.
[4] Foucault and Miskowiec, 'Of Other Spaces', p. 27. Foucault's examples of heterotopias included airports, hospitals, monasteries, prisons, and schools.

Figure 1.1. The solitary hermit has been a common theme in artistic portrayals of monastic life from Late Antiquity until the present day. This sketch shows an early modern imagination of a desert hermit: Hermann Weyer, *Desert Landscape with a Hermit (verso)*, 1615/1620, National Gallery of Art, Washington, DC (this image is in the public domain).

portrayal of St Antony the monk that first conveyed these ideals to an international audience.⁵ Athanasius painted Antony as the exemplary Christian and advocated for a proper ascetic practice in which 'dispossession, solitude and personal austerity were paramount and in which the desert became the locus of true religion'.⁶ *The Life of St Antony* gave birth to the ideal of the solitary hermit and the success of Athanasius' portrayal of Antony led to a literary *imitatio patrum*, where ascetic power was measured against the distance from urban society.⁷ Literary works of fiction such as Jerome's *Life of St Paul* and the tale of Paphnoutios' meeting with the hermit Onnophrios were based on this ideal. The latter work reports how Paphnoutios travelled two weeks through the desert before he came across Onnophrios, a man so holy that he 'had become an angel on earth, and his withdrawn landscape a reflection of heaven'.⁸ In Palestine, in a hagiography that mirrors the *Life of St Antony*, Jerome describes how, in the first half of the fourth century, St Hilarion retreated into the desert and eventually founded the monastic community at Gaza.⁹

Until recently, literary sources and especially hagiographies such as the influential *Apophthegmata Patrum* (for Egypt) and Cyril of Scythopolis' *Lives of the Monks of Palestine* and John Moscus' *Spiritual Meadows* (for Palestine) were used by scholars as the principal evidence for monasteries' economic circumstances. These texts portray ideal Christian lives and the miracles of holy Christian men and women. They were written for the purpose of imitation or to attract pilgrimage to specific sites and were not designed to create an accurate account of the economic lives of the saints and their associated monasteries.¹⁰ Rather than describe work as a revenue-producing activity, the hagiographies describe it as a part of the ascetic lifestyle and as a meditative practice accompanied by prayer.¹¹ In these texts, monastic

---

⁵ *Vita Antonii*; translation in Vivian and Athanassakis, *The Life of Antony*.
⁶ Dunn, *The Emergence of Monasticism*, p. 3. See Sheridan, 'The Development of the Concept of Poverty from Athanasius to Cassius', for a discussion of dispossession in the *Life of St Antony*.
⁷ Goehring, 'The Dark Side of Landscape', p. 443. See also Endsjø, *Primordial Landscapes*.
⁸ Goehring, 'The Dark Side of Landscape', pp. 443–4.
⁹ Deferrari, *The Fathers of the Church*, pp. 245–86. See also Chitty, *The Desert a City*, pp. 13–14.
¹⁰ Papaconstantinou, 'The Cult of Saints' and 'Donation and Negotiation'. See also Blanke, 'Pricing Salvation'.
¹¹ The *Apophthegmata Patrum* describes, for example, how Abba Lucius responded to a group of monks. He stated that 'while doing my manual work, I pray without interruption. I sit down with God soaking my reeds and plaiting my ropes ... So, when I have spent the whole day working and praying, making thirteen pieces of money more or less, I put two pieces of money outside the door and I pay for my food with the rest of the money. He who takes the two pieces of money prays for me when I am eating and when I am sleeping; so, by the grace of God, I fulfil the precept to pray without ceasing.' Translation from Ward, *The Sayings of the Desert Fathers*, pp. 120–1.

production included goods such as baskets and ropes that could be sold or exchanged, which in combination with charitable donations formed the basis of monastic survival.[12] Past scholarship saw monasteries as a burden on contemporary society and an economic and social drain on society's resources. This scholarly stance is perhaps best demonstrated by A. H. M. Jones in his seminal book from 1964 on the economy and social organisation of *The Later Roman Empire*, in which he described a 'huge army of clergy and monks' as 'idle mouths, living upon offerings, endowments and state subsidies'.[13] Derwas Chitty's study on the origins of Egyptian and Palestinian monasticism repeats these views, as does the early work of Peter Brown.[14]

Research carried out over the last two decades on documentary papyri and archaeological remains has suggested a very different economic reality. Although the wealth of monasteries varied considerably, it is possible to reconstruct a picture of some monasteries as important landowners, producers and consumers of goods, as well as significant contributors to the regional economy. New research into documentary sources has shed light on economic aspects not covered by the literary record, including evidence for landholdings, work-contracts, the role of wine and animal husbandry, as well as travel and communication with external monastic and lay communities. At the same time, new archaeological projects using modern techniques and recording methods have uncovered vast built environments that required a substantial capital investment in terms of both construction and maintenance.

The chapters in this volume come together from new research that argues for a need to approach monasteries not just as religious entities in physical seclusion from society, but as the opposite – as active players in the world of Late Antiquity. The volume brings together scholars working across traditional borders of subject and geography, using both archaeology and text within Egypt and Palestine, the latter of which is defined here in the broadest sense, including chapters on Jordan and Syria (Figs 1.2 and 1.3). Our chronological range covers the period from the golden age of monasticism into and well beyond the Arab conquest (roughly fourth to tenth centuries).

Egypt and Palestine are at the forefront of current research on late antique monasticism. The twenty-first century has seen a vast increase in studies that are re-assessing our knowledge base. Scholars are revisiting the

---

[12] The stance taken in, e.g., Chitty, *The Desert a City*, but also reproduced in recent scholarship; see, for example, Milewski, 'Money in the Apophthegmata Patrum'.

[13] Jones, *The Later Roman Empire*, p. 993.

[14] Chitty, *The Desert a City*; Brown, 'The Rise and Function of the Holy Man', p. 83. Brown has since revised his conclusions; see especially Brown, *Treasure in Heaven*. The concept of the 'penniless' monk is also reproduced by modern scholarship relying on the Apophthegmata Patrum; see, for example, Milewski, 'Money in the Apophthegmata Patrum', p. 605.

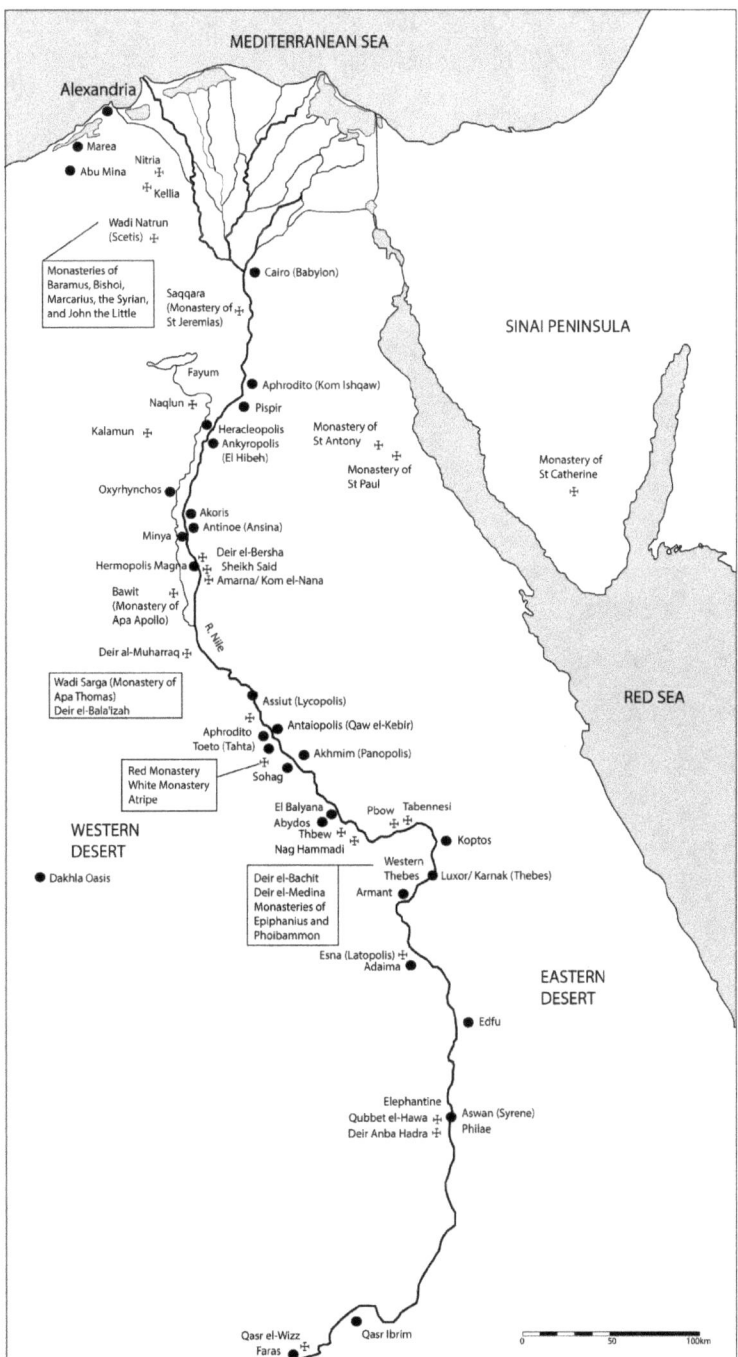

Figure 1.2. Map of Egypt with key sites that are mentioned in the book. Drawn by Louise Blanke.[15]

---

[15] For sites in the Fayum, see Fig. 4.1.

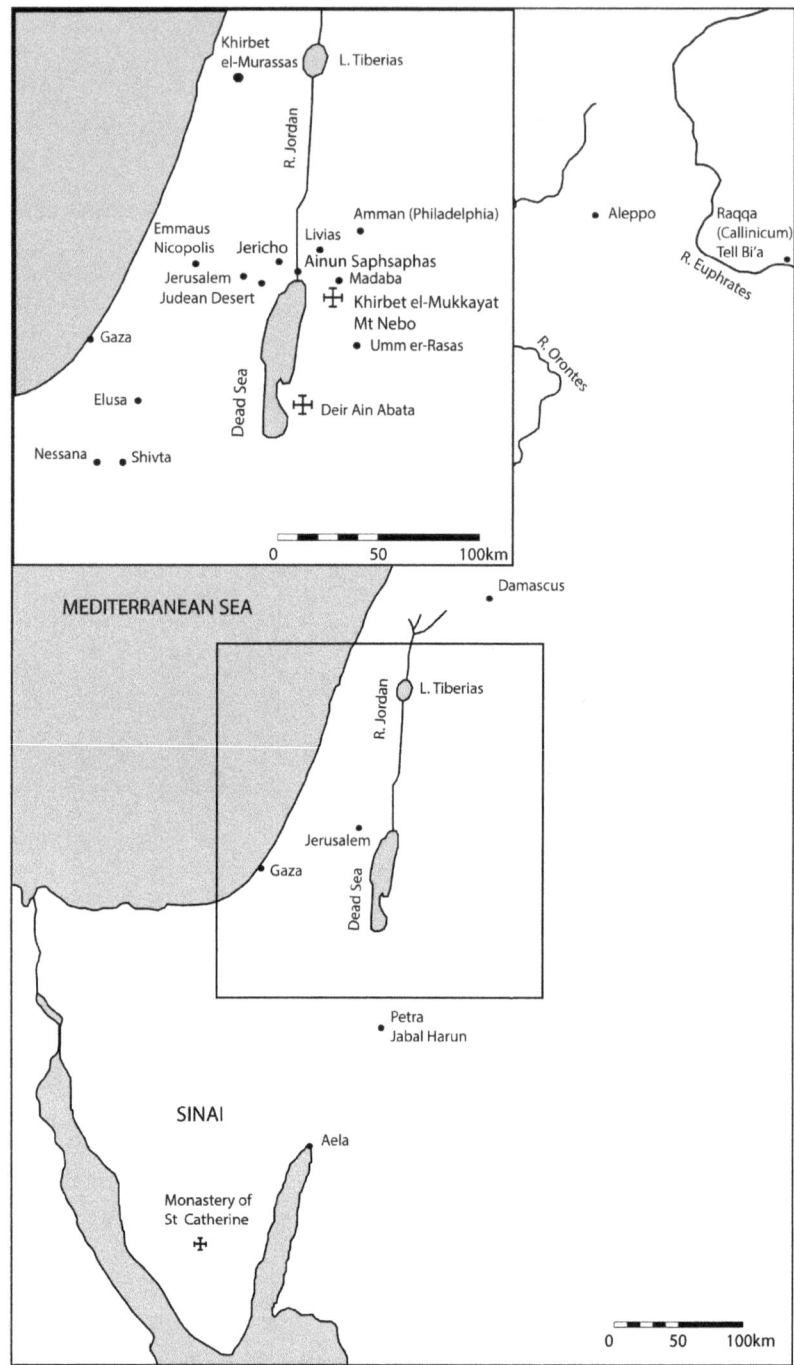

Figure 1.3. Map of Palestine and surrounding area with key sites that are mentioned in the book. Drawn by Louise Blanke.[16]

---

[16] For detailed map of the Jordan Valley, see Fig. 2.1, and for the Mt Nebo area, see Fig. 12.5.

literary sources, asking different questions and extracting new meanings from well-known material, publishing large corpora of documentary papyri, and undertaking archaeological projects that allow us to challenge established ideas and move beyond past biases on monumental church architecture. Egypt and Palestine are unique in this respect, as both regions are unusually rich in historical (textual and material) evidence, which allows us to move beyond stereotypical images derived from the literary sources and to begin to form a more nuanced picture of the complexities of late antique monastic economies. It is our hope that these chapters will inspire scholars of monasticism and help to reshape the agenda for monastic studies in other parts of the late antique world.[17]

As well as being excellent locations to study the evidence for monasticism, bringing together Egypt and Palestine allows broader trends in economic practices to be identified. Our comparative approach enables new questions to be asked of the material in each region and permits us to identify similarities and differences in the organisation of monasteries and their interaction with contemporary society. The authors in this volume identify practices that point towards long-distance networks through which traditions and customs were transmitted from one region to another, while also finding monastic organisation that developed in response to specific local conditions.

At first glance, the economic organisation of monasteries in Egypt and Palestine varies enormously. The proximity to Jerusalem and the association with biblical stories greatly influenced the development of monastic communities at sites in the Holy Land. In Syria and northern Jordan, the remains of stylite pillars and towers and the monastic complexes and pilgrimage sites that surround them testify to a type of asceticism that is not found in Egypt. Indeed, the size and wealth of Egypt's coenobitic federations stand in stark contrast to the smaller communities found near villages throughout Palestine; at Kellia in Egypt's Western Desert, the desert was truly transformed into a city on a scale not found elsewhere in the late antique world.

However, a closer reading of the textual and material remains suggests that, although monasteries and their economic organisation differed enormously, there are also many similarities between our two regions. A disproportionate preservation of textual sources in Egypt and a longer

---

[17] This approach is reflected in recent studies on monasticism in other areas. Notably, chapters in Beach and Cochelin, *Cambridge History of Medieval Monasticism in the Latin West*, include both textual and archaeological approaches to the study of monasticism and take a critical view on the portrayal of monastic life that is found in the literary sources.

tradition of archaeological research of late antique Palestine have informed our understanding of the monastic landscape in both regions. As demonstrated by the contributions to this volume, only by bringing all available evidence together can we begin to reconstruct a fuller picture of the monasteries' economic organisation.

This volume is organised into three sections, each of which represents a key area connected to the economic realities of monastic life, with case studies from both Egypt and Palestine. Section I, 'The Monastic Estate', addresses monastic organisation, landownership, and economic engagement with contemporary society. Section II, 'Production and Consumption of Food and Material Goods', examines revenue-producing activities such as book and wine production, while also re-thinking significant, but less well studied, aspects of the monastic household, such as cooking and baking. Section III, 'Monastic Encounters: Travel, Pilgrimage, and Donations', considers the economic importance of engagements with external communities. Common for all chapters is an insistence on drawing on all relevant sources and a desire to understand the ways in which the monastic economies were embedded within local and regional exchange networks. The following sections discuss the individual contributions within the wider context of monastic studies. Afterwards, the conclusion offers some thoughts on future directions in the study of monastic economies.

The Monastic Estate

The study of Egypt's economy in the Roman and late antique periods has flourished over recent decades. The focus has been directed, in particular, on the great estates, such as that of Aurelius Appianus in the third century and the later Apion estate in the fifth to the early seventh centuries.[18] The nature of these estates, their level of economic sophistication, and their relationship with the public sphere have been the topic of numerous studies. The Apion estate, with its associated archive, has always been at the forefront of discussions of the economy, society, and administration of Late Antiquity, and the volume of publications concerning it has been extensive. Since the turn of the century alone, no less than five monographs dedicated to it, exclusively or in part, have been published.[19]

---

[18] For the estate of Aurelius Appianus, see Rathbone, *Economic Rationalism*.

[19] Mazza, *L'archivio degli Apioni*; Sarris, *Economy and Society*; Banaji, *Agrarian Change*; Ruffini, *Social Networks*; Hickey, *Wine, Wealth, and the State*.

This scholarly focus has been driven by the fortuitous discoveries of archives of Greek papyri, including not only those from the great estates but also the impressive volume of material found in Oxyrhynchus.[20] However, this has created a somewhat one-sided approach to Egypt's economy. Alongside the great estates existed the church (as an institution) – the economic position of which has been studied extensively by Ewa Wipszycka[21] – and then we have the monasteries that were scattered throughout Egypt's urban and rural communities, but are best known from the fringes of the desert along the Nile Valley. The (predominantly) Coptic written material associated with these monasteries has traditionally received less attention than the Greek papyrological evidence for the 'Great Estates' (in part due to the frequently inaccessible nature of their text editions and in part due the lack of translations and commentaries).[22] This situation has created an imbalance, in which the many Christian monasteries have not been properly integrated into past scholarly treatment of the wider economic system of late antique Egypt. Although some aspects of their economy have been studied by scholars, their position in relation to the great estates, the church, and late antique society at large remains mostly unstudied.

The study of the monastic economies has been somewhat slower in the outset, mainly because of the rich corpus of literary sources that were copied through the centuries and constituted the bulk of monastic collections. These texts reflect the religious and intellectual interests of the communities, and they have long defined the key concerns of monastic textual scholarship.[23] Meanwhile, the focus on much past archaeological research has been on monumental architecture and especially on churches, with little attention paid to the infrastructure and productive facilities found within the physical remains of the monasteries.[24] An additional problem, especially in Egypt, is the focus of nineteenth- and early

---

[20] On Oxyrhynchus, see, for example, the collected papers in Bowman *et al.*, *Oxyrhynchus*.

[21] Most recently, Wipszycka, *The Alexandrian Church*.

[22] Many century-old Coptic text editions have no translations (e.g., *O.CrumVC*) or only partial ones (e.g., *O.Crum*, *P.Lond.Copt.* I).

[23] As a case in point, see the volume of scholarship on the literary production of Shenoute, abbot of the White Monastery federation. While editions of Shenoute's texts have been published since the nineteenth century, the past couple of decades have witnessed considerable activity in this area. For example, see Emmel, *Shenoute's Literary Corpus*; Boud'hors, *Le canon 8 de Chénouté*; Layton, *The Canons of Our Fathers*; Brakke and Crislip, *Selected Discourses of Shenoute the Great*. On the library of the White Monastery, see, for example, Orlandi, 'The Library of the Monastery of Saint Shenoute'.

[24] An early exception is the outstanding publication of the monastery of Epiphanius in western Thebes by Winlock and Crum, *The Monastery of Epiphanius*.

twentieth-century scholars working on pre-Christian remains, to the detriment of our understanding of the monasteries' built environment and their estates.

The monastery of Apa Phoibammon (seventh–eighth centuries), built upon the New Kingdom mortuary temple of Hatshepsut at Deir el-Bahri on the west bank of Thebes in the south of Egypt, is a case in point. The monastery's economic activities were first known from a number of papyri, acquired in the mid-nineteenth century. These legal texts include donations of palm trees and livestock to the monastery, as well as the testaments of its early superiors.[25] Despite scholarly interest in this material, when Edouard Naville began working at Deir el-Bahri in 1894, he and his team removed the monasteries' mudbrick architecture without adequate recording in order to expose the remains of the Pharaonic period. Our knowledge of these features therefore relies entirely on photographs taken by Howard Carter, who was part of the team, and earlier drawings by visitors to the site.[26] During this clearance, a large body of ostraca, primarily in Coptic, were found, the majority of which are now in the British Museum.[27] Subsequent work at the site by the Metropolitan Museum of Art (1920s) and the Polish Centre of Mediterranean Archaeology (since the 1960s) has uncovered more material from the monastery.[28]

This situation is not unique to the monastery of Apa Phoibammon, and similar cases are encountered at monastic sites throughout Egypt.[29]

---

[25] The earliest publications of this material appeared already in the 1850s and 1860s; see Goodwin, 'Curiosities of Law' and 'Account of Three Coptic Papyri'. For the testaments, see now Garel and Nowak, 'Monastic Wills', and Garel, *Héritage et transmission*.

[26] This material is collected in Godlewski, *Le monastère de St. Phoibammon*. For the early history of the monastery under its founder Apa Abraham, see Krause, 'Apa Abraham von Hermonthis' – despite subsequent work at the site, this study remains a core reference work, almost seventy years later. See also Garel, *Héritage et transmission*, chapter 3.

[27] The principal publication of the Deir el-Bahri texts is *O.Crum* (published 1902), but see the list of texts in Godlewski, *Le monastère de St. Phoibammon*, pp. 153–63, for texts from or concerning the monastery. However, this list is increasingly in need of an update, with new editions of texts from the site regularly occurring, as the next note indicates.

[28] Many of the ostraca found by the MMA excavations are still unpublished, but see O'Connell, 'Ostraca from Western Thebes' for their archival history, and also sporadic publications of ostraca, including most recently Cromwell, 'Forgive Me, Because I Could Not Find Papyrus', and Dekker, 'Coptic Ostraca Relating to Bishop Abraham'. For texts resulting from the Polish mission, see, for example, Markiewicz, 'Five Coptic Ostraca' and 'New Fragmentary Coptic Texts'.

[29] For example, the monastic complex at Wadi Sarga was excavated in a single season in 1913/14, resulting in the discovery of a considerable body of objects and texts. Almost 400 texts were published in 1922 (*O.Sarga*), many of which deal with the administration of food and wine. Yet, despite this material it has largely not been included in studies on monastic economies, except for one study on wine (Bacot, 'La circulation du vin'). Work has resumed recently on the material and excavation records from the site, but no new excavations are possible as the wadi is

It is therefore frequently difficult to reconstruct the size of monastic estates, in terms of the extent of both their buildings and landholdings. However, several notable publications have addressed this issue, establishing the foundation for future work. In addition to studies focusing broadly on monastic economies, Ewa Wipszycka has produced two substantial volumes in the past decade that bring together archaeology and texts in the study of the life of monastic communities.[30] As well as discussing the physical remains and structure of such institutions, Wipszycka highlights costs involved in their foundation and upkeep, costs that often have to be inferred from the size and quality of what remains, as well as literary allusions, rather than texts that explicitly address this point.[31]

Other studies have focused instead on a single monastery. Over the past two decades, five volumes of editions of Coptic and Greek texts from the monastery of Apa Apollo at Bawit have appeared.[32] In total, over 700 texts have now been published from the site, which date to the seventh and eighth centuries (with a small number of Greek texts dated to the sixth century) and primarily address economic concerns.[33] Many of these texts document the management of the monastery's landholdings and buildings, including sales and leases. A comprehensive synthesis of the monastery's estate is still wanting.[34] However, the monastery of Apa Apollo was clearly a significant landholder in the Hermopolite nome (see also Section II below).[35] Additionally, the texts from the monastery provide evidence for

---

part of a military zone. On recent work, see especially Faiers, 'Wadi Sarga Revisited', O'Connell, 'R. Campbell Thompson's 1913/14 Excavation of Wadi Sarga' and 'Wadi Sarga at the British Museum', and Cromwell, 'Writing Exercises from Wadi Sarga'.

[30] Wipszycka, *Moines et communautés monastiques*; *The Second Gift of the Nile*; and 'Resources and Economic Activities'.

[31] For example, concerning Kellia, Wipszycka reflects in particular on the 'high quality wall paintings' and the hermitages' elaborate layouts, which indicate that 'their inhabitants had substantial material means at their disposal ... given that they could afford to hire highly skilled specialists for constructing and decorating their dwellings' (Wipszycka, *The Second Gift of the Nile*, p. 308). While Wipszycka does not discuss Wadi Sarga in her works, one particular text gives a sense of such costs. O.Sarga 161 is a contract between the monastery and a carpenter to undertake repairs in the monastery, for which he is paid in wheat, barley, wine, and garments.

[32] O.BawitIFAO, P.Bawit Clackson, P.Brux.Bawit, P.Louvre Bawit, P.Mon.Apollo.

[33] The most comprehensive list of texts from the monastery of Apa Apollo is available as an annex to *P.Louvre Bawit*.

[34] Wegner, 'The Bawit Monastery of Apa Apollo', p. 174. The difficulties involved in locating toponyms in the monastery's documents severely hinders a comprehensive synthesis of its estate. However, as increasing attention is given to toponyms, the picture may become clearer in the future. For an example of such work, see Marthot, 'Un village égyptien et sa campagne', as well as her contribution to the current volume (Marthot-Santaniello, Chapter 3).

[35] Detailed discussions of the monastery's estate and economic concerns are provided by Alain Delattre in his substantial introduction to *P.Brux.Bawit*, and Wegner, 'The Bawit Monastery of Apa Apollo'. While Wegner is primarily concerned with the monastery's relations with the

a range of fiscal obligations for which it was liable, as well as the role of individual monks as creditors.[36]

The past decade or so has also seen several archaeological studies that are addressing the physical remains of the monasteries' built environment, examining in depth not only their layout and organisation, but also patterns of production and consumption and how these reflect on the monasteries' economic health and their interaction with extramural society.[37]

Darlene Brooks Hedstrom's archaeological reconstruction of Egypt's monastic landscapes tackles, among other subjects, the misconceptions of Egyptian monasticism arising from nineteenth- and early twentieth-century European engagement with Egypt's past (as described above in relation to the monastery of Apa Phoibammon).[38] She summarises the key textual sources and examines the location of monasteries: from purpose-built settlements the size of large villages, such as Apa Jeremias, which were embedded within economic networks with non-monastic communities, to the monastic reuse of abandoned or unclaimed sites such as quarries, tombs, temples and natural cavities.[39]

Louise Blanke's study of the White Monastery federation analyses the archaeological remains of the three monasteries that were under joint leadership from the time of Shenoute (r. 385–466).[40] The study focuses on the long Late Antiquity but traces the monasteries' activities from their foundation until the present day. The White Monastery (the leading partner of the three federated communities) was an economic powerhouse: textual sources suggest landholdings amounting to 50 km² in the fifth century, while the archaeological remains showcase a richly built environment with an intramural space of 75,000 m², which places the White Monastery among the largest in Egypt.[41] The archaeological remains

---

extramural world, as the majority of these relationships are directly connected to its economy, her study represents the most important work on this aspect of the monastery's life.

[36] On the monastery's fiscal obligations (including land tax and various other taxes introduced after the Arab conquest), see Wegner, 'The Bawit Monastery of Apa Apollo', pp. 189–212. For the monks as creditors, see Papaconstantinou, 'A Preliminary Prosopography of Moneylenders', pp. 634, 638–9, and 646; Wegner, 'The Bawit Monastery of Apa Apollo', pp. 229–42.

[37] Lukas Schachner's doctoral dissertation, 'Economic Production', represents a significant contribution to our understanding of the monastic economies in Egypt and Palestine, but it remains unpublished.

[38] Brooks Hedstrom, *The Monastic Landscape*. See also Brooks Hedstrom, 'Treading on Antiquity'.

[39] See also Brooks Hedstrom, 'Divine Architects'.

[40] Blanke, *An Archaeology of Egyptian Monasticism*.

[41] Only Bawit surpasses the White Monastery in size, with an intramural space of 400,000 m².

further show that oil was produced at a scale far beyond what was consumed within the monastery itself.

The climate of Palestine does not lend itself well to the preservation of papyri. Although rich in literary sources, documents relevant to the economy of monastic complexes survive from only three sites: the main church in the city of Petra, Khirbet Mird near Qumran, and the Sergios-Bakkhos monastery at the village of Nessana in the Negev Desert.[42] The presence of documentary papyri at these three sites suggests that they were commonly found in monastic complexes. However, an abundance of literary sources has largely informed our understanding of Palestinian monasticism,[43] while papyri and archaeological remains have only recently begun to be integrated fully in the study of the monasteries' economic life.[44]

In 1992, Yizhar Hirschfeld published one of the first extensive studies of monastic communities, which attempted to integrate archaeology and literary sources.[45] Building on surveys of the sixty-five monasteries of the Judean Desert, Hirschfeld examined the layout and infrastructure of these settlements, while also studying their daily life and economy. The monasteries varied in size but averaged some twenty monks. From literary sources, Hirschfeld concluded that the monasteries' main source of income was donations in the form of material gifts, bequests, money, and land, while the architectural remains further suggested that the production of oil and wine also contributed to their upkeep.[46]

Hirschfeld's study was ambitious and thorough, but has since been criticised by, for example, Daniel Reynolds for relying too heavily on hagiographical literature in its historical reconstruction, while also seeing the destructive effects of the Sassanian occupation (614–28) and the Arab conquest (638) as the primary causes for the monasteries' gradual

---

[42] For the documents from Petra and Nessana, see respectively *P.Petra* I–V and *P.Ness.* III. It is worth noting that only a few of the Petra papyri contain references to the monastery. *P.Petra* V 55, a will dated to 573, for example, makes reference to 'The house of the High Priest Aaron' as a beneficiary; see the discussion in Frösén, 'The Petra Papyri'. The papyri from Khirbet Mird have yet to be fully published, but a project based at KU Leuven is currently in the process of documenting and conserving the papyri (starting date: 2018). Publications of the papyri include Grohmann, *Arabic Papyri from Khirbet el-Mird*; Malik, 'Une inscription et une lettre'; Van Haelst, *Catalogue des Papyrus Littéraires* and 'Cinq textes provenant de Khirbet Mird'; and Verhelst, 'Les fragments de Castellion'.

[43] See especially Chitty, *The Desert a City*, but also Binns, *Ascetics and Ambassadors*; Dauphin, *La Palestine byzantine*, and Hirschfeld, *The Judean Desert Monasteries*.

[44] Reynolds, 'Monasticism in Early Islamic Palestine', p. 343, but see the contributions by Hamarneh and Caner in this volume.

[45] Hirschfeld, *The Judean Desert Monasteries*.

[46] Hirschfeld, *The Judean Desert Monasteries*, pp. 102–11.

abandonment.[47] These criticisms are relevant for most older studies of Palestinian monasticism, and it is only within the past decade or so that scholars have begun to rely less on the explanatory models provided by the hagiographical literature and engage more critically with the monasteries' material remains.

This approach has been most successful in rural areas that are not associated with biblical sites or home to saints or famous monastic leaders about whom hagiographies were later written. Recent archaeological studies of monasteries in, for example, the Limestone Massif (Syria) and Western Galilee (Palestine) have examined the connection between monastic communities and village sites.[48] With few or no textual sources to guide the scholarly interpretations, the usage of, for example, archaeological landscape survey and the mapping of settlement patterns have proved effective in establishing the close contact between monastic and village communities. Monasteries were often attached to villages – built near or even within village settlements – sometimes with shared facilities for agricultural production, such as oil and wine presses, and evidence suggests that certain significant religious events such as baptism would take place within the monastic churches.[49]

Further reassessment of Palestine's monastic landscapes has been done by, for example, Itamar Taxel, who has examined the variety of monastic settlements and the range of geographical areas in which they are found.[50] Khirbet es-Suyyagh (seventh century) – a farmstead converted into a monastery in the northern Judean foothills – is an example of an agricultural monastery. The farmstead was equipped with oil and wine presses, which were continuously utilised by the monastic settlement. Leah Di Segni has argued that such farmsteads were donated to the church by

---

[47] Reynolds 'Monasticism in Early Islamic Palestine'.

[48] For the Limestone Massif, see Hull, 'The Archaeology of Monasticism' and 'A Spatial and Morphological Analysis of Monastic Sites'. For Western Galilee, see Ashkenazi and Aviam, 'Monasteries, Monks and Villages' and 'Monasteries and Villages'.

[49] Ashkenazi and Aviam, 'Monasteries, Monks, and Villages', especially pp. 289–93. The interdependence of village and monastery is also explored for Deir Ain Abata (Jordan) by Politis, 'The Monastery of Aghios Lot', and for Petra/Jabal Harun (Jordan) by Kouki, 'The Hinterland of a City'.

[50] Taxel's categories include 'urban monasteries of the communal/*coenobion* type (built within or near the borders of large towns and cities); desert monasteries belonging to either the *coenobion* or eremitical/*laura* type; pilgrimage monasteries – *coenobia* built at countryside pilgrim destinations and along pilgrimage routs; and agricultural monasteries – *coenobia* built either independently of villages or on their margins, common in the sown regions and desert fringes'. Taxel acknowledges that there were also hybrid monasteries; Taxel, 'Reassessing the Monastic Phase of Khirbet es-Suyyagh', p. 181; see also Taxel, 'Rural Monasticism' and *Khirbet es-Suyyagh*.

Christian landowners following the Samaritan revolt of 529–30, which left the farm abandoned, but still liable to paying tax.[51]

In this volume, Basema Hamarneh's study on the 'Monastic Estates in Byzantine *Arabia* and *Palaestina* (Fourth–Ninth Centuries)' combines literary, documentary and archaeological sources to reconstruct the complex monastic economies in and around the Holy Land. Hamarneh outlines some of the many ways in which monasteries were organised in the provinces of *Arabia* and *Palaestina*, showing a wide variety in the scale of landownership and monastic possessions, as well as in the personal wealth of monks. Through the use of literary sources (especially hagiographies) and documentary sources (such as the Nessana papyri), she outlines the development of the monastic landscape, showing its range from individual ascetics to large-scale coenobitic communities that flourished especially in the sixth and seventh centuries. The archaeological remains provide further evidence for the significance of monastic sites in the late antique Holy Land, showing that almost every village in the study area supported at least one monastery.

In Egypt, the relationship between villages and monasteries is less well understood. While monasteries are often preserved in the archaeological record due to their location in the dry desert fringe, either villages have not been preserved or the focus of archaeological research has been elsewhere. The archive found in the village of Aphrodito therefore offers a rare opportunity to follow the development of the economic circumstances of several monastic communities over the course of almost two centuries. A sixth-century family archive and administrative documents from an eighth-century village inform Isabelle Marthot-Santaniello's examination of monastic landownership in and near the village of Aphrodito. Land registers reveal that, in the sixth century, seven monasteries owned a substantial amount of all recorded arable land. The monastery of Apa Sourous (known only from textual sources) stands out for its wealth, but monasteries from the region of Panopolis (some 50 km south) also feature as landholders. In the eighth century, almost 100 years after the Arab conquest, the tax records mention new foundations, while other monasteries appear to have maintained their possessions. Other monasteries have disappeared altogether from the records. Interestingly, the monastery of Apa Sourous transitioned to a new status as a large estate.

At Naqlun in Egypt's Fayum Oasis, some 100 hermitages have been excavated by a Polish archaeological mission revealing not only a rich built

---

[51] Di Segni, 'On the Contribution of Epigraphy', pp. 187–8.

environment, but also documentary papyri and ostraca that provide insights into the economic dealings of the desert fathers. Tomasz Derda and Joanna Wegner show how some of the inhabitants at Naqlun had private financial means at their disposal and engaged in business either for themselves or on behalf of the community. The documents reveal how the monks organised both land and sea transport, leant money to laypeople, and invested in wine production. They also offer insights into the significance of kinship in establishing business relations.[52] A collection of miniature vessels found in a storage pit – perhaps intended as souvenirs – suggests an engagement with the pilgrimage industry in which the vessels were exchanged for offerings.

Production and Consumption of Food and Material Goods

As the previous section has demonstrated, the built environment and land holdings of monasteries provide evidence for many economic practices, including the facilities and raw material required for the production and consumption of commodities needed within the communities and exchanged with external groups. The papers in this section focus specifically on these goods and address topics that have been examined in previous studies, revising current knowledge (Dzierzbicka on wine; Achi on books), as well as venturing into newer areas of study (kitchens by Brooks Hedstrom and Kalla; fuel by El Dorry). The abundant textual and archaeological evidence for food and material goods within monasteries provides multiple routes of enquiry, and recent studies that focus on archaeological evidence in particular demonstrate how much potential there is for diverse approaches into the study of production and consumption.[53]

The physical remains of what may be storerooms and ceramic sherds from transport containers, as well as texts referring to commodities, attest to the large number of vessels that must have filled these monasteries, being delivered to and taken away from them, handled by monks and laymen alike. Yet, for a long time, the study of ceramic wares did not receive the level of attention that it requires. As a case in point, the pottery

---

[52] The importance of kinship in monasteries is studied by Schroeder, *Children and Family*, especially pp. 160–90. See also Krawiec, *Shenoute and the Women of the White Monastery*, pp. 161–75.

[53] The chapters in this section address the monastic production and consumption of material goods and do not engage with monastic work and labour, which is a recurring theme in the literary sources. For a recent discussion of these subjects, see Brown, *Treasure in Heaven*.

from the monastery of Apa Thomas at Wadi Sarga received its first preliminary study a century after the site's excavation.[54] This neglect means that questions essential to monastic daily life, and to the monasteries' wider connections, cannot be tackled. As Alain Delattre notes for the monastery of Apa Apollo at Bawit, a large quantity of pottery was required for the monks' needs, but, while it is likely that they were making vessels on site, there is no archaeological evidence for this being the case.[55] A similar situation is found at Kom el-Nana (Amarna) (fifth to seventh centuries). In her study of the glassware and pottery from the site, Jane Faiers notes that there is no evidence for manufacturing during the period in question, and the wares instead are indicative of both short- and long-distance trade.[56] The Egyptian wares show similarities with local wares produced at the city of Hermopolis, suggesting that the monastery was purchasing what it needed for its monastics from here. Other sherds were not local, showing long-distance trade within Egypt (e.g., Aswan and the Fayum), North Africa (Tunisia), as well as the Black Sea region and the eastern Mediterranean. These ceramics therefore provide evidence for connections with a broad geographic range that is not evident from the textual sources.

This is not to say, however, that all monasteries acquired their ceramic wares from external sources. At the monastery of Apa Jeremias, a pottery workshop containing six kilns with two additional kilns found nearby testifies to a large-scale ceramic production. Ceramic wasters found near the kilns inform us of a wide variety of pots produced here, including plates and dishes (tableware), large heavy basins, jugs, as well as *qaddus* pots designed to be used with a water wheel (*saqiyya*).[57]

Though some communities would have to acquire most of the commodities that they consumed from external suppliers (including the vessels required for transportation), other monasteries produced their own goods. While wine seems primarily to be purchased or produced on monastic lands, albeit not by monks (as Dzierbicka's paper demonstrates),

---

[54] Faiers, 'Wadi Sarga Revisited'.
[55] *P.Brux.Bawit* p. 92. Most of the wares studied at the site are Egyptian (Late Roman Amphora 7), with imported wares accounting for only approximately 10 per cent of the total (Van Neer et al., 'Salted Fish Products', p. 149; see also Dixneuf, 'Un lot d'amphores').
[56] Faiers, *Late Roman Glassware and Pottery from Amarna*, p. 9.
[57] Ghaly, 'Pottery Workshops', p. 165; see also Ballet, 'L'approvisionnement des monastères'. Kilns were also identified at Deir el-Dik, at Deir Mari Girgis, at the monastery of St Antony, and at the White Monastery. See the summary of ceramic production at monasteries in Wipszycka, 'Resources and Economic Activities', pp. 183 6, and for St Antony specifically, see Bild et al., 'Excavations at the Monastery of St Antony'.

evidence for wine presses survives from some sites in Egypt, and they are more commonly found at monasteries in Palestine.[58] This difference most likely results from the mode of production, which entails that grapes are pressed into wine at the estates that grow the vines. The pattern of land ownership in Egypt shows how monasteries, such as the White Monastery, often owned a patchwork of agricultural properties, sometimes as much as 70 km from the main site, while monasteries in Palestine, and especially those that had been converted from farmsteads, would have had their agricultural land holdings within their immediate vicinity.[59] More commonly attested in the archaeological record in both Egypt and Palestine are oil presses, with various vegetable oils (olive, sesame, castor) forming part of the monastic diet, as well as being used in lamps.[60] Recent work in particular has brought to light the extent and range of these economic installations.[61]

The study of monastic dietary habits is on the rise. Literary sources, such as monastic rules and hagiographies, provide good insights into the ascetic ideal of the consumption of food, while documentary sources report on the purchase and sale of agricultural production, but less so on the foodstuff consumed within the monasteries.[62] Archaeobotanical and archaeozoological remains, often contained within vessels but also scattered across sites, comprise another relatively recent area of study, providing an important addition to the textual sources for monastic diet. At Bawit, for example, the texts mention calves, sheep, and poultry, and animals were also used for other purposes, providing commodities (e.g., wool) and labour (e.g., transportation). Yet, the excavation reports from the site do not indicate the

---

[58] Hand presses survive from Egypt at the monastery of John the Little in the Wadi Natrun and medieval monasteries, including the thirteenth-century monastery of Abu Maqqar (El Dorry, 'Wine Production in Medieval Egypt', p. 58). For an overview of monastic wine production in Palestine, specifically that linked to the export of Gaza wine, see Decker, 'The End of the Holy Land Wine Trade'.

[59] Future comparative studies of the production and sale of wine could begin to shed light on how well-embedded monasteries were in the Mediterranean economy, drawing upon recent studies in the socio-cultural and economic role of wine in the eastern Mediterranean. See, in particular, Dodd, *Roman and Late Antique Wine Production*, which examines the viticultural practices at Antiochia ad Cragnum (in Anatolia) and Delos in the fifth to seventh centuries.

[60] On oil for lamps, see Mossakowska, 'Les huiles utilisées pour l'éclairage en Égypte'.

[61] See Krastel, Olschok, and Richter's Chapter 11 on Anba Hadra in this volume; see also Blanke, *An Archaeology of Egyptian Monasticism*, pp. 133–7. Crushing basins are found, among other sites, at the monasteries of St Paul and St Antony by the Red Sea (personal observation), as well as at monasteries in the Wadi Natrun. For a comprehensive study of oil and wine presses in Palestine, see Frankel, *Wine and Oil Production*.

[62] For discussion of monastic diets as perceived through the literary sources see, for example, Layton, 'Social Structure and Food Consumption', and Robinson, 'Shenoute's Feast' and *Food, Virtue, and the Shaping of Early Christianity*.

presence of animal bones.[63] The lack of published animal bones is in stark contrast to the volume of fish bones and evidence for fishing found in Egypt (with the Nile providing a ready supply of fresh fish, which could be salted for later consumption).[64] In addition to consumption, ingredients were also required for medicinal use and need to be considered in discussions of the procurement and use of goods. Opium poppy seeds found at Kom el-Nana are most likely to be understood as indicating the costs incurred in the medical care of both monks and laymen.[65]

A final example of recent trends is the study of textile production, from flax cultivation to spinning and weaving of textiles, to the final production of garments.[66] Monasteries were involved in all stages of production, as attested by texts, loom installations and dye shops, and the remains of textiles, worn during life and used for funerary purposes after death, from both Egypt and Palestine.[67] This material introduces gendered aspects to monastic economy. Female monastics are far less well-represented in the written sources, but they played a pivotal role in garment production in the White Monastery federation, as attested by the literary evidence and the existence of dye shops at the women's monastery at Athribis.[68] The presence of Egyptian and Nubian textiles, dating to the ninth century, at the monastery of John the Baptist at Qasr el-Yahud in Jordan possibly indicates a hospital presence at

---

[63] *P.Brux.Bawit* pp. 82–3. Similarly, while animal bones were excavated at Kom el-Nana, they are in considerably smaller quantities than fish bones; see Luff, 'Monastic Diet in Late Antique Egypt'.

[64] For fish at Bawit, see Van Neer *et al.*, 'Salted Fish Products'. A single papyrus, dating to the seventh century and likely from the Assiut area, attests to monastic involvement in fishing, published in Delattre and Vanthieghem, 'Un contrat de location de droit de pêche'. For a comparative example from Palestine, the animal bones from Deir Ain Abata have been exhaustively published and suggest that meat was consumed at the monastery in large quantities; see Beech, 'The Mammal Bones', Beech and Prance, 'The Fish Bones', and Rielly and Beech, 'The Bird Bones'. However, similar to the Egyptian examples, the animal bones from Jabal Harun (Petra, Jordan) suggest that, here, fish were predominant in the monastic diet; see Studer, 'Archaeozoology of Jabal Harun'.

[65] Smith, *Archaeobotanical Investigations*, p. 80. For medical provisions within monasteries, see Crislip, *From Monastery to Hospital*.

[66] Ancient textiles has been a particularly prolific recent field of study, with evidence from monasteries appearing in Mossakowska-Gaubert, *Egyptian Textiles and their Production*, and El-Sayed and Fluck, *The Textile Centre Akhmim-Panopolis (Egypt) in Late Antiquity*. For Palestinian textiles, see for example those found in monks' tombs at Nessana (Shamir, 'Cotton Textiles', §16).

[67] A summary of the evidence from seventh- and eighth-century western Thebes is provided in Cromwell, 'The Threads that Bind Us'. For loom installations at several Egyptian sites, see Sigl, 'Pits with Cross-Bars' and 'Weaving Copts in Amarna'.

[68] The literary evidence is discussed in detail in Krawiec, *Shenoute and the Women of the White Monastery*, pp. 31–50. See Blanke, *An Archaeology of Egyptian Monasticism*, pp. 176–7 for the dye shops.

the site, providing further evidence of the economic impact of monasteries as hospitals, as well as of long-distance pilgrimage and networks across Egypt and Palestine (discussed further in the next section).[69]

As these brief case studies demonstrate, commodities provide plentiful avenues of enquiry into the economic lives of monasteries. While the literary record strongly promotes the ideal of personal poverty, the documentary sources, small finds, and economic installations attest to the range of goods that were produced, bought, and traded, sometimes over long distances, within and between regions. The papers in this section highlight the range of approaches that can be adopted to study this evidence, generating new insights into well-known material and paving the way for entirely new understandings of the economic reality of day-to-day life.

Dorota Dzierzbicka examines the production and consumption of wine in Egyptian monasteries from the sixth to the eighth century, based on information obtained from documentary papyri, inscriptions, and archaeological evidence. Dzierzbicka demonstrates the complexity of wine procurement and its importance for a number of functions within the monastic communities. These included, but were not limited to, religious worship, pious gifts, payment in kind, and monastic consumption. A case study of the documentary papyri from the monastery of Apa Apollo at Bawit suggests a change in the monastery's procurement from the sixth to the eighth century. In the sixth century, vineyards became a part of the monastic estate through donation or bequeathment, and the production was subsidised by wine purchased in large quantities. The seventh and eighth centuries saw a change in the monastery's productive capacity as more vineyards were acquired and the monastery was transformed into a wine-producing estate of some significance.

The consumption of food within ascetic communities was a contested issue, which provoked anxiety among the monastics, encouraged the writing of rules to be followed, and promoted literary ideals to be imitated. The textual focus is often on the consumption of food and the procurement of ingredients, while its production is rarely mentioned. Darlene L. Brooks Hedstrom redresses this imbalance by applying ethnoarchaeological observations and theoretical principles retrieved from household archaeology to a study of the archaeological remains of kitchens, bakeries, storerooms, and dining spaces in Egyptian monasteries. These spaces are often found empty within the archaeological record. Brooks Hedstrom argues that in order to

---

[69] For these textiles, see for example Shamir, 'Tunics from Kasr al-Yahud' and 'Egyptian and Nubian Textiles from Qasr el-Yahud'.

fully appreciate their centrality within the monastic communities, we should imagine them re-cluttered with objects and re-peopled with their ancient users.

The study of the production and consumption of foodstuffs is furthered by Gábor Kalla in Chapter 7 on the refectory and the kitchen at the monastery of Tell Bi'a in Syria. The monastery forms a closed complex of circa fifty rooms with the church, kitchen, and refectory holding a prominent central location. The remains of ovens show how the monastery produced different types of bread, while textual sources and the archaeological remains of storage facilities point towards a monastic engagement with agricultural production. A series of circular benches were excavated in the refectory of Tell Bi'a. These are unique features within Syrian–Palestinian monasticism, linking the site to monasteries in Egypt. Based on the size and layout of the benches, Kalla concludes that the monastery would have been inhabited by forty-eight to sixty-four monastics during its latest phase of use.

In a truly unique contribution to the study of monastic economies, Mennat-Allah El Dorry examines the use of animal dung for fuel in Egyptian monasteries. Animal dung has several significant economic uses, including as fertiliser, building material, and tempering for ceramic production. In agricultural areas where wood is scarce, it further serves as an important source of fuel. Although this function is known from the Pharaonic period to pre-modern Egypt, very little work has been done on its use within the context of monastic settlements. El Dorry draws on inscriptions and titles found in textual sources, as well as archaeobotanical remains, to identify the extent of its usage. El Dorry concludes that dung was an important source of fuel at the two monasteries that have seen adequate archaeobotanical examinations, while the full extent of its usage awaits examination at other monastic sites.

Finally, the ninth- and tenth-century group of illuminated Coptic manuscripts known as the St Michael Collection offers a unique insight into the book culture of medieval Fayum in Egypt. These richly decorated and leather-bound manuscripts represent a costly investment of time and money. Andrea Myers Achi calculates the economics of book production in a detailed study of the materials and labour involved. Achi considers the full range of production from livestock (and their upkeep) required for the parchment, to the use of a skilled workforce and the exchange network of monasteries, scribes, painters, binders, and doners involved in producing and storing the collection. Contemporary papyri offer comparative pricelists, but do not express the spiritual and community value of the monastic 'brand', which would have made the books worth more than their actual monetary costs.

Monastic Encounters: Travel, Pilgrimage, and Donations

The first two sections deal with what are perhaps the most obvious forms of economic interactions in the late antique world. A key question engaging both past and present scholarship concerns the extent to which the wealth of monasteries was dependent on such means (i.e., agricultural and artisanal production and trade) compared to donations and lay gifts. Beat Brenk has argued that late antique monasteries (in Egypt and Palestine) would not have been able to prosper without the financial support of wealthy patrons, and that neither craft production nor agriculture would have sufficed to support the monastic lifestyle.[70] On the contrary, and as already touched upon above, Ewa Wipszycka has argued that documentary sources reveal that the main income of monasteries (in Egypt) was based on the production of cash-crops for sale in local markets.[71] Whether through patronage or trade, it is clear from textual and archaeological sources that engagement with both monastic and lay communities played an important role in the lives of most late antique monasteries.

The traditional scholarly view saw Palestinian monasticism as dependent on wealthy patrons and especially the Christian aristocratic elite. This view has its origins in Eusebius' account of Constantine the Great's (r. 306–37), and his mother Helena's, patronage of churches at Biblical sites, while the empress Eudokia (r. 421–50) and the Emperors Zeno (r. 476–91) and Justinian I (r. 527–65) are also associated with patronage of churches and pilgrimage sites.[72] The influential accounts of aristocratic pilgrims who founded monasteries in and near Jerusalem, such as Melania the Elder, Melania the Younger, and Paula (fourth and early fifth centuries), further shaped this scholarly perception.[73] Similarly, the main interest among

---

[70] Brenk, 'Monasteries as Rural Settlements', especially pp. 472–3.
[71] Wipszycka, 'Resources and Economic Activities', p. 172.
[72] Eusebius, *Life of Constantine* (edition and translation: Winkelmann in Pietri and Rondeau, *Vie de Constantin*); John Moscus, *Spiritual Meadows* (translation: Wortley, *The Spiritual Meadow*); Procopius records that Justinian restored ten monasteries in Palestine and added cisterns to another six (*On Buildings*, 5.9.1–20; translation: Dewing and Downey, *Procopius*). See also Klein, 'Do Good in Thy Good Pleasure unto Zion'; Kosinski, 'The Emperor Zeno's Church Donations'; Krautheimer, *Early Christian and Byzantine Architecture*, p. 111.
[73] Recent discussions of the hagiographical accounts of these women include Chin and Schroeder, *Melania*; Whiting, 'Asceticism and Hospitality'. See also Falcasantos, 'Wandering Wombs, Inspired Intellects'.

scholars studying the material culture of pilgrimage has until recently been on the sites that attracted long-distance travellers (such as Abu Mena in Egypt and Qal'at Sim'an in Syria) and on the flasks and tokens that the pilgrims brought back as religious souvenirs.[74]

According to this traditional view, the international network of wealthy Christian donors collapsed in the early seventh century as a result of, first, the Sassanian occupation (614–28) and, second, the Arab conquest (638). However, refined typologies of especially ceramic evidence and the inclusion of epigraphy from churches are starting to paint a different picture of Christian patronage in the seventh century and later, which suggests that monasteries thrived well beyond the Arab conquest.[75] At the same time, the documentary evidence, especially from Nessana, and the archaeological evidence, for example from Western Galilee, has increased our awareness of the importance of local networks and the embeddedness of monastic communities, not only within long-distance elite networks, but, much more importantly, within their immediate surroundings and their local communities.

In Egypt, the increasing popularity of pilgrimage is attested in writings from the fifth century, when the church father Shenoute famously expressed his disgust at the contemporary Christian obsession with the veneration of martyrs' bones. He condemned the practice of placing their physical remains in churches and chapels and raged against worship associated with shrines. In Shenoute's view, this was the work of demons, as it included singing, feasting, and drinking to a point that led to fornication and even to murder.[76] Ironically, it is well attested that, after his death, Shenoute himself became the object of veneration and an attraction that drew pilgrims to the White Monastery.[77] In light of the many revered figures whose shrines attracted visitors, it is perhaps not surprising that hagiographies describe the roads of Egypt as transformed into rivers, such was the volume of pilgrims travelling the length of the country.[78]

---

[74] See, for example, Anderson, 'An Archaeology of Late Antique Pilgrim Flasks', and Vikan, *Early Byzantine Pilgrimage Art*. Recent studies have begun to challenge this situation; see, for example, Rosenthal-Heginbottom, 'Pilgrim Mementoes'; Collar and Kristensen, *Pilgrimage and Economy*; Kristensen and Friese, *Excavating Pilgrimage*.

[75] Reynolds, 'Monasticism in Early Islamic Palestine', p. 350.

[76] Timbie, 'Once More into the Desert' (on Shenoute's sermon BN 68). See Bitton-Ashkelony, *Encountering the Sacred*, and Yasin, *Saints and Church Spaces*, pp. 15–26, for attitudes towards pilgrimage in the fourth and fifth centuries. See also *Vita Antonii* 1.38 (translation: Vivian and Athanassakis, *The Life of Antony*) for an earlier attestation of this view.

[77] For a summary of pilgrimage to the White Monastery, see Blanke, 'The Allure of the Saint'.

[78] Anonymous travelogues, such as *Historia Monachorum in Aegypto*, are particularly vivid in their description of Egypt's Christian landscape.

Elsewhere in Egypt, the archaeological evidence testifies to the significant contribution made to monastic economies by the steady growth in the provision of religious services. The archaeological remains of the hermitages at Kom 39 and 40 at Qusur Hegeila (Kellia) show that the physical and spiritual needs of visitors were increasingly recognised and catered for from the fifth century onwards.[79] Some monasteries, such as Deir el-Bala'izah (sixth to eighth centuries), were equipped with an extramural guesthouse for visitors.[80] Guesthouses continued to be important centuries later, as attested at Deir Anba Hadra (tenth century), where a large section of the monastery was set aside for visitors. Non-monastics would arrive through a separate entrance in the monastery's east wall and have access to accommodation, kitchens, and the monastery's facilities for worship and prayer (see Krastel, Olschok, and Richter in this volume).

In Palestine, guesthouses were a common feature from the fourth century onwards. They were often connected with pilgrimage routes or sites, since they are frequently found at monasteries that were located on the routes leading to locations associated with saints or biblical stories.[81] A case in point is the monastery of Martyrius in the Judean Desert, which was laid out with an external wing for visitors that comprised accommodation and stables.[82] The monastery's layout suggests that visitors would also have had access to its main church, a tomb (dedicated perhaps to a church father or patron saint), as well as the refectory and bathhouse. An enclosure, about one-third of the size of the total monastery, was set aside for the private use of the monastics.[83]

While the textual and archaeological evidence clearly shows that, in Late Antiquity, monastics and monasteries were hosts and organisers of pilgrimage, they also became the destination of the pilgrims themselves. However, although the presence of visitors is articulated in the archaeological remains of monasteries, it is much more difficult to identify the economic exchanges that were generated by their visits. The interaction

---

[79] See Makowiecka, 'Monastic Pilgrimage Centre at Kellia' for a detailed description of this development. See also Descaeudres, 'Mönche als Pilger und als Pilgerziel'.

[80] The textual and archaeological evidence for guesthouses is summarised in Schachner, 'Economic Production', pp. 285–308.

[81] For travelling (monastics and pilgrims) in late antique Palestine, see Delouis *et al.*, *Les mobilités monastiques*; Dietz, *Wandering Monks*; Whiting, 'Travel in the Late Antique Levant' and 'Monastery Hostels'.

[82] Hirschfeld, *The Judean Desert Monasteries*, pp. 42–6. See also Whiting, 'The Architecture of Monastic Hospitality'.

[83] Guesthouses are also found at major pilgrimage sites such as Qal'at Sim'an, Syria, where monastics were responsible for the upkeep of the site and the provision of food and accommodation for visitors. See Jensen, 'Housing Pilgrims'.

was centred on the monasteries' ability to provide services at the critical stages of life and in the mediation between God and the average Christian.[84] The pricing of these services (such as prayers, baptisms, and burials) is not easily quantifiable, and payment was often made via means other than monetary transactions.[85] Similarly, Achi (Chapter 9) has emphasised the perceived added value that objects produced in monasteries or by monastics may have had compared to those produced in non-monastic settings. We will probably never be able to quantify the value of monasteries' spiritual economy, but the combined literary, documentary, and archaeological evidence shows a clear trend in which the offering of religious services to lay communities became increasingly more prominent throughout and beyond Late Antiquity.

The chapters in Section III examine some of the many ways in which monasteries engaged with the extramural world. Caner studies how monasteries managed the gifts and donations received by laymen, while Bianchi (Mt Nebo, Jordan) and Krastel, Olschok, and Richter (Deir Anba Hadra, Egypt) reconstruct from archaeology and text the roles of pilgrimage and agricultural production in sustaining the monasteries. The section concludes with a study by Tutty of how monastics ventured beyond their communities for the purposes of trade and religious tourism.

An archive of circa 200 documentary papyri from the village of Nessana in the Negev Desert represents one of the largest bodies of papyri that survives outside of Egypt. Among the different topics dealt with in this corpus, a number of texts concern monastic life (and are also discussed in Hamarneh's Chapter 2). One account in particular offers a rare insight into monastic recordkeeping outside of Egypt. The early seventh–century *P. Ness.* III 79 contains a list of gifts and their donors to an unnamed monastery, which is organised in two categories, *prosphorai* (offerings) and *eulogiai* (blessings). Dan Caner argues that the two categories describe very different types of gifts: *prosphorai* were given for specific purposes and came with obligations, whereas the monastics were free to use *eulogiai* as they saw fit (that is, they represent 'restricted' and 'unrestricted' gifts). This document is especially of note in contrast to the Egyptian papyri recording donations, in which *eulogiai* appear less frequently, allowing Caner not only to address the importance of this account for knowledge

---

[84] For a summary of some of these exchanges, see Blanke, 'Pricing Salvation'. See also Brown, *Treasure in Heaven*, p. xiv.

[85] The hagiographical literature supports the idea that some form of payment was expected for the services provided by the pilgrimage sites. See, for example, Papaconstantinou, 'Donation and Negotiation', p. 75.

of early Byzantine monasticism but also our understanding of the practice in Egypt.

Lena Sophie Krastel, Sebastian Olschok, and Tonio Sebastian Richter report on recent examinations of a monastery near the ancient city of Syene (modern Aswan). From the fourth century onwards, Syene comprised a rich Christian landscape with numerous religious institutions, of which Deir Anba Hadra is the best explored. Looking at the archaeological remains of food- and oil-producing facilities, the authors suggest that the monastery's production appears to have been largely designed for its own consumption with little or no engagement in local or regional trade. The epigraphic evidence, however, tells a different story. It reveals how the monastery, through extramural landholdings, provided for the poor while also attesting to an active engagement with visitation in which the monastery capitalised on the provision of spiritual commodities by, for example, encouraging visitors' inscriptions on the monastery walls.

The economic reality of life in this southern Egyptian monastery finds many common features with the community at Mt Nebo in the province of Arabia. Davide Bianchi summarises the economic circumstances of the monastery of the Memorial of Moses, which – similarly to the monastery of Anba Hadra – was largely self-sufficient in agricultural goods, such as bread and wine, but was not involved in surplus production for financial gain. Instead, the monastery engaged in a spiritual economy and relied to an extent on the donations made by pilgrims, local laypeople, and clergy. The monastery was part of a wider network of sites linked with biblical figures of the Old and New Testament and was visited by famous travellers, such as Egeria (fourth century), Peter the Iberian (fifth century), and the Piacenza pilgrim (sixth century).

Drawing on two letter collections (the archive of Nepheros and the Nag Hammadi Codices), as well as several other literary sources, Paula Tutty examines the patterns of travel among fourth-century monastics from these communities in Middle Egypt. Tutty identifies several reasons for travel. Monastics would travel to tend to agricultural land holdings well beyond the monastery and to trade and exchange goods. Senior monastics would visit other monasteries, and at times, individuals or groups of monastics would perform what Tutty describes as *religious tourism* as a part of their monastic training – including travel between Palestine and Egypt (and thereby helping create and maintain the long-distance networks mentioned previously). Depending on the purpose and duration of the journey, monastics would travel by land or on the Nile by boat, with several sources attesting that larger monasteries owned their own boats or barges used for transporting goods as far away as Alexandria. The different methods used and the extent to which monastics travelled also highlights the need to incorporate such communities into broader studies of life in late antique Egypt, with monks representing an important group of travellers that are often overlooked in studies of this period.

Conclusions and Future Perspectives

Together, the chapters in this volume demonstrate the potential of approaching the economies of monasteries in Egypt and Palestine as deeply embedded within the world of Late Antiquity. They show the many ways in which monasteries secured their existence and, in some cases, grew to become major actors in both local and regional economies. Monasteries were not only places that offered opportunities for seclusion from the world; they were also centres of religious power, and the formation and accumulation of their wealth were dependent on their ability to attract monastics and to secure the support of local communities through patronage, pilgrimage, and trade. The patchwork of properties owned by monasteries in Egypt, as illustrated in the Aphrodito archives, reflects not only how land was obtained in the first place, but also the complexities involved in managing the monastic estate. This volume securely displays the level of connectivity that was experienced by both monasteries and monastics through trade, communication, travel, and pilgrimage. Our chapters draw out networks of monastic book production and show how travelling monks contributed to establishing both religious and economic networks. Some monks even travelled as craftsmen, leaving their name in churches in different parts of Egypt.

In this introductory chapter, we have brought together just a small number of examples, from Egypt and Palestine, in order to demonstrate some current trends in studies of monastic economies and to emphasise just how much is still available for future study – both new material being discovered through archaeological fieldwork or archival research and evidence longknown but in need of being revisited. Many questions remain to be answered. The studies in this volume primarily focus on communal monasticism, unsurprisingly so given the abundance of evidence deriving from such communities. One potential direction for future work is the economy of solitary monasticism. While the literary record provides multiple examples of ascetics surviving through divine providence in remote locations (e.g., the inner desert), the archaeological and documentary sources reveal individuals much more closely bound to the world around them, through multiple economic transactions. Perhaps the best-known such monk to come to light in recent decades is Frange, who resided in a cell (a reused ancient tomb) in Sheikh Abd el-Qurna in western Thebes. Through the course of excavating the tomb in the early 2000s, hundreds of Coptic ostraca were found, many of which record Frange's interactions with the world around him (*O.Frangé*). This corpus demonstrates how he procured commodities for his daily needs and the work that he did (textile and book production), as well as his networks that spread throughout western Thebes and across the Nile, which were facilitated through the use of messengers. While several studies of aspects of his life and work have been published, there remains considerable scope for further work, with Frange potentially serving as a model for the economy of hermitic lifestyles.[86]

A firmer integration of monasticism within landscape studies is an important future trajectory. Geography is a significant variable within and between the two regions discussed in this volume. Settlement patterns were formed by local topography and by the availability of raw material. Within Egypt's desert climate, Brooks Hedstrom has demonstrated the variation in monastic settlements based on natural topography and previous site usage.[87] These variations could help illuminate questions that are key to the monastic economies, such as administrative complexity, on-site production, and the relationship with the extramural world, including the extent to which monastics had to travel. Finally, the economy of produce (such as ceramics, oil, and wine) allows for comparisons with non-monastic economies across the late antique Mediterranean world, locating the impact of monastic economies in broader contexts.

Exciting new fieldwork in Egypt and Palestine will also shape future work on monastic economies. Some of this is already noted in the chapters in the current volume, but many projects are underway, including what may, according to the excavators, be the earliest archaeologically attested monastery in Egypt in the Bahariya Oasis.[88] A further possibility for future work involves extending the geographic scope beyond Egypt's southern border, to the Christian kingdoms of Nubia. The study of monasticism in Nubia is still in its infancy, compared to its northern neighbour, but

---

[86] Select publications include Boud'hors, 'Copie et circulation des livres' (Achi in Chapter 9 in the current volume also discusses Frange's book production activities); Cromwell, 'The Threads that Bind Us'; Heurtel, 'Le petit monde de Frangé'. See also the introduction to *O.Frangé*.
[87] Brooks Hedstrom, 'Divine Architects'.
[88] At the time of writing, only initial announcements of the work at the site have appeared, and it remains too soon to confirm either the nature or date of this site, Tell Ganub Qasr el-Aguz.

increasing scholarly attention in this area is already providing material that highlights the economic reality of monastic communities along this region of the Nile Valley.[89] Ultimately, this volume has set out not to create a model that fits all, but to emphasise the variety of the monastic economies and the significance of treating them in their rightful place within the world of Late Antiquity.

Bibliography

Anderson, W. 'An Archaeology of Late Antique Pilgrim Flasks', *Anatolian Studies*, 54 (2004), 79–93.

Ashkenazi, J. and Aviam, M. 'Monasteries, Monks and Villages in Western Galilee in Late Antiquity', *Journal of Late Antiquity*, 5.2 (2013), 269–97.

Ashkenazi, J. and Aviam, M. 'Monasteries and Villages: Rural Economy and Religious Interdependency in Late Antique Palestine', *Vigiliae Christianae*, 71.2 (2017), 117–133.

Bacot, S. 'La circulation du vin dans les monastères d'égypte à l'époque copte' in N. Grimal and B. Menu (eds.), *Le commerce en Égypte ancienne* (Cairo: Institut français d'archéologie oriental, 1998), pp. 269–88.

Ballet, P. 'L'approvisionnement des monastères. Production et reception de la ceramique' in J. den Heijer, S. Emmel, M. Krause, and A. Schmidt (eds.), *Egypt 1350 BC-AD 1800. Art Historical and Archaeological Studies for Gawdat Gabra* (Weisbaden: Reichert Verlag, 2011), pp. 27–33.

Banaji, J. *Agrarian Change in Late Antiquity: Gold, Labour, and Aristocratic Dominance*, 2nd edition (Oxford: Oxford University Press, 2007).

Beach, A. I. and Cochelin, I. (eds.) *Cambridge History of Medieval Monasticism in the Latin West* (Cambridge: Cambridge University Press, 2020).

Beech, M. 'The Mammal Bones' in K. D. Politis (ed.) *Sanctuary of Lot at Deir Ain Abata in Jordan – Excavations 1988-2003* (Amman: Jordan Distribution Agency, 2012), pp. 449–78.

Beech, M., and Prance, C. 'The Fish Bones' in K. D. Politis (ed.) *Sanctuary of Lot at Deir Ain Abata in Jordan – Excavations 1988-2003* (Amman: Jordan Distribution Agency, 2012), pp. 479–502.

Bild, J., El-Antony, Fr. M., Lundhaug, H., Zaborowshi, J., Polliack, M., Gobezieworku, M., and Rubenson, S. 'Excavations at the Monastery of St Antony at the Red Sea', *Opuscula*, 9 (2016), 133–215.

Binns, J. *Ascetics and Ambassadors of Christ: The Monasteries of Palestine 314-631* (Oxford: Oxford University Press, 1996).

---

[89] See especially Obłuski, *The Monasteries and Monks of Nubia*, as well as the collected papers in Gabla and Takla, *Christianity and Monasticism in Aswan and Nubia*.

Bitton-Ashkelony, B. *Encountering the Sacred: The Debate on Christian Pilgrimage in Late Antiquity* (Berkeley and London: University of California Press, 2005).

Blanke, L. 'The Allure of the Saint: Late Antique Pilgrimage to the Monastery of St Shenoute' in T. M. Kristensen and W. Friese (eds.) *Excavating Pilgrimage. Archaeological Approaches to Sacred Travel and Movement in the Ancient World* (Abingdon and New York: Routledge, 2017), pp. 203–23.

Blanke, L. *An Archaeology of Egyptian Monasticism: Settlement, Economy and Daily Life at the White Monastery Federation* (New Haven: Yale Egyptological Publications, 2019).

Blanke, L. 'Pricing Salvation: Visitation, Donation and the Monastic Economies in Late Antique and Early Islamic Egypt' in A. Collar and T. M. Kristensen (eds.) *Pilgrimage and Economy in the Ancient Mediterranean* (Leiden and Boston, MA: Brill, 2020), pp. 228–53.

Boud'hors, A. 'Copie et circulation des livres dans la région thébaine (VIIe–VIIIe siècles)' in A. Delattre and P. Heilporn (eds.), « *Et maintenant ce ne sont plus que des villages . . .* » *Thèbes et sa region aux époques hellénistique, romaine et byanzantine* (Brussels: Association égyptologique Reine Elisabeth, 2008), pp. 150–61 and pls XIV–XV.

Boud'hors, A. *Le canon 8 de Chénouté*, 2 vols (Cairo: Institut français d'archéologie orientale, 2013).

Bowman, A. K., Coles, R. A., Gonis, N., Obbink, D., and Parsons, P. (eds.) *Oxyrhynchus: A City and Its Texts* (London: Egypt Exploration Society, 2007).

Brakke, D., and Crislip, A. *Selected Discourses of Shenoute the Great: Community, Theology, and Social Conflict in Late Antique Egypt* (Cambridge: Cambridge University Press, 2015).

Brenk, B. 'Monasteries as Rural Settlements: Patron-Dependence or Self-Sufficiency?' in W. Bowden, L. Lavan, and C. Machado (eds.), *Recent Research on the Late Antique Countryside* (Leiden and Boston, MA: Brill, 2004), pp. 447–76.

Brooks Hedstrom, D.L. 'Divine Architects: Designing the Monastic Dwelling Place' in R. S. Bagnall (ed.), *Egypt in the Byzantine World 300–700* (Cambridge: Cambridge University Press, 2007), pp. 368–89.

Brooks Hedstrom, D. L. 'Treading on Antiquity: Anglo-American Missionaries and the Religious Landscape of Nineteenth-Century Coptic Egypt', *Material Religion*, 8.2 (2015), 127–52.

Brooks Hedstrom, D. L. *The Monastic Landscape of Late Antique Egypt: An Archaeological Reconstruction* (Cambridge: Cambridge University Press, 2017).

Brown, P. 'The Rise and Function of the Holy Man in Late Antiquity', *The Journal of Roman Studies*, 61 (1971), 80–101.

Brown, P. *Treasure in Heaven. The Holy Poor in Early Christianity* (Charlottesville and London: University of Virginia Press, 2016).

Chin, C. M. and Schroeder, C. T. (eds.) *Melania. Early Christianity through the Life of One Family* (Oakland: University of California Press, 2017).

Chitty, D. *The Desert a City: An Introduction to the Story of Egyptian and Palestinian Monasticism under the Christian Empire* (Oxford: Blackwell, 1966).

Collar, A. and Kristensen, T. M. (eds.) *Pilgrimage and Economy in the Ancient Mediterranean* (Leiden and Boston, MA: Brill, 2020).

Crislip, A. T. *From Monastery to Hospital: Christian Monasticism and the Transformation of Health Care in Late Antiquity* (Ann Arbor: University of Michigan Press, 2005).

Cromwell, J. 'The Threads that Bind Us: Aspects of Textile Production in Late Antique Thebes' in C. Di Biase-Dyson and L. Donovan (eds.), *The Cultural Manifestations of Religious Experience. Studies in Honour of Boyo G. Ockinga* (Münster: Ugarit-Verlag, 2017), pp. 213–24.

Cromwell, J. '"Forgive Me, Because I Could Not Find Papyrus": The Use and Distribution of Ostraca in Late Antique Western Thebes' in C. Caputo and J. Lougovaya (eds.), *Using Ostraca in the Ancient World: New Discoveries and Methodologies* (Berlin: De Gruyter, 2021), pp. 209–34.

Cromwell, J. 'Writing Exercises from Wadi Sarga: O.Sarga II 1–14', *Archiv für Papyrusforschung*, 66.2 (2021), 359–76.

Dauphin, C. *La Palestine byzantine: peuplement et populations* (Oxford: Archaeopress, 1998).

Decker, M. 'The End of the Holy Land Wine Trade', *Strata: Bulletin of the Anglo-Israel Archaeological Society*, 31 (2013), 103–16.

Deferrari, R. J. (ed.) *The Fathers of the Church: Early Christian Biographies* (Washington, DC: The Catholic University of America Press, 1952).

Dekker, R. 'Coptic Ostraca Relating to Bishop Abraham of Hermonthis at Columbia University', *Bulletin of the American Society of Papyrologists*, 57 (2020), pp. 75–115.

Delattre, A. and Vanthieghem, N. 'Un contrat de location de droit de pêche (P. Hamb. Copt. Inv. 10', *Journal of Coptic Studies*, 21 (2019), 19–27.

Delouis, O., Mossakowska-Gaubert, M., and Peters-Custot, A. (eds.) *Les mobilités monastiques en Orient et en Occident de l'Antiquité tardive au Moyen Âge (IVe–XVe siècle)* (Rome: Publications de l'École française de Rome, 2019).

Descaeudres, G. 'Mönche als Pilger und als Pilgerziel' in E. Dassmann and J. Engemann (eds.), *Akten des XII. Internationaen Kongresses für christliche Archäologie* (Münster: Aschendorffsche, 1995), pp. 682–8.

Dewing, H. B. and Downey, G. *Procopius: On Buildings* (Cambridge, MA: Harvard University Press, 1940).

Di Segni, L. 'On the Contribution of Epigraphy to the Identification of Monastic Foundations' in J. Patrich, O. Peleg-Barkat, and E. Ben-Yosef (eds.), *Arise, Walk through the Land. Studies in the Archaeology and History of the Land of Israel in Memory of Yizhar Hirschfeld on the Tenth Anniversary of His Demise* (Jerusalem: Israel Exploration Society, 2016), pp. 185–98.

Dietz, M. *Wandering Monks, Virgins, and Pilgrims: Ascetic Travel in the Mediterranean World, A.D. 300-800* (University Park, PA: Pennsylvania State University Press, 2005).

Dixneuf, D. 'Un lot d'amphores de la première moitié du VIIe siècle à Baouit (Moyenne Égypte). Campagne 2004 – Sondage 3' in A. Boud'hors and C. Louis (eds.), *Études coptes X, Douzième journée d'études (Lyon, 19-21 mai 2005)* (Paris: De Boccard, 2008), pp. 39-49.

Dodd, E. K. *Roman and Late Antique Wine Production in the Eastern Mediterranean* (Oxford: Archaeopress, 2020).

Dunn, M. *The Emergence of Monasticism. From the Desert Fathers to the Early Middle Ages* (Oxford: Blackwell, 2001).

El Dorry, M.-A. 'Wine Production in Medieval Egypt: The Case of the Coptic Church' in M. Ayad (ed.), *Studies in Coptic Culture: Transmission and Interaction* (Cairo: American University in Cairo Press, 2016), pp. 55-63.

El-Sayed, R. and Fluck, C. (eds.) *The Textile Centre Akhmim-Panopolis (Egypt) in Late Antiquity: Material Evidence for Continuity and Change in Society, Religion, Industry, and Trade* (Wiesbaden: Dr Ludwig Reichert, 2020).

Emmel, S. *Shenoute's Literary Corpus*, 2 vols (Leuven: Peeters, 2004).

Endsjø, D. Ø. *Primordial Landscapes, Incorruptible Bodies. Desert Asceticism and the Christian Appropriation of Greek Ideas on Geography, Bodies and Immortality* (New York: Peter Lang, 2008).

Faiers, J. *Late Roman Glassware and Pottery from Amarna and Related Studies* (London: Egypt Exploration Society, 2013).

Faiers, J. 'Wadi Sarga Revisited: A Preliminary Study of the Pottery Excavated in 1913/14' in E. R. O'Connell (ed.) *Egypt in the First Millennium AD: Perspectives from New Fieldwork* (Leuven: Peeters, 2014), pp. 177-89.

Falcasantos, R. S. 'Wandering Wombs, Inspired Intellects: Christian Religious Travel in Late Antiquity', *Journal of Early Christian Studies*, 25.1 (2017), 89-117.

Foucault, M. and Miskowiec, J. 'Of Other Spaces', *Diacritics*, 16.1 (1986), 22-7.

Frankel, R. *Wine and Oil Production in Antiquity in Israel and Other Mediterranean Countries* (Sheffield: Sheffield Academic Press, 1999).

Frösén, J. 'Petra Papyri: Information and Significance' in J. Frösén and Z. T. Fiema (eds.) *Petra: A City Forgotten and Rediscovered* (Helsinki: Amos Anderson Art Museum, 2002), pp. 18-24.

Gabra, G. and Takla, H. (eds.) *Christianity and Monasticism in Aswan and Nubia* (Cairo: American University in Cairo Press, 2013).

Garel, E. *Héritage et transmission dans le monachisme égyptien* (Cairo: Institut français d'archéologie orientale, 2020).

Garel, E. and Nowak, M. 'Monastic Wills: The Continuation of Late Roman Legal Tradition' in M. Choat and M. Giorda (eds.), *Writing and Communication in Early Egyptian Monasticism* (Leiden: Brill, 2017), pp. 108-28.

Ghaly, H. 'Pottery Workshops of Saint-Jeremian (Saqqara)', *Cahiers de la ceramique eqyptienne*, 3 (1992), 161-71.

Godlewski, W. *Le monastère de St. Phoibammon* (Warsaw: PWN-Éditions scientifique de Pologne, 1986).

Goehring, J. E. 'The Dark Side of Landscape: Ideology and Power in the Christian Myth of the Desert', *Journal of Medieval and Early Modern Studies*, 33.3 (2003), 437–51.

Goodwin, C. W. 'Curiosities of Law. 1. Conveyancing among the Copts of the Eighth Century', *Law Magazine and Law Review: Or, Quarterly Journal of Jurisprudence*, 6 (1859), 237–48.

Goodwin, C. W. 'Account of Three Coptic Papyri, and Other Manuscripts, Brought from the East by J.S. Stuart Glennie, Esq.', *Archaeologia*, 39 (1863), 447–56.

Grohmann, A. *Arabic Papyri from Khirbet el-Mird* (Leuven: Publications Universitaires, 1963).

Heurtel, C. 'Le petit monde de Frangé: une micro-société dans la région thébaine au début du 8e siècle' in A. Delattre and P. Heilporn (eds.), « *Et maintenant ce ne sont plus que des villages ...* » *Thèbes et sa region aux époques hellénistique, romaine et byzantine* (Brussels: Association égyptologique Reine Elisabeth, 2008), pp. 163–74.

Hickey, T. *Wine, Wealth, and the State in Late Antique Egypt. The House of Apion at Oxyrhynchus* (Ann Arbor: University of Michigan Press, 2012).

Hirschfeld, Y. *The Judean Desert Monasteries in the Byzantine Period* (New Haven and London: Yale University Press, 1992).

Hull, D. 'The Archaeology of Monasticism: Landscape, Politics, and Social Organisation in Late Antique Syria', unpublished PhD dissertation, University of York, 2006.

Hull, D. 'A Spatial and Morphological Analysis of Monastic Sites in the Northern Limestone Massif, Syria', *Levant*, 40.1 (2008), 89–113.

Jensen, R. 'Housing Pilgrims in Late Antiquity: Patrons, Buildings and Services' in A. Collar and T. M. Kristensen (eds.), *Pilgrimage and Economy in the Ancient Mediterranean* (Leiden: Brill, 2020) pp. 140–59.

Jones, A. H. M. *The Later Roman Empire, 284–602. A Social, Economic and Administrative Survey*, 3 vols (Oxford: Blackwell, 1964).

Klein, K. 'Do Good in Thy Good Pleasure unto Zion: The Patronage of Aelia Eudokia in Jerusalem' in L. Theis, M. Mullet, M. Grünbart, with G. Fingarova and M. Savage (eds.) *Female Founders in Byzantium and Beyond* (Vienna, Cologne, and Weimar: Böhlau Verlag, 2014), pp. 85–95.

Kosinski, R. 'The Emperor Zeno's Church Donations' in E. Dabrowy, M. Dzielskiej, M. Salamona, and S. Sprawskiego (eds.), *Ksiega Pamiatkowa ku Czci Profesora Józefa Wolskiego w Setna Rocnice Urodzin* (Kraków: Hortus Historia, 2010), pp. 635–49.

Kouki, P. 'The Hinterland of a City: Rural Settlement and Land Use in the Petra Region from the Nabataean-Roman to the Early Islamic Period', unpublished PhD dissertation, University of Helsinki, 2012.

Krause, M. 'Apa Abraham von Hermonthis. Ein oberägyptische Bischof um 600', unpublished PhD dissertation, Humboldt University, Berlin, 1956.

Krautheimer, R. *Early Christian and Byzantine Architecture* (New Haven: Yale University Press, 1986).

Krawiec, R. *Shenoute and the Women of the White Monastery: Egyptian Monasticism in Late Antiquity* (Oxford: Oxford University Press, 2002).

Kristensen, T. M. and Friese, W. (eds.) *Excavating Pilgrimage. Archaeological Approaches to Sacred Travel and Movement in the Ancient World* (Abingdon and New York: Routledge, 2017).

Layton, B. 'Social Structure and Food Consumption in an Early Christian Monastery: The Evidence of Shenoute's Canons and the White Monastery Federation A.D. 385–465', *Le Muséon*, 115 (2002), 25–55.

Layton, B. *The Canons of Our Fathers: The Monastic Rules of Shenoute* (Oxford: Oxford University Press, 2014).

Luff, R. M. 'Monastic Diet in Late Antique Egypt: Zooarchaeological Finds from Kom el-Nana and Tell el-Amarna, Middle Egypt', *Environmental Archaeology*, 12.2 (2007), 161–74.

Makowiecka, E. 'Monastic Pilgrimage Centre at Kellia in Egypt' in E. Dassmann and J. Engemann (eds.), *Akten des XII. Internationalen Kongresses für christliche Archäologie* (Münster: Aschendorffsche, 1995), pp. 1002–15.

Malik, J. 'Une inscription et une lettre en Araméen Christo-Palestinien', *Revue Biblique*, 60 (1953), 526–39.

Markiewicz, T. 'Five Coptic Ostraca from Deir el-Bahri', *The Journal of Juristic Papyrology*, 29 (1999), 79–84.

Markiewicz, T. 'New Fragmentary Coptic Texts from Deir el-Bahri', *The Journal of Juristic Papyrology*, 30 (2000), 67–70.

Marthot, I. 'Un village égyptien et sa campagne: étude de la microtoponymie du territoire d'Aphroditê (VIe–VIIIe s.)', unpublished PhD thesis, École Pratique des Hautes Études, Paris, 2013.

Mazza, R. *L'archivio degli Apioni: terra, lavoro e proprietà senatoria nell'Egitto tardo antico* (Bari: Edipuglia, 2001).

Milewski, I. 'Money in the Apophthegmata Patrum', *Studia Ceranea*, 9 (2019), 603–14.

Mossakowska, M. 'Les huiles utilisées pour l'éclairage en Égypte (d'après les papyrus grecs)', *Journal of Juristic Papyrology*, 24 (1994), 109–31.

Mossakowska-Gaubert, M. (ed.) *Egyptian Textiles and Their Production: 'Word' and 'Object'* (Lincoln, NE: Zea E-Books, 2020).

Obłuski, A. *The Monasteries and Monks of Nubia* (Warsaw: Raphael Taubenschlag Foundation, 2019).

O'Connell, E. R. 'Ostraca from Western Thebes. Provenance and History of the Collections of the Metropolitan Museum of Art and at Columbia University', *Bulletin of the American Society of Papyrologists*, 43 (2006), 113–37.

O'Connell, E. R. 'R. Campbell Thompson's 1913/14 Excavation of Wadi Sarga and Other Sites', *British Museum Studies in Ancient Egypt and Sudan*, 21 (2014), 121–92.

O'Connell, E. R. 'Wadi Sarga at the British Museum: Sources for Study (with Annotated Bibliography)' in P. Buzi, A. Complani, and F. Contardi (eds.), *Coptic Society, Literature and Religion from Late Antiquity to Modern Times. Proceedings of the Tenth International Congress of Coptic Studies, Rome, September 17th–22nd, 2012* (Leuven: Peeters, 2016), pp. 1547–66.

Orlandi, T. 'The Library of the Monastery of Saint Shenoute at Atripe' in A. Egberts, B. P. Muhs, and J. van der Vliet (eds.), *Perspectives on Panopolis: An Egyptian Town from Alexander the Great to the Arab Conquest. Acts from an International Symposium Held in Leiden on 16, 17, and 18 December 1998* (Leiden: Brill, 2002), pp. 211–31.

Papaconstantinou, A. 'The Cult of Saints: A Haven of Continuity in a Changing World?' in R. S. Bagnall (ed.), *Egypt in the Byzantine World 300–700* (Cambridge: Cambridge University Press, 2007), pp. 350–67.

Papaconstantinou, A. 'A Preliminary Prosopography of Moneylenders in Early Islamic Egypt and South Palestine', *Travaux et Mémoires*, 16 [=*Mélanges Cécile Morrisson*] (2010), 631–48.

Papaconstantinou, A. 'Donation and Negotiation: Formal Gifts to Religious Institutions in Late Antiquity' in J.-M. Spieser and É. Yota (eds.), *Donations et donateurs dans la société et l'art byzantins* (Paris: Desclée de Brouwer, 2012), pp. 75–93.

Pietri, L. and Rondeau, M.-J. (eds.) *Vie de Consantin* (Paris: Éditions du Cerf, 2013).

Politis, K. 'The Monastery of Aghios Lot at Deir 'Ain 'Abata in Jordan' in F. Daim and J. Drauschke (eds.), *Byzanz – das Römerreich im Mittelalter* (Mainz: Schnell & Steiner, 2011), pp. 155–80.

Rathbone, D. *Economic Rationalism and Rural Society in Third-Century A.D. Egypt: The Heroninos Archive and the Appianus Estate* (Cambridge: Cambridge University Press, 1991).

Reynolds, D. 'Monasticism in Early Islamic Palestine: Contours of Debate' in R. G. Hoyland (ed.), *The Late Antique World of Early Islam: Muslims among Christians and Jews in the East Mediterranean* (Princeton: Darwin Press, 2015), pp. 339–91.

Rielly, K., and Beech, M. 'The Bird Bones' in K. D. Politis (ed.) *Sanctuary of Lot at Deir Ain Abata in Jordan – Excavations 1988–2003* (Amman: Jordan Distribution Agency, 2012), pp. 503–9.

Robinson, D. 'Shenoute's Feast: Monastic Ideology, Lay Piety, and the Discourse of Food in Late Antiquity', *Journal of Early Christian Studies*, 25.4 (2017), 581–604.

Robinson, D. *Food, Virtue, and the Shaping of Early Christianity* (Cambridge: Cambridge University Press, 2021).

Rosenthal-Heginbottom, R. 'Pilgrim Mementoes from the Holy Land: Production, Iconography, Use, and Distribution', *Actual Problems of Theory and History of Art*, 7 (2017), 241–55.

Ruffini, G. *Social Networks in Byzantine Egypt* (Cambridge: Cambridge University Press, 2008).

Sarris, P. *Economy and Society in the Age of Justinian* (Cambridge: Cambridge University Press, 2006).

Schachner, L. A. 'Economic Production in the Monasteries of Egypt and Oriens, AD 320–800', unpublished PhD dissertation, University of Oxford, 2005.

Schroeder, C. T. *Children and Family in Late Antique Egyptian Monasticism* (Cambridge: Cambridge University Press, 2020).

Shamir, O. 'Tunics from Kasr al-Yahud' in L. Cleland (ed.), *The Clothed Body in the Ancient World* (Oxford: Oxbow Books, 2005), pp. 162–8.

Shamir, O. 'Egyptian and Nubian Textiles from Qasr el-Yahud, 9th Century AD' in A. De Moor, C. Fluck, and P. Linscheid (eds.), *Textiles, Tools, and Techniques of the 1st Millennium AD from Egypt and Neighbouring Countries, Proceedings of the 8th Conference of the Research Group 'Textiles from the Nile Valley' (4–6 October 2013, Antwerp)* (Tielt: Lannoo, 2015), pp. 48–60.

Shamir, O. 'Cotton Textiles from the Byzantine Period to the Medieval Period in Ancient Palestine', *Revue d'ethnoécologie [en ligne]*, 15 (2019).

Sheridan, M. 'The Development of the Concept of Poverty from Athanasius to Cassius' in I. Jonveaux, T. Quartier, B. Sawicki, and P. Trianni (eds.), *Monasticism and Economy: Rediscovering an Approach to Work and Poverty* (Rome: Studia Anselmiana, 2019), pp. 35–45.

Sigl, J. 'Pits with Cross-Bars – Investigations on Loom Remains from Coptic Egypt' in K. Endreffy and A. Gulyás (eds.), *Studia Aegyptiaca XVIII. Proceedings of the Fourth Central European Conference of Young Egyptologists* (Budapest: NKTH, 2007), pp. 357–72.

Sigl, J. 'Weaving Copts in Amarna: Further Studies on Coptic Loompits in the Northern Tombs of Tell el-Amarna', *Studien zur Altägyptischen Kultur*, 40 (2011), 357–86.

Smith, W. *Archaeobotanical Investigations of Agriculture at Late Antique Kom el-Nana (Tell el-Amarna)* (London: Egypt Exploration Society, 2003).

Studer, J. 'Archaeozoology of Jabal Harun' in Z. T. Fiema, J. Frösén, and M. Holappa (eds.), *Petra: The Mountain of Aaron II. The Nabataean Sanctuary and the Byzantine Monastery* (Helsinki: Societas Scientiarum Fennica, 2016), pp. 417–66.

Taxel, I. 'Rural Monasticism at the Foothills of Southern Samaria and Judaea in the Byzantine Period: Asceticism, Agriculture, and Pilgrimage', *Bulletin of the Anglo-Israel Archaeological Society*, 26 (2008), 57–73.

Taxel, I. *Khirbet es-Suyyagh: A Byzantine Monastery in the Judaean Shephelah* (Tel Aviv: Emery and Claire Yass Publications in Archaeology, 2009).

Taxel, I. 'Reassessing the Monastic Phase of Khirbet es-Suyyagh: On the Conversion of Farmsteads into Monasteries in Byzantine Palestine' in O. Peleg-Barkat, J. Ashkenazi, U. Leibner, M. Aviam, and R. Talgam (eds.), *Between Sea and Desert: On Kings, Nomads, Cities and Monks. Essays in Honor of Joseph Patrich* (Jerusalem: Kinneret Academic College and Ostracon, 2019), pp. 181–94.

Timbie, J. A. 'Once More into the Desert of Apa Shenoute: Further Thoughts on BN 68' in G. Gabra and H. N. Takla (eds.), *Christianity and Monasticism in Upper Egypt* (Cairo and New York: The American University in Cairo Press, 2008), pp. 169–78.

Van Haelst, J. *Catalogue des papyrus littéraires juifs et chrétiens* (Paris: Publications de la Sorbonne, 1976).

Van Haelst, J. 'Cinq textes provenant de Khirbet Mird', *Ancient Society*, 22 (1991), 297–317.

Van Neer, W., Wouters, W., Rutschowscaya, M., Delattre, A., Dixneuf, D., Desender, K., and Poblome, J. 'Salted Fish Products from the Coptic Monastery at Bawit, Egypt: Evidence from the Bones and Texts' in H. Hüster Plogmann (ed.), *The Role of Fish in Ancient Time. Proceedings of the 13th Meeting of the ICAZ Fish Remains Working Group. Basel/Augst, 4th–9th October 2005* (Rahden: Verlag Marie Leidorf, 2007), pp. 147–59.

Verhelst, S. 'Les fragments de Castellion (Kh. Mird) des évangiles de Marc et de Jean (P^{84})', *Le Muséon*, 116.1/2 (2003), 15–44.

Vikan, G. *Early Byzantine Pilgrimage Art* (Washington, DC: Dumbarton Oaks Research Library and Collection, 2001).

Vivian, T. and Athanassakis, A. N. *The Life of Antony by Athanasius of Alexandria: The Greek Life of Antony, the Coptic Life of Antony and an Encomium on Saint Antony by John Shmūn and a Letter to the Disciples of Antony by Serapion of Thmuis* (Kalamazoo: Cistercian Publications, 2003).

Ward, B. *The Sayings of the Desert Fathers. The Alphabetical Collection* (Kalamazoo: Cistercian Publications, 1975).

Wegner, J. 'The Bawit Monastery of Apa Apollo in the Hermopolite Nome and its Relations with the "World Outside"', *Journal of Juristic Papyrology*, 46 (2016), 147–274.

Whiting, M. 'Travel in the Late Antique Levant: A Study of Networks of Communication and Travel Infrastructure in the 4th–7th Centuries', unpublished PhD dissertation, University of Oxford, 2013.

Whiting, M. 'Asceticism and Hospitality as Patronage in the Late Antique Holy Land: The Examples of Paula and Melania the Elder' in L. Theis, M. Mullett, and M. Grünbart (eds.) *Female Founders in Byzantium and Beyond* (Vienna, Cologne, and Weimar: Böhlau Verlag, 2014), pp. 73–82.

Whiting, M. 'Monastery Hostels in the Byzantine Near East' in Z. T. Fiema, J. Frösén, and M. Holappa (eds.), *Petra: The Mountain of Aaron II. The Nabataean Sanctuary and the Byzantine Monastery* (Helsinki: Societas Scientiarum Fennica, 2016), pp. 108–13.

Whiting, M. 'The Architecture of Monastic Hospitality: Access and Spatial Hierarchies in Monasteries of Byzantine Palestine and Transjordan' in C. Fauchon-Claudon and M.-A. Le Guennec (eds.) *Les lieux de l'hospitalité*, special issue of *Topoi: Orient et Occident* (forthcoming).

Winlock, H. E. and Crum, W. E. *The Monastery of Epiphanius at Thebes. Part I: Archaeological Material; Part II: Literary Material* (New York: Metropolitan Museum of Art, 1926).

Wipszycka, E. *Moines et communautés monastiques en Égypte (IVe–VIIIe siècles)* (Warsaw: The Raphael Taubenschlag Foundation, 2009).

Wipszycka, E. 'Resources and Economic Activities of the Egyptian Monastic Communities (4th–8th Century)', *The Journal of Juristic Papyrology*, 41 (2011), 159–263.

Wipszycka, E. *The Alexandrian Church: People and Institutions* (Warsaw: The Raphael Taubenschlag Foundation, 2015).

Wipszycka, E. *The Second Gift of the Nile: Monks and Monasteries in Late Antique Egypt* (Warsaw: The Raphael Taubenschlag Foundation, 2018).

Wortley, J. *The Spiritual Meadow (Pratrum spirituale) by John Moschus* (Kalamazoo: Cistercian Publications, 1992).

Yasin, A. M. *Saints and Church Spaces in the Late Antique Mediterranean: Architecture, Cult and Community* (Cambridge: Cambridge University Press, 2009).

I.

The Monastic Estate

2 | Monastic Estates in Byzantine *Arabia* and *Palaestina* (Fourth–Ninth Centuries)

BASEMA HAMARNEH

The spread of monasticism in *Arabia* and in *Palaestina Tertia* is attested by written sources and pilgrim accounts from the second half of the fourth century onwards.[1] The introduction of monasticism played a key role in the slow evolutionary process of the Christianisation of local communities and the eradication of pagan cults. Hagiographic narratives reflect that reality by pointing to the part monks played in the religious transformations that took place in marginal lands of the late antique Roman Empire.[2] Significantly, early accounts outline that the shift from paganism to Christianity was a peaceful process.[3] This is mirrored in St Jerome's *Life* of the anchorite St Hilarion, which records the conversion of the pagan population of Elusa in the Negev.[4] Likewise, the sixth-century Greek hagiographic collection of Cyril of Scythopolis, the *Lives of the Monks of Palestine*,[5] shows the successful Christianisation of nomadic populations.[6] According to Cyril, St Euthymius used his charismatic appeal to attract a powerful Arab leader and his tribe to Roman service (*Vita Euthymii* 10).[7] Thus, the conversion of local populations to Christianity was associated with settlement, and led to religious stability with regular clergy and an *indigenous* episcopate in 427.[8] Some sources, however, point to the violence

---

[1] A few decades after the decision of Constantine to build the Church of the Holy Sepulchre in Jerusalem, several monasteries and churches were erected on sites connected with the events of the Old and New Testament. See Armstrong, 'Imperial Church Building'; Armstrong, 'Fifth and Sixth Century Church Buildings', pp. 17–20; Wilken, 'Byzantine Palestine', pp. 214–17 and 233–7; Wilkin, *The Land Called Holy*, pp. 178–81; Patrich, 'Church, State and the Transformation of Palestine', p. 470; Parker, 'The Byzantine Period', p. 136; Stemberger, *Jews and Christians*, pp. 82–5.
[2] Sozomen, 6.34 (Hartranft, *Ecclesiastical History*).
[3] Mostly as part of rhetoric on the victory of Christianity over other religious traditions. See also Frend, 'Monks'.
[4] The *Life* was written around 390; see Figueras, 'Monks and Monasteries', pp. 401–2; Perrone, 'Monasticism', p. 34; Weingarten, *The Saint's Saints*, pp. 106–14. On the Christianisation of *Palaestina Tertia*, see Markschies, 'Stadt und Land', pp. 285–90.
[5] Cyril's writings cover the period 405 to 560. On the textual sources see Dauphin, *Eucharistic Bread*, pp. 21–2; on the limitation of the textual sources see Blanke and Cromwell in Chapter 1.
[6] Binns, *Ascetics*, pp. 156–61; Wood, 'Monks of Palestine', pp. 302–11.
[7] Schwartz, *Kyrillos*, pp. 18–20 (Price, *Cyril of Scythopolis*, pp. 14–17).
[8] Epigraphy provides evidence of such a process in Zoara, where *Equites sagittarii indigenae* (units of cavalry archers recruited from local populations) were quartered; see Fisher et al., 'The Fourth

of monks, following the Theodosian anti-pagan measures, which put an end to the tolerance of public expressions of paganism.[9] A substantial period of time later, Sozomen recounts such events in *Palaestina Tertia*,[10] though he may refer to the actions of the monk Barsauma, who visited Petra between 419 and 422, where he attacked a pagan temple, as well as a Jewish synagogue in Areopolis (er-Rabba).[11] It may be argued that most of these texts were specifically written in order to prove the zeal and the efficiency of monks, and *lato sensu* justify the existence of monastic settlements near villages and towns,[12] thus providing a positive image of the total acceptance of the Christian doctrine by members of older religious identities as pagans and Jews. However, it should be kept in mind that the primary concern of the hagiographers was to create ideal models and demonstrate how deep monasticism had penetrated into the marginal rural societies.[13]

The earliest monastic settlements in *Arabia* and *Palaestina* were connected with ascetic monks who dwelt in solitude in natural cavities adapted to their use along the Jordan River Valley and the Dead Sea: Livias, the Lisan peninsula, Ainun-Saphsaphas, and the Uyun Mousa Valley around

---

Centuries', pp. 82–3. The town appears to have had its own bishop before 369, as may be deduced from the epitaph that mentions the burial of Bishop Apses (see Meimaris and Kritikakou-Nikolaropoulou, *Inscriptions*, pp. 123–4). There are also parallels with the Syriac *Life of Symeon the Sylite the Elder*, who encouraged Arabs to build 'churches among their tents'; see Wood, 'Miaphysite Mission', pp. 350–3.

[9] In June 391, Theodosius issued a law to Romanus, *comes* of Egypt, and to Evagrius, *Praefectus Augustalis*, repeating his previous commands that '[n]o person shall be granted the right to perform sacrifices; no person shall go around the temples; no person shall revere the shrines' (*Codex Theodosianus* 16.10.11; Frankfurter, 'Iconoclasm and Christianization', p. 138). The Syriac *Life of Ahudemmeh* describes vividly the individual application by holy men of the legislation, stating that Ahudemmeh 'destroyed the temples that were used for their sacrifices and burnt the idols they contained. Some Arab encampments resisted him and did not let him approach and did not listen to his preaching. He went away from them and prayed to God, and the stones to which they gave the names of gods were broken. God acted through him to perform signs and prodigies: he expelled demons, purified lepers, healed the sick and drove out the plague [that had been caused by divine] anger, but they [the Arabs] fled from him as from a persecutor' (after Wood, 'Miaphysite Mission', p. 352); Saradi, *The Byzantine City*, p. 356.

[10] See Sozomen 7.15; translation in Hartranft, *Ecclesiastical History*.

[11] For the account of the *Life of Barsauma* (British Library MSS Add. 14732 and 12174), see Nau, 'Deux épisodes'; Piccirillo, *L'Arabia Cristiana*, p. 71; Bowersock, 'Polytheism', pp. 3–9; Blànquez Pérez, 'Bar Sauma', pp. 38–41.

[12] In the *Lives* of Euthymius and Sabas, Cyril of Scythopolis mentions how monasteries were established within walking distance from villages; see Di Segni, 'Monastery, City and Village', pp. 27–8; also see Blanke and Cromwell in Chapter 1.

[13] See, in particular, Festugière, *Antioche* and *Les moines d'orient, culture ou sainteté*. Most of the hagiographic accounts regarding monks are set within the area of influence of the monastery or of the coenobium and mirror the diversity of local society, consisting mainly of peasants; see Patlagean, 'À Byzance', pp. 108–9.

Mt Nebo, mostly in and around Biblical sites.[14] This concentration contributed in creating a sort of religious hinterland prior to the evolution of coenobitic structures. Pilgrim records mention how monks regulated access to the *loca sancta* and offered hospitality, *eulogiai* (i.e., blessings, mostly bread), and religious services.[15] These early *nuclei* were barely anchored to any sort of economic structure or landscape exploitation, the anchorites being dependent on charitable offerings and on wild herbs for their daily diet.[16]

Coenobitic monasticism developed gradually as a natural response to the need to provide proper administration of the holy shrines to the east of the River Jordan, especially following the development of the practice of pilgrimage.[17] Monks contributed to the transformation of the landscape of the Holy Land through building activity and imperial patronage.[18] A similarly anthropogenic landscape was created in the provinces of *Arabia* and *Palaestina*, especially around the most venerated sanctuaries that attracted pilgrims, notably the baptism site at Ainun-Saphsaphas, the shrine of Moses at Mt Nebo, that of Aaron on Mt Hor near Petra, that of St Lot at Zoara, and that of St Elijas the Tishbit at Ajlun (Fig. 2.1). This compelled monks to assume additional duties: producing food and providing hospitality.[19]

---

[14] Some consisted of natural caves adapted for the purpose, either scattered or set within a radius of several hundred metres from the central church, others were isolated and independent hermitages; see Hamarneh, 'Il fenomeno rupestre', pp. 361–5.

[15] The pilgrim Egeria, escorted by monks, visited several holy destinations, such as the summit of Mt Nebo and Ainun-Saphsaphas on the site of *hortus sancti Johannis*. Before ascending Mt Nebo, Egeria recounts visiting monk cells in the valley from whom she received *eulogias*: 'Cum autem ingressi fuissimus ad eos, facta oratione cum ipsis, eulogias nobis dare dignati sunt, sicut habent consuetudinem dandi bis, quos humane suscipiunt'; Piccirillo, 'Pilgrims' Texts', pp. 73–4.

[16] Early monastic biographies underscore how food was provided through holy benevolence, as for example in the *Life* of John of Lycopolis where it is stressed that he 'did not plant anything in the earth'; see Rufus Aquileia, *Historia Monachorum*, cols 391–405. On the subject of providential food, see Dauphin, *Eucharistic Bread*, p. 24 and, on monastic diet, pp. 59–61; also Patrich, 'Daily Life', pp. 129–31, and Layton, 'Social Structure and Food Consumption', pp. 44–5. Being connected to the passions of the flesh (Kislinger, 'Christians of the East', p. 199), food consumption was regulated by strict rules. Ascetic monks had to fight carnal temptations by eating raw and cold foods and avoiding body-warming foodstuffs such as wine and meat (Rousselle, *Porneia*, pp. 172–5). Eating habits varied regionally across the empire, and there were clear differences between the coenobites and the solitary monks, who often relied on poorer food (Patlagean, *Pauvreté économique*, pp. 48–9); also see Robinson, *Food*, pp. 123–8; and Blanke and Cromwell in Chapter 1.

[17] Hamarneh, 'Between Hagiography and Archaeology', pp. 41–2.

[18] Dauphin, 'Mosaic Pavements'; Hunt, *Holy Land Pilgrimage*, pp. 221–48; Sivan, 'Pilgrimage'; Perrone, 'Monasticism in the Holy Land', pp. 35–6; Bar, 'Population', p. 315.

[19] Archaeological evidence shows how early monasteries were connected by roads and paths, notably the route from Livias to Esbous that connected the baptism site, Wadi el-Carit, the shrine of St Elijas, St Lot, and Mt Nebo. See also Klostermann, *Das Onomastikon*, p. 136, l. 5 and p. 12, l. 20, Egeria, *Itinerarium* X, 8; Piccirillo, 'La strada romana', p. 288. In the same way, several monasteries of the Judean Desert were served by the road from Jerusalem to Jericho.

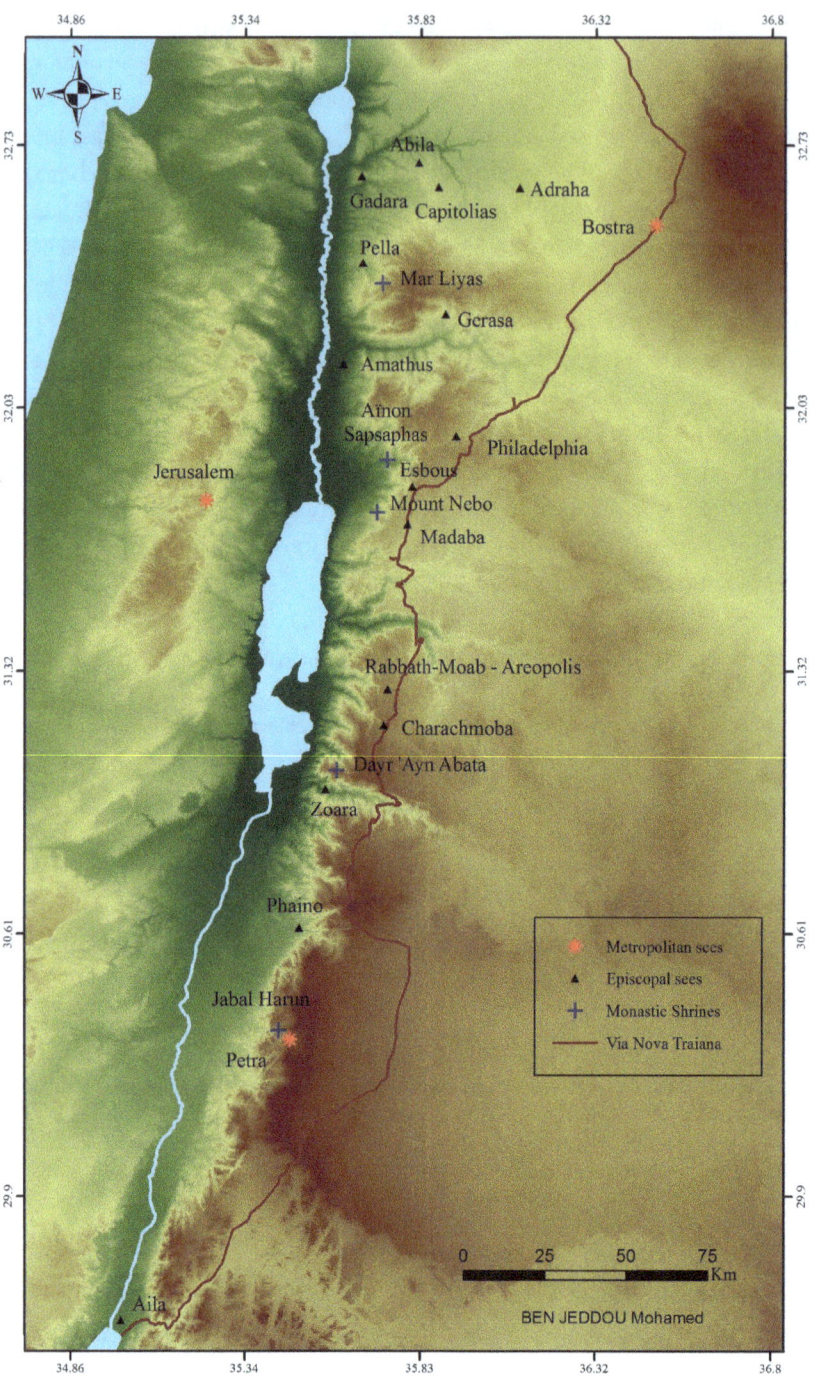

Fig. 2.1. Main coenobitic monasteries east of the River Jordan (by M. Ben Jeddou).

Monastic Territorial Organisation

Monasteries can be considered as units of a complex organic system based on sophisticated logistics to appropriate and provide a continuous supply of food and water, this in turn leading to the transformation of the natural landscape and the development of large coenobitic compounds.[20] Monastic institutions assimilated the common forms of economic life of the provinces to the east of the River Jordan, which were based primarily on agriculture.[21] From the second half of the fifth century, most of the monasteries evolved into well-run agricultural estates within the context of a wider rural economy.[22] Their integration into the social and economic landscape of *Arabia* and *Palaestina Tertia* is traceable from the growing number of monasteries, as revealed by archaeology especially on the outskirts of rural settlements.[23] In parallel, the fifth- and sixth-century monastic foundations in the Judean Desert and in the Negev were part of the process of settlement and population of marginal lands.[24]

Hagiographic accounts provide insights into the gradual formation of monastic property by mentioning how patronage, private donations – often through miraculous mediation – triggered the development of the monastic, built environment.[25] Cyril of Scythopolis provides several significant examples. In *Vita Euthymii*, he mentions the conversion and healing of Terebon the Saracen, whose uncle gave all his belongings to build and enlarge the monastery of Euthymius (*Vita Euthymii* 10).[26] Peter, another Saracen,

---

On this last aspect, see Wilkinson, 'Christian Pilgrims'; Hirschfeld, *The Judaean Desert Monasteries*, pp. 55–8, Tzaferis, 'Early Christian Monasticism', p. 318; Bar, 'Population', p. 315; Di Segni, 'Monastery, City and Village', pp. 27–8, n. 10. Some monasteries, as that of Martyrius, held a hostelry, a large garden, and a bathhouse; see Magen and Talgam, 'The Monastery of Martyrius', p. 93; for additional examples, see Patrich, 'Daily Life', p. 135, n. 39.

[20] See the discussion below.

[21] Some monks, before joining monastic life, came from villages and were familiar with agriculture. John Moschus in *Pratum spirituale* mentions an old monk of Choziba who used to work secretly by night in the field of a poor man of his village; see *Pratum* 24 (Wortley, *Spiritual Meadow*, p. 16). In another passage, Moschus refers to monks assisting in wheat-harvesting works in Scetis and how they were even hired as day-labourers by local peasants; see *Pratum* 183 (Wortley, *Spiritual Meadow*, pp. 152–3).

[22] The wide distribution of monasteries in *Palaestina* indicates that they should be regarded as a consequence of the general economic expansion and cannot be considered as *the cause* of local prosperity; see Bar, 'Population', p. 316.

[23] For the area to the west of the Jordan, see Hirschfeld, *The Judaean Desert Monasteries*, pp. 10–17; Tzaferis, 'Early Christian Monasticism', p. 318; on the agricultural *coenobia*, compare Avni, *The Byzantine–Islamic Transition*, p. 201. For an overview of the relation between villages and monasteries to the east of the Jordan, see Hamarneh, 'Monasteries in Rural Context' and below.

[24] Bowersock *et al.*, *Late Antiquity*, p. 584.

[25] Avi-Yonah, 'The Economics', p. 44; Neary, 'Constantinople', p. 148.

[26] Schwartz, *Kyrillos*, pp. 20–21 (Price, *Cyril of Scythopolis*, pp. 16–17).

contributed by paying workmen to build a great cistern in the garden, a bakery, three cells, and an oratory or a church, for the new Laura of Euthymius (*Vita Euthymii* 15).[27] In the *Life* of Sabas, Cyril recounts the purchase of monastic cells and lodgings in Jerusalem, and in Jericho, in one of the gardens that Sabas had bought for his monasteries (*Vita Sabae* 31).[28]

The account of the Piacenza pilgrim, around 570, mentions a young lady called Mary, whose husband had died on the very night of the wedding: 'She bore it with courage, and within a week she had set all his slaves free, and given away all his property to the poor and to monasteries.' The woman then disappeared from the city and was seen living as a wandering hermit 'in the desert across the Jordan'.[29]

In the first half of the sixth century, Sophronius, the abbot of the monastery of Theodosius, received a generous donation from the imperial official Mamas, his relative, which he used to expand the monastery fourfold and to acquire property and annual revenues (*Vita Theodosii* 5).[30] The Petra Papyrus Inv. 6a, dated to 573(?), registers a donation *propter mortem*, in which Obodianos son of Obodianus, lying ill, promised half of his belongings to the Holy House of the Saint High Priest Aaron.[31] Kerykos, son of Petros,

---

[27] Schwartz, *Kyrillos*, p. 24, l. 15 (Price, *Cyril of Scythopolis*, p. 20). Donations in kind were also very common. Cyril of Scythopolis records a woman who hired two weavers to make two curtains for the monasteries of Kastellion and the Cave (*Vita Sabae* 80: Schwartz, *Kyrillos*, p. 186, l. 5; Price, *Cyril of Scythopolis*, p. 194). Similarly, he recounts how visitors from Jerusalem gave thirty animal loads of wine, bread, grain, oil, honey, and cheese offerings to the Great Laura during a famine (*Vita Sabae* 58: Schwartz, *Kyrillos*, p. 160, l. 5; (Price, *Cyril of Scythopolis*, p. 169).

[28] Schwartz, *Kyrillos*, p. 240, l. 20 (Price, *Cyril of Scythopolis*, p. 267). The guesthouse at Jericho, with the gardens and water supply, in addition to the guesthouse in the Laura were purchased with the inheritance Sabas received from his mother Sophia (*Vita Sabae* 25: Schwartz, *Kyrillos*, p. 109, l. 10; Price, *Cyril of Scythopolis*, p. 118). Avi-Yonah, 'The Economics', p. 44.

[29] Wilkinson, *Jerusalem Pilgrims*, p. 144. Leontios of Damascus in the life of St Stephen the Sabait recounts of a noble woman and her two daughters who left all their belongings and lead wandering hermit lives near the mountains of Cutila. The story reflects the *Leitmotiv* of the renunciation to proper wealth and assets to embrace ascetic life, and how the esteem for such an ideal persisted into the eighth century; see *Life of St Stephen*, 50 (Pirone, *Vita*, pp. 247–51); Piccirillo, 'Dall'archeologia', p. 108.

[30] Mamas was a eunuch and served Emperor Anastasius first as *cubicularius* and later as *praepositus*; see Schwartz, *Kyrillos*, p. 240, l. 15 (Price, *Cyril of Scythopolis*, p. 267).

[31] For the Greek text and the commentary of the Papyrus see Frösén, 'Gift after Death', pp. 115–27. The term may not solely refer to the monastery on Jebel Harun but also to a 'house' belonging to the coenobitic structure set in the vicinity. Two epigraphic discoveries may contribute to this interpretation, the first being a lintel inscription discovered in Hesban (Esbous), which refers to the church as the 'saving house' or the 'house of salvation' in which the abbot George, mentioned in the text, served, these terms designating perhaps the church attached to the monastery (Di Segni, 'Varia Arabica', p. 585). A second case is that of the inscription of the monastery of Kaianus in Wadi Uyun Mousa, in which 'the house of the deacon' is mentioned. The latter may refer to the small monastic clusters belonging to the main community on Mt Nebo and located in Wadi Uyun Mousa (see Di Segni, 'The Greek Inscriptions', pp. 454–7), in

presbiteros and abbot of the monastery, represented the receiving entity.³² The donor set the condition that his mother, Thaaious, should be nourished and clothed as long as she lived.³³ The incomplete draft or annotation of a will in *P.Petra* R 86a also refers to an act of donation of a property to a hospice or hospital, whereas a vineyard in Zadakathon near Petra³⁴ and other assets were possibly left in favour of the monastery of Aaron.³⁵ Monasteries in fact ran charitable institutions: in Mishrefe (modern Mitzpe Shivta) near Sobaita (modern Shivta) there may have been located a desert inn, described in circa 570 by the anonymous Piacenza pilgrim as 'a fort, the guesthouse (*xenodochium*) of Saint George', situated twenty miles from Elusa to the south, 'which provides something of a refuge for passers-by and gives food for hermits'.³⁶ The Laura of Euthymius miraculously fed 400 Armenian pilgrims stopping there on their way to the Jordan (*Vita Euthimii* 17).³⁷ The coenobium of Theodosius was particularly devoted to social welfare activities. It comprised a hospital, a lunatic asylum, an old-age home, and a guesthouse for foreign brothers (*Vita Theodosii* 34),³⁸ a pilgrim hostel and a hospital in Jericho (*Vita Theodosii* 34–5).³⁹ On Palm Sunday, Assumption, and Dedication Feast, it fed the poor of the countryside and of the city (*Vita Theodosii* 38–9).⁴⁰ The monastery of St Hilarion near

---

analogy with the 'houses' of St Pachomius; see Veilleux, *Pachomian koinonia*, p. 147; Patrich, *Sabas*, p. 19.

³² The remaining part of the same donation was left to the *xenodochion* of the Saint and Triumphant martyr Cyricus in Petra; see Frösén and Miettunen, 'Aaron in Religious literature', p. 12. Frösén, 'The Petra Papyri', p. 22.

³³ After the woman's death an additional sum of ten *solidi* was to be given to the abbot. See Gagos and Frösén, 'Petra Papyri', p. 477.

³⁴ Property donation to shrines was a common practice in similar contexts in Egypt, as for example the Coptic document *P.KRU* 18, dated to the first third of the eighth century. The text mentions John, the steward of the shrine of Apa Phoibammon (Deir el-Bahri), selling parts of a house previously donated to the church; see Till, *Die koptischen Rechtsurkunden*, pp. 116–18. Other papyri, dated to the same period, such as *P.KRU* 107–9, mention donations of fields to the monastery; Till, *Die koptischen Rechtsurkunden*, pp. 190–2.

³⁵ The text is not fully conserved. Nonetheless it mentions several times the monastery of Aaron, being possibly the recipient of a substantial part of the donation, together with other pious institutions as a hospice or hospital named in the verso of the same papyrus; Arjava and Lehtinen, 'Draft', p. 104; also Gagos and Frösén, 'Petra Papyri', p. 481.

³⁶ Wilkinson, *Jerusalem Pilgrims*, p. 145; Figueras, 'Monks and Monasteries', p. 422. On monastic hostels, see Whiting, 'Monastery Hostels', pp. 109–10.

³⁷ Schwartz, *Kyrillos*, p. 27, l. 5 (Price, *Cyril of Scythopolis*, pp. 22–23); Stone, 'Holy Land', p. 95.

³⁸ Usener, *Der heilige Theodosius*, pp. 40–2.   ³⁹ Usener, *Der heilige Theodosius*, pp. 40–1.

⁴⁰ The monastery also provided 100 tables a day to beggars and those reduced to indigence in times of famine (*Vita Theodosii* 36: Usener, *Der heilige Theodosius*, p. 43); see the discussion in De Segni, 'Monk and Society', p. 34; Avi-Yonah, 'The Economics', p. 46; Neary, 'Constantinople', p. 147.

Gaza also ran a hostelry in the sixth century.[41] In the year 600, Pope Gregory the Great sent wool blankets for fifteen beds and a sum of money for the hostelry (*xeneion*) of the monastery of St Catherine in Sinai, which was built by an Isaurian.[42] In 603, he also, in a letter written to Abba Philippe, mentions a sum of money given by Abba Probus to build a guesthouse (*xenodochium*) in Jerusalem to which the Pope added 50 *solidi* of his own funds.[43]

In several cases, monasteries were involved directly in real property sales and rentals. Monastic land sales and registrations are mentioned in the Petra papyri. In the deed *P.Petra* III 25, dated 558/9, Philumenos, presbyter/hegumenos[44] of the church or monastery of Saint and Martyr Theodore of Ammatha, bought for his ecclesiastic institution, from a deacon, a hamlet (*epoikion*), or a property, then registered in the archive of the tax receivers (*hypodektai*) of Petra,[45] consisting of one and one-ninths *iugerum* (an area unit equivalent of 240 roman feet in length and 120 feet in width) of well-irrigated land together with agricultural labour (γεωργία),[46] located near the village of *Augustopolis*.[47] Part of that property is described in the document as *patrimonium* being subject probably, in this specific case, to the imperial treasury instead of the fiscal system of Petra.[48]

---

[41] Elter and Hassoune, 'Un complex de continuité', p. 200.

[42] Piccirillo, 'Gregorio Magno', p. 324. The donation is mentioned by the pilgrim Ludholfus de Suchem–Westfalia in the fourteenth century, who states that the generosity of the Pope allowed provision of hospitality to 400 monks (Deycks, *De itinere Terrae Sanctae*, p. 67).

[43] Piccirillo, 'Gregorio Magno', p. 325.

[44] The presbyter had a second title that is not possible to decipher, owing to the poor conservation of the papyrus. It is, however, evident that he performed a special function within his religious community that allowed him to conduct business transactions such as that described; see *P.Petra* V p. 80.

[45] Justinian, according to *Novella* 7.12, forbade monasteries from acquiring infertile land. In case of low profitability, the contract was to be void, and the abbot or hegumenos in charge of the transaction was personally liable for the loss; see also Kaplan, *Les propriétés*. The responsibility of tax collecting was laid on each city by its name, as in similar contexts in Late Antique Egypt; see Bagnall, *Egypt in Late Antiquity*, pp. 157–60.

[46] The reference to agricultural labour (γεωργία) appears also in *P.Petra* III 30 and *P.Petra* IV 48. It may also stand for a private long-term (emphyteutic) lease, as in *P.Petra* V 86r; see Koenen et al., 'Introduction', pp. 4 and especially 7–10.

[47] See *P.Petra* V pp. 79–88. Similar cases are documented in Egypt, such as *P.KRU* 113, which mentions the donation of tools and irrigation equipment to the monastery of Apa Phoibammon (Deir el-Bahri); see Till, *Die koptischen Rechtsurkunden*, p. 194.

[48] The latter were estates or lands whose revenues were allocated to the personal expenses of the rulers in compliance with Justinianic legislation. However, it should be kept in mind that the Imperial House was one of the largest landowners in *Palaestina*; see Jones, *The Later Roman Empire*, pp. 415–16.

According to Cyril of Scythopolis, the monastery of Theoctistus owned fields in common with the Laura of Euthymius. The monks worked these lands together until 485, when the fields were divided (*Vita Cyrilli* 7).[49] Sabas' monastery had a garden located farther away to the north and irrigated from a gorge (*Vita Ioanii Heychastesis* 26).[50] The monks of Marda had a garden located six miles away from the Laura, which they used to grow vegetables.[51] At the turn of the seventh century, Anthony of Choziba narrates how the monks of Choziba had gardens outside the walls of their monastery (*Vita Georgii Chozibitae* 6; *Miracula Beatae Virginis in Choziba* 4).[52] In the Passion of the Twenty Martyrs of Mar Saba (*Martyrium SS. XX patrum Sabaitarum* 28),[53] Saracens forced the brethren of the monastery of St Saba into the garden of their abbot.[54] Theodorus of Petra, in the *Vita Theodosii*, mentions a fenced wheat field and a village that provided the necessary supply of food produce to the monastery.[55]

Securing food for the monastic community, for the poor, and for farmers of nearby villages was one of the major concerns of eminent figures of the monastic community.[56] Sabas performed miracles during the drought and the plague of locusts (*Vita Sabae* 58),[57] and Euthymius prayed for rain during drought (*Vita Euthymii* 25).[58] These episodes clearly express the importance of agriculture in the daily life of the communities and the almost symbiotic relationship between village and monastery. Monks, however, regulated access to their land: in the written sources, there are even a few cases of disputes between the monks and shepherds over land use for pasture and grazing,[59] probably because monasteries also practised animal husbandry. John Moschus in *Pratum spirituale* mentions a monk

---

[49] Schwartz, *Kyrillos*, p. 226 (Price, *Cyril of Scythopolis*, p. 249).
[50] Schwartz, *Kyrillos*, p. 221, l. 10 (Price, *Cyril of Scythopolis*, p. 240).
[51] *Pratum* 158 (Wortley, *Spiritual Meadow*, p. 131).
[52] Used mainly to grow vegetables; see Di Segni, *Nel deserto*, pp. 100 and 128–9.
[53] Papadopoulos-Kerameus, *Sbornik*, p. 22; in the recent edition by Shoemaker, *Three Christian Martyrdoms*, p. 109, the term is incorrectly translated as the courtyard of the hegumenos's cell; see also Koenen et al., 'Introduction', p. 15.
[54] The term used, ζηρόκηπος, may indicate literally a dry garden or an unirrigated orchard that receives water from rain and runoff; see also below, note 155.
[55] *Vita Theodosii*; see Usener, *Der heilige Theodosius*, pp. 80 and 85; Di Segni, 'Monastery, City and Village', p. 30.
[56] It cannot be excluded that villagers were tenants of the monastery; see Di Segni, 'Monastery, City and Village', p. 30.
[57] Schwartz, *Kyrillos*, p. 160, l. 5 (Price, *Cyril of Scythopolis*, p. 169).
[58] Schwartz, *Kyrillos*, p. 39, l. 5 (Price, *Cyril of Scythopolis*, p. 35).
[59] Cyril of Scythopolis describes how the monks at the monastery of the Cave complained when flocks of goats and sheep were put to graze on the lands of the monastery; see *Vita Sabae* 59 (Schwartz, *Kyrillos*, p. 160, l. 15; Price, *Cyril of Scythopolis*, pp. 169–70).

engaged in pig farming at Phasaelis.[60] Contention and hostility are mentioned in the life of Porphyry of Gaza, whose servant Barochus was soundly beaten when he tried to collect dues from some farmers.[61] The landed estates of the church were the reason for disputes between the abbot of the monastery and the citizens of Emmaus–Nicopolis.[62]

After joining a community, monks could still own private property and probably had personal funds,[63] which they could use for private donations. Moschus states that an elder, living near the River Jordan, was visited twice by robbers who took away three gold pieces (*Pratum* 212).[64] Abba Auxanion of Pharan, lying ill in Jerusalem, sent back six gold pieces that he received from the hegumenos of the Laura of Saba, because he already possessed ten gold pieces himself (*Pratum* 42).[65]

Greek inscriptions discovered in an ecclesiastical context flesh out this aspect: for example, the sixth-century inscription found at the monastery of Khirbet ed-Deir, according to which two monks donated funds for the altar table of the church.[66] In the church of St George in Nessana, which was not a monastic church, a column was dedicated to the Saint, by George the hegumenos and his wife.[67] According to the Nessana papyri, Bishop George, prevented by illness from attending the festival of St Sergius,[68] made arrangements for a donation *in absentia* through the abbot of the monastery.[69]

In *Provincia Arabia*, mosaic inscriptions in Greek often refer to donations by monks either of monastic churches or of churches in urban and in rural settlements alike. Although there is a diversity of examples, the texts

---

[60] *Pratum* 92 (Wortley, *Spiritual Meadow*, p. 74).

[61] The farmers, reported to be pagan, did not accept the authority of the Christian landowners; *Vita Porphyrii* 22–23 (Hill, *The Life of Porphyry*, p. 29); Avi-Yonah, 'The Economics', p. 47.

[62] Cotelerius, *Ecclesiae Graecae* Monumenta, p. 411; Avi-Yonah, 'The Economics', p. 48.

[63] In *Vita Hilarionis*, dated to the fourth century, it is said that Saint Helarion was invited to visit the vineyard of a monk named Sabas, and after the saint had blessed the vineyard, it produced a triple yield, namely 300 jars of wine: *Vita Hilarionis ab Hieronymo* XVII, 7 (Bastiaensen and Smit, *Vita*; Schachner, 'Wine-Production', p. 158. A division of inheritance between three brothers in the Nessana papyri explicitly mentions parts of the property that were assigned to Victor the monk, one of the three heirs; see also *P. Ness.* III 31 (especially the commentary on p. 99).

[64] Wortley, *Spiritual Meadow*, pp. 190–1.

[65] Wortley, *Spiritual Meadow*, pp. 32–3; Avi-Yonah, 'The Economics', p. 47.

[66] Di Segni, 'The Inscriptions', p. 99.   [67] *P.Ness.* II 7.

[68] The church of Sergius and Bacchus was probably the most important in the town, to which people from numerous villages, towns, and cities, including Elusa and Birosaba, used to bring offerings on the feast of the Patron Saints. It was probably served by a community of monks; see *P.Ness.* III 79 (on this text, see also Caner in Chapter 10); Figueras, 'Monks and Monasteries', p. 425.

[69] *P.Ness.* III 50 is dated to the seventh century.

in which the hegumenos is listed *ex ufficio* (as in monastic churches) will not be considered here.[70]

The euergetism of hegumenoi and monks in rural, or at least not monastic, churches is part of a long tradition in *Arabia* and *Palaestina* as an act of public self-assertion, it may as well substantiate the significant bond between monks and the surrounding rural religious landscape. A hegumenos is attested in the pavement of the church of St John the Baptist in Khirbet es-Samra;[71] Iulianus the monk in the chapel of Priest John at Khirbet al-Mukhayyat;[72] and Cassiseus the monk in the inscription of the Upper Church of Kayanos in Wadi Uyun Mousa.[73] A monk is mentioned in the inscription of the chapel attached to the Church of the Apostles in Madaba dated to the first decade of the seventh century,[74] and three monks are listed in the Holy Sophia Church of Rihab dated to 605.[75] In Nessana, the dedicatory inscription of the monastic church of St Sergius mentions the donation by a rich family from Emesa in 609.[76] It may be argued that the offering was made when one of the family members, Sergius, became a monk.

In the church of St Cosma and Damianos in Khirbet Daria, the *chorepiscopos* (country-bishop) Kassiseos of the monastery of St Gellon in the seventh century is listed among the donors,[77] while on the mosaic pavement of the church of St Stephen at Umm er-Rasas dated to 756, a vignette set near the *presbiterium* displaying a monk from Phisga (Mt Nebo) may well indicate a private contribution.[78]

Some Nessana papyri, such as *P.Ness.* III 44–7 and 53 seem to deal with the private affairs of Patrick, the hegumenos of the monastery of St Sergius, who was a major land-owner in his own right and paid taxes on his private possessions.[79] Additional evidence is provided by the Nessana papyri referring to a plot of land as belonging to 'Victor, son of the Very

---

[70] As in Mt Nebo (Piccirillo, *Madaba*, p. 153), Deir Ain Abata and Mar Elijas.

[71] The church of St John the Baptist, or church number 79, built in 639, was situated within the boundaries of the village and was part of an ecclesiastical complex consisting of four churches; see Gatier, 'Exploration', p. 389; Hamarneh, *Topografia cristiana*, pp. 73–4.

[72] Piccirillo, *Madaba*, p. 192.

[73] Piccirillo, *Madaba*, pp. 209–10; Piccirillo, 'Monks and Monasteries'; Piccirillo, 'The Monastic Presence', 196–7.

[74] Piccirillo, *Madaba*, p. 106.   [75] Piccirillo, *Giordania settentrionale*, pp. 68–9.

[76] Figueras, 'Monks and Monasteries', p. 429; see also Caner in Chapter 10.

[77] The inscription is not published; see Karasneh, 'Khirbet Dariya', p. 30; Piccirillo, *L'Arabia cristiana*, p. 225; Hamarneh, *Topografia cristiana*, p. 287.

[78] Phisga is the biblical name of Mt Nebo; see Piccirillo, *Madaba*, pp. 288–9; Piccirillo, 'The Monastic Presence', pp. 195–6.

[79] *P.Ness.* II 6.

Honourable Sergius Aladias, monk'.[80] In all probability some monks in Nessana and elsewhere in the Negev conducted their own agricultural and commercial activities, either of importance or of a modest kind,[81] a situation that may also have been common to the east of the River Jordan.

In Shelomi, in Western Galilee, the Greek inscription in one of the rooms of a building enabled its identification with an 'ecclesiastical farm'. The use of the title hegumenos in the inscription suggests that this farm belonged to a monastery. The excavator, Claudine Dauphin, has argued that this was an emphyteutic property.[82] Tell Zira'a near Gadara may offer a similar case, since the recently discovered inscription mentions works carried out in 709 by the *deuterarios* and some monks.[83]

Agriculture was also practised by monks in *Arabia* and in *Palaestina*. Excavations and surveys have actually revealed in most cases that a monastery was found next to *every* village of Byzantine sites in Jordan.[84] These were mostly small or medium-sized monasteries with water cisterns and winepresses located on the outskirts of large or small villages and perfectly integrated into their topography, supporting the hypothesis that each village supported at least one monastery.[85] The main task of these monasteries, in addition to pastoral and assistance

---

[80] P.Ness. III 31; see also the churches or monasteries listed in P.Ness. III 90 and 91; Figueras, 'Monks and Monasteries', p. 430.

[81] Basket making and rope twining were among the occupations of early Byzantine monasteries, providing a supplementary source of income (see Hirschfeld, *The Judaean Desert Monasteries*, pp. 104–5). In the *Life* of Sabas (*Vita Sabae* 44), the monk Aphrodisius, obliged to penitential seclusion, for thirty years received palms each month from the *oikonomos* (for the term see below) and made or supplied over ninety woven baskets (Schwartz, *Kyrillos*, p. 135, l. 5; Price, *Cyril of Scythopolis*, p. 144). John Moschus recounts a story of a monk going to Alexandria to sell his handicraft; see *Pratum* 194 (Wortley, *Spiritual Meadow*, p. 169). Cordage and basketry were among the organic finds in the excavation of the monastery of Lot in Deir Ain Abata (Politis, 'Basketry') and in cells 3 and 4 in 'Ain Abu Mahmud (Patrich, 'Daily Life', p. 134, fig. 13).

[82] The inscription is dated to 736 of the Era of Tyre, hence 610 (Dauphin, 'A Byzantine Ecclesiastical Farm'). On the Shelomi ecclesiastical farm as an emphytheotic property, see Dauphin, 'Une propriété monastique', pp. 44–6; Dauphin and Kingsley, 'Ceramic Evidence', pp. 65–8.

[83] The *deuterarius* can be considered as second-in-command to the hegumenos, replacing him in case of absence or illness, and thus also fulfilling administrative tasks (as in *Vita Euthymii* 48: Schwartz, *Kyrillos*, p. 70, l. 13; Price, *Cyril of Scythopolis*, p. 67). For the inscription of Tell Zira'a, see Zerbini, 'The Area II Inscription'. The office of the *deuterarios*, according to Feissel, is mentioned in the Greek inscription n. 81 of the church in Khirbet es-Samra in *Provincia Arabia* (Gatier, 'Exploration', p. 390–1, n. 81; Feissel, *Chroniques*, p. 271, no. 864). A *deuterarius* is listed in the sixth-century inscription of the apse in the monastery of St Catherine in Sinai (Ševčenko, 'Sinai Monastery', p. 263, n. 7). See Festugière, *Les moines d'Orient 3,1*, p. 125, n. 157; Meimaris, *Sacred Names*, pp. 249–50; Patrich, *Sabas*, p. 17.

[84] See Hamarneh, 'Monasteries in Rural Context'.

[85] Similar cases are discussed in Ashkenazi and Aviam, 'Monasteries and Villages', pp. 122–3.

duties, was probably to administer church property, labour, produce and revenues, and possible re-investments in ecclesiastical buildings.[86]

The Arab authors of the Abbasid period describe an advanced stage of monastic development.[87] According to various historians, *coenobia* had extensive land and property, while some monks are reported to have maintained private possessions while residing in monasteries. Vivid images give life to monasticism in Egypt, Syria, and the middle Euphrates. Al-Waqidi (d. 822) in *Futuh Bilad esh-Sham* recounts a story involving a monk who had his own farm (*mazraa*) not far from his coenobium, located between Aleppo and Sir.[88] Abu al-Faraj al-Isfahani (d. 967) in *Kitab al-Aghani*,[89] the two geographers al-Bakri (*Mu'jam ma ist'jam*) and Yaqut al-Hmaoui (*Mu'jam al-Buldan*), and later in the fourteenth century al-Umari (*Masalik al-Absar*) devote long descriptions to monasteries and monks.[90] Most of the accounts do not focus on monasteries as Christian religious structures, but rather as places of affable and generous hospitality. Monks welcomed caliphs, princes, governors, and travellers with food, wine, and shelter for the night, and received generous compensations.[91] Several monasteries described by al-Isfahani, Yaqut, and later al-Umari, in Hira, along the Tigris and Euphrates rivers, Anatolia, Syria, and Egypt featured landed property, fruit trees, gardens, vineyards, and cultivated fields. Although east of the River Jordan is not included in these narratives, one may argue that this type of economic system was not only long lasting (harking back to Byzantine rule), but also common for the entire eastern Mediterranean basin.

---

[86] Villagers were in some cases (such as at Shelomi) tenants of the monastery (see Dauphin, 'Une propriété monastique', pp. 44–8; Dauphin and Kingsley, 'Ceramic Evidence', pp. 62–7). On rural monasticism in *Arabia* and *Palaestina Tertia*, see Hamarneh, 'Monasteries in Rural Context', pp. 282–3. A similar symbiotic relationship is detectible in Western Galilee. For examples and discussion, see Ashkenazi, 'Holy Man', pp. 754–5.

[87] The landscape was studded with monastic settlements that probably included facilities to welcome travellers and traders along the commercial routes. Several stories in Prophet Mohamed's biography mention encounters with a monk or monks; see Millar, 'Christian Monasticism'; Griffith, 'St. John of Damascus', p. 42. According to one of these stories, which refers to the *hanafiya*, Zayd Ibn 'Amr met a monk at Mayfa'a (Umm er-Rasas), who prophesied the advent of Mohamed in Mecca; see Griffith, 'Mayfa'ah', p. 51; Shahid, *Byzantium and the Arabs*, p. 189.

[88] Al-Waqidi, vol. 1, p. 331 (Nassau, *The Conquest of Syria*).

[89] Isfahani's general work on monasteries, the *Kitab al-Diyarat*, is known only from quotations by other authors. Some information on monasteries is included in his other work *Kitab al-Aghani*; see also Shahid, *Byzantium and the Arabs*, pp. 159–60.

[90] See Shahid, *Byzantium and the Arabs*, p. 157.

[91] On this specific aspect see Bowman, *Monastic Life*, pp. 154–60.

Admittedly, under Islamic rule the physical conditions of the monasteries in *Arabia* and in *Palaestina Tertia* varied. Some lost their importance and were abandoned, due to the decline in pilgrimage and patronage. According to Patrich, the number of active monasteries and hermitages decreased drastically by 72 per cent.[92] Others, instead, showed continuity, as witnessed by Leontius of Damascus in the life of St Stephan the Sabaite, dated to the ninth century, who mentions the monastery of al-Quweismeh near Philadelphia-Amman and hermit cells near the Dead Sea. The mosaic Greek inscriptions from the pavement of the monastery of the Theotokos in Ain al-Kanisah near Mt Nebo, dated to 762, provide further evidence for the continuity of the monastic tradition in the Umayyad period. The two texts mention members of the monastic and ascetic hierarchy such as Abraham who was both hegumenos and archimandrite of the whole desert, a monk, a stylite, and a recluse.[93]

Models of Management

Beginning with the examination of the model of management, one may note that the administration of monastic properties varied considerably depending on the importance and the spread of the possessions, on whether it was a large or small monastery, and finally on the origin and process of constitution of its fortune.

At an early stage, *coenobia* were probably small in size, as can be evinced indirectly by the fact that most financial matters were dealt with on the spot by the abbot. Hagiographic sources mention financial offerings that were received by the abbot himself in the coenobium of Choziba, in that of Theoctistus, and in that of Penthucla, near the River Jordan.[94] In Justinianic legislation that dealt with coenobitic monasteries, no specific mention is made of the *oikonomos*.[95] However, the office is listed in the lives of Euthymius (*Vita Euthymii* 39–48),[96] Cyriacus (*Vita Cyriacus* 6),[97] and Sabas (*Vita Sabae* 46).[98]

---

[92] According to *Commemoratorium de casis Dei*, the number of the monastic population of the Judean Desert was around 500; see Levy-Rubin and Kedar, 'A Spanish Source'; Patrich, 'Impact of the Muslim Conquest', pp. 212–13; Bowman, *Monastic Life*, pp. 117–25.

[93] Piccirillo, 'Le due iscrizioni', pp. 525–7; Di Segni, 'The Greek Inscriptions', pp. 448–50.

[94] *Vita Sabae* 9 (Schwartz, *Kyrillos*, p. 92, l. 20; Price, *Cyril of Scythopolis*, p. 101); *Pratum* 13 (Wortley, *Spiritual Meadow*, p. 11); Patrich, *Sabas*, p. 177.

[95] Granic, 'Die Rechtliche Stellung', p. 29. The *oikonomos* is mentioned in the case of a church; see *Codex Iustinianus I*, 3, 55, paragraph 2; Nov. 7, paragraph 12; Patrich, *Sabas*, p. 177.

[96] Schwartz, *Kyrillos*, p. 58, l. 24 and 69,10 (Price, *Cyril of Scythopolis*, pp. 55 and 66).

[97] Schwartz, *Kyrillos*, p. 226, l. 5 (Price, *Cyril of Scythopolis*, p. 249).

[98] Schwartz, *Kyrillos*, p. 137, l. 15 (Price, *Cyril of Scythopolis*, pp. 146–7).

The management of monastic possessions was probably divided into general and local administration. Heading general administration was the hegumenos or the *oikonomos*, who was in charge of supervising the local managers, as the superintendents residing in the estates.[99]

Inscriptions in churches that record donations emphasise the charitable disposition of members of the monastic elite. In *Arabia* and in *Palaestina*, the titles of hegumenos and *oikonomos* are often referred to as being responsible for building monastic churches,[100] although the office of the hegumenos/abbot seems to prevail. According to the lintel inscription of Hesban, George, the most God-fearing presbyter and abbot of the house of salvation, probably provided the necessary funds for the renovation of the church.[101]

In the monastery of Mt Nebo, several inscriptions reflect over time various phases of construction works within the monastic fabric. They refer to: Alexius, priest and abbot, in the sanctuary, or *presbyterium*;[102] Elia priest and hegumenos (abbot) in the Diaconicon-Baptistery dated to 530/1;[103] Martirius, priest and hegumenos, in the new baptistery of Mt Nebo dated to 597/8;[104] Martirius and Theodore, priest and hegumenos, the main donors of the chapel of the Theotokos in the seventh century;[105] Rabebos, priest and hegumenos, in the oriental wing; and 'our father', probably Abbot Procapis, in the funerary chapel on the slopes of the north terrace.[106] The dedicatory Greek inscription of the monastic church of St Lot at Deir Ain Abata, dating to 573, lists additionally the offices of the *epitropos* (manager of the estates) and the *oikonomos* (manager of finances).[107]

Special attention must be paid also to the office of the *oikonomos*, who had among his duties the superintendence of all the finances of the diocese, church, or monastery on behalf of the bishop of a diocese or of an individual ecclesiastical structure.[108] These duties may have included the administration of revenues of fields, vineyards, or any other property for a limited time, one year, or three at most; the economic surplus was possibly destined either for alms or for financing construction, decoration, or renovation

---

[99] Lefort, 'Rural Economy', pp. 293–5.
[100] See Di Segni, 'Epigraphic Documentation', pp. 149–52.
[101] Mattingly and Burgh, 'Lintel Inscription'; Di Segni, 'Varia Arabica', p. 585.
[102] Piccirillo, *Madaba*, p. 153; see also the contribution of Bianchi on Mt Nebo in Chapter 12.
[103] Piccirillo, *Madaba*, p. 157.   [104] Piccirillo, *Madaba*, p. 163.   [105] Piccirillo, *Madaba*, p. 165.
[106] Piccirillo, *Madaba*, pp. 170–2.
[107] The title may designate the duties of the management of ecclesiastical property; see Meimaris and Kritikakou-Nikolaropoulou, 'The Greek Inscriptions', pp. 395–7. The monastery of Lot probably had important income and landed property that required the involvement of both estate and finance managers.
[108] See Meimaris, *Sacred Names*, pp. 256–9; Di Segni, 'The Greek Inscriptions', p. 453.

works.[109] The Greek inscriptions found in churches to the east of the River Jordan attest to the involvement of the *oikonomos* in numerous building projects. For the current purposes, only monastic contexts will be considered to trace specific administrative and management functions of the office. The inscription of the monastery of Kayanos at Uyun Mousa remembers the zeal of Salaman, who held the office of deacon and *oikonomos* and probably took charge of the financial matters for the construction of the monastic church, which was under the influence of the monastery of Mt Nebo.[110] In 661, the martyrion of St Sergius in Rihab was mosaicked during the stewardship of the presbyter Stephen;[111] in 663, the chapel of martyr Philemon in Rihab was renovated by Stephanos, deacon and abbot.[112] A similar context can be evinced by the mention of Stefanos the *oikonomos* who donated a chancel screen to the monastic church of Umm er-Rasas located next to the stylite tower.[113] The office is also attested in 717/18, as Tsobeos, priest and *oikonomos*, was engaged in the renovation of the monastic church of al-Quweismeh (dioceses of Philadelphia-Amman).[114] Similar administrative functions were probably assigned to the *paramonarius*, typically a cleric and an overseer of an estate.[115] This office is assigned to three monks mentioned in the dedicatory inscription of the church of Holy Sofia in Rihab.[116]

The Monastic Estates According to Archaeology

The distribution of monastic sites shows an advanced exploitation of the agrarian landscape, though it is important to differentiate the areas according to their agrogeological potential (such as soil composition and altitude) and the impact of environmental factors such as drought or insufficient rainfall. Admittedly, reconstructing the impact and the extension of monastic land possessions is not easy, neither territorially nor

---

[109] In some cases, a right was established to appoint an administrator (*oikonomos* or *paramonarios*) by testors for the church or monastery endowed, according to the type of charitable activity, particularly if the endowment was a property or 'in coin'; see *Corpus Inscriptionum Judaicarum* nos. 1, 3, 45 (Frey, *Corpus*); Di Segni, 'The Greek Inscriptions', p. 460, n. 50.
[110] Di Segni, 'The Greek Inscriptions', p. 453.
[111] Feissel and Gatier, 'Bulletin Epigraphique', no. 544.
[112] Feissel and Gatier, 'Bulletin Epigraphique', no. 544.   [113] Piccirillo, *Madaba*, p. 303.
[114] Piccirillo, 'Quweismeh', p. 334.   [115] Meimaris, *Sacred Names*, pp. 259–60.
[116] Piccirillo, *Giordania settentrionale*, pp. 68–9.

chronologically.[117] Some areas that have not undergone extensive urbanisation in recent decades still show traces of individual plots of land associated with adjacent monastic settlements, but this association becomes difficult to prove if monasteries developed on the edges of rural villages. In most cases, agricultural plots were ordinarily located within or near the monasteries, as evidenced by surveys,[118] or set some distance away, the latter being most probably dependent upon the system of private donations or purchase and may be deduced solely from literary sources. In this regard, Cyril of Scythopolis narrates that the monastery of Theoctistus in the Judean Desert owned fields approximately five kilometres away, near the monastery of Euthymius (*Vita Cyrilli* 7), and the Petra papyri deal with land given to monasteries located in villages in *Palaestina Tertia*.

Surveys and excavations in *Palaestina* have yielded some good examples of land exploitation systems, including Khirbet ed-Deir in the Judean Desert, where cultivated plots were identified in the adjacent *wadi* bed, some of which were delimited by a retaining wall.[119] Reliance on terraced field cultivation, as in the monastery of Deir Qal'a in western Samaria,[120] was more frequent. The remains of a similar agricultural system were also discovered on the slopes around the monastery of Deir Ain Abata on the Jordanian bank of the Dead Sea,[121] near the monasteries at El-Qasrein,[122] at Khirbet Siyar al-Ghanam ('the Shepherds Field') outside of Bethlehem,[123] and at Khan el-Ahmar in the Judean Desert. In the latter monastery, stone walls surrounded two of the plots that have been identified as gardens.[124]

Although in *Arabia* and *Palaestina Tertia* extensive investigations and surveys were limited to a few sites, the available information allows one to recognise a common pattern roughly corresponding to what has been observed west of the River Jordan. At Umm er-Rasas, small, walled land plots extend near the monastic complex built in the proximity of the stylite tower (Fig. 2.2). An analogous distribution may be observed in the northeastern *wadi*, where plots are organised around two small monasteries

---

[117] The common run-off cultivation system, which is well-documented in the area, has a long employment history, though modern structures seem to be poorer than the ancient ones; see Lavento et al., 'Runoff Cultivations', p. 225.
[118] For Israel, see the extensive survey in Hirschfeld, *The Judaean Desert Monasteries*, p. 200.
[119] For a detailed description, see Hirschfeld, *Khirbet Ed-Deir*, pp. 91–4.
[120] Hirschfeld, 'Deir Qal'a', pp. 158–63.   [121] Politis, 'Excavations', p. 228.
[122] Hirschfeld, 'List of the Byzantine Monasteries', p. 44.   [123] Corbo, *Gli scavi*, pp. 254 5.
[124] Hirschfeld, 'Euthymius', p. 359.

Fig. 2.2. The monastic complex near the stylite tower of Umm er-Rasas (courtesy APAAME, photograph by D. L. Kennedy).

provided with a fenced area, parallel walls, cisterns, and winepresses.[125] Terracing predominates also around Mt Nebo,[126] but this was not the sole agriculturally exploited area; in fact, it cannot be excluded that the monastery relied on the farming of land in the fertile *wadi* bed of Uyun Mousa (Fig. 2.3).[127] This allows one to suggest that Abbot Rabebos, who is mentioned in the inscription of the Lower Church of Kayanos,[128] could have been the same person recorded in the inscription of the small funerary chapel in the oriental wing of Mt Nebo monastery.[129] Likewise, the monastery of Ain Qattara, on the southern slopes of the *wadi* towards the hot springs of Hamamat Ma'in, was provided with a cistern and other elements

---

[125] Bujard, *Kastron Mefaa*, pp. 114–15. The close proximity of the rural settlement of Umm er-Rasas prevents determination of the exact extent of monastic landed property, as compared to that of individual villagers and common village land. Aerial photograph mapping around Umm er-Rasas shows that small plots were cultivated at a distance of 500 m from the site, medium sized plots at 700 m, large plots at 1 km, and very large plots at 2 km. At a general level this can be considered as an indication of the intensification of land use and may also hint to the concentration of landed properties into fewer hands, either ecclesiastic or lay.

[126] Saller, *Memorial of Moses*, pp. 197–9.

[127] Small monasteries are located at Ain Jammaleh, Ain Judedideh, Ain el-Kanisah, and the monastery of Kayanos. To the south and to the south-west of the monastery of Kayanos, two other small monasteries can still be seen with areas probably used for vineyards; see Piccirillo, *Madaba*, pp. 201–2 and 205–16. A monastery in Wadi 'Afrit must also be added, for which see Piccirillo, 'Campagna', pp. 350–8.

[128] Piccirillo, *Madaba*, p. 213. [129] Piccirillo, *Madaba*, pp. 169–70. See also Bianchi, Chapter 12.

Fig 2.3. Valley of Uyun Mousa (photograph by D. Bianchi).

compatible with terrace agriculture, as well as a cistern and an area delimited by a wall that may have served as a vegetable garden.[130]

In Jebel Harun, near Petra, extensive *wadi* agriculture was practised some distance away from the monastery (Fig. 2.4).[131] The survey around Jebel Harun yielded evidence, about four kilometres south-west of Petra, of water run-off harvesting systems to the west, which may have been used in earlier epochs.[132] Archaeological remains showed structures related to run-off farming, a method based on a system of dams in the *wadis* and terrace walls on hillsides to collect rainwater and direct it into the small field plots on the lower slopes and in *wadi* beds.[133] This integrated, complex cultivation system, which made use of several tributary *wadis*, may initially have been part of a single estate dated to the Nabatean period, either royal or temple property.[134] It cannot be excluded that the existent field system was later

---

[130] The monastery was identified by Piccirillo, but has not been excavated to date; see Piccirilo, *Madaba*, pp. 248–9. A fenced garden is also reported as part of the monastery of Martyrius (Khirbet el-Murassas) in the Judean Desert; Magen and Talgam, 'Monastery of Martyrius', p. 93.

[131] Lavento and Huotari, 'Water Management', p. 103.

[132] Lavento et al., 'Ancient Water Management', pp. 166–7; Lavento et al., 'Terrace Cultivation', p. 148.

[133] Mayerson, 'Ancient Agricultural Regime', pp. 231–49; Kouki, 'Production Sites', p. 247–8.

[134] Frösén et al., 'Jabal Harun Project Report', pp. 498–9; Lavento et al., 'Runoff Cultivations', pp. 219–24.

Fig. 2.4. Aerial view of the monastery of Aaron near Petra (courtesy APAAME, photograph by R. Bewley).

exploited, totally or partially, by the monastery of Aaron (Jebel Harun), from the late fifth century, perhaps with reliance on less-demanding crops.[135]

Cereals were grown, mainly wheat and barley, pulses, vines, and olives.[136] The semi-arid regions produced barley, since it needed less rainfall and thus tolerated higher soil salinity levels.[137] Wheat is reported as being cultivated in Nessana,[138] and in the Madaba plain, since hagiographic accounts mention some wealthy landowners of the city providing the monasteries of Sabas with grain and pulses (*Vita Sabae* 45).[139] There was a constant supply of products between *Arabia* and *Palaestina*. Cyril of Scythopolis mentions an incident that occurred to a camel rider while transporting grain bought at Machaeros to the monastery in Wadi en-Nar in the Judean Desert (*Vita Sabae* 81).[140] In *Vita Gesasimi* 8, a Saracen driver of a camel caravan is forced to abandon the camels after crossing the

---

[135] Lavento *et al.*, 'Terrace Cultivation', p. 151.
[136] Zohary, *Plants of the Bible*, p. 41; Patlagean, *Pauvreté économique*, p. 38; on some aspects of wine production in monasteries see Schachner, 'Wine-Production', pp. 163–8.
[137] Wheat cultivation requires a minimum of 400 mm annual rainfall, whereas barley needs a minimum of 200 mm; see Zohary, *Plants of the Bible*, p. 26; Broshi, 'Diet of Palestine', p. 43.
[138] Mayerson, 'Ancient Agricultural Regime', pp. 227–30.
[139] Schwartz, *Kyrillos*, p. 136, l. 4 (Price, *Cyril of Scythopolis*, p. 145).
[140] Schwartz, *Kyrillos*, p. 186, l. 15 (Price, *Cyril of Scythopolis*, p. 195).

Jordan.[141] The Nessana papyri bear witness to the trade of other produce, such as dates with Egypt, operated through the mediation of a monk.[142] Dates were probably bought near the Dead Sea: Leontius of Damascus, in the *Life of St Stephen the Sabaite*, dated to the eighth century, mentions monks buying dates for the Laura from the Ghor (Dead Sea area).[143]

The analysis of plant remains in the excavations of the monastery of St Lot at Deir Ain Abata has shown the predominance of barley, both for human consumption and as fodder, owing to its ability to withstand drought and the saline conditions of the environment of Ghor es-Safi.[144] In marginal areas, there was therefore greater reliability on barley yields.[145] In a different region and under a milder climate, the cultivation of wheat and barley is attested archaeologically by the identification of seeds retrieved by soil-flotation in the ecclesiastical farm at Shelomi in Western Galilee.[146] In *Palaestina Tertia*, some monasteries may have grown wheat, though it was not the dominant crop in the region.[147] Barley seeds predominated in the Petra region in the Late Roman contexts at ez-Zantur,[148] and in the late Byzantine–early Islamic strata in the monastery on Jebel Harun.[149] Archaeological evidence for grain processing is limited to a few threshing floors in the Jebel Harun area and in the Udhruh region. These areas of bedrock were cleared of stones; some were partially walled and

---

[141] Di Segni, *Nel deserto*, pp. 71–2. The monks of the Judean Desert had to buy grain in *Arabia*, since the environmental conditions were not suitable for its cultivation; see Hirschfeld, *The Judaean Desert Monasteries*, pp. 82–5. Saracen camel-drivers are attested in the sources as carrying grain from *Arabia* to the Holy City and to the Great Laura of Sabas (*Vita Sabae* 45, 81: Schwartz, *Kyrillos*, p. 136, p. 187, l. 15; Price, *Cyril of Scythopolis*, pp. 145 and 195); Di Segni and Tsafrir, 'Ethnic Composition', p. 453.

[142] The quantity varied between one donkey load and ninety-three-and-a-half baskets. The payment included the price for the dates and cleaning. See *P.Ness.* III, p. 278, n. 91.

[143] See the *Life* of St Stephen, 36 (Pirone, *Vita*, p. 193). Dried and ground dates were added to barley flour to produce the so-called 'desert bread', then dried to extend preservation. Dembinska, 'Food Consumption', pp. 435–8; Tenhunen, 'The Macrofossil Analysis', pp. 461–2. Evidence for the importance of dates in the monastic diet can be evinced from the donation of palm trees and the fruit produce to the monastery of Apa Phoibammon in Egypt, mentioned in *P.KRU* 110–11, dated to the eighth century (Till, *Die koptischen Rechtsurkunden*, pp. 192–4).

[144] Politis, 'Excavations at Deir 'Ain 'Abata', p. 231; Hoppé, 'Plant Remains', pp. 518 and 521.

[145] Charles, 'Cereals', p. 25; Tenhunen, 'The Macrofossil Analysis', pp. 460–2.

[146] It belonged to a monastery in the Tyre region, but was worked by lay tenant farmers by emphyteotic contract; see Dauphin, 'A Byzantine Ecclesiastical Farm'; Kaplan, *Les hommes*, pp. 164–9.

[147] Villeneuve suggested that grain culture prevailed in south *Palaestina* (Villeneuve, 'L'économie rurale', pp. 121–2). Although in the semi-arid and arid zones of *Palaestina Tertia*, whose alluvial and brown soils are more appropriate for the growing of barley, which requires less water, wheat was probably cultivated in 'better' and more humid years.

[148] Karg, 'Pflanzenreste', p. 358.

[149] Tenhunen, 'FJHP 2000'; Lavento et al., 'Runoff Cultivations', pp. 225–6.

occasionally paved with flagstones. They are not easy to date; in some cases, their location close to ancient building remains suggests they might be contemporaneous.[150]

Various pulses, such as dried lentils and broad beans, chickpeas, and lupin were probably cultivated or purchased for consumption as they formed an important part of the diet.[151] Lentils and other unidentified legumes have been found in archaeobotanical samples from both ez-Zantur and Jebel Harun in Late Roman, Byzantine, and early Islamic strata.[152] Sabas' monasteries received pulses from wealthy landowners of Madaba (*Vita Sabae* 45). Arab manuscript number 692, kept in St Catherine's Monastery in Sinai, mentions an endowment by Emperor Justinian of wheat, barley, and lentils for the daily diet of the monks.[153] According to a mosaic inscription in a room in the monastery of Mar Elijas in Jordan, dated to 775/6, the room was decorated with mosaics thanks to the offering of a pulse merchant and his wife.[154]

The Petra papyri mention gardens owned by local families that probably grew fruit,[155] but no specific monastic garden has been detected so far east of the River Jordan. Archaeobotanical remains from ez-Zantur show that the cultivation of fig trees and date palms, in addition to vines and fruit trees, was common in the area of Petra.[156]

Olives represented one of the most important items in the Byzantine diet, as may be deduced from the archaeobotanical samples from Jebel Harun[157] and from olive stones from Mt Nebo. Crushed olive stones identified in Late Roman contexts at ez-Zantur were most likely pressing waste used as fuel.[158] There are no examples of olive presses in monastic contexts, except for an oil press in the village that developed to the south-east of the Theotokos Monastery at Khirbet adh-Dharih.[159] The remains of several olive presses dated to the Nabatean, and Byzantine–early Islamic periods, probably reused

---

[150] The lack of archaeological materials is a major dating obstacle (Abudnah, 'Settlement Patterns', p. 203).
[151] Dar, 'Food and Archaeology', p. 330.
[152] See Karg, 'Pflanzenreste', p. 358 and Tenhunen, 'FJHP 2000'.
[153] Mouton and Popescu-Belis, 'La fondation du monastère', p. 188, lines 64–6.
[154] On this inscription, see Di Segni, 'Varia Arabica', pp. 579–80.
[155] *P.Petra* II 17, *P.Petra* III 27, and *P. Ness.* III 31.20, 28, refer to a plantation of trees that did not require irrigation; see Koenen *et al.*, 'Introduction', p. 15; see also Tenhunen, 'The Macrofossil Analysis', pp. 462–4.
[156] Karg, 'Pflanzenreste', p. 358, the chart; Jacquat and Martinoli, 'Vitis vinifera', p. 29.
[157] For the archaeobotanical study, see Tenhunen, 'FJHP 2000'.
[158] Karg, 'Pflanzenreste', p. 357.
[159] Villeneuve and Al-Muheisen, 'Nouvelles recherches', pp. 1528–31; in a recent publication Villeneuve argued that Khirbet adh-Dharih was mainly an estate; Villeneuve, 'Dharih', pp. 323–7.

and rebuilt, have been found in Wadi Musa, as well as in the Khirbat an-Nawafla area,[160] but the latter cannot be directly linked to monastic settlements. Olive groves probably grew on the western slopes of Jebel ash-Shara, such as in the valley of Wadi Musa and southern Palestine, since taxes to be paid to the Arab conquerors in the seventh century by the city of Elusa were calculated in oil and wheat, and registered in Arabic on *P.Ness.* III 62–4.[161]

Archaeological traces of viticulture and winepresses associated with monasteries were recorded in twenty-three cases.[162] Although this data may suggest a well-rounded economy, it does not imply considerable demand, nor a direct connection to the open market.[163] The modest dimensions of these structures may indicate that monastic communities were self-sufficient in basic requirements, especially if we consider the importance of wine in liturgical celebrations. In *Palaestina*, the evidence points instead in some cases to larger wine production, as evidenced by the large dimension of the vats.[164] In fact, the construction of winepresses in monasteries is documented by Greek inscriptions, as in Tell Ashdod, in which a winepress (ἡ ληνός) was built from the foundations together with the monastery in 529 by the abbot.[165]

Conclusions

Papyri and other written sources combine to produce a picture of a flourishing economy, especially in the sixth and seventh centuries, when monasteries received endowments in land and real estate, but also

---

[160] 'Amr *et al.*, 'Wadi Musa', pp. 233–4.   [161] *P.Ness.* III pp. 227–33.
[162] See monasteries with winepress facilities listed in Hamarneh, 'Monasteries', 289–91.
[163] According to a recent study by Ashkenazi and Aviam, monasteries in *Palaestina* were integrated into the rural economy and were a central factor in oil and wine production, and thus contributed to the economic boom of the Levant in general and of Palestine in particular; see Ashkenazi and Aviam, 'Monasteries and Villages', p. 118; also Decker, *Tilling*, pp. 48–51; Avni, *The Byzantine-Islamic Transition*, p. 201. Further evidence for the church role in transport of goods is provided by the shipwreck of Yassı Ada, dated to 625/6, which contained mainly *amphorae* transporting wine and oil from the eastern Mediterranean. An inscription on a steelyard (*Georgiou presbuterou nauklerou*) may suggest that the ship's captain Georgios worked for the church, and the involvement of the church in the transport can also be evinced from numerous graffiti on the *amphorae*. Additional data are provided by several globular and cylindrical *amphorae* much like those on the ship that were brought to light in the excavation of a church complex at Samos that also had a winepress. See van Alfen, 'New Light', p. 212; Whittaker, 'Late Roman Trade', pp. 168–9.
[164] Hirschfeld, *The Judaean Desert Monasteries*, pp. 106–9 and 204–5.
[165] The sale of surplus wine was probably an important source of income for the monastery; see Schachner, 'Wine-Production', pp. 164–5; Di Segni, 'Tel Ashdod', pp. 32–3. In a similar way, the members of the monastery at el-Kufr in Hauran built a wine cellar (οἰνοθήκη) by the care of their abbot; see Ewing, 'Greek and Other Inscriptions', p. 276, n. 152; Di Segni, 'Tel Ashdod', p. 33; Di Segni, 'Late Antique Inscriptions', p. 303.

administered various charitable institutions that required adequate management and infrastructural organisation. Monastic communities experienced a degree of material comfort that is reflected in architecture, in mosaic pavements, and in liturgical furniture, all of which attest to an advanced level of local civic and ecclesiastical patronage. Land division in plots, terrace agriculture, and winepresses were uncovered on several sites and in monastic complexes, while hagiographic texts mention cereal crops and vegetables, which formed the basis of the monks' diet. Monastic estates developed greatly thanks to donations, and thus were well inserted into the local economy by either managing ecclesiastical land on an intensive scale or, more frequently, practising subsistence agriculture on small plots of land or on terraced fields according to a pattern that was probably common east and west of the River Jordan.

It seems difficult at this stage to determine if the monasteries of *Arabia* and *Palaestina* (to the east of the River Jordan) were actually engaged in surplus production to any degree. The largest number of small and medium-sized monasteries was located in the vicinity of rural settlements, reaching an almost symbiotic relationship with villages, probably owing to the monks' pastoral and assistance duties in local societies. This position gradually involved more sophisticated tasks, such as running or administering Church property, tenants, crops, and revenues. Over time, monasteries received endowments in land: the Nessana and Petra papyri mention property ownership and real estate as part of private and ecclesiastical affairs. Despite the abundance of laws and references in literary sources, the scale of monastic involvement in real property sales, rentals and produce in *Arabia* and *Palaestina Tertia* in the period from the sixth to the eighth century remains unknown, but can be considered widespread and well-rooted. Significant elements provided by the lives of monastic figures and mosaic Greek inscriptions indicate a great degree of contact between village societies and monks, either ascetic or monastic. These holy men,[166] the 'locus of the supernatural' and 'mediators between earth and heaven', assumed new functions in the society of their time by contributing to the creation of an alternative network of power, which was not grounded in urban-based structures, but was certainly far from immaterial.

---

[166] Brown, 'Rise and Function'; Brown, 'Saint as Exemplar'; Rapp, 'Reflections'; Di Segni, 'Monk and Society', p. 31; Ashkenazi, 'Holy Man', pp. 746–8.

Bibliography

Abudnah, F. 'Settlement Patterns and Military Organisation in the Region of Udhruh (Southern Jordan) in the Roman and Byzantine Periods I–II', unpublished PhD thesis, University of Newcastle upon Tyne, 2006.

'Amr, K., al-Momani, A., al-Nawafleh, N., and al-Nawafleh, S. 'Summary Results of the Archaeological Project at Khirbat an-Nawafla/Wadi Musa', *Annual of the Department of Archaeology of Jordan*, 44 (2000), 231–55.

Arjava, A., and Lehtinen, M. 'Draft or Annotations' in A. Arjava, J. Frösén, and J. Kaimio (eds.), *The Petra Papyri V* (Amman: American Center of Oriental Research, 2018), pp. 103–8.

Armstrong, G. T. 'Imperial Church Building in the Holy Land in the Fourth Century', *Biblical Archaeologist*, 30 (1967), 90–102.

Armstrong, G. T. 'Fifth and Sixth Century Church Buildings in the Holy Land', *The Greek Orthodox Theological Review*, 14.1 (1969), 17–30.

Ashkenazi, J. 'Holy Man Versus Monk. Village and Monastery in the Late Antique Levant: Between Hagiography and Archaeology', *Journal of the Economic and Social History of the Orient*, 57 (2014), 745–65.

Ashkenazi, J. and Aviam, M. 'Monasteries and Villages: Rural Economy and Religious Interdependency in Late Antique Palestine', *Vigiliae Christianae*, 71 (2017), 117–33.

Avi-Yonah, M. 'The Economics of Byzantine Palestine', *Israel Exploration Journal*, 8 (1958), 39–51.

Avni, G. *The Byzantine–Islamic Transition in Palestine. An Archaeological Approach* (Oxford: Oxford University Press, 2014).

Bagnall, R. S. *Egypt in Late Antiquity* (Princeton: Princeton University Press, 1993).

Bar, D. 'Population, Settlement and Economy in Late Roman and Byzantine Palestine (70–641 AD)', *Bulletin of the School of Oriental and African Studies*, 67.3 (2004), 307–20.

Bastiaensen, A. A. R. and Smit, J. W. *Vita di Martino; Vita di Ilarione; In memoria di Paola* (Milan: Mondadori, 1975).

Binns, J. *Ascetics and Ambassadors of Christ. The Monasteries of Palestine, 314–631* (Oxford: Oxford University Press, 1994).

Blànquez Pérez, C. 'Bar Sauma Versus Dushara: The Christianisation of Petra and its Surroundings' in A. de Francisco Heredero, D. Hernàndez de la Fuente, S. Torres Prieto (eds.), *New Perspectives on Late Antiquity in the Eastern Roman Empire* (Newcastle upon Tyne: Cambridge Scholars, 2014), pp. 32–47.

Bowersock, G. W. 'Polytheism and Monotheism in Arabia and the Three Palestines', *Dumbarton Oaks Papers*, 51 (1997), 1–10.

Bowersock, G. W., Brown, P., and Grabar, O. (eds.) *Late Antiquity: A Guide to the Postclassical World* (Cambridge, MA: Harvard University Press, 1999).

Bowman, B. *Christian Monastic Life in Early Islam* (Edinburgh: Edinburgh University Press, 2021).

Broshi, M. 'The Diet of Palestine in the Roman Period – Introductory Notes', *The Israel Museum News*, 5 (1986), 41–56.

Brown, P. 'The Rise and Function of the Holy Man in Late Antiquity', *Journal of Roman Studies*, 61 (1971), 80–101.

Brown, P. 'The Saint as Exemplar in Late Antiquity', *Representations*, 2 (1983), 1–25.

Bujard, J. *Kastron Mefaa, un bourg a l'époque byzantine travaux de la Mission archéologique de la fondation Max van Berchem a Umm al-Rasas, Jordanie (1988–1997)* (Fribourg: Fondation Max van Berchem, 2016).

Charles, M. P. 'Introductory Remarks on the Cereals', *Bulletin on Sumerian Agriculture*, 1 (1984), 17–31.

Corbo, V. *Gli scavi di Khirbet Siyar al-Ghanam (Campo dei pastori) e i monasteri dei dintorni* (Jerusalem: Franciscan Press 1995).

Cotelerius, J. B. *Ecclesiae Graecae Monumenta*, I (Paris: Luteciae Parisiorum, 1677).

Dar, S. 'Food and Archaeology in Romano-Byzantine Palestine' in J. Wilkins, D. Harvey, and M. Dobson (eds.), *Food in Antiquity* (Exeter: University of Exeter Press, 1995), pp. 326–35.

Dauphin, C. 'Mosaic Pavements as an Index of Prosperity and Fashion', *Levant*, 12 (1980), 112–34.

Dauphin, C. 'Une propriété monastique byzantine en Phénicie Maritime: le domaine agricole de Shelomi' in V. Kremmydas, C. A. Maltezou, and N. M. Panagiōtakēs (eds.), *Aphieroma ston Niko Svorono (Mélanges Nicolas Svoronos)* I (Rethymno: Panepistēmio tēs Krētēs, 1986), pp. 36–50.

Dauphin, C. 'A Byzantine Ecclesiastical Farm at Shelomi' in Y. Tsafrir (ed.), *Ancient Churches Revealed* (Jerusalem: Israel Exploration Society, 1993), pp. 43–8.

Dauphin, C. *Eucharistic Bread or Thistles? The Diet of the Desert Fathers in Late Antique Egypt and Palestine* (Lampeter: Trivium Publications, University of Wales, 2009).

Dauphin, C. and Kingsley, S. A. 'Ceramic Evidence for the Rise and Fall of a Late Antique Ecclesiastical Estate at Shelomi in Phoenicia Maritima' in C. G. Bottini, L. Di Segni, and L. D. Chrupcala (eds.), *One Land – Many Cultures. Archaeological Studies in Honour of S. Loffreda* (Jerusalem: Franciscan Printing Press, 2003), pp. 61–74.

Decker, M. *Tilling the Hateful Earth: Agricultural Production and Trade in the Late Antique East* (Oxford: Oxford University Press, 2009).

Dembinska, M. 'A Comparison of Food Consumption between Some Eastern and Western Monasteries in the 4th–12th Centuries', *Byzantion*, 55 (1985), 431–62.

Deycks, F. *Ludolphi, rectoris ecclesiae parochialis in Suchem De itinere Terrae sanctae liber* (Stuttgart: Litterarischer Verein, 1851).

Di Segni, L. *Nel deserto accanto ai fratelli. Vite di Gerasimo e di Giorgio di Choziba* (Magnano: Edizioni Qiqajon, 1991).

Di Segni, L. 'The Greek Inscriptions' in M. Piccirillo and E. Alliata (eds.), *Mount Nebo. New Archaeological Excavations 1967-1997* (Jerusalem: Stadium Biblicum Franciscanum, 1998), pp. 425-67.

Di Segni, L. 'Epigraphic Documentation on Building in the Provinces of *Palaestinae* and *Arabia* 4th-7th c.' in J. H. Humphrey (ed.), *The Roman and Byzantine Near East*, vol. 2: *Some Recent Archaeological Research*, special edition of *Journal of Roman Archaeology*, 31 (1999), 149-78.

Di Segni, L. 'The Inscriptions' in Y. Hirschfeld (ed.), *The Early Byzantine Monastery at Khirbet ed-Deir in the Judaean Desert: The Excavations in 1981-1987*, Qedem, 38 (Jerusalem: Institute of Archaeology, The Hebrew University of Jerusalem, 1999), pp. 97-106.

Di Segni, L. 'Monk and Society' in J. Patrich (ed.), *The Sabaite Heritage in the Orthodox Church from the Fifth Century to the Present* (Leuven: Peeters, 2001), pp. 31-6.

Di Segni, L. 'Monastery, City and Village in Byzantine Gaza', *Proche-Orient Chrétien*, 55 (2005), 24-51.

Di Segni, L. 'Varia Arabica. Greek Inscriptions from Jordan', *Liber Annuus*, 56 (2006), 578-92.

Di Segni, L. 'The Greek Inscriptions from Tel Ashdod: A Revised Reading', *'Atiqot*, 58 (2008), 31-6.

Di Segni, L. 'Late Antique Inscriptions in the Provinces of *Palaestina* and *Arabia*: Realities and Change' in K. Bolle, C. Machado, and C. Witschel (eds.), *The Epigraphic Cultures of Late Antiquity* (Stuttgart: Franz Steiner Verlag, 2017), pp. 287-615.

Di Segni, L. and Tsafrir, Y. 'The Ethnic Composition of Jerusalem's Population in the Byzantine Period (312-638 CE)', *Liber Annuus*, 62 (2012), 405-54.

Elter, R. and Hassoune, A. 'Un complex de continuité entre del IVe et VIIIe siècles: le cas du monastère de Saint-Hilarion à Tell Umm er-'Amr' in A. Borrut, M. Debié, A. Papaconstantinou, D. Pieri, and J. P. Sodini (eds.), *Le Proche-Orient de Justinien aux Abbassides. Peuplement et dynamiques spatiales* (Turnhout: Brepols, 2011), pp. 187-204.

Ewing, W. 'Greek and Other Inscriptions Collected in the Hauran', *Palestine Exploration Quarterly*, 27.1 (1895), 246-54.

Feissel, D. *Chroniques d'épigraphie byzantine 1987-2004* (Paris: Association des amis du Centre d'histoire et civilisation de Byzance, 2006).

Feissel, D. and Gatier, P.-L. 'Bulletin Epigraphique 2005-2015. Syrie, Phenicie, Palestine, Arabie', *Revue des études grecques*, 129 (2016), available online: https://igls.mom.fr/be-2005-2015.

Festugière, A. J. *Antioche païenne et chrétienne, Libanius, Chrysostome, et les moines de Syrie* (Paris: E. de Boccard, 1959).

Festugière, A. J. *Les moines d'orient, culture ou sainteté. Introduction au monachisme oriental* (Paris: Éditions du Cerf, 1961).

Festugière, A. J. *Les moines d'orient 3,1. Les moines de Palestine: Cyrille le Scythopolis, Vie de Saint Euthyme* (Paris: Éditions du Cerf, 1962).

Figueras, P., 'Monks and Monasteries in the Negev Desert', *Liber Annuus*, 45 (1995), 401–50.

Fisher, G., Lewin, A., and Whately, C. 'The Fourth Centuries: Allies and Enemies' in G. Fisher (ed.), *Arabs and Empires Before Islam* (Oxford: Oxford University Press, 2015), pp. 74–88.

Frankfurter, D. 'Iconoclasm and Christianization in Late Antique Egypt: Christian Treatments of Space and Image' in J. Hahn, S. Emmel, and U. Gotter (eds.), *From Temple to Church: Destruction and Renewal of Local Cultic Topography in Late Antiquity* (Leiden: Brill 2008), pp. 135–59.

Frend, W. H. C. 'Monks and the End of Greco-Roman Paganism in Syria and Egypt', *Cristianesimo nella storia*, 11 (1990), 469–84.

Frey, J. B. *Corpus Inscriptionum Judaicarum* 2 vols (Vatican City: Pontificio Ist., 1936–52).

Frösén, J. 'The Petra Papyri: Information and Significance' in J. Frösén and Z. Fiema (eds.), *Petra. A City Forgotten and Rediscovered* (Helsinki: Amos Anderson Art Museum, 2002), pp. 18–24.

Frösén, J. 'Gift after Death' in A. Arjava, J. Frösén, and J. Kaimio (eds.), *The Petra Papyri V* (Amman: American Center of Oriental Research, 2018), pp. 108–36.

Frösén, J., Fiema, Z. T., Haggrén, H., Koistinen, K., Lavento, M., and Peterman, G. L. 'The Finnish Jabal Harun Project Report on the 1997 Season', *Annual of the Department of Antiquities of Jordan*, 42 (1998), 483–502.

Frösén, J. and Miettunen, P. H. 'Aaron in Religious Literature, Myth and Legend' in J. Frösén and Z. T. Fiema (eds.), *Petra: The Mountain of Aaron I. The Church and the Chapel* (Helsinki: Societas Scientiarum Fennica, 2008), pp. 5–26.

Gagos, T. and Frösén, J. 'Petra Papyri', *Annual of the Department of Antiquities of Jordan*, 42 (1998), 473–81.

Gatier, P. L. 'Exploration, épigraphie et histoire' in J. B. Humbert and A. Desreumaux (eds.), *Fouilles de Khirbet es-Samra en Jordanie. La voie romaine, le cimetière. Les documents èpigraphiques* (Turnhout: Brepols, 1998), pp. 361–431.

Granic, B. 'Die Rechtliche Stellung und Organisation der Griechischen Kloster nach dem Justinianischen Recht', *Byzantinische Zeitschrift*, 29 (1929), 6–34.

Griffith, S. H. 'Mayfa'ah: un sito dimenticato nella primitiva tradizione islamica' in M. Piccirillo and E. Alliata (eds.), *Umm al-Rasas Mayfa'ah I. Gli scavi del complesso di Santo Stefano* (Jerusalem: Stadium Biblicum Franciscanum, 1994), pp. 51–3.

Griffith, S. H. 'The Mansur Family and St. John of Damascus: Christians and Muslims in Umayyad Times' in A. Borrut and F. M. Donner (eds.), *Christians and Others in the Umayyad State* (Chicago: Oriental Institute of the University of Chicago, 2016), pp. 29–51.

Hamarneh, B. *Topografia cristiana ed insediamenti rurali nel territorio dell'odierna Giordania nelle epoche bizantina ed islamica: V–VIII sec.* (Vatican City: Pontificio Istituto di Archaeologia Cristiana, 2003).

Hamarneh, B. 'Monasteries in Rural Context in Byzantine Arabia and Palaestina Tertia: A Reassessment' in L. D. Chrupcała (ed.), *Christ Is Here! Studies in Biblical and Christian Archaeology in Memory of Fr Michele Piccirillo ofm.* (Milan: Edizioni Terra Santa, 2012), pp. 275–96.

Hamarneh, B. 'Il fenomeno rupestre nell'Oriente Bizantino: il caso delle province di Arabia e di Palaestina Tertia' in J. Lopéz-Quiroga and A. Tejera (eds.), *In concavis petrarum habitaverunt. El fenómeno rupestre en el Mediterráneo Medieval: De la investigación a la puesta en valor* (Oxford: Archaeopress, 2014), pp. 361–74.

Hamarneh, B. 'Between Hagiography and Archaeology: Pilgrimage and Monastic Communities on the Banks of the River Jordan' in F. Daim, J. Pahlitzsch, J. Patrich, C. Rapp, and J. Seligman (eds.), *Pilgrimage to Jerusalem. Journeys, Destinations, Experiences across Times and Cultures* (Mainz: Verlag des Römisch-Germanischen Zentralmuseums, 2020), pp. 41–56.

Hartranft, C. D. *The Ecclesiastical History of Sozomen* (Grand Rapids: Eerdmans, 1890–1900).

Hill, G. F. *The Life of Porphyry Bishop of Gaza by Mark the Deacon* (Oxford: Clarendon Press, 1913).

Hirschfeld, Y. 'List of the Byzantine Monasteries in the Judaean Desert' in G. C. Bottini, L. Di Segni, and V. C. Corbo (eds.), *Christian Archaeology in the Holy Land New Discoveries* (Jerusalem: Franciscan Print. Press, 1990), pp. 1–89.

Hirschfeld, Y. *The Judaean Desert Monasteries in the Byzantine Period* (New Haven: Yale University Press, 1992).

Hirschfeld, Y. 'Euthymius and His Monastery in the Judean Desert', *Liber Annuus*, 43 (1993), 339–71.

Hirschfeld, Y. *The Early Byzantine Monastery at Khirbet Ed-Deir in the Judean Desert: The Excavations in 1981–1987* (Jerusalem: Institute of Archaeology, The Hebrew University of Jerusalem, 1999).

Hirschfeld, Y. 'Deir Qal'a and the Monasteries of Western Samaria' in J. Humphrey (ed.), *The Roman and Byzantine Near East*, vol. 2 (Ann Arbor: Journal of Roman Archaeology, 2002), pp. 155–89.

Hoppé, C. 'The Macroscopic Plant Remains' in K. D. Politis (ed.), *Sanctuary of Lot at Deir 'Ain 'Abata in Jordan. Excavations 1988–2003* (Amman: American Center of Oriental Research, 2012), pp. 518–22.

Hunt, E. D. *Holy Land Pilgrimage in the Later Roman Empire, AD 312-460* (Oxford: Clarendon Press, 1982).

Jacquat, C. and Martinoli, D. 'Vitis vinifera L.: Wild or Cultivated? Study of the Grape Pips Found at Petra, Jordan; 150 B.C.-A.D. 40', *Vegetation History and Archaeobotany*, 8 (1999), 25-30.

Jones, A. H. M. *The Later Roman Empire, 284-602. A Social, Economic, and Administrative Survey*, 3 vols (Oxford: Blackwell, 1964).

Kaplan, M. *Les propriétés de la couronne et de l'église dans l'empire byzantin (Ve-VIe siècles)* (Paris: Publications de la Sorbonne, 1976).

Kaplan, M. *Les hommes et la terre à Byzance du 6 au 11 siècle* (Paris: Publications de la Sorbonne, 1992).

Karasneh, W. 'Excavations of the Church of Khirbet Dariya/az-Za'tara/Samad 1995', *Annual of the Department of Antiquities of Jordan*, 41 (1997), 21-35 [in Arabic].

Karg, S. 'Pflanzenreste aus den nabatäischen und spätrömischen Schihcten' in A. Bignasca, N. Desse-Berset, R. Fellmann Brogli, R. Glutz, S. Karg, D. Keller, B. Kolb, C. Kramar, M. Peter, S. G. Schmid, C. Schneider, R. A. Stucky, J. Studer, and I. Zanoni (eds.), *Petra ez Zantur I. Ergebnisse der Schweizerisch-Liechtensteinischen Ausgrabungen 1988-1992* (Mainz: P. von Zabern, 1996), pp. 355-8.

Kislinger, E. 'Christians of the East. Rules and Realities of the Byzantine Diet' in A. Sonnenfeld (ed.), *Food. A Culinary History from Antiquity to the Present* (New York: Columbia University Press, 1999), pp. 194-205.

Klostermann, E. *Das Onomastikon der Biblischen Ortsnamen (Eusebius Werke III,1)* (Leipzig: J. C. Hinrich, 1904).

Koenen, L., Kaimio, J., Kaimio, M., and Daniel, R. W. 'Introduction. Terms Pertaining to Dwellings and Agriculture' in L. Koenen, J. Kaimio, M. Kaimio, and R. W. Daniel (eds.), *The Petra Papyri II* (Amman: American Center of Oriental Research, 2013), pp. 1-22.

Kouki, P. 'Production Sites' in P. Kouki and M. Lavento (eds.), *Petra: The Mountain of Aaron III. The Archaeological Survey* (Helsinki: Societas Scientiarum Fennica, 2013), pp. 247-51.

Lavento, M. and Huotari, M. 'A Water Management System around Jabal Harûn, Petra - Its Design and Significance' in C. Ohlig, Y. Peleg, and T. Tsuk (eds.), *Cura Aquarum in Israel. Proceedings of the 11th International Conference on the History of Water Management and Hydraulic Engineering in the Mediterranean Region, Israel 7-12 May 2001* (Siegburg: Deutschen Wasserhistorischen Gesellschaft, 2002), pp. 93-106.

Lavento, M., Huotari, M., Jansson, H., Silvonen S., and Fiema, Z. T. 'Ancient Water Management System in the Area of Jabal Haroun, Petra' in H. D. Bienert and J. Häser (eds.), *Men of Dikes and Canals* (Berlin: Verlag Marie Leidorf, 2004), pp. 163-72.

Lavento, M., Kouki, P., Silvonen, S., Ynnilä, H., and Huotari, M. 'Terrace Cultivation in the Jabal Harun Area and Its Relationship to the City of Petra in Southern Jordan', *Studies in the History and Archaeology of Jordan*, 9 (2007), 145–56.

Lavento, M., Silvonen, S., and Kouki, P. 'Runoff Cultivations and Hydraulic Structures' in P. Kouki and M. Lavento (eds.), *Petra: The Mountain of Aaron III. The Archaeological Survey* (Helsinki: Societas Scientiarum Fennica, 2013), pp. 212–29.

Layton, B. 'Social Structure and Food Consumption in an Early Christian Monastery', *Le Muséon*, 115 (2002), 25–55.

Lefort, J. 'The Rural Economy 7th–12th Centuries' in A. E. Laiou (ed.), *The Economic History of Byzantium from the Seventh through the Fifteenth Century* (Washington, DC: Dumbarton Oaks, 2002), pp. 231–310.

Levy-Rubin, M. and Kedar, B. Z. 'A Spanish Source on Mid-Ninth-Century Mar Saba and a Neglected Sabaite Martyr' in J. Patrich (ed.), *The Sabaite Heritage: The Sabaite Factor in the Orthodox Church – Monastic Life, Theology, Liturgy, Literature, Art and Archaeology (5th Century to the Present)* (Leuven: Peeters, 2001), pp. 63–72.

Magen, Y. and Talgam, R. 'The Monastery of Martyrius at Ma'ale Adummim (Khirbet el-Murassas) and its Mosaics' in G. C. Bottini, E. Alliata, and L. Di Segni (eds.), *Christian Archaeology in the Holy Land. New Discoveries. Archaeological Essays in Honour of Virgilio C. Corbo* (Jerusalem: Franciscan Print. Press, 1990), pp. 91–152.

Markschies, C. 'Stadt und Land. Beobachtungen zu Ausbreitung und Inkulturation des Christentums in Palästina' in H. Cancik and J. Rüpke (eds.), *Römische Reichsreligion und Provinzialreligion* (Tübingen: Mohr Siebeck, 1998), pp. 265–97.

Mattingly, K. and Burgh, T. W. 'Lintel Inscription from Tall Hisban, Field M, Square 5, 2001', *Andrews University Seminary Studies*, 43.2 (2005), 247–60.

Mayerson, P. 'The Ancient Agricultural Regime of Nessana and the Central Negeb' in H. D. Colt (ed.), *Excavations at Nessana*, I (London: British School of Archaeology in Jerusalem, 1962), pp. 211–69.

Meimaris, Y. E. *Sacred Names, Saints, Martyrs and Church Officials in the Greek Inscriptions and Papyri Pertaining to the Christian Church of Palestine* (Athens: National Hellenic Research Foundation, 1986).

Meimaris, Y. E. and Kritikakou-Nikolaropoulou, K. I. *Inscriptions from Palaestina Tertia, Ia: The Greek Inscriptions from Ghor es-Safi (Byzantine Zoora)* (Athens: National Hellenic Research Foundation, 2005).

Meimaris, Y. E. and Kritikakou-Nikolaropoulou, K. I. 'The Greek Inscriptions' in K. D. Politis (ed.), *Sanctuary of Lot at Deir 'Ain 'Abata in Jordan* (Amman: American Center of Oriental Research, 2012), pp. 393–416.

Millar, F. 'Christian Monasticism in Roman Arabia at the Birth of Mahomet', *Semitica et Classica*, 2 (2009), 97–115.

Mouton, J. M. and Popescu-Belis, A. 'La fondation du monastère Sainte Catherine du Sinaï selon deux documents de sa bibliothèque: codex Arabe 692 et rouleau Arabe 955', *Collectanea Christiana Orientalia*, 2 (2005), 141–205.

Nassau, W. (ed.) *The Conquest of Syria, Commonly Ascribed to Abou 'Abd Allah Mohammad b. 'Omar al-Waqidi*, 3 vols (Calcutta: Asiatic Society, 1854–60).

Nau, F. 'Deux épisodes de l'histoire juive sous Théodose II (423 et 438) d'après la vie de Barsauma le Syrien', *Revue des études juives*, 83 (1927), 184–206.

Neary, D. 'Constantinople and the Desert City: Imperial Patronage of the Judaean Desert' in N. S. M. Matheou, T. Kampianaki, and L. M. Bondioli (eds.), *From Constantinople to the Frontier. The City and the Cities* (Leiden: Brill, 2016), pp. 142–58.

Papadopoulos-Kerameus, A. *Sbornik palestinskoĭ i siriiskoĭ agiologii* (St Petersburg: Izd. Imp. pravoslavnago palestinskago ob-va, 1907).

Parker, S. T. 'The Byzantine Period: An Empire's New Holy Land', *Near Eastern Archaeology*, 62.3 (1999), 135–80.

Patlagean, E. 'À Byzance: ancienne hagiographie et histoire sociale', *Annales. Économies, Sociétés, Civilisations*. 23e année, N. 1 (1968), 106–26.

Patlagean, E. *Pauvreté économique et pauvreté sociale à Byzance, 4e–7e siècles* (Paris and La Haye: De Gruyter Mouton, 1977).

Patrich, J. 'Church, State and the Transformation of Palestine – the Byzantine Period (324–640 CE)' in T. E. Levy (ed.), *The Archaeology of Society in the Holy Land* (New York: Facts on File, 1995), pp. 470–87.

Patrich, J. *Sabas. Leader of Palestinian Monasticism. A Comparative Study in Eastern Monasticism, Fourth to Seventh Centuries* (Washington, DC: Dumbarton Oaks Papers, 1995).

Patrich, J. 'The Impact of the Muslim Conquest on Monasticism in the Deser of Jerusalem' in A. Borrut, M. Debié, A. Papaconstantinou, D. Pieri, and J. P. Sodini (eds.), *Le Proche-Orient de Justinien aux Abbaside: peuplement et dynamiques spatiales* (Turnhout: Brepols, 2011), pp. 205–18.

Patrich, J. 'Daily Life in the Desert of Jerusalem' in O. Delouise and M. Mossakowska-Gaubert (eds.), *La vie quotidienne des moines en Orient et en Occident (IVe–IXe siècle)*, vol. I: *L'état des sources* (Cairo: l'Institut français d'archéologie orientale IFAO, 2015), pp. 125–50.

Perrone, L. 'Monasticism in the Holy Land: From the Beginnings to the Crusaders', *Proche-Orient Chrétien*, 45 (1995), 31–63.

Piccirillo, M. 'Campagna archeologica a Khirbet el-Mukhayyat (città di Nebo)', *Liber Annuus*, 23 (1973), 322–58.

Piccirillo, M. *Chiese e mosaici della Giordania settentrionale* (Jerusalem: Franciscan Print. Press, 1981).

Piccirillo, M. 'Le chiese di Quweismeh – Amman', *Liber Annuus*, 34 (1984), 329–40.

Piccirillo, M. *Chiese e mosaici di Madaba* (Jerusalem: Franciscan Print. Press, 1989).

Piccirillo, M. 'Monks and Monasteries in Jordan from the Byzantine to the Abbassid Period', *Al-Liqa' Journal*, 1 (1992), 17–30.

Piccirillo, M. 'Le due iscrizioni della cappella della Theotokos nel wadi Ayn al-Kanisah – Monte Nebo', *Liber Annuus*, 44 (1994), 521–38.

Piccirillo, M. 'La strada romana Esbus-Livias', *Liber Annuus*, 46 (1996), 285–300.

Piccirillo, M. 'The Monastic Presence' in M. Piccirillo and E. Alliata (eds.), *Mount Nebo: New Archaeological Excavations 1967–1997* (Jerusalem: Stadium Biblicum Franciscanum, 1998), pp. 193–219.

Piccirillo, M. 'Pilgrims' Texts' in M. Piccirillo and E. Alliata (eds.), *Mount Nebo: New Archaeological Excavations 1967–1997* (Jerusalem: Stadium Biblicum Franciscanum, 1998), pp. 71–83.

Piccirillo, M. *L'Arabia Cristiana. Dalla Provincia imperiale al primo periodo islamico* (Milan: Jaca Book, 2002).

Piccirillo, M. 'Gregorio Magno e le Province orientali di Palestina e Arabia', *Liber Annuus*, 54 (2004), 321–41.

Piccirillo, M. 'Dall'archeologia alla storia. Nuove evidenze per una rettifica di luoghi comuni riguardanti le province di Palestina e di Arabia nei secoli IV-VIII d.C.' in A. C. Quintavalle (ed.), *Medioevo Mediterraneo: l'Occidente, Bisanzio e l'Islam dal Tardoantico al secolo XII. VII Convegno Internazionale di Studi* (Milan: Electa, 2007), pp. 95–111.

Pirone, B. *Leonzio di Damasco. Vita di santo Stefano Sabaita* (Cairo and Jerusalem: Franciscan Centre of Christian Oriental Studies, 1991).

Politis, K. D. 'Excavations at Deir 'Ain 'Abata 1988', *Annual of the Department of Antiquities of Jordan*, 33 (1989), 227–33.

Politis, K. D. 'The Basketry and Cordage' in K. D. Politis (ed.), *Sanctuary of Lot at Deir 'Ain 'Abata in Jordan* (Amman: American Center of Oriental Research, 2012), pp. 375–7.

Price, R. M. *Cyril of Scythopolis: The Lives of the Monks of Palestine* (Kalamazoo: Cistercian Publications, 1991).

Rapp, C. 'For Next to God You Are My Salvation: Reflections on the Rise of the Holy Man in Late Antiquity' in J. Howard-Johnston and P. A. Hayward (eds.), *The Cult of Saints in Late Antiquity and the Early Middle Ages: Essays on the Contribution of Peter Brown* (Oxford: Oxford University Press, 1999), pp. 63–82.

Robinson, D. *Food, Virtue, and the Shaping of Early Christianity* (Cambridge: Cambridge University Press, 2020).

Rousselle, A. *Porneia. On Desire and the Body in Antiquity* (Oxford and New York: Basil Blackwell, 1988).

Rufus Aquileia, *Historia Monachorum Seu Liber De Vitis Patrum*, 1, *De Sancto Joanne*, ed. J. P. Migne, *Patrologiae Latinae* 21 (Paris: Garnier, 1849).

Saller, S. *The Memorial of Moses on Mount Nebo*, 2 vols (Jerusalem: Franciscan Press, 1941).

Saradi, H. *The Byzantine City in the Sixth Century. Literary Image and Historical Reality* (Athens: Distributed by the Society of Messenian Archaeological Studies, 2006).

Schachner, L. A. '"I Greet You and Thy Brethren. Here Are Fifteen Shentasse of Wine": Wine-Production in the Early Monasteries of Egypt and the Levant', *Aram*, 17 (2005), 157–84.

Schwartz, E. *Kyrillos von Skythopolis* (Leipzig: Hinrichs Verlag, 1939).

Ševčenko, I. 'The Early Period of the Sinai Monastery in the Light of Its Inscriptions', *Dumbarton Oaks Papers*, 28 (1966), 255–64.

Shahid, I. *Byzantium and the Arabs in the Sixth Century: Toponymy, Monuments, Historical Geography and Frontier Studies*, vol. 2.1 (Washington, DC: Dumbarton Oaks Research Library and Collection, 2002).

Shoemaker, S. J. *Three Christian Martyrdoms from Early Islamic Palestine* (Provo, UT: Brigham Young University Press, 2016).

Sivan, H. 'Pilgrimage, Monasticism, and the Emergence of Christian Palestine in the 4th Century' in R. Ousterhout (ed.), *The Blessings of Pilgrimage* (Urbana: University of Illinois Press, 1990), pp. 54–65.

Stemberger, G. *Jews and Christians in the Holy Land: Palestine in the Fourth Century*, trans. R. Tuschling (Edinburgh: T & T Clark, 2000).

Stone, M. 'Holy Land Pilgrimage of Armenians before the Arab Conquest', *Revue Biblique*, 93.1 (1986), 93–110.

Tenhunen, T. 'FJHP 2000: Macrofossil Analysis. The 1998–2000 Finnish Harûn Project: Specialized Reports', *Annual of the Department of Antiquities of Jordan*, 45 (2001), 386–7.

Tenhunen, T. 'The Macrofossil Analysis: Evidence for Dietary and Environmental Conditions' in Z. T. Fiema, J. Frösén, and M. Holappa (eds.), *Petra: The Mountain of Aaron II. The Nabataean Sanctuary and the Byzantine Monastery* (Helsinki: Societas Scientiarum Fennica, 2016), pp. 454–77.

Till, W. C. *Die koptischen Rechtsurkunden aus Theben* (Vienna: Kommissionsverlag der Österreichischen Akademie der Wissenschaften, 1964).

Tzaferis, V. 'Early Christian Monasticism in the Holy Land and Archaeology' in J. Patrich (ed.), *The Sabaite Heritage in the Orthodox Church from the Fifth Century to the Present* (Leuven: Peeters, 2001), pp. 317–21.

Usener, H. (ed.) *Der heilige Theodosius, Schriften des Theodoros und Kyrillos* (Leipzig: Teubner, 1890).

van Alfen, P. G. 'New Light on the 7th-c. Yassı Ada Shipwreck: Capacities and Standard Sizes of LRA1 Amphoras', *Journal of Roman Archaeology*, 9 (1996), 189–213.

Veilleux, A., *Pachomian koinonia: The Lifes, Rules and Other Writings of Saint Pachomius and His Disciples. Pachomian Chronicles and Rules*, vol. 2 (Kalamazoo: Cistercian Publications, 1981).

Villeneuve, F. 'L'économie rurale et la vie des campagnes dans le Hauran antique (Ier siècle avant J.C.–VIème siècle après J.C.): une approche' in J. M. Dentzer (ed.), *Hauran I. Recherches archéologiques sur la Syrie du Sud a l'époque hellénistique et romaine* (Damascus: Bibliotheque Archeologique Et Historique, 1985), pp. 63–136.

Villeneuve, F. 'Dharih (Jordanie Méridionale): village chrétien puis musulman (IVe–Ixe siècles) dans les ruines d'un sanctuaire nabatéen' in A. Borrut, M. Debié, A. Papaconstantinou, D. Pieri, and J. P. Sodini (eds.), *Le Proche-Orient de Justinien aux Abbassides. Peuplement et dynamiques spatiales* (Turnhout: Brepols, 2011), pp. 315–27.

Villeneuve, F. and Al-Muheisen, Z. 'Nouvelles recherches à Khirbet edh-Dharih (Jordanie du Sud, 1996–1999)', *Comptes-Rendus des Séances de l'Académie des Inscriptions et Belles-Lettres*, 144. 4 (2000), 1525–63.

Weingarten, S. *The Saint's Saints. Hagiography and Geography in Jerome* (Leiden: Brill, 2005).

Whiting, M. 'Appendix. Monastery Hostels in the Byzantine Near East' in Z. T. Fiema, J. Frösén, and M. Holappa (eds.), *Petra: The Mountain of Aaron II. The Nabataean Sanctuary and the Byzantine Monastery* (Helsinki: Societas Scientiarum Fennica, 2016), pp. 108–13.

Whittaker, C. R. 'Late Roman Trade and Traders' in P. Garnsey, K. Hopkins and C. R. Whittaker (eds.), *Trade in the Ancient Economy* (Berkeley: University of California Press, 1983), pp. 163–211.

Wilken, R. L. 'Byzantine Palestine – Christian Holy Land', *The Biblical Archaeologist*, 51.4 (1988), 214–37.

Wilken, R. L. *The Land Called Holy: Palestine in Christian History and Thought* (New Haven: Yale University Press, 1992).

Wilkinson, J. 'Christian Pilgrims in Jerusalem during the Byzantine Period', *Palestine Exploration Quarterly*, 108 (1976), 75–101.

Wilkinson, J. *Jerusalem Pilgrims before the Crusades* (Warminster: Aris & Phillips, 2002).

Wood, P. 'Miaphysite Mission in the Jazira: The Life of Ahudemmeh' in G. Fisher (ed.), *Arabs and Empires before Islam* (Oxford: Oxford University Press, 2015), pp. 350–7.

Wood, P. 'The Monks of Palestine' in G. Fisher (ed.), *Arabs and Empires before Islam* (Oxford: Oxford University Press, 2015), pp. 302–11.

Wortley, J. (ed.) *The Spiritual Meadow (Pratum Spirituale) by John Moschus* (Minnesota: Liturgical Press, 2008).

Zerbini, A. 'The Area II Inscription' in U. Rothe, A. Zerbini, and F. Kenkel (eds.), *Excavations in Area III on Tall Zar'a*, edition of *Annual of the Department of Antiquities of Jordan*, 58 (2017), 268–70.

Zohary, M. *Plants of the Bible. A Complete Handbook to All the Plants with 200 Full-Color Plates in the Natural Habitat* (Cambridge: Cambridge University Press, 1982).

3 | Monastic Estates in Transition from Byzantine to Islamic Egypt: Evidence from Aphrodito

ISABELLE MARTHOT-SANTANIELLO

Introduction

A wide variety of religious institutions are attested in late antique Egypt, from small local shrines that occur only once in the documentation to wealthy, densely populated establishments that still function today. Papyri often offer a snapshot of the situation in a given time, but opportunities are rare to examine the economic role, follow the evolution, and compare the fate of several monasteries in a specific place over more than a hundred years. Aphrodito's papyri provide one of these exceptional sets of data.

If the village of Aphrodito, modern Kom Ishqaw (located between Assiut and Sohag), has become famous among scholars of late antique Egypt, it is due to the huge volume of papyri found there in the first half of the twentieth century, written mostly in Greek, but also in Coptic and Arabic.[1] These papyri can be divided into two distinct groups, which differ in terms of their date and also their content. The Byzantine group is the most famous: it covers the sixth and early seventh centuries, comprises more than 600 texts, mostly private papers, and is often referred to as the 'Dioscorus archive', after the individual who features most prominently in the corpus.[2] The Umayyad group is limited to a shorter span of time, the end of the seventh to the beginning of the eighth century, and gathers the professional papers, about 400 texts, of the village administrator, Basileios.[3] Both groups constitute the largest archives of their time and offer a remarkable source of evidence on the Egyptian countryside,

---

Preliminary remarks on the transformation of monastic estates in Aphrodito were included in my doctoral dissertation, Marthot, 'Un village égyptien' (the publication of which is forthcoming), which were further developed as part of the project 'Change and Continuities from a Christian to a Muslim Society – Egyptian Society and Economy in the 6th to 8th Centuries' (SNSF-sponsored project 162963), Basel University. An online database on Aphrodito papyri (aphrodito.info) is in preparation.

[1] More than a thousand documents have been found. The papyri were discovered by villagers in at least three different finds; for detail, see Marthot, 'La toponymie d'un village', 161–2.

[2] For a list of the papyri from the Dioscorus archive, see Fournet, *Les archives de Dioscore*, pp. 307–43. For the presence of several sub-archives, in addition to the one strictly belonging to Dioscorus, see Fournet, 'Sur les premiers documents juridiques coptes (2)'.

[3] The earliest stage of Basileios' archive is formed by papers related to his predecessors, among whom is Epimachos; see, e.g., *P.Lond.* IV 1512.5 (709). A list of these papyri, divided by language, is available in Richter, 'Language Choice', pp. 197–208.

with a unique level of detail and from the rare point of view of a village (Greek *kome*) and not a city (Greek *polis*). Although a large part of the Aphrodito papyri were published more than a century ago, it is only in recent decades that several major works have provided a better understanding of the Byzantine component. The evidence for several monasteries taking part in the rural economy, both distant and local, as well as the existence of a pious foundation by the father of Dioscorus himself, has attracted the attention of editors and historians, producing a large bibliography upon which the present research draws.[4] The Umayyad papyri are, however, more difficult to interpret, and have thus not been exploited to the same extent.[5] Moreover, there have been very few attempts to bring together the two sets of information and compare the picture of the countryside that they offer before and after the Islamic conquest.[6] Specifically, these documents illustrate changes in the status of monasteries in the early eighth century whose scale can only be evaluated by taking into account the available evidence from the previous centuries. To understand the evolution of monasteries in Aphrodito, this paper focuses on the key element of their landholdings, specifically on which monasteries (local and distant, recent and well-established) owned what land in the village in the Byzantine period, and what picture can be drawn from the available data about monastic estates in the eighth century that can contribute to the study of this period of transition.

Methodological Approach

Getting an overview of the massive amount of data from Aphrodito can be difficult. To search for religious institutions attested in Aphrodito, geographical repertories such as Stefan Timm's monumental work or thematic syntheses such as the one produced by Arietta Papaconstantinou that focus on the worship of saints are useful. Regarding Aphrodito, the figures given by Timm (thirty churches, thirty-eight monasteries, and twenty-six *topoi*)[7] and Papaconstantinou (twenty-six religious establishments dedicated to saints,

---

[4] See, for example, the short presentation in Wipszycka, *Moines et communautés*, pp. 87–8.
[5] See, however, the following works by Janneke de Jong: the edition of P.Würzb. inv. 122–129 in *P. Würzb.* II; de Jong, 'A Summary Tax Assessment'; and de Jong, 'Who Did What'. I would like to thank Janneke for her invaluable comments on a preliminary version of the present paper.
[6] An exception is H. I. Bell, who edited papyri from both groups in *P.Lond.* IV and V, and enriched his commentary with diachronic remarks; another rare and inspiring example is Rémondon, 'P. Hamb. 56'. Despite its title, Ruffini, *Life in an Egyptian Village*, is focused on the documentation from the sixth and early seventh centuries and only alludes to the eighth century texts in the first chapter and conclusion.
[7] Timm, *Das christlich-koptische Ägypten*, pp. 1443–55 (s.v. Kôm Išqāw).

excluding the institutions named after their founders)[8] are all too high for the number of institutions in a single village. Papaconstantinou underlined two parameters that could explain this abundance: first, the establishments are not all mentioned during the entire period and therefore may not have functioned simultaneously; second, some may have been located outside the village itself. These are indeed elements to bear in mind, but more generally it should be emphasised that these authors and their predecessors adopted an inclusive approach, collecting any possible mention that may refer to a religious institution. Therefore, their lists contain institutions that are mentioned in the Aphrodito papyri but cannot be proved to be located in the village itself or even in the village's territory. Among the monasteries attested in the Aphrodito papyri, several, as will be seen, were clearly located in other nomes.

The main reason for this overestimation is, however, of another nature: it comes from an ambiguity in the definition of the object. These lists include not only institutions that are explicitly designated as *monasterion* but also proper names qualifying the desert (*oros*) and even the vague word for 'place' (*topos*). A discussion on these terms and a revised list of the religious institutions that were in Aphrodito's territory, necessitating a thorough examination of each reference in the texts, is currently in preparation. For the current purpose, I consider only the monasteries that can confidently be identified as landowners in the village, whether they were located in the village territory or acted from other nomes. This study is limited to monasteries and thus excludes other religious institutions, such as churches, 'holy places', *martyria*, and hospices (*xeneon, xenodocheion*). The study of these institutions would be fruitful as well, since some also owned land in the village, and a glimpse of their evolution in the eighth century can be caught, but it goes beyond the scope of the present discussion.[9]

Landowning Monasteries in Sixth-Century Aphrodito

In dealing with the Dioscorus archive, it should always be borne in mind that it is a private, family archive. Therefore, if a landowner appears several times, it does not necessarily mean that he was important at the village level, only that he had strong business relations with Dioscorus' family.[10]

---

[8] Papaconstantinou, *Le culte des saints*, pp. 296–8.
[9] For an example of a study that includes all the types of religious institutions, see MacCoull, 'Monastic and Church Landholding'.
[10] The Dioscorus archive is the object of network analysis in Ruffini, *Social Networks*, especially pp. 152–60 on Dioscorus' circle.

Fortunately, two documents provide descriptive, though incomplete, data on the village, its landlords, and its taxpayers. The first one was written around 524 and is a land register, a 'cadastre', recording all the land in the village territory for which landlords had to pay taxes called *astika* to the nearby city of Antaiopolis, the capital of the nome in which Aphrodito was located.[11] Each entry contains the name of the landlord, the tenant(s), and the surface area owned, divided into four land categories (arable, reed, orchard, vineyard), but not necessarily the location of the plot.[12] A summary at the end of the document shows that the total for the land taxed with *astika* was 1,375 arouras, which corresponded to a quarter of the total taxable surface of the village (5,200 arouras), the three remaining quarters being the object of the *kometika* tax that was directed to the village treasury.[13] According to which criteria land was assigned to *astika* or *kometika* tax is still debated; it would be too simplistic to schematise that the *astika* tax was paid by landlords living in the city and the *kometika* by the village landlords, as we will see with monasteries.[14] This document mentions eight monasteries as landowners.[15] Leslie MacCoull closely examined the figures concerning all the religious institutions, and noted that some land was in co-ownership with people who seemed to be 'well-off, well-educated'.[16] As for the tenants, she underlined how the same individuals often cultivated land for several institutions and other landowners. Joanna Wegner has provided an even more thorough examination of the social interaction between monasteries and lay people attested in the document.[17]

On the question of landownership repartition, the editor, Jean Gascou, underlined that the seven richest monasteries owned one-third of the total of

---

[11] SB XX 14669, reedited in Gascou, *Fiscalité et société*, pp. 247–305, and MacCoull, 'Why and How'.

[12] For a detailed study of the legal ground of these entries, see Mirković, 'Count Ammonios'.

[13] Gascou, *Fiscalité et société*, p. 257. The actual size of Aphrodito's territory has been questioned by Zuckerman, *Du village à l'Empire*, pp. 221–2, who collected evidence for a Great House of a former prefect that could have represented nearly three-fifths of the taxable land of Aphrodito. This issue is too large to be discussed here, but see the grounds for reservation in Bagnall, 'Village Landholding', p. 188.

[14] Gascou, *Fiscalité et société*, p. 258.

[15] Other monasteries are mentioned in the text, but not as landowners: a monk of the monastery of Apa Psempnouthes is a tenant (line 222), and payments are made for the *topos* of the monastery of Psintase (line 247).

[16] MacCoull, 'Monastic and Church Landholding', p. 245. I would advise caution, however, in MacCoull's link between the presence of reed land and economical specialisation in ropemaking, or the existence of vineyards leading to the sale of surplus. These land categories can be detached from the reality of how they were used, and evidence is lacking concerning monastic production.

[17] Wegner, 'Monastic Communities', pp. 77–87.

the recorded arable land, i.e., the land subject to the *astika* tax.[18] The cadastre attests, however, considerable variation in the size and division of monastic holdings, highlighting several profiles of monastic institutions (see Table 3.1).

The four most important landowning monasteries are known from other sources to be one local institution (Apa Sourous) and three Panopolite establishments (Apa Zenobios, Smine, and Apa Shenoute), while the other four are more difficult to characterise. Among all of them, the monastery of Apa Sourous stands out as being registered as having 300 arouras of arable land, twice the amount owned by all the other monasteries combined. Corresponding to 22 per cent of the total amount of land registered in the entire cadastre, this figure makes it the largest landowner in the whole document.[19] It can certainly be identified as a local institution due to the fact that, in 565, two Aphroditan villagers are known to be the descendants of

Table 3.1: *Monastic holdings according to the Aphrodito Cadastre.*

Landowning monastery	Amount of aroura possessed	Percentage of the total amount[20]	Number of entries[21]	Average quantity of aroura per entry[22]
Apa Sourous	300	22	42	7.14
Apa Zenobios	67	5	15	4.46
Smine	33	2.5	9	3.66
Apa Shenoute	19.5	1.5	2	9.75
Porbis	12	1	3	4
Ama Termouthia	3.25	0.25	1	3.25
Oasites	5 (in co-ownership with Apa Sourous)	0.35	1	5
Tarouthis	1 (in co-ownership with Dioscorus' father)	0.05	1	1

[18] See Gascou, *Fiscalité et société*, pp. 258–60 for the three other categories. It may be relevant to keep in mind that an unknown number of entries is missing at the beginning of the document; see Gascou, *Fiscalité et société*, p. 251. The comparison between the amounts preserved and the final recapitulation indicates that these entries correspond to approximately 110 arouras, among which a portion may have belonged to monasteries.

[19] Ruffini, 'Aphrodito before Dioscorus', pp. 228–30. The most recent text on this monastery is published in Stolk, 'A Byzantine Business Letter'.

[20] Rounded figures; the total of *astika* land is the aforementioned 1,375 arouras, among which the detail for 110 arouras is lost; see n. 18.

[21] The total number of preserved entries is 186, documenting 1,265 arouras; see n. 18.

[22] The average quantity of aroura per entry for the preserved part of the document is 6.8 (see previous note and n. 18).

its founder.[23] Ruffini reconstructed the history of the family and made the hypothesis that Sourous was likely born in the first half of the fifth century.[24] The monastery not only owned the most arouras, it occupied forty-two entries, with an average of 7.14 arouras per entry.[25] These entries do not necessary mean that it owned forty-two separate plots of land, but proves that its landholding was not managed as one estate but was split into medium-size parcels (or shares) in the hands of numerous tenants.

Next in size are the three monasteries located in the Panopolite nome, which have much smaller holdings: Apa Zenobios is registered for 67 arouras (5 per cent of the total),[26] Smine for half that amount, 33 arouras (2.5 per cent),[27] and Apa Shenoute, the White Monastery near Sohag, for 19.5 arouras (1.5 per cent).[28] The latter only occurs in two entries, giving an average of 9.75 arouras per entry. This amount suggests holdings of only a couple of properties, but properties that would have been important in size, as opposed to the two other Panopolite monasteries that, with an average of 4.46 and 3.66 arouras per entry, more likely possessed a rather high number of small parcels.

Two other monasteries do not occur elsewhere in the Aphrodito papyri: Porbis, probably an institution located in another nome, maybe the Hermopolite or the Apollonopolis Minor nome, is registered for modest possessions (twelve arouras in three entries),[29] whereas nothing is known about Ama Termouthia (the reading of which is unsure), registered for only 3.25 arouras (line 76). The last two could also be local establishments:

---

[23] See *P.Cair.Masp.* I 67110.27.

[24] Ruffini, 'Aphrodito before Dioscorus', p. 229. It could even be earlier, since Ruffini based his argument on the use of the word *progonos* for Sourous combined with the fact that this word was used in another case, possibly for the maternal grandfather, who would thus be the nearest possible kin. The word could, however, refer also to another ancestor, e.g., a maternal great-grandfather. On the paternal side, the closest available candidate is a great-great-grandfather: the father of the anonymous father of Biktor. See Ruffini, 'Aphrodito before Dioscorus', p. 229: 'Biktor and his anonymous father certainly date to the mid-fifth century, if not earlier.' Sourous cannot have been the anonymous father of Biktor, since the end of the name in the genitive is clearly –ου in *P.Cair.Masp.* I 67110.10.

[25] See *SB* XVI 14669.4 and commentary to this line on p. 282. Twenty-six of these entries give the name of the place (*topos*) in question.

[26] Lines 44, 51, 54, 67, 167, 215, 219, 233–5, 244–5, 252, 265, 275, and 289; seven place names are mentioned. For the bibliography on this monastery, see the commentary to line 44 on p. 283.

[27] Lines 45, 81, 88, 121, 128, 135, 152, and 249–51. Five place names are preserved. Five of these entries are with the same tenant, Palos son of Patais, who also worked for other landlords, among which there is a church; see Ruffini, *A Prosopography*, p. 403 s.v. Palos 4, likely to be identical to Palos 6 (Palos *georgos*), who is recorded as paying on behalf of this monastery in the fiscal register *P.Aphrod.Reg.* 208.

[28] Lines 49 and 144. No place name is mentioned in these entries.

[29] Lines 12 (see the commentary on p. 282), 282, and 290.

Tarouthis appears in five entries in which it has the unexpected position as the tenant, except for a small plot of a little less than one aroura for which it is both co-landlord and co-tenant (lines 105–7).[30] Tar(r)outhis is known as a village in the Hermopolite nome, and I have argued elsewhere that there is no evidence for a homonymic village in the Antaiopolite nome and that it should not be confused with the well-attested village of Terythis.[31] The mention in the cadastre could, however, refer not to a village but to a local monastery that is not otherwise attested, at least under this name, in the rest of the Byzantine documentation on Aphrodito, but it does reappear in the eighth century, as will be seen.[32] Finally, the monastery of the Oasites is mentioned only once in the cadastre (line 55), for a small plot in co-ownership with Apa Sourous. It is present in a second text in which it owns one-third of an oil press in the village.[33] This monastery is also mentioned once in the eighth-century papyri, in an unusual context from which it is unclear whether it still owned land in the village or not.[34] It is more likely that it was not a local institution, but rather an absentee landowner.[35] Since monasteries are prominent characters in the cadastre, owning one-third of the *astika* land, it would be logical that they were similarly notable among *kometika* taxpayers. However, no similar register survives that lists the *kometika* land. There is, though, evidence that the monasteries, as landlords, were liable for *kometika* taxes, but not in the expected proportion.

The second document in which an overview of wealth distribution in the village can be found provides the opportunity to complete the cadastre: a fiscal register recording the payment of the *kometika* taxes in gold to the village treasury.[36] The document was made soon after the cadastre, and it is complete, except for minor damage. It offers a different picture. Only three monasteries feature among the taxpayers. Two are Panopolite establishments also present in the cadastre: Apa Zenobios appears in seven entries

---

[30] The monastery is the tenant in lines 97, 99–101, 102–3, and 104. No place name is preserved.

[31] Marthot, 'Homonyms Causing Confusion', pp. 489–90.

[32] It is all the more surprising that there is no other mention of this monastery in the archive, since the cadastre indicates that it was in a business relationship with Dioscorus' father. One would therefore expect to find it mentioned in the family's private accounts.

[33] *P.Flor.* III 285.4 (552). [34] *P.Lond.* IV 1419.1255. This point is developed further below.

[35] In support of this status is *P.Flor.* III 285.4 (552), in which this monastery is not said to be 'located' (*diakeimenos*) but 'possessing' (*kektemenos*) in Aphrodito's territory; for this argument concerning another religious institution, see Fournet, 'Quittances de loyer', p. 47. Another argument, as we will see, is that this monastery is not among the five main institutions of the village in the eighth-century documentation. If it is, indeed, a local institution, it must have been of humble size.

[36] Published in Zuckerman, *Du village à l'Empire* (see p. 37 for the nature of the document).

and pays a total of 5.5 *solidi*, while Smine occupies nine entries but pays only 4.5 *solidi*. The last monastery is recorded only once (and the amount is lost), under the name Treges, which is known from another text to be a microtoponym.[37] This suggests that this monastery was a local establishment that disappeared soon after the tax register was drawn, or was usually called by another name. Regarding the share of monasteries in the register, its editor stresses: 'Ces sommes les placent, certes, parmi les grands propriétaires des *kometika*, mais elles ne représentent, ensemble, que 3% des impôts fonciers inscrits au Registre.'[38] This is a large discrepancy with the situation drawn from the cadastre, but it is mainly the result of the absence of the Apa Sourous monastery. This absence led the editor of the register to conclude that all the landholdings of this monastery had been inscribed as *astika* land when the cadastre was compiled.[39] The second most important monastery in the cadastre, Apa Zenobios, owns, as we have seen, about 5 per cent of the *astika* land, which is more in line with its share in the register: important but not unequalled. Roger Bagnall analysed the figures in the register and calculated that 'the total tax yield for the village comes to the equivalent of about ... 1.4 *solidi* per individual', which means that the two Panopolite monasteries paid three to almost four times the average amount.[40] He also used the data of the register to address, among other issues, the question of the 'institutional ownership by religious foundations' and established that 'ecclesiastical establishments own just 6.3 per cent of the land in the category of the *kometika* ... far less than their percentage of land in the account of the *astika*, which is about thirty-eight per cent, although it remains a significant total'.[41] The two Panopolite monasteries represent 40 per cent of the contributions by religious institutions, the rest (3.7 per cent of the total) is formed by nine churches and one or more oratories. Bagnall draws a comparison with Temseu Skordon, a Hermopolite village from which a sixth-century tax register has also survived: in this text, only one religious institution is mentioned, the Holy Church, but it owned a greater proportion of land (more than

---

[37] *P.Cair.Masp.* II 67239.5 (summer 546 or 553), an agricultural lease in which Treges is the name of a *kleros* in which the rented field is located. For the meaning of *kleros* as a subdivision of the countryside, see Marthot, 'La toponymie d'un village', p. 164.

[38] Zuckerman, *Du village à l'Empire*, p. 228.

[39] Zuckerman, *Du village à l'Empire*, p. 228: 'À peine deux ans avant le Registre, la totalité des terres appartenant alors au monastère d'apa Sourous a été classée par le *censitor* Iôannês parmi les ἀστικά ; nous ignorons si c'était le souhait des moines ou si l'établissement est devenu trop important pour être géré, sur le plan fiscal, par le Trésor villageois. Pour des raisons que nous ne connaissons pas non plus, Iôannês était moins rigide à l'égard des propriétés d'apa Zénobe et de Smin.'

[40] Bagnall, 'Village Landholding', p. 183.   [41] Bagnall, 'Village Landholding', p. 184.

15 per cent). As Bagnall states, 'individual priests, however, play a more important part in land ownership at Aphrodito ... than at Temseu Skordon'.[42]

This was the situation in the years 524–5, and for the rest of the sixth and the entire seventh century, evidence is scattered in letters and petitions, accounts, land leases, and rent-receipts.[43] The main event to be tracked is the foundation of a monastery by Apollos, the father of Dioscorus. Ewa Wipszycka studied this dossier,[44] and the forthcoming editions of Coptic letters and reeditions of Greek documents will improve our understanding of the monastery's organisation.[45] Wipszycka declares: 'Tout comme la plupart des monastères de l'époque, le monastère d'Apa Apollôs vivait de la terre. Au début de son existence, il possédait la terre donnée par le fondateur; plus tard, il reçut des parcelles d'autres donateurs.'[46] The landholdings that the monastery certainly had are less visible in the archive than one would expect. In addition to possible building extensions inside the monastery itself,[47] it owned a farm building (*epaulis*) in the southern part of the village,[48] and, according to a petition, it received six arouras, the locations of which are not specified other than that they were next to small plots (*gedia*) already belonging to the monastery.[49] P.Strasb. gr. inv. 1668 (dated between 567 and 573) is a damaged petition written by Dioscorus in his function as administrator of his father's monastery. It probably also

---

[42] In Aphrodito, fourteen priests owned 11 per cent of the property, while five accounts (one of which is not certainly related to a church title) take up 6.5 per cent at Temseu Skordon. 'In both cases, they own more than their *per capita* share of the property, but in Aphrodito there is one cleric per 16 landowners, in Temseu Skordon only one per 72 landowners' (Bagnall, 'Village Landholding', p. 185).

[43] A first overview of 'Monastery-owned land' was given in Keenan, 'Notes on Absentee Landlordism', pp. 157–9.

[44] Wipszycka, 'Le monastère d'Apa Apollôs'.

[45] See the twenty-one Coptic letters in PhD dissertation of Vanderheyden, 'Les lettres coptes', the publication of which is forthcoming (among the twenty-one, P.Louvain Lefort.Copt. 20b could be related to irrigation work to be undertaken for the benefit of the monastery), and the (re)editions by Jean-Luc Fournet mentioned in the following notes.

[46] Wipszycka, 'Le monastère d'Apa Apollôs', p. 263. She follows by saying: 'Les parcelles appartenant à la communauté monastique de Pharoou étaient prises à bail par des membres de l'élite du village, qui les sous-louaient à des paysans.' This assumption is not based on direct textual evidence but on comparison with other monasteries. *SB* XX 14626 (forthcoming reedition by Jean-Luc Fournet) attests that the monastery had sheep and a *ktetor* (owner) status, but no information on specific landholdings can be drawn from the text.

[47] *P.Cair.Masp.* I 67096 (573) and commentary in Wipszycka, 'Le monastère d'Apa Apollôs', pp. 268–70.

[48] P.Cair. SR 3733 (3) dated 563, edited in Fournet, 'Un document inédit'.

[49] *P.Cair.Masp.* I 67003.15, dated 567 (forthcoming reedition by Jean-Luc Fournet).

mentions the monastery's holdings, both buildings and fields, but more specific information is not provided, given its state of preservation.[50]

Turning to Apa Sourous, the largest landowner in the cadastre is also the best represented by stray documents: a letter shows that the monastery could benefit from help and support from the powerful landlord Count (*comes*) Ammonios when it encountered issues with its tenants.[51] The estate accounts of the same Ammonios keep track of one financial transaction of obscure nature with or related to the monastery.[52] Leases and rent-receipts attest that the monastery owned, in addition to a pottery workshop,[53] several kinds of landholdings in different parts of the village territory (*pedias*):[54] a naked field without irrigation equipment (mere *arourai*)[55] and a large agricultural exploitation including a vineyard (*ktema*),[56] both in the western *pedias*, one smaller property qualified as *organon* in the northern *pedias*, and another (if not identical) referred to as *georgion*.[57] Concerning this last landholding, there is only one indication of its size: the rent is ninety-two artabas of wheat, which suggests a property of around twenty arouras.[58]

---

[50] Forthcoming publication by Jean-Luc Fournet.

[51] P.Oslo inv. 523 (sixth century) edited in Stolk, 'A Byzantine Business Letter': Count Ammonios writes this letter to help the Apa Sourous monastery resolve a conflict with the tenants of one of its properties, which included a vineyard.

[52] *P.Cair.Masp.* II 67139 VI v° 3 (dated 542–6) mentions an important money payment (two *solidi* minus four *carats*) in favour of Apa Sourous' barley to Artemidoros *singularis*, who is known from other documents to be the administrator of the monastery; see below n. 55. For a discussion of the hypothesis developed in Thomas, *Private Religious Foundations*, p. 73, that this payment may have been somehow related to 'the institution's tax obligations', see Wegner, 'Monastic Communities', pp. 56–8.

[53] *P.Cair.Masp.* I 67110 (dated 565).

[54] On the organisation of the Aphrodito countryside and the vocabulary referring to its components, see Marthot, 'La toponymie d'un village', pp. 163–7.

[55] *P.Lond.* V 1704 (sixth century): the name of the monastery is lost but can be restored based on the mention of the administrator Artemidoros, line 4, as Φλ(αυίου) Ἀρτεμιδώρ[ου σ] ιγ(γουλαρίου), 'Flavius Artemidoros *singularis*'; see Gascou, 'Les Pachômiens', p. 278.

[56] *P.Mich.* XIII 667 (dated 565).

[57] Both are rented by Dioscorus: for the *organon*, see *P.Cair.Masp.* I 67087 (543) and Keenan, 'Village Shepherds'; for the *georgion*, see *P.Cair.Masp.* II 67133 (542). For *organon* and *georgion* used to qualify the same property, see *P.Cair.Masp.* III 67307 (539) line 4 ([τ]οῦ ὑπὸ σὲ τῆς ἁγίας ἐκκλησίας ὀργάνου, 'the *organon* of the holy church in your hands') and 8 (τοῦ αὐτοῦ ὑπὸ σὲ γεωργίου, 'the said *georgion* in your hands').

[58] See *P.Michael.* 43 from 526 in which a twenty-eight-aroura property (*georgion*) has an annual rent of five artabas (2/3 wheat and 1/3 barley) per aroura, and see commentary by Keenan, 'Aurelius Phoibammon', p. 147 and note 7. The rate is similar twenty years later: in *P.Hamb.* I 68 from 548, the rent of the arable land is four artabas of wheat and one artaba of barley per aroura. In order to avoid converting one artaba of barley into wheat, a general order of magnitude can be reached as follows: at a rate of four artabas of wheat per aroura (i.e., barley is negligible), ninety-two artabas correspond to twenty-three arouras; at a rate of five artabas per aroura (i.e., barley counts like wheat), the said ninety-two artabas correspond to 18.4 arouras.

It could even be bigger, since the receipt does not specify, as is usually the case, that the payment is for the full rent. The lease of the larger exploitation (*ktema*) is in fact an agreement on changes in contract terms: the tenant, Phoibammon, Dioscorus' cousin, is already exploiting the *ktema*,[59] and he agrees to pay all the taxes of any kind rather than the monastery. No exact amount is given; there is only a reference made to the codex of the *censitor* Ioannes. There is, however, no obvious link with a property mentioned in the cadastre, which is also considered to be an abstract of Ioannes' codex.[60] The tenant also has to provide a fixed complementary rent: twenty artabas of wheat and fifty *aggeia* of wine (of six *sextarii* each), which seems a small amount for such a property.[61] The contract includes the provision that the amphorae have to be provided by the monastery, which, as we have already seen, happened to own a pottery workshop. While not unparalleled, this type of renting agreement is rare.[62]

Although it can be demonstrated from the cadastre and the tax register that the monastery of Apa Zenobios was an important landowner, no further text documenting its properties is known.[63] This is not the case for the two other Panopolite institutions. The monastery of Smine appears in two unusual situations: first, in 527, Apollos, Dioscorus' father, rented a property (*georgion*) that belongs to a count (whose name is lost) but was 'in the hands of the holy monastery for a long and impossible to remember time'.[64] It is thus an example of a sub-lease. It is, however, possible that the landholding was not in Aphrodito but in the neighbouring village of

---

[59] P.Mich. XIII 667.3 (dated 565), read ὑπ' ἐμὲ κτή[ματος τ]οῦ αὐτοῦ ἁγίου μοναστηρίου, 'the *ktema* of the said holy monastery in my hands' instead of ὑπ[ογ]ε[γρ(αμμένου)] κ[τ]ή[ματος το]ῦ αὐτοῦ ἁγίου μοναστηρίου, 'the *ktema* described below of the said holy monastery' (forthcoming publication by Florence Lemaire).

[60] Gascou, *Fiscalité et société*, pp. 249–50.

[61] For a comparison with another vineyard lease from Aphrodito, see P.Cair.Masp. I 67104.12 (dated 530), in which the annual rent is 120 *aggeia* of 7 *sextarii* per aroura.

[62] Among the corpus of about a hundred leases and rent-receipts from the Dioscorus archive gathered by Florence Lemaire for her PhD thesis, the only similar agreements are P.Cair.Masp. III 67300 (dated 527) and P.Lond. V 1695 (dated 530), two successive leases for the same *ktema*, owned in common by two sisters, Sibylla and Heraeis daughters of Mousaios, who are both said to be 'most well-born' (*eugenestate*). P.Lond. V 1841 (dated 536), also being edited by Florence Lemaire, is the lease of a *ktema*: the rent consists of the payment of all the taxes only in the absence of flood; otherwise, an equal share of the crops is planned.

[63] The Coptic letter P.Cair.S.R. 3733.5bis is addressed to Apa Termoute, the superior of the Apa Zenobios monastery, but it is not concerned with landholdings; see Vanderheyden, 'Les lettres coptes', text 4. P.Hamb. I 68 (dated 548) is the lease of a *ktema* located in the *kleros* Pherko and belonging to a monastery whose name is lost, but which could be Apa Zenobios, as the cadastre (line 265) records a landholding in Pherko. However, this is a fragile hypothesis.

[64] P.Lond. V 1690 + P.Heid. V 353.8–9; forthcoming reedition by Florence Lemaire. See also Gascou, 'Les Pachômiens', p. 280 and n. 15.

Pakerke in the Panopolite nome.⁶⁵ The second text relates to Aphrodito: in 565, Dioscorus sold to the monastery three arouras of unirrigated land, which are said to be included in a 'big' *georgion* belonging to the monastery and located in the *kleros* Hieras in the southern *pedias*.⁶⁶ The price of the sale is the payment of the *astika* taxes on fourteen arouras that Dioscorus owned in the *pedias* of the neighbouring village of Phthla. How Dioscorus happened to acquire this small plot in the first place is unclear: had he bought it from the monastery and later sold it back or was it the result of a shared inheritance? It is also intriguing that no duration date for the payment of the taxes in Phthla is mentioned: it would not be a satisfactory deal for the monastery if it were unlimited. Was it understood that the agreement would end with Dioscorus' death? The document is silent about this.

The monastery of Apa Shenoute is further attested as a landowner not in Aphrodito but in the neighbouring villages: unirrigated land (*arourai*) leased to Dioscorus' cousin, Phoibammon, in Phthla,⁶⁷ and an equipped property (*ktema*) in Thmonechte.⁶⁸ About this last landholding, it is mentioned in the lease that the previous tenant was the father of the current tenant.

One last monastery is attested as a landowner in Byzantine Aphrodito, the monastery of Genealios, which appears in the lease *P.Hamb.* I 68 (548): the object of the lease is located next to its property (*ktema*) in the *kleros* Pherko in the southern *pedias*. This establishment is attested only one other time: it is registered in an undated list of taxpayers, *P.Cair.Masp.* III 67288 VI v° 4. It may have been located outside Aphrodito's territory.

Thus, the Byzantine documentation from Aphrodito attests a small dozen of landowner monasteries with several profiles, from long-distant institutions owning a couple of plots in the village and the neighbourhood, to one humble, newly founded establishment. Compared to the others, Apa Sourous' monastery stands out by its wealth, which made it a major actor of the village economy. Even in this last case, the monastic estate looks

---

⁶⁵ Florence Lemaire suggests, at line 11: διακειμένου ἐπ[ὶ π]εδ[ιάδ(ος) κώμης Πα]κερκ[ῆτος], 'located in the *pedias* of the village of Pakerke'.

⁶⁶ *P.Lond.* V 1686 (dated 565).

⁶⁷ *P.Ross.Georg.* III 48 is a rent-receipt for the eighth indiction (dated by Florence Lemaire to summer 544). It acknowledges that the rent in wheat and barley has been paid in full, without further information. Pap.Lond. inv. 2836 (dated to 539 or 542 by Florence Lemaire) is likely to be another receipt for the same landholding: four artabas of wheat and four artabas of barley have been paid, which would point to a very modest property, although there is no indication that this amount was the full rent.

⁶⁸ *P.Cair.Masp.* II 67242 descr. (dated 547), forthcoming edition by Florence Lemaire.

fragmented, made of little bits of land that were most likely acquired by donations and without visible attempts to rationalise the management. There are, however, rare hints of entrepreneurial attitudes, but they happen to come from another institution, the Smine monastery. One example of a sub-lease and another of purchase may indicate economical strategies, although the latter relates to land located inside a property already belonging to the institution, so it reflects rationalism rather than expansion. To have their land cultivated, monasteries do not seem afraid to conclude special agreements, specifically in relation with the payment of taxes, nor to hire the children of previous tenants. For a distant landlord, perpetuating business agreements with trustworthy local families through the generations is common sense. For the villagers, the prospect of stable work relations, which would not be jeopardised by personal difficulties or succession problems, may have been a motive to prefer monasteries to individuals as landlords. Otherwise, no specific interest in cultivating monastic land can easily be spotted: as with any absentee landlord, the question of transporting the rent to the landlord's place can be an issue worth negotiating in the lease, since, for example, Apa Shenoute is located a little more than fifty kilometres south of Aphrodito. Texts documenting Aphrodito in the seventh century are rare, and when the sources start again to be extensive, the situation for landowner monasteries has evolved.

Aphrodito in the Eighth Century

The eighth-century papyri from Aphrodito are administrative documents that were most likely kept in the office of the village administrator. They do not contain leases, receipts, private letters, or drafts of petitions like Dioscorus' papers.[69] They provide, however, information on the fiscal organisation of the village, which reveals major changes from the Byzantine period. At this time, the village was no longer under the authority of the pagarch of the Antaiopolite nome (which had been joined with the Apollonopolite Minor nome). Neither did it become the head of a nome with its own pagarch and authority over surrounding villages. Ruled by an official called 'administrator' (*dioiketes*), who was directly accountable to the governor's office in the new capital Fustat, the village kept the same territory and became an independent administrative unit.[70] Its territory

---

[69] See Marthot and Vanderheyden, 'Désigner et nommer', pp. 218–20.
[70] See Marthot, 'Un village égyptien', pp. 187–212. Coptic texts refer to the administrator of Aphrodito (Coptic Djkoou) by borrowing the Greek word *pagarchos* and never *dioiketes*.

became divided into fiscal units called *choria*:[71] the village itself, three 'campaigns' (*pediades*), eight 'hamlets' (*epoikia*), and five monasteries.[72] This last category comprises five establishments: Abba Hermauos, Pharoou, Taroou, Barbarou, and Hagia Maria (Saint Mary).

Among these five monasteries, two clearly recall establishments encountered in the Byzantine documentation: Pharoou is the institution founded by Dioscorus' father, and Taroou, sometimes spelled Taroout(-),[73] may be identified with the Tarouthis monastery mentioned in the cadastre. Nothing is known of a Byzantine past for Barbarou (sometimes spelled Barbariou)[74] and Hagia Maria.[75] The last monastery, Abba Hermauos, however, appeared discretely in the Dioscorus archive through a mention of an *eukterion* (oratory) of Apa Hermauos in a list of taxpayers[76] and two references to priests. In a famous petition from the inhabitants of Aphrodito to the empress Theodosia, Palos, a priest and *oikonomos* of Saint [Apa] Hermauos, signs with the help of a monk named Ioannes.[77] In Count Ammonios' accounts, an unnamed 'priest of Apa Hermauos' occurs twice, immediately after entries related to inhabitants from Peto,[78] and a third instance may refer to the same priest Palos.[79] There is, thus, a possibility that the mention of a 'monastery of Peto' in the same text refers to the same institution as Apa Hermauos.[80]

However, whereas a pagarch rules over a city and villages, the Coptic formula is 'pagarch of Djkoou, its hamlets and its campaigns'; see, for example, *P.Lond.* IV 1494.8 (dated 709).

[71] On this new fiscal unit, see Gascou, 'Arabic Taxation', pp. 672–3.

[72] Besides these territory divisions, there were two fiscal groups called 'the men who are in Babylon' (*P.Lond.* IV p. XV) and 'the men of Saint Mary', who were 'clearly distinct' from Saint Mary's monastery (*P.Lond.* IV p. XVI). As such, they are not included in the present study.

[73] *P.Lond.* IV 1419.639,1144,1150,1153 (dated 716/17); see also Taloou at line 1299.

[74] *Chrest.Wilck.* 256, 1 and 3 (dated 709).

[75] There was at least one church in the village dedicated to the Virgin Mary; see Papaconstantinou, 'Les sanctuaires', pp. 86–7, numbers 13–14. The question whether there were one or two monasteries in the eighth century is not as simple as it appears in Cadell, 'Nouveaux fragments', p. 155 (5) and deserves a more detailed treatment.

[76] *P.Cair.Masp.* III 67288 VI v° 5 (sixth century).

[77] *P.Cair.Masp.* III 67283 III 21 (before 547). On this text, see *P.Mich.Aphrod.*, pp. 10–15 and Ruffini, *Social Networks*, pp. 177–9. Note that all the other ecclesiastical individuals mentioned in this document are priests of churches and *hagioi topoi* (holy places): they occur together in a previous section (II 1–10) and are all literate enough to sign for themselves. This could be a hint that Apa Hermauos was a humble institution.

[78] *P.Cair.Masp.* II 67138 III v° 11 and 67139 V v° 25 (dated 541–6).

[79] In *P.Cair.Masp.* II 67139 V v°4, δ(ιὰ) Π[.....]. πρε(σβυτέρου) ἄπα Ἑρμαῶτος, it is very tempting to read Πα[λῶτο]ς, especially as an Apa Palos occurs on the recto of this account (V r° 20) in relation with a cistern (*lakkos*) of Pekusios, while a 'cistern of Peto' occurs in *P.Cair.Masp.* II 67138 II r° 28, and a Pekusis, along with his son Pous, is a known inhabitant of Peto; see *P.Cair.Masp.* II 67139 V v° 5. Palos 15, 16, and 19 in Ruffini, *A Prosopography*, could be the same priest from Peto.

[80] *P.Cair.Masp.* II 67138 II v° 19 and 67139 II v° 14. On the importance of Peto for Count Ammonios, see Ruffini, *Social Networks*, p. 175.

Information on monastic properties is mainly found in the codex *P. Lond.* IV 1419, of which lines 1269–311 are concerned with tax payments from the five monasteries-*choria*. Additional indications are given elsewhere in the tax registers when payments are made by individuals for a place (*topos*) in favour of a monastery: it is, then, likely that the monastery is (one of) the landlord(s) of the place. In *P. Lond.* IV 1419, the entry about Pharoou occupies only one line (1292), recording a total of 111 *solidi* and 44 artabas without further detail. There is no trace elsewhere of any landholding for this monastery in the eighth century, suggesting that it had neither significantly flourished nor expanded since its foundation. No property is mentioned either for Abba Hermauos (lines 1293–8): its entry, the total of which is 189 *solidi*, 8 *keratia*, and 67 artabas, lists only payments by individuals. Two places, however, are indicated in the rest of the documentation as properties of this monastery.[81] Landholdings are listed for the three last monasteries: Hagia Maria, Barbarou, and Taloou (for Taroou). Hagia Maria has to pay 114 *solidi* but only a small amount of wheat (twelve artabas). It owned properties in seven *topoi* (lines 1269–80). Barbarou pays 110 *solidi* but forty-six artabas for nine different *topoi* (lines 1281–91). Taloou's total is lost; it is registered for ten *topoi* (lines 1299–311).

Further systematic investigations are still needed to fully understand the tax contributions of each *chorion*. The five monasteries seem nevertheless to be minor contributors to the village taxation. A first hint has been provided above, with the section of *P.Lond.* IV 1419.1269–311 dedicated to them and recording both humble and similar amounts (from 110 to 189 *solidi* with Taroou's total missing), suggesting that they were of equivalent importance. Further evidence is given by a series of *entagia* (orders of payment) preserved for the fiscal year 709/10, whose data is gathered in Table 3.2, with the monasteries noted by an asterisk.[82]

The two smaller monasteries are asked to pay only one per cent of what the largest *epoikion* Pakaunis paid. Even the most heavily taxed monastery, Hagia Maria, pays five times less than the said *epoikion*. A list of taxes in wheat required for a fifth indiction shows that, out of a total of 1,500 artabas, the village itself is asked for 755, but the 'monasteries'

---

[81] Payment in favour of this monastery for the *topos* Panuchatou in *P.Lond.* IV 1419.1057, and for the *topos* Neos Ktema (the 'New Property') in *SB* XX 15099.151.

[82] On this group of texts, see Cadell, 'Nouveaux fragments', pp. 143–4 and 153–5.

Table 3.2: *Amounts required by the central administration for the fiscal year 709/10.*

Text	Chorion	Amount in solidi	Amount in artabas of wheat
SB I 5644	Pakaunis	498	128
SB I 5638	Five eastern *pediades*	461	270
SB I 5653	Three western *pediades*	400	250
SB I 5654	Two western *pediades*	253	235
SB I 5645	Emphuteuton	131	
P.Cair.Arab. III 160	Psurou	104	11
SB I 5650	Hagia Maria*	98	88
SB I 5655	Name lost (Sakoore ?)	98	
SB I 5652	Men of Hagia Maria	47	
SB I 5646	Bounon	47	5
P.Cair.Arab. III 161	Hagios Pinouton	37	
SB I 5648	Poimen	30	18
P.Cair.Arab. III 162	Oros of Hagia Maria in the East*[83]	30	
P.Cair.Arab. III 163	Abba Hermaous*	28	
SB I 5647	Keramiou	25	
Chrest.Wilck. 256	Barbariou (*sic*)*	10	
SB I 5649	Taurinou (= Taroou)*	5	
SB I 5651	Pharoou*	5	

(*ta monasteria*), grouped all together in one entry, have to pay only fifty artabas.[84]

These entries gathering all the 'monasteries' together led Harold Idris Bell, the editor of *P.Lond.* IV, to wonder if they may concern more institutions than the usual five monasteries-*choria*. Bell pointed out that there were at least two cases in which there are entries both for '*ta monasteria*' and for each of the five monasteries-*choria*, with totals showing that the former is not the addition of the latter.[85] These observations suggest that other, small monasteries existed, which appear only occasionally in the rest of the documentation. There are, indeed, scattered mentions of other monasteries: Abba Charisios,[86] Abba/Saint Psempnouthes,[87] the mysterious (because otherwise

---

[83] Distinct from Hagia Maria; see n. 75.   [84] *P.Lond.* IV 1415 v° 13–17.
[85] *P.Lond.* IV p. XVI referring to *P.Lond.* IV 1416.72–9 (dated 732–4) and *P.Lond.* IV 1445.2–5 (eighth century).
[86] *P.Lond.* IV 1419.1003.
[87] *P.Lond.* IV 1419.1002 (payer) and 363 (beneficiary). As already mentioned, a monk of the monastery of Apa Psempnouthes is a tenant in the cadastre (line 222), which suggests that the institution was not far from the village.

unattested) 'Abba Entiou',[88] 'Ken[-]riou' (a very doubtful reading),[89] and Saint Psoios,[90] but nothing is known about these institutions.

Since the monastery of Apa Sourous was of such importance in the sixth century, we would expect it to have become a *chorion* in the new organisation of Aphrodito in the eighth century. The monastery, now called Abba Sourous, does not disappear from the documentation, but its presence is reduced to the already mentioned *P.Lond.* IV 1419, which joins with *SB* XX 15099 (dated 716/17), a long codex concerned with land taxes in which Abba Sourous is mentioned twenty times. In general in this codex, an individual is registered first for payments in his own name for a given place (*topos*) and then for payments in favour of the *ousia* of Abba Sourous for the same place.[91] The word *ousia*, referring to large estates in the sixth century, is rarely present in the eighth-century papyri from Aphrodito, and almost all the occurrences relate to the *ousia* of Abba Sourous.[92] The only element to complete this picture is *P.Lond.* IV 1416 (dated 732–4), a fragmentary register of various content, in which the 'codices of the *ousiai* of the pagarchy' are mentioned (line 25).[93] This would suggest that the *ousiai* were in different registers and were administered differently, in a type of independence from the village officer. As a possible comparison, *ousia* is used in texts from the Hermopolite monastery of Apa Apollo at Bawit, where it apparently refers to geographical divisions of the estate.[94]

The monastery of the Oasites, which owned a small plot in the cadastre and a part of an oil factory in 552, appears in *P.Lond.* IV 1419.1255 among the *adespota ktemata*, 'properties without a landlord' managed by the village administration. In the same section, in lines 1258 and 1260, a place (*topos*) named 'of the Oasites' is mentioned, probably identical to a field known from the Byzantine period in an agricultural account written by Dioscorus, *P.Cair.Masp.* III 67325 I 25 v° 5 (dated 554–61). It is unlikely that the monastery itself has become a property without a landlord; it is

---

[88] *P.Lond.* IV 1419.437 and restored line 1382. I give the attested form in the genitive instead of a speculative nominative ending.

[89] *P.Lond.* IV 1419.9 (in the genitive; see previous note).

[90] *P.Lond.* IV 1444.3 (eighth century).   [91] For example, *P.Lond.* IV 1419.867–8.

[92] Twice it appears to refer to the estate of the Governor (*symboulos*): that of Abd el-Aziz in *P.Lond.* IV 1447.172 (dated 685–705) and one explicitly located in Damascus in *P.Lond* IV 1414.81 and 151. Finally, *ousia* occurs three times with a name that is not attested elsewhere in the Aphrodito documentation: Prinkop(-) in *P.Lond.* IV 1419.967; Stephanaket[-] in *SB* XX 15099.267 (dated 716/17); and Kallinikos in *P.Lond.* IV 1419.1346.

[93] Κωδίκω(ν) τῶ(ν) οὐσι(ακῶν) τῆ(ς) παγαρχ(ίας): in a note, Bell expressed his doubts about the resolution of the abbreviation and a possible reference to a fiscal category of land. Since the adjective *ousiakos* is not certainly attested after the Byzantine period, it could be *ousi(on)*.

[94] *P.Brux.Bawit* 31.

more reasonable to suspect, if not a confusion of the scribe, at least an elliptic formula meaning 'the [place which used to belong to the] monastery of the Oasites'. Evidence is too thin to decide whether this monastery was part of Aphrodito's 'small monasteries' mentioned above or a distant institution which had gradually lost its properties in the village's territory.[95]

The monastery of Abba Shenoute is also present in *P.Lond.* IV 1419.1328–48, in association with the rare word *orgon*, the meaning of which is unclear. It probably owned a *topos* Panouhool, which may have been located between Aphrodito and Thmonechte, a neighbouring village in which it already had landholdings in the Byzantine period.

Another Panopolite establishment reappears, without much information, in *SB* XX 15099.152, in which a payment is made in favour of the account (*onoma*) of 'Zminos', which must relate to the Smine monastery. While encountering payments for a *topos* Smine,[96] the question arises whether monasteries could give their names to properties they (co-)owned. There are indeed attestations of *topoi* named after three out of the five monasteries-*choria*,[97] but some are also named after Abba Senouthios (Apa Shenoute),[98] Hagios Phoibammon,[99] and Abba Senobios. The latter of these could be the Panopolite Apa Zenobios, especially since there is one taxpayer who is registered for this *topos* and for another, Piah Kaloou, which is probably identical to the *topos* Kalau that belonged to Apa Zenobios in the cadastre.[100] It is not impossible, however, that these place names may have retained the memory of former – and so not actual – landlords. There is no evidence that the Apa Zenobios monastery still owned land in eighth-century Aphrodito. In fact, evidence on this point started and stopped with the cadastre and the register, so in the years 524–5.

Thus, in the new organisation of Aphrodito, as it appears in the early eighth century, five monasteries had acquired the administrative status of *chorion*. Further investigation is needed to determine the exact implications of this new status in terms of internal hierarchical structure and of relation to the 'world outside', but its fiscal responsibilities are clear. If they were indeed an official component of the village organisation, these

---

[95] See above, n. 35.
[96] The same woman pays for the *topos* Zminos in *P.Lond.* IV 1420.46 (dated 706) and Tsminos in *P.Lond.* IV 1424.14 (dated perhaps to 714).
[97] *Topos* Barbarou in *P.Lond.* IV 1416.33 (dated 732–4); *topos* of Abba Hermauos in *P.Lond.* IV 1419.338; *topos* Talou (for Taroou) among others in *P.Lond.* IV 1419.1314.
[98] *P.Lond.* IV 1421.73,79,109,120 (dated 705).
[99] Among others, *P.Lond.* IV 1419.1305, payment by Taloou monastery.
[100] *P.Lond.* IV 1419.572–3 and *SB* XX 14669.235 (dated circa 524).

monasteries paid the smallest amounts of tax, showing that they were not the richest part of the village population. The short list of the landholdings that can be attributed to them confirms this modest share in the rural economy. Some distant monasteries managed to retain some properties, but, judging by the remaining evidence, the tendency would rather be of a decline or maintenance, rather than of an expansion. The only monastery that owned a significant portion of the village territory in the Byzantine period, Apa Sourous, became an estate, the taxation of which escaped the village treasury. The exact extent of this estate is, however, difficult to evaluate because of the incompleteness of the sources. The resulting image is certainly not of a village economically in the hands of various monasteries.

Conclusion

Thanks to a large quantity of texts originating from one single village over two centuries, precise elements can be identified concerning monasteries as landowners in Aphrodito. It is, however, striking how little correspondence from the monastic properties themselves is known from the time between the two archives. A change in designation may obscure some identifications: because of an especially rich documentation, the monastery founded by Dioscorus' father can be identified, whether it is referred to as 'of the Christ-bearing Apostle', 'of Apa Apollos', or 'of Pharoou'. This shows that the same institution, in coeval texts, can receive three different designations: the name of its dedicatee, that of its founder, and that of the place where it stood. The same goes for the White Monastery, which is called Apa/Abba Senouthios/Shenoute after its founder or Tripe/ Atrep(-) after Tripheion, the former sanctuary of the goddess Triphis, on or around which it was built.[101] It is likely that competing designations were possible not only for the monasteries, but also for the name(s) of the properties they owned. Nevertheless, regardless of this point, there remains little evidence of properties belonging to monasteries throughout the centuries.

The comparison of the two archives clearly shows three patterns of evolution for monastic estates: distant institutions maintained a discreet presence in Aphrodito and its surroundings, the White Monastery in apparently a more stable way than the two other Panopolite establishments of Apa Zenobios and Smine, while local Tarouthis/Taroou and the recently

---

[101] Marthot, 'Homonyms Causing Confusion', p. 489.

founded Pharoou continued to be of modest size and played an active part in the new post-conquest fiscal organisation, as opposed to the other local, and more wealthy, monastery of Sourous, which acquired a different status as *ousia*. This latter transformation raises the question of whether the process of becoming an independent estate had not already started in the early sixth century when all Apa Sourous' land was liable for the *astika* and not the *kometika* tax. A better understanding of Aphrodito's landowners in general and of the specific changes visible in the eighth-century archive should, in the future, refine the picture of monasteries as landowners. Analysis of the data from the texts and archaeological remains would provide invaluable input, but only if the present restrictions imposed on surveys in this area are no longer in place.[102]

More generally, a close examination of Aphrodito's documentation proves that the number and importance of monasteries in and around the village has been widely overestimated so far by scholars. Impressed by the development of monastic estates founded in the third and fourth centuries and already flourishing in the sixth century, there has been a tendency to multiply what could be taken for allusions to religious institutions, reaching untenable figures for a mere village. Generalisations have also led to the spread of the idea that 'the monasteries' were prime actors in the village economy, while in fact this statement can only be applied to one specific establishment, the monastery of Apa Sourous. All the other institutions have a rather discreet role, and interest on monasteries should not overshadow the role of other components of the rural society, such as, for example, professional associations and local intermediaries of distant landowners, in this complex period of political and administrative change.

Bibliography

Bagnall, R. S. 'Village Landholding at Aphrodito in Comparative Perspective' in J.-L. Fournet (ed.), *Les archives de Dioscore d'Aphrodité cent ans après leur découverte, histoire et culture dans l'Égypte byzantine* (Paris: Études d'archéologie et d'histoire ancienne, 2008), pp. 181–90.

Cadell, H. 'Nouveaux fragments de la correspondance de Kurrah ben Sharik', *Recherches de Papyrologie*, 4 (1967), 107–60.

de Jong, J. H. M. 'A Summary Tax Assessment from Eighth Century Aphrodito' in A. Nodar and S. Torallas Tovar (eds.), *Proceedings of the 28th Congress of*

---

[102] Present restrictions are due to military reasons.

Papyrology; 2016 August 1–6; Barcelona (Barcelona: Publicacions de l'Abadia de Montserrat, Universitat Pompeu Fabra, 2019), pp. 577–85.

de Jong, J. H. M. 'Who Did What in Eighth-Century Aphrodito? P.Würzb.inv. 122–127, Greek Tax Documents and Some Observations on Prosopography' in *Documents and Manuscripts in the Arab-Islamic World: The Seventh International Society for Arabic Papyrology (ISAP) Conference (Berlin, 20–23 March, 2018)* (forthcoming).

Fournet, J.-L. 'Un document inédit des archives de Dioscore d'Aphrodité au Musée Égyptien' in M. Eldamaty and M. Trad (eds.), *Egyptian Museum Collections around the World. Studies for the Centennial of the Egyptian Museum* (Cairo: The American University in Cairo Press, 2002), vol. I, pp. 397–407.

Fournet, J.-L. (ed.), *Les archives de Dioscore d'Aphrodité cent ans après leur découverte, histoire et culture dans l'Égypte byzantine* (Paris: Études d'archéologie et d'histoire ancienne, 2008).

Fournet, J.-L. 'Quittances de loyer du topos d'apa Michel d'Antaiopolis', *Bulletin of the American Society of Papyrologists*, 45 (2008), 45–58.

Fournet, J.-L. 'Sur les premiers documents juridiques coptes (2): les archives de Phoibammôn et de Kollouthos' in A. Boud'hors and C. Louis. (eds.), *Études coptes XIV. Seizièmes journées d'études coptes, Genève, 19–21 juin 2013* (Paris: De Boccard, 2016), pp. 115–41.

Gascou, J. *Fiscalité et société en Égypte byzantine* (Paris: Association des amis du Centre d'histoire et civilisation de Byzance, 2008).

Gascou, J. 'Les Pachômiens à Aphrodité' in J.-L. Fournet (ed.), *Les archives de Dioscore d'Aphrodité cent ans après leur découverte, histoire et culture dans l'Égypte byzantine* (Paris: Études d'archéologie et d'histoire ancienne, 2008), pp. 275–82.

Gascou, J. 'Arabic Taxation in the Mid-Seventh-Century Greek Papyri' in C. Zuckerman (ed.), *Constructing the Seventh Century* (Paris: Association des amis du Centre d'histoire et civilisation de Byzance, 2013), pp. 671–7.

Keenan, J. G. 'Aurelius Phoibammon, Son of Triadelphus: A Byzantine Egyptian Land Entrepreneur', *Bulletin of the American Society of Papyrologists*, 17 (1980), 145–54.

Keenan, J. G. 'Notes on Absentee Landlordism in Aphrodito', *Bulletin of the American Society of Papyrologists*, 22 (1985), 137–69.

Keenan, J. G. 'Village Shepherds and Social Tension in Byzantine Egypt' in N. Lewis (ed.), *Papyrology*, Yale Classical Studies 28 (Cambridge: Cambridge University Press, 1985), pp. 245–59.

MacCoull, L. S. B. 'Why and How Was the Aphrodito Cadaster Made?', *Greek, Roman, and Byzantine Studies*, 50 (2010), 625–38.

MacCoull, L. S. B. 'Monastic and Church Landholding in the Aphrodito Cadaster', *Zeitschrift für Papyrologie und Epigraphik*, 178 (2011), 243–6.

Marthot, I. 'Homonyms Causing Confusion in Toponymy: Examples from Aphrodito and the Antaiopolite Nome' in P. Schubert (ed.), *Proceedings of* the 26th International Congress of Papyrology (Geneva: Droz, 2012), pp. 487–90.

Marthot, I. 'Un village égyptien et sa campagne: étude de la microtoponymie du territoire d'Aphroditê (VIe–VIIIe s.)', unpublished PhD thesis, École Pratique des Hautes Études, Paris, 2013.

Marthot, I. 'La toponymie d'un village de Moyenne-Égypte et de sa campagne aux VIe et VIIIe siècles apr. J.-C., le cas d'Aphroditê dans l'Antaiopolite d'après les papyrus grecs' in Y. Gourdon and Å. Engsheden (eds.), *Études d'onomastique égyptienne, méthodologies et nouvelles approches* (Cairo: Institut français d'archéologie orientale, 2016), pp. 161–75.

Marthot, I. and Vanderheyden, L. 'Désigner et nommer en grec ou en copte ? Bilinguisme toponymique de la campagne d'Aphroditê du VIe au VIIIe s.' in C. Somaglino and S. Dhenin (eds.), *Décrire, imaginer, construire l'espace. Toponymie égyptienne de l'Antiquité au Moyen-Âge* (Cairo: Institut français d'archéologie orientale, 2016), pp. 217–31.

Mirković, M. 'Count Ammonios and Paying Taxes in the Name of Somebody Else in the Cadastre from Aphrodito' in T. Gagos (ed.), *Proceedings of the 25th International Congress of Papyrology* (Ann Arbor: The University of Michigan Library 2010), pp. 565–72.

Papaconstantinou, A. 'Les sanctuaires de la Vierge dans l'Égypte byzantine et omeyyade. L'apport des textes documentaires', *Journal of Juristic Papyrology*, 30 (2000), 81–94.

Papaconstantinou, A. *Le culte des saints en Égypte des Byzantins aux Abbassides. Apport des inscriptions et des papyrus grecs et coptes* (Paris: CNRS Éditions, 2001).

Rémondon, R. 'P. Hamb. 56 et P. Lond. 1419 (notes sur les finances d'Aphrodito du VIe siècle au VIIIe)', *Chronique d'Égypte*, 40 (1965), 401–30.

Richter, T. S. 'Language Choice in the Qurra Dossier' in A. Papaconstantinou (ed.), *The Multilingual Experience in Egypt, from the Ptolemies to the Abbasids* (Farnham: Ashgate, 2010), pp. 189–220.

Ruffini, G. 'Aphrodito before Dioscorus', *Bulletin of the American Society of Papyrologists*, 45 (2008), 225–39.

Ruffini, G. *Social Networks in Byzantine Egypt* (Cambridge: Cambridge University Press, 2008).

Ruffini, G. *A Prosopography of Byzantine Aphrodito* (Durham, NC: American Society of Papyrologists, 2011).

Ruffini, G. *Life in an Egyptian Village in Late Antiquity: Aphrodito before and after the Islamic Conquest* (Cambridge: Cambridge University Press, 2018).

Stolk, J. V. 'A Byzantine Business Letter and Account from the Collection of the Oslo University Library', *Archiv für Papyrusforschung*, 59.2 (2013), 391–400.

Thomas, J. P. *Private Religious Foundations in the Byzantine Empire* (Washington, DC: Dumbarton Oaks, 1987).

Timm, S. *Das christlich-koptische Ägypten in arabischer Zeit, eine Sammlung christlicher Stätten in Ägypten in arabischer Zeit, unter Ausschluss von*

Alexandria, Kairo, des Apa-Mena-Klosters (Dēr Abū Mina), der Skētis (Wādi n-Naṭrūn) und der Sinai-Region, 7 vols (Wiesbaden: L. Reichert, 1984–2007).

Vanderheyden, L. 'Les lettres coptes des archives de Dioscore d'Aphroditê (VIe siècle; Égypte)', unpublished PhD thesis, École Pratique des Hautes Études, Paris, 2015.

Wegner, J. 'Monastic Communities in Context: Social and Economic Interrelations of Monastic Institutions and Laymen in Middle Egypt (6th–8th centuries)', unpublished PhD thesis, University of Warsaw, 2017.

Wipszycka, E. 'Le monastère d'Apa Apollôs: un cas typique ou un cas exceptionnel?' in J.-L. Fournet (ed.), *Les archives de Dioscore d'Aphrodité cent ans après leur découverte, histoire et culture dans l'Égypte byzantine* (Paris: Études d'archéologie et d'histoire ancienne, 2008), pp. 261–73.

Wipszycka, E. *Moines et communautés monastiques en Égypte, IVe–VIIIe siècles* (Warsaw: Raphael Taubenschlag Foundation, 2009).

Zuckerman, C. *Du village à l'Empire: autour du registre fiscal d'Aphroditô (525/526)* (Paris: Association des amis du Centre d'histoire et civilisation de Byzance, 2004).

4 | The Naqlun Fathers and Their Business Affairs: Private Assets and Activities of the Monks in a Semi-Anchoritic Community in the Late Antique Fayum

TOMASZ DERDA AND JOANNA WEGNER

Egyptian Monasticism in the Fourth to Eighth Centuries

In the period from the fourth to eighth centuries, monastic settlements could be found throughout Egypt, both in the remote desert regions east and west of the Nile Valley and in the more familiar border zones between desert and cultivated land.[1] Monastic presence permeated the landscape, extending into villages, towns, cities, and suburban districts. It also adapted and redefined pagan sacred spaces (necropoleis and – to a lesser extent – temples) or ancient industrial installations (quarries).[2]

Various settlement forms reflected the wide range of ways in which the monastic vocation was fulfilled. The literary sources expound the three 'models' of monastic life: the anchoritic (solitary-eremitic), the coenobitic (communal and commensal), and the semi-anchoritic (solitary-eremitic, but organised around a communal centre in which the Eucharist and common meals took place). These labels are useful terminological approximations, but they do not cover the actual diversity of solutions applied in organising monastic lives, and should not be treated as referring to clear-cut models.

The variety of social and economic arrangements among the monks and within communities was equally great. Renunciation of worldly affairs played an important role in monastic ideology, but separation from 'the world outside' was never complete, especially in the economic sphere.[3] Social and economic links with 'the world', which occupy a marginal role in the literary discourse focused on spirituality, come to

---

[1] Wipszycka, *Moines et communautés monastiques*, pp. 107–10.
[2] Brooks Hedstrom, *The Monastic Landscape*; O'Connell, 'Tombs for the Living'; O'Connell, 'Excavation of Wadi Sarga'; Wipszycka, *Études sur le christianisme*, pp. 281–336; Wipszycka, *Moines et communautés monastique*; Wipszycka, *Second Gift*.
[3] Goehring, *Ascetics, Society, and the Desert*, pp. 39–52 and 89–109; Wipszycka, 'Resources'; Wipszycka, *Second Gift*, pp. 457–89; for a case study, see Wegner, 'The Bawit Monastery'.

the fore in documentary texts related to monasticism that emerge in substantial numbers from the sixth century onwards.[4] Documents on papyrus and potsherds (ostraca), preserved due to the extreme aridity of the desert regions of Egypt, were drawn up by and for monastic communities and their members to clarify property rights and contractual obligations, and to regulate the flow of money, goods, and services. The monasteries we see in the documents were often landowning institutions with serious fiscal and managerial concerns.

A striking feature of monastic life, as recorded in the documents, is the access to material resources enjoyed by individual monks. Property possession was an ambiguous matter in the monastic movement.[5] Hermits had to rely on the work of their own hands to survive and did possess private means at their disposal. In coenobitic monasteries, individuals were essentially prohibited from possessing property and depended on communal resources. Documentary papyri bring to light examples of property-possessing monks who were either anchorites or community members. The former are represented, among others, by the somewhat waspish Frange – the resident of a reused Pharaonic tomb in the eighth-century Thebaid, who earned his living by weaving and producing books, and left dozens of letters that provide a unique insight into his activities and mentality (*O.Frangé*). Property-possessing community members are found, for example, in the Middle Egyptian monasteries of Bawit and Deir el-Bala'izah.[6] The documentary dossiers of these two communities contain private loan contracts concluded by monks in their own name with other monks, laypeople, and the monks' own monasteries. Almost all of these contracts feature individual monastic creditors[7] and give a solid testimony to the financial independence of monks within communities.[8]

---

[4] The earliest monastic documentary dossiers, composed mainly of letters dealing with both spiritual and material affairs, date to the fourth century. Legal and administrative texts are, however, later. For an overview of monastic documentary papyri and ostraca, see Wipszycka, *Moines et communautés monastiques*, pp. 80–99; Wipszycka, *Second Gift*, pp. 266–83.

[5] Bagnall, 'Monks and Property'.

[6] For Bawit, see Wegner, 'The Bawit Monastery'. For Bala'izah, see *P.Bal.* II 103, 106, and 110; other Bala'izah documents referring to financial dealings of the monks are *P.Bal.* II 114, 124, and 157.

[7] In *P.Mon.Apollo* 38, the creditor is the monastery of Apa Apollo, while the debtor is one of its monks.

[8] Markiewicz, 'The Church, Clerics, Monks and Credit'.

The Monastery of Deir el-Naqlun in the South-Eastern Fayum

The Site and the Finds: Architecture and Papyri

Access to private financial resources is an important feature of the small dossier of Greek documentary papyri discovered in the monastery of Deir el-Naqlun. The site, located in the south-eastern Fayum (Fig. 4.1), has been excavated since 1986 by Polish archaeologists under the direction of Włodzimierz Godlewski. It has witnessed monastic occupation from the fifth century AD, when the first hermitages associated with the site were established. The thriving monastery of Archangel Gabriel today continues the long monastic tradition of the place. The area of Polish archaeological activity in Naqlun comprises: a) the plateau east of the modern monastery; b) a group of circa eighty cave hermitages east of the plateau; and c) a group of nine to ten hermitages west of the plateau, separated from the rest of the site by a modern road (Fig. 4.2). Only seven hermitages in the east (numbers 1, 2, 6, 25, 44, 50, 89) and two hermitages in the west (85 and 87) were excavated. The works on the plateau focused on buildings dating from the sixth to at least the eleventh century.

Among the earliest structures discovered in Naqlun are two western hermitages, 85 and 87, dated to the fifth century.[9] They were built close to the Bahr el-Gharaq canal, which was (and still remains) the main watercourse in the area and marked the boundary between desert and cultivated land.[10] Monastic occupation of the range of low desert hills (Gebel Naqlun) east of the plateau began around the same period: a fifth-century date is proposed for hermitage 44, the northernmost of the eastern group, hermitage 6 in the southern section of the gebel, as well as hermitages 50 and 89.[11] The remaining excavated hermitages in Gebel Naqlun were constructed in the sixth century and witnessed activity until the medieval period, as indicated by Coptic and Arabic documents found in them.[12] All of the eastern hermitages were artificial caves hewn in the soft rock of the gebel. Excavated structures on the plateau date from the sixth to the eleventh

---

[9] Godlewski, 'Naqlun: Excavations 1995', p. 85; Godlewski, 'Excavating the Ancient Monastery', p. 157; Godlewski, 'Naqlun (Nekloni): Preliminary Report 2006', p. 204; Godlewski, 'Naqlun 2007', p. 238.

[10] Derda and Wegner, 'Naqlun in the Fifth–Seventh Century'.

[11] Godlewski, 'Naqlun: The Hermitage of Phibamo'; Godlewski *et al.*, 'Deir el-Naqlun 2014–2015', p. 279; Wipszycka, *Moines et communautés monastiques*, p. 137; Godlewski, 'Naqlun 2016'; Danys, 'Pottery Finds', p. 182; Lichocka, 'Roman and Early Byzantine Coins'.

[12] Godlewski, 'Excavating the Ancient Monastery', p. 157; Urbaniak-Walczak, 'P. Naqlun inv. 12/89'.

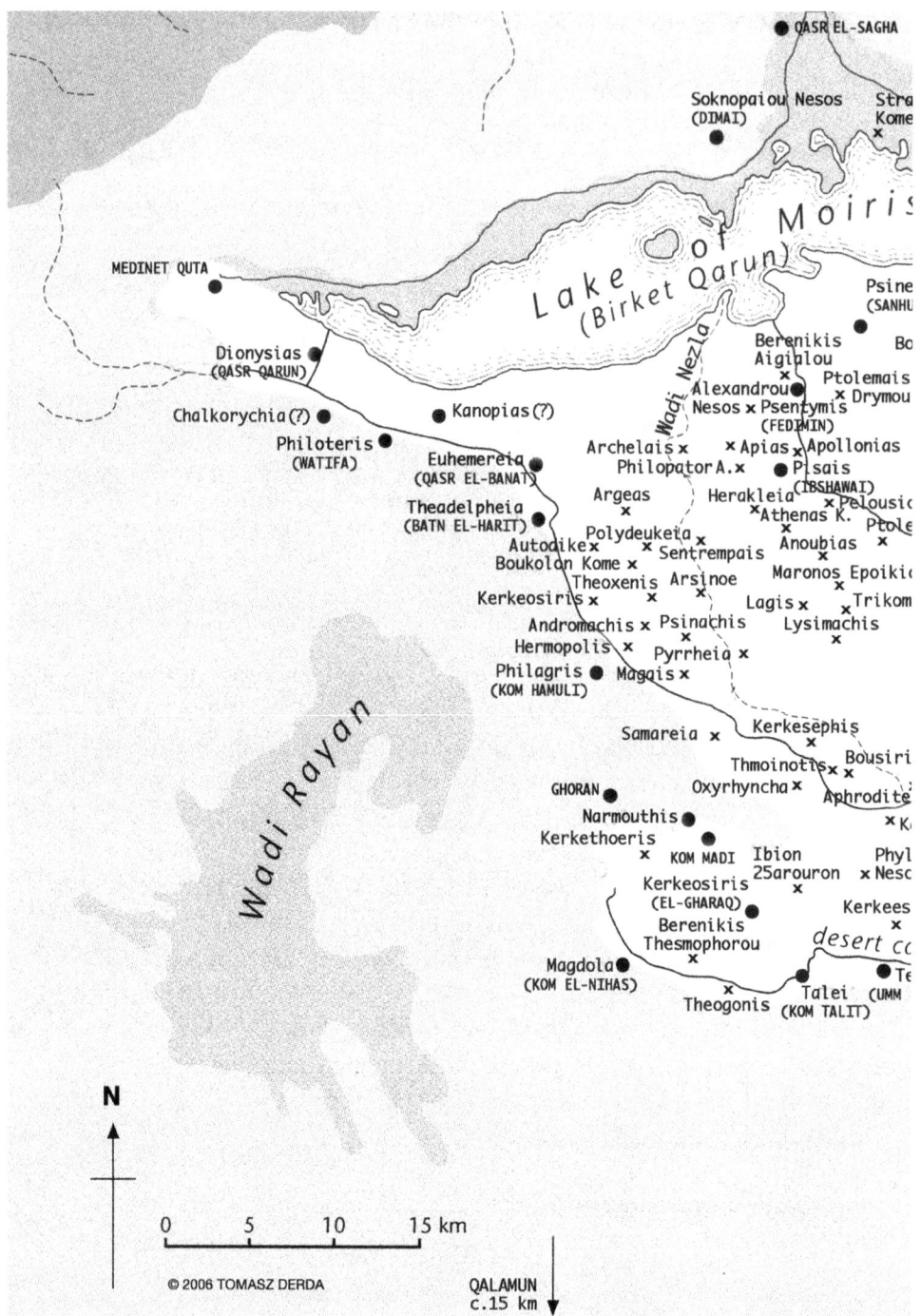

Fig. 4.1. Map of the Fayum.

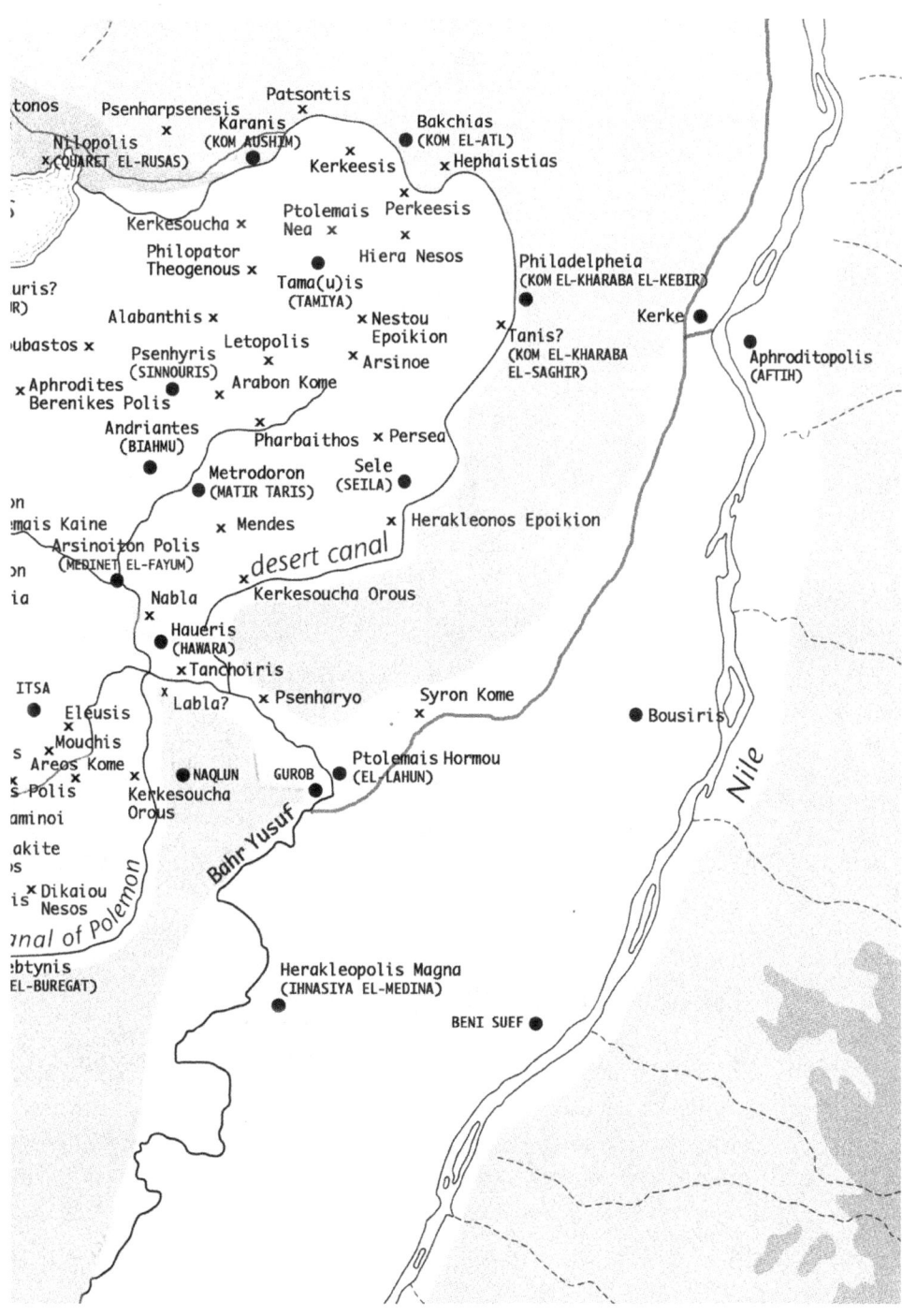

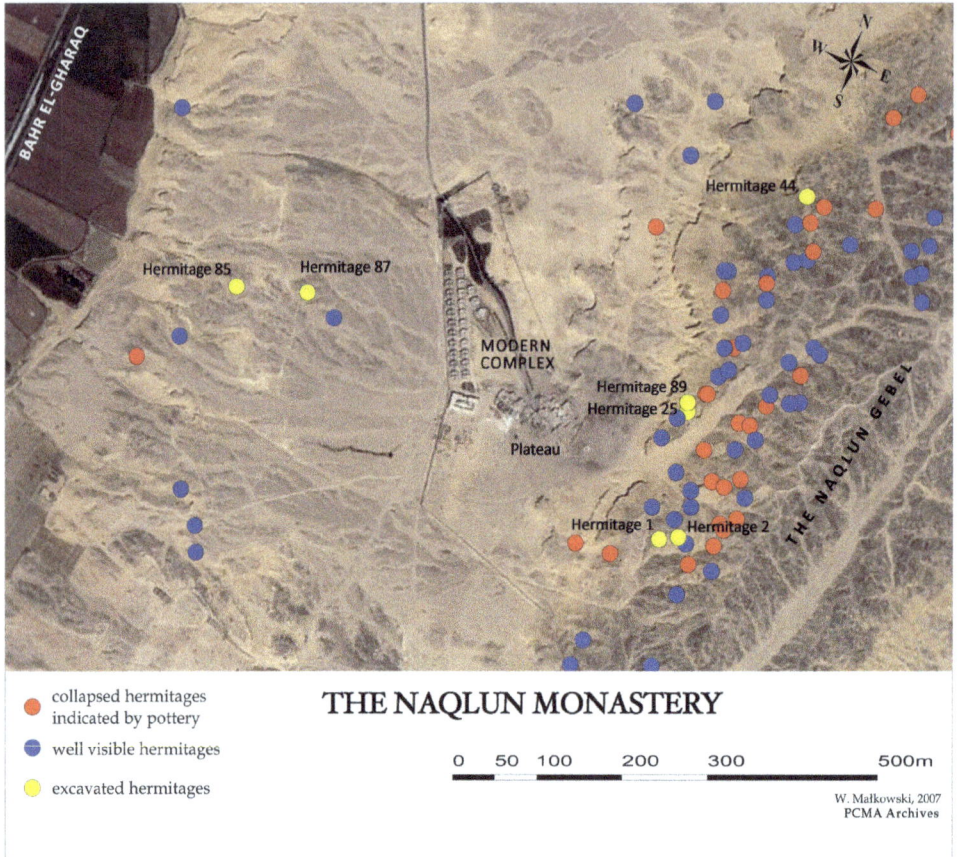

Fig. 4.2. The Naqlun monastery. © Wiesław Małkowski and PCMA Archives.

century; of these, the earliest (sixth–seventh century) are buildings A, AA 20, the first phase of buildings E and J, and the bottom layers of the rubbish dump in sector B.[13]

Apart from architectural structures and related artefacts (mainly pottery, baskets, and leather and wooden objects), the excavations yielded a number of documentary papyri. The earliest phase of the monastery's existence (fifth–seventh centuries) is documented by texts written mostly in Greek – evidently the community's main language in this period.[14] With few exceptions, the papyri can be dated only on palaeographic grounds,

---

[13] Godlewski et al., 'Deir el-Naqlun', pp. 181–8; Godlewski, 'Naqlun: Excavations 1999', pp. 126–31; P. Naqlun II p. 7; Derda and Dzierzbicka, 'Refuse Dump', p. 212.

[14] The Naqlun documents are referred to by their consecutive numbers: P.Naqlun I 1–14; P Naqlun II 15–34; P.Naqlun 35–38 = Derda and Wegner, 'New Documentary Papyri'; P. Naqlun 39 [= P.Gascou 29] = Derda and Wegner, 'Letter from Tebetny'.

which limits our ability to use them for building diachronic narratives. The texts come from various locations scattered across the site: the earliest layers of the refuse dump in sector B on the plateau, sector D on the plateau, and hermitages 2, 6, 25, 87, and 89. Our knowledge of the archaeological context of these finds markedly increases their informative value and allows even for the poorly preserved or apparently unrelated texts to be incorporated – sometimes, admittedly, only in a hypothetical manner – into our reconstruction of the structure of the monastic settlement in the Byzantine period.

The Shape of the Naqlun Community in the Fifth–Seventh Centuries

The source base available for a reconstruction is lacunose, but a brief outline of the community's basic development can be drawn nonetheless.[15] The fifth-century phase of the monastic settlement by the canal is obscure. Hermitages 85 and 87 were exceptionally well-equipped and fully autonomous units (see below); nothing indicates that the monks who inhabited them perceived themselves as members of a community.

A topographic and organisational shift seems to have occurred with the passage of time: from the sixth century onwards, the occupation concentrated in the eastern cave hermitages[16] and on the plateau. Large structures – building A (18.5 m by 13.0 m) and the adjacent complex AA – emerged; elements of architectural decoration, most probably from the as yet unidentified communal church, were found on the plateau and in the church of Archangel Gabriel.[17] The interpretation of archaeological vestiges on the plateau is difficult, as the buildings were not only refashioned multiple times but also damaged by later medieval burials. However, it seems that some sort of communal hub crystallised there in the sixth century.

---

[15] For a more detailed reconstruction, see Derda and Wegner, Πατέρες τοῦ ἁγίου Νεκλονίου.

[16] Occupation later than the sixth century is attested in the eastern group of hermitages in Gebel Naqlun. The excavated western hermitages 85 and 87 were abandoned by the sixth century. West of the plateau and close to the western group of hermitages, a cemetery was discovered, with burials dated to the sixth century and later (Zych, 'Cemetery C'; Godlewski, 'Naqlun (Nekloni): Season 2004'; Godlewski, 'Naqlun 2007'). This may point to the cessation of monastic occupation of the western part of the site in the later period, but, due to the state of excavation of this area, final judgement has to be suspended.

[17] Godlewski, 'The Hermitages'; Godlewski et al., 'Deir el-Naqlun', pp. 181–8; Godlewski, 'Naqlun: Excavations 1999', pp. 128–30; Godlewski, 'Naqlun: Excavations 2000', pp. 151–4; Godlewski, 'Naqlun: Excavations 2002', pp. 160–8. Grossmann, Christliche Architektur, p. 513 interprets building A as a church that had undergone several alterations.

P.Naqlun 39, a letter from the villagers of a Fayumic village Tebetny to the Naqlun monks, dated on palaeographic grounds to the sixth–seventh centuries, hints at a monastic 'board of representatives' comprising a presbyter and three deacons.[18] The addressees are asked to mediate between Tebetny and the nearby village of Oxyrhyncha, and to dispatch some monks to Tebetny for an unclear purpose (maybe as labourers during harvest).[19] The clerical representatives most probably resided and operated on the plateau where our text was found in the refuse dump. The *Life of Samuel of Kalamoun* by Isaac the Presbyter – a ninth-century narrative about a Miaphysite monk Samuel who spent some time in Naqlun during the 630s[20] – depicts the community as a semi-anchoritic *laura* composed of cave hermitages and a religious and administrative centre (ⲙⲟⲛⲁⲥⲧⲏⲣⲓⲟⲛ).[21] The author's orientation in the topography of Naqlun was fairly good, and his work is considered a reliable source.[22]

The papyri found in the hermitages mention distinct monastic units within the community called *Oros Kellon* ('mountain of cells'). These units could have their own superiors, which suggests a model of dispersed leadership characteristic of *laura*-type communities.[23] No indications of

---

[18] Edition in Derda and Wegner, Πατέρες τοῦ ἁγίου Νεκλονίου. The address reads as follows: 'To our beloved and fathers Agathius/Agathes the presbyter and Apa Paul, and Apa Neilammon and Apa Aanios the deacons, and to all the monks of the holy Neklonion' (τοῖς ἀγαπητοῖς καὶ πατράσιν ἡμῶν Ἀγαθίῳ (or Ἀγαθήτι) πρεσβυτέρῳ καὶ ἄπα Παύλῳ καὶ ἄπα Νειλαμμῶνι καὶ ἄπα Ἀανίῳ διακόνοις καὶ πᾶσι τοῖς μονάζουσι ἁγίου Νεκλονίου; lines 1–9, standardised transcription).

[19] The harvest context is made clear in the last sentence of the letter: 'Since you know that it is the time of the harvest in the fields' (ἐπεὶ οἴδατε ὅτι ὁ καιρὸς γὰρ τῶν καρπῶν ἐν τῷ ἀγρῷ ἐστιν; lines 39–41, standardised transcription).

[20] Edition and English translation in Alcock, *The Life of Samuel*.

[21] Samuel, who came to Naqlun after fleeing Scetis, lived initially in the *monasterion*, whence he was driven out by throngs of visitors attracted by his holiness (*Life* 8). *Life* 9 reads: '[H]e made for himself a cave on the east side of the monastery (ⲙⲟⲛⲁⲥⲧⲏⲣⲓⲟⲛ), about a mile away, and nobody knew of it. The holy Apa Samuel would shut himself up for the whole week ... When he reached Saturday and Sunday, he would go to the monastery (ⲙⲟⲛⲁⲥⲧⲏⲣⲓⲟⲛ) to celebrate the Mass' (for Coptic, see Alcock, *The Life of Samuel*, pp. 8–9). The *monasterion* was also a place in which the visitors and pilgrims could meet with Samuel. In a later episode of the *Life*, the patriarch Cyrus – Samuel's sworn doctrinal enemy – seeks to force the Monothelete doctrine upon the inhabitants of the Fayum by persuading the monks of the region to embrace it first. The soldiers, whom Cyrus sends to pave the way for his arrival, come to the Naqlun *monasterion* and meet there an *oikonomos*, the only community member left on guard, as other brothers, encouraged by Samuel, had fled into the mountains to avoid trouble (*Life* 10: 'They did not find a single monk, except only the one who serves. The soldiers hastily seized him, took him with them and met the Colchian [i.e., Cyrus] on the road at the mouth of the canal ... The steward (ⲡⲟⲓⲕⲟⲛⲟⲙⲟⲥ) said, "I do not know why they [the other monks] have gone."' For Coptic, see Alcock, *The Life of Samuel*, p. 10).

[22] Wipszycka, *Second Gift*, pp. 395–7.

[23] *P.Naqlun* II 21.5–8: τῷ εὐλαβ[εστ]άτῳ ἄπα Νείλῳ μονάζο[ντι κ]αὶ προεστὼς [read προεστῶτι] Πύργου κα[ὶ τοῦ] ἁ[γί]ου Φοιβάμμ(ωνος) [Ὄρους] Κελλῶν: 'to the most pious Apa Neilos, monk

a structured, uniform spiritual leadership over the whole community have yet been found in the Naqlun material.

The Economic Circumstances of the Naqlun Community

Data concerning the material foundations of the Naqlun community is scarce. The inhabitants of cave hermitages in the gebel had private financial means at their disposal, just like their predecessors from hermitages 85 and 87 (see below). However, the abovementioned indications of the existence of a communal centre of the *laura* suggest that we should search for a source of assets belonging to the community as a whole and managed on its behalf by designated people. Unfortunately, nothing in the material excavated so far can be unequivocally proved to relate to the communal assets of the monastery.

Papyrological dossiers from other monasteries, including those at Bawit, Deir el-Bala'izah, and Wadi Sarga, contain administrative documents that reflect managerial practices on the estates belonging to the communities. Three documents of this kind were discovered in Naqlun, but their interpretation is fraught with difficulties. *P.Naqlun* I 7 and 8 were found in hermitage 25, where a certain pious monk had reused them for writing down religious texts based on the Book of Psalms;[24] both were written by professional scribes.[25] *P.Naqlun* I 7 lists disbursements of wheat to various people, including a stableman, a camel driver, a baker, and two anchorites. *P.Naqlun* I 8 is a list of land parcels stating their type, acreage, and expected yield, which could be used to calculate rents. The document features the term *koinon*, which can designate a community of cultivators.[26] *P.Naqlun* I 9, found on the

---

and *proestos* of the [monastery] of the Tower and of St Phoebammon of the Mountain of the Cells'; *P.Naqlun* II 22. 4–5: υἱὸς ἀβᾶ Ἀπαναγίῳ μων[ά]ζωγτι [read ἀββᾶ Ἀπανακίου μονάζοντος] μὲν ἐν Πύργ[ο]υ κ[α]ὶ ἀναχ[ω]ρ(ητῆ) αὐτοῦ: 'son of Abba Apanagios, monk in the *monasterion* of the Tower and its anchorite'; 8–10: τῷ εὐλαβεστ]άτῳ ἀβᾶ Μηνᾷ μωνάσ[ο]υτι [read μονάζοντι] [ἀπὸ τ]οῦ μοναστηργίου [read μοναστηρίου] Κωθαυ Ὄρος [read Ὄρους] Κελλῶν: 'to the most pious Abba Menas from the *monasterion* of Kothau on the Mountain of the Cells'; see Derda and Wegner, 'Πατέρες', pp. 81–3, 91–2. Although it predates the Naqlun documents by approximately two centuries, *P.Lond.* VI 1913, addressed to the *proestotes* of the Melitian *laura* of Hathor, provides the best analogy for such an organisational solution.

[24] Psalm 108 (edited as *P.Naqlun* I 3), of which lines 4–11, 14–17, and 24–31 are preserved, was written to fill the free space left on the recto side of the papyrus roll by the scribe of *P.Naqlun* I 7; the verso of the roll preserves lines 3–24 of Psalm 103 (*P.Naqlun* I 4). The verso of *P.Naqlun* I 8 preserves lines 9–20 of Psalm 65, and lines 1–8 of Psalm 98 (edited together as *P.Naqlun* I 5).

[25] *P.Naqlun* I p. 97.

[26] It is known, among others, from the dossier of the Oxyrhynchite estate of the senatorial family of Flavii Apiones (see Gascou, *Fiscalité et société*, pp. 172–3, Hickey, *Wine*, pp. 65–7, with further references).

plateau, is a transactions account listing people representing trades connected mainly with luxurious items (e.g., dealers in roses and purple-dye, goldsmiths, and producers of unguents). The men give and receive[27] money and products (Chian mastic, marjoram wine, or 'Cnidian berries'), but to whom and from whom we do not know. The document mentions *pittakia*[28] (payment orders or receipts) used in the transactions, which suggests a certain level of documentation of the procedures.

What is, however, the documents' connection with the monastery? They could have ended up at Naqlun as wastepaper obtained by monks for reuse from the functionaries of a local estate.[29] Another possibility is that the documents were drawn up at Naqlun by monastic administrators. This would have far-reaching consequences for our image of the community: the character of the documents indicates an advanced organisation system, with complex accounting procedures applied in land management, and possible circulation of luxurious products between the monastery and 'the world'. From the dossiers of Bawit, Deir el-Bala'izah, and Wadi Sarga, we learn that monastic communities could be well-organised institutions leasing land to farmers and remunerating monastic and lay workers,[30] making use of the services of professional scribes.[31] However, until more

---

[27] The composition of the text presents interpretational problems. The entries begin either with ἔχω followed by a name in genitive, or ἔχι (read: ἔχει) followed by the nominative. See, e.g., lines 6 and 7: / ἔχω Ἰούδα χρυ(σοχοῦ) δ(ιὰ) Θεοδώρου Σωτερίχ(ου) νο(μίσματα) β· δ´ κ̣[- - -] | ἔχ[ι] Θεόδωρος Σωτερίχ(ου) δ(ιὰ) Ἰούδα χρυ(σοχοῦ) νο(μίσματα) β· δ´ κ̣[- - -]: 'I have got [from?] Judas goldsmith, through Theodore son of Soterichos – 2 1/6(?) 1/4 *solidi*; Theodore son of Soterichos has got through Judas goldsmith – 2 1/6(?) 1/4 *solidi*.' It seems that entries beginning with ἔχω refer to the acquisition of products and money, while those beginning with ἔχει refer to expenditures.

[28] *P.Naqlun* I 9.4, 22, 24, 30, 37, 38, 39, 40, 41.   [29] See *P.Naqlun* I pp. 97–8.

[30] A system of payments in kind for people connected with a monastic institution (including the members of the community itself) is known from the seventh- to eighth-century dossier of the monastery of Apa Apollo at Bawit. A large group of brief dispatches by monastic superiors (the so-called 'our Father' documents; see *P.Bawit Clackson*) and orders of payment (see *P.Brux. Bawit* pp. 157–225) record disbursements of various products to monks and laymen. For an explicit attestation of payments to monks, see *P.Brux.Bawit* 28.2: (ὑπὲρ) μισθ(οῦ) μοναζ(όν)-τ(ων) *vac.* ? (νομίσματα) ι *vac.* ? σί(του) (ἀρτάβαι) ρ ('for salary of the monks, 10 *solidi*, 100 artabae of wheat'). If, however, we treat *P.Naqlun* I 7 as a spurious document originating from an estate, the disbursements for the anchorites are most probably to be understood as pious donations (compare the accounts of Apionic *pronoetai* that mention disbursements to various monasteries and groups of monks, e.g., *P.Oxy.* XVI 1913.58: 40 artabae of wheat for monks of Pruchthis and Berku).

[31] See *P.Bawit Clackson* 29, a monastic superior's order for the dispatch of barley to an 'office of the *notarios*'; a *notarios* named Anoup receives an unknown product in another superior's order from Bawit, *P.Bawit Clackson* 71. An unpublished letter from hermitage 6, Nd.15.084, addressed to a monk of the Naqlun community, suggests the presence of such a person in the monastery in the sixth century. The sender asks the addressee to pass his greetings to a *notarios*, who does not bear any monastic titles but seems to be connected with the community.

documents are discovered to clarify the situation, the possibility that the presence of the three accounts in Naqlun is merely a result of wastepaper circulation should hold our reasoning in check.

The Monastery and Its Surroundings: Naqlun in Context

If nothing certain can be said of the monastic economic hinterland of Naqlun, the documents do allow us to catch glimpses of the relations between the monastery and its wider surroundings. In the sixth and seventh centuries, the south-eastern Fayum did not witness the disappearance of rural settlements on a scale attested on the northern fringes of the region.[32] The rich toponomastic repertoire of the Byzantine Fayumic papyri gathered by Wessely (*Stud.Pal.* X and XX) reflects a persistently dense network of villages. The region saw an expansion of aristocratic landownership.[33] An *ousia*, perhaps a unit of an estate, is attested in the village of Kerkesoucha Orous (*Stud.Pal.* X 262.8),[34] which can possibly be identified with Qalamshah or Qalamshah Esba – the modern settlements closest to the Deir el-Naqlun site.[35] Papyri mention estates and aristocratic presence in Tebetny, known from the aforementioned letter, *P.Naqlun* 39.[36] The village was located circa ten kilometres from Arsinoe; the other location mentioned in the letter, Oxyrhyncha, was most probably located nearby (see Fig. 4.1).[37] The context of *P.Naqlun* 39 is unclear, but it is possible that the monastic intervention requested by the villagers from Tebetny had at its base some sort of practical interest on the monastery's part, rather than being just an exercise of religiously sanctioned authority.

The sources preserve attestations of various monasteries in the Fayum in the Byzantine and early Arab period, but the full map of monastic settlements in the region is impossible to establish.[38] A semi-anchoritic *laura* (*Labla*) located in the vicinity of the Hawara pyramid is attested in three papyri dated to the beginning of the sixth century (see Fig. 4.1).[39]

---

[32] Keenan, 'Deserted Villages'; Rathbone, 'Towards a Historical Topography'; Rathbone, 'Surface Survey'; Banaji, *Agrarian Change*, p. 179.
[33] Banaji, *Agrarian Change*, pp. 145–6 and 179. See also Palme, 'Die *domus gloriosa*'; Gonis, 'Notes on the Aristocracy', p. 209.
[34] ρμς ἀπὸ χω(ρίου) Κερκεσούχω(ν) Ὄρου(ς) οὐσια( ); '146 from the *chorion* of Kerkesoucha Orous, *ousia*'. The word *ousia* is routinely used to designate substantial landed property.
[35] Derda and Wegner, 'Naqlun in the Fifth–Seventh Century', pp. 185–6.
[36] *Stud.Pal.* X 138; *P.Flor.* I 11; *Stud.Pal.* X 252.
[37] Derda and Wegner, 'Letter from Tebetny', commentary to lines 12 and 16 of *P.Naqlun* 39.
[38] Abbot, *The Monasteries*; Gabra, *Christianity and Monasticism*.
[39] *P.Dubl.* 32–4; McGing, 'Melitian Monks'.

A monastic community established by Samuel of Kalamoun[40] received 'reinforcements' in the form of fourteen monks who moved to the new monastery from Naqlun (*Life* 26). The transfer of monks to Kalamoun is the only trace of contacts between Naqlun and another monastic settlement, apart from the rather vague indication in *P.Naqlun* II 28 (see below).

More is known concerning relations with 'worldly' settlements, even though the information is still quite patchy. The inhabitants of the Naqlun hermitages provided credit to people from villages in the Arsinoite nome (see below).[41] The monks also had contacts with people further afield: the papyri provide mentions of various locations, including Heracleopolis, Psenneris, and Chaireu Polis near Alexandria.[42] In Nd.15.084 (hermitage 6), the addressee is requested to come to 'the city' (perhaps Arsinoiton Polis or Heracleopolis) to visit the sender.[43] A person from a city (again, more than one option is possible) maintained communication with a high-ranking man from the monastery, most probably Bishop Nicholas who resided in Naqlun at some point in the sixth century.[44] The same bishop corresponded through his secretary with a local official and had dealings with three lay individuals called *kyra* Joannia and *kyrioi* Philoxenus and Timothy (see below). The image that emerges from this scattered evidence suggests a monastery with a network of contacts that was fairly broad in social and geographic terms. As we shall see, these contacts were mostly of a commercial/business nature.

Private 'Businesses' of the Monks of Naqlun

With the Naqlun documentation, we move from monastic economy to economies of the monks. Again, what we see are isolated snapshots rather than cohesive clusters of evidence. We see one anchorite living in

---

[40] Wipszycka, *Moines et communautés monastiques*, p. 217.

[41] *P.Naqlun* II 21: the debtor, Makarios son of Jacob, is from Alexandrou Nesos, a village tentatively placed far from Naqlun, in the ancient *meris* of Themistos, close to the southern shore of Lake Qarun. Eleusina (Eleusis), the place of origin of the debtor in *P.Naqlun* II 22, was closer to the monastery, on the way from Arsinoiton Polis. The name of the *kome* from which the third creditor, Victor son of Joseph, came is not preserved. For the proposed locations of the villages, see Fig. 4.1.

[42] Heracleopolis: *P.Naqlun* II 28; in addition to the explicit mention of the city, the papyrus also speaks of a 'brother' – probably a monk – travelling between a *polis* and the monastery (Naqlun?). Psenneris: *P.Naqlun* II 27. Chaireu Polis: *P.Naqlun* II 29.

[43] Line 1: καταξιώσῃ ⟨ἡ⟩ [ὑ]μετέ[ρα title] ἐλθεῖν ἕως τῆς πόλεως πρὸς ὑμᾶς ('May your [title] deem it worthy to come to the city to us').

[44] *P.Naqlun* II 25. The letter reports unrest in a city, which most probably led to the incineration of a civic building (*praetorium*).

hermitage 2 in the gebel purchasing pieces of clothing and paying for their transport (*P.Naqlun* I 11; sixth century). The monk paid three *solidi* – not a negligible sum – for the garments and their delivery.[45] *P.Naqlun* II 27 (plateau, refuse dump; sixth century) records transactions involving money and unknown products; the letter accompanied a dispatch of salted and fresh fish – a gift for the addressee or a purchase made on his behalf.[46] The Naqlun monks and their correspondents were also active in organising transport. In *P.Naqlun* II 28 (plateau, refuse dump; sixth century), someone in the community is requested to keep an eye on pack animals that circulated between Naqlun and a city, most probably Heracleopolis.[47] *P.Naqlun* II 29 (plateau, refuse dump; sixth century) speaks of searching for a ship in Chaireu near Alexandria. Except for the clearly private garment purchase in *P.Naqlun* I 11, however, we cannot be sure whether these financial and logistical dealings were of an individual character or were effectuated on behalf of the community, albeit through private channels of communication.

Monastic 'Businessmen' from Hermitage 89

The situation is clear in the three contracts discovered in the storage pit of hermitage 89 in the gebel. Towards the end of the sixth century, two monks of the Naqlun community – Apa Neilos, monk and *proestos* of Pyrgos and St Phoibammon, and Apa Menas of the *monasterion Kothau*[48] – provided credit to Arsinoite villagers (see above, n. 41). Two of the documents: *P.Naqlun* II 21 (Apa Neilos) and 22 (Apa Menas) are 'ordinary' loans of money. In the former, the capital sum is not preserved, but the interest stated at 600 myriads of denarii suggests that the borrowed sum amounted to approximately two *solidi*. *P.Naqlun* II 22 states the

---

[45] The items were delivered to him by a man named Joseph; see lines 1–3: † γνῶσις ὀνελασίων [read: ὀνηλασίων] παρ' ἐμοῦ Ἰωσὴφ χρυ(σίου) νο(μισμάτιον) (καὶ) τρίμισα ἕξ ('List of items brought on donkey-back from me, Joseph, one golden *solidus* and six tremisses') .

[46] *P.Naqlun* II 27.7–8.

[47] *P.Naqlun* II 28: 'Keep (?) these (animals?) for two(?) days, until the brother comes and takes [them] back to the city (Heracleopolis?). If possible, I ask you to bother to come to Heracleopolis, so that I can tell you [my] answer. And since the man I sent with two animals is a stranger – as he is Alexandrian – do not entrust him with them (sc. the animals), but send him off tomorrow.'

[48] See above, n. 23. The loan featuring Abba Menas as the creditor (*P.Naqlun* II 22) ended up with Neilos' papers most probably through the agency of Apa Apanakios, the father of the debtor, who could introduce his son to his fellow monk (see van Minnen, 'Review of *P.Naqlun* II', p. 222). Apanakios himself was a monk in *Pyrgos* (μονάζων ἐν Πύργῳ) and could be the immediate successor of Neilos as resident of hermitage 89 (Derda and Wegner, 'Πατέρες', p. 83).

capital at one *solidus* less three-quarter carats, without an explicitly mentioned interest. These sums correspond with data on monastic loans gathered by Markiewicz: most of the loans in the papyrological record in which the creditors are monks amounted to circa two *solidi*.[49]

The third document, *P.Naqlun* II 23, is a so-called sale on delivery.[50] Here, Apa Neilos pays Aurelius Victor the price of 200 *kouri* of wine, which Victor should deliver in jars provided by himself.[51] Sales on delivery were frequent arrangements in wine distribution. The sellers (debtors) used the money to invest in production or pay the taxes, while the buyers (creditors) received for a lower price goods they could either consume or resell. A number of documents feature monks as buyers in such transactions.[52] Some uncertainty remains as to whether they acted as private persons or representatives of their communities; the private interpretation, however, seems to prevail.[53] As far as we know, *P.Naqlun* II 23 is the only attestation of a monk's involvement in this kind of transaction in the Arsinoite record.

The document points to links with the capital of the nome, Arsinoe. The man who subscribes for the illiterate debtor and the witness are said to hail from the city;[54] the debtor himself was of village origin.[55] We can only speculate why people from Arsinoe were engaged in the transaction. Perhaps Victor tried to obtain the loan in the capital, which was the natural place to look for credit (city-based creditors are frequent in loans in

---

[49] Markiewicz, 'The Church, Clerics, Monks and Credit', p. 182.
[50] See Dzierzbicka, *ΟΙΝΟΣ*, pp. 249–50; Jakab, 'Guarantee and Jars'; Hickey, *Wine*, pp. 192–3.
[51] Contrary to the usual practice; see Gallimore, 'A Contract', pp. 161–3.
[52] Markiewicz, 'The Church, Clerics, Monks and Credit', pp. 184–7 and 199–202; see also Kruit, 'Three Byzantine Sales'; Wegner, 'The Bawit Monastery', pp. 229–37; Dzierzbicka in Chapter 5.
[53] Concerning the Bawit monastery of Apa Apollo, which so far has yielded the richest documentation on the subject, Markiewicz draws the general conclusion that 'lending and borrowing in Apa Apollo seems to have been principally a private affair' (Markiewicz, 'The Church, Clerics, Monks and Credit', p. 190). For instance, in *P.Amst.* I 47 and 48 – two sales on future delivery of considerable amounts of wine (more than 250 *knidia* and 450 *knidia* respectively) – the creditor/buyer is Serenus, the archimandrite of the monastery of Apa Apollos; nothing, however, indicates that the archimandrite was acting in the name of the whole community. Legal deeds concluded with the participation of monastic representatives usually state such circumstances in an explicit manner.
[54] *P.Naqlun* II 23.14–17: [- - -] υἱός το[ῦ] μακαρίου Ἰσὰκ ἀπὸ τῆς Ἀρσινοιτῶν [πόλεως ἔγραψα ὑπὲρ αὐ]τοῦ ἀγραμμάτου ὄντος. †† (hand 3) Αὐρήλιος Γεώργ[ιος υἱὸς τοῦ - - -] ἀπὸ τῆς Ἀρσινοιτῶν πόλεως μαρτυρ[ῶ ὡς πρόκειται]: 'son of the late Isaac from Arsinoiton Polis, I wrote for him since he is illiterate; Aurelius Georgios son of [...] from Arsinoiton Polis, I witness the aforesaid'. *P.Naqlun* II 23 is the only one of the three contracts from hermitage 89 in which a witness appears.
[55] *P.Naqlun* II 23.7–9: ἐμοῦ παρέχον[τος τὰ κοῦφα - - -] καὶ ἀποκαταστοῦντος [read: ἀποκαταστατοῦντος] ἰς [read: εἰς] [τ]ὸν [- - - ἐκ τῆς(?)] ἡμετέρας κ[ώ]μης: 'with me undertaking the provision of empty jars and the restoration [...] from our village'. Since the whole clause refers to Victor, we can assume that the village in question was his place of origin.

general).⁵⁶ We cannot exclude that Apa Neilos himself was in the city when Victor was seeking credit, and that the whole transaction took place there. The idea of an anchorite travelling to a city is not at odds with what we know from our documents: the letter Nd.15.084 (see above) contains a request, addressed to an anchorite, to do just that.

Neilos could play a part in the redistribution of wine within his community or outside it.⁵⁷ Even without certainty in this respect, we can say that, by lending money on interest, he displayed an entrepreneurial streak. Was Menas from *P.Naqlun* II 22, whose loan comprised no interest, less entrepreneurially minded? This is impossible to say; the edition suggests that the lack of interest may be due to the fact that the borrower was introduced to Menas by another monk.⁵⁸ However, it is also possible that the interest was simply hidden in the sum stipulated in the document, as was often the case in Byzantine loans.⁵⁹

The Riddle of Hermitage 89's Ceramic Assemblage

The same hermitage 89 in which Neilos' and Menas' documents were found yielded finds that shed light on the activities of the hermitage's inhabitant.⁶⁰ In the storage pit, together with the aforementioned contracts sealed between two layers of clay floor, the archaeologists found an assemblage of approximately sixty handmade miniature vessels, of which circa thirty were almost completely preserved (Fig. 4.3). It ended up in the storage pit as a result of a one-time clean-up. Based on the date of *P.Naqlun* II 22 (593), the *terminus ante quem* for the find can be set at the end of the sixth or the beginning of the seventh century.⁶¹ The publication of the find was being prepared by the Polish ceramic specialist Tomasz Górecki before his premature death; the following presentation is based on his personal communication, for which we remain deeply grateful.

---

[56] See Bagnall, *Egypt in Late Antiquity*, pp. 74–5.
[57] The same was most probably true of Apa Serenus from Bawit (see above, n. 53); the amounts of wine purchased by Serenus or Neilos were too large to be destined for immediate individual consumption. On this subject, see also Wegner, 'Monks and Monasteries in Egypt', pp. 94–5. For wine in Naqlun, see Dzierzbicka in Chapter 5.
[58] *P.Naqlun* II p. 113.
[59] Markiewicz, 'The Church, Clerics, Monks and Credit', p. 188; see also Bagnall, 'Price'.
[60] Godlewski, 'Deir el-Naqlun 1991', pp. 51–3; Derda, 'Polish Excavations at Deir el-Naqlun', pp. 128–9; *P.Naqlun* II pp. 88–90.
[61] *P.Naqlun* II pp. 90–91.

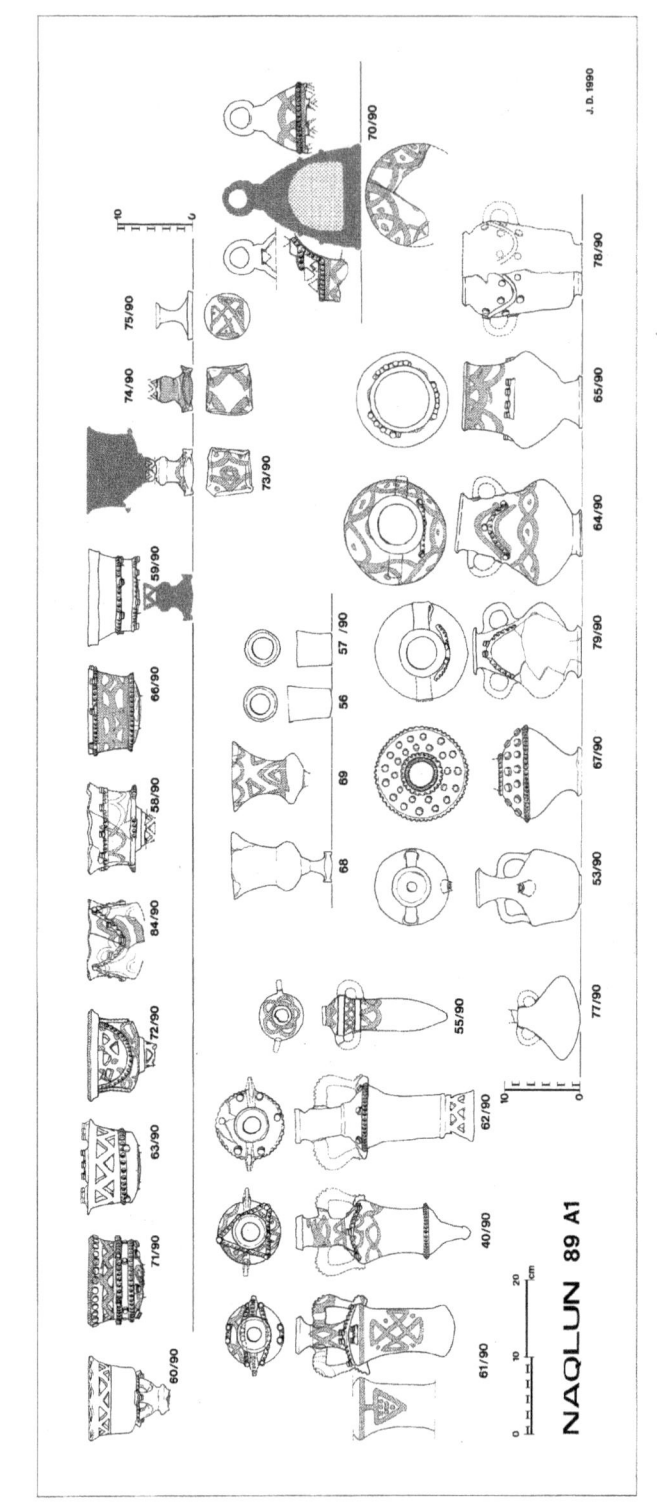

Fig. 4.3. The ceramic assemblage from hermitage 89. Drawn by Jarosław Dobrowolski. © PCMA Archives.

Miniature vessels were found on other archaeological sites, but their number is usually small.[62] The assemblage of hermitage 89 most probably came from a monk's small pottery workshop. All of the more complete pieces had little defects (chips or cracks). There were also several loose elements, mostly parts of handles and feet, chipped off during or even before firing. Technically speaking, the quality of the vessels was poor. They were made of crudely prepared Nile clay of high porosity. Laboratory analyses showed that the firing process was achieved in low temperature (circa 700°C). This could be done in a small furnace, which could be a makeshift construction, e.g., a hole in the ground covered with a large vessel turned upside down. As the firing process could cause discomfort to the hermit, the furnace could have been located away from the hermitage; it could subsequently have disappeared in a landslide without a trace.

The vessels display a great diversity of forms and decoration and, despite their technical defects, were a product of a talented and imaginative potter. They imitate forms such as censers, Gaza amphorae, cooking pots, and Late Roman bottles. The potter wanted to make his miniature copies as faithful as possible, adding parts necessary in large vessels but superfluous in miniatures (e.g., four handles on cooking pots). His models included vessels made of clay, metal, and glass; the rich decoration repertory (painting, incision, openwork, appliqué) observed in the miniatures also reflected the techniques applied to full-size vessels (e.g., openwork metal censers).

Why, however, were the vessels made? The diversity of their forms suggests that the potter wanted to give them unique traits. This, and the richness of their decoration, may indicate that the vessels were conceived of as 'fancy' items, maybe 'souvenirs' intended for visitors who came to the monastery, exchanged for offerings. Bottles and amphorae could contain oil blessed by a monk (due to clay porosity, the vessels could hold only denser substances), while censers could be used according to their original purpose, e.g., for burning incense in front of a holy image kept at home. It is possible that what we see is only the defective fraction of a larger produce, the successful part of which had left the monastery with the visitors. The question remains whether the produce was particular to the monk from hermitage 89 or was intended for distribution on behalf of the community.

[62] For example, the monastic settlement in Kellia: Egloff, *Kellia*, pp. 137–9; Kasser, *Explorations*, fig. 491. The miniature jars in the latter publication are interpreted as containers for oils used in liturgical contexts. Miniature vessels also appear in Elephantine and in Sudan, in the church at Banganarti and in Dongola. Examples from sites other than Naqlun are standardised and were made on a pottery wheel; their connection with the examples from hermitage 89 is doubtful. The information on miniature vessels in Egypt and Nubia and the references come from personal communication with Katarzyna de Lellis-Danys, for which we are deeply grateful.

Equally questionable is the economic dimension of this produce; if the 'souvenir' hypothesis has some truth to it, the symbolic value of the exchange for which the vessels were destined would probably outweigh the practical one. The ceramic assemblage, however, may also be indicative of the process of professional training, or of a mere pastime of an imaginative anchorite (the amateurish features of the production fit especially well with the last option).

The Bishop's Business and an Overzealous *Comes*: *P.Naqlun* I 12 and the Dossier of Nicholas from the Naqlun Plateau

The Naqlun material contains a small dossier connected with an individual named Nicholas, who, as indicated in the texts, was a bishop living in the monastery towards the end of the sixth century.[63] Bishop Nicholas may have been a monk of the Naqlun monastery before his episcopal ordination and continued to live in Naqlun after it. His episcopal see is unknown; simple geography suggests either Arsinoe or Heracleopolis, located in equal (and not excessively large) distance from Naqlun. A Heracleopolite connection of Naqlun is attested in *P.Naqlun* II 28 (see above). Still, there are no firm grounds for locating Nicholas in the network of Egyptian bishoprics.

Nicholas' dossier is composed almost exclusively of correspondences.[64] Its central piece, *P.Naqlun* I 12, is a letter which, despite being signed by Nicholas only, contains communications from two persons: Nicholas and a certain Apa Hor, the latter being most probably the right hand and secretary of the former. It remained unsent and ended up in the plateau refuse dump, perhaps because its chaotic structure was finally deemed improper. Nicholas does not bear any titles in the letter, but the connection with the homonymous bishop of *P.Naqlun* II 32–4 is almost certain. The argument for the identification rests on the profile of the individual involved and the rarity of his name. *P.Naqlun* I 12 is addressed to a local official, *comes* Basilius, and refers to communication with people of some

---

[63] On Nicholas, see Derda and Wegner, 'Πατέρες'. For bishops in Egyptian monasteries, see Giorda, 'Bishops-Monks'. The texts connected with Nicholas (definitely and hypothetically) are: *P.Naqlun* I 12; *P.Naqlun* II 32–4; *P.Naqlun* 35; *P.Naqlun* II 25–6; *P.Naqlun* I 10. All the documents were retrieved from the refuse dump on the plateau.

[64] Some of the pieces are connected with the bishop only in a tentative manner. *P.Naqlun* II 25 is a report on local unrest and the ensuing trials (see above, n. 44). *P.Naqlun* II 26 speaks of disturbances in the Apollonopolite, Lycopolite, and Hypselite nomes. The texts touch upon political matters that surface only rarely in the monastic correspondence.

standing (the two men and a woman mentioned in the letter are respectfully called *kyrioi* and *kyra*). The second 'speaker' in the letter, Apa Hor, intervenes immediately after Nicholas and voices concerns caused to 'our father' by the addressee's actions. It is logical to assume that this 'father' was none other than Nicholas himself.

The immediacy with which Basilius is addressed in the letter and the cursory introduction of both Hor and Nicholas suggest that the three men were acquainted. In the main body of the document, Nicholas asks Basilius to deliver documents (*apochai*) to *kyrios* Timothy – a purchaser of plots of vineland in hamlets[65] – and pass the response of *kyra* Joannia concerning a matter known to both correspondents and thus also unmentioned. From the interpretational point of view, Joannia's case is lost to us, but we may speculate about the reasons for Nicholas' involvement with Timothy. One possibility is that the former could be the one who sold the *choria* to the latter; if this was so, the plots were certainly his private property, since he would not have been legally able to dispose of the monastery's unalienable property.

Apa Hor's subscription to the letter adds to the confusion. As far as we can reconstruct the situation, it seems that the *comes* had visited a place and provided some people with wine without informing anyone.[66] Nicholas and Apa Hor saw it as inappropriate; Apa Hor urged Basilius to receive compensation in the form of a certain number of *kouri* of must equalling the amount of originally delivered wine. Again, we miss the key information, which is: where did Basilius go and who received wine from him? If

---

[65] *P.Naqlun* I 12: 'Would your Dearness kindly give *kyrios* Timothy two receipts (*apochai*) which you have, namely one [from] the *epimeletes*, the other [from] the *grammateus*. For he (Timothy?) appropriated (or: bought) the vineyards (*choria*) in the *epoikia*. And please let me also know through the person who is with you and who is coming to us the answer of *kyra* Joannia as I told your Dearness and *kyrios* Philoxenus.' The interpretation of the verb ᾠκειώσατο used to describe Timothy's action is not easy; we are tempted, however, to assume that he acquired the plots in a lawful manner. Only in such a case would Nicholas be willing to help Timothy obtain some necessary documents. On *choria* as a designation of vineyards, see Dzierzbicka, ΟΙΝΟΣ, p. 58.

[66] 'And I, Apa Hor, am greatly surprised at your presumption (*phronesis*) that you came and went and did not [say or do] anything [to or for] me about the matter of the list of wine [supplies] (*gnosis ton oinarion*). What has happened [in the matter] of those who are mentioned as having received wine from you? But you do well to accept at once the same number of *kouri* of must and not to check (or: not to ask about) the price, so that we can pay you in this form at least.' The edition in *P.Naqlun* I translates *phronesis* as 'prudence'. 'Presumption', however, seems a better option, given the chiding tone of the letter (see Liddell and Scott, *Lexicon*, s.v. φρόνησις, A.5: 'arrogance, pride'). In the only Byzantine papyrological attestation of the word, it is used with a clearly negative intention: *SB* V 7655.23–5 (Hermopolite nome, first half of the sixth century): αὐτὸς ἔγραψέν μοι ἐπιστολὴν πρεπουσα<ν> τῇ ὄψει αὐτοῦ καὶ τῇ φρονήσει τῇ ματαίᾳ· καὶ ἐπειδὴ παιδίον ἐστὶν καὶ μῶρος ... : 'he wrote me a letter fitting his countenance and his vain presumption; and because he is child-like and dull ... '.

Basilius came to Naqlun and donated wine to monks,[67] Nicholas' reaction could result from his annoyance at the fact that something was happening in the monastery that was beyond his control. In this case, the second part of the letter would reflect Nicholas' concerns as monastic supervisor. However, would an act of even unwanted pious generosity warrant this somewhat hostile reaction? The link connecting Basilius with Nicholas' private affairs may point in a different direction. Basilius certainly kept documents (the *apochai* mentioned earlier in the letter), most probably of a fiscal nature, which were of some importance to Nicholas.[68] Could this be because of his capacity as Nicholas' administrator? If so, we can imagine him visiting a unit of Nicholas' estate and distributing wine, e.g., to estate workers. From the letter, it would appear that the delivery was made from Basilius' own stocks, exposing him to losses that Nicholas was determined to reimburse. Such generosity on Basilius' part may seem suspicious to us (as it certainly did to Nicholas and Hor); it is, however, possible that he was eager to relieve his venerable superior in the circumstances of shortage (notice that the reimbursement in must seems to be somewhat embarrassing to Apa Hor, who writes 'so that we can pay you in this form at least'). In doing so, however, he would have taken one step beyond what was expected of him. The vagueness of the document makes it impossible to choose between the two interpretations; nevertheless, *P.Naqlun* I 12 still provides an interesting insight into the way in which a high-ranking member of a monastic community (if not yet a bishop) could conduct his affairs. One could even say, with a hint of colourful exaggeration, that the letter, with its slightly emotional tone, allows us to catch a glance of Nicholas' 'management ethics'.

Concluding Remarks

The material from Naqlun allows us to sketch some portraits of the monks who inhabited the hermitages and the plateau in the fifth to seventh centuries. These people lived in a landscape well-defined in physical and geographic terms, but still rather poorly recognised as an institution and economic unit. Placing these individuals in a larger picture is difficult when

---

[67] Religious institutions could have their own accounts drawn up with the intention of regulating wine distributions. See *P.Iand.* VIII 154 (provenance unknown, circa 600) – a wine account listing clerics, members of religious associations, and other people associated with an unknown church, entitled *gnosis oinou*; cf. *gnosis ton oinarion* in *P.Naqlun* I 12.

[68] For *apoche*, see Preisigke, *Wörterbuch*, s.v.

the said larger picture is in itself basically a construct deduced from fragmentary premises. This does not mean that we should give up on trying – and try we shall.

The first striking overall feature of the Naqlun archaeological and papyrological testimonies is the widespread independence of individuals throughout the first two centuries of the community's existence. Architecturally, this is most pronounced in the fifth-century hermitages, 44, 85, and 87. All had dedicated spaces for the reception of visitors;[69] hermitage 85 had its own church, thanks to which its inhabitants could retain full independence also in the religious sphere.[70] Therefore, even the desire to participate in the Eucharist did not have to interfere with the inhabitants' seclusion. The later hermitages in the gebel were less elaborate than the fifth-century examples, but they could still provide the monks with all they needed on an everyday basis: rooms for living and working, prayer niches, ventilated storage pits, courtyards, and kitchens (see Fig. 4.4). Dedicated reception halls are, however, unattested in this period.[71] Some of the hermitages were designed for more than one inhabitant, but their layout still guaranteed a degree of privacy, with separate modules destined for individual monks repeating the same basic pattern.[72] Papyrological sources bring into relief the private financial and managerial dealings of some Naqlun monks from the hermitages (Apa Neilos and Menas of hermitage 89) and the plateau (Nicholas).

The correspondence-based networks of contact attested in the papyri, which extended outside the nome boundaries, also seem highly personalised. The best example is, unsurprisingly, the case of Nicholas. The *comes*, two *kyrioi* and a *kyra*, and the *epimeletes* and *grammateus* listed in *P.Naqlun* I 12 provide glimpses of some elements of what seems to be the bishop's or superior's local network. On the other hand, *P.Naqlun* II 22 points to the potential significance of kinship bonds in establishing business relations.

---

[69] In the fifth-century phase of its occupation, hermitage 44 in the gebel had a spacious room with benches along the walls, accessible separately from the hermitage and from the outside. Finds from the hermitage (magical texts in Coptic and medical instruments) suggest that its inhabitant was a physician/healer who could offer his services to the local populace. The presence of a reception hall could therefore be conditioned by his individual needs (Godlewski, 'Naqlun: The Hermitage of Phibamo'; Mossakowska-Gaubert, 'L'anachorète', pp. 184–5; Wipszycka, *Moines et communautés monastiques*, p. 137; Wipszycka, *Second Gift*, pp. 298–9). Hermitage 85 had a room with benches interpreted as a reception hall: Mossakowska-Gaubert, 'L'anachorète', p. 188; see also Godlewski, 'Naqlun (Nekloni): Preliminary Report 2006', p. 205 and Wipszycka, *Second Gift*, p. 298.

[70] See Godlewski, 'Naqlun (Nekloni): Preliminary Report 2006'; Godlewski, 'Naqlun 2007'.

[71] Mossakowska-Gaubert, 'L'anachorète', pp. 183–8.

[72] The best examples are hermitage 1, built for two monks, and hermitages 2 and 25, destined for three inhabitants (see Godlewski *et al.*, 'Deir el-Naqlun'; Wipszycka, *Moines et communautés monastiques*, pp. 133 and 135; Wipszycka, *Second Gift*, pp. 293–5).

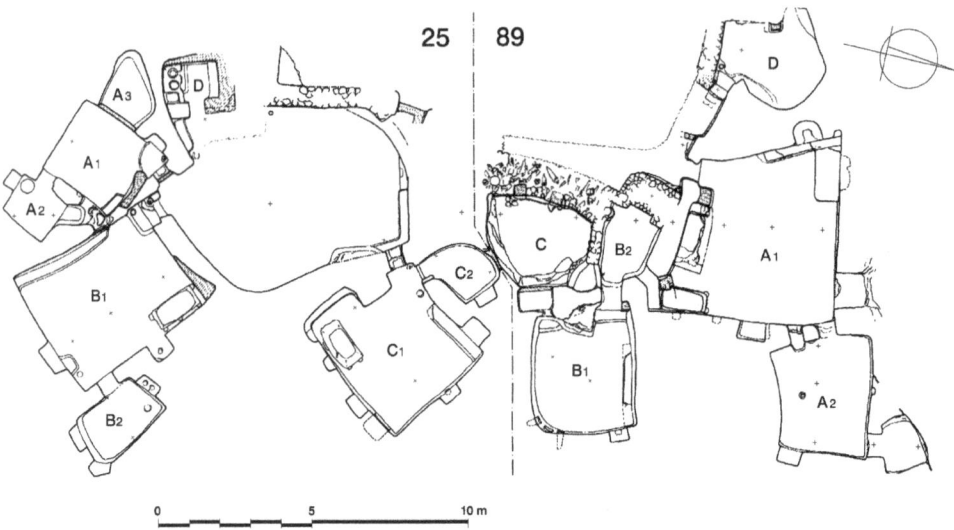

Fig. 4.4. Plan of hermitages 25 and 89. Drawn by Jarosław Dobrowolski.

The debtor and his representative are two brothers, sons of a Naqlun monk; it is impossible not to see this connection as the reason behind their choice of the source of credit.

The Naqlun fathers whom we see through the prism of the papyri and archaeological remains seem to have formed a relatively affluent group. All of the excavated hermitages in Naqlun were constructions that required professional skills for their erection; such skills were most probably outsourced by hiring workers from 'the world outside'. The neat and complex hermitages 85 and 87, partially delved in bedrock and partially built of stone and brick, with their walls finely plastered, bear testimony to decent planning and careful execution.[73] The cave hermitages may seem desolate in their present state of dilapidation (Gebel Naqlun consists of a rock formation which is prone to collapse), but they certainly were not so while they were occupied. The walls of the hermitages were carefully plastered, the ventilation systems of the storage pits were ingeniously conceived,[74] and the kitchens were fairly well equipped.[75] For a small

---

[73] See Godlewski, 'Naqlun (Nekloni): Preliminary Report 2006'; Godlewski, 'Naqlun 2007'.

[74] A well-preserved shaft was discovered in hermitage 6. It began in the south-western end of the storage pit, ran 1.8 m through the rock and ended above the walking level in the hermitage's courtyard; see Godlewski et al., 'Deir el-Naqlun 2014–2015', p. 279.

[75] See, for example, Godlewski et al., 'Deir el-Naqlun', pp. 192–3 (hermitage 1); Godlewski et al., 'Deir el-Naqlun (Nekloni), 1988–1989', p. 207, fig. 6 (hermitage 25); Godlewski et al., 'Deir el-Naqlun 2014–2015', pp. 281–6 (hermitage 6).

selection of texts, the Naqlun dossier is relatively rich in mentions of money; again, most of these mentions come from contexts that seem private. Admittedly, the sums are not particularly large,[76] but their very presence testifies to a relatively common access to cash in an essentially rural and geographically marginal setting. We must not, however, be tricked into envisaging the Naqlun settlement as a place of pious retirement for a handful of well-off individuals. We do not know exactly how many monks lived in Naqlun at any given moment; the number of hermitages can be deceptive, as it is improbable that all of them were inhabited at the same time. The *Life of Samuel* gives us a baffling proportion of 120 monks to 200 *kosmikoi* (lay inmates, most probably servants) in Naqlun in the 630s. As usual in literary sources, the neatly rounded figures are suspicious; however, given the coherent and sensible character of the narrative, the number itself, and more importantly, the proportion, do not seem to be blatantly far-fetched.[77] Some of these monks would have lived in the *monasterion* on the plateau. As already said, the interpretation of the architecture in this part of the monastery is very difficult. It is possible that the buildings in the monastic 'centre' hosted monks who could not afford the construction and maintenance of hermitages. Less fortunate monks must have been present in the community but were doomed to oblivion, living a life that left no legible material traces and having no need for written documentation. Even in a monastery not everyone could afford to have a history.

As we have seen, the monastery neighboured a densely populated environment. However, only the Tebetny letter bears testimony to a 'community-to-community' relation between the monastery and a rural human grouping. Other contacts seem personal and accidental; the same can be said about relations with higher-ranking members of society, for which our testimonies are limited to Nicholas' network and a letter dispatched most probably from a chancellery of an official,[78] which mentions a person bearing the aristocratic title *paneuphemos* – again connected with Nicholas' dossier. We know, however, that aristocrats and their estates were present in the region, in Kerkesoucha Orous and Tebetny – the former being physically close to the Naqlun community, and the latter

---

[76] Three *solidi* paid for garments in *P.Naqlun* I 11; loan of one *solidus* minus three-quarter carats in *P.Naqlun* II 22; loan calculated at around two *solidi* in *P. Naqlun* II 21; transactions amounting to four *solidi* in *P.Naqlun* II 27.

[77] The account is considered credible by Wipszycka, *Second Gift*, pp. 396–7.

[78] This is suggested by the address on the verso, executed in an elegant handwriting typical of officials' correspondence (see *P.Naqlun* II p. 127).

having an established connection with the monastery. Maybe it was from these estates that *P.Naqlun* I 7, 8, and 9 came to Naqlun.

Finally, we need to return to the question posed in the first paragraph of this brief conclusion. What was the relation of individual monks to the communal framework in the period when this framework had already emerged (presumably around the turn of the sixth century, thus roughly in the period when the Tebetny letter was composed, and before Samuel's brief stay in Naqlun)?[79] The *Life of Samuel* reveals something of the scale of the monastic enterprise in Samuel's days. The monastery welcomed visitors and supported 200 laypeople, and the only technical monastic designation used in the account is, perhaps not accidentally, *oikonomos*. Someone had to cater for the pilgrims, organise the work, and regulate the remuneration of lay servicepeople; the crystallising practical needs of the community would lead to the appointment of a steward. The Bawit dossier of the monastery of Apa Apollo, slightly later than the Naqlun documents (seventh–eighth centuries), shows how many of the monastic inmates could be involved in administrative tasks in a community.[80] Naqlun was smaller than Bawit and did not yet have to face some of the fiscal challenges brought about by the Arab takeover; but the organisational problems would at best have been scaled down, not entirely non-existent or substantially different. From the Tebetny villagers (*P.Naqlun* 39) we learn that the superior in Naqlun could dispatch his monks outside the monastery to fulfil some tasks; therefore, the monks were expected to sacrifice their time and energy on behalf of their community. We can hypothesise that if the monastery was to be run smoothly, such contributions would have been commonplace; at the same time, financial independence of at least some of the inmates would have relieved the pressure on the communal infrastructure (whether only nascent or already developed). The vague and hypothetical character of the connection between the communal and the individual aspect of life in Naqlun in the period immediately preceding the Arab conquest is most frustrating for the historian and papyrologist. The wish to clarify such a crucial issue for a monastery that, in all probability, was one of the more prominent religious centres of the region in the Byzantine period should provide a strong incentive for continued research on the site.

---

[79] For the date of Samuel's sojourn in Naqlun, see Derda and Wegner, 'Naqlun in the Fifth–Seventh Century', p. 193.
[80] Wegner, 'The Bawit Monastery'; Wegner, *Monastic Communities in Context*, pp. 232–8.

Bibliography

Abbot, N. *The Monasteries of the Fayyum* (Chicago: University of Chicago Press, 1937).

Alcock, A. *The Life of Samuel of Kalamun by Isaac the Presbyter* (Warminster: Aris and Philips, 1983).

Bagnall, R. S. 'Price in "Sales on Delivery"', *Greek, Roman, and Byzantine Studies*, 18 (1977), 85–96.

Bagnall, R. S. *Egypt in Late Antiquity* (Princeton: Princeton University Press, 1993).

Bagnall, R. S. 'Monks and Property: Rhetoric, Law, and Patronage in the Apophtegmata Patrum and the Papyri', *Greek, Roman, and Byzantine Studies*, 42 (2001), 7–24.

Banaji, J. *Agrarian Change in Late Antiquity: Gold, Labour, and Aristocratic Dominance* (Oxford: Oxford University Press, 2001).

Brooks Hedstrom, D. L. *The Monastic Landscape of Late Antique Egypt. An Archaeological Reconstruction* (Cambridge: Cambridge University Press, 2017).

Danys, K. 'Pottery Finds from Hermitage EE.50 in Naqlun. Preliminary Assessment of the Assemblage', *Polish Archaeology in the Mediterranean*, 26.1 (2017), 173–84.

Derda, T. 'Polish Excavations at Deir el-Naqlun 1986–1991: Interdependence of Archaeology and Papyrology' in A. Bülow-Jacobsen (ed.), *Proceedings of the 20th International Congress of Papyrologists, Copenhagen, 23–29 August 1992* (Copenhagen: Museum Tusculanum Press, 1994), pp. 124–30.

Derda, T. and Dzierzbicka, D. 'Refuse Dump in Sector B in Naqlun: Excavation Report 2008–2009', *Polish Archaeology in the Mediterranean*, 21 (2012), 212–21.

Derda, T. and Wegner, J. 'New Documentary Papyri from the Polish Excavations at Deir el-Naqlun (P.Naqlun 35–38)', *Journal of Juristic Papyrology*, 44 (2014), 117–31.

Derda, T. and Wegner, J. 'Letter from Tebetny to the Monks of Naqlun Concerning Fieldwork (*P.Naqlun 39*)' in J.-L. Fournet and A. Papaconstantinou (eds.), *Mélanges Jean Gascou. Textes et études papyrologiques (P.Gascou)* (Paris: Association des Amis du Centre d'Histoire et Civilisation de Byzance, 2016), pp. 133–50.

Derda, T. and Wegner, J. 'Πατέρες τοῦ ἁγίου Νελονίου. Functionaries of the Naqlun Monastery in the First Two Centuries of Its Existence' in A. Łajtar, A. Obłuski, and I. Zych (eds.), *Aegyptus et Nubia Christiana. The Włodzimierz Godlewski Jubilee Volume on the Occasion of His 70th Birthday* (Warsaw: Polish Centre of Mediterranean Archaeology, 2016), pp. 73–97.

Derda, T. and Wegner, J. 'Naqlun in the Fifth–Seventh Century: Papyrological and Literary Evidence' in M.-P. Chaufray, I. Guermeur, S. Lippert, and V. Rondot (eds.), *La Fayoum. Archéologie – Histoire – Religion. Actes du sixième colloque international, Montpellier, 26–28 octobre 2016* (Wiesbaden: Harrassowitz, 2018), pp. 183–98.

Dzierzbicka, D. *ΟΙΝΟΣ: Production and Import of Wine in Graeco-Roman Egypt* (Warsaw: The Raphael Taubenschlag Foundation, 2018).

Egloff, M. *Kellia: la poterie copte: quatre siècles d'artisanat et d'échanges en Basse-Égypte* (Geneva: University of Geneva, 1977).

Gabra, G. (ed.) *Christianity and Monasticism in the Fayoum Oasis* (Cairo: The American University in Cairo Press, 2005).

Gallimore, S. 'A Contract for the Advanced Sale of Wine', *Bulletin of the American Society of Papyrologists*, 49 (2012), 151–65.

Gascou, J. *Fiscalité et société en Égypte byzantine* (Paris: Association des Amis du Centre d'Histoire et Civilisation de Byzance, 2008).

Giorda, M. 'Bishops-Monks in the Monasteries: Presence and Role', *Journal of Juristic Papyrology*, 39 (2009), 115–49.

Godlewski, W. 'Deir el-Naqlun 1991', *Polish Archaeology in the Mediterranean*, 2 (1991), 48–53.

Godlewski, W. 'Naqlun: Excavations 1995', *Polish Archaeology in the Mediterranean*, 7 (1996), 82–8.

Godlewski, W. 'Naqlun: Excavations 1999', *Polish Archaeology in the Mediterranean*, 11 (2000), 125–32.

Godlewski, W. 'Naqlun: The Hermitage of Phibamo' in K. M. Ciałowicz and J. A. Ostrowski (eds.), *Civilisations du bassin méditerranéen. Hommages à Joachim Śliwa* (Kraków: Jagiellonian University, Institute of Archaeology, 2000), pp. 91–8.

Godlewski, W. 'Naqlun: Excavations 2000', *Polish Archaeology in the Mediterranean*, 12 (2001), 149–61.

Godlewski, W. 'Naqlun: Excavations 2002', *Polish Archaeology in the Mediterranean*, 13 (2002), 159–70.

Godlewski, W. 'Excavating the Ancient Monastery at Naqlun' in G. Gabra (ed.), *Christianity and Monasticism in the Fayoum Oasis* (Cairo: The American University in Cairo Press, 2005), pp. 156–71.

Godlewski W. 'Naqlun (Nekloni): Season 2004', *Polish Archaeology in the Mediterranean*, 16 (2005), 181–90.

Godlewski, W. 'The Hermitages, Cemetery and the Keep in the Early Sixth Century' in S. Lippert and M. Schentuleit (eds.), *Graeco-Roman Fayum: Texts and Archaeology. Proceedings of the Third International Fayum Symposion, Freudenstadt, May 29–June 1, 2007* (Wiesbaden: Harrasowitz, 2008), pp. 101–12.

Godlewski, W. 'Naqlun (Nekloni): Preliminary Report 2006', *Polish Archaeology in the Mediterranean*, 18 (2008), 195–206.

Godlewski, W. 'Naqlun 2007. Preliminary Report', *Polish Archaeology in the Mediterranean*, 19 (2010), 229–44.

Godlewski, W. 'Naqlun 2016. Hermitage EE.50: Preliminary Report', *Polish Archaeology in the Mediterranean*, 26.1 (2017), 161–72.

Godlewski, W., Danys, K., and Maślak, S. 'Deir el-Naqlun 2014–2015. Preliminary Report', *Polish Archaeology in the Mediterranean*, 25 (2016), 265–88.

Godlewski, W., Derda, T., and Górecki, T. 'Deir el-Naqlun (Nekloni), 1988–1989, Second Preliminary Report', *Nubica*, 3.1 (1994), 201–63.

Godlewski, W., Herbich, T., and Wipszycka, E. 'Deir el-Naqlun (Nekloni) 1986–1987: First Preliminary Report', *Nubica*, 1–2 (1990), 171–207.

Goehring, J. E. *Ascetics, Society, and the Desert. Studies in Early Egyptian Monasticism* (Harrisburg: Trinity Press International, 1999).

Gonis, N. 'Notes on the Aristocracy of Byzantine Fayum', *Zeitschrift für Papyrologie und Epigraphik*, 166 (2008), 203–10.

Grossmann, P. *Christliche Architektur in Ägypten* (Leiden: Brill, 2002).

Hickey, T. M. *Wine, Wealth, and the State in Late Antique Egypt: The House of Apion at Oxyrhynchus* (Ann Arbor: University of Michigan Press, 2012).

Jakab, E. 'Guarantee and Jars in Sales of Wine on Delivery', *Journal of Juristic Papyrology*, 29 (1999), 33–44.

Kasser, R. (ed.) *Explorations aux Qouçoûr el-Izeila* (Leuven: Peeters, 1999).

Keenan, J. G. 'Deserted Villages: From the Ancient to the Medieval Fayum', *Bulletin of the American Society of Papyrologists*, 40 (2003), 119–39.

Kruit, N. 'Three Byzantine Sales on Future Delivery: *SB* XVI 12401 + 12402, *SB* VI 9051, *P. Lond.* III 997', *Tyche*, 9 (1994), 67–88.

Lichocka, B. 'Roman and Early Byzantine Coins from Naqlun' in N. Bonacasa, M. Casini, and A. Etman (eds.), *The Culture of the Oasis from the Antiquity to the Modern Age: El Kharga, 22–27 October 1998* (Cairo: Istituto italiano di cultura del Cairo, 2000), pp. 245–7.

Liddell, H. G. and Scott, R. *A Greek–English Lexicon. Ninth Edition with Revised Supplement* (Oxford: Oxford University Press, 1996).

McGing, B. 'Melitian Monks at Labla', *Tyche*, 5 (1990), 67–94.

Markiewicz, T. 'The Church, Clerics, Monks and Credit in the Papyri' in A. Boud'hors, J. Clackson, C. Louis, and P. Sijpesteijn (eds.), *Monastic Estates in Late Antique and Early Islamic Egypt: Ostraca, Papyri, and Essays in Memory of Sarah Clackson* (Cincinnati: The American Society of Papyrologists, 2009), pp. 178–202.

Mossakowska-Gaubert, M. 'L'anachorète et ses visiteurs', *Journal of Juristic Papyrology*, 42 (2012), 165–94.

O'Connell, E. R. 'Tombs for the Living. Monastic Reuse of Monumental Funerary Architecture in Late Antique Egypt', unpublished PhD thesis, University of California Berkeley, 2007.

O'Connell, E. R. 'R. Campbell Thompson's 1913/14 Excavation of Wadi Sarga and Other Sites', *The British Museum Studies in Ancient Egypt and Sudan*, 21 (2014), 129–92.

Palme, B. 'Die *domus gloriosa* des Flavius Strategius Paneuphemos', *Chiron*, 27 (1997), 95–125.

Preisigke, F. *Wörterbuch der griechischen Papyrusurkunden, mit Einschluss der griechischen Inschriften, Aufschriften, Ostraka, Mumienschilder usw. aus Ägypten*, edited by E. Kissling, vol. I (Berlin: Selbstverlag der Erben, 1925).

Rathbone, D. 'Towards a Historical Topography of the Fayum' in D. M. Biley (ed.), *Archaeological Research in Roman Egypt: The Proceedings of the Seventeenth Classical Colloquium of the Department of Greek and Roman Antiquities, British Museum, Held on 1–4 December 1993* (Ann Arbor: Journal of Roman Archaeology, 1996), pp. 50–6.

Rathbone, D. 'Surface Survey and the Settlement History of the Ancient Fayum' in C. Basile (ed.), *Archeologia e papiri nel Fayum, Storia della ricerca, problemi e prospettive, Atti del convegno internazionale Siracusa, 24–25 maggio 1996* (Syracuse: Istituto internazionale del papiro, 1997), pp. 7–20.

Urbaniak-Walczak, K. 'P.Naqlun inv. 12/89: Ein Fragment eines Syllabars aus Naqlun (Faijum)', *Journal of Juristic Papyrology*, 24 (1994), 145–8.

van Minnen, P. 'Review of *P.Naqlun II*', *Bulletin of the American Society of Papyrologists*, 46 (2009), 219–23.

Wegner, J. 'The Bawit Monastery of Apa Apollo in the Hermopolite Nome and Its Relations with the "World Outside"', *Journal of Juristic Papyrology*, 46 (2017), 147–274.

Wegner, J. *Monastic Communities in Context: Monasteries, Economy, and Society in Late Antique Egypt* (Leuven: Peeters, 2021).

Wegner, J. 'Monks and Monasteries in Egypt between Household and Estate: A Case Study from Bawit', *Journal of Juristic Papyrology*, 51 (2021), 83–104.

Wipszycka, E. *Études sur le christianisme dans l'Égypte de l'antiquité tardive* (Rome: Institutum Patristicum Augustinianum, 1996).

Wipszycka, E. *Moines et communautés monastiques en Égypte (IVe-VIIIe siècles)* (Warsaw: The Raphael Taubenschlag Foundation, 2009).

Wipszycka, E. 'Resources and Economic Activities of the Egyptian Monastic Communities (Fourth–Eighth Century)', *Journal of Juristic Papyrology*, 41 (2011), 159–263.

Wipszycka, E. *Second Gift of the Nile. Monks and Monasteries in Late Antique Egypt* (Warsaw: The Raphael Taubenschlag Foundation, 2018).

Zych, I. 'Cemetery C in Naqlun: Preliminary Report on the Excavation in 2006', *Polish Archaeology in the Mediterranean*, 18 (2008), 230–46.

II.
―――

Production and Consumption of Food
and Material Goods

5 | Monastic Vintages: The Economic Role of Wine in Egyptian Monasteries in the Sixth to Eighth Centuries

DOROTA DZIERZBICKA

Wine was a vital element of the economy of late antique Egypt, and as such it features prominently in the surviving archaeological and textual sources. The cultivation of vineyards was a task that required substantial investment and special effort, and the vine was a labour-intensive and high-risk crop, but in return it could bring high yields. Thus, wine was cultivated as a cash crop by profit-seeking landowners. However, wine also played an important role in everyday life and was a staple commodity ubiquitous in Egypt by Late Antiquity. Even landowners who chose not to invest heavily in viticulture usually owned some vine land to gain a degree of self-sufficiency in wine.[1] Others who could not afford vineyards could lease a plot for a share of the yield or rely on purchases.

Which of these strategies was preferred by monastic landowners and how did monasteries procure wine? The sources presented below concern monastic ownership of vineyards, as well as alternative ways in which communities of monks acquired wine. First, however, it is necessary to briefly discuss the nature of our sources and then the uses of wine in a monastic setting,[2] as they are crucial for understanding why this commodity played such a vital part in the life of monastic economies.

Nature of the Sources

To establish the role of wine in monastic economies we must consider a variety of sources. The Egyptian landscape features working monasteries on ancient sites and the remains of abandoned monastic centres: imposing ruins in the desert of Middle Egypt, sand-covered mounds hiding mud-brick structures on

---

I thank Joanna Wegner for her inspiring and important comments, which helped improve this paper. I am also grateful to Jennifer Cromwell for sharing with me the results of her work on Wadi Sarga material. Words of gratitude are also due to the anonymous reviewers for their useful insights.

[1] For example, the Apions; see Hickey, *Wine, Wealth, and the State*, pp. 147–8.
[2] For a more detailed discussion of wine consumption and usage in monasteries, see Dzierzbicka, 'Wine Consumption'.

the edge of the Delta and Fayum, as well as vestiges of monastic dwellings in ancient tombs and temples of Upper Egypt. These ruins yielded material evidence for the use of wine, such as amphorae and jar stoppers, and some archaeological remains possibly related to production, such as pottery kilns and storage facilities.

However, direct evidence for wine making at Egyptian monasteries has not been found in the material record. Excavations at various monastic sites have been conducted since the late nineteenth and early twentieth centuries, and we must rely on this early documentation for information. As time passed, the ruins have suffered further destruction. Modern excavations, in turn, provide a wealth of useful data on the lives of the communities, but as far as wine is concerned the material finds have generated more questions than answers.

Fortunately, clues lacking in archaeological sources can, to an extent, be found in complementary textual evidence. Several monastic sites have proven to be rich sources of Greek and Coptic documentary texts, providing vivid details of the economic lives of their communities. Other monasteries appeared in dossiers and individual texts recovered from other sites or acquired on the antiquarian market. It is the textual record, therefore, that provides the most useful information for the study of the role of wine in monastic economies.

The principal sites that provide relevant data occupy the middle section of the Egyptian Nile Valley, stretching from the southern tip of the Delta to modern-day Sohag. An outlier to the south is Deir Anba Hadra (also, erroneously, known as the monastery of St Simeon) near Aswan.[3] This paper scrutinises archaeological evidence, texts, and inscriptions from the monastery of Apa Jeremias at Saqqara, the Hermopolite monastery of Apa Apollo in Bawit, the monastery of Apa Thomas at Wadi Sarga near Assiut, the monastery of Apa Apollo at Deir el-Bala'izah (about twenty kilometres to the south of Wadi Sarga), and monasteries of the Pachomian federation near Sohag. In addition, documentary texts mention vineyard-owning monasteries that have not been matched to specific locations: the monastery of Pouinkoreus, another monastery of Apa Jeremias in the Hermopolite nome, as well as several monasteries in the Herakleopolite, Antaiopolite, and Panopolite nomes.

Monasteries as Consumers of Wine

Wine was an indispensable element of religious worship in monasteries, and the amounts needed for this purpose were sometimes fairly substantial. A lengthy inscription carved in stone on a wall at the monastery of Apa

---

[3] For Deir Anba Hadra, see Krastel, Olschok, and Richter, Chapter 11.

Jeremias in Saqqara is a list of wine to be used on designated days of the liturgical year (fifty-two Sundays and thirty-one feasts).[4] The total for the year is 122 jars. Not only did monastic communities as a whole need wine for religious purposes, so did individual monks. In a letter written by the priest and anchorite Moses, who inhabited a tomb in western Thebes in the first half of the eighth century (*O.Frangé* 752.16–17), the sender asks for wine so that he can make a *prosphora* (pious gift) during a feast.[5]

Wine was also part of food rations included in payments to various specialists and service providers hired outside the monastery. We have such an account of payments in wine issued during five consecutive days of the month of Mesore (10–14 August), sometime in the eighth century, at the Hermopolite monastery of Apa Apollo in Bawit (*P.Mon.Apollo* 45). Also at this monastery, jars of wine go to a church and to persons with ecclesiastical titles ('our great father'; a priest), but they are also distributed to various laypersons possibly working for the monastery, for instance to smiths (line 23). There are many more testimonies of such disbursements from Bawit. For instance, *P.Mon.Apollo* 46 is a similar account, and *P.Mon.Apollo* 47 is a receipt for one jar of wine for a mason.

We have more specific information on wine issued as part of payments in contracts from the monastery of Apa Thomas in Wadi Sarga.[6] *P.Sarga* 161 is a labour contract with a carpenter. The abbot of the monastery agrees to pay him twenty-five artabas of wheat, twenty-five *lahe*-measures of wine, a further two jars of wine, some barley and fodder, and some pieces of clothing for a year of work. In *P.Sarga* 164, a contract with a salt dealer, the monastery of Apa Thomas agrees to pay the man a monthly wage consisting of cash and alimentary rations, including a *lakoote*-measure of wine. Salaries partly paid in commodities are nothing out of the ordinary on secular estates in Graeco-Roman and Byzantine Egypt, and clearly monasteries upheld this long-established practice.[7]

As for the monks themselves, it is without a doubt that anchorites and members of coenobitic communities alike consumed wine at least on

---

[4] Quibell, *Excavations at Saqqara*, pp. 69–70, no. 226.
[5] The tomb, known as Theban Tomb 29 (hereafter TT 29), was inhabited by two monks, Moses and Frange, whose activities are well documented by the hundreds of ostraca found therein. For this dossier, see the introduction by Boud'hors and Heurtel to *O.Frangé*, vol. I, pp. 9–32. For the meaning of *prosphora* as a pious gift, see the commentary to lines 2–3 of *P.Oxy.* LXVII 4620.
[6] At Wadi Sarga, wine was even handed out in exchange for fodder given to the camels transporting a shipment of wine in *P.Sarga* 139.
[7] For *opsonion*, or disbursements in kind issued as part of salaries, see, for example, Rathbone, *Economic Rationalism*, pp. 91–102 and Hickey, *Wine, Wealth, and the State*, pp. 132–6. For wine issued as part of salaries and on top of payments in Graeco-Roman and Byzantine Egypt, see Dzierzbicka, ΟΙΝΟΣ, pp. 237–43.

occasion. There were various dietary restrictions that came with being a monk, and there were probably as many regulations as there were monasteries. The strict precepts of Shenoute prohibited wine consumption to healthy monks of his congregation, but, besides this exceptional case, wine was generally not forbidden. Moreover, its consumption was recommended to monks who were sick or weak.[8] Wine was issued to monks on various occasions. An account from Deir el-Bala'izah mentions the issue of wine 'for the table of the superior' and 'for our table'.[9] Documents from Wadi Sarga also refer to issues of wine to male and female monastics, both for personal use and for their communities.[10]

Archaeological investigations on various monastic sites have yielded an abundance of amphorae originally used for wine.[11] The jars themselves are not direct evidence for wine consumption; they served as containers for a variety of foodstuffs, and even those originally meant for wine were often reused. Monks also collected empty wine vessels from surrounding villages and brought them to their cells after filling them with water. However, monastic sites also yielded mud stoppers used to seal the contents of wine amphorae at their place of origin.[12] Imprints of amphora rims visible on some of these plugs correspond in dimensions to the amphora repertoire

---

[8] On monastic drinking, see Pachomius, *Instructions* 1.46 (Lefort, *Oeuvres de S. Pachôme*, pp. 19–20; Veilleux, *Pachomian Koinonia III*, p. 35). Shenoute implies that the sick must request wine themselves, as indicated by rules 156 and 189–191 (numbering according to Layton, *The Canons of Our Fathers*, pp. 152-3 and 164-5). On the use of wine in monastic infirmaries, see Crislip, *From Monastery to Hospital*, pp. 33-4 and 74-5. Those visiting the sick could also occasionally partake in the same wine, as indicated by *Apophthegmata Patrum* Rho (An Abba of Rome) 1 (ed. Cotelier, *Ecclesiae Graecae Monumenta* 1, p. 658, reprinted in Migne, *Patrologia Graeca* (hereafter *PG*) 65 (cols. 387–388); Ward, *Sayings of the Desert Fathers*, p. 209). For requests for wine on account of illness in the dossier of Frange in western Thebes (TT 29), see *O. Frangé* 98 and 99. See also *P.Naqlun* I 9 for a mention of wine flavoured with marjoram (σαμψούχινος οἶνος), a herb occurring in medical texts, for instance in a medical handbook from the Apa Jeremias infirmary in Saqqara (Erichsen, 'Aus einem koptischen Arzneibuch', folio B recto, 106).

[9] *P.Bal.* II 312.8, 10 (seventh–mid-eighth century).

[10] For example, *P.Sarga* 92.5, 8-9; 168.4; 169.8; 170.5; 186.6, 10 (sixth–early eighth century); for instructions on consumption of wine among female ascetics, see Pseudo-Athanasius, *De virginitate* 12 (*PG* 28, 263 D and 264 A) and 22 (*PG* 28, 278 D and 280 A); translations in Shaw, 'Pseudo-Athanasius'.

[11] For instance, at Naqlun the Polish archaeological team under the direction of W. Godlewski excavated a sixth–seventh-century dump consisting mostly of kitchen refuse (Dzierzbicka, 'Refuse Dump in Sector B in Naqlun'), which included numerous fragments of wine amphorae from different production sites in Egypt and beyond (Danys-Lasek, 'Deir el-Naqlun 2010 and 2011').

[12] The monastery of Apa Jeremias at Saqqara (Quibell, *Excavations at Saqqara*, pp. 4, 24, 27-30); the monastery of Epiphanius at Thebes (Winlock and Crum, *Monastery of Epiphanius*, pp. 79–81); Wadi Sarga (O'Connell, 'R. Campbell Thompson's 1913/14 Excavation', p. 128); Kellia (Egloff, *Kellia*, pp. 33-5); Bawit (Lyon-Caen, 'Bouchons d'amphore').

found on the sites, enabling them to be matched to different variants of vessels produced along the Nile Valley, as well as in the Delta region. Thus, amphora stoppers found amid refuse are direct evidence of wine consumption on monastic sites.

Monasteries as Vineyard Owners

Whether for individual consumption, liturgical purposes, or payments, monastic communities needed wine. The larger the monastery, the more wine it was likely to need. It was the second most common commodity transported from different villages to the monasteries, as we learn from delivery requests, orders of payment, lists, and receipts, primarily from Wadi Sarga and Bawit.[13]

At the monastery of Apa Thomas in Wadi Sarga, documentary evidence from the sixth to eighth centuries mentions camels carrying wine from vineyards to the monastic complex.[14] Caravans of up to forty camels (*P. Sarga* 194) brought as much as 200 measures of wine per day (*P.Sarga* 255 and 257), and some consignments of wine travelled by boat all the way from the Herakleopolite nome (*P.Sarga* 135), or even the Fayum (e.g., *P.Sarga* 235 and 236). The total supply of wine to the monastery has been estimated as 25,665 litres per annum, but in the light of recent research it was certainly higher.[15]

In Bawit, the monastic administration had a system of managing deliveries of wine, which may have totalled circa 50,000 litres or even circa 100,000 litres per year.[16] Up to thirty-one caravans of camels transported over 1,000 measures of wine daily at vintage time (*P.Louvre Bawit* 28). How was this wine procured? Did all or part of it come from monastic estates?

It is widely assumed that monasteries, especially the more affluent ones, owned vineyards, but in fact there are few direct attestations of this. In addition, it seems that monasteries gradually gained possession of vineyards throughout the period under consideration, so ways of obtaining wine likely changed from century to century (see below, Continuity and

---

[13] Bacot, 'La circulation du vin'.   [14] *P.Sarga* 121-4; 209-381.

[15] Bacot, 'La circulation du vin', p. 273. Jennifer Cromwell's current research on unpublished Wadi Sarga texts adds another forty wine receipts to the corpus, so Bacot's estimate needs to be reconsidered.

[16] For the first figure, see *P.Brux.Bawit* pp. 93-5; for the second, I cite Delattre's unpublished paper 'Agricultural Management and Food Production at the Monastery of Bawit', presented at the conference 'Monastic Economies in Egypt and Palestine, 5th-10th Centuries CE' (16-17 March 2016, Oxford). See also below.

Change in Monastic Wine Acquisition Strategy: The Case of Bawit). Some monasteries appear as suppliers of substantial amounts of wine: for instance, the Pachomian monastery of Pouinkoreus in the Hermopolite nome sold 1,500 *knidia*-jars of wine to a bishop (*P.Cair.Masp.* II 67168; sixth century).[17] This document is a receipt issued by Theodoros, bishop of Pentapolis, who had paid for the wine in advance, and the consignment was delivered to him at Alexandria. Because contracts of sale of wine for future delivery were typically drawn up between vineyard owners and wholesale buyers, the document is an indirect testimony of vineyards in possession of the monastery.[18]

In the sixth century, vineyards on monastic estates do not seem to be the result of purchase or investment on the part of the monastery. Rather, they were donated to the community in a developed and productive state.[19] In the mid-sixth century, the monastery of Apa Jeremias in the Hermopolite nome received one aroura of vine land from Flavius Phoibammon, who was a chief medical officer (*archiatros*) at Antinoe.[20] The plot was part of an estate he had inherited from his father, and it was located at Ibion Sesembythis in the Hermopolite nome. The vineyard was equipped with a full range of irrigation machinery.

We find information on vineyards belonging to monasteries and other religious institutions of Aphrodito in *SB* XX 14669 (524/5), a fiscal register of money taxes on one category of land in the village (*astika*, or plots for which taxes were payable to the office in the city of Antaeopolis rather than in the village office at Aphrodito).[21] Out of nine monasteries mentioned in the document, six owned vineyards. However, this monastic vine land, which amounted to only a little over twelve arourae, is a small fraction of the collective figure for vine land in Aphrodito, estimated by Zuckerman as 252.5 arourae.[22] The largest monastic landowner in the document with

---

[17] If we follow the conclusion in Mayerson, 'The Enigmatic Knidion', that a *knidion* was a measure equal to four *sextarii*, or circa 2.2 litres, then we end up with 3,300 litres of wine – a yield of about three and a half arourae of vine land (assuming an average yield of 33.3 hectolitres per hectare after *P.Cair.Masp.* I 67104).

[18] See Jakab, 'Guarantee and Jars', and further references therein.

[19] There are sales of land to monasteries (e.g., *P.Mon.Apollo* I 24), but they do not mention vineyards. For donations of land in the seventh and eighth centuries, see Steinwenter, 'Aus dem kirchlichen Vermögensrechte der Papyri'. Plots were also transferred to monasteries by property owners who had joined the communities (*P.Mon.Apollo* I 25, eighth century). For monastic landed property in general, see Richter, 'Cultivation of Monastic Estates'.

[20] *P.Cair.Masp.* II 67151, circa 545/6.

[21] For the text, see Zuckerman, *Du village à l'empire*; Gascou, 'Le cadastre d'Aphroditô'; Bagnall, 'Village Landholding at Aphrodito'; MacCoull, 'Monastic and Church Landholding'. For monastic estates in Aphrodito, see Marthot-Santaniello, Chapter 3.

[22] Three-fifths of arable land in Aphrodito belonged to a major landowner, *comes* Ammonios, and the remaining two-fifths were divided between two categories: *kometika* – plots for which taxes

nearly 300 arourae of *astika* (one-fifth of the total land covered by the cadastre) in forty-nine parcels, the monastery of Apa Sourous, owned five and two-thirds of an aroura of vineyards. A pottery workshop in the monastery of Apa Sourous mentioned in a different document written several decades later (*P.Cair.Masp.* I 67110 from 565) was probably part of the same private foundation established and endowed by the founder, a member of a wealthy Aphroditan family.[23] The second most substantial vineyard measured four and three-quarters of an aroura and belonged to the Pachomian monastery of Smin from Panopolis, a major landowner in Aphrodito. It is important to note that the twelve arourae of vine land are attested only in one land category, in one village, in a fragmentary text. The monasteries could have also owned vineyards in other nomes. Nonetheless, this small figure may in fact be representative for the sixth century.

Archaeological evidence for wine pressing found thus far in Egyptian monasteries is scarce. Monneret de Villard reported finding a grape-processing installation within the walls of the monastery of Deir Anba Hadra in Aswan, but his identification of structure no. 19 as a wine press is not convincing.[24] However, investigations of a team from the German Archaeological Institute uncovered remains of burnt matting covered in grape pulp that seem to have constituted wine press refuse.[25] These materials left over from pressing and apparently used as fuel may have come from an unidentified installation within the monastic walls.

Some monasteries were equipped with workshops for the production of pottery containers.[26] Such communities may have been engaged in wine production, but this is not a rule. For instance, potters figure in registers of crafts performed in monasteries belonging to Shenoute's congregation.[27] Apparently the needs of this community were large enough to warrant launching pottery production, but the use of these amphorae is still uncertain. While several installations uncovered in the White Monastery are

---

were paid in the village office; and *astika* – plots for which taxes were paid in the city office. From Zuckerman's collective figures for the whole village, it appears that monasteries held under 5 per cent of all the land. Monasteries most probably owned slightly more land than can be calculated from the entries that list their names. Dues for their plots may have been paid by middlemen, and it was they who went on the record (Zuckerman, *Du village à l'empire*).

[23] Gascou and MacCoull, 'Le cadastre d'Aphroditô', p. 137; Ruffini, 'Aphrodito before Dioskoros', pp. 228–30.

[24] Monneret de Villard, *Il Monastero de S. Simeone*, vol. 1, pp. 84–6.

[25] I am indebted to Tonio Sebastian Richter, Mennat-Allah El Dorry, and Sebastian Olschok from the project *Deir Anba Hadra. Sociocultural and Economic Significance of a Holy Place in Upper Egypt from the Late Ancient to the Early Mamluk Period* for sharing this information with me.

[26] Ballet, 'L'approvisionnement des monastères'; Mahmoud, 'Organisation des ateliers de potiers'.

[27] Kuhn, *Letters and Sermons of Besa*, p. 33.

testimony to oil pressing on the premises, no direct evidence for wine manufacture has been found.[28] Nonetheless, given the community's vast landholdings, vineyard ownership should not be ruled out. In such a case, amphorae made by the community could have been used for packaging wine produced on monastic land beyond the walls of the monastery.

Archaeological remains discovered in Saqqara at the monastery of Apa Jeremias also testify to amphora production.[29] Six kilns dated to the sixth–seventh centuries have been found at the monastery (two more medium-sized kilns discovered further to the west were also mentioned in the publication without further detail). The kilns served for the manufacture of a variety of ceramic forms including amphorae, which were also found in an unfired state. The amphorae were imitations of type LRA 1 (i.e., Late Roman Amphora 1; Egloff 164) made from coarse alluvial Nile silt and covered in red slip.

The internal diameters of the kilns found at the monastery at Saqqara ranged from 1.0 to 2.6 m. Their capacity is difficult to determine based on archaeological evidence alone, but helpful data is found in *P.Lond.Copt.* I 695 (sixth–eighth centuries), an account of jars produced in a pottery at Psabt in the Fayum. On the basis of the numerical data preserved in this document, Terry Wilfong estimated an output of 160–214 jars per kiln in a single firing.[30] The thirteen kilns listed in the account produced a total of 10,440 amphorae in a session consisting of five firings. Using these figures, the maximum output of the six published Saqqara kilns may be estimated to be around 6,400 amphorae per production session, which would have taken at least five days. The number of amphorae produced may have been much smaller, however, as we cannot be sure that all the kilns were operational simultaneously and that all six were used for firing amphorae.

The timing and volume of amphora production was frequently correlated with local wine production. After firing, empty jars were transported to winepressing installations, which were usually at or near vineyards.[31] The production and firing of amphorae was performed in days preceding the vintage, and the quantity of jars depended on the amounts ordered by

---

[28] Brooks Hedstrom *et al.*, 'White Monastery Federation Project', pp. 351–7. The interpretation of some features as possible *garum* production facilities has recently been refuted in Blanke, *Archaeology of Egyptian Monasticism*, p. 85.

[29] Ghaly, 'Pottery Workshops of Saint-Jeremia'.

[30] Wilfong, 'A Coptic Account of Pottery'. On firing amphorae in general, see Gallimore, 'Amphora Production', pp. 170–7.

[31] This was common practice throughout the Graeco-Roman period in Egypt; see, e.g., *P.Cair.Zen.* III 59366.15–18 (241 BC, Philadelphia); *SB* XIV 11960 (second half of the second century, Oxyrhynchite nome); *P.Flor.* II 175.26–32 (255, Theadelphia).

wine producers, who may have been, for instance, lessees of monastic land.³² The production of amphorae at Saqqara may also have been connected with other types of activity, for instance oil production.³³

The monastery of Apa Jeremias stored wine, but no industrial-scale storage facilities are attested on the site: one vaulted room (no. 1889) in a service area of the monastery was identified as a wine cellar.³⁴ This identification was based on finds, which included amphora sealings and sherds, as well as the characteristics of the room itself: the lack of structures within, only mud plaster on the walls and a niche for a lamp. It would have been well suited for the assigned function, as wine is best stored in cool and dark conditions with a minimal temperature fluctuation. This long room, measuring approximately two by eight metres, would have provided enough space for about 150 amphorae with a maximum body diameter of thirty centimetres.³⁵ Therefore, it seems to have served for storing wine for the current needs of the monastery. Furthermore, the wine may have been obtained from various sources, not just through monastic production. The ceramic finds from the site also included LRA 7 jars produced elsewhere in the Nile Valley, as well as imported LRA 1 of Cypriot or Cilician origin.³⁶

Monastic production of wine amphorae may be attested in a Coptic ostracon found in the temple in Akoris, in rooms that housed a pottery workshop.³⁷ The ostracon begins as follows: 'In the name of God and Archangel Michael, this is a list of *koupha* from the pottery workshop.' According to Wipszycka, the reference to Archangel Michael at the beginning of the list of produced vessels could indicate that the workshop belonged to a monastic community whose patron was Michael and which was installed inside the temple.

Evidence for vineyards in possession of the monastery of Apa Apollo at Bawit dates from the seventh to eighth centuries. *P.KölnÄgypt.* II 41 (for more on which, see below) is an eighth-century letter written by a monk concerning preparations for the vintage in several vineyards. *P.Vat.Aphrod.*

---

[32] Hickey, *Wine, Wealth, and the State*, pp. 72–3.
[33] On agricultural products in Egyptian amphorae, see Dixneuf, *Amphores égyptiennes*, pp. 197–211.
[34] Quibell, *Excavations at Saqqara*, p. 27 and pl. I.
[35] For the dimensions of the room, see the plan in Quibell, *Excavations at Saqqara*, pl. I. The amphora types found in the monastery included LRA 1 and LRA 7 amphorae, which reach such diameters (Dixneuf, *Amphores égyptiennes*, pp. 163 and 174–5).
[36] For local and imported pottery found at Wadi Sarga, including LRA 1 amphorae, see Faiers, 'Wadi Sarga Revisited'.
[37] Morelli and Schmelz, 'Gli ostraca di Akoris'.

13 (675–725),³⁸ a list of requisitions imposed on Bawit by the Arab administration, is a clear indication of vineyard ownership. Among various products it calls for *hepsema* (boiled wine) and raisins. The volume of boiled wine is relatively small (144 *sextarii*, so between twenty and fifty jars),³⁹ but the required amount of raisins is thirteen artabae, or approximately 400 kg.⁴⁰ Additionally, *P.Mon.Apollo* I 45 (eighth century) is an account of wine expenditure from Bawit associated by its editor, Clackson, with requisitions through the mention of a *shaliou*, a local official involved in the collection of taxes and other levies. In this document (lines 4, 12, 15), the *shaliou* of Ptene is credited with three separate payments of boiled wine, possibly requisitioned by the Arab administration as provisions.⁴¹

At Bawit, wine was produced on monastic property, but not at the monastery itself.⁴² No presses have been found on the site to date, and the presence of storerooms with large numbers of wine jars cannot be viewed as evidence of wine production on the spot.⁴³ Also, the fact that numerous transport ostraca testify to the delivery of wine in jars in the month of Thoth (29 August to 27 September), a few days to a few weeks after the vintage, suggests that treading, pressing, and primary fermentation took place outside the monastery, most likely at or near the vineyard.

Ostraca from the monastery of Apa Thomas at Wadi Sarga often refer to wine arriving at the monastery or disbursed to various persons (*P.Sarga* 121–7, 133, 135, 213–344; see also the commentary on pp. 10–12). These documents, however, cannot stand alone as proof of wine production on the property of the monastery, since deliveries could, in theory, have been purchases in bulk or repayments of loans in kind, as is well attested elsewhere. However, the monastery of Apa Thomas certainly owned vineyards. A document which attests to wine production on land belonging to the monastery at Wadi Sarga is *P.Sarga* 344 (seventh century?), a receipt for a tax paid in wine. The relevant fragment is translated as follows: '15 *hats* [a measure of unknown capacity] of wine we have received from you, on

---

³⁸ See *BL* VIII: 503. For this text, see Gonis, 'Two Fiscal Registers', pp. 21–5.
³⁹ Capacities known for jar types in papyri of the Late Roman and Byzantine periods range from three to eight *sextarii*; Kruit and Worp, 'Geographical Jar Names', p. 106.
⁴⁰ An *artaba* is slightly more than 30 kg. Since the weight of dried fruit would have decreased by approximately 75 per cent (Christensen and Peacock, 'Harvesting and Handling', p. 194), 400 kg of raisins would have been obtained from circa 1,600 kg of grapes. In turn, 1,600 kg of grapes would provide circa 12.3 hectolitres of wine (Robinson, *Oxford Companion to Wine*, pp. 780–1), which in Egyptian conditions would have been the yield of 0.37 ha or 1.34 arourae of vine land (assuming the average yield of 33.3 hectolitres per hectare after *P.Cair.Masp.* I 67104).
⁴¹ See also orders to issue *hepsema* to persons with Arabic names in Delattre, 'Le monastère de Baouît'.
⁴² *P.Brux.Bawit* 85–6.   ⁴³ *P.Brux.Bawit* 50.

account of the tax [*demosion*] of the fields of Tahomo for the crop of the 1st indiction. Paid on Thoth 9.'[44] In addition, the fact that monks took the trouble to transport wine all the way from the Fayum and the Herakleopolite nome implies that the vine land located there was monastic property.[45]

Management of Monastic Vineyards

We have no evidence for the cultivation of vineyards directly by monasteries. *P.KölnÄgypt.* II 41 from Bawit is a fragmentary letter in which the monk Pamoun informs Apa Enoch about the expected harvest from vineyards cultivated with the aid of *ampelourgoi*, vineyard specialists. The letter is written close to the time of the vintage and refers to the supply of empty jars (*koupha*). Pamoun plans to send the scribe Apollo to help with accounting during the harvest. Despite the apparent active interest of the monastery in these vineyards and organisation of the vintage, this letter is not an indication that the plots in question were under direct management. Procuring jars and assessing the yields would also have been the landowner's task if the vineyards were leased out. The mention of *ampelourgoi* makes it likely, in fact, that the plots in question were cultivated by tenants, as was the case on the Apion estate,[46] and the editor, Schenke, is probably correct in associating the monk's activity with the collection of *aparche*, the first-fruits from leased vineyards.[47]

Several contracts show monastic vineyards leased to tenants. Unlike affluent landowners in Egypt in Late Antiquity, who seem to have preferred to lease their vineyards in exchange for fixed rent in cash, monasteries seem to have relied on sharecropping leases.[48] In such agreements, the lessor and lessee divided the yield from the leased plot into two shares. The tenants, where the information survives, were mostly inhabitants of villages located close to the vineyards in their care. Their responsibility was vineyard work, while other tasks and financial responsibilities remained in the hands of the landowner.

A sixth-century document from the Hermopolite nome, *P.Giss.* I 56, is a ten-year lease of a monastic vineyard with irrigation machinery for

---

[44] Translation by the editors (Crum and Bell).
[45] I am grateful to Jennifer Cromwell for pointing this out.
[46] Hickey, *Wine, Wealth, and the State*, p. 77.
[47] For a discussion of the term *aparche* and summary of the scholarly debate on this subject, see Wipszycka, *Moines et communautés monastiques*, pp. 556–65, especially p. 560 for *aparche* paid in wine.
[48] Banaji, *Agrarian Change*, p. 125.

a 50 per cent share in the yield. In *P.Mich.* XIII 667 (Aphrodito, mid-sixth century), a plot of land belonging to the monastery of Apa Sourous was leased for fixed rent instead of a share, but the payment was to be delivered in wheat and wine (fifty *angeia* jars, each holding seven *sextarii*, or 3.8 litres – a total of 190 litres). The tenant, Phoibammon, is also obliged to take care of proper irrigation and vine-pruning. If, as in the case of Apa Jeremias and Apa Sourous, the wine-growing plots received from donors were equipped with irrigation machinery, pottery kilns, and other facilities, then the monastery did not need to invest a great deal in order to keep the vineyard productive. The burden of labour and care for the vineyard was assumed by the tenant.

Monasteries that leased their vineyards in exchange for part of the produce received wine in the form of must several days after the initial phase of grape processing at the winery. The time of the vintage varied from year to year, but typically occurred in a period that ranged from mid-Mesore to mid-Thoth (August and the first half of September) and lasted up to three weeks.[49] Winepressing installations in Egypt were typically located in rural areas, close to the vineyards.[50] Freshly pressed must remained in the vat (typically a plastered basin sunk into the ground) through the first phase of fermentation that lasted no more than a few days. For the second stage, which no longer involved the release of as much carbon dioxide as the first one, the new wine was decanted into ceramic jars for further maturing and storage. Once packaged, the wine could be transported from the vineyard to the monastery.

Alternative Ways of Procuring Wine

Certainly not all monasteries had vineyards. Even monastic centres that owned vine land did not always collect enough wine to meet the needs of their communities. In such cases, it was necessary to supplement domestic production with wine from other sources. When in need of wine, anchorites like Moses (an inhabitant of TT 29 mentioned above) could count on charity, but the same could not be a solution for entire monasteries.

---

[49] *CPR* V 26 (late fifth century, Skar, Hermopolite nome), col. 6 contains an account recording deliveries of wine from the *topos* of Tyrrannou on 12–16 Mesore (6–12 August). *SB* XII 10990 from Abu Mina (Wortmann, 'Griechische Ostraka aus Abu Mena') lists receipts for payments of food and wine to teams of grape-pickers (τρυγηταί) from 28 Mesore to 20 Thoth (24 August–17 September) and to grape treaders from 15 to 25 Thoth (12–22 September). For the Fayum, see Rathbone, *Economic Rationalism*, p. 250.

[50] Dzierzbicka, 'Wineries and their Elements'.

Laypersons donated wine and other foodstuffs to monasteries, but the irregular nature of such offerings made them an unreliable source of consumables in the long run.[51] In accounts of expenditures *pietatis causa* from the Apion archive, churches receive wine from the estate, no doubt for liturgical purposes, but monasteries are recorded only as recipients of vinegar.[52] An exception is a document in which Serenos, the wine steward of the Apion estate, issued 360 double jars (*dipla*) of wine and at least sixty double jars of vinegar to the *monasterion* at Pela, but in this case at least part of the issue was purchased by the monastery.[53]

A way for individual monks to acquire wine was through tenancy. In one early sixth-century lease document from Aphrodito, *P.Flor.* III 279 (514), the tenant is a monk who agrees to work in a vineyard and water a reed bed belonging to an Aphroditan landlord for four years in exchange for a share of the yield. Monasteries did not necessarily provide members of their communities with wine for consumption.[54] Such leases undertaken by individual monks could help them provide for themselves. Any wine the tenant did not consume on his own could be sold, exchanged for other goods, given as *prosphora*, or distributed as charity.[55]

We have good evidence for monasteries simply meeting their need for wine with purchases. Monastics are attested as buyers in contracts of sale of wine with deferred delivery. The purchases take the form of cash loans arranged to be repaid in wine.[56] In one example, *P.Bad.* IV 55 (sixth–seventh centuries), the archimandrite of the monastery of Hipponon in the Herakleopolite nome purchases wine with payment in advance from a man in the Oxyrhynchite nome.[57] The amounts purchased were sometimes considerable. In two sixth-century documents from the monastery of Apa Apollo in Bawit, *P.Amst.* I 47 (537) and *P.Amst.* I 48 (sixth century), we see the archimandrite as the buyer of fifty and then another 450 jars of wine.[58]

---

[51] Wipszycka, *Moines et communautés monastiques*, pp. 494–5.
[52] Hickey, *Wine, Wealth, and the State*, pp. 104–5 and tables 4.3–4.5. However, monastic churches do receive wine; see, for example, the evidence of jar inscriptions from Kellia (discussion with references in Wipszycka, *Moines et communautés monastiques*, p. 496).
[53] *PSI* VIII 953.12–13 (567/8).   [54] *P.Brux.Bawit* p. 99.
[55] For the importance of the distribution of foodstuffs to the poor, see, e.g., Wipszycka, *Moines et communautés monastiques*, p. 497.
[56] This category of documents is referred to as sales of wine for future or deferred delivery, sales with payment in advance, sales on delivery, or loans with payment in kind; see Harrauer 'Sechs byzantinische Weinkäufe'; *P.Heid.* V; Kruit, 'Three Byzantine Sales'; and Gallimore, 'A Contract for the Advanced Sale of Wine'.
[57] Kruit and Worp, '*P.Bad.* IV 55: Ein neuer Text'.
[58] However, the contracts of sale of wine for future delivery featuring archimandrites as buyers do not explicitly refer to them as agents acting on behalf of a monastic institution. It is a common-sense assumption that they acted as such, and it is an attractive and plausible hypothesis that the

Loans in which the borrowed sum was to be repaid in wine feature not only monastic superiors, but also individual monks as lenders or buyers. It is difficult to determine if they too represented their monasteries or conducted private operations, but the latter is more likely.[59] In one such loan contract (*SB* XVI 12267), the parties involved are a monk from Bawit and a man from the nearby village of Sentryphis. In another, Neilos, a monk from Naqlun, was to receive 200 *kouri* of wine as repayment for a sum he had lent to Aurelius Victor.[60] According to this document, Victor was to provide the jars and deliver the wine to Neilos, i.e., to Naqlun. In *P.Bal.* 114 and 116 (seventh–eighth centuries), in turn, all the parties involved in the loans to be repaid in wine are monks.

It is impossible to tell on the basis of the available sources if, in the sixth century, monasteries such as those in Bawit and Naqlun owned vineyards of their own at all. If there were vineyards on monastic property, perhaps they did not produce enough wine to satisfy the needs of the communities. It also cannot be excluded that monasteries (or individual monks) treated retail sales of wine as a source of revenue. Purchases of wine in advance were a way to pay less for new wine that could later be re-sold at higher prices after it had matured at the monastery.

Some monasteries, for instance Bawit, seem to have had substantial cash surpluses,[61] and as holders of ready cash,[62] they were convenient business partners for wine producers: a monastery could be an alternative to a wine merchant, and similarly could buy wine in bulk with advance payment. The producer received cash needed to pay taxes and wages, and the monastery received wine at wholesale prices, in a quantity that would meet its needs and of a quality that was guaranteed by the seller.

We do not know when the wine purchased with payment in advance was claimed by monasteries. Sales of wine on delivery do not specify when the purchased goods were to be delivered. As Jakab convincingly explains, Mesore was indicated in these documents as the month of the vintage in which the newly made wine became the property of the buyer, but in contracts with guarantee clauses the physical delivery was deferred until

---

wine was purchased for the community and not for use in the archimandrites' own, private affairs. A shadow of a doubt remains, however, especially since the issue of discerning between the monastery's funds and the monks' funds in such dealings is a complex one. In order to fully grasp the mechanism of the institutional procurement of wine to monasteries like Bawit or Naqlun, we need a more profound understanding of the economic organisation of communities in which individual monks retained the right to own property and manage business affairs.

[59] Wipszycka, *Moines et communautés monastiques*, p. 548.   [60] *P.Naqlun* II 23 (590–6?).
[61] *P.Brux.Bawit* pp. 98–9; Wipszycka, *Moines et communautés monastiques*, p. 546.
[62] Markiewicz, 'Church, Clerics, Monks and Credit', pp. 199–202.

the wine was ready and fit for use.⁶³ Jakab argues that, by including the guarantee clause in the contract, the seller undertook to store and take care of the wine until the specified month, usually Tybi (from 27 December to 25 January) or Phamenoth (from 25 February to 26 March).⁶⁴

Continuity and Change in Monastic Wine Acquisition Strategy: The Case of Bawit

Scholars have consistently argued that wine played an important role in the economy of the monastery of Apa Apollo in Bawit.⁶⁵ Although, as mentioned above, the evidence for vineyards owned by the monastery is scarce, there are many texts that refer to large transports of new wine or freshly pressed must from vineyards to the monastery. On the other hand, bulk purchases of wine are also well attested for Bawit.

A diachronic view is useful in trying to make sense of the evidence on wine deliveries and vineyard ownership in Bawit. The problem is the diverse nature of the sources: for the sixth century, we have contracts of purchase with deferred delivery, but no contemporary receipts reveal details of the collection of the wine. Purchases of wine in the sixth century indicate that either the monastery owned no vineyards or the yields of monastic vine land did not meet the needs of the community.

Several contracts related to wine supply to the monastery and dated to the sixth century preserve clauses concerning the supply of jars and terms of guarantee.⁶⁶ Where the clauses are extant, the monastery is the supplier of jars, while the seller guarantees the good quality of the wine until it is claimed by the buyer.⁶⁷ As one can assume on the basis of similar documents from

---

⁶³ Jakab, 'Guarantee and Jars'.
⁶⁴ For a recent and exhaustive overview of the scholarly debate on this subject and for bibliography, see Gallimore, 'A Contract for the Advanced Sale of Wine', pp. 158–164.
⁶⁵ P.Mon.Apollo p. 27; P.Brux.Bawit pp. 85–6.
⁶⁶ P.Amst. I 47 (537): purchase with deferred delivery (archimandrite), clauses not preserved; P. Amst. I 48 (sixth century): purchase with deferred delivery (archimandrite), monastery provides new jars, guarantee until Phamenoth; P.Athen Xyla 6 (sixth century): purchase with deferred delivery, monastery provides new jars, guarantee until the end of Phamenoth; SB XVI 12267 (540): loan of wine (monk); SB XXII 15595 (590): purchase with deferred delivery or loan to be repaid in wine (monk), buyer provides jars, guarantee until Phamenoth; P.Lond. V 1899 (600): purchase with deferred delivery? (P.Louvre Bawit, Appendix), clauses not preserved.
⁶⁷ In sixth-century contracts from Bawit, the quality of the wine is guaranteed by the seller until Phamenoth (March). However, over half a year (from the vintage in August until the end of March) is a long time for storing wine in Egypt, especially when we compare it to other contracts with guarantee clauses only until Tybi. The monastery certainly needed wine for disbursements on a day-to-day basis (P.Brux.Bawit p. 177), and keeping the supply closed up at the vineyard until

the Oxyrhynchite nome, the place of pickup was usually the vineyard ('at the vat'), and the buyer was responsible for organising the transport.[68]

In turn, the corpus of ϣⲓⲛⲉ ⲛⲥⲁ ostraca (formulaic waybills) from Bawit shows the process of conveying wine to the monastery, but these documents are dated to the seventh and eighth centuries, a time for which we have indications of both vineyard ownership and purchases with deferred delivery. Perhaps Bawit acquired vineyards during the apex of its activity in the seventh and eighth centuries – possibly after the Arab conquest, in the aftermath of which the population and wealth of monasteries are known to have increased.[69] For this period, we have the most explicit evidence for vineyard ownership in the form of documents related to requisitions and tax payment in kind (boiled wine and raisins), as well as *P.KölnÄgypt.* II 41, a letter concerning preparations for the vintage.

The purchases with deferred delivery and the ϣⲓⲛⲉ ⲛⲥⲁ ostraca could be treated as testimonies of two different realities: an earlier one in which the monastery purchases its wine, and a later one in which its wine supply comes from its own vineyards. As mentioned above, Alain Delattre estimates on the basis of the corpus of ϣⲓⲛⲉ ⲛⲥⲁ ostraca that the monastery in Bawit received circa 50,000 or even 100,000 litres of wine per year in the seventh and eighth centuries. However, we cannot be certain that all this wine came from vineyards owned by the monastery; the collection procedure may have been the same for all wine that was to be picked up at the vineyards, regardless of property rights and details of contractual arrangements.

If all this wine were to come from monastic property, however, the area under vines in possession of the monastery would be considerable by Egyptian standards. Even assuming a relatively high yield of 33.3 hectolitres per hectare, as attested in *P.Cair.Masp.* I 67104, 100,000 litres of wine would mean ownership of a minimum of 100 arourae of vineyards

---

spring could potentially lead to shortages. Fermentation took no more than a few weeks to complete, and even relatively new wine was fit for use, for instance as a means of payment. Possibly, Mesore and Phamenoth (or Tybi in other contracts) were liminal dates between which the pickup could be arranged at the buyer's discretion. The buyer would then have claimed the wine at will, even though the seller remained liable for its quality for some months to come. I do not, however, feel qualified to consider the matter from a legal point of view.

[68] Kruit, 'Meaning of Various Words', p. 269. Also, an Arsinoite sale of wine for future delivery dated to the sixth century has the place of delivery indicated as 'at the vat', ἐν τῷ ἐποικ[ίῳ] (line 4); Gallimore, 'A Contract for the Advanced Sale of Wine' (Vienna P.Vindob.G. 40267). The Hermopolite formula of these documents does not include information on the exact place of pickup (Kruit, 'Local Customs'). In exceptional cases, when the seller is to supply the jars and bring the wine to the buyer (e.g., *P.Naqlun* II 23), these terms are explicitly stated in the document; *contra* Bacot, 'La circulation du vin', p. 271 and n. 11, whose citation appears to be erroneous.

[69] Wipszycka, *Moines et communautés monastiques*, p. 501.

(1 aroura = 0.2756 ha). Since the landowner usually took only part of the yield and left the rest to crop-sharing tenants and labourers, the total area under vines could have even been twice as high. By comparison, the minimal area of vineyards belonging to the Theadelphia unit of the Appianus estate is tentatively placed at 100 arourae,[70] while the total area under vines on the Apion estates is estimated to be 825–1,250 arourae.[71] Two-hundred arourae of vine land would certainly place the monastery of Apa Apollo in Bawit among the major landowners of the Hermopolite nome.

The ϣⲓⲛⲉ ⲛⲥⲁ ostraca, however, do not offer any indication as to the process through which the wine was acquired. As shown above, there were several ways to obtain wine: from their own vineyards, either directly managed or leased out; through purchase with deferred delivery; by undertaking a sharecropping lease. From the monastery of Apa Apollo, we have a few lease contracts, and none concern vineyards, but the shortage of these documents may be due to the preservation of the evidence.[72] Several sales with deferred delivery dated to the seventh and eighth centuries are preserved from Bawit, and the continuation of this commercial practice is well attested through the eighth century.[73]

Where preserved, the conditions of contracts from the sixth century (see n. 67 above) do not provide a basis for differentiating between deliveries of wine purchased through payment in advance and deliveries of produce from monastic vineyards. In both cases, the monastery most likely had to procure the jars and organise transport.[74] The delivery of purchased wine could also take place at the same time as the delivery of wine from monastic vineyards: the contracts from the seventh and eighth centuries are not preserved well enough to determine if they contained guarantee clauses. However, according to contracts without this clause, wine would have been delivered immediately after the vintage,[75] like the wine attested in the ϣⲓⲛⲉ ⲛⲥⲁ ostraca.

---

[70] Rathbone, *Economic Rationalism*, p. 38. [71] Hickey, *Wine, Wealth, and the State*, p. 153.

[72] P.Mon.Apollo I 26; P.HermitageCopt. 13 (eighth century). Indirect attestation of a land lease is also found in a letter concerning renewal of a lease of fodder land: P.Pierpont Morgan Library Inv. M 662 b (6a) verso (Delattre et al., 'Papyrus coptes', pp. 39–42).

[73] P.Louvre Bawit 16 (seventh–eighth century): purchase with deferred delivery (monk); P.Mon. Apollo 35 (eighth century): purchase with deferred delivery (monk?); P.Mon.Apollo 44 (eighth century): loan agreement? (editor's view), sale on payment? (Markiewicz, 'Church, Clerics, Monks and Credit', table, pp. 199–202); P.Mich.Copt. 21 (eighth century?): purchase with deferred delivery?

[74] Jars: analogous to sixth-century documents P.Amst. I 48, P.Athen.Xyla 6, and SB XXII 15595; transport: as in Oxyrhynchite documents, see n. 68 above.

[75] Jakab, 'Guarantee and Jars'.

It seems that in the seventh and eighth centuries, Bawit owned vineyards, and indeed it is likely that some or most of the wine evidenced in the ⲱⲓⲛⲉ ⲛⲥⲁ ostraca came from vine land owned by the monastery. However, wholesale purchase with deferred delivery, a wine acquisition strategy that likely prevailed at the monastery in the sixth century, remained in use in Bawit also in the seventh and eighth centuries. The orders of transport show an administrative *modus operandi* for dealing with wine belonging to the monastery, but not necessarily produced on monastic land. After all, wine bought with payment in advance was also the property of the monastery. Thus, whether the transported wine was solely the produce of monastic estates remains an open question until further evidence comes to light.

Conclusion

As the presented evidence shows, new wine that arrived at a monastery need not have come from vineyards owned by that monastery. Receipts for must prove, nonetheless, that further stages of wine production sometimes took place in monasteries, which must have had the proper storage space for maturing wine, as well as specially trained staff, either monks or individuals hired for the purpose.[76]

Monasteries, even the most affluent ones, were usually not profit-seeking landowners who heavily invested in viticulture in the period under consideration. In the sixth century, the attested monastic vineyards (for instance those of Apa Jeremias and Apa Sourous) were donated or bequeathed by wealthy benefactors to serve the monastery as a source of income. However, they were not the result of an economically rational business plan. As bequests, they were likely to be already fully developed and furnished with necessary facilities, so they also did not require substantial investment on the part of the monastics. Over the seventh and eighth centuries, however, some monasteries, such as Apa Apollo in Bawit or Apa Thomas in Wadi Sarga, may have acquired more vineyards and developed into wine-growing estates of some significance.

The monastic vineyards were leased for rent or on a crop-sharing basis. The internal needs of monastic communities could also be met through

---

[76] In an earlier article (Dzierzbicka, 'Wine Consumption', p. 101), I referred to *P.Sarga* 55–56 and Maspero and Drioton, *Fouilles exécutées à Baouît*, no. 60 as attestations of monastic wine pressers, yet further consideration has persuaded me that ⲓⲟⲙ in these texts rather refers to the men's Fayumic origin than to a wine press (see also *P.Brux.Bawit* p. 48). Therefore, direct monastic involvement in the process of wine making remains unconfirmed thus far.

purchases from other wine producers or loans to be repaid in wine. For this reason, the mentions of transport of wine or must from a vineyard to a monastery need not imply monastic ownership of the plot itself. The reality of monastic economies in late antique Egypt was far more complex.

On a more general note, one is struck by the limited geographic spread of wine-producing monasteries. In terms of the total volume of textual material from late antique Egypt, it is the Theban area that dominates all other regions, but the amount of information from sites in that area that is relevant for the study of monastic vineyard ownership remains negligible. I think this is not incidental, but it cannot be attributed to a single causal factor. One contributing element could be the regional economy and, indirectly, geography. Wine was consistently produced and sold in the Theban region, but seems to have played a minor part in the economy, possibly due to the paucity of land suitable for vineyards. In Middle Egypt, where the valley on both sides of the Nile and the Bahr Yusuf spreads far and wide, there was ample room for the cultivation of both grain and the vine, while, in the narrow strip of cultivated land in the Theban area, even artificially irrigated land was frequently under cereals. Another factor may have been the size, nature, and wealth of the monastic communities. Monasteries attested as vineyard owners in Middle Egypt appear to have been very large, wealthy communities with considerable landed property. The monasteries of the Theban region, in turn, were mostly small and did not own large estates. Lastly, a chronological factor may be considered. The monasteries of the Theban region are active primarily in the sixth and seventh centuries, and the only larger community surviving until the eighth century is the monastery of Apa Phoibammon (at Deir el-Bahri). Meanwhile, if the pattern proposed above for the monasteries of Apa Apollo at Bawit and Apa Thomas at Wadi Sarga holds true, the later seventh and the eighth centuries were the time when the volume of evidence for monastic vineyard ownership increased beyond the anecdotal.

Bibliography

Bacot, S. 'La circulation du vin dans les monastères d'Egypte' in N. Grimal and B. Menu (eds.), *Le commerce en Egypte ancienne* (Cairo: Institut français d'archéologie orientale, 1998), pp. 269–88.

Bagnall, R. S. 'Village Landholding at Aphrodito in Comparative Perspective' in J.-L. Fournet and C. Magdelaine (eds.), *Les archives de Dioscore d'Aphrodité cent ans après leur découverte. Histoire et culture dans l'Égypte byzantine.*

Actes du colloque de Strasbourg (8–10 décembre 2008) (Paris: De Boccard, 2008), pp. 181–90.

Ballet, P. 'L'approvisionnement des monastères. Production et réception de la céramique' in M. Eaton-Krauss, C. Fluck, and G. J. M. van Loon (eds.), *Egypt 1350 BC to AD 1800: Art Historical and Archaeological Studies for Gawdat Gabra* (Wiesbaden: Reichert, 2011), pp. 27–33.

Banaji, J. *Agrarian Change in Late Antiquity: Gold, Labour, and Aristocratic Dominance* (Oxford: Oxford University Press, 2001).

Blanke, L. *An Archaeology of Egyptian Monasticism: Settlement, Economy and Daily Life at the White Monastery Federation* (New Haven: Yale Egyptological Publications, 2019).

Brooks Hedstrom, D. L., Bolman, E. S., Abdel Rahim, M., Mohammed, S., McCormack, D., Herbich, T., Pyke, G., Blanke, L., Musacchio, T., and Khalifa, M. 'The White Monastery Federation Project: Survey and Mapping at the Monastery of Apa Shenoute (Dayr al-Anba Shinūda), Sohag, 2005–2007', *Dumbarton Oaks Papers*, 65/66 (2011–12), 333–64.

Christensen, L. P. and Peacock, W. L. 'Harvesting and Handling' in L. P. Christensen (ed.), *Raisin Production Manual. University of California, Agricultural and Natural Resources Publication 3393* (Oakland: University of California, 2000), pp. 193–206.

Cotelier, J. B. *Ecclesiae Graecae Monumenta*, vol. 1 (Paris: Muguet, 1677).

Crislip, A. T. *From Monastery to Hospital. Christian Monasticism and the Transformation of Health Care in Late Antiquity* (Ann Arbor: University of Michigan Press, 2005).

Danys-Lasek, K. 'Deir el-Naqlun 2010 and 2011, Including Deposit of Pottery from Building K.1', *Polish Archaeology in the Mediterranean*, 23.1 (2014), 543–642.

Delattre, A. 'Le monastère de Baouît et l'administration arabe' in A. T. Schubert and P. M. Sijpesteijn (eds.), *Documents and the History of the Early Islamic World* (Leiden: Brill, 2015), pp. 43–9.

Delattre, A., Pilette, P., and Vanthieghem, N. 'Papyrus coptes de la Pierpont Morgan Library I. Cinq documents du monastère de Baouît', *Journal of Coptic Studies*, 17 (2015), 33–53.

Dixneuf, D. *Amphores égyptiennes. Production, typologie, contenu et diffusion (IIIe siècle avant J.-C.–IXe siècle après J.-C.)* (Alexandria: Centre d'études alexandrines, 2011).

Dzierzbicka, D. 'Wineries and Their Elements in Graeco-Roman Egypt', *Journal of Juristic Papyrology*, 35 (2005), 9–91.

Dzierzbicka, D. 'Refuse Dump in Sector B in Naqlun: Excavation Report 2011', *Polish Archaeology in the Mediterranean*, 23.1 (2014), 192–203 (with appendix by B. Czaja).

Dzierzbicka, D. 'Wine Consumption and Usage in Egypt's Monastic Communities (6th–8th c.)' in A. Łajtar, A. Obłuski, and I. Zych (eds.), *Aegyptus et Nubia*

Christiana. The Włodzimierz Godlewski Jubilee Volume on the Occasion of His 70th Birthday (Warsaw: PCMA UW, 2016), pp. 99–111.

Dzierzbicka, D. ΟΙΝΟΣ. Production and Import of Wine in Graeco-Roman Egypt (Warsaw: The Raphael Taubenschlag Foundation, 2018).

Egloff, M. Kellia. La poterie copte: quatre siècles d'artisanat et d'échanges en Basse-Egypte, 2 vols (Geneva: Georg, 1977).

Erichsen, W. 'Aus einem koptischen Arzneibuch', Acta Orientalia, 27 (1963), 23–45.

Faiers, J. 'Wadi Sarga Revisited: A Preliminary Study of the Pottery Excavated in 1913/14' in E. O'Connell (ed.), Egypt in the First Millennium AD. Perspectives from New Fieldwork (Leuven: Peeters, 2014), pp. 177–92.

Gallimore, S. 'Amphora Production in the Roman World. A View from the Papyri', Bulletin of the American Society of Papyrologists, 47 (2010), 155–84.

Gallimore, S. 'A Contract for the Advanced Sale of Wine', Bulletin of the American Society of Papyrologists, 49 (2012), 151–66.

Gascou, J. 'Le cadastre d'Aphroditô (SB XX 14669)' in J. Gascou (ed.), Fiscalité et société en Egypte byzantine (Paris: Association des amis du Centre d'histoire et civilisation de Byzance, 2008), pp. 247–305.

Gascou, J. and MacCoull, L. S. B. 'Le cadastre d'Aphroditô', Travaux et Mémoirs, 10 (1987), 103–58.

Ghaly, H. 'Pottery Workshops of Saint-Jeremia (Saqqara)', Cahiers de la céramique égyptienne, 3 (1992), 161–71.

Gonis, N. 'Two Fiscal Registers from Early Islamic Egypt (P. Vatic. Aphrod. 13, SB XX 14701)', Journal of Juristic Papyrology, 30 (2000), 21–9.

Harrauer, H. 'Sechs byzantinische Weinkäufe' in R. Pintaudi (ed.), Miscellanea papyrologica. Papyrologica Florentina VII (Florence: Gonnelli, 1980), pp. 109–26.

Hickey, T. M. Wine, Wealth, and the State in Late Antique Egypt: The House of Apion at Oxyrhynchus (Ann Arbor: University of Michigan Press, 2012).

Jakab, E. 'Guarantee and Jars in Sales of Wine on Delivery', Journal of Juristic Papyrology, 29 (1999), 33–44.

Kruit, N. 'Local Customs in the Formulas of Sales of Wine for Future Delivery', Zeitschrift für Papyrologie und Epigraphik, 94 (1992), 167–84.

Kruit, N. 'The Meaning of Various Words Related to Wine', Zeitschrift für Papyrologie und Epigraphik, 90 (1992), 265–76.

Kruit, N. 'Three Byzantine Sales for Future Delivery', Tyche, 9 (1994), 67–88.

Kruit, N. and Worp, K. 'Geographical Jar Names: Towards a Multidisciplinary Approach', Archiv für Papyrusforschung, 46.1 (2000), 65–146.

Kruit, N. and Worp, K. 'P.Bad. IV 55: Ein neuer Text', Zeitschrift für Papyrologie und Epigraphik, 137 (2001), 215–19.

Kuhn, K. H. (ed.), Letters and Sermons of Besa (Leuven: Secrét. du Corpus SCO, 1956).

Layton, B. The Canons of Our Fathers: Monastic Rules of Shenoute (Oxford: Oxford University Press, 2014).

Lefort, L. T. (ed.), *Oeuvres de S. Pachôme et de ses disciples* (Leuven: L. Durbecq, 1956).

Lyon-Caen, C. 'Bouchons d'amphore et bouchons de jarre du site de Baouit: problématique et premier récolement' in A. Boud'hors and C. Louis (eds.), *Études coptes X. Douzième Journée d'Études (Lyon 19–21 mai 2005)* (Paris: De Boccard, 2008), pp. 63–75.

MacCoull, L. S. B. 'Monastic and Church Landholding in the Aphrodito Cadaster', *Zeitschrift für Papyrologie und Epigraphik*, 178 (2011), 243–6.

Mahmoud, F. 'Organisation des ateliers de potiers en Égypte du Bas-Empire à la conquête arabe. Les productions céramiques égyptiennes' in N. Bosson and A. Boud'hors (eds.), *Actes du Huitième Congrès international d'Études coptes. Paris, 28 juin–3 juillet 2004*, vol. I (Leuven: Peeters, 2007), pp. 267–78.

Markiewicz, T. 'The Church, Clerics, Monks and Credit in the Papyri' in A. Boud'hors, J. Clackson, C. Louis, and P. Sijpesteijn (eds.), *Monastic Estates in Late Antique and Early Islamic Egypt. Ostraca, Papyri, and Essays in Memory of Sarah Clackson (P. Clackson)* (Cincinnati: American Society of Papyrologists, 2009), pp. 178–204.

Maspero, J. and Drioton, E. *Fouilles exécutées à Baouît* (Cairo: Institut français d'Archéologie orientale, 1931).

Mayerson, P. 'The Enigmatic Knidion: A Wine Measure in Late Roman / Byzantine Egypt?', *Zeitschrift für Papyrologie und Epigraphik*, 141 (2002), 205–9.

Migne, J.-P. (ed.) *Patrologia Graeca*, 161 vols (Paris: Imprimerie Catholique, 1857–66).

Monneret de Villard, U. *Il Monastero de S. Simeone presso Aswan*, vol. 1: *Descrizione Archeologica* (Milan: Pontificia Archvescoville S. Giuseppe, 1927).

Morelli, F. and Schmelz, G. 'Gli ostraca di Akoris n. 19 e 20 e la produzione di koufa nell'area del Tempio Ovest', *Zeitschrift für Papyrologie und Epigraphik*, 139 (2002), 127–37.

O'Connell, E. R. 'R. Campbell Thompson's 1913/14 Excavation of Wadi Sarga and Other Sites', *British Museum Studies in Ancient Egypt and Sudan*, 21 (2014), 121–92.

Quibell, J. E. *Excavations at Saqqara (1908–09, 1909–10). The Monastery of Apa Jeremias* (Cairo: Institut français d'Archéologie orientale, 1912).

Rathbone, D. *Economic Rationalism and Rural Society in Third-Century A.D. Egypt. The Heroninos Archive and the Appianus Estate* (Cambridge: Cambridge University Press, 1991).

Richter, T. S. 'Cultivation of Monastic Estates in Late Antique and Early Islamic Egypt. Some Evidence from Coptic Land Leases and Related Documents' in A. Boud'hors, J. Clackson, C. Louis, and P. Sijpesteijn (eds.), *Monastic Estates in Late Antique and Early Islamic Egypt. Ostraca, Papyri, and Essays in Memory of Sarah Clackson (P. Clackson)* (Cincinnati: American Society of Papyrologists, 2009), pp. 205–15.

Robinson, J. (ed.), *Oxford Companion to Wine*, 3rd edition (Oxford: Oxford University Press, 2006).

Ruffini, G. 'Aphrodito before Dioskoros', *Bulletin of the American Society of Papyrologists*, 45 (2008), 225–40.

Shaw, T. M. 'Pseudo-Athanasius. Discourse on Salvation to a Virgin' in R. Valantasis (ed.), *Religions of Late Antiquity in Practice* (Princeton: Princeton University Press, 2000), pp. 82–99.

Steinwenter, A. 'Aus dem kirchlichen Vermögensrechte der Papyri', *Zeitschrift der Savigny-Stiftung für Rechtsgeschichte. Kanonistische Abteilung*, 75 (1958), 1–34.

Veilleux, A. *Pachomian Koinonia III. Instructions, Letters, and Other Writings of Saint Pachomius and His Disciples* (Kalamazoo: Cistercian Publications, 1982).

Ward, B. *The Sayings of the Desert Fathers: The Alphabetical Collection*, revised edition (Kalamazoo: Cistercian Publications, 1984).

Wilfong, T. G. 'A Coptic Account of Pottery from the Kilns of Psabt (P.Lond.Copt. 1.695)', *Bulletin of the American Society of Papyrologists*, 45 (2008), 247–59.

Winlock, H. E. and Crum, W. E. *The Monastery of Epiphanius at Thebes* (New York: Cambridge University Press, 1926).

Wipszycka, E. *Moines et communautés monastiques en Égypte (IVe–VIIIe siècles)* (Warsaw: The Raphael Taubenschlag Foundation, 2009).

Wipszycka, E. 'Resources and Economic Activities of the Egyptian Monastic Communities (4th–8th Century)', *Journal of Juristic Papyrology*, 41 (2011), 159–263.

Wortmann, D. 'Griechische Ostraka aus Abu Mena', *Zeitschrift für Papyrologie und Epigraphik*, 8 (1971), 41–69.

Zuckerman, C. *Du village à l'empire. Autour de Registre Fiscal d'Aphrodito* (Paris: Association des Amis d'Histoire et Civilisation de Byzance, 2004).

6 | Cooking, Baking, and Serving: A Window into the Kitchen of Egyptian Monastic Households and the Archaeology of Cooking

DARLENE L. BROOKS HEDSTROM

Food preparation and consumption were very much on the minds of those living in monastic communities from the very beginning of asceticism. Antony, as we learn from Athanasius, set a standard with his minimal diet of bread, salt, and water as a young ascetic.[1] Yet, his diet changed as he aged. It also changed in response to a higher number of encounters with visitors.[2] He became self-sufficient in caring for a small garden outside of his home, where he grew grain and vegetables. Although Antony is a role model for ascetic eating, Athanasius speaks very little about how Antony prepared his food, how he baked his bread, or how his relationship to cooking and food changed after becoming a monk.

A clearer picture of the importance of Egyptian monastic cooking appears in the Coptic *Regulations of Horsiesios* (circa 380), which outlines specific behaviours within the homosocial communities overseen by Pachomius in Upper Egypt.[3] The *oikonomos*, or house steward, is responsible for ensuring good tasting and fresh food.[4] For example, bread and beans should not sit in old water, for the foul smell of the food will dissuade monks from eating. Similarly, monks must not waste vegetables and dates, which may spoil quickly. The rules also outline the need to tend to the kitchen's fires by not using too much wood; to avoid creating smoke; to cook food slowly so as not to burn it; and not to

---

Initial ideas for this paper were presented at the 2012 Byzantine Studies Conference in Boston; the 2014 Spring Symposium for Byzantine Studies at Dumbarton Oaks; the 2015 St Shenoute Society Conference in Los Angeles; and the 2015 American Schools of Oriental Research annual meeting in Atlanta. A fellowship at Dumbarton Oaks in Byzantine Studies provided time for research during 2015. This chapter is part of a forthcoming monograph *Feeding Asceticism: The Archaeology of Byzantine Monastic Cooking* (Amsterdam: ARC Humanities).

[1] Athanasius, *Life of Antony* 8; Greek text in Bartelink, *Vie d'Antoine*, pp. 150–6; Coptic text in Garitte, *S.Antonii Vitae*, pp. 10–12; English translation of the Sahidic Coptic and Greek *Life* in Vivian and Athanassakis, *The Life of Antony*, pp. 72–5.

[2] *Life of Antony* 50; Greek text in Bartelink, *Vie d'Antoine*, pp. 268–72; Coptic text in Garitte, *S. Antonii Vitae*, pp. 56–7; English translation in Vivian and Athanassakis, *The Life of Antony*, 164–7.

[3] *Regulations of Horsiesios*, Coptic text in Lefort, *Oeuvres de S. Pachôme*, pp. 82–99; English translation in Veilleux, *Pachomian Koinonia II*, pp. 197–223.

[4] *Regulations of Horsiesios* 22; Lefort, *Oeuvres de S. Pachôme*, pp. 88–9; Veilleux, *Pachomian Koinonia II*, p. 205.

complain if one is appointed to serve in the bakehouse with the ovens.[5] Those who serve in the preparation of food should exhibit care for the utensils, bowls, and pots. Monks are told not to 'damage any of the dishes' and to 'not allow ... a kettle or anything else on the fire to be damaged leaving it there without water, or by not stirring'.[6] While the rules offer explicit guidelines for monastic behaviour, we do not learn anything about the physical nature of the kitchens or the bakehouses where food was prepared.

The extensive archaeological remains of Egypt's monastic communities present new evidence for where food was prepared, baked, and later served. The kitchens and bakeries demonstrate the value of the built environment for employing theoretical readings in household archaeology and in the archaeology of cooking. Both approaches will provide new avenues for understanding variations in ascetic communities in Egypt and offer a more informed view of the literary and documentary sources. By placing monastic communities in the same category as other domestic, residential communities, which have been examined with good results, we can better understand how monastic kitchens may serve as windows into the economic life of a community, in terms of human labour, physical space, and ingredients. Kitchens, bakeries, storerooms, and dining spaces are frequently neglected as sources since they are less glamorous and more utilitarian.

The importance of food for any society, even one based on ascetic principles, is vital for daily living. Although monastic literature presents a discourse of fasting and limited diets, the archaeological evidence reveals a slightly different story – a story of multiple kitchens, food preferences, visiting guests with differing diets, private kitchens, and communal eating halls. Documentary sources speak of fish sauces, various breads, deliveries of dung and firewood, the ownership of bakeries and mills, and experienced cooks. Read together with archaeobotanical remains, ceramic assemblages, and the physical spaces in which food was prepared and later served, the documentary sources bring life to material once dismissed as less informative for writing an economic history of monastic life. Regardless of the size of the monastic community, each monastic settlement had some features to assist in the storage, cooking, and eating of food. Thus, a close examination of kitchens, bakeries, courtyards, and refectories will enhance our understanding of the social and economic realities of monastic life in Egypt. In sum, an eye toward the kitchen provides an inside view of monasticism not previously considered and demonstrates the value of

---

[5] *Regulations of Horsiesios* 23, 30, and 50; Lefort, *Oeuvres de S. Pachôme*, pp. 88–90 and 96; Veilleux, *Pachomian Koinonia II*, p. 205.

[6] *Regulations of Horsiesios* 23 and 26; Lefort, *Oeuvres de S. Pachôme*, pp. 88–90; Veilleux, *Pachomian Koinonia II*, p. 205.

reading monastic settlements as big households with the same challenges of monitoring staff, managing utensils and storage, and finding enough space to feed the residents and any visiting guests.

The Benefits of Ethnohistory and Household Archaeology

A central purpose in reading archaeological evidence is to consider how spaces and objects relate to the people who used them. Archaeology is a discipline that seeks to be scientifically objective with a more comprehensive adoption of methods that distance us from speculative interpretations of the past. However, the trade-off is that in our efforts to look at the microscopic level of materials, we may lose sight of how individuals interacted with the built environment and the materials they used within distinct spaces.

Ethnoarchaeology and household archaeology provide an effective tool for the study of production, sociocultural interactions, and consumption habits. They are fields that are very temporally grounded, in contrast to archaeology, which is the study of materials preserved from multiple periods and not from a solitary moment in time.[7] How is it possible to use a methodology that is based in a limited present to interpret a multiperiod past? I would posit that the study of early twentieth-century monastic communities in Egypt offers a useful framework for reassessing the archaeological record by placing individuals and things back into spaces usually deemed empty.

For instance, the 1930–31 ethnohistorical photographs of the monks from the monastery of St Antony by the Red Sea present a record of monastic use of space that is not attested in written documentation for the community. When Thomas Whittemore, one of the founders of the Byzantine Institute of America, led an expedition of Byzantinists to the monastery and to the nearby monastery of St Paul in 1930, his intent was to document the medieval Christian paintings preserved in the churches of the two monasteries.[8] While there, Whittemore took photographs of the environs in addition to monks making bread, grinding coffee beans, spinning wool, crafting metal, and milling flour. He also made a silent-film

---

[7] David and Kramer, *Ethnography in Action*, pp. 50–1.

[8] Whittemore's papers of the expedition, along with photographs, are housed in the Image Collections and Field Archives at Dumbarton Oaks in Washington, DC. An online exhibit of some of the material is 'Before Byzantium: The Early Activities of Thomas Whittemore (1871–1931)', Image Collections and Field Archives (ICFA), available at www.doaks.org/resources/online-exhibits/before-byzantium.

documenting activities within an open courtyard and an alleyway.⁹ Read together, the ethnohistorical film and photographs offer a reminder that the empty spaces on an archaeological site plan are sterilised spaces. They are, for the most part, stripped of the things that once gave the space multiple meanings and functions. Bjornar Olsen highlights the imbalance in current archaeology whereby the things of the past have been removed from contexts to declutter the archaeological report.¹⁰ In doing so, we see spaces, such as a kitchen or an open-air courtyard, as spaces devoid of people and things. The photo of a small courtyard at St Antony's in 1931 shows men preparing bread for the bakehouse (Fig. 6.1). Monks prepare the loaves of bread on the long boards. The dough sits in metal basins, and long boards are used for laying out flattened loaves of bread for easy transport to the monastery's bakery. The courtyard contains three work areas set up simply by the addition of the large, portable boards for the preparation of loaves. Four kneaders are assisted by three others, who carry the shaped loaves of bread to the bakehouse. Based upon their clothing, the

Fig. 6.1. Preparing bread at St Antony's Monastery, 1930–1. The Red Sea Monasteries, Egypt. Dumbarton Oaks, Image Collections and Fieldwork Archives. Washington, DC, Trustees for Harvard University. ICFA.BI_DO.REDSEA.

---

⁹ The 8:55 minute film is available at www.doaks.org/resources/online-exhibits/a-truthful-record /history/red-sea-monastery.
¹⁰ Olsen, *In Defense of Things*, pp. 22–3.

men represent three different groups at the monastery: monks dressed in black and wearing a small cap; men wearing lighter coloured *gallabiya*, possible novice monks; and a single man wearing a shirt, vest, and short pants. All indications point to his status as a hired labourer working at the monastery for the monks.[11] We can observe the portable nature of the tools needed for making bread (the kneading boards that double as wooden trays for carrying the loaves and the metal basins) and the lack of any production-specific elements present in the courtyard. If we remove the individuals from the scene, and indications of their positions within the community, along with the materials needed to make the loaves, we are left with an open-air courtyard that appears unused and unimportant to daily life. Whittemore's photo is a reminder of Olsen's call for archaeologists to reclutter space. And, I would argue, we need to repeople the spaces as well. It is not enough to put objects back in a courtyard or kitchen; we can benefit from also considering the movements of individuals cooking, baking, and preparing food.

The ethnohistorical foundation is necessary for two reasons. First, the study of monastic archaeology in Egypt is woefully in need of greater theorisation, as is Byzantine archaeology more generally. The necessity to present specialist reports is entirely necessary, as so little exists in terms of well-studied typologies based on both relative and absolute dating methods. The result is that we miss the opportunity to consider the intersection of architecture, ceramics, metal objects, textiles, and those who lived in daily contact with these materials. Second, the field of monastic archaeology in the East Mediterranean was focused in large part on stone churches, chapels, mosaic floors, and baptisteries. These features are recognisable as Christian constructions and thus reflections of monastic life. However, by privileging specific components of a monastery, we neglect the components of the communities such as latrines, courtyards, or even kitchens, which may reveal far more about monasticism than previously thought.

Household archaeology, like ethnoarchaeology, offers archaeologists fruitful avenues for using material culture to consider complex social questions, with the recognition that we are able to only work with the artefacts of society and cannot fully reconstruct the demographic and behavioural aspects of an anthropological study.[12] As a development of settlement and processual archaeology, household archaeology evolved as a methodology for constructing order and divisions within a site that may

---

[11] Quataert, 'Clothing Laws, State, and Society'.
[12] Wilk and Rathje, 'Household Archaeology'.

follow social norms of a past community.[13] With the advent of postprocessual archaeology, which seeks to modify and challenge the heavily structuralist and positivist readings of archaeological material from the previous generations, household archaeology now considers a greater variation in how households functioned and in how individuals interacted within the built environment.[14] This theoretical overview is important before proceeding because monastic spaces are not traditionally read as complex households. I would contend that monastic settlements emerge as new households in the Byzantine world and warrant an examination within a theoretical framework if we are to understand why, for example, the kitchen or dining space has importance in our reconstruction of monasticism.

Monasteries, therefore, become excellent examples of Homi Bhabha's *third space*, in which the communities are spaces where social values and cultures overlap: monasteries are where the culture of the world and the culture of heaven are fused together.[15] Egyptian monastic settlements are spaces where residents constantly negotiated between what it means to be a member of a homosocial community and to be engaged with economic activities and social meetings with those outside the community. Despite the physical separation from biological households, the spiritual household develops upon very similar lines, as is evinced in the documentary and literary sources.

The relationships are almost impossible, however, to discern from the archaeological record, as most settlements are 'household series' – meaning the settlements are reused, modified, and abandoned without clear lines as to who lived in a space and exactly when.[16] Since monastic sites contain a multitude of household series over time, it is necessary to be acutely sensitive to the fact that our archaeological evidence is not a frozen moment in time. Rather, these sites have witnessed several periods of use that we might never fully articulate or separate out during excavation. In the case of looking at kitchens, bakehouses, and dining areas, household archaeology is a heuristic tool to make us aware of the limits of the physical evidence, while simultaneously suggesting that spatial relationships may reveal important insights as to how individuals, over generations, interacted and negotiated movement within a space. The question I seek to explore in this chapter is *how* household archaeology, aided by ethnoarchaeology, facilitates a more holistic reading of what it means to cook food, bake bread, and serve meals within a monastic context.

[13] Steadman, 'Recent Research in the Archaeology of Architecture'.
[14] Souvatzi, *A Social Archaeology of Households*, pp. 23–4.
[15] Bhabha, *The Location of Culture*, p. 36.
[16] Alexander, 'Mesoamerican House Lots and Archaeological Site Structure', pp. 80–1.

Diverse Sources for Early Monastic Cooking

The vital importance of food and controlling access to it emerges vividly in the *Apophthegmata Patrum* (*Sayings of the Desert Fathers*) and in the writings of John Cassian, Palladius, and others. While monastic literature offers memorable stories centred around monks and their food, these accounts are intensely structured by their authors and reflect later redactions of oral traditions about how ascetics navigated real desires and anxieties about food, drink, and fasting.[17] Monks made wine and baked bread. They cooked beans and boiled vegetables. They harvested grain, salted fish, and tended to gardens. They were all aware of the need to be good hosts to those who visited them and to offer better food during such visits. And when monks aged or became ill, monastic diets changed as food and the proper balance of particular ingredients offered medical or homeopathic benefits in regulating the wetness and heat of the body.[18] Monastic diets could differ dramatically, and apparently temptingly so, such that being ill required tests to ensure monks were not feigning illness for better food.[19] Being sick granted one access to a richer array of food and drink, such as wine, meat, and fish broth.[20] Healthy monks, in contrast, ate less frequently and with a more restricted diet. Being sick certainly afforded one special privileges, and thus it is not surprising that we encounter rules that address monks feigning illness at the White Monastery in Upper Egypt in order to have access to a more variegated diet.[21]

While concerns about food and what someone was or was not eating appear in monastic literature, the preparation of the food that was eaten is discussed little, if at all.[22] In looking at documentary evidence from papyri and ostraca, few texts record monastic recipes, daily menus, or monastic opinions about the quality or quantity of food consumed. Letters and monastic orders record the transport of ingredients and goods such as bread, wine, different types of oil, wheat, vegetables, and firewood for monks and non-monastics. However, the sources do not, in general, address the next step in the process whereby ingredients became food,

---

[17] Dauphin, 'The Diet of the Desert Fathers'; Regnault, *La vie quotidienne des Pères du Désert*.
[18] Grimm, 'From Feasting to Fasting', pp. 157–79; Shaw, *The Burden of the Flesh*, pp. 53–63.
[19] Crislip, *From Monastery to Hospital*, p. 20; Crislip, *Thorns in the Flesh*, pp. 36–58.
[20] Jerome, *Praefatio* 5 and *Praecepta* 45–46; Latin text in Boon, *Pachomiana Latina*, pp. 7 and 24–25; English translation in Veilleux, *Pachomian Koinonia II*, pp. 143 and 152.
[21] Krawiec, *Shenoute and the Women of the White Monastery*, pp. 35–6.
[22] Such mundane topics, such as food preparation, were, as Johannes Koder states, 'commonplace or self-evident', and therefore the evidence we wish to see 'barely exists' for Byzantium; Koder, '*Stew and Salted Meat*', p. 61.

and some food goods were used as payments and parts of deliveries, but how they all worked together to become meals is less clear. Therefore, we need to compile a wide array of sources to consider how ingredients became monastic meals and moved from the kitchen to the monastic table.

Three bodies of evidence are generally considered for examining the role of food consumption and production within a monastic context. The first two are the ones employed most often in the study of monasticism: texts and visual culture. The third is archaeology, which will be discussed extensively in what follows.

Monastic literature, such as hagiography, monastic foundations or *typika*, religious travelogues, and a growing collection of monastic documentary evidence, especially from Egypt, offers great insight into the agricultural and economic practices at monastic estates. Letters, wills, and contracts between monastic and non-monastic communities offer a far more nuanced history of the relationship between food production and monastic self-sufficiency than what appears in the highly idealised accounts of monastic living. A second collection of resources is a loose confederation of visual evidence of Late Roman and Byzantine kitchens, bakeries, and dining facilities represented in manuscripts, mosaics, ivories, wall paintings, and icons. For example, the sixth-century *Vienna Genesis* includes illuminated scenes showing Jacob preparing bread and lentils for Esau.[23] We see Isaac working with a fire and using tools, and then, to the right, he offers food at a table to his brother. The scene illustrates a raised, u-shaped fire pit, and Isaac holds a pot and a poker to tend to the fire. The scene provides an early Byzantine representation of a physical stove, cooking utensils, and a general sense of how a cook may have interacted with physical features within a kitchen. Although the image does not represent a *monastic* kitchen, the image can be instructive when read alongside some monastic literary accounts about the role of cooks and servers from the sixth century.[24]

A similar scene of a cook with the u-shaped fire pit is visible in the 1931 photograph of a monk at the kitchen at St Antony's Monastery by the Red Sea (Fig. 6.2). He sits on a mud brick installation of an oven, with a floor-level niche for holding fuel. A large cauldron sits on the opening of the oven. Left of the monk is a *kanun*, a floor level stove, with a u-shape to allow for easy access to stoking the fire. A large bronze vat sits atop the fire and a small coffee or tea pot sits in the embers at the opening. Behind the monk, the wall holds additional kitchen utensils, which he uses during meal preparation.

---

[23] *Vienna Genesis*, fol. 8 and 15; see Wellesz, *The Vienna Genesis*, pl. 4.
[24] Bourbou, *Health and Disease*, p. 128.

Fig. 6.2. Monastic kitchen at St Antony's Monastery, 1930–1. The Red Sea Monasteries, Egypt. Dumbarton Oaks, Image Collections and Fieldwork Archives. Washington, DC, Trustees for Harvard University. ICFA.BI_DO.REDSEA.0016.

The ethnohistorical evidence offers a glimpse into the continuity of cooking methods and tools used over several centuries, and specifically within a monastic context. Whittemore's photograph shows a cook sitting in his kitchen, surrounded by utensils, a food bench, and a stove, with food being prepared. The image provides an interesting comparison to the sixth-century illumination, which shows the same type of stove and cooking utensils. Another page from the *Vienna Genesis* illustrates how we might contextualise monastic anxieties about cooking, eating, and presentation by looking at the scene of Pharaoh's feast in Egypt. The illuminator shows guests reclining at a table that would be common to Late Roman and early Byzantine elites (Fig. 6.3).[25] Musicians entertain them while servers bring food and drink to the table. The image represents the luxury of eating that was available to wealthy Byzantine elites, with patterned textiles, including an elbow bolster, a flute player with a percussionist, and servants – this style of elite dining was at odds with the new monastic table at which the monks were to sit and be separated physically one from another.[26]

---

[25] Sixth-century Byzantine illuminated manuscript illustrating Pharaoh's banquet from the *Vienna Genesis*: Wiener Genesis, fol. 17ᵛ; see Zimmermann, *Die Wiener Genesis*, pl. 26.

[26] El Dunbabin, *The Roman Banquet*, pp. 141–3.

Fig. 6.3. Sixth-century Byzantine illuminated manuscript illustrating Pharaoh's banquet from the *Vienna Genesis*. Wiener Genesis, fol. 17^v. Österreichische Nationalbibliothek, Wien.

Someone who was familiar with the luxury of reclining was Evagrius of Pontus (d. 399). After his adoption of the monastic life and relocation to Kellia in Egypt's Delta, Evagrius apparently continued to have memories of his previous life, as did other monastics. His community was one made of several independent buildings in which two to fifteen monks might live together with their own kitchen facilities and without the supervision of a superior, as was the case with Pachomian and Shenoutean monasticism in Upper Egypt. Evagrius's *Talking Back* records how he and others struggled with desires for prepared food and meals, as displayed in the *Vienna Genesis*. In looking at the 'thoughts' to rebuke gluttony in *Talking Back*, several of the sixty-nine responses deal specifically with memories and the sensorial experience of well-cooked dishes, lavish tables spread with food, and the presence of delicacies and wines. Evagrius recalls the tactile pleasures of holding cups, reclining at a table, and sharing a meal with family.[27] To curtail and combat such memories and desires, Evagrius urges his fellow monastics to turn to Scripture for pointed verses to rebuke pleasure. Being part of a new community required the establishment of new household rules that were shaped by ascetic values – values that required a break with the past, both in thought and in action with regards to eating.

In Upper Egypt, we can look at Pachomian and Shenoutean monastic communities of the fifth century to ascertain specific behavioural changes for combatting old memories of eating and dining. For example, the *Rules*, copied by Jerome in 404 AD, provide an overview of monastic behaviours about sixty years after the death of Pachomius.[28] By establishing new habits for encountering food, such as regulating diet, preparing food, and the importance of communal and regulated eating, monks physically changed their position in relationship to food from reclining to the seated position and specifically without touching or looking at one another.[29] Early Byzantine eating could be a highly intimate event, but homosocial living required a physical distance from others to ensure the sexual purity of the community. The physical separation from other diners and the limitation on eating whatever one wanted was strictly enforced and taught by each housemaster.[30] Superiors supervised both the eating of food and the preparation of food, and they were not allowed to have special food or cook their own meals.[31] Even the distribution of the sweets upon the conclusion of the meal required waiting until one was in the privacy of the monastic house to consume it in solitude.[32]

---

[27] Evagrius, *Talking Back* I. 30 and 41; Greek and Syriac text in Frankenberg, *Euagrios Ponticus*, pp. 478–81; English translation in Brakke, *Evagrius of Pontus*, pp. 59 and 62.
[28] Rousseau, *Pachomius*, pp. 48–53.
[29] Jerome, *Praecepta* 30; Boon, *Pachomiana Latina*, p. 20; Veilleux, *Pachomian Koinonia II*, p. 150.
[30] Jerome, *Praecepta* 31; Boon, *Pachomiana Latina*, p. 21; Veilleux, *Pachomian Koinonia II*, p. 150.
[31] Jerome, *Praecepta* 35; Boon, *Pachomiana Latina*, pp. 21–2; Veilleux, *Pachomian Koinonia II*, p. 151.
[32] Jerome, *Praecepta* 37–8; Boon, *Pachomiana Latina*, pp. 22–3; Veilleux, *Pachomian Koinonia II*, p. 151.

Difficulties in managing the distribution of food and its preparation also appear in the fifth-century writings of Shenoute. His communities dealt with a variety of concerns relating to food, including monks stealing food from the storeroom, jealousies over the food eaten by the sick, and complaints when servers gave larger and tastier portions to friends and not to others.[33] Even in the general refectory within communal monasteries, monks reportedly envied the food of others. Leaders of communal monasteries recognised the practical need to have separate eating areas for the sick, whose richer meals would certainly engender envy and grumbling by others.[34] From the monastic sources, we learn about food anxiety and its importance for both physical and spiritual health. However, monastic authors did not address in any detail where food was prepared, what ingredients were used, and whether there was a tradition of apprenticeship in the kitchen.

Since the visual and textual sources reflect very particular interests in food, eating, and cooking, the archaeological remains of Byzantine monastic kitchens is the third and most vital body of evidence that complements and amplifies what we might learn from Byzantine visual and written sources. The first complex monastic kitchens were found at Kellia in the Delta and illustrate that monastics were not living only on water and small biscuits. The bread ovens and multi-burner stoves illustrate that monks had private kitchens in their dwellings. The physical remains of kitchen facilities are greatly enhanced by recent floral and faunal studies of food recovered from monastic sites, such as John the Little in Wadi el-Natrun, the monastery of Apa Apollo at Bawit in Middle Egypt, and a monastery at Kom el-Nana at Amarna.[35] This evidence demonstrates that monastic communities had access to a much more complex array of food and condiments than what we can reconstruct from the incomplete literary and documentary evidence. My aim in what follows is not to look at food from the microscopic level of archaeobotany and archaeozoology, nor from the meta-narrative of monastic ascetic diet as espoused by the written sources, but rather to look at food from a middle space in which the practical space of the kitchen offers a unique vantage point to consider how monasteries functioned as a household. I consider food not from its traditional place as a cornerstone for monastic behaviour and spiritual discipline, nor from the ubiquitous ceramic corpus of pots and pans, but rather from within the monastic kitchen where the actual food was made.

[33] Krawiec, *Shenoute and the Women of the White Monastery*, pp. 35–6.
[34] Layton, 'Social Structure and Food Consumption'.
[35] El Dorry, 'Monks and Plants'; Luff, 'Monastic Diet in Late Antique Egypt'.

The Physical Remains of Egyptian Monastic Kitchens

What makes a kitchen and bakehouse different from a cooking area? Defining exactly what spaces are and mean is important because some archaeologists may call any space that has an oven a kitchen, whereas others simply refer to the feature as a hearth or fireplace, and still others avoid giving a function or identity to any particular space without epigraphic support. Few definitions or descriptions are found in our sources about the differences between a kitchen and another space within a monastic settlement. This might be exactly where part of the problem lies, in that excavators are uncertain how to refer to particular spaces, as monastic authors do not describe them with enough detail for us to know what things are in Egyptian monasticism. I define a kitchen in this study as a space that is demarcated by the presence of three or four walls to physically separate a space for cooking with at least one stove with direct heat. The area is usually confined enough that few other, additional activities could take place in the space. A kitchen is also a physical space set aside *within* a larger structure. The kitchen, therefore, becomes an integral part of the monastic built environment. If the space does not include a hearth or stove, but only an oven, it is a bakehouse. A cooking area, in contrast to a kitchen and bakehouse, is a part of a larger physical space, usually an open-air courtyard. The space was often centralized and accessible from several houses and pathways as a communal area. In general the courtyard is a multi-functional space with an oven or hearth relegated to one corner of the courtyard. A cooking area may also occur outside the walls of a building and in the areas between buildings, such as alleyways. By comparing the spaces, a kitchen is therefore a built-space within a structure for the primary or sole purpose of food preparation with direct heat. A bakery is an area whose primary function is for baking bread with indirect heat and is likely not used as frequently as the stoves or hearths found in a kitchen.

In looking at excavations of monastic settlements since the early twentieth century, the bread oven is the most frequently identified cooking feature commented on in relation to the archaeology of cooking. The circular, bee-hive structure is easily recognised due to its shape and size, ranging from 50to100 cm in diameter, with later medieval ovens spanning over 150 cm. The preservation height varies, but its basic circular form was unmistakable in the field even when monastic cooking was of little interest to the excavators. The ovens are made from accessible materials: mud, clay coils, broken ceramic body sherds, and mud bricks. Depending upon the period, some fired bricks are used in lieu of mud bricks. The continual firing of the internal surface through indirect and direct heat strengthened the feature, increasing its longevity and preservation long past the settlement's occupation. Additionally, the accumulation of ash in the ovens further secured the identification of the oven as a function-specific feature.

David Depraetere's study of 113 bread ovens from early Ptolemaic times until the period following the Arab conquest (i.e., the late fourth century BC to the seventh/eighth centuries AD) demonstrated the use of four basic designs of Egyptian ovens.[36] Specifically for the late antique period, he examined the presence of ovens at three monastic and seven nonmonastic settlements. All bread ovens required indirect heat for the baking of bread and would be too large to be used for other food preparation. In my own study, I added six more monastic sites in order to create a more comparable set of settlements in terms of size, preservation, and diversity of ovens. This expanded dataset results in a total of eighty-two ovens from nonmonastic sites and sixty-five ovens from monastic settlements. The comparison of the placement of ovens at the different settlements produced important differences. At non-monastic residential settlements, 84 per cent of the ovens (N=68) were placed in corners of open-air courtyards or alleyways, and only 16 per cent (N=14) were found within interior rooms. The vast majority of nonmonastic ovens were therefore located in courtyards often owned by several families, as attested in Roman and Byzantine legal documents.[37] In looking at the sixty-five ovens found at nine monastic sites, the placement of the ovens shifted so that 83 per cent (N=54) were located within enclosed rooms, kitchens, frequently alongside a stove installation, and only 17 per cent (N=11) were found in open spaces or courtyards. Therefore, monastic settlements demonstrate a significant architectural and technological shift by placing the bread oven inside a room within a building rather than in an open cooking area.

In addition to the placement of bread ovens within settlements, a closer examination of the size and location of kitchens, bakeries, and places for eating enhances our knowledge of the built environment. The spaces themselves provide a unique perspective on the economic activities of the monastery. Due to the incomplete nature of the archaeological evidence, it is rare for the surviving monastic remains to still possess all the spaces associated with meal production. A brief survey of a few Egyptian sites

---

[36] Depraetere, 'A Comparative Study'.
[37] See the ovens at Karanis, for example, in Husselman, *Karanis Excavations*, p. 49.

highlights the diverse spatial configuration of monastic communities and how we might use the size, location, and presence of some rooms to gain better insight into the economy of cooking and baking.

Many of the monastic sites provide archaeological evidence of kitchens that integrate a bread oven alongside a stove installation with several burners. At Kellia, the famous site of the Desert Fathers, over 1,500 separate dwellings, each with over twenty-five rooms, contained at least one room equipped with stoves and ovens built against each other in order to create a kitchen. In particular, the use of the *kanun* appears most often as the source of direct heat for cooking. The kitchens were a key feature of the spatial design of the monastic residence, which could house five to ten monks, whereas larger dwellings might have over twenty. At QR195, the residence in its final stage had seven kitchens, of which five had bread ovens, in addition to two separate bakeries with one oven each.[38] Private kitchens were also found at the monastery of John the Little in Wadi el-Natrun, where the dwellings have a similar design to those found at Kellia. One residence, Building 64, contains two separate kitchens (area 2.4 m^2; 4.4 m^2), each with ovens, and a third space (area 13 m^2) with two bread ovens.[39]

At the monastic community at Naqlun in the Fayum, over eighty geostructures were carved from the shale and pebble cliffs of Gebel Naqlun.[40] Most of the monastic dwellings had private kitchens and less frequently a bread oven, which might be placed in a separate room from the kitchen. Hermitage 87 is an example of a residence with two rooms dedicated to preparing food on the south-east side of an open-air courtyard. Room 10 (area 11 m^2) includes a single bread oven and is adjacent on the north side of the private kitchen Room 12 (area 10 m^2) with a two-burner stove (Fig. 6.4).[41] The two rooms are entered by separate doorways on the east side of the courtyard and are not linked to any other rooms on the south-east side of the residence. At Naqlun, storage was not in the form of separate rooms, but rather as rectangular bins cut directly into the floors of various rooms of the residence.

At the sites of Esna and Adaima in Upper Egypt, monks elected to build their dwellings as semi-subterranean geostructures in the desert. A staircase, at ground level, led down to an open-air courtyard. Various rooms were built entirely underground with windows located on exterior walls that face the courtyard, to allow light into the spaces. The private kitchens were equipped

---

[38] Henein and Wuttmann, *Kellia*, vol. 1, p. 209.
[39] Pyke and Brooks Hedstrom, 'The Afterlife of Sherds'.
[40] Brooks Hedstrom, *The Monastic Landscape in Late Antique Egypt*, pp. 265–72.
[41] Godlewski, 'Naqlun 2007', pp. 237–8 and fig. 9.

Fig. 6.4. Room 10 in Hermitage 87 at the monastic site of Naqlun in the Fayum Oasis; Godlewski, 'Naqlun 2007', p. 238, fig. 9. Photo courtesy of W. Godlewski, archive PCMA.

with small stoves, bread ovens, and chimneys, since the room would need to have ventilation for smoke and heat (Fig. 6.5).[42] Unlike the residences at Naqlun, the dwellings at Esna and Adaima had separate storage rooms and even a few rooms with cisterns to provide water. None of the three sites revealed any specific location for the eating of meals, although built-in benches along the walls of a small room, where a monk might spend his day working and praying, could also serve as a place for eating a meal. Thus, these three sites do not have any room that could be identified as a refectory.

A more complex story of food preparation and eating is found at the Theban necropolis, where a complex web of modest monastic settlements nestled alongside two substantial monasteries, the monastery of Apa Phoibammon at Deir el-Bahri and the monastery of Apa Paul at Deir el-Bachit.[43] For example, the small residence built at the tomb MMA 1152 (just south of the monastery of Apa Phoibammon) contained a one-room kitchen (area 7.2 m^2). Equipped with three depressions for holding fuel for

---

[42] Sauneron and Jacquet, *Les ermitages chrétiens*, vol. 1, pp. 18–24 and pl. VIII; Sauneron, 'The Work of the French Institute', pl. XXXI.

[43] Godlewski, *Le monastère de St Phoibammon*, pp. 79–88. Burkard et al., 'Die spätantike/koptische Klosteranlage'; Eichner and Fauerbach, 'Die spätantike/koptische Klosteranlage'.

Fig. 6.5. Kitchen with stove and oven in Hermitage 18 at 'Adaima in Upper Egypt; Sauneron, 'The Work of the French Institute of Oriental Archaeology in 1973-1974', pl. XXXI. Photograph of the kitchen in Hermitage 18. Photograph by J.-F. Gout. Courtesy of IFAO.

heating cooking pots, the kitchen was unroofed and connected to an open courtyard.[44] At the larger *topos* of Apa Epiphanius, near the monastery of Apa Phoibammon, at Sheikh abd el-Qurna, monks built two bakeries – one in the West Court and one in Room 19 in the East Terrace.[45] The west oven was found outside the central buildings and built in a courtyard, perhaps reflecting earlier designs for communal baking. In contrast, the east oven was built into Room 19 (area 19.8 m^2), reflecting the shift to having ovens within enclosed spaces of the monastic structures. Both of these two sites share greater parallels with the spatial configuration of the monasteries at Adaima, Esna, and Naqlun.

At the monastery of Apa Paul, monks ate food in a large refectory (area 89 m^2) with six built-in circular tables, with ringed seating around pairs of tables.[46] The refectory increased in size over three phases, reflecting an increase in the community's population. At its maximum capacity, with monks sitting next to each other but not touching, the dining hall could host

---

[44] Górecki, 'Sheikh abd el-Gurna', p. 177. See Antoniak, 'Preliminary Remarks', p. 245; Garel, 'Ostraca of Victor the Priest'.
[45] Winlock and Crum, *The Monastery of Epiphanius I*, pp. 53–4.
[46] Eichner and Fauerbach, 'Die spätantike/koptische Klosteranlage', pp. 144–5.

approximately sixty-six monks at one sitting. Although a formal bakery and kitchen has not been found at the site, the refectory and various storage rooms with large ceramic bins point to significant food requirements.[47] This refectory points to its communal nature as a site needing a large eating area to accommodate more monks and suggests that, as a monastery increased in size, the ability to prepare and consume food was no longer in the hands of the residents, but in the hands of assigned cooks and bakers.

A similar development is evident at the massive communal monastic settlement at the monastery of Apa Jeremias at the mountain of Memphis.[48] Over the course of excavations in the early twentieth century, nine ovens were identified during excavations. All were located within rooms and were clustered in three distinct areas of the site. The first set of ovens was found by the main church, perhaps reflecting the production of bread for those attending the liturgy.[49] A second set of ovens was placed by three spaces designed to accommodate large numbers of individuals: a communal refectory, the monastery's infirmary, and a meeting hall. A third set of ovens was found in the residential quarters on the west side of the settlement, where an oven occupied a single room. Each of the three areas suggests different types of baking activities, based upon their spatial location to other facilities: a church, the refectory and communal hall, and private monastic residences.

Finally, at the site of Wadi Sarga in Middle Egypt, the monks at the monastery of Apa Thomas used at least five ovens located in four different areas of the site, but little evidence of private kitchens, such as those found at Naqlun or at Kellia, has been found (Fig. 6.6). Thanks in large part to the photographs, detailed notebooks, and sketches produced by archaeologist R. Campbell Thompson, it is possible to differentiate between the ovens and hearths at the site – a level of observation not common in documentation from early twentieth-century excavations.[50] The residential quarters of the settlement are built with rooms next to each other, and we do not see separate residences. The spatial layout here reflects monks living in an extended apartment complex, and it may be possible that four wings of the North Houses were responsible for the food preparation for this complex.[51]

---

[47] For an analysis of the ceramic corpus and its relationship to food production, see Beckh, *Zeitzeugen aus Ton die Gebrauchskeramik*, pp. 3–10.
[48] Brooks Hedstrom, *The Monastic Landscape of Late Antique Egypt*, pp. 225–37.
[49] A small room with ovens was found at the old monastery of Moses the Black in Wadi el-Natrun; see Innemée, 'Excavations at Deir Al-Baramus'.
[50] O'Connell, 'R. Campbell Thompson's 1913/14 Excavation'.
[51] Brooks Hedstrom, 'Thinking about Monastic Food'.

Fig. 6.6. 'Fireplace in Room 50i' from R. Campbell Thompson's 1913/14 excavation of the monastery of Apa Thomas in Wadi Sarga. AESAR.719. Courtesy of the Trustees of the British Museum.

The examples provided above of the great diversity of monastic spaces for cooking, baking, and eating illustrate that monastic communities did not necessarily follow a strict layout in terms of where food was prepared. However, in comparison with earlier Greco-Roman settlements and contemporary late antique non-monastic sites, it is clear that monastic communities embedded their food production areas within their residences. Any comparison of the location or presence of kitchens is therefore complicated by the sheer fact that kitchen spaces with features with direct heat are not prominent until we see the physical construction of new monastic settlements, in which kitchens serve as a central component of monastic spatial configurations.[52]

The reasons for the lack of kitchens are many, but I believe three potential reasons may help explain the lack or underrepresented nature of stoves excavated in kitchens. First, the physical form of a mud brick counter with u-shaped hearths was not a part of earlier domestic designs, and yet the feature becomes a diagnostic element of Byzantine monastic sites and then appears more regularly in later Islamic period settlements

[52] Brooks Hedstrom, 'Monks Baking Bread and Salting Fish', pp. 203–4.

Fig. 6.7. Kitchen from Building 48 from John the Little in Wadi Natrun. The kitchen includes a circular oven and a stove with a triple-*kanun* built above a niche for holding fuel. Photo: D. Brooks Hedstrom.

(Fig. 6.7). Second, cooks could use portable ceramic braziers that were moved between rooms and open spaces. Several examples exist from ancient Egypt, and possibly their forms were not recognised or documented as they resemble ceramic coarseware with carbon residue. And third, the physical size of the small u-shaped hearth or stove, the *kanun*, could be easily destroyed or removed during excavations. The function of these embedded features could also be overlooked as being less significant than the more prominent bread ovens during excavations, especially those conducted in the first decades of the archaeology of monastic sites. In the end, the construction of monastic kitchens is a fairly new technology in the archaeology of Byzantine cooking, and the presence of the kitchens at monastic settlements makes the feature an essential component of monastic site design.[53] As monastic communities expanded either through the increase in the number of monks in residence or through the community's popularity with pilgrims, we can see a direct correlation with the increase in cooking facilities at the sites, illustrating the economic growth of the monastery. By providing food for guests, for the infirm, and for special

---

[53] See the discussion of Byzantine cuisine and food in works such as Dalby, *Flavours of Byzantium*; Dalby, *Siren Feasts*; Dalby, *Dangerous Tastes*.

feast days, which may draw larger and larger numbers, some monasteries expanded greatly, such as Kellia and the monastery of Apa Jeremias, whereas other sites saw modest changes in the addition of later ovens, such as at the monastery of John the Little or at the monastery of Apa Thomas.

Conclusion

After the meals were cooked, where did monks eat? The usual answer is the refectory – a place for eating. However, this is not necessarily true in many monastic sites in Egypt, where the space for eating varied greatly and is often unrecognisable in the archaeological record. Communal monasteries, such as those found at Bawit, Saqqara, and Sohag, existed at the same time as independent confederations of the monastic dwellings at Kellia, Naqlun, Thebes, and Wadi el-Natrun. Of these first millennium monastic sites, only a few have spaces one may confidently identify as refectories. The clearest form is the room with circular tables and ring benches, as excavated at the monastery of Apa Paul, possibly the largest monastic site in western Thebes. At the monastery of Apa Jeremias, a large hall may be a refectory, as it is located by two other large halls and near a kitchen, but the space lacks tables and seating. Epigraphic evidence from the rooms at Apa Jeremias suggests that the space was a refectory, the *place of eating*, although some scholars have questioned this identification.[54] Once we move away from monastic communal sites, we cannot definitively identify rooms set aside for eating. In most cases, we are looking at multi-functional spaces in which monks worked, prayed, entertained guests, and ate all in the same space.

One way to approach the study of the archaeology of monastic cooking is by turning our focus to the physical space of the kitchen. It is a room that is dedicated to the shaping of monastic meals and taste in an environment in which personal preferences are curtailed to better serve the community's goals, whether it be in a small group of a few monks or in the large communal setting with hundreds of monks.[55] By considering how the built kitchen impacted the individual monk and how he or she experienced food, we can benefit by considering the *somatic* nature of the monastic settlement. This allows us to consider how bodies reacted to and were acted

[54] Burkard *et al.*, 'Die spätantike/koptische Klosteranlage', fig. 2.
[55] Brooks Hedstrom, 'Monks Baking Bread and Salting Fish'.

upon within their built environments.[56] Did the kitchen create a *somatic* landscape whereby cooking and baking produced smells that would signal the changing of the day's tasks or engender a sensorial awareness of the liturgical calendar as food changed in relationship to feast days? In order to study the archaeology of cooking, rather than the archaeology of food, I have used the methodologies employed by monastic archaeologists working in Europe to inform my reading of taste and food production processes.[57] I do this because Byzantine archaeologists have been, for the most part, reluctant to embrace the theoretical shifts within archaeology that other colleagues employ in the study of homosocial communities. The study of monasticism as a field of Byzantine archaeology is well poised to ask new questions about the built environment and what we might deduce by doing so. The kitchen with its ovens and stoves offers just one example of how a shift in focus may produce greater insights into what it was like to live in a monastic community.

Employing theoretical models, such as household archaeology, draws together a variety of concerns correlated to social relationships around a household's identity through the analysis of archaeology and ethnohistorical material. The identity of a monastic community could and may be shaped by the physical structures that were built, in large part, specifically for monastic living. The monastic movement required new habitations and ones in new locations to be set apart from the traditional and biological households. The importance of consumption habits within the family setting played a role in reinforcing one's identity in a monastery or in a nonmonastic family. The shift to a new residence required significant changes to help redefine one's experience as being different from that of the past.[58] By considering the construction of kitchens, bakeries, and dining areas, the archaeology of cooking places the cooks, bakers, and consumers at the centre, and this work then complements the vital archaeobotanical and microarchaeological work being undertaken at comparable monastic sites.[59]

---

[56] The archaeology of taste, as Yannis Hamilakis explains, is a way to shift our understanding into one that 'begins with the human body, or rather the *trans-corporeal, somatic landscape*' and is 'culturally defined'; Hamilakis, 'Archaeology of the Senses', p. 212 (emphasis original); see also Hamilakis, 'The Past as Oral History'. All built environments are somatic landscapes, and a sensitivity to rereading the landscape as one that acts upon the body is providing new avenues for environmental readings of the archaeological evidence; see Christophersen, 'Performing Towns'.

[57] Brooks Hedstrom, 'Models of Seeing and Reading Monastic Archaeology'. For evidence from Western monastic sites, see Bond, 'Production and Consumption of Food and Drink'; Courtney, 'Excavations in the Outer Precinct'.

[58] Madella et al., *The Archaeology of Household*, pp. 119–56.

[59] Matthews, 'About the Archaeological House', p. 560.

Three conclusions emerge from this analysis of the archaeological evidence for monastic kitchens in Egypt. First, the presence of monastic kitchens as circumscribed spaces may be private kitchens, rather than communal kitchens found at larger settlements. The small kitchen may reflect the particular food preferences and ascetic habits of individuals that we cannot observe in large communal monasteries where supervision of eating, cooking, and presentation was under the review of specific monastic leaders. A private kitchen offers an archaeological indicator of the nature of monasticism practised within a community for which we may not have any documentary or literary evidence. Second, the archaeological evidence for a range of oven styles and monastic kitchens is unique to the material remains of Egyptian monasticism. While kitchens and ovens are identified in monasteries in Palestine, the use of mud brick counters with a *kanun* for a small hearth is a mark of Egyptian monastic designs. The regional variety may stem from the level of preservation and the quality of the raw materials used in construction. For example, we have better evidence for refectories in the Levant simply due to the presence of mosaic donor inscriptions that label the spaces of refectories, whereas mosaic floors within expressly monastic contexts in Egypt are rare.[60] Third, the physical relocation of ovens and kitchens to interior spaces within Egyptian monastic sites marks a departure from the modes of cooking and baking in previous centuries. It is also important to note that, as we move forward into the medieval Islamic periods, more ovens and kitchens are found inside houses, indicating that monastic architecture may have influenced later urban planning. While the presence of kitchens does not necessarily reveal a propensity for luxury, the importance of cooking food for the ascetic table required greater attention than what may have been the case in non-monastic settings. We know from faunal and floral analysis at Kom el-Nana and at John the Little that monks had access to a more varied diet than what we might be led to believe if we rely only upon the testimony of monastic authors.[61]

One way to examine a study of monastic kitchens is through the history of specific foods as it relates to Christian practice – those forbidden, those

---

[60] Hirschfeld, *The Judean Desert Monasteries*, pp. 63–5.
[61] One way to determine if monks were eating a more varied diet is to conduct carbon and nitrogen stable isotope analysis of carbonate and bone collagen extracted from the skeletons of monks to identify whether they were eating more meat and fish, for example, than what is recorded. Byzantine monastic burials at St Stephen's community in Jerusalem demonstrated higher ratios of nitrogen isotopes, proving monks were eating nonplant protein, despite the textual accounts that claim they ate only vegetables and bread. Gregoricka and Guise Sheridan, 'Ascetic or Affluent?'.

permitted, and those restricted.[62] Known more commonly as the archaeology of food, this approach places food at the centre of the study. We learn little about how the meals were experienced – or how food moved from the fire pit in a small dwelling or a large communal monastery to a table. The archaeological evidence of Egyptian monastic kitchens provides ample evidence for undertaking further study of the archaeology of *cooking*. While related to food, the archaeology of cooking is concerned with the type of *human processes* that transform ingredients into meals and, in this case, how monastic cooks and bakers participated in the making of the sensorial meal that drew together smells, sights, taste, and touch.

A focus on the spatial placement and design of monastic kitchens provides new avenues for considering the economic component for building, remodelling, and expanding monastic housing. For example, at Kellia we can trace the addition of rooms, but also the construction of kitchens and their size as indicators of an increase in residents or visitors to the community. Therefore, one way to trace the growth, or even the decline, of a community is by looking at the archaeological components of kitchens, the number of stoves with hearths, and the size of bread ovens. Even the placement of the kitchen, either in an apartment or with access to an infirmary or a communal hall for eating, offers evidence for assessing the economic changes in terms of who may be living at the community versus how the community serves visitors or pilgrims.

The financial resources needed for food production, the transport of goods, and the fuel needed to prepare food, along with the human labour involved in making and serving food, are important aspects for considering the quantitative elements of monastic life. The physical space given to food preparation and storage may also provide information that is not found in our written sources, whether documentary or literary in nature. In discussing the practicalities of moving the Byzantine army across Anatolia in 1071 to Mantzikert, John Haldon *et al.* highlight the challenges we face in building a reliable, economic model, as our written sources do not always tell us all that we wish to know about the past: 'Numbers in ancient and medieval texts are notoriously problematic – sometimes entirely plausible and seemingly trustworthy ... sometimes entirely incredible, yet at the same time not always to be cast aside or ignored.'[63] Haldon *et al.* turn to environmental science and ethnohistorical research to build a more robust model of the premodern landscape in Anatolia to consider 'demography,

---

[62] Grimm, *From Feasting to Fasting*, pp. 85 106.
[63] Haldon *et al.*, 'Marching across Anatolia', p. 209.

settlement patterns, land use and resource allocation, distribution, and consumption' as an army of 30,000–40,000 men and their animals ate their way across to Mantzikert.[64]

While monastic communities were not moving armies, the multidisciplinary approach that Haldon employs is an effective illustration of how we might use the kitchen space as a venue for calculating food needs, fuel, and the capacity of kitchens to produce the calorific needs for those living in a monastery, regardless of its size. Both Ewa Wipszycka and Louise Blanke have used such an approach to consider the bread production described at the White Monastery in Sohag. They conclude that the historical numbers are not viable considering the number of ovens, let alone a storage facility that would hold a year's worth of bread loaves for the community and visitors.[65] To extend this analysis to consider monastic communities as a whole involves spatial analysis, experimental archaeology, in terms of the amount of fuel needed to heat ovens, to test the production of bread and portions with similar cooking facilities, and to examine the possible sources of ingredients needed to help create the food outlined in our sources.

What is remarkable about Haldon's work is that, until now, the most important military campaign in Byzantine history was not studied for its practical, economic logistics. The fixation upon the political and military components overshadowed any interest in the particulars of how an army might move across the land. Similarly, I would argue that food production and the monastic kitchen has also lacked such robust investigation. More commonly, the study of monastic food has focused on diet rather than on the logistics of making meals and the economic requirements for production. However, in order to undertake the examination of a physical kitchen, much like the roads and landscape of Anatolia, the analysis requires the research of many individuals, whose expertise in ecohistory, environmental science, demography, and ethnohistory can work together to inform our reading of the written sources. In the end, there is much to be explored in terms of how the physical kitchen can be examined to write a complex account of monastic living and how the room for cooking may be a window into richer analysis of the economic cost of and need for food preparation.

---

[64] Haldon *et al.*, 'Marching across Anatolia', p. 210.
[65] Wipszycka, 'Resources', pp. 186–90; Blanke, *An Archaeology of Egyptian Monasticism*, p. 138.

Bibliography

Alexander, R. T. 'Mesoamerican House Lots and Archaeological Site Structure: Problems of Inference in Yaxcaba, Yucatan, Mexico, 1750–1847' in P. Allison (ed.), *The Archaeology of Household Activities* (New York: Routledge, 1999), pp. 78–100.

Antoniak, I. 'Preliminary Remarks on the Coptic Ostraca from Seasons 2003 and 2004', *Polish Archaeology in the Mediterranean*, 16 (2005), 244–7.

Bartelink, G. J. M. (ed.) *Athanase d'Alexandrie: Vie d'Antoine* (Paris: Les Éditions du Cerf, 1994).

Beckh, T. *Zeitzeugen aus Ton Die Gebrauchskeramik der Klosteranlage Deir el-Bachit in Theben-West (Oberägypten)* (Berlin: De Gruyter, 2013).

Bhabha, H. *The Location of Culture* (London: Routledge, 1994).

Blanke, L. *An Archaeology of Egyptian Monasticism: Settlement, Economy and Daily Life at the White Monastery Federation* (New Haven: Yale Egyptology, 2019).

Bond, J. 'Production and Consumption of Food and Drink in the Medieval Monastery' in G. Keevill, M. Aston, and T. Hall (eds.), *Monastic Archaeology: Papers on the Study of Medieval Monasteries* (Oxford: Oxbow Books, 2001), pp. 54–87.

Boon, A. *Pachomiana Latina. Règle et épîtres de s. Pachôme, épître de s. Théodore et 'Liber' de s. Orsiesius. Texte latin de s. Jérôme* (Leuven: Universiteitbibliotheek, 1932).

Bourbou, C. *Health and Disease in Byzantine Crete (7th–12th Centuries AD)* (Farnham: Ashgate Publishing Limited, 2010).

Brakke, D. *Evagrius of Pontus. Talking Back. A Monastic Handbook for Combating Demons* (Collegeville, MN: Liturgical Press, 2009).

Brooks Hedstrom, D. L. 'Models of Seeing and Reading Monastic Archaeology', *Cistercian Studies Quarterly*, 48.3 (2013), 299–315.

Brooks Hedstrom, D. L. 'Monks Baking Bread and Salting Fish: An Archaeology of Early Monastic Ascetic Taste' in M. Mullett and S. Ashbrook Harvey (eds.), *Knowing Bodies, Passionate Souls: Sense Perceptions in Byzantium* (Washington, DC: Dumbarton Oaks Press, 2017), pp. 183–206.

Brooks Hedstrom, D. L. *The Monastic Landscape in Late Antique Egypt: An Archaeological Reconstruction* (Cambridge: Cambridge University Press, 2017).

Brooks Hedstrom, D. L. 'Thinking about Monastic Food: Theory, Practice, and the Archaeology of Spatial Design' in M.-A. El Dorry (ed.), *Continuities and Transitions: Approaches to Studying Food and Drink in Egypt and Sudan* (Cairo: Institut français d'archéologie orientale, forthcoming).

Burkard, G., Mackensen, M., and Polz, D. 'Die spätantike/koptische Klosteranlage Deir el-Bachit in Dra' Abu el-Naga (Oberägypten)', *Mitteilungen des deutschen archäologischen Instituts, Abteilung Kairo*, 59 (2003), 41–65.

Christophersen, A. 'Performing Towns. Steps towards an Understanding of Medieval Urban Communities as Social Practice', *Archaeological Dialogues*, 22.2 (2015), 109–32.

Courtney, P. 'Excavations in the Outer Precinct of Tintern Abbey', *Medieval Archaeology*, 33 (1989), 99–143.

Crislip, A. *From Monastery to Hospital: Christian Monasticism and the Transformation of Health Care in Late Antiquity* (Ann Arbor: University of Michigan Press, 2005).

Crislip, A. *Thorns in the Flesh: Illness and Sanctity in Late Ancient Christianity* (Philadelphia: University of Pennsylvania Press, 2012).

Dalby, A. *Siren Feasts: History of Food and Gastronomy in Greece* (London and New York: Routledge, 1997).

Dalby, A. *Dangerous Tastes: The Story of Spices* (Berkeley: University of California Press, 2002).

Dalby, A. *Flavours of Byzantium* (Totnes: Prospect, 2003).

Dauphin, C. 'The Diet of the Desert Fathers in Late Antique Egypt', *Bulletin of the Anglo-Israel Archaeological Society*, 19–20 (2001-2), 39–63.

David, N. and Kramer, C. *Ethnography in Action* (Cambridge: Cambridge University Press, 2001).

Depraetere, D. D. E. 'A Comparative Study on the Construction and the Use of the Domestic Bread Oven in Egypt during the Graeco-Roman and Late Antique/Early Byzantine Period', *Mitteilungen des deutschen archäologischen Instituts, Abteilung Kairo*, 58 (2002), 119–56.

Eichner, I. and Fauerbach, U. 'Die spätantike/koptische Klosteranlage Deir el-Bachit in Dra` Abu el-Naga (Oberägypten)', *Mitteilungen des deutschen archäologischen Instituts, Abteilung Kairo*, 61 (2005), 139–52.

El Dunbabin, K. M. D. *The Roman Banquet: Images of Conviviality* (Cambridge: Cambridge University Press, 2003).

El Dorry, M.-A. 'Monks and Plants: A Study of Foodways and Agricultural Practices in Egyptian Monastic Settlements', unpublished PhD dissertation, Münster, 2015.

Frankenberg, W. (ed.) *Euagrios Ponticus* (Berlin: Weidmannsche Buchhandlung, 1912).

Garel, E. 'The Ostraca of Victor the Priest Found in the Hermitage MMA 1152' in T. Derda, A. Łajtar, and J. Urbanik (eds.), *Proceedings of the 27th International Congress of Papyrology, Warsaw 29.07–3.08 2013* (Warsaw: University of Warsaw, 2016), pp. 1041–54.

Garitte, G. *S. Antonii Vitae versio Sahidica* (Paris: E Typographeo Reipublicae, 1949).

Godlewski, W. *Deir El-Bahari V. Le monastère de St Phoibammon* (Warsaw: PWN, 1986).

Godlewski, W. 'Naqlun 2007: Preliminary Report: Excavations', *Polish Archaeology in the Mediterranean*, 19 (2007), 229–79.

Górecki, T. 'Sheikh abd el-Gurna Coptic Hermitage', *Polish Archaeology in the Mediterranean*, 15 (2003), 173–9.

Gregoricka, L. A. and Guise Sheridan, S. 'Ascetic or Affluent? Byzantine Diet at the Monastic Community of St. Stephen's, Jerusalem from Stable Carbon and Nitrogen Isotopes', *Journal of Anthropological Archaeology*, 32.1 (2013), 63–73.

Grimm, V. *From Feasting to Fasting, the Evolution of a Sin: Attitudes to food in Late Antiquity* (London: Routledge, 1996).

Haldon, J, Gaffney, V., Theodropoulos G., and Murgatroyd, P. 'Marching across Anatolia: Medieval Logistics and Modeling the Mantzikert Campaign', *Dumbarton Oaks Papers*, 65 & 66 (2011–12), 209–35.

Hamilakis, Y. 'The Past as Oral History: Towards an Archaeology of the Senses' in Y. Hamilakis, M. Pluciennik, and S. Tarlow (eds.), *Thinking through the Body: Archaeologies of Corporeality* (New York: Kluwer/Plenum, 2002), pp. 121–36.

Hamilakis, Y. 'Archaeology of the Senses' in T. Insoll (ed.), *The Oxford Handbook of the Archaeology of Ritual and Religion* (Oxford: Oxford University Press, 2011), pp. 208–25.

Henein, N. H. and Wuttmann, M. *Kellia: l'ermitage copte QR 195*, 2 vols (Cairo: Institut français d'archéologie orientale, 2000).

Hirschfeld, Y. *The Judean Desert Monasteries in the Byzantine Period* (New Haven: Yale University Press, 1992).

Husselman, E. M. *Karanis Excavations of the University of Michigan in Egypt, 1928–1935: Topography and Architecture* (Ann Arbor: Kelsey Museum of Archaeology, 1979).

Innemée, K. C. 'Excavations at Deir Al-Baramus 2002–2005', *Bulletin de la Société d'archéologie Copte*, 44 (2005), 55–68.

Koder, J. '*Stew and Salted Meat* – Opulent Normality in the Diet of Every Day?' in L. Brubaker and K. Linardou (eds.), *Eat, Drink, and Be Merry (Luke 12:19): Food and Wine in Byzantium: Papers of the 37th Annual Spring Symposium of Byzantine Studies, in Honour of Professor A. A. M. Bryer* (Aldershot: Ashgate, 2007), pp. 59–72.

Krawiec, R. *Shenoute and the Women of the White Monastery: Egyptian Monasticism in Late Antique Egypt* (Oxford: Oxford University Press, 2002).

Layton, B. 'Social Structure and Food Consumption in an Early Christian Monastery: The Evidence of Shenoute's Canons and the White Monastery Federation A.D. 385–465', *Le Muséon*, 115 (2002), 25–5.

Lefort, L. T. *Oeuvres de S. Pachôme et de ses disciples* (Leuven: Durbecq, 1956).

Luff, R. M. 'Monastic Diet in Late Antique Egypt: Zooarchaeological Finds from Kom el-Nana and Tell el-Amarna, Middle Egypt', *Environmental Archaeology*, 12 (2007), 161–74.

Madella, M., Kovacs, G., Berzseny B., Briz I, and Godino, I. (eds.) *The Archaeology of Household* (Oxford: Oxbow, 2013).

Matthews, R. 'About the Archaeological House: Themes and Directions' in B. J. Parker and C. P. Foster (eds.), *New Perspectives on Household Archaeology* (Winona Lake: Eisenbrauns, 2012), pp. 559–66.

O'Connell, E. R. 'R. Campbell Thompson's 1913/14 Excavation of Wadi Sarga and Other Sites', *British Museum Studies in Ancient Egypt and Sudan*, 21 (2014), 121–92.

Olsen, B. *In Defense of Things: Archaeology and the Ontology of Objects* (Lanham: AltaMira Press, 2010).

Pyke, G. and Brooks Hedstrom, D. L. 'The Afterlife of Sherds: Architectural Re-use Strategies at the Monastery of John the Little, Wadi Natrun' in B. Bader and M. Ownby (eds.), *Functional Aspects of Egyptian Ceramics in Their Archaeological Context* (Leuven: Peeters, 2012), pp. 307–26.

Quataert, D. 'Clothing Laws, State, and Society in the Ottoman Empire, 1720–1829', *International Journal of Middle East Studies*, 29 (1997), 403–25.

Regnault, L. *La vie quotidienne des Pères du Désert en Égypte au IVe siècle* (Paris: Hachette, 1990).

Rousseau, P. *Pachomius: The Making of a Community in Fourth-Century Egypt* (Berkeley: University of California Press, 1985).

Sauneron, S. 'The Work of the French Institute of Oriental Archaeology in 1973–1974: 'Adaima', *Bulletin de l'Institut Français d'Archéologie Orientale*, 74 (1973–4), 186–95.

Sauneron, S. and Jacquet, J. *Les ermitages chrétiens du désert d'Esna*, 4 vols (Cairo: Institut français d'archéologie orientale, 1972).

Shaw, T. M. *The Burden of the Flesh: Fasting and Sexuality in Early Christianity* (Minneapolis: Fortress Press, 1998).

Souvatzi, S. *A Social Archaeology of Households in Neolithic Greece: An Anthropological Approach* (Cambridge: Cambridge University Press, 2008).

Steadman, S. R. 'Recent Research in the Archaeology of Architecture: Beyond the Foundations', *Journal of Archaeological Research*, 4.1 (1996), 51–93.

Veilleux, A. *Pachomian Koinonia II. Pachomian Chronicles and Rules* (Kalamazoo: Cistercian Publications, 1981).

Vivian, T. and Athanassakis, A. N. *The Life of Antony: The Coptic Life and the Greek Life* (Kalamazoo: Cistercian Publications, 2003).

Wellesz, E. *The Vienna Genesis with an Introduction and Notes* (New York: Faber and Faber, 1960).

Wilk, R. and Rathje, W. L. 'Household Archaeology', *American Behavioural Scientist*, 25/6 (1982), 617–39.

Winlock, H. E. and Crum, W. E. *The Monastery of Epiphanius at Thebes. Part I, The Archaeological Material; The Literary Material* (New York: Metropolitan Museum of Art, 1926).

Wipszycka, E. 'Resources and Economic Activities of the Egyptian Monastic Communities (4th–8th Century)', *The Journal of Juristic Papyrology*, 41 (2011), 159–263.

Zimmermann, B. *Die Wiener Genesis im Rahmen der antiken Buchmalerei* (Wiesbaden: Reichert, 2003).

7 | The Refectory and the Kitchen in the Early Byzantine Monastery of Tell Bi'a (Syria): The Egyptian and Palestinian Connections

GÁBOR KALLA

In memoriam Eva Strommenger (1927–2022)

One of the most intensively explored monastic complexes of Syria is located at the site Tell Bi'a, near modern Raqqa. The monastery was erected on the ruins of Tuttul, a flourishing political-religious centre in the Bronze Age (third to second millennium BC), which was uninhabited when the construction works started in the sixth century.

The excavation of Tuttul took place under the leadership of Eva Strommenger between 1980 and 1995.[1] The main goal of the excavation was the investigation of the Bronze Age city, covering an area of approximately fifty hectares and including several mounds. The main effort was concentrated on the centre of the site on mound E (Hügel E), where several palaces were found. The remains of the monastery extended over the Middle Bronze Age Palace (Palast A), and its excavation was necessary to reach the Bronze Age levels. After the first mosaic was found in 1990, further investigation of the monastery resulted in a separate project with the leadership of the author. The circumstances for a more extensive exploration of the building complex were fortunate; the walls lay directly under the surface and stood 0.8 m high at some points, although at other places only the foundations were discovered. Following some smaller scale investigations, during the course of three seasons of excavation led by the author (1990, 1992, 1993), approximately 3,000 m² of the architectural complex were excavated. This is an estimated 70–80 per cent of the whole monastery, but the exact dimensions of the complex are unknown (Fig. 7.1). The fully excavated southern part was heavily eroded, and it seems likely that, due to the lie of the land, not much more was preserved on the steep slope. On the eastern and western side, the external wall could be found, and – according to surface observations – an unexcavated area of 60 by 20 m on the northern side is all that remains. Consequently, we may reckon with a monastic complex 60 by 80 m (almost 5,000 m²) in size.

---

[1] For a summary of the excavations, see Krebernik and Strommenger, '1980–1995: Tuttul'. The results of the excavations are published in the series *Ausgrabungen in Tall Bi'a / Tuttul* (edited by Eva Strommenger and Kay Kohlmeyer; 1998–). My publication of the monastery is currently in preparation.

Fig. 7.1. Ground plan of the excavated area of the Tell Bi'a monastery.

Early Syrian Monasticism

Early Syrian monasticism is not as well researched as its Palestinian or Egyptian counterparts. There have been remarkably few focused excavations, and the known examples come mainly from the architectural surveys of well-preserved buildings, without any detailed investigation. It is probably for this reason that, despite the richness of the written sources, we know so little about the material culture, and why no comprehensive analysis and study has been carried out yet. Early Byzantine cloisters beyond Tell Bi'a are known almost only from western and southern Syria and the region of Tur Abdin (modern south-east Turkey). However, it is known that other regions played an important role in monastic life as well, and thus our knowledge is rather one sided. This proves to be a significant problem, as coenobitic monasteries appear in various shapes and sizes, with few generic types appearing, and the layout of the different rooms and chambers is often unique, meaning that their function – without inbuilt installations – is often impossible to determine.[2]

According to the written sources, numerous forms of monasticism coexisted in Syria during the third and fourth centuries, including: recluses (solitary hermits), stylites (hermits living on top of columns), and different types of communal monasticism.[3] The archaeological remains of the reclusive hermits comprise towers in deserted places, in which they often secluded themselves, and the columns upon which they lived.[4] Alongside such extreme individual asceticism, the organisation of communities started in different regions of Syria (Mesopotamia, Euphratensis, Osrhoene; modern north Iraq, north-east Syria, south-west Turkey), with the fundamental driving role of Manichean and Egyptian monasticism, which reached Syria via Palestine. As a result, a new form came to life, in which outstanding spiritual leaders collected the hermits and created a semi-coenobitic community type, the *hirta*. While similar to the *laura*, a significant difference was that, though the monks lived in their own cells separately, in a *hirta* they prayed together once every day, but in a *laura* only once a week.[5] Unfortunately, the amount of archaeological data concerning this form of monasticism is minimal. Yet, it is possible that the poorly preserved, sparsely excavated remains of a separately standing church and the scattered one-roomed cells with burials between them actually are the traces of a *hirta*.

The increasing number of monks, which often reached 100 people in some communities, made it necessary to establish a more complex internal organisation. The turning point was the appearance of St Ephraim towards the end of the fourth century, whose example had a huge impact on Syrian Christianity. By the fifth and sixth centuries, coenobitic monasteries ruled the region.[6] As a result of the introduction of the Basilian and Pachomian rules, local regulations were created, of which twenty-three are known. However, in reality almost every community had its own unique customs, so these regulations can only be used with caution in the interpretation of the archaeological data.[7] Furthermore, the main purpose of the earliest of these rules, introduced through various theological traditions (Miaphysite/

---

[2] Brenk, 'Frühes Mönchtum', p. 66.
[3] An outstanding summary of the written sources of Syrian monasticism is Vööbus, *History of Asceticism*.
[4] Peña, Castellana, and Fernandez, *Les reclus syrien*; Peña, *Christian Art*, p. 105.
[5] Vööbus, *History of Asceticism*, vol. 2, pp. 115–17; Patrich, *Sabas*, pp. 23–4. For lauras in Palestine, see Hirschfeld, *The Judean Desert Monasteries*, pp. 18–33.
[6] Vööbus, *History of Asceticism*, vol. 2, pp. 70–110 and vol. 3, pp. 27–50.
[7] For a translation of the regulations, see Vööbus, *History of Asceticism*, vol. 3; also Patrich, *Sabas*, pp. 25–8.

Syrian Orthodox and Nestorian), such as the Canons of Rabbula, was to separate the monks from their secular surroundings, family, and personal belongings.[8]

Therefore, a new external architectural style was developed, a closed monastery with peripheral walls. Interestingly, in the case of numerous early Syrian monasteries, this tendency is not visible; communities based on the earlier tradition of scattered cells somehow endured. Instead of a closed architectural unit, the monastic complex was created from individual buildings joined around a courtyard, with the absence of a symmetrical layout and in many cases with a strong openness towards pilgrims and guests, for example, the monasteries of Ed-Deir, Qasr el-Banat, Turmanin, and Breij.[9] Beside the church itself, the most characteristic unit of the monasteries was a huge, two-storey building, most probably used for the everyday life of the monks, providing a space for the dormitories and the refectory. Often, one or more additional storeys were erected, which served as guesthouses. This custom was mainly common in central pilgrim destinations, such as Qal'at Sem'an and its neighbouring region. Their specific feature is their portico, which was erected from huge monolithic stones. Though the traces of economic activity, such as oil presses or cisterns, were preserved on several occasions, the original functions of the rooms are hardly distinguishable. Interestingly, in none of the excavated monasteries has a refectory or kitchen been identified. It is possible that they were instead located on upper levels.

The Monastery of Tell Bi'a

The scientific value of the monastery at Tell Bi'a lies not only in the fact that it was almost completely excavated, but also in its unique features when compared to other Syrian monasteries. While these were erected with the use of ashlar stones, the significant feature of this building complex is that the whole structure was built of mudbricks – stones were only applied on installations that experienced intense use (e.g., doorsteps, larger doorways, and baked bricks for external benches), or probably for elements of static

---

[8] Thomas and Hero, *Byzantine Monastic Foundation Documents*, pp. 38–41.
[9] Brenk, 'Frühes Mönchtum', especially p. 77; Peña, *Christian Art*, p. 113. Early, well-documented monasteries are almost exclusively known from western and southern Syria. For examples, see Butler, *Early Churches*, pp. 83–112; Lassus, *Sanctuaires chrétiens*, pp. 264–88; Tchalenko, *Villages antiques*. The monasteries of the region Tur Abdin were completely rebuilt in later periods, or their ruins are not visible; Bell, *The Churches and Monasteries*; Palmer, *Monks and Masons*. However, it has to be kept in mind that no archaeological excavations have been carried out at these sites.

importance (e.g., the corners of the church). No other monastery built from mudbrick is known from the early Byzantine period from Syria or Palestine. Although the use of mudbrick in monastic architecture is mostly known from Egypt,[10] its presence in Syria is perhaps not surprising. It is possible that the use of mudbrick was influenced by Mesopotamian architectural tradition, which is also observable in Tell Tuneinir (near Hasseke, north-western Syria), where a mudbrick church was erected in the twelfth century,[11] which also suggests that the use of mudbrick in the sacral architecture of Syria was more widespread than previously thought.

Another significant feature of the building complex of Tell Bi'a is that it belongs to a different architectural tradition than the other monasteries known from western and southern Syria, where all the complexes were built in ashlar masonry. These complexes consisted of: several buildings with a loose connection to one another; a church with no or very little adjoining architecture; a refectory and kitchen that did not form an individual, easily identifiable unit; and a limited number of ground level rooms (in most cases fewer than ten), probably due to the presence of several storeys. On the contrary, the Tell Bi'a monastery was constructed with a clear plan, and a ground floor layout, which consisted of fifty rooms that formed a closed complex, from which the church – even though it was heavily built around – and the block of the refectory and kitchen clearly stood out. Additionally, numerous installations were preserved, which were essential in the identification of the function of rooms and chambers. Overall, in this case, the everyday life of the monastery can be reconstructed outstandingly well.

The Beginning

More than a thousand years after the original site of Tell Bi'a was abandoned, mound B was used during Hellenistic and Roman times as a cemetery by the inhabitants of Nikephorion (later Callinicum).[12] Later, burials also appeared on the highest mound, mound E. It was probably one

---

[10] Grossmann, *Christliche Architektur*, passim.
[11] Fuller and Fuller, 'A Medieval Church'. An earlier monastery was found as well, but it was already built in stone. Only limited data has been published from this excavation; see Fuller and Fuller, 'Archaeological Discoveries'.
[12] The important Hellenistic city of Nikephorion (modern Mishlab, part of the city of Raqqa) was founded by Seleucus I Nicator (321–281 BC) 800 m south of Tell Bi'a. Seleucus II Callinicus (246–26 BC) later enlarged the city, and it was probably renamed to Callinicum after him. Due to the inhabitation of the place, few investigations have been carried out here, and the Hellenistic city is barely known except for the town walls (al-Khalaf and Kohlmeyer, 'Untersuchungen').

of these burials that made the place holy in the eyes of Christians, and was why hermits started to settle here. Another important aspect behind the selection of the place was that, in this time period, ruins were commonly used as the foundations of new monasteries.[13] In this case, features such as standing walls could not play a significant role, for the old mudbrick walls were not visible anymore. However, a considerable amount of old pottery and figural terracotta slabs belonging to these older occupations were found during the excavations.

The small, one-roomed buildings found in the layers under the monastery and the foundations of the antecedent of the later church suggest that, prior to the construction of the building, in the fifth century a *hirta*-type community may have existed here, which was later reorganised as a coenobitic one. After the removal of the previous structures, in the sixth century a new coenobitic monastic complex was erected on the top of mound E, with a view of the teeming city below. The identification of the complex was rather difficult, as the written sources mention four monasteries around Raqqa. According to the inscriptions' editor, Manfred Krebernik, the Tell Bi'a complex can be identified as the monastery of Mar Zakkai.[14]

The Location

The location of the building provided an ideal way of living for the monks. As Alice-Mary Talbot has made clear, the following factors were all important in choosing the appropriate site when founding a monastery: fertile land, good water supply, temperate climate, peaceful surroundings, security, and the natural beauty of the landscape (here, an artificial landscape).[15]

The waters of the Euphrates and especially the Balih rivers may have secured the requirements for the agricultural needs. The surrounding area of the monastery was a closed karst depression that was irrigated from the Balih River, creating a fertile land,[16] while the ruins of the Bronze Age city of Tuttul provided a fair-sized (fifty hectare) inner area, surrounded and defended by high city walls and ramparts. The ruins of the ancient city walls and ramparts still survive up to 15 m today, meaning that at the time of the

---

[13] For the selection of the location for the Syrian monastery, see Vööbus, *History of Asceticism*, vol. 2, pp. 163–72. From these criteria, the most important was the monastery as a memorial place for the dead.

[14] It could be the original home monastery of the famous person, Johannes bar Qursos, later bishop of Tella; see Krebernik, 'Schriftfunde'.

[15] Talbot, 'Byzantine Monastic Horticulture'.

[16] W. Schirmer in Miglus and Strommenger, *Stadtbefestigungen*, pp. 7–8.

foundation of the monastery the place was still a closed territory. Furthermore, the soil of the tell is exceptionally fertile. Thus, and also due to its high ash-content, it has commonly been used for land reclamation from the third millennium until today.[17] Therefore, it may also have been ideal for horticulture. Even if the entire area inside the ancient city walls had not been cultivated at once, the enclosed structure of the monastery may have been surrounded by spacious terraced gardens, at least on the central mounds (E and F).

The Building Complex

The inner layout of the monastery of Tell Bi'a is so far unique in the Syrian territory, with the closest parallel coming from Palestine. The monastery of Martyrius (Khirbet el-Murassas, modern Ma'ale Adummim) was founded in 474 and lies 6 km from the city of Jerusalem (Fig. 7.2).[18] The orthogonal ground plan, as well as the arrangement of the functional units, shows remarkable similarity to the Tell Bi'a monastery. In both cases, the layout follows a uniform plan: the perimeter walls enclose a square space; the refectory and kitchen lie north-west of a central court; the church, as well as the entrance, is located to the east of the court; the living quarters occupy the south-western wing; and the economic units are located in the north-eastern wing. Although some details differ, these two monasteries, on the whole, can be regarded as close parallels, and this type of layout also forms an individual group in the monastic architecture of Palestine.[19] Their ground plans were of similar scale as well, although one has to admit that we are dealing with an elusive point here, since in the case of Martyrius we also have to take into account a more extensive floor-plan over two storeys, which explains why the Tell Bi'a monastery had – despite its smaller external size – twice as many rooms.[20]

---

[17] Today, this land use is one of the greatest threats to the cultural heritage, because local farmers often destroy the archaeological sites to get fertiliser. In the case of Tell Bi'a, during the excavation, farmers regularly came with cars to transport the refuse. This activity has grown during the recent civil war, and part of the site is now destroyed not only because of the illicit digging for antiquities, but for the fertile soil. For the use of the earth from tells for soil fertiliser and on its effects on the archaeological remains, see Wilkinson, *Archaeological Landscapes*, pp. 117–18.

[18] For the monastery of Martyrius, see Magen and Talgam, 'The Monastery of Martyrius'; Hirschfeld, *The Judean Desert Monasteries*, pp. 42–5.

[19] See Hirschfeld, *The Judean Desert Monasteries*, fig. 25.

[20] Compared to the Tell Bi'a monastery's suspected 5,000 m² floor plan, the monastery of Martyrius was rather large, at 5,200 m², not including the hostelry (see Hirschfeld, *The Judean Desert Monasteries*, p. 43). It is possible that the Tell Bi'a monastery also had a hostelry, on the unexcavated north-eastern side, considering that hostelries usually were a key element of these buildings in western Syria. Currently, though, we have no evidence for one.

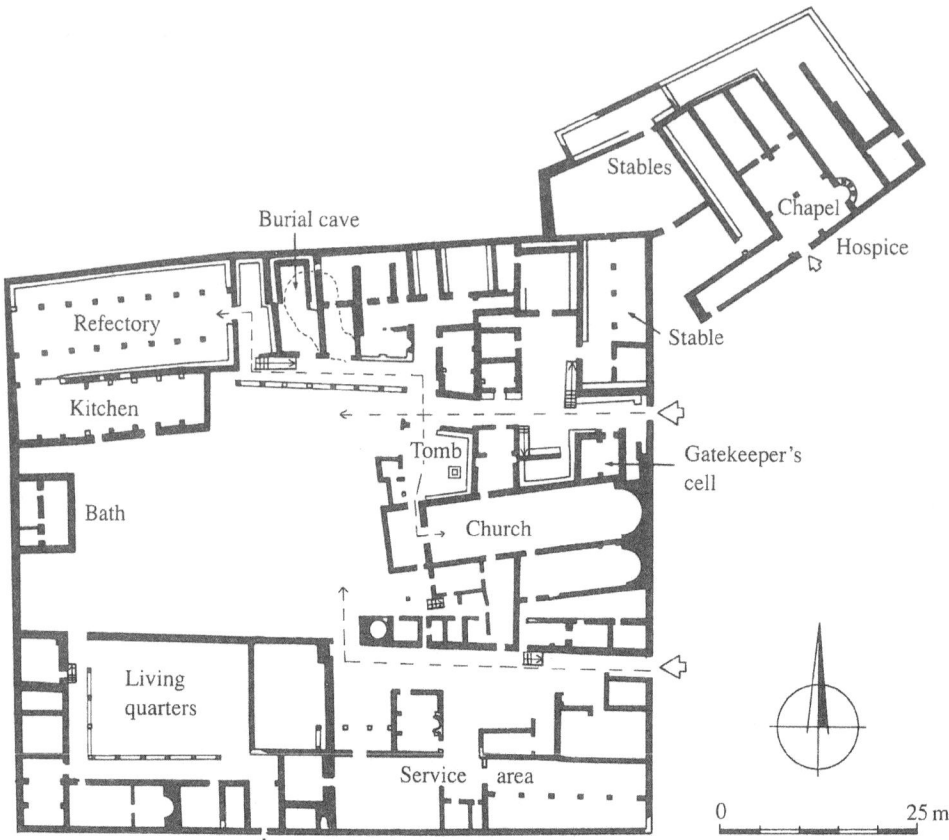

Fig. 7.2. Monastery of Martyrius (Khirbet el-Murassas, after Hirschfeld, *The Judean Desert Monasteries*, p. 43).

These features become even more interesting in that the ground plans of the churches represent two different traditions. The church of Martyrius has a longitudinal layout, while the church in the Tell Bi'a monastery has a transversal (broad room) plan, with three closed rooms (sanctuary and *pastophoria*) on the east side. Its parallels are well known from the Syrian Orthodox (Miaphysite) monasteries of Tur Abdin in modern south-east Turkey.[21] However, similarities to the overall layout of the monastery are not found in these sites. These parallels are not that surprising, since it is well-known that, despite ideological differences, communities devoted to

---

[21] On the church of the Tell Bi'a monastery and its parallels, see Kalla, 'A Holy Place'. For the monastery churches of the Tur Abdin region, see Bell, *Churches and Monasteries*; Palmer, *Monks and Masons*.

different denominations often employed the very same craftsmen and artisans for the construction of their religious buildings and decorations.[22]

During the construction of the building-complex, comprising more than fifty rooms, the builders adjusted the plan to the shape of the mound, and thus certain rooms and units were arranged on different terrace-levels (Fig. 7.3). For example, the church occupied the most elevated point of the mound, while the surface sloped towards the north and the west so significantly that, sometimes, the difference in the floor-levels reaches 3.5 meters.

In the area of the church, two main building phases can be distinguished, and in the case of the refectory, three phases can be recognised. Fortunately, the inscriptions of the mosaics allow us to date the phases of the church: according to the inscription in the narthex, the construction of the presently known complex can be dated to 509, while the inscription in the sanctuary signifies a larger-scale alteration that took place in 595.[23]

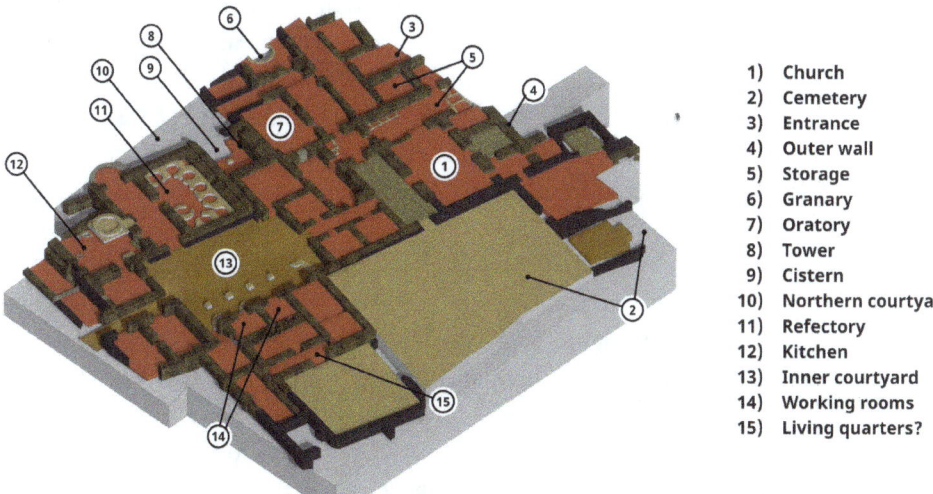

1) Church
2) Cemetery
3) Entrance
4) Outer wall
5) Storage
6) Granary
7) Oratory
8) Tower
9) Cistern
10) Northern courtyard
11) Refectory
12) Kitchen
13) Inner courtyard
14) Working rooms
15) Living quarters?

Fig. 7.3. 3D model of the Tell Bi'a monastery (drawing: Lőrinc Tímár).

---

[22] See, for example, the mosaicists and workshops in Palestine, who worked for both synagogues and churches, and the used iconographical themes were similar in many instances; see Hachlili, *Ancient Mosaic Pavements*, pp. 254–80.

[23] Krebernik, 'Schriftfunde'. For the mosaics, see Kalla, 'Das ältere Mosaik' and 'Christentum', pp. 135–41.

The Monastery as Household

Monasteries should also be investigated as household units. From the viewpoint of household archaeology, the following aspects have to be considered. According to the now classic article by Robert Wilk and William Rathje,[24] households have three different aspects: the social, the material, and the behavioural. Monasteries, additionally, are probably the best example for demonstrating that one also has to reckon with a further, fourth aspect: the symbolic. From a social viewpoint, monasteries represent a special group of households, in which members of the co-residential group are not relatives, yet inner hierarchy and division of labour are conspicuous. Thinking in terms of the social aspect, the internal relational networks of the monasteries are well documented in the written sources, although it has recently become clear that the pictures which can be drawn from these documents are often idealised.[25] The discipline of archaeology, however, is apt for exhibiting unique characteristics and differences.

The material and behavioural aspects of a household comprise various aspects of sustenance, production, and consumption. In comparison with smaller households that use multifunctional spaces, larger households, such as the Pachomian types of coenobiums, separate the different activities by architectural means, constructing specialised rooms. Such rooms are identified in the Tell Bi'a complex, as indicated on Fig. 7.3. Liturgical activities, storage, diverse forms of work, as well as food preparation, cooking, and consumption all took place in separate units.[26] Churches and refectories, as symbols of community life, occupied prominent and extraordinary positions. It is not a coincidence that generally the refectory is the second largest unit after the church – although, the size of the kitchens is also significant. Coenobite refectories are both religious and secular in their nature, with an emphasis on the former.[27] The ritualised practice of meals, regulations concerning them,[28] and Christian symbols appearing on the walls (in this case, a Byzantine cross in a niche) suggest that the refectory was the most important religious space after the church. Nevertheless, communal meals are also among the most important

---

[24] Wilk and Rathje, 'Household Archaeology'. From the vast literature of household archaeology, see the recent studies collected in Müller, *Household Studies*. See also the contribution by Brooks Hedstrom, Chapter 6.

[25] See, e.g., Brooks Hedstrom, 'Redrawing a Portrait', p. 34.

[26] For the Syrian Orthodox regulations, see Vööbus, *History of Asceticism*, vol. 3; Palmer, *Monks and Masons*, pp. 81–91, although the known sources lack the complete picture.

[27] Popović, 'The Trapeza', pp. 296–303; Popović, 'Dividing the Indivisible', pp. 48–9.

[28] Veilleux, *Pachomian Koinonia II*, pp. 28–39.

cohesive practices of a household, and thus dining rooms concurrently display social and symbolic aspects.

The Refectory

In the Tell Bi'a monastery, the refectory (Room 37) and the kitchen (Room 3) interconnected with a corridor (Room 36), constituting an enclosed wing in the north-western part of the complex (Figs 7.4–7.5), between the central and the northern courts. Northwards from the kitchen lies a partly excavated room (Room 48), its floor level approximately one metre lower than the floor of the corridor and the northern court, probably accessible only from the west, through another corridor (Room 1). Its position suggests that it was used as a cellar. From the southern part of the kitchen opened another room (Room 2), without any installations, which raises the question of its function. This was the only room besides the kitchen that was always kept warm, through the circulation of hot air from the fireplaces of the kitchen. At the previously mentioned monastery of Martyrius, in the same position between the living quarters and the kitchen, a bath-house was unexpectedly found, which was established for the sick monks.[29] Though in the Tell Bi'a case no traces suggesting a bath have been

Fig. 7.4. The refectory and the kitchen from the north.

---

[29] The three roomed bathhouse had a caldarium (hot room) with a hypocaust floor, such as Roman baths had. This is one of the few known bathhouses from a Byzantine monastery; see

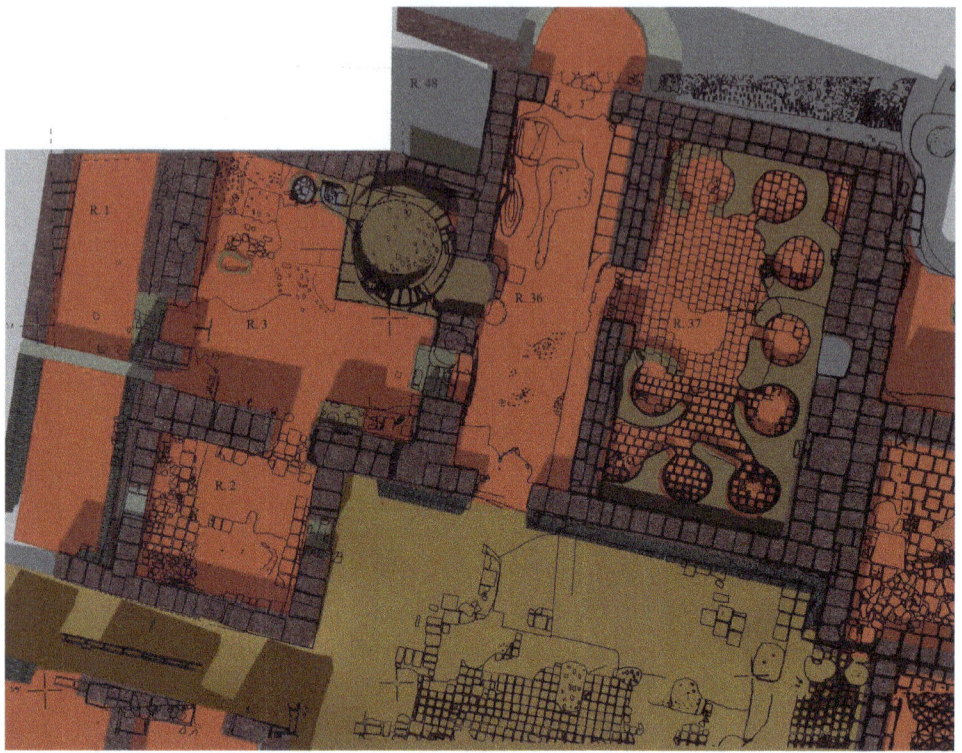

Fig. 7.5. The refectory and the kitchen.

unearthed, one can imagine that it had a function similar to a medieval warming-house (*calefactorium*), in which monks could warm themselves on colder winter days.[30] A different solution is that, as an appendix of the kitchen, it played a role in the preparation of the cooked food.

The symbolic significance of the refectory is underlined by its traditional Mediterranean gable roof and its terracotta tile covering (*imbrices* and *tegulae*). As the only non-flat roofed room, except for the church and perhaps the kitchen,[31] the whole kitchen-refectory wing most likely formed

---

Magen and Talgam, 'The Monastery of Martyrius', p. 106. Another example of a monastic bathhouse is that in the monastery of St Hilarion at Gaza. However, in this case, the bathhouse is situated in the hospital (see Elter and Hassoune, 'Le complexe du bain').

[30] The warming-houses in monasteries of the Middle Ages are often near the kitchen. For these calefactories, see Hecht, 'Calefactorium'. The difference is that these have individual heating, while Tell Bi'a did not – in the Syrian climate, it was probably sufficient to use the heat from the kitchen.

[31] As suggested by the concentrated appearance of iron nails from wooden frameworks and roof tile (*tegulae*) fragments in the immediate vicinity of the church and refectory in Tell Bi'a. In other parts of the monastery, very few pieces of them were found.

a separate block, which emerged visibly from the monastery complex. The alterations of the refectory are of remarkable importance (Fig. 7.5). The original dimensions of the room were about 10.1 m by 6.3 m (63.6 m^2), closely corresponding to that of the nave (*naos, heikal*) of the church (10.7 m by 6.2 m; 66.3 m^2). At the time of the construction of the cloister-complex (509), it did not contain any inbuilt elements, nor built-up benches. It is possible that the floor was paved with mosaic, since a few, relatively intact pieces were found in the northern court, near the refectory.[32]

It is possible that mobile furniture was used. According to Peter Grossmann, we can also assume that in many Egyptian refectories there was no furniture at all: the monks simply sat on the floor during the meals, possibly seating themselves in circles.[33] However, bearing the ground-plan structure in mind, it may be conjectured that, at least at first, the Palestinian influence was the dominating one. The question arises whether marble tables, many of which have been found in Palestinian monasteries, could have been constructed from tabletops with mobile supports.[34] In this case, tables could have been surrounded by light chairs or benches.

During the second phase (Fig. 7.6), sometime between 509 and 595, the eastern wall was strengthened with a mantle, slightly narrowing the available space. The supposedly damaged floor mosaic was replaced with a baked brick pavement. Upon the latter, six horseshoe-shaped benches were built in the southern part of the room, while in the northern part the builders left an empty space. Presumably in 595, or around that time (Figs 7.4, 7.5, and 7.6), when some of the walls of the church were relocated, the western wall was rebuilt 0.7 m eastwards and three further circular benches were constructed, while a previous one was removed. At this point, the room held altogether eight benches, measuring circa 0.5 m in width, with an internal diameter of 1.4 m and a height of 0.35 m. The benches were built of mudbrick (Fig. 7.5), covered with a reddish layer of mud and then with indurated plaster, constructing a hard and highly durable surface. The

---

[32] The situation could be similar to the church, where sometime in the middle of the sixth century the floor of the nave and the sanctuary was removed, and only the sanctuary got a new mosaic floor. The Chalcedonian/non-Chalcedonian controversy may stand behind this situation, influencing the acceptable iconography and meaning that the previous floor was not suitable (see Kalla, 'A Holy Place'). Another possible explanation is that the mosaic floor had already deteriorated, but there were no resources to renew it, so it was replaced with floor tiles.

[33] Grossmann, *Christliche Architektur*, p. 291.

[34] On the typical marble tables with multiple lobes (polylobed tables) found in Palestinian monasteries with literature, see Habas, 'The Marble Furniture', pp. 123–5.

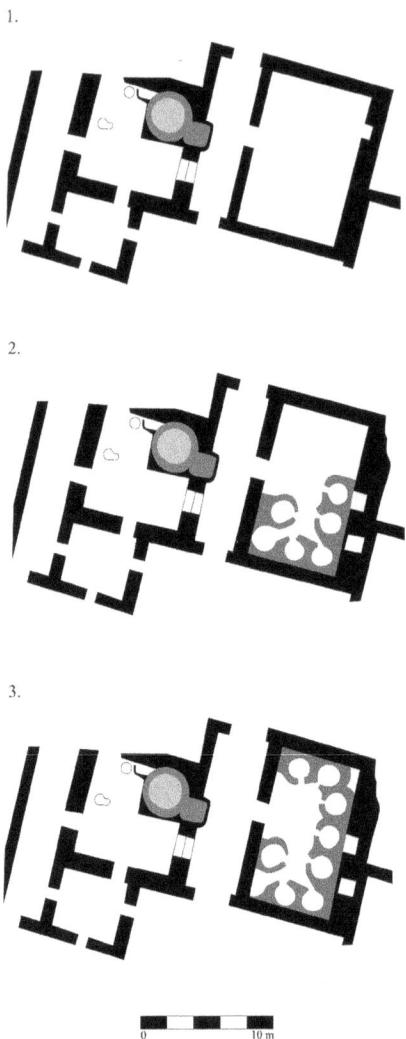

Fig. 7.6. Building phases of the refectory and its installations (Drawing: Fruzsina Németh).

given circles abutted and, by the last phase, almost completely covered the room, leaving an empty space only in front of the door.

The benches assumed permanent relationships among the coenobites, for whom their seat's location also indicated their rank in the community.[35] The abbot and the elders could have sat at the top of the table, in this case, at the central bench of the eastern side, under the niche decorated with

---

[35] Each monk had his permanent seat; see *Rules of Pachomius* 34 (Veilleux, *Pachomian Koinonia II*, p. 150).

a painted Byzantine cross. The other circular benches also had a table head, who said grace at the beginning of the meal.[36] In the centre of the eastern wall of the refectory, a 1.3 m wide niche was carved, which was closed-off with a semi-circular vault. Similar to the whole room, the niche was white and decorated with a Byzantine cross within a wreath. This was the only wall painting found in the complex. Another niche on the same wall, slightly higher up, may have functioned as a storage place for the holy scriptures read during dining.

The Egyptian and Nubian Parallels of Tell Bi'a's Circular Benches

The excavated circular benches in the refectory of the Tell Bi'a monastery are, to date, a unique phenomenon in the Syrian–Palestinian region. The refectory of the contemporary eastern Syrian monastery in Tell Tuneinir lacks traces of inbuilt structures,[37] and at other places it is hard to even identify the refectory itself.

The custom of the use of circular mudbrick benches stems, in all likelihood, from Egypt, since all the known examples from this period have been discovered here (throughout the entire country, and also in Nubia).[38] Here, two types of benches became common in refectories: a long type and a circular type. According to Grossmann, circular benches represent an older tradition.[39]

As a matter of fact, only a few examples have survived. The earliest one, dating to the mid-seventh century from the monastery of Apa Jeremias (Saqqara), in the Old Refectory (Fig. 7.2), provides the closest parallel for the Tell Bi'a refectory. The badly preserved circular benches (inner diameter: 1.5 m) were built close together, making passage among them difficult. Their fabric is mudbrick (in this case, sludge brick) covered with hard plaster. The width of the room is also similar to that of Tell Bi'a (5.5 m), although the length is not comparable as the refectory was only partially excavated.[40] The circular benches of the refectory of Deir el-Bachit (Fig. 7.3) have been preserved in the most intact state. Here, six such benches (inner diameter 1.60–1.72 m) were found in a T-shaped irregular

---

[36] On customs and manners of the Syrian Orthodox monasteries, see Palmer, *Monks and Masons*, p. 82.
[37] Fuller and Fuller, 'Archaeological Discoveries', p. 73.
[38] An excellent overview of the Egyptian examples is provided by Grossmann, *Christliche Architektur*, pp. 286–92.
[39] Grossmann, *Christliche Architektur*, p. 287.
[40] Grossmann and Severin, 'Reinigungsarbeiten', pp. 162–3, Abb. 1; Grossmann, *Christliche Architektur*, pp. 289–90.

room, arranged in twin-groups. Their construction is also of mudbrick covered with hard pink plaster. The point of interest here is the existence of massive inner table-bases.[41] Based on the ceramic survey, the use of these structures can be dated to between the seventh and ninth centuries.[42]

In Grossman's view, circular benches were also in use in the so-called Small Refectory of Apa Shenoute at Sohag, which can be dated broadly to the same period. However, following Louise Blanke's recent study of the monastery, Grossman's identification was incorrect, and the so-called benches are later constructions.[43] Not far from Sohag lies another member of the White Monastery federation, the women's monastery at Atripe. The refectory was divided into two aisles by six pillars. Here, the circular benches were similarly narrow, as with the following examples from Deir Anba Hadra, but their dimensions were more considerable.[44] At the complex of Deir Anba Hadra near Aswan (dated from the twelfth century) the space of the refectory was split into two naves by columns (Fig. 7.6), and against the walls at both sides of the room, seven benches in total remained, exhibiting an irregular arrangement.[45]

The refectory of Qasr el-Wizz in Nubia (Fig. 7.5), dated to the ninth to tenth centuries, is much better preserved than those at the Apa Jeremias and Apa Shenoute monasteries. The rectangular room was divided into four quadrants by a central pillar, and yielded four separate circular benches.[46] The benches' dimensions are not uniform, with inner diameters ranging between 1.5 and 1.8 m, and their width and height being 0.35 m and 0.45 m respectively. Recent Polish excavations in Ghazali revealed dining rooms with sizes and characteristics similar to the Qasr el-Wizz refectory. Its refectory had a rectangular plan, a central pillar, and five circular benches.[47]

To summarise, circular benches seem to be most common, while the variant of closely adjacent structures occurs only at the monastery of Apa Jeremias in Saqqara. This closer pattern may have been the earlier form,

---

[41] Eichner and Fauerbach, 'Die spätantike/koptische Klosteranlage', pp. 143–6, Abb. 2, Taf. 22–4; Eichner, 'Aspekte des Alltagslebens', p. 163, Abb. 6.

[42] Beckh, *Zeitzeugen aus Ton*.   [43] Blanke, *Archaeology of Egyptian Monasticism*, pp. 80–2.

[44] See El-Sayed and El-Masry, *Athribis I*.

[45] Walters, *Monastic Archaeology*, p. 100, pl. 19; Grossmann, *Christliche Architektur*, p. 291. On the recent German excavations at the site, see Krastel, Olschok, and Richter, Chapter 11.

[46] Scanlon, 'Excavations at Kasr el-Wizz I', pl. 33.1, plan 1; Scanlon, 'Excavations at Kasr el-Wizz II', pp. 21–2.

[47] I thank Artur Obłuski for providing a photo showing this feature, and for confirming its similarity. I also thank Dorota Dzierzbicka who brought the Ghazali refectory to my attention. Obłuski's monograph on Nubian monasticism (which became accessible to me only after completion of my study) devotes a chapter to the refectories. According to him, all Nubian refectories were furnished with circular or sigma-shaped benches. In addition to information from Qasr el-Wizz and Ghazali, he also discusses circular benches in the refectories of the monasteries in Kom D and Kom H in Dongola; Obłuski, *Monasteries and Monks*, pp. 169–82.

which the Tell Bi'a builders adjusted in its refectory. Tell Bi'a has provided the earliest known examples of circular benches, but this may be due to the accident of discovery. Their appearance here may signify conceptual changes. We know that during the mid-sixth century, many conflicts pervaded the monastic life in Syria,[48] and the more prominent Egyptian influence could also be ascribed to this fact. The Egyptian sources document well the movement of Syrian monks to Egypt, the best-known example being the later takeover of the Deir es-Suryani monastery in the Wadi Natrun.[49] Moreover, the appearance of the circular benches in Tell Bi'a may also indicate some changes in monastic order.[50]

Another feature is also attested in the Tell Bi'a refectory. A brick pavement is missing inside some circles, suggesting the existence of a onetime built-up table.[51] A similar table-base was also observed inside one of the two circular benches at the middle court.[52] Although table tops have not been found here, examples from Palestine and Greece also testify to the use of table tops.[53] These polylobed tables were made of marble and other stones, with a characteristic row of carved lobes (arches or circles) on the edges. Their upper faces were smooth, while their lower surfaces were roughly worked. Three types are known: sigma-formed, round, and square.[54] At Tell Bi'a, circular, possibly sigma types must have been used, which fit the approximately 1 m diameter negative spaces in the middle of the circular benches.

---

[48] At this time, Johannes bar Qūrsōs, the later bishop of Tella, was dispelled from the Mār Zakkai monastery in Callinicum (perhaps this complex); see Menze, 'The Regula ad Diaconos', pp. 46–8.

[49] Van Rompay and Innemée, 'La présence des syriens'.

[50] Approximately in the same period, the iconographical programme of the church was reorganised, when the floor mosaics of the nave and the sanctuary were removed and replaced by new representations. These changes were probably due to the new leaders of the community (see Kalla, 'A Holy Place').

[51] In Deir el-Bachit, in the middle of the circular benches, massive inner table-bases were also preserved; Eichner and Fauerbach, 'Die spätantike/koptische Klosteranlage', pp. 143–6, Abb. 2, Taf. 22–4; Eichner, 'Aspekte des Alltagslebens', p. 163, Abb. 6.

[52] Two circular benches were uncovered at the southern section of the middle court (Room 6), in front of the refectory entrance, before the living quarters. Their location raises several problems: is it possible that they were used during receptions of high-ranked guests? Regardless, inside one of them, traces of a table base remained.

[53] Kalla, 'Das Refektorium', pp. 259–61. Libi Habas raises the possibility that, in monasteries in Israel, not only the altars but also dining tables had polylobed tabletops. This type of tabletop is known from several refectories in Israel; see Habas, 'The Marble Furniture', pp. 123 and 125. In Greece, for example, in Vatopedi/Athos the stone tabletops still stand in their original place (Orlandos, Μοναστηριακή αρχιτεκτονική, Abb. 64). Barskii's drawing from the seventeenth century is particularly interesting for the function of the Megiste Lavra refectory in Athos (Strzygowski, 'Der sigmaförmige Tisch', p. 75; Kalla, 'Das Refektorium', Abb. 4). On the use of polylobed tables in Greek refectories, see Strzygowski, 'Der sigmaförmige Tisch'; Popović, 'The Trapeza', p. 299.

[54] Habas, 'The Marble Furniture', p. 123, pl. 2. For a well-executed summary of eastern Mediterranean polylobed tables, see Roux, 'Tables chrétiennes'.

Estimating the Number of Monks

In investigating the social aspect of the monastery, determining the size of the community is an important task; that is, one has to estimate the size of the household. Circular benches offer a great opportunity to do so (Fig. 7.5). On their basis, several scholars have attempted to estimate such populations; their results, however, show great divergence, even though the sizes of the benches vary within a quite narrow range: an inside diameter between 1.4 and 1.8 m (although we should note the particularly great size of 2.1 m at Deir Anba Hadra), and 0.35–0.50 m in width. George Scanlon supposed that, at Qasr el-Wizz, five to six persons may have sat together in a circle, and thus reckoned with 20–24 total inhabitants.[55] Ina Eichner and Ulrike Fauerbach, on the basis of personal experiment (and working with roughly same-sized benches), assumed that 11–12 persons may have sat on one bench in the refectory of Deir el-Bachit.[56] After a similar experiment at Tell Bi'a, I expect six to seven persons per bench.[57] If we assume that one person needed at least 40–50 cm of space, the theoretical number of the seats at Deir el-Bachit decreases, meaning that, even considering the larger circles, at most nine to ten persons may have sat together in a circle.[58] Table 7.1 collects this information. Note that the possible number of users of refectories is scaled up (i.e., it does not simply multiply the number of benches by the number of possible sitters), to take fluctuation in personnel into account. Despite these differences, the size of the community can essentially be estimated on the basis of the benches. According to the number and size of the latter, the monastery of Tell Bi'a may have had 36–54 monks during the second phase, and 48–64 during its latest period.

Table 7.1 reveals that there is only a loose connection between the size of the refectory and the number of monks. In some cases, the available space was not fully taken advantage of, while at other monasteries the rooms were more packed with benches.

---

[55] Scanlon, 'Excavations at Kasr el-Wiz II', p. 21.
[56] Eichner and Fauerbach, 'Die spätantike/koptische Klosteranlage', p. 143.
[57] Kalla, 'Das Refektorium', p. 263.
[58] On the picture published by Eichner, 'Aspekte des Alltagslebens', Abb. 6, monks are shown sitting very close together, pointing to the problem of personal space in eastern monasteries. The question emerges whether the twelve-people units around tables (see Grossmann, *Christliche Architektur*, p. 290), proposed by Cassianus, also mentioned by Eichner and Fauerbach, 'Die spätantike/koptische Klosteranlage', p. 143, was a custom here.

Table 7.1. *Circular benches in refectories and estimations of their users.*

Monastery	Refectory dimensions	No. benches	Inner diameter	Height	Width	No. places / bench	No. persons
Tell Bi'a (last period)	10.1 × 5.4 m (54.5 m²)	8	1.4 m	0.35 m	0.5 m	6–9	48–64
Apa Jeremias	? × 5.5 m	x-4	1.5 m	–	–	6–9	x+24–36
Qasr el-Wizz	5.75 × 7.25 m (41.7 m²)	4	1.5–1.8 m	0.43 m	0.35 m	6–10	24–40
Deir el-Bachit	8 × 5 m + 3 × 5 m + 5 × 6 m (85 m²)	6	1.6–1.7 m	–	–	7–10	42–60
Deir Anba Hadra	17 × 8 m (136 m²)	8?	1.55–2.1 m	–	–	8–12	64–96

The Kitchen

Among the multiple activity areas, the kitchen, usually quite a sizeable room, was devoted to food preparation. The central kitchen served as an effective solution for cooking the coenobites' meals, leaving the cook's great influence on shaping the taste of the community.[59] The *Rules of Pachomius* forbade cooked meals being prepared outside the cloister, and everyone had to consume the same meal.[60] It is not, however, clear how general the different, rather strict rules were, and to what extent they were actually followed. The Canons of Shenoute, for example, restricted the consumption of cooked food to once per week.[61]

At Tell Bi'a, the refectory and the kitchen were connected by a corridor (Figs 7.4–7.5), which ran between the central and the northern courts. Its original brick pavement is now lost. At the north-eastern part of the room, two hollows are visible in the crude floor screed, which may have been used for the setting of large water containers. The kitchen, lying 0.5 m deeper, was accessible by a staircase and only a few traces of the original baked-brick floor pavement survive. The room itself is 7 by 7 m; its shape, however, is not a regular square.

---

[59] On the role of cooks shaping monastic taste, see Brooks Hedstrom, 'Monks Baking Bread', especially p. 185.

[60] *Rules of Pachomius* 80 and 35 (translation in Veilleux, *Pachomian Koinonia II*, pp. 159 and 151). See also Brooks Hedstrom, 'Monks Baking Bread'. I refer here to the Egyptian canons, because the Syrian canons say little about food regulations, except for the prohibition of consuming wine; see, for example, the Canons of Rabbula, rule 4 (Vööbus, *History of Asceticism*, vol. 3, p. 71).

[61] Layton, *The Canons of Our Fathers*, p. 52 (Rule 179).

The prominent feature of the south-eastern side of the room is the round bread oven, circa 3 m in diameter, which stood on a 0.6 m high brick socket (Fig. 7.7). The oven was laid immediately under the surface, and thus only the base of its baking surface, made from large-sized gravel, has survived. Its wall was built with roof tiles (*tegulae*) and fragments of baked bricks. The direction of the opening could not be determined, and its covering was probably beehive shaped. This type of oven is well known from Palestine (e.g., Khirbet ed-Deir),[62] but is found in Egypt, as well.[63] In terms of function, it was used for baking bread in large quantities.

At least three further baking and cooking furnishings were brought to light in the kitchen (Fig. 7.7). Immediately next to the large oven, an open fireplace suitable for cooking (0.8 by 0.8 m) and a tannur-like round oven (0.7 m in diameter),[64] with thin walls and sunk 0.2 m into the ground, were discovered. A third, pear-shaped oven, also sunk into the ground, stood at the western side of the room. As indicated by traces on the floor, a rectangular, inbuilt platform stood at the north-western corner, the material of which (stone or baked bricks) were removed long ago.

Fig. 7.7. The kitchen from the north.

[62] Hirschfeld, 'The Architectural Remains', pp. 74–6, figs 118–20. Compare the intact sixth-century domed oven of the St Catherine monastery in Sinai (Forsyth and Weitzmann, *The Monastery of St. Catherine*, pl. 22A–B.)

[63] On Egyptian bread ovens, see Brooks Hedstrom, 'Monks Baking Bread', pp. 197–204.

[64] Oven type Ia in Depraetere, 'A Comparative Study', pp. 121–2, fig. 1.

Additionally, a working surface or another cooking place may also have been erected in here. There are no traces that grinding occurred in the kitchen; instead, this procedure was most probably performed in a room lying southwards from the central court. The simultaneous use of the oven and the tannur suggests that the monks consumed different types of bread: flatbread and leavened bread. This is unsurprising, since bread constituted the most basic food product.[65]

The 1.1 m thick walls suggest that the kitchen may have been raised above its surroundings in the same way as a tower, with the large airspace allowing for the diversion of smoke and the supply of fresh air. This prominent architecture created a strong, clearly visible signal regarding the importance of the refectory–kitchen wing: along with the church and the tower, this part of the building complex was elevated above the surrounding flat-roofed rooms.

Water Supply and Irrigation

The water used for cleaning the kitchen was diverted through an enclosed pipe, sunk into the floor. The water-supply of the kitchen, as well as that of the whole building, was provided by rainwater, carefully collected in cisterns. One such cistern was constructed under the tower, standing east from the refectory, which collected the water flowing down from the roof of the north-eastern part of the cloister and from the northern court, by means of a drainpipe sunk into the pavement (Fig. 7.8). The location of the cistern under a tower was similar to that of the upper cistern at Khirbet ed-Deir.[66]

A drainpipe, leading from the central court, diverted water outside from the building, possibly to a cistern that was used for the irrigation of the garden. In the case of Tell Bi'a, the possible terraces on the slope of the hill were already completely demolished by erosion, but in the Palestinian monasteries watered gardens and the cisterns and water channels belonging to them are easily recognisable.[67] Another type of irrigation system is shown by ceramics that reflect an Egyptian influence: qawadi-pots, which were found in large numbers. They may have been used with a saqqiya-type water-lifting device, as was

---

[65] On the importance of bread baking in monastic contexts, see Hirschfeld, *The Judean Desert Monasteries*, pp. 85–6. Compare *Rules of Pachomius* 116–17; translation in Veilleux, *Pachomian Koinonia II*, p. 163.
[66] Hirschfeld, 'The Architectural Remains', pp. 59–62, fig. 43 and 87–91.
[67] Hirschfeld, *The Judean Desert Monasteries*, pp. 105–7 and 148–61.

Fig. 7.8. Aqueduct of the northern court and the cistern under the tower.

the case in the Egyptian examples.[68] These devices suggest a water canal system, which led the water of natural ambient rivers, in this case the Balikh River, to the fields. Later Arabian sources commemorate the flourishing gardens and water channels of the monasteries near Raqqa, such as Tell Bi'a.[69]

Storage

Inbuilt elements shed considerable light on the different means and spaces of storage, especially at the units lying north from the church (Fig. 7.2). Room 49 yielded a large, round, free-standing silo, 3 m in diameter, and two further, smaller sized round silos built against the wall. Inbuilt bins of different sizes are also characteristic elements (Rooms 27 and 32), which are similar to those discovered at Deir el-Bachit.[70] The high number of complete and fractured amphorae indicate the volume of wine and oil stored here.

---

[68] On qawadi-pot use, see Winlock and Crum, *The Monastery of Epiphanius*, pp. 64–5, pl. XVIII. In the ceramic study of the Deir el-Bachit monastery, Beckh, *Zeitzeugen aus Ton*, pp. 47–8, suggests the multifunctionality of this type of pot, but notes that originally they were used as parts of water wheels.

[69] Krebernik, 'Schriftfunde', pp. 51–7.

[70] Eichner and Fauerbach, 'Die spätantike/koptische Klosteranlage', pp. 149–50.

Discussion and Conclusion

Though we have no direct written sources about the economy of Tell Bi'a, as survives in the papyrological record for its Egyptian counterparts, the canons and lives of saints refer to the lands, gardens, handcrafting, and trading activities of Syrian communities.[71] Similarly to Palestine and Egypt, in Syria the originally small eremitic groups started to grow during the fifth century, and the financial status of the large and most populous monasteries changed as a result of the spread of coenobitism and its growing popularity. With the consolidation of coenobitism, and with the help of the wealth and donations of the novices, the small, mostly poor communities became strong economic centres. For the maintenance of the communities, which often housed more than a hundred people, a steady source of income was provided by multiple sources: pilgrims and travellers, as well as the products and incomes of the gardens, orchards, plantations, fields, and herds.[72] The Canons of Rabbula consider it obvious that work in the gardens and the fields belonged to the daily routine of the Syrian coenobitic monks. They also permitted business activity, if it was to satisfy their own needs, but only if it occurred outside of the monastery.[73] A flourishing economy is indicated in the architecture of Syrian monasteries, whose building complexes were similar in appearance to palaces, and which were made affordable through generous donations.[74]

The archaeological remains of the Tell Bi'a monastery suggest a well-organised economic and social unit that suited the coenobitic lifestyle, which became common in the fifth to sixth centuries. The community's population would have been between forty-eight and sixty-four persons, as indicated by the refectory. This figure places it among the moderately larger of the Syrian monasteries. According to Yizhar Hirschfeld, in the case of Palestinian monasteries, there lived an average of twenty monks in

---

[71] On the economic life of the early monasteries, see Brenk, 'Monasteries as Rural Settlements', pp. 455–60. For Palestine, see Hirschfeld, *The Judean Desert Monasteries*, pp. 102–11.

[72] Vööbus, *History of Asceticism*, vol. 2, pp. 140–6. Against this growing wealth came opposition from critics, who were mainly against the personal properties and business operations of the monks, which detracted them from their original goal, the spiritual life. Alexander, a member of an important new trend, tried to reset the old poverty, prohibiting personal property and the work monks could undertake. Consequently, different wings of coenobitism came to life in Syria; see Vööbus, *History of Asceticism*, vol. 2, pp. 146–58. In light of later events, it is obvious that this return to poverty was practised by a minority only.

[73] Canons of Rabbula, rules 6, 7, 10, 11 (Vööbus, *History of Asceticism*, vol. 3, pp. 71–3).

[74] Vööbus, *History of Asceticism*, vol. 2, p. 145. Sometimes, the emperors and the members of the royal family aided the construction works. For donations to monasteries, see Vööbus, *History of Asceticism*, vol. 2, pp. 173–6.

smaller, fifty in medium, and 150 in large communities.[75] This was probably the case with the Syrian monasteries as well, though the written sources only mention the outstandingly large ones.[76]

The floor space of the Tell Bi'a monastery was rather large (approximately 4,800 m^2) compared to other known complexes. It was twice the size of Qasr el-Banat (circa 2,300 m^2), which also belonged to the larger buildings,[77] and was not much smaller than the biggest Palestinian monasteries, namely Martyrius (5,200 m^2) and Theodosius (7,000 m^2), excluding their hostelries.[78] However, Tell Bi'a's refectory (in the last period 54.5 m^2) was significantly smaller than, for example, Martyrius (318 m^2), which furthermore had two storeys. Similar differences occur in the case of the kitchen, which was 49 m^2 at Tell Bi'a and 126 m^2 at Martyrius, again with two storeys.[79]

Tell Bi'a is located in fertile territory. In particular, the choice of the top of the mound for its construction suggests that the building complex was surrounded by gardens and orchards, which provided vegetables and fruits for daily meals. This assumption is confirmed by the fact that they collected rainwater and stored it in cisterns, using it in part to water the gardens, as well as the presence of qawadi-pots, which suggest the use of irrigation canals.

It is impossible to determine how much income their own work and the leased lands generated, because the extent of Tell Bi'a's landowning is unknown. According to the storage capacity, we can suggest that the fields of the monastery were considerable. Without the key data, though, we can only talk about a minimum amount, because the majority of the storage buildings are located in the area of the complex that was not excavated. If we reconstruct the larger, 3 m wide silo of Room 49 to 2 m in height, then it alone could store 14,000 litres of grain. The bins and amphorae also suggest a surplus. The monastery could complement its income with handcraft and trade – the sources also mention business activities involving the local population. The pottery and glass vessels found at the site probably derived from exchanges with the local communities.[80]

---

[75] Hirschfeld, *The Judean Desert Monasteries*, pp. 78–9.
[76] In the middle of the fifth century in Qartmīn (Tur Abdin), 400 monks lived in numerous separate units, while in Apamea (western Syria) 400 monks lived in two monasteries (Hawkins, Mundell, and Mango, 'The Mosaics', p. 279). At another time, also at Apamea, a community of 250 people is mentioned (Patrich, *Sabas*, p. 25).
[77] After the layout published by Butler, *Early Churches*, pp. 93–4, ill. 96.
[78] See Hirschfeld, *The Judean Desert Monasteries*, p. 49, table 3. As mentioned at the beginning of this chapter, it is possible that there was a hostelry on the unexcavated north-eastern side of Tell Bi'a.
[79] See Hirschfeld, *The Judean Desert Monasteries*, p. 49, table 3. There is no comparable data from Syria.
[80] The glass vessels were probably used during the Eucharist, as the sherds mostly came from the service rooms north of the church. On handcraft, see Brenk, 'Monasteries as Rural Settlements', p. 448.

The building of the complex was most probably not financed from the income of the monastery. For example, the church and its mosaics were most likely financed by rich donors, which seems to be confirmed by the Greek inscription on the first mosaic (509) of the church's anteroom (narthex). During the second building phase (595), the new mosaic floor of the sanctuary may also have been renewed from donations. This mosaic stands out not only because of its fine depictions, but by the use of gold-covered tesserae. The mosaic of one of the burial chapels south from the church also suggests that the donators were the inhabitants of Callinicum, who were buried here.[81]

Concerning the monastery's external contacts, and its place in a wider network, key information is provided primarily by the complex's architecture. While the church layout and written sources make it clear that this was a Syrian Orthodox community, the original architectural plan points to Palestinian contacts. During the middle of the sixth century, changes implemented in the refectory (six and later two further circular benches) followed Egyptian antecedents. We do not, however, know much about the details of the connections. The textual sources suggest that some monks came from Egypt to Syria,[82] while Syrian monks visited the burials of Egyptian saints, and translated Egyptian literature into Syriac.[83] However, these connections in Tell Bi'a, due to the paucity of its material culture, are barely traceable. The only exceptions are the qawadi-pots, which are distinctly of Egyptian character.

Despite the rules surrounding dining, which were stricter than those in Egypt, the complex furnishings of the kitchen (Fig. 7.9) reveal that written sources present an idealised picture of food consumption in the monastery.[84] As Mary Harlow and Wendy Smith have made clear in this regard,[85] compared to the 'frugal' consumption of Colin Walters,[86] the botanical finds reflect a multi-coloured picture in Egypt.[87] Darlene Brooks Hedstrom demonstrates

---

[81] The inscriptions of the first mosaic mention Orestas and Kyros in a central position between two bird figures. The leaders of the monastery were mentioned on a Syrian inscription on a *tabula ansata*. For the inscriptions, see Krebernik, 'Schriftfunde', pp. 41–51. For the mosaics, see Kalla, 'Das ältere Mosaik', and Kalla, 'Christentum', pp. 135–41.

[82] For example, Alexander Akoimetos, an Anatolian monk of great influence, was followed by monks speaking four different languages (Syrian, Greek, Latin, Egyptian) to his newly founded community (see Vööbus, *History of Asceticism*, vol. 2, pp. 187–8 and 193). Egyptian monks also arrived at the famous monastery of Qartmin (see Vööbus, *History of Asceticism*, vol. 2, p. 227).

[83] The Syrian sources do not mention the financial background of these pilgrim routes.

[84] Brenk, 'Monasteries as Rural Settlements', pp. 448–50.

[85] Harlow and Smith, 'Between Fasting and Feasting'.

[86] Walters, *Monastic Archaeology*, pp. 205–17.

[87] No carbonised seeds or other visible botanical remains were found on the excavations of Tell Bi'a. As a consequence of the constant and exhaustive cleaning of the refectory and the kitchen with water, such finds were not even expected in the first place. The monastery's dining trash was moved to a garbage dump outside the excavated area.

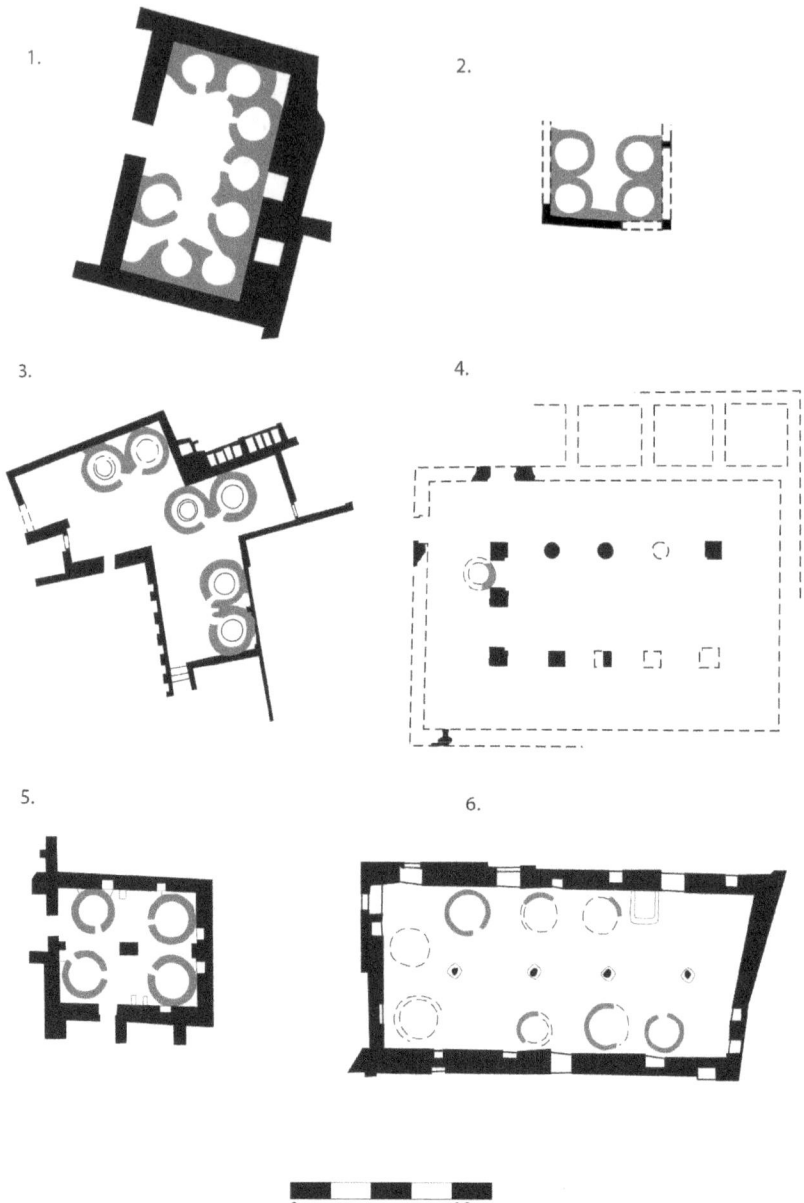

Fig. 7.9. The refectories with circular benches. 1. Tell Bi'a; 2. Apa Jeremiah/Saqqara; 3. Deir el-Bakhit; 4. Apa Shenute/Sohag; 5. Qasr el-Wizz; 6. Deir Anba Hadra (Drawing: Fruzsina Németh).

the importance of combining written sources with archaeology in order to identify taste differences among distinct monasteries.[88] Lacking adequate

[88] Brooks Hedstrom, 'Monks Baking Bread'.

amounts of data, we cannot provide such a detailed account of the local taste at Tell Bi'a. However, furnishings apt for multiple culinary processes, as well as the character of the infrastructure, clearly suggest that the monastic diet varied between 'fasting and feasting' in Syria, just as it did elsewhere.

The investigation of the Tell Bi'a monastery provides a much more vivid picture of the climax of Syrian monasticism than has previously been possible, offering an insight into monastic economy and details of daily life. It was the first site in Syria where a refectory and kitchen – the central elements of monastic households – were excavated. According to these data, it is possible to estimate the size of the community, and to draw a picture about the complexity of its dining customs. The most significant indicator of the economic prosperity is its architecture and decoration;[89] the white painted mudbrick walls of Tell Bi'a were especially spectacular. Though the church was built and decorated from donations, the building of the extended complex also went with considerable expenses, which the community was able to cover on the basis of its own wealth.

Bibliography

al-Khalaf, M. and Kohlmeyer, K. 'Untersuchungen zu ar-Raqqa-Nikephorion – Callinicum', *Damaszener Mitteilungen*, 2 (1985), 133–62.

Beckh, T. *Zeitzeugen aus Ton. Die Gebrauchskeramik der Klosteranlage Deir el-Bachît in Theben-West (Oberägypten)* (Berlin: de Gruyter, 2013).

Bell, G. *The Churches and Monasteries of the Tur 'Abdīn*, 2nd edition, with an introduction and notes by Marlia Mundell Mango (London: Pindar Press, 1982).

Blanke, L. *An Archaeology of Egyptian Monasticism: Settlement, Economy and Daily Life at the White Monastery Federation* (New Haven: Yale Egyptological Publications, 2019).

Brenk, B. 'Frühes Mönchtum in Syrien aus archäologischer Sicht' in E. M. Ruprechtsberger (ed.), *Syrien. Von den Aposteln zu den Kalifen* (Mainz: von Zabern, 1993), pp. 66–81.

Brenk, B. 'Monasteries as Rural Settlements: Patron-Dependence or Self-Sufficiency?' in W. Bowden, L. Lavan, and C. Machado (eds.), *Recent Research on the Late Antique Countryside* (Leiden: Brill, 2004), pp. 447–76.

Brooks Hedstrom, D. 'Redrawing a Portrait of Egyptian Monasticism' in D. Blanks, M. Fressetto, and A. Livingstone (eds.) *Medieval Monks and Their World:*

---

[89] See Brenk, 'Monasteries as Rural Settlements', p. 449.

Ideas and Realities. Studies in Honor of Richard E. Sullivan (Leiden: Brill, 2006), pp. 11–34.

Brooks Hedstrom, D. 'Monks Baking Bread and Salting Fish: An Archaeology of Early Monastic Taste' in S. Ashbrook Harvey and M. Mullett (eds.) *Knowing Bodies, Passionate Souls: Sense Perceptions in Byzantium* (Washington, DC: Dumbarton Oaks, 2017), pp. 183–206.

Butler, H. C. *Early Churches in Syria: Fourth to Seventh Centuries* (Princeton: Department of Art and Archaeology of Princeton University, 1929).

Depraetere, D. 'A Comparative Study on the Construction and the Use of the Domestic Bread Oven in Egypt during the Graeco-Roman and Late Antique/Early Byzantine Period', *Mitteilungen des Deutschen Archäologischen Instituts. Abteilung Kairo*, 58 (2002), 119–56.

Eichner, I. 'Aspekte des Alltagslebens im Paulskloster (Deir el-Bachît) von Theben-West / Oberägypten anhand archäologischer Belege' in F. Daim and J. Drauschke (eds.), *Hinter den Mauern und auf dem offenen Land: Leben im Byzantinischen Reich* (Heidelberg: Römisch-Germanisches Zentralmuseum, 2016), pp. 159–70.

Eichner, I. and Fauerbach, U. 'Die spätantike/koptische Klosteranlage Deir el-Bachit in Dra' Abu el-Naga (Oberägypten). Zweiter Vorbericht', *Mitteilungen des Deutschen Archäologischen Instituts, Abteilung Kairo*, 61 (2005), 139–52.

El-Sayed, R. and El-Masry, Y. (eds.) *Athribis I, General Site Survey 2003–2007. Archaeological and Conservation Studies: The Gate of Ptolemy IX: Architecture and Inscriptions* (Cairo: Institut français d'archéologie orientale, 2012).

Elter, R. and Hassoune, A. 'Le complexe du bain du monastère de Saint Hilarion à Umm el-'Amr, première synthèse architecturale', *Syria*, 85 (2008), 129–44.

Forsyth, G. H. and Weitzmann, K. *The Monastery of St. Catherine at Mount Sinai: The Church and Fortress of Justinian* (Ann Arbor: University of Michigan Press, 1973).

Fuller, M. and Fuller, N. 'A Medieval Church in Mesopotamia', *Biblical Archaeologist*, 57.1 (1994), 38–45.

Fuller, M. and Fuller, N. 'Archaeological Discoveries at Tell Tuneinir, Syria', *Journal of Assyrian Academic Studies*, 12 (1998), 69–82.

Grossmann, P. *Christliche Architektur in Ägypten* (Leiden, Boston, MA, and Cologne: Brill, 2002).

Grossmann, P. and Severin, H.-G. 'Reinigungsarbeiten im Jeremiaskloster bei Saqqara. 4. vorläufiger Bericht', *Mitteilungen des Deutschen Archäologischen Instituts, Abteilung Kairo*, 38 (1982), 155–93.

Habas, L. 'The Marble Furniture' in Y. Hirschfeld (ed.), *The Early Byzantine Monastery at Khirbet Ed-Deir in the Judean Desert: The Excavations in 1981–1987* (Jerusalem: Hebrew University of Jerusalem, 1999), pp. 119–32.

Hachlili, R. *Ancient Mosaic Pavements: Themes, Issues, and Trends* (Leiden and Boston, MA: Brill, 2008).

Harlow, M. and Smith, W. 'Between Fasting and Feasting: The Literary and Archaeobotanical Evidence for Monastic Diet in Late Antique Egypt', *Antiquity*, 75 (2001), 758–68.

Hawkins, E. J. W., Mundell, M. C., and Mango, C. 'The Mosaics of the Monastery of Mār Samuel, Mār Simeon, and Mār Gabriel near Kartmin', *Dumbarton Oaks Papers*, 27 (1973), 279–96.

Hecht, K. 'Calefactorium' in *Reallexikon zur Deutschen Kunstgeschichte, Bd. III* (Stuttgart: A. Druckenmüller, 1952), pp. 308–12

Hirschfeld, Y. *The Judean Desert Monasteries in the Byzantine Period* (New Haven and London: Yale University Press, 1992).

Hirschfeld, Y. 'The Architectural Remains of the Monastery' in Y. Hirschfeld (ed.), *The Early Byzantine Monastery at Khirbet Ed-Deir in the Judean Desert: The Excavations in 1981–1987* (Jerusalem: Hebrew University of Jerusalem, 1999), pp. 9–96.

Kalla, G. 'Das ältere Mosaik des byzantinischen Klosters in Tall Bi'a', *Mitteilungen der Deutschen Orient-Gesellschaft*, 123 (1991), 35–9.

Kalla, G. 'Christentum am oberen Euphrat. Das byzantinische Kloster von Tall Bi'a', *Antike Welt*, 30.2 (1999), 131–42.

Kalla, G. 'Das Refektorium und die Küche des byzantinischen Klosters in Tall Bi'a' (Syrien)' in G. Kovács (ed.), *'Quasi liber et pictura'. Studies in honour of András Kubinyi on his Seventieth Birthday* (Budapest: Eötvös Loránd University, 2004), pp. 257–64.

Kalla, G. 'A Holy Place from Mudbrick. The Sixth-Century Church in the Monastery of Tall Tall Bi'a, Syria', *ARAM Periodical*, 30 (2018), 147–60.

Krebernik, M. 'Schriftfunde aus Tall Bi'a 1990', *Mitteilungen der Deutschen Orient-Gesellschaft*, 123 (1991), 41–70.

Krebernik, M. and Strommenger, E. '1980–1995: Tuttul (Tall Bī'a). Ausgrabungen in der Stadt des Gottes Dagan' in G. Wilhelm (ed.), *Zwischen Tigris und Nil* (Mainz: Zabern, 1998), pp. 126–37.

Lassus, J. *Sanctuaires chrétiens de Syrie* (Paris: Geuthner, 1947).

Layton, B. *The Canons of Our Fathers: Monastic Rules of Shenoute* (Oxford: Oxford University Press, 2014).

Magen, Y. and Talgam, S. 'The Monastery of Martyrius at Ma'ale Adummim (Khirbet el-Muraṣṣaṣ) and Its Mosaics' in G. C. Bottini, L. di Segni, and E. Alliata (eds.), *Christian Archaeology in the Holy Land: New Discoveries* (Jerusalem: Franciscan Printing Press, 1990), pp. 91–152.

Menze, V. 'The Regula ad Diaconos: John of Tella, His Eucharistic Ecclesiology and the Establishment of an Ecclesiastical Hierarchy in Exile', *Oriens Christianus*, 90 (2006), 44–90.

Miglus, P. A. and Strommenger, E. *Stadtbefestigungen, Häuser und Tempel. Ausgrabungen in Tall Bi'a / Tuttul VIII* (Saarbrücken: Saarbrücker Druckerei und Verlag, 2002).

Müller, M. (ed.) *Household Studies in Complex Societies: (Micro)Archaeological and Textual Approaches* (Chicago: The Oriental Institute, 2015).

Obłuski, A. *The Monasteries and Monks of Nubia* (Warsaw: Taubenschlag Press, 2019).

Orlandos, A. K. Μοναστηριακή αρχιτεκτονική, 2nd edition (Athens: Estia Publication, 1958).

Palmer, A. *Monks and Masons on the Tigris Frontier* (Cambridge: Cambridge University Press, 1990).

Patrich, J. *Sabas, Leader of Palestinian Monasticism. A Comparative Study in Eastern Monasticism, Fourth to Seventh Centuries* (Washington, DC: Dumbarton Oaks, 1995).

Peña, I. *The Christian Art of Byzantine Syria* (Reading: Garnet, 1996).

Peña, I., Castellana, P., and Fernandez, R. *Les reclus syrien. Recherches sur les anciennes formes de vie solitaire en Syrie* (Jerusalem: Franciscan Printing Press, 1980).

Popović, S. 'The Trapeza in Cenobitic Monasteries: Architectural and Spiritual Contexts', *Dumbarton Oaks Papers*, 52 (1998), 281–303.

Popović, S. 'Dividing the Indivisible: The Monastery Space – Secular and Sacred', *Recueil des travaux de l'Institut d'études byzantines*, 44 (2007), 47–65.

Roux, G. 'Tables chrétiennes en marbre découvertes à Salamine' in *Salamine de Chypre IV: Anthologie Salaminienne* (Paris: de Boccard, 1973), pp. 133–96.

Scanlon, G. T. 'Excavations at Kasr el-Wizz: A Preliminary Report I', *The Journal of Egyptian Archaeology*, 56 (1970), 29–57.

Scanlon, G. T. 'Excavations at Kasr el-Wizz: A Preliminary Report. Part II: The Monastery', *The Journal of Egyptian Archaeology*, 58 (1972), 7–42.

Strzygowski, J. 'Der sigmaförmige Tisch und der älteste Typus des Refektoriums', *Wörter und Sachen*, 1 (1909), 70–80.

Talbot, A-M. 'Byzantine Monastic Horticulture: The Textual Evidence' in A. Littlewood, H. Maguire, and J. Wolschke-Bulmahn (eds.), *Byzantine Garden Culture* (Washington, DC: Dumbarton Oaks, 2002), pp. 37–67.

Tchalenko, G. *Villages antiques de la Syrie du Nord*, 3 vols (Paris: Geuthner, 1953–8).

Thomas, J. and Hero, A. C. (eds.) *Byzantine Monastic Foundation Documents I* (Washington, DC: Dumbarton Oaks, 2000).

Van Rompay, L. and Innemée, K. 'La présence des syriens dans le Wadi al-Natrun, Egypte: à propos des découvertes récentes de peintures et de textes muraux dans l'église de la Vierge du couvent des syriens', *Parole de l'Orient*, 23 (1998), 167–202.

Veilleux, A. *Pachomian Koinonia. Vol. II: Pachomian Chronicles and Rules* (Kalamazoo: Cistercian Publications, 1981).

Vööbus, A. *History of Asceticism in the Syrian Orient. A Contribution to the History of Culture in the Near East*, 3 vols (Leuven: Peeters, 1958–88).

Walters C. C. *Monastic Archaeology in Egypt* (Warminster: Aris & Phillips, 1974).

Wilk, R. R. and Rathje, W. L. 'Household Archaeology', *American Behavioral Scientist*, 25.6 (1982), 617–39.

Wilkinson, T. J. *Archaeological Landscapes of the Near East* (Tucson: The University of Arizona Press, 2003).

Winlock, H. E. and Crum, W. E. *The Monastery of Epiphanius at Thebes, Part I: The Archaeological Material; The Literary Material* (New York: Metropolitan Museum of Art, 1926).

8 | It's a Dung Job: Exploring Fuel Disc Production in Egyptian Monasteries

MENNAT-ALLAH EL DORRY

Introduction

Fuel is one of the most basic commodities needed by humans. Throughout Egypt's history, different types of fuel were available. Wood (or charcoal), by-products of plant processing (such as straw after cereals are cleaned), production wastes (from, for example, grape or oil-pressing), and wild vegetation were commonly utilised as fuel. But, above all, animal dung was the most common fuel in the past.

Although animal dung fuel is argued to be among the preferred forms of fuel for ancient societies, a thorough investigation of its history and economy in Egypt is still lacking. The present contribution will review the history of this class of fuel in Egypt, with a focus on its production and use in Coptic monasteries. While a modest amount of knowledge has come to us through Coptic literary and documentary sources, ethnographic and archaeological evidence provides additional information that forms a more complete picture for this first assessment of the exploitation of animal dung as fuel.

Fuel Choices and Favouring Animal Dung

The choice of fuel depends on multiple factors. In arid environments, wood is scarce, and if present, its exploitation as timber is preferred. In such environments, shrubs and bushes, which have small twigs that are ideal for lighting small fires (such as campfires), can be used alongside other fuels. Wild vegetation, when dried, burns up quickly and provides efficient kindling for fires. Crop-processing wastes, for example cereal straw and the weeds growing among crops, or in modern times the sheaths and cobs of corn, cottonwood, and sugarcane stalks, are an excellent source of kindling or as complementary fuels in agricultural societies.¹ Olive pressings, and to a lesser degree grape pressings, can also be exploited as fuel where olive oil or wine are produced.² Where wood supply is sparse, dung fuel is a convenient and effective fuel, especially in agricultural and rural societies in which animal husbandry forms an important part of daily life.³ Very often, fires may include more than one type of fuel.⁴ The choice of fuel would be dictated by availability, but may also be influenced by the burning properties of each type of fuel.

Animal dung is a multipurpose commodity. In addition to being a very important source of fertiliser in Egypt,⁵ it can be employed in the construction and repairs of structures,⁶ in the making of mudbricks,⁷ and in controlling oxygen-flow through ovens by sealing holes.⁸ It can be used for tempering ceramics,⁹ possibly even in the glazing of faience.¹⁰ The inclusion of dung in ancient Egyptian medicinal recipes and in Coptic magical and alchemical manuscripts is also attested. In these texts, excrement from a wide range of animals was exploited.¹¹

Fuel discs made of cattle dung provide a cheaply produced and easily stored fuel that emits a high and steady heat when burnt, which means that the fire can be left unattended while carrying out other tasks.¹² Dung discs emit relatively little smoke and can be used alongside other forms of fuel.¹³ Animal dung can be used as fuel for domestic cooking installations;¹⁴

---

[1] Crop-processing wastes may also be used in non-agricultural societies, in which chaff may be traded on its own as an independent commodity; see Bagnall, *Egypt in Late Antiquity*, p. 156; van der Veen, 'Economic Value of Chaff'.
[2] Foxhall, 'Snapping Up the Unconsidered Trifles'; Miller, 'Sweeter than Wine'; Smith, 'Fuel for Thought'.
[3] Charles, 'Fodder from Dung'; Miller and Smart, 'Intentional Burning of Dung'.
[4] Smith, 'Fuel for Thought'; Zapata Peña *et al.*, 'Wood and Dung as Fuel'.
[5] Foaden and Fletcher, *Text-book of Egyptian Agriculture, vol. 1*, p. 241.
[6] In southern Kenya: Shahack-Gross, 'Herbivorous Livestock Dung', p. 212. In Egypt, I have personally observed this in the eastern Delta.
[7] Marinova *et al.*, 'Plant Economy'.
[8] van der Spek, *The Modern Neighbors of Tutankhamun*, p. 265.
[9] Hamdan *et al.*, 'Ancient Egyptian Pottery'. I am grateful for feedback from both Gillian Pyke and Meredith Brand on this point.
[10] Matin and Matin, 'Egyptian Faience Glazing'.
[11] Nunn, *Ancient Egyptian Medicine*; Richter, 'Coptic Alchemical Texts'. I am grateful to Tonio Sebastian Richter for drawing my attention to these Coptic manuscripts.
[12] Lancelotti and Madella, 'The "Invisible" Product', p. 953.
[13] Blackman, *Fellāhīn*, pp. 154–5; Lancelotti and Madella, 'The "Invisible" Product', p. 953; Rizqallah and Rizqallah, *La préparation du pain*, p. 148; Sillar, 'Dung by Preference', p. 46.
[14] Zapata Peña *et al.*, 'Wood and Dung as Fuel', pp. 165–7.

industrial furnaces, for example, for pottery[15] or even for souvenir scarabs in modern Egypt;[16] for public baths;[17] and for heating indoor spaces during winter.[18] Multiple experiments have documented the temperatures of wood- and dung-fuelled fires. While kindling material (such as crop-processing by-products or wild vegetation) light up and burn very quickly, wood produces a hot flame (which can reach up to 900–1,000°C) that lasts longer than kindling and heats ovens quickly.[19] As for dung-fuelled fires, archaeobotanist Delwen Samuel's experiments in Middle Egypt showed that they may reach a maximum of 640°C in twelve minutes, gradually falling to 100°C after forty-six minutes.[20] Further experiments by Freek Braadbaart and colleagues have documented that cow dung may reach 800°C (without specifying how long it took to reach that temperature).[21] It thus proves difficult to generalise when it comes to the temperatures reached by different fuel types. Varying environmental conditions, the amount of moisture in the fuels, and the heating installations (open or closed fires, for example) greatly affect the temperatures of the fire: another study by Ruth Shahack-Gross showed that fresh animal dung burned in open-air fires reached a temperature of 630°C, which did not go below 400°C for some two or three hours after lighting.[22] Additionally, there is often inconsistency in presenting the results of experimental fire lighting, with scholars not always describing the exact conditions, such as the structure of the fire, complimentary fuels used, and whether or not they continued feeding the fire after it was lit.[23] It is evident that there is a real need for more research on the burning properties of the different fuel types that were available in ancient Egypt. Such a study would necessitate ethnographic observations and experimental burning to explore how, and for which purposes, different fuels were used.

---

[15] Zapata Peña *et al.*, 'Wood and Dung as Fuel', pp. 169–71. However, little is known about dung-fuelling pottery kilns in Egypt. Dung fuel was not documented by either Jacques Hivernel or Nessim Henry Henein in their ethnographic accounts of pottery production in Egypt (Hivernel, *Balat*; Henein, *Poterie et potiers*). On this point, I have benefited greatly from discussions with Gillian Pyke and Meredith Brand.

[16] van der Spek, *The Modern Neighbors of Tutankhamun*, p. 265.

[17] Bouchaud, 'Heating the Greek and Roman Baths'.

[18] Rizqallah and Rizqallah, *La préparation du pain*, pl. II.

[19] Stiner *et al.*, 'Differential Burning', p. 227.   [20] Samuel, 'Their Staff of Life', p. 276, table 12.1.

[21] Braadbaart *et al.*, 'Fuel, Fire and Heat'.

[22] Shahack-Gross, 'Herbivorous Livestock Dung', p. 212.

[23] Aldeias, 'Experimental Approaches', p. 194, table 1. Another example of experimental firing that gives a variety of temperatures is Kenoyer, 'Experimental Studies'.

The Use of Animal Dung Fuel in Egypt: An Ethnographic Overview

Animal dung fuel is used worldwide and is an especially common form of fuel in Africa,[24] Asia,[25] South America,[26] and Europe.[27] Its use has been documented in Egypt in multiple ethnographic records. Although the reports mentioned below are not an exhaustive list of animal dung-fuel references in ethnographic literature on Egypt, they present the most prominent and detailed studies. Alexander Henry Rhind (1862) described how women living in Thebes kneaded cattle dung to create fuel cakes.[28] Carl Benjamin Klunzinger, who lived in Egypt in the 1860s and 1870s, noted that it was the chief source of fuel owing to the scarcity of firewood.[29] He documented how young boys tending to the oxen that operated water wheels collected their dung for fuel.[30] He also described how cakes of animal dung were plastered on house walls to dry.[31]

Although not strictly an ethnographic account, a textbook from 1908, written by the agriculturalists George P. Foaden and Fred Fletcher and directed at Egyptian agriculture students, also tackles the topic. The authors assert that 'in every village a considerable proportion of excrement is so employed', but add that only the poorest of classes do so, while the elites used wood.[32] They also added that it was more commonly used in the summer, while maize stalks and cottonwood were used more often in autumn and winter.[33] While they do not cite a reason, it is likely a matter of convenience: in autumn and winter, the maize and cotton harvest has just ended, and much of these crops' wastes are available for use. In the 1920s and 1930s, Winifred Blackman, an Egyptologist/anthropologist, documented the social and religious lives of multiple Middle Egyptian villages. She observed how dung cakes were produced (usually by children)

---

[24] Tunisia: Smith, 'Fuel for Thought'; Morocco: Zapata Peña *et al.*, 'Wood and Dung as Fuel'; Northern Nigeria: Hill, *Rural Hausa*; Portillo *et al.*, 'Domestic Patterns'; South Africa: Becker, *Inland Tribes*.

[25] Uzbekistan: Gur-Arieh *et al.*, 'An Ethnoarchaeological Study of Cooking Installations'; India: Jeffery *et al.*, 'Taking Dung-Work Seriously'; Turkey: Anderson and Ertung-Yaras, 'Fuel, Fodder and Faeces'; Iran: Miller and Smart, 'Intentional Burning of Dung'; Syria: Bottema, 'Composition of Modern Charred Seed Assemblages'; Tibet: Ekvall, *Fields on the Hoof*, pp. 50–1; China (Tibetan and Mongolian deserts): Teichman, *Travels of a Consular Officer*, p. 113.

[26] Peru: Winterhalder *et al.*, 'Dung as an Essential Resource'.

[27] Valamoti, 'Towards a Distinction'. [28] Rhind, *Thebes*, p. 295.

[29] Klunzinger, *Upper Egypt*, p. 144. [30] Klunzinger, *Upper Egypt*, p. 137.

[31] Klunzinger, *Upper Egypt*, p. 124.

[32] Foaden and Fletcher, *Text-book of Egyptian Agriculture*, vol. 1, p. 255.

[33] Foaden and Fletcher, *Text-book of Egyptian Agriculture*, vol. 1, p. 255.

and stored (on roof tops), describing cow dung as the 'ordinary household fuel'.[34] In 1938, the Jesuit Priest, Father Habib Ayrout, published his doctoral dissertation, through which he documented buffalo dung collection (by women or children) and production (in which children were also involved), and described household fires as being a mix of corn stalks and cotton plants, in addition to the dung.[35] Nessim Henry Henein, an architect by training, documented life in the Upper Egyptian village, Mari Girgis, in the 1960s/70s, including the production of dung discs. Here, dung was collected by young girls and formed into discs ca. 25 cm in diameter by the women.[36] Like Klunzinger, he noted that they were plastered on the walls of houses and left to dry.[37] He wrote that the dried discs were considered the best form of fuel, especially for bread.[38] A more bread-specific ethnographic account, also from the 1970s, is by Fawzeya Rizqallah and Kamel Rizqallah.[39] Their work, documenting the production of bread in el-Sharqiyyah governorate in the eastern Delta, provides the most detail on the procurement of dung (whether through women collecting the dung or dung being purchased) and disc production (formed by women into discs of around 40 cm in diameter and 2 cm in thickness).[40] They described the types of dung that were employed (from cows, water buffalos, horses, and donkeys), the tempering needed, the drying process, and the storage.[41] They also described how dung was sold in sets of four cakes, of which five sets (twenty cakes) were needed for each oven firing.[42]

More recently, an Egyptian report estimated that three-quarters of fuel used in rural communities in Egypt largely comprised animal dung and crop-processing wastes (i.e., straw/chaff and contaminating weeds).[43] Animal dung fuel has clearly been a major fuel in Egypt for millennia.

Producing Fuel Discs from Animal Dung

Multiple factors are at play in the choice of which animal species' dung can be used. For example, availability is a key issue: yak dung is used in Tibet;[44] in some parts of the world sheep dung is preferred;[45] and cattle dung may

---

[34] Blackman, *Fellāhīn*, pp. 27–8, 154–5, 211.
[35] Ayrout, *The Egyptian Peasant*, pp. 50–1, 59, 127.   [36] Henein, *Mārī Girgis*, p. 49.
[37] Henein, *Mārī Girgis*, p. 49.   [38] Henein, *Mārī Girgis*, pp. 49, 169.
[39] Rizqallah and Rizqallah, *La préparation du pain*.
[40] Rizqallah and Rizqallah, *La préparation du pain*, p. 11.
[41] Rizqallah and Rizqallah, *La préparation du pain*, pp. 11–12.
[42] Rizqallah and Rizqallah, *La préparation du pain*, pp. 11–12.
[43] Alaa El-Din *et al.*, 'Rural Energy in Egypt'.   [44] Xiao *et al.*, 'Indoor Air Pollution'.
[45] Wallace and Charles, 'What Goes In', p. 19.

also be used where available.[46] In some cases, even dung from wild animals may be used.[47] For fuel resources, the dung from cattle, such as cows, buffalos, and oxen, is generally preferred: as ruminants with four chambered-stomachs, these bovines produce dung that lends itself well to forming porous discs with better burning properties.[48]

In Egypt, according to the aforementioned ethnographic accounts, dung is most often collected by children from where animals are located, whether grazing areas, water wheels, or stables. The excrement is tempered with chaff and other plant material to reach the desired consistency. It is then formed, usually by women, into discs typically between 30 and 40 cm in diameter and a few centimetres in thickness.[49] They are often left to dry in courtyards on a layer of chopped straw to prevent them from sticking to the ground, or they can be plastered onto house walls until they are dry.[50] Drying might require anywhere from a few days to over a week, depending on the season.[51] The discs can then be piled and stored, usually on top of the flat roofs of village houses, until needed. Villagers who do not have access to animals can either resort to buying dung discs or collecting dung of lesser quality, such as that of goats or sheep.[52]

A History of Animal Dung Use in Ancient Egypt

The use of dung as fuel has been documented from sites in Egypt throughout its history. The sources for animal dung in ancient Egypt include archaeobotanical remains, material finds from archaeological sites, and textual evidence.

Animal dung used as fuel has long been seen as the primary source of botanical remains in archaeological contexts.[53] Consequently, many ancient Egyptian sites have evidence of animal dung fuel, often recovered in a charred form from cooking installations. These remains may be in the form of amorphous dung fragments, dung pellets, or fodder remains that

---

[46] Miller and Smart, 'Intentional Burning of Dung'.
[47] Miller, 'Seed Eaters of the Ancient Near East', p. 525.
[48] Wallace and Charles, 'What Goes In', p. 19; Sillar, 'Dung by Preference'.
[49] Blackman, *Fellāhīn*, pp. 154–5; Rizqallah and Rizqallah, *La préparation du pain*, p. 11.
[50] Henein, *Mārī Girgis*, p. 169; Klunzinger, *Upper Egypt*, p. 124; Rizqallah and Rizqallah, *La préparation du pain*, p. 11.
[51] Rizqallah and Rizqallah, *La préparation du pain*, p. 11.
[52] Rizqallah and Rizqallah, *La préparation du pain*, p. 11; van der Spek, *The Modern Neighbors of Tutankhamun*, p. 265.
[53] Charles, 'Fodder from Dung'; Marinova *et al.*, 'Bioarchaeological Research on Animal Dung'; Miller and Smart, 'Intentional Burning of Dung'.

have passed through an animal. Some of these sites stand out and include an Old Kingdom (ca. 2469–2150 BC) settlement in Kom el-Hisn in the western Delta, where wood charcoal was scarce in the samples, whereas dung fragments and fodder species were far greater, pointing to the use of animal dung fuel.[54] Dung, with the occasional piece of wood, was the prominent fuel at Tell el-Maskhuta, east of the Nile Delta (ca. 1640–1550 BC).[55] A storage of unused fuel was recovered from kitchen spaces at Amarna (ca. 1349–1323 BC), including both sheep dung and straw, in addition to what may be dung discs.[56] At Tell el-Retaba in the eastern Delta, which dates to the late New Kingdom/Third Intermediate Period (ca. 1295–712 BC), dung was the dominant fuel for larger heating installations, and cereal processing by-products with some shrubs seem to have been preferred in regular ovens.[57] A more systematic study on the use of fuel from Egypt was carried out by the archaeobotanist Charlène Bouchaud, who investigated the fuelling of Ptolemaic and Roman baths across Egypt. Her results show that fuel selection was dictated by the available natural vegetation and remains of agricultural activities (for example, crop-processing by-products and vine pruning), while animal dung was only used at two sites. The first of these sites is the Ptolemaic baths and Roman Thermae at Karnak, dating to the second century BC and second-to-fourth centuries AD. The second site is the Roman Baths at the fortress of Xeron (first–third centuries AD), where charcoal and camel dung were used as fuel.[58]

As for textual references from ancient Egypt, a few do exist. These include hieratic ostraca mentioning donkey-loads of dung being delivered to Deir el-Medina, which Jaroslav Černý concluded were meant as fuel, as they are often mentioned alongside wood for burning.[59] Another example is a Ramesside ostracon that acknowledges the receipt of rushes and dung followed by two donkey loads of wood.[60] Papyrus Anastasi IV (British Museum EA 10249) mentions dung along with grass as a stored good.[61] A Saite demotic text also mentions the exchange of dung.[62] A later attestation of possible dung transport comes from a Greek text from AD 131, in

---

[54] Moens and Wetterstrom, 'Agricultural Economy'; Wetterstrom and Wenke, 'Kom el-Hisn's Plant Remains'.
[55] Crawford, 'Weeds'. [56] Peet and Woolley, *The City of Akhenaten: Part I*, p. 64.
[57] Malleson, 'Archaeobotanical Investigations at Tell el-Retaba', pp. 194–5.
[58] Bouchaud, 'Heating the Greek and Roman Baths'.
[59] Černý, 'Some Coptic Etymologies', pp. 36–7; Janssen, *Commodity Prices*, pp. 36–7; see also O. DeM 131 in Černý, *Catalogue des ostraca hiératiques*, p. 5, pl. 10.
[60] Caminos, *Late-Egyptian Miscellanies*, p. 167 (citing O.IFAO 101, v° 2–3).
[61] Caminos, *Late-Egyptian Miscellanies*, p. 167. [62] Cruz-Uribe, 'A Saïte Request for Payment'.

which a certain Heron was contracted to transport either dung or perhaps *sebakh*.⁶³ The intended use of this material is not known.

Coptic Textual Evidence

Mentions of animal dung in texts deriving from monastic contexts are uncommon, and often do not indicate its use as fuel. Three Coptic words are used to refer to dung. The first is ϩⲁⲥ (*has*), which refers to animal dung or bird droppings, and is exclusive to medical recipes.⁶⁴ Its use in connection with fuel or economic activity in monasteries is not known to me. The second term, ϩⲟ(ⲉ)ⲓⲣⲉ (*hoeire*),⁶⁵ is etymologically connected to the ancient Egyptian word *Hyrt*, which features regularly in Deir el-Medina ostraca in connection with the delivery of animal dung as part of the village's fuel supply.⁶⁶ ϩⲟ(ⲉ)ⲓⲣⲉ appears commonly in Biblical texts, and its use is not exclusive to animal excrement, but includes human waste as well.⁶⁷ It does not, however, appear in documentary texts, and there is no known link to monastic activities.⁶⁸

The third term is ⲥⲟⲧ (*sot*), which occurs in two different constructions: ⲧⲁⲗⲟ ⲥⲟⲧ, 'dung-lifter' (or loader), and ⲡⲁⲡⲥⲟⲧ, 'the one of the dung'. The first expression appears on a limestone stela from the monastery of Apa Jeremias in Saqqara in reference to a certain 'Paul, who loads dung' (ⲁⲛ[ⲡⲁ] ⲩⲗⲉ ⲉϥⲧⲁⲗⲟ ⲥⲟⲧ).⁶⁹ This entry is part of a list of men, several of whom bear the title 'brother', suggesting that Paul himself was a monk. The appearance of 'the one who loads the dung' among other personnel, such as the one who stokes the oven, the cattle feeder, the one who keeps measure, and the father of laundry, suggests that loading the dung was a specific assignment among tasks that needed to be carried out at the monastery. A manuscript

---

⁶³ Delia, 'Carrying Dung'. *Sebakh* are the decomposed remains of earlier settlements, formed of decayed mudbricks mixed with organic debris resulting from the former exploitations of a particular settlement site.

⁶⁴ Crum, *Coptic Dictionary*, p. 709a–b. I am grateful to Tonio Sebastian Richter for bringing this term to my attention.

⁶⁵ Crum, *Coptic Dictionary*, p. 697b. The word ⲥⲟⲧ also appears in Borgia, *De miraculis Sancti Coluthi*, p. 181.

⁶⁶ Černý, 'Some Coptic Etymologies', pp. 36–7; Černý, *Etymological Dictionary*, p. 291. I am grateful to Arto Belekdanian for his help with the hieratic texts.

⁶⁷ For example, Ez. 4:15, Zeph. 1:17, Lev. 4:11, Is. 30:22; I thank Alain Delattre for discussing these sources with me.

⁶⁸ Alain Delattre kindly confirmed this point, adding that this term is only attested in non-literary sources as part of a toponym.

⁶⁹ Quibell, *Excavations of Saqqara*, p. 72 (no. 227, line 18).

that clearly shos the use of ⲥⲟⲧ as fuel comes from an alchemical manuscript, where a concoction is heated up 'in a tempered fire of dung' (ϩⲛ ⲟⲩⲕⲱϩⲧ ⲉϥⲕⲉⲣⲁ ⲛⲥⲟⲧ).[70]

The second expression, ⲡⲁⲛⲥⲟⲧ, also occurs at the monastery of Apa Jeremias in Saqqara on a limestone stela dedicated to two deceased people.[71] The stela mentions a *papa* Aloudj of the dung' (ⲡⲁⲡⲁ ⲁⲗⲟⲩϫ ⲡⲁⲛⲥⲟⲧ), suggesting again that this task was one undertaken by a monk.[72] A *dipinto* from the same monastery also mentions somebody who is ⲡⲁⲛⲥⲟⲧ, but the name of the individual is lost.[73] Beyond Saqqara, the title occurs in a papyrus from Bawit, *P.Bawit Clackson* 27, probably dating to the eighth century: the monastery's superior orders a certain Apa Johannes to pay Apa Abraham, who is 'of the dung', for an undesignated service. It is possible that the payment was for his services in delivering (or cleaning out) dung.

Another type of dung-related title or task is ⲃⲁⲣⲱϩ (*barôh*).[74] Its exact meaning is disputed, but it seems to refer to a 'cattle-feeder' or 'fodder-seller', who is sometimes also mentioned in connection with dung.[75] Alain Delattre suggests an association between both feeding cattle and collecting their waste. This is further supported by *P.Brux.Bawit* 12, in which the ⲃⲁⲣⲱϩ is said to have transported ⲥⲟⲧ.[76] The same responsibility is perhaps also documented in the abovementioned Greek text, where a man named Heron was contracted to transport either dung or *sebakh*.[77]

The tasks associated with individuals bearing titles derived from ⲥⲟⲧ revolve around dung. Could it have been human dung, indicating that 'he-of-the-dung' (ⲡⲁⲛⲥⲟⲧ) was in charge of cleaning out latrines? Crum states that ϩⲟ(ⲉ)ⲓⲣⲉ refers to either animal or human excrement, but he does not address this point for ⲥⲟⲧ. Nevertheless, the term does not appear in contexts in which it may denote human waste, and it was probably exclusively related to animal dung.[78] The term ⲃⲁⲣⲱϩ, at least, can be securely attributed to animal dung, as it is connected to foddering cattle. On this basis alone, it would appear that dung-related assignments were occasionally part of the repertoire of monastics tasks.

---

[70] Richter, 'Coptic Alchemical Texts'.
[71] According to Wietheger, *Das Jeremias-Kloster zu Saqqara*, p. 312 (no. 25).
[72] Quibell, *Excavations of Saqqara*, p. 94 (no. 302, line 7).
[73] Quibell, *Excavations of Saqqara*, p. 100 (no. 322b, line 1).
[74] Crum, *Coptic Dictionary*, p. 44b; *P.Brux.Bawit* pp. 198–201.   [75] *P.Brux.Bawit* pp. 198–201.
[76] Alain Delattre has kindly brought this reference to my attention.
[77] Delia, 'Carrying Dung'.
[78] Tonio Sebastian Richter and Alain Delattre have kindly discussed this point with me.

Archaeology of Dung-Fuel

Methodological Problems

Identifying dung or dung discs in the archaeological record is fraught with difficulties.[79] They often disintegrate and are not immediately recognisable to the unfamiliar eye. Nevertheless, different modes of analysis can help detect the presence of dung, notably archaeobotanical analysis, which may reveal plant species that are common components of animal feed. These remains often still have bits of dung adhering to their surfaces. Different types of chemical analysis may also be used to identify the presence of dung. One example is phytoliths analysis, which detects animal dung and also identifies the species of animal, as well as their diets.[80] Unless archaeological remains are analysed for plant remains that were once part of the feed, or analysed for isotopes, lipids, aDNA, or other forms of investigative methods, it may be difficult to recognise the presence of dung.[81] With the exception of archaeobotanical analysis, no investigative methods have been undertaken on monastic archaeological sites in Egypt to ascertain the presence and use of animal dung. Much of what is discussed here, therefore, is reliant on what little archaeobotanical analysis has been undertaken, in addition to observing animal dung remains on archaeological sites.

Archaeobotany

Archaeobotanical analysis can aid the identification of the used form of fuel, although with limitations. When fuels, usually wood, vegetable material, or animal dung (or a mix of multiple fuels) are burned, most of them are reduced to ashes. However, some items survive, such as chunks of charcoal, or the sturdy parts of plant remains, such as seeds and twigs.[82] When animal dung is used, parts of the undigested animal fodder and even lumps of dung are often preserved. Therefore, the examination of residues in fireplaces can reveal the types of fuel used. Such examination begins by sieving ashes and deposits from heating contexts using very fine geological sieves with a minimum mesh size of half a millimetre. This size is small enough for fine ash and sand to be separated from any plant remains larger than half a millimetre. These plant remains can then be analysed under

---

[79] Linseele et al., 'Species Identification', pp. 5–6.
[80] Lancelotti and Madella, 'The "Invisible" Product'; Shahack-Gross, 'Herbivorous Livestock Dung', p. 206, especially table 1.
[81] Linseele et al., 'Species Identification'; Shahack-Gross, 'Herbivorous Livestock Dung'.
[82] Hillman, 'Reconstructing Crop Husbandry Practices', p. 131.

a microscope and their species identified. Other relevant items, such as animal dung remains, can also be observed under the microscope. In the case of animal dung fuel, a sample will have both animal dung and plant species that are often part of animal feed.[83] When other forms of fuel are employed, such as crop processing waste or wood, these can also be identified among a sample. As multiple fuels are often simultaneously used, and other non-fuel material also ends up in the fire, isolating individual fuelling episodes may not be straightforward, but it is not impossible.[84]

Animal Dung in Monastic Contexts

Several monastic sites have yielded remains of animal dung, either through archaeobotanical remains that reveal dung and species typical of fodder or through the observation of dung itself. These sites are Deir Anba Hadra in Aswan, the monastery of Apa Jeremias in Saqqara, Kom el-Nana in Middle Egypt (Amarna), and the monastic settlement of John the Little in Wadi el-Natrun.

Deir Anba Hadra on the western bank of the Nile opposite Aswan was first excavated in the 1920s by the Italian architect Ugo Monneret de Villard, and over the last few years the site has been reinvestigated by the Freie Universität of Berlin and the German Archaeological Institute.[85] The monastery's chronology is still under investigation, but it is believed that its earliest history dates to the fourth century AD.[86] The complex includes a church, a keep, and the so-called economic complex, an area with mills, vats, ovens, and other structures related to different crafts and production processes. In this economic area, at least three mills were surrounded by compacted dung layers, partially covered with a stone slab. The tentative interpretation of this configuration is that the animals drawing the mill deposited their excrement while working, which accumulated to a point that it was necessary to place a slab on top of the dung to prevent the animals from getting stuck in their own waste. If this interpretation is correct, it would mean that the dung was, in this context at least, not a valuable enough commodity for the inhabitants of the complex to collect and use elsewhere. Further dung accumulations were found around a stabling area, also in the economic complex near troughs, but

---

[83] See, for example, Wallace and Charles, 'What Goes In'; Valamoti, 'Towards a Distinction'.
[84] Anderson and Ertung-Yaras, 'Fuel, Fodder and Faeces'.
[85] On the renewed work at Deir Anba Hadra, see Krastel, Olschok, and Richter, Chapter 11.
[86] Personal communication from Sebastian Olschok. See also Krastel, Olschok, and Richter, Chapter 11.

a connection with fuel cannot be established here either. The archaeobotanical samples studied from the site so far do not indicate that animal dung was used as fuel: species typical of animal fodder were not found and no charred dung was recovered. This may have more to do with the taphonomic conditions of the site: Monneret de Villard removed most contexts during his excavations and discarded their fill outside the monastic complex. No cooking installations were subsequently recovered with their fill *in situ*, and we therefore cannot estimate the types of fuel that were used.

In the fifth-century AD monastery of Apa Jeremias in Saqqara, a room thought to be a stabling space (Room 1723) was found covered with a layer of dung. Little detail was recorded concerning its size, and further investigations were not carried out to analyse the species of animal(s) or the fodder(s) consumed. Additionally, as with Deir Anba Hadra, dung remains were found around a mill where animals treaded.[87] Whether or not this dung was meant to be used as fuel cannot be ascertained. The contents of the recovered cooking installations were not described in James Edward Quibell's publications of the monastery, and it is impossible to determine whether they contained animal dung fuel.

A more detailed picture of the use of dung fuel is to be found at the fifth-to-seventh-century AD monastic settlement of Kom el-Nana. Here, a round dung disc was recovered from a space identified as an animal stall.[88] Additionally, Wendy Smith, who analysed the archaeobotanical material from the site, concluded that cereal chaff would have been used as fuel alongside animal dung.[89] She noted the presence of compacted vegetal material in some of the ovens, which she identified as herbivore dung.

Another yet more explicit image of animal dung fuel can be obtained from the monastic settlement of John the Little. As part of the Yale Monastic Archaeological Project excavations at the site, a ninth–tenth century residence was excavated, in which seventeen cooking installations were discovered. Two types were found: ovens and *kanuns* (the latter are open-topped stove-like structures).[90] The fuels used in the ovens and *kanuns* form the corpus of archaeobotanical remains recovered from the site. The plant material includes a high number that are typical of fodder, which may have been part of the animal feed and hence the fuel. Given that amorphous lumps of dung were found adhering to the surface of many plant remains, it can be concluded that the material came from animal

---

[87] Quibell, *Excavations of Saqqara*, p. 30.
[88] Smith, *Archaeobotanical Investigations*, p. 41, fig. 3.10.
[89] Smith, *Archaeobotanical Investigations*, p. 41; Smith, 'Fuel for Thought', pp. 194–5.
[90] Pyke and Brooks Hedstrom, 'The Afterlife of Sherds'.

dung. Combined with their discovery in heating installations, this suggests that these amorphous lumps and plant material come from animal dung that was used as fuel. The larger ovens contained more fodder-type plants and animal dung bits than the smaller *kanuns*, which contained more local vegetation. This distinction could indicate that each of the two types of structure, as a result of their diverse purposes, required different fuels. In addition to the archaeobotanical remains, a round disc of about 30 cm was found next to one of the ovens.[91] Dung discs are usually kept within reach of the ovens immediately before being deposited in the fire chamber of a heating installation.[92] This disc was examined for archaeobotanical remains, but it was largely formed of chopped straw, and further analysis of its contents is lacking. In addition to the disc, a space potentially identified as an animal pen (Room 14) had a dung layer covering its floor.[93] The layer, approximately 10 cm thick, was briefly analysed for botanical remains, and proved to be comprised by chaff. Further analysis is still required to ascertain whether or not this dung is the source of the dung fuel used in the ovens. In other words, if the dung cakes were made from this dung, they may have similar contents, unless the fuel-cakes were made using dung from a different season and hence different flora. A local in-house production may be suggested for the excavated residence at the monastic settlement of John the Little: an animal pen had a dung deposit, and dung discs were used as fuel in the nearby heating installations.[94]

Archaeological evidence for the use of dung as fuel elsewhere is more ambiguous. Serge Sauneron mentioned that the heating installations in the Esna hermitages were fuelled with wood and twigs. He presumed that the wood would have been complemented by cow or camel dung, but does not mention the recovery of any dung.[95] A closer inspection of the ash layers from the Esna hermitages would have revealed either archaeobotanical remains associated with dung, or even amorphous fragments that could be identified as such. At Kellia, charcoal and twigs were common in the samples, leading the archaeologists to conclude that they were the chief fuel.[96]

Archaeobotanical analysis in the monastic settlements of John the Little and Kom el-Nana, the only two monastic sites with systematic archaeobotanical sampling, have shown that dung fuel was unequivocally the main

---

[91] El Dorry, 'Monks and Plants', pp. 123–6. I am grateful to Mohamed Khalifa for his valuable input, which confirmed this item as a dung disc.
[92] This was not explicitly mentioned in any of the aforementioned ethnographic accounts, but I have observed this practice in Luxor.
[93] El Dorry, 'Monks and Plants', pp. 123–6.   [94] El Dorry, 'Monks and Plants', pp. 123–6.
[95] Sauneron, *Les ermitages chrétiens*, p. 22.   [96] Weidmann, *Kellia*, p. 437.

fuel source.⁹⁷ At John the Little, the surviving plant materials are predominantly ones that are typically parts of animal feed, and there are large amounts of dung fragments, many of which are less than a centimetre in length.

Economic Value

Animal dung was a steady feature in the everyday economy of villages throughout most of Egypt's history. In an agricultural society such as Egypt, copious amounts of dung were produced by animals, which had to be dealt with somehow. In the first instance, it had to be cleaned up, whether by children in the villages or, in a monastic context, the brethren. Texts from monasteries indicate that individuals among the brethren were assigned with specific dung-related tasks. The presence of titles pertaining to these duties indicates that dung was a commodity that needed to be administered in some manner. The titles also suggest that the dung-related tasks consumed enough time to necessitate dedicated staffing.

In general, villagers with no access to dung could have been provisioned with it, or could have bought it, as textual evidence from ancient Egypt indicates. For example, Deir el-Medina's inhabitants were provisioned with dung among other fuel-stuffs, demonstrating that dung played a part in the trade and economy of these settlements. The economic value of animal dung is further supported by modern ethnographic evidence from el-Sharqiyyah in the eastern Nile Delta, where dung discs were available for purchase in sets of four to be used as fuel. Although the textual data from ancient Egypt is limited to the New Kingdom through to the Hellenistic Period, and the ethnographic data to nineteenth- and twentieth-century Egypt, it is likely that the economic value of animal dung continued for most of Egypt's history. By contrast, the exchange of animal dung as an economic commodity in Egyptian monastic settlements remains unclear.

Once obtained, how dung was used was an important economic decision on the part of cattle owners and farmers. More specifically, the decision to burn dung for fuel required weighing certain economic factors, at the forefront of which is whether or not dung is better used as fertiliser. Although nutrient-rich soil was provided by the annual inundation of the Nile, farmyard manure – including animal dung – still played a key role in fertilisation.⁹⁸ Foaden and Fletcher claim that early twentieth-century

---

[97] El Dorry, 'Monks and Plants', p. 243; Smith, *Archaeobotanical Investigations*; Smith, 'Fuel for Thought'.
[98] Foaden and Fletcher, *Text-book of Egyptian Agriculture, vol. 1*, pp. 236ff.

Egyptian farmers were aware of this loss, but made this difficult economic decision in the absence of better fuel alternatives.[99] This was an economic decision in which more factors may have played a part, and the issue is worthy of further exploration in the future.

What is clear, however, is that animal dung was a main category of fuel at least in the two major monastic sites at which archaeobotanical analysis has been undertaken: the settlements of John the Little and Kom el-Nana. Is there sufficient evidence from monastic settlements to suggest that animal dung, especially fuel discs, played an economic role? Neither dung nor fuel discs are a commodity that appear in receipts to and from monks or monasteries. This absence may suggest that the dung disc was a locally produced and used commodity, one that was not traded between distant sites, requiring documentation of delivery. The presence of titles related to the management of dung resources would conform with this local production scenario. This would be conceivable especially in larger, more communal monasteries in which cattle constituted part of the economy, and their dung would have been available for use by the community. As for monks living in seclusion, the situation remains unclear. Although most of the secluded brethren are said to have sustained themselves on nothing but bread rations and raw vegetables, occasionally they required fuel to cook.[100] How they obtained their fuel is unknown, but local vegetation (whether wild species or wastes of cultivated flora), animal dung, and occasionally wood would have been the only available fuels. An 'in-house' production of dung can therefore be suggested for monasteries, at least for those with a communal lifestyle and landholdings with livestock. This would have necessitated specialist personnel, such as 'he-of-the-dung', those who load dung, or the ⲃⲁⲣⲱϩ, but such titles have rarely left their mark in written documentation. A similar scenario was suggested for the excavated residence at the monastic settlement of John the Little, where dung may have been locally sourced from the animal pen, locally manufactured, and used in the same location.[101]

Conclusion

Little is known about fuel in Egypt in Late Antiquity, and even less is understood about the availability of animal dung for fuel. Ethnographic evidence from Egypt shows that animal dung is a vital form of fuel in rural

---

[99] Foaden and Fletcher, *Text-book of Egyptian Agriculture*, vol. 1, p. 255.
[100] El Dorry, 'Monks and Plants'; Smith, *Archaeobotanical Investigations*.
[101] El Dorry, 'Monks and Plants', pp. 123–6.

societies. The dung, usually collected by children, is shaped by women into discs that provide a slow and steady heat, which does not need to be constantly tended. The use of animal dung as fuel has its history in ancient Egypt, either where multiple sites have yielded textual evidence (such as Deir el-Medina) in support of it or where archaeobotanical evidence proves its use. Evidence from Coptic textual evidence suggests that dung-related tasks (perhaps collection or manufacturing of fuel-discs) was a large enough endeavour to require administering, as evident through titles related to dung. The archaeological and archaeobotanical remains from two monastic sites, Kom el-Nana and John the Little, have proven the use of animal dung as an important fuel source at both settlements.

This first assessment of animal dung fuel in Egyptian monasteries has underlined the importance of exploring the exploitation of this fuel type. Understanding the economic value of animal dung, particularly its use as fuel, is intricately tied with the availability of fuels and an awareness of animal husbandry. On the one hand, the list of fuels available in Egypt is clear: crop processing wastes, wild vegetation, animal dung, and occasionally wood. On the other hand, the availability varies from one site to another, and each monastery may have had different patterns of fuel-usage, depending on accessibility to fuels, which varies seasonally and depending on what needed to be heated. Furthermore, knowing what livestock was present at a given site is necessary, as it provides an idea of what type of animal dung would have been available for fuelling and of the amounts produced. These are the next steps in an assessment of the economics involved with producing and using animal dung discs as fuel.

An examination of the history of agriculture in Egypt, which includes ethnographic accounts of animal and plant husbandry, is also required in order to reconstruct the decision-making process of how animal dung was used. Further to that, experimental burning of different fuels in Egypt is needed. Combined with ethnographic investigations, this would afford a better understanding of which fuels were used and for which purposes.

This review is meant to draw attention to animal dung fuel discs, especially in terms of textual evidence. Greater care is necessary during excavations to observe and identify animal dung in monastic settlements, regardless of whether the dung was used as fuel or not. This approach will allow a wider understanding of animal dung and its exploitation in monasteries. By shedding light on this valuable commodity, which has been almost entirely neglected in studies of the economy and daily life in Egypt. I hope to encourage the collection of further textual, archaeological, and ethnographic data for future work.

Bibliography

Alaa El-Din, M. N., Rizk, I., El-Lakkani, H., Abdel-Nabey, M., El-Sabbah, M., and El-Shimi, S. A. 'Rural Energy in Egypt: A Survey of Resources and Domestic Needs' in Agricultural Research Centre, Alexandria University (ed.), *International Congress on the State of the Art on Biogastechnology, Transfer and Diffusion* (Alexandria: Ministry of Agriculture, 1984), pp. 17–24.

Aldeias, V. 'Experimental Approaches to Archaeological Fire Features and their Behavioural Relevance', *Current Anthropology*, 58.S16 (2017), S191–S205.

Anderson, S. and Ertung-Yaras, F. 'Fuel, Fodder and Faeces: An Ethnographic and Botanical Study of Dung Fuel in Central Anatolia', *Environmental Archaeology*, 1 (1998), 99–109.

Ayrout, H. H. *The Egyptian Peasant* (Cairo: The American University in Cairo Press, 2005).

Bagnall, R. S. *Egypt in Late Antiquity* (Princeton: Princeton University Press, 1993).

Becker, P. *Inland Tribes of Southern Africa* (New York: Granada Publishers, 1979).

Blackman, W. S. *The Fellāhīn of Upper Egypt* (Cairo: American University in Cairo Press, 2000).

Borgia, S., *De miraculis Sancti Coluthi et reliquiis actorum Sancti Panesniu martyrum thebaica fragmenta duo alterum auctius alterum nunc primum ... Accedunt fragmenta varia notis inserta omnia ex Museo Borgiano Veliterno, deprompta et illustrata opera ac studio F. Augustini Antonii Georgii* (Rome: Antonius Fulgonius, 1793).

Bottema, S. 'The Composition of Modern Charred Seed Assemblages' in W. van Zeist and W. A. Casparie (eds.), *Plants and Ancient Man: Studies in Palaeoethnobotany* (Rotterdam: A Balkema, 1984), pp. 207–12.

Bouchaud, C. 'Heating the Greek and Roman Baths in Egypt. Papyrological and Archaeobotanical Data' in B. Redon (ed.), *Collective Baths in Egypt 2. New Discoveries and Perspectives* (Cairo: Institut français d'archéologie orientale, 2017), pp. 323–49.

Braadbaart, F., Poole, I., Huisman, H. D. J., and van Os, B. 'Fuel, Fire and Heat: An Experimental Approach to Highlight the Potential of Studying Ash and Char Remains from Archaeological Contexts', *Journal of Archaeological Science*, 39.4 (2012), 836–47.

Caminos, R. A. *Late-Egyptian Miscellanies* (Oxford: Oxford University Press, 1954).

Černý, J. *Catalogue des ostraca hiératiques non littéraires de Deir el-Médineh* (Cairo: Institut français d'archéologie orientale, 1937).

Černý, J. 'Some Coptic Etymologies' in O. Firchow (ed.), *Ägyptologische Studien: Festschrift Hermann Grapow zum 70. Geburtstag gewidmet* (Berlin: Akademie-Verlag, 1955), pp. 30–7.

Černý, J. *Coptic Etymological Dictionary* (Cambridge: Cambridge University Press, 1976).

Charles, M. P. 'Fodder from Dung: The Recognition and Interpretation of Dung-Derived Plant Material from Archaeological Sites', *Environmental Archaeology*, 1 (1998), 111–22.

Crawford, P. 'Weeds as Indicators of Land-Use Strategies in Ancient Egypt' in K. Neumann, A. Butler, and S. Kahlheber (eds.), *Food, Fuel and Fields. Progress in African Archaeobotany* (Cologne: Heinrich-Barth-Institute, 2003), pp. 107–21.

Crum, W. E. *A Coptic Dictionary* (Oxford: Clarendon Press, 1939).

Cruz-Uribe, E. 'A Saïte Request for Payment', *The Journal of Egyptian Archaeology*, 71 (1985), 129–33.

Delia, D. 'Carrying Dung in Ancient Egypt: A Contract to Perform Work for a Vineyard', *Bulletin of the American Society of Papyrologists*, 23.1–2 (1986), 61–4.

Ekvall, R. B. *Fields on the Hoof: Nexus of Tibetan Nomadic Pastoralism* (New York: Waveland Press Inc, 1983).

El Dorry, M.-A., 'Monks and Plants: A Study of Plant Based Foodways and Agricultural Practices in Egyptian Monasteries', unpublished PhD thesis, University of Münster, 2015.

Foaden, G. P. and Fletcher, F. *Text-book of Egyptian Agriculture*, vol. 1 (Cairo: National Printing Department, 1908).

Foxhall, L. 'Snapping Up the Unconsidered Trifles: The Use of Agricultural Residues in Ancient Greek and Roman Farming', *Environmental Archaeology*, 1 (1998), 35–40.

Gur-Arieh, S., Mintz, E., Boaretto, E., and Shahack-Gross, R. 'An Ethnoarchaeological Study of Cooking Installations in Rural Uzbekistan: Development of a New Method for Identification of Fuel Sources', *Journal of Archaeological Science*, 40.12 (2013), 4331–47.

Hamdan, M. A., Martinez, S. M., Vallès, M. T. G., Nogués, J. M., Hassan, F. A., Flower, R. J., Aly, M. H., Senussi, A., and Ebrahim, E. S. 'Ancient Egyptian Pottery from the Subsurface Floodplain of the Saqqara–Memphis Area: Its Mineralogical and Geochemical Implications', *Archaeometry*, 56.6 (2013), 987–1008.

Henein, N. H. *Mārī Girgis, village de Haute-Égypte*, 2nd edition (Cairo: Institut français d'archéologie orientale, 1988).

Henein, N. H. *Poterie et potiers d'Al-Qasr: oasis de Dakhla* (Cairo: Institut français d'archéologie orientale, 1997).

Hill, P. *Rural Hausa: A Village and a Setting* (Cambridge: Cambridge University Press, 1972).

Hillman, G. C. 'Reconstructing Crop Husbandry Practices from Charred Remains of Crops' in R. Mercer (ed.), *Farming Practice in British Prehistory* (Edinburgh: Edinburgh University Press, 1981), pp. 123–62.

Hivernel, J. *Balat: étude ethnologique d'une communauté rurale* (Cairo: Institut français d'archéologie orientale, 1996).

Janssen, J. J. *Commodity Prices from the Ramesside Period: An Economic Study of the Village of Necropolis Workmen at Thebes* (Leiden: Brill, 1975).

Jeffery, R., Jeffery, P., and Lyon, A. 'Taking Dung-Work Seriously: Women's Work and Rural Development in North India', *Economic and Political Weekly*, 24.17 (1989), WS32-7.

Kenoyer, J. M. 'Experimental Studies of the Indus Valley Technology at Harappa' in A. C. Parpola and P. Koskikallio (eds.), *South Asian Archaeology 1993* (Helsinki: Suomalainen Tiedeakatemia, 1994), pp. 345-62.

Klunzinger, C. B. *Upper Egypt: Its People and Its Products: A Descriptive Account of the Manners, Customs, Superstitions and Occupations of the People of the Nile Valley, the Desert and the Red Sea Coast, with Sketches of the Natural History and Geology* (New York: Scribner, Armstrong, 1878).

Lancelotti, C. and Madella, M. 'The "Invisible" Product: Developing Markers for Identifying Dung in Archaeological Contexts', *Journal of Archaeological Science*, 39.4 (2012), 953-63.

Linseele, V., Reimer, H., Baeten, J. de Vos, D., Marinova, E., and Ottoni, C. 'Species Identification of Archaeological Dung Remains: A Critical Review of Potential Methods', *Environmental Archaeology*, 18.1 (2013), 5-17.

Malleson, C. 'Archaeobotanical Investigations at Tell el-Retaba. Ramesside Fortress and 3rd Intermediate Period Town (Area 9). Polish-Slovak (PCMA) Mission Seasons 2010-2014', *Ägypten und Levante*, 25 (2015), 175-200.

Marinova, E., Linseele, V., and Kühn, M. 'Bioarchaeological Research on Animal Dung – Possibilities and Limitations', *Environmental Archaeology*, 18.1 (2013), 1-3.

Marinova, E., van Loon, G. J. M., De Meyer, M., and Willems, H. 'Plant Economy and Land Use in Middle Egypt during the Late Antique/Early Islamic Period – Archaeobotanical Analysis of Mud Bricks and Mud Plasters from the Area of Dayr al Barshā' in A. G. Fahmy, S. Kahlheber, and A. C. D'Andrea (eds.), *Windows on the African Past: Current Approaches to African Archaeobotany* (Frankfurt am Main: Africa Magna Verlag, 2012), pp. 120-36.

Matin, M. and Matin, M. 'Egyptian Faience Glazing by the Cementation Method Part 2: Cattle Dung Ash as a Possible Source of Alkali Flux', *Archaeological and Anthropological Sciences*, 8.1 (2016), 125-34.

Miller, N. F. 'Seed Eaters of the Ancient Near East: Human or Herbivore?', *Current Anthropology*, 37.3 (1996), 521-28.

Miller, N. F. 'Sweeter than Wine', *Antiquity*, 82 (2008), 937-46.

Miller, N. F. and Smart, T. L. 'Intentional Burning of Dung as Fuel: A Mechanism for the Incorporation of Charred Seeds into the Archaeological Record', *Journal of Ethnobiology*, 4.1 (1984), 15-28.

Moens, M.-F. and Wetterstrom, W. 'The Agricultural Economy of an Old Kingdom Town in Egypt's West Delta: Insights from the Plant Remains', *Journal of Near Eastern Studies*, 47.3 (1988), 159–73.

Nunn, J. F. *Ancient Egyptian Medicine* (Norman: University of Oklahoma Press, 2002).

Peet, T. E. and Woolley, L. C. *The City of Akhenaten: Part I: Excavations of 1921 and 1922 at el-'Amarneh* (London: The Egypt Exploration Society, 1951).

Portillo, M., Valenzuela, S., and Albert, R. M. 'Domestic Patterns in the Numidian Site of Althiburos (Northern Tunisia): The Results from a Combined Study of Animal Bones, Dung and Plant Remains', *Quaternary International*, 275 (2012), 84–96.

Pyke, G. and Brooks Hedstrom, D. L. 'The Afterlife of Sherds: Architectural Reuse Strategies at the Monastery of John the Little, Wadi Natrun' in B. Bader and M. Ownby (eds.), *Aspects of Egyptian Ceramics within their Archaeological Context* (Leuven: Peeters, 2012), pp. 307–25.

Quibell, J. E. *Excavations of Saqqara (1908-9, 1909-10): The Monastery of Apa Jeremias* (Cairo: Institut français d'archéologie orientale, 1912).

Rhind, A. H. *Thebes, Its Tombs and Their Tenants, Ancient and Present: Including a Record of Excavations in the Necropolis* (London: Longman, Green, Longman, and Roberts, 1862).

Richter, T. S. 'Coptic Alchemical Texts', in Sources of Alchemy and Chemistry. Sir Robert Mond Studies in the History of Early Chemistry, Ambix Supplements (in preparation).

Rizqallah, F. and Rizqallah, K. *La préparation du pain dans un village du Delta Égyptien (province de Charqia)* (Cairo: Institut français d'archéologie orientale, 1978).

Samuel, D. 'Their Staff of Life: Initial Investigations on Ancient Egyptian Bread Baking' in B. J. Kemp (ed.), *Amarna Reports V* (London: Egypt Exploration Society, 1989), pp. 253–90.

Sauneron, S. *Les ermitages chrétiens du désert d'Esna I: archéologie et inscriptions* (Cairo: Institut français d'archéologie orientale, 1972).

Shahack-Gross, R. 'Herbivorous Livestock Dung: Formation, Taphonomy, Methods for Identification, and Archaeological Significance', *Journal of Archaeological Science*, 38.2 (2011), 205–18.

Sillar, B. 'Dung by Preference: The Choice of Fuel as an Example of How Andean Pottery Production Is Embedded within Wider Technical, Social, and Economic Practices', *Archaeometry*, 42.1 (2000), 43–60.

Smith, W. 'Fuel for Thought: Archaeobotanical Evidence for the Use of Alternatives to Wood Fuel in Late Antique North Africa', *Journal of Mediterranean Archaeology*, 11.2 (1998), 191–205.

Smith, W. *Archaeobotanical Investigations of Agriculture at Late Antique Kom el-Nana (Tell el-Amarna)* (London: Egypt Exploration Society, 2003).

Stiner, M. C., Kuhn, S. L., Weiner, S., and Bar-Yosef, O. 'Differential Burning, Recrystallization, and Fragmentation of Archaeological Bone', *Journal of Archaeological Science*, 22.2 (1995), 223–37.

Teichman, E. *Travels of a Consular Officer in North-West China* (Cambridge: Cambridge University Press, 1921).

Valamoti, S. M. 'Towards a Distinction between Digested and Undigested Glume Bases in the Archaeobotanical Record from Neolithic Northern Greece: A Preliminary Experimental Investigation', *Environmental Archaeology*, 18.1 (2013), 31–42.

van der Spek, K. *The Modern Neighbors of Tutankhamun: History, Life, and Work in the Villages of the Theban West Bank* (Cairo: American University in Cairo Press, 2011).

van der Veen, M. 'The Economic Value of Chaff and Straw in Arid and Temperate Zones', *Vegetation History and Archaeobotany*, 8 (1999), 211–24.

Wallace, M. and Charles, M. 'What Goes in Does Not Always Come out: The Impact of the Ruminant Digestive System of Sheep on Plant Material, and Its Importance for the Interpretation of Dung-Derived Archaeobotanical Assemblages', *Environmental Archaeology*, 18.1 (2013), 18–30.

Weidmann, D. *Kellia: Kôm Qouçoûr 'îsâ 1. Fouilles de 1965 à 1978* (Leuven: Peeters, 2013).

Wetterstrom, W. and Wenke, R. J. 'Kom el-Hisn's Plant Remains' in R. J. Wenke, R. Redding, and A. J. Cagle (eds.), *Kom el-Hisn (ca. 2500–1900 BC): An Ancient Settlement in the Nile Delta of Egypt* (Atlanta: Lockwood Press, 2016), pp. 205–54.

Wietheger, C. *Das Jeremias-Kloster zu Saqqara unter besonderer Berücksichtigung der Inschriften* (Altenberge: Oros, 1992).

Winterhalder, B., Larsen, R., and Thomas, R. B. 'Dung as an Essential Resource in a Highland Peruvian Community', *Human Ecology*, 2.2 (1974), 89–104.

Xiao, Q., Saikawa, E., Yokelson, R. J., Chen, P., Li, C., and Kang, S. 'Indoor Air Pollution from Burning Yak Dung as a Household Fuel in Tibet', *Atmospheric Environment*, 102 (2015), 406–12.

Zapata Peña, L., Leonor Peña-Chocarro, J. J. I. E., and Urquijo, J. G. 'Wood and Dung as Fuel' in K. Neumann, A. Butler, and S. Kahlheber (eds.), *Food, Fuel and Fields. Progress in African Archaeobotany* (Cologne: Heinrich-Barth-Institute, 2003), pp. 163–75.

9 | Illuminating the Scriptoria: Monastic Book Production at the Medieval Monastery of St Michael

ANDREA MYERS ACHI

Introduction

By the ninth century, Egyptian Christian monastic institutions prospered, as indicated by the expansion of many monasteries into large settlements that owned land with dependent tenants.[1] These monasteries participated in a thriving book culture, represented by the survival of approximately 4,000 Coptic manuscripts and manuscript fragments dating from the fourth to the eleventh centuries.[2] A combination of the financial health of monastic communities and the vigour of their craft production sustained the creation of these manuscripts. Also, individual monks were economic agents active in book production.[3] Monks and monasteries shared their books with other monasteries in their regions and throughout Egypt.[4] The forty-seven manuscripts of the St Michael Collection (dating from 823 to 914) reveal aspects of monastic book production ranging from acquisition of materials to the practices of scribes and painters, as well as aspects of book culture, from the dedication of books to sharing them across a regional network of monasteries.

The thriving culture of book production in the medieval Fayum Oasis was part of the larger economic structure of monasteries in the region. The physical remains of the monasteries associated with St Michael in the Fayum have not been identified. They are only known from the colophons of the manuscripts from the St Michael Collection. The St Michael Collection

---

[1] The work of Ewa Wipszycka, in particular, is the most comprehensive. While she focuses on other aspects of craft production in monastic contexts, mainly on Late Antique material, her work also provides a framework for inserting medieval book production into the structure of monastic economic endeavours; see Wipszycka, *Moines et communautés*, and Wipszycka, 'Resources and Economic Activities'. For additional discussion of the economic activities of monasteries in this period, see Swanson, *Coptic Papacy*, p. 11; Richter, 'The Cultivation of Monastic Estates'; and Papaconstantinou, 'Egypt'.

[2] This figure comes from Emmel, 'Coptic Manuscripts', p. 44. For parchment manuscripts and fragments, trismegistos.org, a metadata database, lists 895 records for the same period. Though the St Michael Collection is included in Trismegistos' records, the database focuses on texts written before AD 800; as Emmel notes, most of the extant Coptic manuscripts date to after the ninth century.

[3] For a discussion of this, see Goehring, *Ascetics*, p. 45.

[4] For a description of the area and its monasteries, see Coquin, 'Monasteries of the Fayyum'.

is the earliest extant group of painted Coptic manuscripts; the collection is impressive because it has remained together as a cohesive whole. Though documentary evidence confirms the existence of other monastic libraries in medieval Egypt, fragments of actual manuscripts are rarely discovered together in their find spots. The study of the St Michael Collection helps reconstruct the contents of early medieval monastic libraries and provides important insights into book production in medieval Egypt.

Evidence from the St Michael Collection confirms that monastic book production centres existed in Egypt, at least in the ninth and tenth centuries. The level of uniform organisation and structure across these institutions in the Fayum is not known, as it is difficult to discern which monastery might have had a formal book production centre or only intermittently produced manuscripts for neighbouring monastic communities. By focusing solely on the St Michael Collection, this study builds on the comprehensive research that has been done on Egyptian book production over the last decade. The study of this unique collection allows the cost of these manuscripts to be estimated, using inferences about the materials, time, and effort required to produce them. In addition, I apply digital network analysis tools to the information contained in the colophons; the results of this analysis enhance our understanding of the relationships among patrons, books, monasteries, and scribes in the ninth and tenth centuries in the Fayum Oasis. I argue that, within the context of the Egyptian monastic economy, the production of these books was not expensive. Yet, the cost of books in the medieval period was still perceived to be high.

Politically, ninth- and tenth-century Egypt is considered a 'tumultuous' century, when the dynasties of the Tulunids (868–905), the Abbasids (905–35), and the Ikhshidids-Kafurid (935–69) ruled.[5] During his reign, Ahmad ibn Tulun (868–84) imprisoned the Coptic Patriarch Michael III (880–907). The Patriarch was released for 20,000 dinars, which indicates that the Coptic Church had access to such funds for a ransom. In 914 (also the date of the last dated manuscript in the St Michael Collection), the armies of the Fatimid caliph and imam el-Mahdi attempted an unsuccessful invasion of Egypt.[6] In this transitional period between political dynasties, the Fayum region was crowded with monasteries; at least thirty-five monasteries existed in the area by the eighth century.[7] In addition to demographic changes in the region,

---

[5] The following historical summary is outlined in the discussion of Patriarch Michael III in Swanson, *Coptic Papacy*, p. 44.

[6] Swanson, *Coptic Papacy*, p. 44.

[7] For a description of the region and its monasteries, see Coquin, 'Monasteries of the Fayyum'. See also Timm, *Das christlich-koptische Ägypten*, who identifies the place names of monasteries and churches in the Fayum Oasis and across Egypt.

sociolinguistic shifts were prevalent. Although Coptic was the vernacular language of most Egyptians, parts of the population were bilingual in Egyptian and Greek (to varying extents and levels of proficiency), and later, Arabic.[8] In the Coptic texts of the St Michael Collection, however, some colophons and marginal notations are in Greek, which suggests that some monks were comfortable with both Coptic and Greek for copying or reading the manuscripts. In order to avoid religious or even ethnic connotations in the description of the ninth and tenth centuries, I use the term 'medieval Egypt'.

Overview of the St Michael Collection

The narrative of the collection's provenance is as compelling as it is suspicious. According to the manuscripts' dealers, in 1910 Egyptian farmers found a hoard of bound books in a stone vat outside the village of el-Hamuli in the Fayum.[9] A year later, additional manuscripts with similar bindings were added to the hoard. In 1912, all items were sold to J. Pierpont Morgan.[10] Though the farmers claimed they retrieved the books from the 'ruins of an ancient monastery dedicated to St Michael', no excavation has confirmed the precise location of the monastery.[11] In fact, even in the colophons, the location of the monastery of St Michael is not clear; its physical location appears to change over time.[12] Nonetheless, the find-spot's name remains with the

---

[8] Richter, 'Language Choice', p. 190. On Greek–Coptic bilingual scribal activity, see Cromwell, *Recording Village Life*. For a general discussion on Coptic and Greek in the papyrological record, see Fournet, 'Multilingual Environment'.

[9] Scholars repeat this unverified provenance consistently. A more detailed narrative concerns a tenth-century monk who hid the manuscripts in the stone vat in order to protect them from raiders. This story first appears on page xiii in Henri Hyvernat's 1919 publication, *A Check List of Coptic Manuscripts in the Pierpont Morgan Library*. As recently as 2014, Luijendijk, *Forbidden Oracles*, p. 41, quoting Leo Depuydt and Hyvernat, says of the manuscripts, 'They were apparently found in a "stone vat" as if they were disposed there by the Coptic fathers in anticipation of a raid.' See also, Depuydt, *Catalogue of Coptic Manuscripts*, p. lviii.

[10] As a conservation effort, the Morgan Library and Museum (formerly the Pierpont Morgan Library) sent the manuscripts to the Vatican Library in 1912. At the time, most of the manuscripts retained their original (and fragile) leather bindings. In order to make the manuscripts accessible to scholars, the Vatican removed the bindings from the text blocks of the manuscripts and trimmed the folios to an average size of 13 by 9 inches (33.0 by 22.9 cm). The conservators put the manuscripts in modern red leather bindings. The manuscripts returned to the Morgan Library in 1929. Personal communication with Morgan Library staff, 15 June 2017.

[11] Depuydt, *Catalogue of Coptic Manuscripts*, p. xlv.

[12] The monastic community dedicated to the Archangel Michael in the Fayum Oasis seemed to have moved their physical location, over time, for multiple place names associated with this monastic community are present in the colophons. The social structure of the community (and the physical structures in which they lived) likely evolved over the hundred-year period that the

group, which is also often referred to as the Hamuli manuscripts. In addition, colophons identify three place names that participated in the production of the manuscripts in the St Michael Collection: the monastery of Kalamon, and the towns of Ptepouhar and Touton. Overall, these place names, in conjunction with a monastery of St Michael, represent a combination of literacy, craft production, and monastic resources. Illuminating understudied Christian arts and texts from medieval Egypt, the St Michael Collection is significant because of its comprehensiveness and state of preservation. The manuscripts were copied in neat book hands, mostly in the Sahidic dialect of Coptic. Nearly half of the books are compilations of narratives about saints, martyrs, and church fathers. Songbooks, homilies, lectionaries, and selections of scriptures from the Old and New Testaments are also included.

Almost all the books had original intricate leather bindings, which were removed and are now separately stored at the Morgan Library.[13] Most manuscripts preserve their decorative initials, marginalia, and borders (in shades of reds, browns, yellows, greens, and some purples and gold). Twenty-seven painted frontispieces with both figural and ornamental decoration retain the same colour palette. Compared to other contemporary Egyptian manuscripts, which were often bound in wooden book-covers and were rarely decorated, the St Michael Collection represents a costly investment of time and money.

Producing a book required a great amount of resources, time, technology, and skills; each book in the collection needed a variety of materials, such as parchment and leather (for binding), as well as source materials for copying liturgical texts. In addition to a network of skilled craftsmen, such as translators, scribes, painters, binders, and correctors, a thriving livestock industry supported the demand for parchment and leather.[14] All of these materials, as well as skilled work and agricultural considerations for growing feed for animals, affected the value of the books.

Different monastic individuals were responsible for the copying, painting, and binding of books.[15] For example, a sixth-century letter on parchment

---

books were produced. For this reason, 'a' monastery of St Michael is distinguished from 'the' St Michael Collection.

[13] The bindings and many of the paintings in the St Michael Collection can be found online at www.themorgan.org.

[14] For a comprehensive discussion of the various skilled workers involved in producing a medieval manuscript, see Clemens and Graham, *Introduction to Manuscript Studies*, pp. 3–64. See also Alexander, *Medieval Illuminators*, pp. 36–51.

[15] See the following studies for contextualisation of the production of the St Michael Collection: Lowden, 'Book Production'; Emmel, 'Coptic Manuscripts'; Bagnall, *Early Christian Books*; Kotsifou, 'Books and Book Production'; Kotsifou, 'Bookbinding and Manuscript Illumination'.

presents the joint decision-making process involved in adding gold paint to a manuscript.[16] Anne Boud'hors' work on scribes and book production in western Thebes provides an important approach to analysing documentary evidence for multiple craftsmen.[17] The multiple perspectives of the St Michael Collection further enhance our understanding of book production in medieval Egypt.

The colophons confirm that mainly monks were involved in the various tasks of producing books for their own communities, but the extent to which monasteries had formal scriptoria with precise divisions of labour is not yet clear. Thus, Chrysi Kotsifou avoids the term 'scriptorium', as it is problematic for the discussion of Egyptian monastic book production.[18] In order to circumvent an association with large scale and organised scriptoria, she suggests the alternative terms 'book production workshops' and 'book production centers'. Maria Agati, however, is less rigid in the application of the term scriptorium. The most common meaning given to the term is that of a group of writers (scribes) and, more generally, craftsmen of the book who get together in a particular place and give themselves rules to follow, in the manufacture or copying of books and their adaption to their own uses (internal) or as required by a patron. What counts is that such a collaboration is not occasional, but lasts over time, so that the books produced in that place will have features in common, both palaeographical and codicological.[19]

Even if medieval Egyptian book production centres do not parallel the scale and processes of scriptoria from other regions in the Mediterranean, robust and consistent book-producing communities certainly existed in medieval Egypt. The St Michael Collection reflects the consistency highlighted by Agati. While there is not yet archaeological evidence for a physical place designated for book production in medieval Egypt, the manuscripts in the St Michael Collection were the products of a network of craftsmen associated with specific book production centres.[20] For the sake of clarity, I term these centres 'workshops'. What is not clear, however, is the relationship between the economic structure of monasteries and monastic book production workshops.

The documentary record is mostly silent on the topic of book prices, and consequently, the precise cost of labour and materials for books in medieval

---

[16] For a discussion of this letter, see Kotsifou, 'Books and Book Production'.
[17] Boud'hors, 'Copie et circulation'.
[18] Kotsifou, 'Bookbinding and Manuscript Illumination', p. 216, n. 15.
[19] Agati, *The Manuscript Book*, p. 249.
[20] In her definition, Agati does not mention physical space as a criterion for a scriptorium.

Egypt remains unclear. In his overview on book production in the Byzantine world, John Lowden recognises a general problem for understanding economic aspects of book production: 'the fiscal records and/or guild regulations that make a detailed study possible'. He notes that the best way to address the lack of sources is to focus on the objects themselves.[21] Just as important as the monetary cost of production are the time and effort required to produce them and the number of monks required to work on them. From another perspective, Roger Bagnall's calculation of early Christian book prices provides a methodological framework with which one can evaluate the potential cost of the St Michael Collection.[22] By adapting this calculation, a central contribution of the present study is the estimation of the cost of production of these manuscripts, using inferences about the materials, time, and effort required to produce them.

The St Michael Collection also had a spiritual value that reinforced the role of orality and writing in monastic contexts. As has been highlighted by Kim Haines-Eitzen's concern with the intertwining of 'the oral and written' texts, 'orality shaped the use of texts'.[23] Reading the text out loud and listening to its contents made the manuscripts an important component of the monastic experience, shaping the texts as oral utterance and linking the reader to the text's author.[24] Writing played an equally valuable role in the monastic experience. In this respect, Derek Krueger's premise that 'writing was a vehicle for the expression of piety' is also relevant.[25] In the St Michael Collection, the scribes often compiled discrete texts into one codex. These multiple-text codices seem to have been holy gifts to both the monastic readers and listeners; they represented acts of penance on the part of the scribes, who practised scribal humility through the copying of the late antique texts; the texts and the practice of copying connected the monks to their predecessors.

Economics of Producing Books in Monasteries

Written texts were an integral part of monastic life. While Egyptian monastic writings highlight the importance of memory and orality, the abundance of ostraca (pottery sherds and limestone flakes that were used as writing surfaces) and inscriptions found in monastic cells signify the importance of writing to monks and point to a significant level of literacy within some monasteries.[26]

---

[21] Lowden, 'Book Production', p. 462. [22] Bagnall, *Early Christian Books*, p. 51.
[23] Haines-Eitzen, 'Textual Communities', pp. 246 and 249.
[24] Krueger, *Writing and Holiness*, p. 4. [25] Krueger, *Writing and Holiness*, p. 6.
[26] Layton, 'Monastic Rules of Shenoute'.

Hoards of textual objects found in monasteries reflect the network of textual communities that supported their production. Objects on which texts were written varied in cost, production, and function; for example, the cost-production value of an ostracon was significantly less than a parchment codex. Inevitably, monastic economy and book production are linked, but the cost, making, and use of textual objects in their monastic contexts can be difficult to parse. To understand these terms, what follows is a review of the evidence concerning monastic economy and book production in late antique and medieval Egypt. This review will lead to a broad understanding of the relationship between monasteries, economic exchanges, and books.

There are significant lacunae in the literary, documentary, and archaeological evidence for monastic economy and book production, and only when they are examined together can one fully appreciate these gaps. For example, literary texts idealise withdrawal and renunciation of social obligations, whereas documentary texts and archaeological evidence reveal the prosperity of many Egyptian monasteries. Therefore, although literary texts highlight the need for both spatial and social distance from the outside world, the St Michael Collection's colophons and manuscripts – the combination of texts and the physical materials on which texts are written – point to connections among monasteries, individual monks and their immediate families.[27] This section does not provide an exhaustive review of the connections between each category and monastic economy. Rather, it reflects on a variety of aspects concerning economic relationships and book production between Egyptian monks and their surrounding communities. It also suggests how we can use this information to understand the context in which manuscripts of the St Michael Collection were produced.

Literary Evidence for Book Cost and Production

The literary evidence highlights the importance of textual objects as commodities for monastic communities. Four stories in the *Apophthegmata Patrum* discuss the cost and value of books. The story of Apa Gelasios depicts an elder monk, who owned a leather-bound Bible worth eighteen *solidi*.[28] A thief stole the book and tried to sell it for a higher price. Theodore of Pherme sold three

---

[27] Russell, *Lives of the Desert Fathers*, p. 18. These connections are also found in the colophons of the St Michael Collection.

[28] AlphAP [=*Alphabetic Apophthegmata Patrum*], 145; Greek text in Migne, *Patrologia Graeca* (hereafter *PG*) 65; Gelasius 1 in Ward, *Sayings of the Desert Fathers*, p. 46.

books and gave the money from the sale to the poor.[29] In another story, thieves stole Theodore's books. The theft of these books implies their value to both the thieves and the monks.[30] Despite Serapion's criticism of libraries, he also owned books.[31] When he went to a brothel to convert a prostitute, he read from his psalter and epistle.[32] Likewise, to Epiphanius, books were both useful and edifying.[33] In another literary text, *Pratum spirituale*, Abba John narrates a story of an anchorite named Theodore who wants to purchase a New Testament book but cannot afford it. Abba John helps him and says:

> I made inquiries and discovered that Abba Peter, who became Bishop of Chalcedon, possessed such a book. I went and spoke with him and he showed me a copy of the New Testament written on extremely fine skins. I asked him how much it was and he told me: 'Three pieces of gold.' But then he added: 'Is it you, yourself who wants to buy it, or somebody else.' I said: 'Believe me, father, it is an anchorite who wants it.' Then Abba Peter said to me: 'If the anchorite wants it, take it to him gratis. Here too are three pieces of gold. If he does not like the book, there are the three pieces of gold; buy him what he wants.' I took up the book and brought it to the anchorite. He took it and went off into the wilderness.[34]

Theodore later decides to earn money and purchase the book. Receiving a per diem of five copper coins, he performs labour-intensive jobs and continues in this way until he saves the equivalent of three *solidi* in copper. Though these amounts do not derive from documents of actual cost or purchase price, they suggest that monks considered the books to be of high value.

The literary evidence also suggests that monks produced books in their monasteries. Many monks were trained to be book producers. For example, in the biography of Anba Youna, a passage describes a monk named Pesynthius, who, at the age of eleven, learned copying and binding.[35] Like weaving and basket-making, copying texts seems to be one of the many labour tasks monks could perform. At the White Monastery, for

---

[29] *AlphAp*, 187; Greek text in *PG* 65; Theodore of Pherme 1 in Ward, *Sayings of the Desert Fathers*, p. 73.
[30] *AlphAp*, 195; Greek text in *PG* 65; Theodore of Pherme 29 in Ward, *Sayings of the Desert Fathers*, p. 78.
[31] *AlphAp*, 414; Greek text in *PG* 65; Serapion 2 in Ward, *Sayings of the Desert Fathers*, p. 278.
[32] *AlphAp*, 414; Greek text in *PG* 65; Serapion 1 in Ward, *Sayings of the Desert Fathers*, pp. 276–8.
[33] *AlphAP*, 165; Greek text in *PG* 65; Epiphanius 8 in Ward, *Sayings of the Desert Fathers*, p. 58.
[34] *The Life of Theodore the Anchorite* in Wortley, *The Spiritual Meadow*, pp. 110–11. Bagnall, *Early Christian Books*, p. 51, calculates that the resulting value of a complete Bible at 15.6 *solidi*, which is comparable to the cost of Gelasios' Bible.
[35] As quoted in Wipszycka, 'Resources and Economic Activities', p. 183 and Doresse, 'Monastères coptes', pp. 337–9. Binding was associated with the production of leather goods in general. The techniques used to decorate leather shoes and leather book covers seem to be similar.

example, the monks' structured days revolved around praying and producing goods or doing 'handiwork' (ϩⲱⲃ ⲛϭⲓϫ).[36] Based on the rules of Shenoute, the leader of the White Monastery, Layton reconstructs the daily schedule of monks. Throughout the day, the monks alternated between praying and doing handiwork.[37] The results of the 'handiwork' were commodities such as baskets, socks, and other textiles, as well as the copying of books. This evidence provides an interesting parallel to what is found in the colophons of the St Michael Collection. The scribes often describe copying as 'little handiwork' (ⲡⲁⲕⲟⲩⲓ ⲛϩⲱⲃ ⲛϭⲓϫ). Zachary of Kalamon requests the reader to 'Bear with me and my little handiwork.'[38] At the end of MS M.580 (Papnoute's *Life of St Onnophrius the Anchorite* and Julius of Aqfahs' *Martyrdom of St Apa Epima*), Basil and Peter remark, 'Bear with us and our little handiwork, lest we be mistaken with a word. We wrote according to the copy that was before us.'[39] The consistent use of this term – in the colophons and Shenoute's monastic rules – suggests copying of manuscripts was a part of monastic commodity production. The most significant costs, then, were in the book materials, but these costs are not listed in the literary texts.

Documentary Evidence for Book Production

Monastic communities recognised the cost-production value of books, even if they did not pay for them (in the case of donors providing books). The documentary texts indicate that monks were trained to make books within their monasteries, and they likely did not pay for the raw materials with money. Either the animal skins were donated, or they were exchanged for other commodities produced in the monastery, such as wine or grain.[40] Locally raised animals were often used for the creation of parchment, yet acquisition of sufficient parchment stock for a book project was an endeavour that might have taken months, if not years. In a seventh-century letter

---

[36] Literally in English, handcraft; see Crum, *Coptic Dictionary*, p. 654a.
[37] Layton, 'Rules, Patterns, and the Exercise of Power', pp. 52–3.
[38] Colophon in Hagiographic Miscellany, MS M.586. For catalogue information, see Depuydt, *Catalogue of Coptic Manuscripts*, p. 360.
[39] Colophon in Hagiographic Miscellany MS M.580 For catalogue information see, Depuydt, *Catalogue of Coptic Manuscripts*, p. 360.
[40] I do not have evidence for this exchange, but other scholars have come to similar conclusions; see Wipszycka, 'Resources and Economic Activities', p. 236. It is likely, however, that some commodities were paid for with money.

from a monastic context in Thebes, the writer, Pesynthius, explicitly requests goatskins:

> Be so good and go unto the dwelling of Athanasius, the son of Sabinus, the craftsman, and get good goat skins, either three or four, or whatsoever you shall find of good (ones); and do bring them to me, that I may choose one therefrom for this book. But hasten and bring them. And if Athanasius desires to bring them, and he comes, [let him] bring them. If you find not (skins) with him, [...] another craftsman and bring [them].[41]

This letter suggests two possibilities: either goatskins were collected, prepared, and then stored, rather than commissioned for a specific project, or the scribe needed one additional good goatskin for his project. Overall, the letter highlights a critically important aspect of monastic economy: monks often worked with laymen to procure the materials they needed.[42]

Still, the documentary evidence from monastic contexts does not indicate the specific costs of the material needed to produce a book.[43] Documentary evidence from Roman Egypt, however, points to the potential value of parchment. Specifically, tax registrations from Roman Egypt give a general price for sheep and goats.[44] For example, from the Oxyrhynchite nome, a tax registration (to a *strategus* from a group of herders) mentions a higher number of sheep (used for their wool) than goats.[45] This suggests that there were more sheep than goats in this and perhaps other pastoral communities in Egypt.[46] Since the quantity of skins needed to make a book was so high, it is likely that parchment was made from both sheepskins and goatskins, rather than goatskins exclusively. Sheep, however, were expensive. One lease agreement from the Heroninos archive suggests that herders would lease flocks of sheep from

---

[41] *P.Mon.Epiph.* 380; the translation is the editor's, with some slight modifications. See also, Kotsifou, 'Bookbinding and Manuscript Illumination', p. 229.

[42] Goehring, *Ascetics*, p. 47; Goehring, 'Monasticism in Byzantine Egypt', p. 398. Gascou, 'Economic Activities of Monasteries'.

[43] This section uses prices from Roman Egypt; see below for consistency in prices across the late antique and medieval periods.

[44] For a discussion of the price of sheep and goats, see Keenan, 'Pastoralism in Roman Egypt'.

[45] *P. Oxy.* LV 3778, discussed in Keenan, 'Pastoralism in Roman Egypt', p. 177. For example, in the letter, six livestock owners recorded that they had seventy-eight sheep, three goats, lambs, and kids. This document indicates the neighbourhood where the herd will graze and promises the payment of taxes.

[46] In general, flocks likely had more sheep than goats. One could try to confirm this through analysing the sheep and goat bones at potential book production centres; however, since sheep and goat bones appear identical in most archaeological assemblages, it is difficult to differentiate the species through on-site faunal analysis; see Cool, *Eating and Drinking*.

large estates for as much as 2,000 drachmas.[47] Since third-century wage rates for agricultural labour were sixty to sixty-eight drachmas a month, this rental amount was considerable.[48] This system allowed the herders to maintain large quantities of animals and have a consistent cash flow from wool production. The lessees could keep whatever wool the sheep produced, but they also had the responsibility to ensure the sheep remained healthy and the herd remained intact. The value of these animals was mainly in their fleece. From the Aphrodito archive of Dioscorus son of Apollo, a sixth-century papyrus mentions one-third of a *solidus* for a purchase of wool.[49] Using additional information from *P.Lond.* V 1695 and *P.Cair.Masp.* III 67300, James Keenan calculates that this purchase equates to 5.4 kg of wool.[50] This calculation could be a baseline for the value of sheep and thus for the possible value of parchment in a non-monastic setting.

Multiple variables must be considered to estimate the cost of parchment and other materials. Calculation begins with the most valuable part of the sheep: its wool. Over the expected life span of 10.5 years, one sheep can produce 0.90 to 13.6 kg of wool a year.[51] Thus, a sheep with an average life expectancy and average production capacity could produce 76.2 kg of wool over its lifetime. Using Keenan's calculation (5.4 kg of wool equals one-third of a *solidus*), the estimated minimum value of an average sheep, based entirely on its wool, would have been approximately 4.7 *solidi*. This represents a gross value, not a net value, taking into account the sheep's consumption and sheepskin utility. The context for understanding these numbers is found in the weight of wheat. A family of eight ate around 36–44 *artabas* of wheat a year.[52] Ten artabas of wheat equal one gold *solidus*; thus, 3.6 to 4.4 *solidi* were needed for a family's wheat consumption for one year. On this basis, sheep could be worth more than the amount needed to feed a large family for one year. But did monastic use of sheepskin, or even goatskin, reflect this considerable value?

The cost-production value of wool (renewable) compared to the cost-production value of parchment (non-renewable) was significantly different. Further, the prices available represent a leap from Roman Egypt to Egypt in the ninth and tenth centuries. Thus, I here assume consistency in relative worth rather than prices. Even if the monastic book producers did

---

[47] Rathbone, *Economic Rationalism*; Keenan, 'Pastoralism in Roman Egypt', p. 185. Similar documents support these conclusions; Keenan cites *P.Alex.Giss.* V and *P.Lond.* III 851, 885a, and 848v.
[48] Bowman, *Egypt after the Pharaohs*, p. 238.   [49] *P.Cair.Masp.* II 67127.
[50] Keenan, 'Pastoralism in Roman Egypt', p. 196 (who notes the weight as 12 lb).
[51] McFadden *et al.*, 'Effect of Prenatal Androgens' (who give a range of 2–30 lb).
[52] Bagnall, *Egypt in Late Antiquity*, p. 116.

not purchase sheepskin, they would have recognised a sheep's relative worth. As such, I present a working model of potentially real prices that allows the building of a secure set of costs (open to variation) that reflect a book's relative worth, which I term 'perceived value'.

The Cost of Books in the Documentary Record

Regardless of any perceived value, documentary texts allude to the purchase and donation of manuscripts. In a colophon from Edfu, a scribe states, 'The cost of copying and binding was settled by a pious deacon.'[53] How much the unnamed pious deacon paid for these tasks is not recorded; however, other texts provide evidence that can be used to calculate the extent to which monastic labour subsidised the cost of producing books. For example, scholars turn to the fourth-century *Edict of Diocletian on Maximum Prices* to calculate the cost of scribal labour.[54] The copying of 100 lines (at a high-quality level) would have cost approximately twenty denarii.[55] On this basis, according to Bagnall, it would have cost 27,355 denarii, or ten *solidi*, for the copying of the 136,667 lines of the Bible.[56] Some scribes of the St Michael Collection recorded the lines they copied. For example, on the last folio of MS M.570, a scribe writes: 'The fourteen Epistles of the Holy Apostles, 5,574 *stichoi* [lines].'[57] MS M.570 is about the average size of a manuscript in the St Michael Collection; it has eighty-five leaves with about thirty-five lines per side, or seventy lines per leaf. The scribe, then, was mostly accurate in his tallying of lines (5,574 lines divided by 85 leaves equals 66.36 lines per leaf). Based on this metric, which depends on prices at the levels in the Diocletianic Edict, it would have cost an average of 1,115 denarii, or two-fifths of a *solidus*, for the copying of each manuscript in the St Michael Collection (52,405 denarii, or about 19.9 *solidi*, for the whole collection).

Turning from the cost of copying to the cost of a completed book, Bagnall explains that the cost of parchment was likely 20 per cent of the total book cost. Following this model, the parchment for one Bible with 850

---

[53] Cockerell, 'Development of Bookbinding Methods', pp. 11–12.
[54] Lowden, 'Book Production'. See below for the consistency in anachronistic price lists.
[55] Sections 1.1a and 7.38.
[56] The exact cost of copying, however, likely varied across production centres; see Bagnall, *Early Christian Books*, p. 56. Though the *Edict of Diocletian on Maximum Prices* gives costs for copying, it is possible that these late antique prices do not convert neatly to ninth-to-tenth-century currency; see also Koenen, 'Ein Mönch als Berufsschreiber'. In a monastic context, the perception of this cost might have been in the spiritual value of copying, not its monetary value.
[57] Colophon for MS M.570.

leaves would have cost 3.2 *solidi*.[58] Therefore, the base (perceived) price of the parchment in the St Michael Collection (2,481 leaves) would be 9.3 *solidi*. The additional cost of bookbinding – the materials and labour – could be one tremis, i.e., one-third of a *solidus*.[59] As such, forty-seven bindings in the St Michael Collection would have added 15.5 *solidi* to the cost of the collection.[60] So far, this calculation includes the cost of copying (19.9 *solidi*), parchment (9.3 *solidi*) and bindings (15.5 *solidi*): 44.7 *solidi* in total. If the parchment represents 20 per cent of the entire collection, then the collection would be around 60.8 *solidi*. Thus, the other aspects of book production, such as paints, painting, and decoration of the binding, would cost 16.1 *solidi*.

The tasks of copying, painting, and binding were carried out by specialists.[61] A sixth- or seventh-century documentary papyrus describes the various phases of preparation of parchment. To prepare the parchment for writing, the scribe is instructed:

> You shall merely place the soft pumice upon it and shall wipe it and write on it, but you shall pumice it on both sides before you write at all upon it. Then you shall spread upon it a little white-lead mixed with a little alum, they were pounded together and tied in a linen cloth, so that only the powder reach it; (then) you shall wipe it and write on it.[62]

Not only does this text describe some aspects of the parchment making process before copying, it also indicates that scribes might undertake several phases of the labour necessary for producing the book.

Decorating the book was another aspect of the production process. P.Yale inv. 1318, a fourth- or fifth-century letter, describes a presbyter who received a book for painting:

> I, the presbyter Heraclius, acknowledge that I have received from you the book for painting, on the condition that I return it to you within a month without subterfuges.[63]

---

[58] Bagnall, *Early Christian Books*, pp. 50–69 (chapter 3: 'The Economics of Book Production').
[59] Bagnall, *Early Christian Books*, p. 57. This hypothetical price comes from the cost of a Bible's leather cover, and it does not take into account the potential variance in binding quality.
[60] According to Bagnall, these prices would be relatively the same in Egypt up until the mid-tenth century (personal communication, 15 April 2013).
[61] Papaconstantinou, 'Egypt', p. 212.
[62] Crum, 'A Coptic Recipe', p. 169. The text was formerly in Cheltenham in the Phillipps collection; the current location and inventory is unknown.
[63] Parássoglou, 'A Book Illuminator'. Also discussed in Kotsifou, 'Bookbinding and Manuscript Illumination', p. 239; Kotsifou, 'Books and Book Production', pp. 49–50.

Here, we get a sense of the time it might take to illustrate a book, although it is not possible to state whether this is a lightly or heavily decorated book. The letter acted as a receipt of sorts, so it is interesting that the text does not mention payment for the paintings, which would provide an impression of the relative worth of book decoration. In a fifth- or sixth-century letter (written on parchment rather than the usual papyrus), a monastic copyist named Peschot requests decoration for a book that he is sending to two other monks, Kolluthus and Timotheus:[64]

> As for the book that I sent you, see to it that it is illustrated. Pay serious attention to the sheets: choose good ones and do not scratch them ... Give the book to someone who knows the art of book illumination; and if it has already been prepared, if I have not yet come north, send it south ... tell the illustrator to make some small decorations, either a gate or a wheel.[65]

Within these texts, we witness a community of book producers corresponding with each other. These texts suggest that in each case, the scribe was not the artist for the project but outsourced the illustrations.

To summarise, the documentary texts show that scribes acted as project managers in the book production process: they prepared parchment for copying and sent out manuscripts for paintings. It is possible that scribes continued to act as project managers throughout the medieval period. The extent of the oversight that monasteries had in this process is not, however, clear. Based on the documentary texts alone, we do not know if individual monks or monasteries organised the book production process. A practice of institutional oversight would separate scribes occasionally copying books from established book production workshops.

Archaeological Information for the Presence of Books

While excavations have provided information on the daily lives of monks, the archaeological record does not reveal much about book production.[66] Since books were potentially expensive to produce outside the monastic

---

[64] *P.Köln.* 10213; Weber, 'Zur Ausschmückung koptischer Bücher'. Discussed in Browne, 'Ad P. Colon. Inv.Nr. 10.213'.

[65] Translation in Parássoglou, 'A Book Illuminator', p. 365; see also Browne, 'Ad P. Colon. Inv.Nr. 10.213', p. 52.

[66] A notable exception is from the Polish Centre of Mediterranean Archaeology excavation in western Thebes, MMA 1152, where tools and leather bits might represent the materials of craftsmen involved in book binding. Górecki, 'Sheikh Abd El-Gurna', p. 303. Thank you to Jennifer Cromwell for pointing me to this reference.

setting, monastic libraries are either evidence of book production within the monastic environment or of the donation of books to a monastery. When a hoard such as the St Michael Collection is found, one can only assume a library, repository, or archive existed. The monks of St Michael's may have used these liturgical books for church services and feasts days and stored them when not in use.

Archaeological evidence confirms the existence of other monastic libraries in medieval Egypt, but fragments of actual manuscripts are rarely preserved together. A significant number of the extant Coptic manuscripts are associated with monasteries and their libraries by their colophons, although the manuscripts themselves are dispersed throughout various collections in Europe and the Coptic Museum in Cairo. Many Egyptian monasteries probably had collections similar to the one associated with a monastery of St Michael, but most simply did not survive into modern times. The British Library has a collection of manuscripts from the monastery of St Mercurius in Old Cairo. Written between the late tenth and twelfth centuries, the collection includes biblical and apocryphal writings, homilies, and passions. The White Monastery in Sohag had an extensive library, but scholars are still trying to piece together the physical location of the library and its relationship with the extant manuscripts from the monastery.[67]

According to Tito Orlandi, the library at the White Monastery 'became with time by far the largest Coptic library ever known'.[68] Walter Crum stated that the library is located 'in the small room to the north of the central apse [of the White Monastery church], entered from the north apse by a narrow passage'. Inscribed on the walls were vertical lists of books, which Crum believed 'indicate the relative positions once occupied by special chests or shelves'. He explained, 'It would seem that the New Testament manuscripts were arranged along the north side of the room, the homiletic and historical works along the east, the biographical works along the west. Against the south wall, where only one text is legible, may have stood the Old Testament.'[69] Orlandi reinterpreted the Coptic inscriptions and identified the following additional books: fifty-nine copies of the Tetraevangelion and possibly ten volumes not yet bound on the north wall, and on the west wall, eight books of Shenoute, twenty copies of the *Life of Pachomius*, two copies of the *Life of Moses of Abydos*, a homily on the

---

[67] This room is below the second-floor room known as the 'Candle Room' in Davis et al., 'Left Behind'.
[68] Orlandi, 'Library of the Monastery of Saint Shenute'.
[69] Crum, 'Inscriptions from Shenoute's Monastery'.

resurrection of the body, the *Life of Shenoute*, and thirteen copies of the Psalms.[70]

The descriptions of the books in spaces of various functions in monastic contexts indicate that books were not always stored together. While this discussion of libraries does not directly speak to monastic economy and book production, it does demonstrate that the materials, resources, and effort required to create a monastic library were significant.

Colophons and Book Value in the St Michael Monastic Community

General definitions of 'value' and 'valuable' stress the monetary worth of goods and their relative worth. Value, of course, cannot be defined in one sentence. From an economic perspective, value and markets are linked. According to the standard economic definition of value: 'The central role of markets is to determine the price of goods. A price is the value of the good in terms of money.'[71] This definition becomes an issue when the market is not clearly defined.

Because of the scanty available documentary evidence on socio-economic concerns for medieval monasteries in the Fayum, it is difficult to assess the market for Coptic manuscripts and whether the collection was expensive for the monastic community to produce. In this section, I first describe the monastic book production workshops associated with a monastery of St Michael, and then I address potential values of the St Michael Collection, which required many resources and skills.[72]

This section also considers the spiritual value of the collection to its community through the texts of the colophons. The colophons represent a significant factor in the analysis of value, and I emphasise their expression of repentance and ascetic labour. Network analysis tools visualise the connections of the people who made and commissioned the manuscripts. These relationships of scribes, painters, donors, monastic leaders, and monks of the Fayum Oasis represent a supraspecific monastic community associated with the St Michael Collection. The purpose of the following analysis is not to argue that every monk in a monastery of St Michael would recognise all aspects of a book's value. Rather, these values highlight the manuscripts' importance as material objects in their monastic contexts.

[70] Orlandi, 'Library of the Monastery of Saint Shenute', pp. 213–15.
[71] Samuelson and Nordhause, *Economics*, p. 31.
[72] Kotsifou, 'Bookbinding and Manuscript Illumination', p. 220.

Book Production Centres in the St Michael Collection

The colophons mention three locations of book production: the monastery of Kalamon (Deir el-Kalamun) and the towns of Ptepouhar (unknown location) and Touton (Tebtunis, Umm el-Buraigat). Locating these sites is difficult, as only Touton is associated with an excavated archaeological site. Though the precise locations of the other sites are not known, the monastery of Kalamon is mentioned in documentary records. A combination of archaeological data and textual evidence from medieval sources can help identify the approximate geographical locations of the sites in the Fayum. The proximity of the sites encouraged the monastic book culture and textual communities of the region.

Monastery of Kalamon

Founded when fourteen monks left the monastery of Naqlun to join the anchorite Samuel, the monastery of Kalamon was large compared to other monasteries in the Fayum. Within its walls, the monastery contained twelve churches and four towers, and medieval Arab writers described the massive monastic estate as thriving until the fourteenth century.[73] Not much is known about the monks of the monastery other than the original monk, Samuel, and Abba Isaac, the author of the *Life of Samuel of Kalamon*.[74]

Scholars do not agree on the exact place of the ancient monastery. Gilberto Bagnani argues that this monastery was once at the modern site of Umm el-Buraigat. Archaeological evidence for another monastic site named Touton (discussed below) was also found at Umm el-Buraigat, so Bagnani suggests that the site held two monasteries with book production workshops.[75] Bagnani published this hypothesis in 1934. Since then, scholars have discovered in the textual sources that both sites, Touton and the monastery of Kalamon, were described as large and at the south-west tip of the Fayum Oasis; two archaeological sites fit this description. Leo Depuydt suggests that the monastery of Kalamon could have been at Narmouthis (Medinet Madi), since there are two large mounds at the archaeological location.[76] In the Wadi Mawalih, which is in south-west Fayum, the remains of a large monastery are still visible, and this location also fits the description of the monastery of Kalamon given by Arab authors.[77] Bagnall and Rathbone, however, note that

---

[73] Abbott, 'Monasteries of the Fayyūm'. [74] Alcock, *Life of Samuel of Kalamun*.
[75] Bagnani, 'Gli scavi di Tebtunis'.
[76] Depuydt, *Catalogue of Coptic Manuscripts*, p. cxi states that the site is located about fifteen miles south of the southernmost tip of the Fayum and thirty miles west of the Nile.
[77] Meinardus, *Two Thousand Years*, p. 275.

the remains of a monastery of St Samuel are located at the south end of Wadi Rayan, near Magdola (Medinet en-Nehas). Controlled by St Samuel in the seventh century, this monastery was destroyed in the ninth century and then rebuilt.[78]

Two non-biblical miscellanies (MS M.588 and MS M.586) in the St Michael Collection were made at the monastery of Kalamon. The colophons were both signed by Zachary, 'the calligrapher of the monastery of Kalamon'. Zachary copied MS M.588, *Encomium on St Mercurius*, in 842 and MS M.586, a hagiography on St Mercurius, in 844, and he also painted his name on the frontispieces of both manuscripts. The production of Zachary's two books within two years of each other suggests the length of time that it took to copy and paint a manuscript. The manuscripts have decorated frontispieces depicting large crosses with splayed ends, bordered with small diagonal finials, filled with complex interlacing in shades of yellow and red and inscribed with ιγ̄| χ̄γ and q̄θ.[79] However, they are not copied stroke for stroke, and there are noticeable differences between the two crosses. On the frontispiece of MS M.588 the interlace of the cross is rounded and resembles the curves of woven thread, while on the frontispiece of MS M.586, a hagiography on St Mercurius, the interlace of the cross is sharp and geometrical. Furthermore, the first cross has two hanging lamps suspended from chains, while the other cross has three hanging lamps. The crosses have similar dimensions, so the difference between the number of lamps is not due to spatial constraints. The variation in the crosses suggests that the frontispieces were not directly copied from a model. The headpieces in both manuscripts and the ornament between the two manuscripts are similar overall. In MS M.586, however, the marginal ornament and initials are rarely infilled with paint, and their decoration is made with faint applications of ink. For both manuscripts, Zachary left some portions of the paintings unfinished.

As the only manuscripts with colophons mentioning the monastery of Kalamon, MS M.588 and MS M.586 are uniquely important to the corpus of the St Michael Collection. The monastery of Kalamon is the only named monastery associated with book production in the St Michael Collection. All the other scribes of the St Michael Collection present themselves as being 'from' or 'belonging to' specific towns or villages in the Fayum but not 'of' institutions (such as a monastery or a church). The manuscripts made at the monastery of Kalamon share key characteristics: their genre

---

[78] Bagnall and Rathbone, *Egypt from Alexander to the Early Christians*, p. 147.
[79] For images, see the manuscript file at themorgan.org.

and the style of the frontispieces. The differences in the manuscripts, however, point to Zachary's process of book production and are helpful to the analysis of manuscripts without colophons. The manuscripts provide a foundation for us to understand book production workshops in the Fayum Oasis. The paintings in these manuscripts differ significantly from the paintings in manuscripts from other production sites such as Ptepouhar and Touton, whose decorative programmes are described in the next two sections.

Ptepouhar

The only mention of Ptepouhar's place name seems to be in colophons of Coptic manuscripts; medieval Arab writers do not mention the monastery.[80] In 891, Apa Isaac of Ptepouhar copied and painted a manuscript specifically for the monastery of St Michael: *The Encomium on the Four Bodiless Beasts* (MS M.612). Later, around 893, he presumably copied an unidentified manuscript; its colophon, however, was used as a pastedown in another manuscript (MS M.578) in the St Michael Collection. MS M.578 shares decorative conventions with MS M.612, and it was likely made at Ptepouhar as well. MS M.612, however, is the only manuscript in the collection securely connected with the production site.[81]

In this manuscript, the headpieces, placement of the enlarged initials, vine scrolls, and four-legged animals present a set of decorative conventions used by Isaac of Ptepouhar.[82] The headpiece has triangular and bulbous spearhead finials and is filled in with yellow interlace over a black background with half-circle borders. The middle folios of the manuscript include significant portions of unpainted marginal animals and ornament, suggesting that it was not important for painters to colour each motif. Some of the characteristics of MS M.612 resemble those of other production centres, including Touton, such as the metal-like interlocking gold and brown ornament in both the frontispieces and headpieces in the manuscripts. As a result of the similarity with the Touton manuscripts, Theodore Petersen suggests that Isaac and the scribes from Ptepouhar were trained in Touton or were 'good imitator[s] of the Touton Style'.[83]

---

[80] Crum, 'Bibliography: Christian Egypt', p. 206. In addition to the two manuscripts discussed in this section, Ptepouhar is mentioned in a colophon from a manuscript now stored in the Coptic Museum. Crum believes that this manuscript is from the same find as the St Michael Collection.
[81] MS M.578 and two other manuscripts with similar palaeographic and painting styles (MS M.611 and MS M.585).
[82] See image file for MS. M612 on themorgan.org. [83] Petersen, 'Paragraph Mark', pp. 323–4.

Touton

Touton (Tebtunis) is associated with the site Umm al-Buraigat. The area thrived from the Pharaonic to medieval periods and was known as a textual community. The archaeological remains reflect a thriving Christian community in the ninth and tenth centuries. The site includes a monastic complex with large painted churches and mud-brick towers.[84] In the ninth and tenth centuries, scribes and painters of Touton were certainly connected to other monastic communities in the Fayum (Table 9.1). The colophons of the St Michael Collection identify seven different men from Touton who were either scribes or painters, working on manuscripts associated with various monasteries in Egypt.[85] The painters of Touton produced manuscripts for several monasteries in the region, including at least eight manuscripts (ca. 890–914) for the monastery of St Michael and five (ca. 920–40) for the White Monastery in Sohag.[86] Not all of the monastery of St Michael manuscripts made in Touton were originally dedicated to the monastery. A biblical miscellany, for example, was donated to an unidentified monastery dedicated to the Holy Virgin, but at some point it made its way to the monastery of St Michael.[87] In the colophons of these second-hand manuscripts, copyists erased the names of the original recipients and added 'monastery of St Michael'.

The corpus of extant manuscripts from Touton exhibits a group of characteristics that together make up what I refer to as the 'Touton Style', a term used to describe characteristic palaeographic features on manuscripts from Touton.[88] In the following discussion, I extend the list of characteristic features to include painting style. Visual analysis reveals that the colour palette of the manuscripts is remarkably consistent, with red, yellow-orange, brown, and green paints used throughout the group.

---

[84] For most recent bibliography, focusing on mainly Greco-Roman remains, see Bagnall and Rathbone, *Egypt from Alexander to the Early Christians*, pp. 142–52; Begg, 'New Potential from Old Archives'; Begg, 'Papyrus Finds at Tebtunis from the Bagnani Archives'; Litinas, *Tebtynis III*; Hadji-Minaglou, *Tebtynis IV*; Rondot et al., *Tebtynis II*; Gallazzi, 'Due campagne di scavo a Umm-el-Breigât'; Gallazzi, 'La ripresa degli scavi a Umm-el-Breigât'; Keenan, 'Deserted Villages'.

[85] The colophons do not state a division in the tasks of copying and painting.

[86] See Orlandi, 'The Library of the Monastery of Saint Shenute', pp. 215–19. About the relationship between the two monasteries, he writes, 'Both groups of manuscripts display the same style of writing and decoration, but, interestingly, there is no chronological overlap between these two groups of manuscripts, although there is a scribal continuity between them. There may thus have been a shift in clientele from the Monastery of St Michael to the White Monastery around 915.' Two of the St Michael manuscripts are now stored in the Coptic Museum in Cairo: MS 3820 and MS 3811.

[87] *Miscellany*, Morgan Library and Museum, New York, MS M.593.

[88] Depuydt has used this term to describe Touton's palaeographic characteristics. See Table. 9.2 for a list of criteria for attribution for Touton and the other book production centres discussed in this chapter.

Table 9.1. *Touton manuscript information.*

MS	Date	Description	Scribe	Illustrator	Donor
613	December 31, 867 AD	9 leaves (2 columns, 31 lines) 334 x 260 mm	Moses and Khael	Moses and Khael	By Ama Phelabia, daughter of Kurillos, from Pichai; to the monastery of St Michael
580	889/90 AD	59 leaves (2 columns, 30–31 lines) 357 x 375 mm	Basil	Petros	By Archi-Apa Epima and his son Ouanabre; to the monastery of St Michael
593	892/893 AD	50 leaves (2 columns, 33–35 lines) 352 x 266 mm	John	Petros	To the monastery of the Holy Virgin St Mary
577	August 30, 895 AD	51 leaves (2 columns, 31 lines) 337 x 259 mm	Samouel	Samouel	By Petros, son of Severos, from Narmoute, together with Nonna, his daughter, to the monastery of St Michael
574	897/898 AD	91 leaves (1 column, 31–34 lines) 280 x 218	Basili and Samouel	Basili and Samouel	By koinobiarch and archimandrate Papa Iohannes, oikonomos of the monastery of St Michael
600	905/906 AD	64 leaves (2 columns, 31 lines) 353 x 274 mm	(N/A)		
604	n/a	77 leaves (2 columns, 29–31 lines) 346 x 265 mm	Petros	Petros	To the monastery of St Michael
597	913/14 AD	75 leaves (2 columns, 30–32 lines) 351 x 268 mm	Kalamon and Stephen	Kalamon and Stephen	In Honor of the Holy Virgin

Human figures are frontal, flat, and nimbed, and most have red circular marks on their cheeks, foreheads, and hands. The painters paid attention to details, such as the use of schematic lines, folds of the figures' necks, and the

Table 9.2. *Criteria for attributions of book production centres.*

Monastery of Kalamon	Ptepouhar	Touton	Monastery of St Michael
Frontispiece decorative programme: Cross with hanging lamps, *nomina sacra* I͞Y |X͞Y and q͞ē. Scribe's name on frontispiece.	Headpiece with triangular and bulbous spearhead finials. Unpainted middle folios. Consistent placement of enlarged, initials, vince scrolls, and four-legged animals on first folio. Multiple-text codex.	Colour palette of red, bright yellow-orange, brown, and green. Leaf-shaped finials (used on floral paragraph scrolls). Headpieces with guilloche motifs. Human figures have red circular marks on their cheeks, foreheads, and hands. Schematic lines; folds on figures' necks.	All colophons recording donation to monastery of St Michael of the Desert (Phantou). Single topic text. Most do not have frontispieces. Stylised birds and four-legged animals. Ornamented initials with guilloche motif. Rinceau motifs. Fantastical creatures in margins.

wrinkles on their hands. The paintings in the manuscripts are consistent, despite some variations in quality.

Specific textual and scribal choices emerge over the period. First, the subjects of the Touton manuscripts made for the monastery of St Michael were mostly hagiographical. Second, many of the manuscripts contain scribal errors that would have hindered their readability in a public context. Analysis of such features will help identify Touton as the production centre for manuscripts in the St Michael and other collections.

Value of the Materials: Cost

The colophons in the St Michael Collection do not explicitly state the monetary value of the manuscripts, so it is impossible to know the precise amount that the scribes at the three book production workshops charged the donors of the St Michael Collection. As the average size of the manuscripts in the St Michael Collection is 34.3 by 24.6 cm, around sixty sheets of parchment were needed for one large manuscript.[89] This would have required thirty sheepskins or goatskins.[90] Thus, the collection of forty-seven manuscripts, consisting of 2,481 leaves of parchment, required, at the very least, 1,240.5 sheep or goats.[91] To date, I have not found any documentary medieval source that clarifies the cost of sheep or goats in Egypt. Most scholars, however, concede that the production of animal hides was a by-product of animal slaughter for consumption.[92] In other words, the price of livestock and the price of their skins following slaughter were likely different. Parchment was also recycled from manuscripts. A tenth-century Syriac manuscript of John Chrysostom's homilies contained a parchment palimpsest with a seventh-century Latin grammatical treatise and a fifth-century Latin text attributed to Granius Licinianus.[93] This reuse suggests that parchment was expensive and that the book producer used cost-saving techniques to keep costs low.

Books were often rededicated from one monastery to another. The colophons indicate that fourteen manuscripts, or one-third of the St Michael Collection, were donated to other churches or monasteries before making their way to the monastery of St Michael (Table 9.3). Some of the original monasteries' names were erased entirely. The remaining names include the monastery of Apa Epima of Pshante at Narmouthis (three manuscripts), the monastery of St Apa Sansneos of Terso-the-Deserted, the Small Church of Apa Timothe at Tmouou, and the church of St Michael and the monastery of St George Martyr at Narmouthis. Partially restored names include the monastery of Our Holy Father (name erased), the monastery of the Holy Virgin St Mary at an unknown place (the place name is in lacuna), and the monastery of Selbane in Honour of the Virgin (location similarly lost in lacuna) in the Fayum. This rededication of at least 33 per cent of the manuscript collection suggests that the monastery of St Michael may have acquired second-hand manuscripts because the initial cost of producing the manuscripts may have been prohibitive.

Other materials contributed to the value – real and perceived – of books. Expensive colours are attested in the documentary texts. In a letter from eighth-century Thebes, a monk says, 'you will decorate a book for my father Krauteous, a lectionary for a golden dove, [...] draw/paint the golden

---

[89] Buzi and Emmel, 'Coptic Codicology', p. 143. [90] Mathisen, 'Paleography and Codicology'.
[91] Lowden, 'Book Production', p. 463. [92] Lowden, 'Brook Production', p. 463.
[93] London, British Library, Add. MS 17,212 (fols 1–8, 10–13); see Peter Toth, 'Palimpsests: The Art of Medieval Recycling', 14 September 2016 (https://blogs.bl.uk/digitisedmanuscripts/2016/09/palimpsests-the-art-of-medieval-recycling.html).

Table 9.3. *Manuscripts that were not donated to a monastery of St Michael.*

Morgan	Genre	Original Owner
M587	Biography and History – Non-Biblical Characters	A Monastery with its name erased, then to St Michael
M609	Miscellany	Church of St Michael
M603	Biography and History – Biblical Characters	Church of St Michael
M569	Bible – New Testament	Church of the Blessed Theotokos Mary of T–T (Perkithoout?)
M571	Bible – New Testament	Monastery of Apa E[...] (possibly Apa Epima of Narmoute)
M596	Miscellany	Monastery of Apa Epima of Psante at Narmoute
M594	Commentaries, Homilies – Attributed	Monastery of Apa Epima of Psante at Narmoute
M572	Bible – New Testament	Monastery of St George Martyr at Narmoute
M570	Bible – New Testament	Monastery of Our Holy Father ... (name erased)
M598	Miscellany	Monastery of St Apa Sansneos of Terso-the-Deserted
M593	Biography and History – Biblical Characters	Monastery of the Holy Virgin St Mary at (...)
M597	Biography and History – Biblical Characters	Monastery of Selbane in Honor of the Virgin at (...) in the Fayum
M573	Bible –Lectionary	Small Church of Apa Timothe at Tmouou

image upon it'.[94] This text indicates that precise instructions were given to a scribe or painter both in content – lectionary – and in the material – gold paint. Many of the bindings in the St Michael Collection contained gilded parchment over red leather. A gold pigment was also used for the manuscript paintings. The pigment, mimicking gold, could heighten the perceived value of a manuscript.[95]

It is difficult to assess the cost of the leather bindings of the books. Almost all the manuscripts in the collection were discovered with their original covers, and the group represents the single most comprehensive corpus of Coptic bindings that have survived today.[96] The Morgan Library's curatorial notes explain that many bindings were cut from

---

[94] Kotsifou, 'Bookbinding and Manuscript Illumination', p. 239. The gold 'dove' refers to payment for the lectionary; on this term, see Cromwell and Grossman, 'Condition(al)s of Repayment', p. 158.

[95] See the essays in Panayotova, *Colour*. Though the inks used in the St Michael Collection manuscripts have not been scientifically tested, the results of such a test could potentially add to the analysis of the manuscripts' value.

[96] Due to their fragile state, the bindings are not made available to researchers; I therefore rely on the curatorial notes for this discussion.

a 'single piece of red leather and sewn over the gilt parchment'.[97] The bookbinder adorned the binding with small circles, crosses, rosettes, and geometric designs. The technical skill required to make the bindings could have added value to the books.

How should production values be factored into the cost of books produced in a monastic context for monastic use? Scribes, painters, other craftsmen, and patrons would decide the parameters of the project, such as texts to be included, layout, and degree of decorative elements. The production of the manuscript was based in part on the availability and affordability of materials.[98] Parchment, leather, and inks could have been purchased, exchanged, or made within the monastery. The sequence of work had to be determined in advance, as well. If the scribe was not also the artist, he had to allocate space for the marginal ornaments, decorative initials, headpieces, and tailpieces.[99]

Although the extant evidence concerning medieval book production in Egypt does not allow for a calculation of the St Michael Collection's monetary cost, the colophons indicate that the manuscripts were not free. Donors of all types – monks, priests, laymen, and laywomen – contributed to the production of the St Michael Collection. Monks are often described as 'ordering' books 'through their own labours'; some were 'responsible for the production of [a] book' or took 'care of it' and then gave the book to the monastery of St Michael.[100] Others seem to use the donation as an offering to God; Ama Phelabia, for example, 'gave [the book] to the church of Holy Archangel Michael of Phantau for the salvation of her soul'.[101] At the White Monastery, goods were often exchanged for commodities: '[He will be] paid [in] gold, bronze, baskets, sacks, books, and any other product in return for grain and wool and every kind of thing that we obtain.'[102] It is tempting to think that the production of books, too, could be exchanged for wool, grain, or even the donor's labour. As mentioned above, this connection between monks and laymen is also evident later in the colophons of the St Michael Collection.

Overall, even if a book was purchased with grain and not gold, the book could still be considered valuable: it had a relative worth. In the next two sections, I consider other types of values that the books might have had to the monastic communities of St Michael.

---

[97] 'Coptic Bindings', The Morgan Library and Museum, www.themorgan.org/collection/coptic-bindings.
[98] Newton, 'The Scriptorium and Library at Monte Cassino'.
[99] Lowden, 'Book Production', p. 465.   [100] Colophon of MS M.588; colophon of MS M.612.
[101] Colophon of MS M.613.
[102] XM 464–65; Layton, 'Rules, Patterns, and the Exercise of Power', p. 49.

Value of Their Labour: Spiritual

The relationships between the twenty-eight scribes named in the colophons are essential for understanding not only the scribal networks that were active in the Fayum Oasis, but also the time and effort needed to produce the books in the St Michael Collection. The colophons document in detail how the process of compiling the collection was a community endeavour.

The scribes Basil and Samuel eloquently described the gravity of the task of copying:

> Father, Son, and Holy Spirit protect the God-loving Father John the *oikonomos* of the monastery of the Archangel Michael in the mountains [Phantau] of Sophes district Fayum because he has provided this Hermeneiai for his Monastery ... Pray for me, that God may grant me the knowledge and in the small seconds my hands perceive grace! I still realise that I am learning. For humble Deacon Basil and Deacon Samuel, who is my son, are the students from Touton in Fayum. May our minds not have been inattentive, lest we be mistaken in a single word because we have written from the copy before us. Suffer for us, forgive us! [Written in the year] 614, the era of holy martyrs.[103]

This colophon indicates that around 897/8, Father John donated a Hermeneia to his monastery. At least two men, Basil and Samuel, copied and decorated the book. Asking the reader to forgive them for any mistakes, the scribes admit that they are still students from the book production workshop at Touton.

Throughout the colophons in the St Michael Collection, the scribes used a formula to describe the copying of books as a penance. They speak of making a *metanoia*, a term for repentance that can be loosely translated as penance:

> Bless me. I make a *metanoia*. Bear with me and my little handiwork, for I am not very skilled. Remember me so that God might have mercy on me. Amen.[104]
>
> Bless me. I make a *metanoia*, my clerical fathers. I, Isaac, the scribe who belongs to Ptepouhar. Bear with me and my feeble little handiwork, for I am not yet very skilled. ... but I received instruction from your holy prayers. Age of the Martyrs 609. I wrote these books.[105]
>
> Bless me. I make a *metanoia*. Bear with me, for I am not very skilled. I am a mere pupil. I have written this from a copy in front of me.[106]

---

[103] *Hermeneiai with Various Hymns*, Morgan Library and Museum, New York, MS M.574; translation adapted from Quecke, *Untersuchungen zum koptischen Stundengebet*, pp. 94–5.
[104] Colophon in MS M.586 written by Zakharias; translated in Alcock, 'Colophons', p. 6.
[105] MS M.612, written in 892. Alcock, 'Colophons', p. 12.
[106] MS M.583, written in 848 by Theodore. Alcock, 'Colophons', p. 7.

The purpose of the manuscripts, then, seems to have been both an act of penance on the part of the scribes and a holy gift to the monastic readers and listeners. This common theme of *metanoia* and the lack of skill suggests that copying was a pious, difficult task. Following Krueger's concern with scribal holiness, I emphasise that the colophons highlight the act of copying books as integral to the books' function within the monastic community.[107] These monks sustained a textual preservation project through their acts of penance (despite their acknowledged mistakes).

Value of the Book Producing Network: Community

The knowledge of the scribes and donors who helped produce the books provided additional value to the St Michael Collection. The colophons specifically request the reader to remember the scribes and donors; in many respects, this act of remembering the scribes, painters, donors, and monasteries was a goal of the colophons. The connections among the scribes, painters, and monasteries described in the colophons are often challenging to disentangle. These connections emerge fully once the entire collection is analysed as a group, but it is still difficult to discern the relationships between the lists of peoples and place names. Social network analysis, however, can highlight connections that are not readily discernible and visually organise the various individuals who were involved in the production of the manuscripts in the St Michael Collection.

Through these connections, we can assess the community value of books, which relied on the role of the monastic community's memory of the book producers. For example, Fig. 9.1 visualises information from the colophons about relationships between patrons and monasteries in the Fayum Oasis. The clusters here plotted represent scribes of the St Michael Collection who either worked together or worked at the same monastery. Of the thirty-three colophons in the St Michael Collection, twenty-two had named donors. For the most part, each patron donated only one manuscript to the monastery of St Michael. The shades of dark grey represent monasteries that produced books, and the tones of light grey represent patrons who commissioned books from those monasteries; the darker the shade, the higher the degree to which the monasteries are connected by the patrons of the books. Touton has the most commissions from named patrons, so it is the deepest shade of grey.

---

[107] Krueger, *Writing and Holiness*, p. 6.

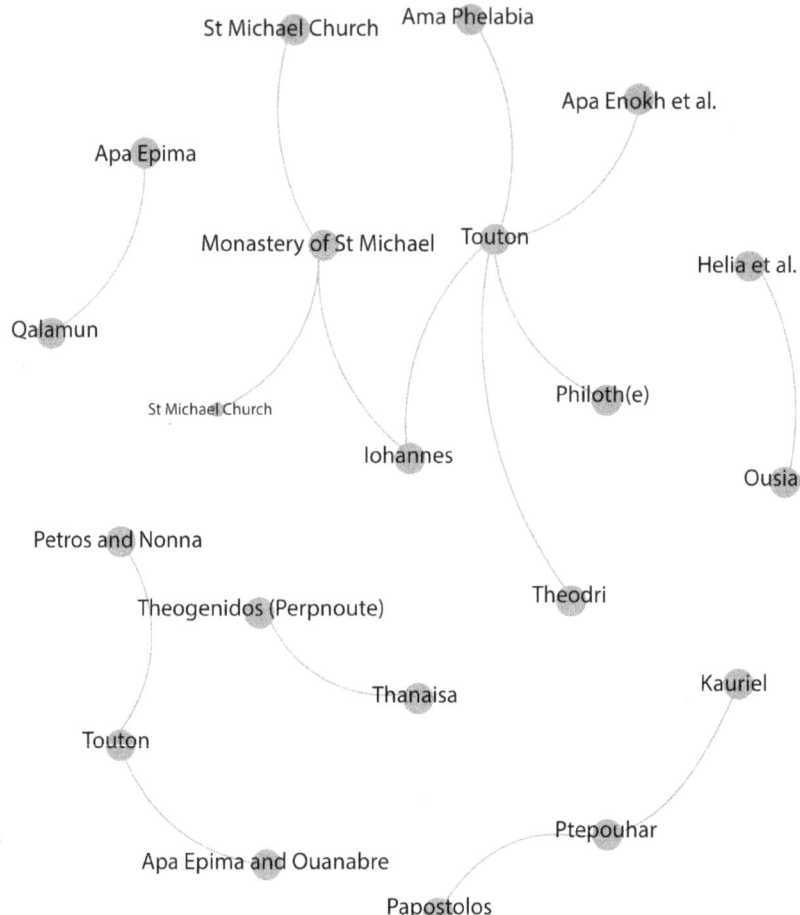

Fig. 9.1. Information from the colophons about relationships between patrons and monasteries in the Fayum Oasis.

The visualisations also help disentangle the relationships between patrons and manuscripts. Initially, I assumed that there might be a correlation between the number of people donating a manuscript and its size, since a large book would presumably be more expensive than a small book. As many as eight patrons contributed to one manuscript, a Catholic epistle, originally donated to the monastery of St George Martyr at Narmouthis, not the monastery of St Michael (Fig. 9.2).[108] Despite the many people contributing to this donation, this manuscript, with only sixteen parchment sheets, is one of the smaller

---

[108] MS M.572's colophon: Apa Enokh, Papa Abraham, Papa Samuel, Papa Seureos, Deacon Apaioulei [or Apa Ioulei] son of Apa Semon, the novices Deacon Khouleip and Deacon [NN], together with the other minor brothers, the reader Ab[raham], and Deacon Khouleip.

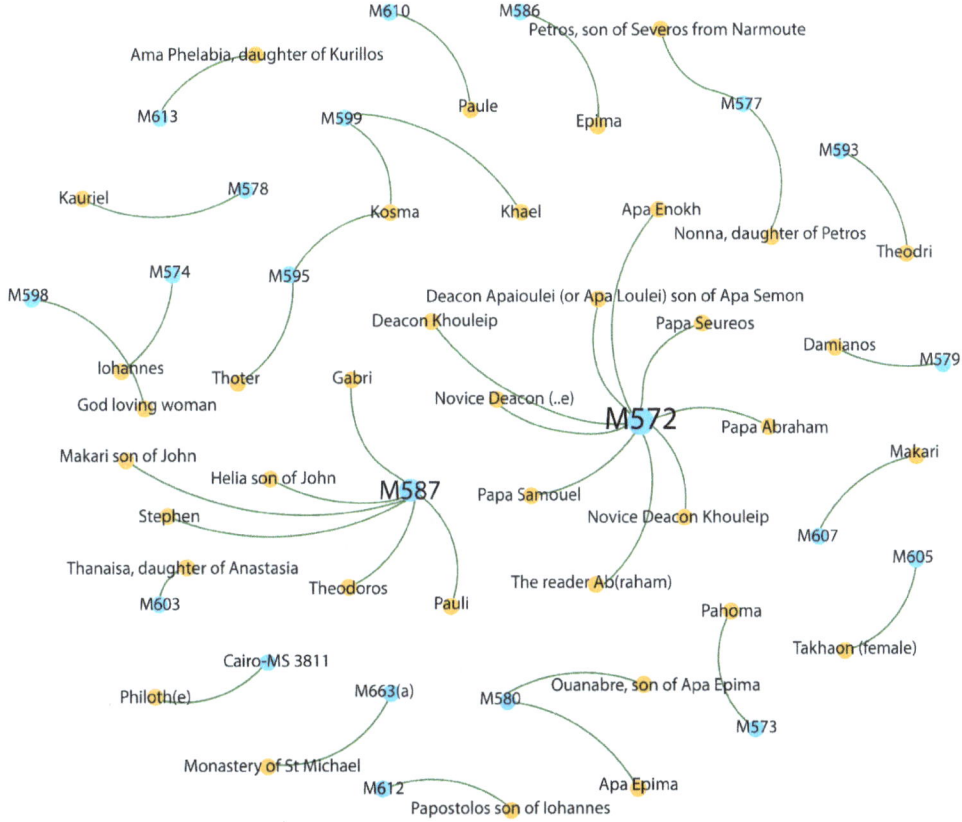

Fig. 9.2. Relationships between patrons and manuscripts.

manuscripts in the collection. Moreover, it contains almost no decoration. This suggests that – at least for the St Michael Collection – there is no consistent correlation between manuscript size, decoration, and the number of patrons donating a single manuscript. For the most part, each patron only gave one manuscript to the monastery of St Michael.

The monks recognised the names in the colophons, and, together, these names represent the manuscript community of the southern Fayum Oasis (Fig. 9.3). The visualisations reveal both connections among the manuscripts' communities and the communities' importance to the production of the St Michael Collection. The spiritual and community value of the collection made the books worth more than their actual monetary costs.

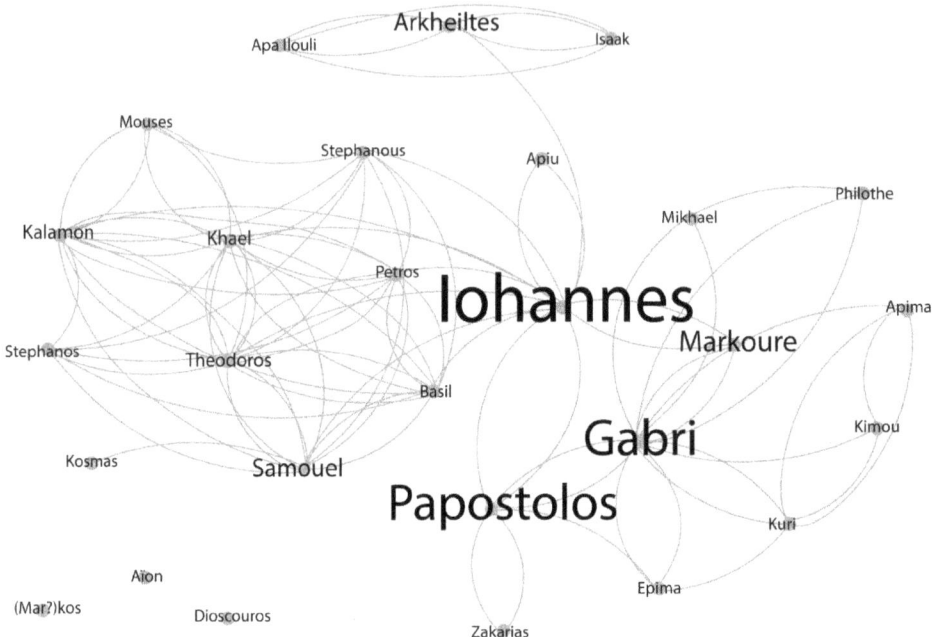

Fig. 9.3. Network of book producers in the Fayum Oasis.

Conclusions

Part of the importance of the St Michael Collection lies in the fact that the manuscripts have remained together as a group in the Morgan Library and Museum in New York.[109] The St Michael Collection reveals characteristics of medieval monastic libraries in the Fayum and possibly in other regions of Egypt. Similar intact collections are exceedingly rare. Many Egyptian monasteries probably had collections similar to the one associated with the monastery of St Michael, but they simply have not survived to modern times. Traces of those collections are preserved in the colophons of manuscripts dispersed throughout various collections in Europe and in the Coptic Museum in Cairo. Taken together, these manuscripts attest to the existence of an extended, thriving, and networked monastic book culture in the Fayum in the ninth and tenth centuries.

The St Michael Collection sheds light on crucial aspects of monastic book production, such as the high value of the materials, the technical skills of

---

[109] Depuydt, *Catalogue of Coptic Manuscripts*, p. lvii.

manuscript painters, and book culture (such as how generations of scribes and painters in far-flung monasteries collaborated to build monastic libraries). In this study, I have acknowledged that the cost-production value of manuscripts might not reflect true monastic expenditures or the spiritual value of the books, which is especially evident in the colophons' use of the word *metanoia*. The colophons reveal an extended community of scribes, painters, and donors who were monks and laymen. The authors of the colophons articulate their own perceptions of the monetary and spiritual value of these books. The nature of the Fayum book production centres cannot be fully deciphered with the St Michael Collection alone, yet the Collection demonstrates that they thrived and endured. Throughout the economic, religious, and political upheaval of Egypt in the ninth and tenth centuries, the monks of St Michael's enlisted the help of their monastic brothers elsewhere to create a set of liturgical manuscripts for their monastery.

Bibliography

Abbott, N. 'The Monasteries of the Fayyūm', *The American Journal of Semitic Languages and Literatures*, 53.1 (1936), 13–33.

Achi, A. 'Illuminating the Scriptorium: The St. Michael Collection and Monastic Book Production in the Fayyūm Oasis, Egypt during the Ninth and Tenth Centuries', unpublished PhD thesis, New York University, 2018.

Agati, M. L. *The Manuscript Book: A Compendium of Codicology* (Rome: 'L'ERMA' di Brettschneider, Roma, 2017).

Alcock, A. *The Life of Samuel of Kalamun by Isaac the Presbyter* (Warminster: Aris & Phillips, 1983).

Alcock, A. 'Colophons of Coptic Manuscripts Part One: Fayyum', online publication, available at www.academia.edu/30732203/Colophons_of_Coptic_Manuscripts_Part_One_Fayyum.

Alexander, J. *Medieval Illuminators and Their Methods of Work* (New Haven: Yale University Press, 1992).

Bagnall, R. S. *Early Christian Books in Egypt* (Princeton: Princeton University Press, 2009).

Bagnall, R. S. *Egypt in Late Antiquity* (Princeton: Princeton University Press, 1993).

Bagnall, R. S. and Rathbone, D. *Egypt from Alexander to the Early Christians: An Archaeological and Historical Guide* (Los Angeles: The J. Paul Getty Museum, 2014).

Begg, D. J. I. '"It Was Wonderful, Our Return in the Darkness with ... the Baskets of Papyri!" Papyrus Finds at Tebtunis from the Bagnani Archives, 1931–1936', *Bulletin of the American Society of Papyrologists*, 35 (1998), 185–210.

Begg, D. J. I. 'New Potential from Old Archives' [unpublished paper presented at the conference 'Ancient Lives: The Tebtunis Papyri in Context', Berkeley, 2000].

Boud'hors, A. 'Copie et circulation des livres dans la région thébaine' in A. Delattre and P. Heilporn (eds.), *'Et maintenant ce ne sont plus que des villages': Thèbes et sa région aux région époques hellénistique, romaine et byzantine Actes du colloque tenu à Bruxelles les 2 et 3 decembre 2005* (Brussels: Association égyptologique Reine Elisabeth, 2008), pp. 149-62.

Bowman, A. K. *Egypt after the Pharaohs: 332 BC-AD 642: From Alexander to the Arab Conquest* (Berkeley and Los Angeles: University of California Press, 1996).

Browne, G. M. 'Ad P. Colon. Inv.Nr. 10.213', *Zeitschrift für Papyrologie und Epigraphik*, 14 (1974), 51-2.

Buzi, P. and Emmel, S. 'Coptic Codicology', in A. Bausi, P. G. Borbone, F. Briquel-Chatonnet, P. Buzi, J. Gippert, C. Macé, M. Maniaci, Z. Melissakis, L. E. Parodi, and W. Witakowski (eds.), *Comparative Oriental Manuscript Studies: An Introduction* (Hamburg: Comparative Oriental Manuscript Studies, 2015), pp. 137-53.

Clemens, R. and Graham, T. *Introduction to Manuscript Studies* (Ithaca: Cornell University Press, 2008).

Cockerell, D. 'The Development of Bookbinding Methods – Coptic Influence', *The Library*, 4.1 (1932), 1-19.

Cool, H. E. M. *Eating and Drinking in Roman Britain* (Cambridge: Cambridge University Press, 2006).

Coquin, R.-G. 'Monasteries of the Fayyum' in A. S. Atiya (ed.), *The Coptic Encyclopedia* (New York: Maxwell Macmillan International, 1991), pp. 1650b-1651b.

Cromwell, J. *Recording Village Life: A Coptic Scribe in Early Islamic Egypt* (Ann Arbor: University of Michigan Press, 2017).

Cromwell, J. and Grossman, E. 'Condition(al)s of Repayment: *P.CLT* 10 Reconsidered', *The Journal of Egyptian Archaeology*, 96 (2010), 149-60.

Crum, W. E. 'Inscriptions from Shenoute's Monastery', *The Journal of Theological Studies*, 5.20 (1904), 552-69.

Crum, W. E. 'A Coptic Recipe for the Preparation of Parchment', *Society of Biblical Archaeology*, 27 (1905), 166-70.

Crum, W. E. 'Bibliography: Christian Egypt', *Journal of Egyptian Archaeology*, 5 (1918), 201-15.Crum, W. E. *A Coptic Dictionary* (Oxford: Oxford University Press, 1939).

Davis, S. J., Pyke, G., Davidson, E., Farag, M., and Schriever, D., with contributions by Blanke, L. 'Left Behind: A Recent Discovery of Manuscript Fragments in the White Monastery Church', *Journal of Coptic Studies*, 16 (2014), 69-87.

Depuydt, L. *Catalogue of Coptic Manuscripts in the Pierpont Morgan Library* (Leuven: Peeters, 1993).

Doresse, J. 'Monastères coptes aux environs d'Armant en Thébaide', *Analecta Bollandiana*, 67 (1949), 327–49.

Emmel, S. 'Coptic Manuscripts' in A. Bausi, P. G. Borbone, F. Briquel-Chatonnet, P. Buzi, J. Gippert, C. Macé, M. Maniaci, Z. Melissakis, L. E. Parodi, and W. Witakowski (eds.), *Comparative Oriental Manuscript Studies: An Introduction* (Hamburg: Comparative Oriental Manuscript Studies, 2015), pp. 44–6.

Fournet, J.-L. 'The Multilingual Environment of Late Antique Egypt: Greek, Latin, Coptic, and Persian Documentation' in R. S. Bagnall (ed.), *Oxford Handbook of Papyrology* (Oxford: Oxford University Press, 2009), pp. 418–51.

Gallazzi, C. 'La ripresa degli scavi a Umm-el-Breigât (Tebtynis)', *Acme*, 48 (1995), 3–24.

Gallazzi, C. 'Due campagne di scavo a Umm-el-Breigât (Tebtynis), 1995 e 1996', *Acme*, 50 (1997), 15–30.

Gascou, J. 'Economic Activities of Monasteries' in A. S. Atiya (ed.), *The Coptic Encyclopedia* (New York: Maxwell Macmillan International, 1991), pp. 1639a–1645b.

Goehring, J. E. *Ascetics, Society, and the Desert: Studies in Early Egyptian Monasticism* (Harrisburg: Trinity Press International, 1999).

Goehring, J. E. 'Monasticism in Byzantine Egypt' in R. S. Bagnall (ed.), *Egypt in the Byzantine World, 300–700* (New York: Cambridge University Press, 2007), pp. 390–407.

Górecki, T. 'Sheikh Abd El-Gurna: Hermitage in Tomb 1152 and Chapel in Tomb 1151', *Polish Archaeology in the Mediterranean*, 19 (2010), 297–303.

Hadji-Minaglou, G. *Tebtynis IV: les habitations à l'est du temple de Soknebtynis* (Cairo: Institut Français d'Archéologie Orientale, 2007).

Haines-Eitzen, K. 'Textual Communities in Late Antique Christianity' in P. Rousseau (ed.), *A Companion to Late Antiquity* (Chichester: Blackwell, 2009), pp. 246–57.

Hyvernat, H. *A Check List of Coptic Manuscripts in the Pierpont Morgan Library* (New York: Privately printed, 1919).

Keenan, J. 'Pastoralism in Roman Egypt', *Bulletin of the American Society of Papyrologists*, 26.3/4 (1989), 175–200.

Keenan, J. 'Deserted Villages: From the Ancient to the Medieval Fayyum', *Bulletin of the American Society of Papyrologists*, 40 (2003), 119–39.

Keenan, J. 'Fayyum Villages in SPP XX 229' in J. Frösén, T. Purola, and E. Salmenkivi (eds.), *Proceedings of the 24th International Congress of Papyrology, Helsinki, 1–7 August, 2004* (Helsinki: Societas Scientarum Fennica, 2004), pp. 486–96.

Koenen, L. 'Ein Mönch als Berufsschreiber. Zur Buchproduktion im 5./6. Jahrhundert', in *Festschrift zum 150 jährigen Bestehen des Berliner Ägyptischen Museums* (Berlin: Akademie-Verlag, 1974), pp. 347–54.

Kotsifou, C. 'Bookbinding and Manuscript Illumination in Late Antique and Early Medieval Monastic Circles in Egypt' in J. P. Monferrer-Sala, H. Teuele, and

S. Torallas Tovar (eds.), *Eastern Christians and Their Written Heritage: Manuscript, Scribes, and Context* (Leuven: Peeters, 2012), pp. 213–44.

Kotsifou, C. 'Books and Book Production in the Monastic Communities of Byzantine Egypt' in W. Klingshirn and L. Safran (eds.), *The Early Christian Book* (Washington, DC: The Catholic University of America Press, 2007), pp. 48–68.

Krueger, D. *Writing and Holiness: The Practice of Authorship in the Early Christian East* (Philadelphia: University of Pennsylvania Press, 2011).

Layton, B. 'Rules, Patterns, and the Exercise of Power in Shenoute's Monastery: The Problem of World Replacement and Identity Maintenance', *Journal of Early Christian Studies*, 15.1 (2007), 45–73.

Layton, B. 'The Monastic Rules of Shenoute' in J. Clackson, A. Boud'hors, C. Louis, and P. Sijpesteijn (eds.), *Monastic Estates in Late Antique and Early Islamic Egypt: Ostraca, Papyri, and Essays in Memory of Sarah Clackson (P.Clackson)* (Cincinnati: The American Society of Papyrologists, 2009), pp. 170–7.

Litinas, N. *Tebtynis III: Vessels' Notations from Tebtynis* (Cairo: Institut français d'archéologie orientale, 2000).

Lowden, J. 'Book Production' in J. Haldon, E. Jeffreys, and R. Cormack (eds.), *Oxford Handbook of Byzantine Studies* (Oxford: Oxford University Press, 2008), pp. 462–72.

Luijendijk, A.-M. *Forbidden Oracles? The Gospel of the Lots of Mary* (Tübingen: Mohr Siebeck, 2014).

McFadden, D., Pasanen, E. G., Valero, M. D., Roberts, E. K., and Lee, T. M. 'Effect of Prenatal Androgens on Click-Evoked Otoacoustic Emissions in Male and Female Sheep (Ovis Aries)', *Hormones and Behavior*, 55.1 (2009), 98–105.

Mathisen, R. 'Paleography and Codicology' in S. A. Harvey (ed.), *The Oxford Handbook of Early Christian Studies* (Oxford: Oxford University Press, 2008), pp. 140–68.

Meinardus, O. F. A. *Two Thousand Years of Coptic Christianity* (Cairo: American University in Cairo Press, 1999).

Migne, J.-P. (ed.) *Patrologia Graeca*, 161 vols (Paris: Imprimerie Catholique, 1857–66).

Newton, F. *The Scriptorium and Library at Monte Cassino, 1085–1105* (Cambridge: Cambridge University Press, 1999).

Orlandi, T. 'The Library of the Monastery of Saint Shenute at Atripe' in A. Egberts, B. P. Muhs, and J. van der Vliet (eds.), *Perspectives on Panopolis: An Egyptian Town from Alexander the Great to the Arab Conquest* (Leiden: Brill, 1998), pp. 211–31.

Panayotova, S. *Colour: The Art and Science of Illuminated Manuscripts* (Turnhout: Brepols, 2016).

Papaconstantinou, A. 'Egypt' in S. F. Johnson (ed.), *The Oxford Handbook of Late Antiquity* (Oxford: Oxford University Press, 2012), pp. 195–223.

Parássoglou, G. M. 'A Book Illuminator in Byzantine Egypt', *Byzantion*, 44 (1974), 362–8.

Petersen, T. C. 'The Paragraph Mark in Illuminated Coptic Manuscripts' in D. Miner (ed.), *Studies in Art and Literature for Belle Da Coasta Greene* (Princeton: Princeton University Press, 1954), pp. 295–330.

Quecke, H. *Untersuchungen Zum Koptischen Stundengebet* (Leuven: Université catholique de Louvain, 1970).

Rathbone, D. *Economic Rationalism and Rural Society in Third-Century AD Egypt: The Heroninos Archive and the Appianus Estate* (Cambridge: Cambridge University Press, 1991).

Richter, T. S. 'The Cultivation of Monastic Estates in Late Antique and Early Islamic Egypt: Some Evidence from Coptic Land Leases and Related Documents' in A. Boud'hors, J. Clackson, C. Louis, and P. Sijpesteijn (eds.), *Monastic Estates in Late Antique and Early Islamic Egypt: Ostraca, Papyri, and Essays in Memory of Sarah Clackson (P.Clackson)* (Cincinnati: The American Society of Papyrologists, 2009), pp. 205–16.

Richter, T. S. 'Language Choice in the Qurra Dossier' in A. Papaconstantinou (ed.), *The Multilingual Experience in Egypt, from the Ptolemies to the Abbasids* (Farnham: Ashgate Publishing, Ltd., 2010), pp. 189–220.

Rondot, V., Boutros, R., and Soukiassian, G. *Tebtynis II: le temple de Soknebtynis et son dromos* (Cairo: Institut français d'archéologie orientale, 2004).

Russell, N. *The Lives of the Desert Fathers: The Historia Monachorum in Aegypto* (Collegeville, MN: Cistercian Publications, 1981).

Samuelson, P. and Nordhause, W. *Economics* (New York: McGraw-Hill, 1948).

Swanson, M. N. *The Coptic Papacy in Islamic Egypt: (641–1517)* (Cairo: American University in Cairo Press, 2010).

Timm, S. *Das christlich-koptische Ägypten in arabischer Zeit, eine Sammlung christlicher Stätten in Ägypten in arabischer Zeit*, 7 vols (Wiesbaden: L. Reichert, 1984–2007).

Ward, B. *The Sayings of the Desert Fathers: The Alphabetical Collection* (Kalamazoo: Cistercian Publications, 1984).

Weber, M. 'Zur Ausschmückung Koptischer Bücher', *Enchoria*, 3 (1973), 53–62.

Wipszycka, E. *Moines et communautés monastiques en Égypte* (Warsaw: University of Warsaw and Raphael Taubenschlag Foundation, 2009).

Wipszycka, E. 'Resources and Economic Activities of the Egyptian Monastic Communities (4th–8th Century)', *Journal of Juristic Papyrology*, 41 (2011), 159–263.

Wortley, J. (ed.) *The Spiritual Meadow (Pratum Spirituale) by John Moschus* (Minnesota: Liturgical Press, 2008).

III.

Monastic Encounters: Travel,
Pilgrimage, and Donations

10 | Distinguishing Offerings from Blessings in Early Byzantine Monasticism: The Significance of *P.Ness.* III 79 (ca. 600 AD)

DANIEL F. CANER

This essay explores an important aspect of early monastic economies: the management of lay donations. It is now recognised that the 'road to riches' for many early Byzantine monasteries was paved by the receipt of lay donations: as Michel Kaplan has recently summarised, 'outside of Egypt, work as a source of revenues for the monasteries of the Roman East ... occupied a secondary place after alms and donations'.[1] It is also clear that not all lay donations were given for the same purposes.[2] Nonetheless, while general discussions of the role of lay donations in early Byzantine monastic economies certainly exist,[3] few have explored how monks managed such gifts after their receipt, or what ethical or practical considerations might have shaped their practices.[4] I therefore examine here a monastic papyrus

---

[1] Kaplan, 'The Economy of Byzantine Monasteries', p. 360; see also López, *Shenoute of Atripe and the Uses of Poverty*, pp. 46–72; Gascou, 'Monasteries', p. 1641.

[2] Caner, *The Rich and the Pure*; Davies and Fouracre, *The Languages of Gift*; Silber, 'Echoes of Sacrifice?'.

[3] For example, Klein, 'Von Hesychie zu Ökonomie'; Wipszycka, 'Resources and Economic Activities'; Wipszycka, *Moines et communautés monastiques*, pp. 471–565; Wipszycka, *Les ressources et les activités économiques des églises*, pp. 29–32.

[4] A notable exception is Papaconstantinou, 'Donation and Negotiation', which uses Egyptian papyri to differentiate offerings (προσφοραί) from bequests or grants (δωρεαί), arguing (pp. 76–80) that the former were 'essentially in kind and were intended as contributions towards the day-to-day expenses and management of the institutions, including their charitable activity', while the latter 'increased the economic assets of the institution through the transfer of profit-bearing items'. This argument is important but also problematic: since formal testamentary documents required use of a generic legal term to describe assets or privileges being transferred for an endowment, this formal legalese (*doreai*) obscures the specific religious identity and intent of such gifts. Furthermore, although no extant papyrus document attests an immovable gift of land or house itself being designated as a *prosphora*, hagiography includes episodes where offerings provide long-term assets, such as a new building (Cyril of Scythopolis, *Vita Euthymii* 50 [translation: Price, *Cyril of Scythopolis*]; Gerontius, *Vita Melaniae Iunioris* 49 [translation: Clark, *Life of Melania the Younger*]. In fact, some of the papyri cited to show the distinctiveness of *doreai* (*P.Cair.Masp.* I 67003, II 67151, 67312) specify that these were being given to endow long-term performances of liturgical *prosphorai*, closely connecting (or blurring any hard distinction between) these categories of gifts. Indeed, since *P.Cair.Masp.* III 67324 specifies that *prosphorai* given in kind were to be used to fund such liturgical performances, we might speculate that the bequests given to

discovered in early seventh-century Palestine that distinguishes between two types of Christian religious gifts – offerings (*prosphorai*), on the one hand, and blessings (*eulogiai*), on the other. This is the only extant papyrus that distinguishes between these two types of gifts within the same document. To help explain this and other features, I shall first analyse the document itself, and then for comparanda I will draw attention to concerns and resulting 'best practices' attested in both early Byzantine hagiography and modern non-profit organisations.

To justify this somewhat anachronistic approach, let me recall an observation of a late, great historian of ancient Mediterranean economies. In the last publication of his career, Moses Finley lamented how few studies of classical cities had shed any light on how the ancient economies of those cities had actually worked. The problem was methodological: most studies just summarised whatever data could be mined from ancient sources without invoking models for interpreting the resulting data through comparison and contrast. Such an approach, based on the explicit use of models, was necessary, he argued, both because there was not nearly enough information to reconstruct any ancient economy, and because scholars tended to fill in the gaps with implicit assumptions about how such economies worked anyway.[5] Far better, he maintained, that we be explicit about our assumptions and the paradigms behind them from the start; this would provide a clear basis for comparison and contrast, and might even reveal aspects of ancient economies that were previously unimagined.

What Finley says about reconstructing the economies of ancient cities is applicable to the study of ancient monastic economies as well. Papyrus 'archives' present a largely random and fragmentary mass of evidence. The numerical data contained in this evidence cannot be added up to reconstruct any monastery's economy, but the terminology it uses should alert us to underlying programmatic concerns. As John Philip Thomas observes, 'Byzantine sources give every indication of being very careful about [distinguishing between various] incomes, fees and emoluments' religious foundations received, adding that this 'deserves close attention ... and promises rich rewards for future investigation'.[6] A Greek monastic papyrus known as *P.Ness*. III 79 presents just such an opportunity for investigation.

endow liturgical *prosphorai* in *P.Cair.Masp.* I 67003, II 67151, and II 67312 were similarly considered to be *prosphorai* (see Thomas, *Private Religious Foundations*, p. 76: 'Some of these [*prosphorai*] donations may actually have been contractual fulfillments of earlier testamentary benefactions that come under the designation of *prosphora mortis causa*'). So, it may be that no sharp distinction between *doreai* and *prosphorai* existed outside of the legal sphere.

[5] Finley, *Ancient History*, pp. 61–6.   [6] Thomas, *Private Religious Foundations*, p. 4.

Its monastic authors carefully distinguished between the donations their monastery had received as offerings (προσφοραί, *prosphorai*) and the donations it had received called blessings (εὐλογίαι, *eulogiai*), separating the two types of donations in different registers within the same document. Because its combined reference to and separation of these types of donations is unique in the extant papyrological record, and because it does not provide any explanation about the meaning or purpose behind this differentiation, it presents an interpretative challenge that requires drawing parallels from models both ancient and modern.

My intention, however, is not merely to show that *P.Ness.* III 79 is unique, but also to show that it is uniquely revealing. It demonstrates that monastic stewards in early Byzantine monasteries saw a categorical difference between donations called offerings and donations called blessings. This has not been recognised before, partly because donations called 'blessings', whether called *eulogiai* in Greek or *smou* (ⲥⲙⲟⲩ) in Coptic, are seldom mentioned in papyri.[7] *P.Ness.* III 79 provides singular documentary proof that *eulogiai* constituted a distinct category of Christian gift in the Byzantine monastic mind – distinct from, but closely related to, Christian *prosphorai*.

Here, I shall propose that these two types of donations were carefully differentiated in this document because the stewards knew that in the case of offerings their monastery was expected to use them following the specific wishes of their donors, but in the case of blessings it was not. To substantiate this, I will invoke not only early Byzantine hagiography, which illustrates some of the ethical norms and expectations that monks at Nessana might have known, but also modern distinctions that non-profit organisations draw today between 'restricted' and 'unrestricted' gifts. This distinction helps non-profits clarify obligations and uses associated with benefactors' donations. Of course, the restricted/unrestricted gift analogy can only go so far in suggesting why early Byzantine monks distinguished between offerings and blessings. Nonetheless, using this model to illumine the ancient distinction is worthwhile, insofar as one point of using any model is to determine how much something less familiar corresponds to, or differs from, a more familiar ideal or practice. And what early Byzantine monasteries and modern non-profits had in common was a need to secure or maintain their donors' goodwill by making clear from the start how their donations were going to be used.

---

[7] Not to say that they are completely unattested in papyri; for references, see Caner, *The Rich and the Pure*, p. 156.

P.Ness. III 79 and the St Sergius Monastery at Nessana

P.Ness. III 79 is one of nearly 200 papyri discovered in the 1930s in the ruins of Nessana (Auja el-Hafir/Nitzana) in modern Israel's southern Negev Desert. Nessana was one of the six so-called 'dead cities' that flourished in the arid Late Roman province of Third Palestine south-east of Gaza during the early Byzantine era. Like those other desert towns, it owed its unprecedented growth at this time to the nearby Gaza wine trade, its own specialisation in dry farming, and its location on an important pilgrimage route from Jerusalem to Mount Sinai. Inhabited up to the ninth century, it reached its peak expansion during the seventh century, when it must have bustled with an estimated 2,000 people, several caravanserais, and at least three churches.[8]

Despite being heavily quarried to serve as an Ottoman army base during World War I, Nessana remains the most revealing of all the Negev dead cities due to the discovery there of two separate papyri collections. The recovered documents are mostly in Greek (some are in Arabic or Syriac), and all were written between the fifth and eighth centuries. The larger of the collections, which includes *P.Ness.* III 79, was found in a niche of a wall of a church dedicated to Sts Sergius and Bacchus on the town's acropolis. Together with its adjacent baptistery, this sizeable church (also known as the North Church) was renovated with the addition of a small monastery in the early seventh century. Measuring 21 m by 14 m, its central building enclosed an atrium and a separate interior chapel. Two more enclosed spaces (or 'annexes') ran along the western and eastern sides of this building; the western annex had five rooms. Regrettably, the excavation report says nothing about either their use or their chronological relation to the monastery's central building.[9] It is safe to say, however, that the monastery could have housed just a handful of monks, and that it should be identified with 'the monastery of St Sergius' mentioned in *P.Ness.* III 79.

Called 'An Account of Offerings to the Church of St Sergius' by its editor Casper Kraemer, *P.Ness.* III 79 actually contains at least four distinct registers, each recording donations given to the St Sergius church or its monastery over two, probably successive, years (for Kraemer's text and translation, see the Appendix below). The papyrus, 88 cm long, is not entirely preserved; some of its bottom and all its right side are missing, so

---

[8] Colt, *Excavations at Nessana*; Gutwein, *Third Palestine*; Urman, 'Nessana Excavations'; Ruffini, 'Village Life'; and Trombley, 'From *Kastron* to *Qaṣr*'.
[9] Urman, 'Nessana Excavations', pp. 11*–21*.

we do not know what materials were given and recorded in each register (except wine, mentioned in lines 66–67), or in what quantities. Moreover, the text becomes increasingly mutilated as it approaches the right side. Nonetheless, the bottom is more fully preserved, so that much can be reconstructed from the entries there,[10] and enough remains of the document over all to show that consistent patterns of categorical recordkeeping were practised and maintained throughout.

'Categorical recordkeeping' is the correct description, because what makes *P.Ness.* III 79 unique is that it explicitly distinguishes between two specific categories of Christian gifts, designated *prosphorai* and *eulogiai*, with each entered into a separate register by the same (it appears) scribal hand. After an initial, nearly illegible register (ll. 1–24), we find a second register, entitled 'Account of receipts of *prosphora* to the monastery for the m[. . . .]',[11] followed by a list of donors (ll. 25–43), some of whose names are followed by notations starting with the Greek preposition *eis*, 'for', indicating the purpose of the gift. After this register comes a third register, entitled 'Account of receipts of *eulogia* to the monastery of St Sergius', followed by another set of donors (ll. 44–55); then a fourth register, entitled 'Account of receipts of *eulogia* for the festival of St Sergius', which lists only one donor (ll. 56–7); and then a final list – possibly a fifth register – marked ιδ ('14/4'), which Kraemer considered an abbreviation for the date, 'Fourth Indiction', i.e., the fourth year in a fifteen-year tax cycle. These final entries present a series of gifts (ll. 58–67). Their categorical type is not specified. Because they include a Theodore son of Stephan whose name is also found among the *prosphora* donors in the second register (ll. 58, 27), and because they resemble the entries of that second register by including notations in

---

[10] I thank the Pierpont Morgan Library for sending me photographs to inspect *gratis*. Not being a specialist in Greek palaeography, I cannot discern all the letters that appear with dots in Kraemer's edition. My interpretation completely relies on his edition and expertise. In
a personal communication, Peter van Minnen expressed scepticism that the document can be interpreted as I do, because he suggests 1) that the last register (Section V, lines 59 forward), which contains several '*eis*' phrases indicating purpose, could be a continuation of the previous *eulogia* register (Section IV); and 2) that these may indicate what the *eulogiai* of previous register were spent on; and 3) that the dashes of the prior register (Section III) could have included more such phrases, now lost; and 4) that I have over-interpreted the check marks, which could have been made just for adding up donations. While possible, van Minnen's objections themselves are speculations, requiring inferences that are not clearly supported in the document. Lacking a comparable papyrus that lists and marks both *prosphorai* and *eulogiai*, I must make an inductive argument based on contemporary hagiography. I believe *P.Ness.* III 79 sufficiently conforms to hagiographical distinctions to make my interpretation credible; readers must decide for themselves if it is reasonable or convincing.

[11] The translations I provide for the headings and other details of the Greek text are more literal than those in Kraemer's original translation, which is reproduced in the Appendix.

the form of prepositional phrases after the names of several of its donors (ll. 58, 62, 64, 66–7), it is plausible that these final entries recorded *prosphora* donations as well, received a year or so later than those recorded in the previous *prosphora* register. All the previous registers seem to have been written by the same hand in the same year. Because *P.Ness*. III 79 was written on the verso of a document firmly dated to 596/7 – thereby establishing the *terminus post quem* for *P.Ness*. III 79 – and because the fourth indiction mentioned in the final heading of *P.Ness*. III 79 could have fallen in 600/1, Kraemer dated the writing of all the contents of *P.Ness*. III 79 to the final years of the sixth century and first year of the seventh, namely ca. 596/7–600/1.[12]

Kraemer observes that the different headings that the steward or scribe chose to use in *P.Ness*. III 79 'leave no doubt that [their] phraseology was designed to reflect a distinction between *eulogiai* and *prosphorai*'.[13] He also notes that this use of different headings implies that these donations had different intended purposes. This inference is supported by the fact that, whereas many of the individual *prosphorai* entries add phrases with the preposition *eis*, which, as noted above, seems to have indicated the specific purpose for which each of those so marked had been given (ll. 25, 27–9, 31, 35, 37, 39, 43; cf. 58, 62, 64, 66–7), none of the *eulogiai* entries have such notations, except for a general indication in the headings that they were either 'for the monastery of St Sergius' or 'for the festival of St Sergius' (a feature discussed below).

Indeed, additional scribal markings found beside entries throughout the document suggest that these two categories of donations were managed differently. Nearly all the *prosphorai* and *eulogiai* entries are preceded by a down stroke, probably acknowledging receipt (or promise) of a gift from its named donor. But, otherwise, the marks differ markedly and consistently between the two types of donations: whereas almost all *prosphorai* entries have two (ll. 26, 28, 30, 33, 34, 41–3), three (27, 32, 36, 37, 39, 40), or even four (31) more strokes besides the entry, only one single *eulogia* entry has an extra stroke (l. 46). This suggests that the recordkeeper felt more concern to record gifts received from – or actions taken for – donors of *prosphorai* than donors of *eulogiai*. *P.Ness*. III 79 thus presents an intriguing pattern of donative categories, recordkeeping, and stewardship practices. What does it mean?

---

[12] *P.Ness*. III pp. 229 and 232 n. 58. The Duke Databank of Documentary Papyri and the Trismegistos Database (TM 39302) both date it circa 600–25, without explanation.

[13] *P.Ness*. III p. 229.

Previous Conjectures Regarding Nessana Offerings and Blessings

Casper Kraemer and Frank Trombley have both offered conjectures about how these categories should be interpreted. Regarding *prosphorai*, the prepositional phrases added to the donor's name specify that they had been given to the monastery variously 'for the women's quarters' (ll. 25, 29, 31, 62; cf. 26, 32, 33), 'for the atrium' (ll. 27, 39, 40, 58), and 'for the house/household [*oikos*] of Jumahir' (ll. 28, 35, 37, 43), as well as (if the last register also records *prosphorai*) 'for the house/household of Zunayn' (l. 64), '[for the house/household] of Abdella' (l. 66), '[for the house/household] of John, son of Quthaim' (l. 67).[14] Because Kraemer believed that all these offerings referred to commemorative liturgies ('masses') performed for the dead, he translates the second register as 'Account of Receipt of Masses to the Monastery'. Regarding the *eulogiai*, he simply remarks that these were given to fund the monastery or its saints' day celebrations, adding that such gifts otherwise went into the general fund of the church. He bases this proposal on another papyrus, *P.Ness*. III 80, an 'Account of the Receipt of *Eulogiai* of St Sergius' (l. 1: λ(ό)γ(ος) τõν εὐλογιõν τοῦ ἁγί(ου) Σεργί(ου)). Dated to a thirteenth indiction (which Kraemer argues fell in 684/5), this records donations of wheat given as *eulogiai* by nine donors in quantities of 2 to 10 *modii*, averaging 3.7 *modii* per donor (approximately 432 kg in all). As with the *eulogiai* in *P.Ness*. III 79, these are all recorded without specifying a particular purpose and without scribal markings. Kraemer simply considered them to be donations to the monastery church. Frank Trombley, however, proposes that they represent 'an unofficial ecclesiastical tax on the wealthier members' of the Nessanite community. He bases this both on the large quantities of wheat involved, and on the similarity of this list to yet another Nessana document (*P.Ness*. III 81) that records wheat rendered to the state by Nessanites in the same year, apparently as taxes.[15]

To my knowledge, only Kraemer and Trombley have discussed these donative registers. Before turning to my own interpretation, let me explain my objections to theirs, starting with Trombley's assertion that the *eulogiai* represented a kind of 'ecclesiastical tax'. Of course, we can never know

---

[14] Kraemer and others have interpreted the dashes written after the names in lines 23, 26, 32, 33, 40, and 54 as 'ditto' marks, meaning that its sense should be derived from the preceding entry. This would increase the entries for *prosphorai* specifically earmarked for the *matronikia* (as would be the case in ll. 26, 32, 33) and atrium (l. 40).

[15] Trombley, 'From *Kastron* to *Qaṣr*', p. 186, referring to text in *P.Ness*. III p. 235.

whether gifts given to monks, clerics, or their institutions masked some kind of forced payment, tribute, or 'tax'. References in seventh-century papyri to first fruits (*aparchai*) collected by Egyptian monks from the laity in the Nile Valley have similarly been suspected of representing a compulsory tithe.[16] Indeed, church documents, as well as a fifth-century imperial law, attest that *prosphorai* were occasionally demanded by clerics as payments for liturgical services and that *eulogiai* were occasionally given as bribes.[17] Yet, it is also clear that those cases represented abuses of expected norms. Indeed, certain norms regarding *eulogiai* are evinced elsewhere in the Nessana papyri.

The Nessana papyri refer to Christian gifts of *eulogiai* in two other documents. One is an early seventh-century letter (*P.Ness*. III 50.5) written by a bishop of Aela (modern Eilat/Aqaba) to the abbot of the Sergius monastery, requesting that the abbot provide a *eulogia* at a festival of St Sergius in his absence. The other is an account by itinerant traders (*P.Ness*. III 89.24) that records their gift of a gold *solidus* as a *eulogia* at the basilica at Mount Sinai, where they had gone to fulfil a vow.[18] These documents show that the term 'blessing' was used and recognised in the Nessana region to designate a genuine religious gift. Moreover, if the *eulogiai* recorded in *P.Ness*. III 80 had reflected ecclesiastical payments complementing the state tax payments recorded in *P.Ness*. III 81 for the same year, we might expect that the donors found in one list would closely match those found in the other list, when in fact only one donor (Stephan son of Hanun) is listed as contributing in both cases. It therefore appears that the *eulogiai* registered in *P.Ness*. III 80 simply reflect the type of donations recorded in *P.Ness*. III 79 (as well as in *P.Ness*. III 50 and 89). In fact, we know from the Palestinian hagiographer Cyril of Scythopolis that it was customary for sizeable *eulogiai* to be given by lay donors to monasteries in the Judean Desert each year on an annual basis (Cyril of Scythopolis, *Vita Euthymii* 47, *Vita Iohannis Hesychastis* 20, *Vita Theodosii* 3;[19] cf. *P.Ness*. III 52.6). It is therefore reasonable to conclude that *P.Ness*. III 80 also represents documentation of such annual lay donations. This does not explain the significance of *eulogiai* gifts, per se, but it does support Kraemer's assumption that they represented genuine religious gifts rather than a compulsory tax.

---

[16] *P.Mon.Apollo* pp. 17–23; see also Wipszycka, 'Resources and Economic Activities'; Schenke, 'Monastic Control over Agriculture and Farming'; Thomas, *Private Religious Foundations*, p. 77.

[17] Patlagean, *Pauvreté économique*, pp. 293–4; Batiffol, *Études de liturgie et d'archéologie chrétienne*, pp. 247–64.

[18] *P.Ness*. III pp. 144–5 and 255–7.

[19] See the relevant sections in Price, *Cyril of Scythopolis*.

Nevertheless, Kraemer's assumption that the *P.Ness.* III 79 *prosphorai* all represent gifts specifically given to fund 'masses for the dead' (i.e., commemorative liturgies) cannot stand. Most of these entries specify that such offerings had been given for more immediate, concrete purposes ('for women's quarters', 'for the atrium'). Only those given 'for the house' of Jumahir (and perhaps of Zunayn, Abdella, and John) seem to have been given expressly for the specific purpose of funding commemorative liturgies for the individuals or households cited.[20] That said, Kraemer is almost certainly correct that donors who gave such offerings would have expected to receive liturgical commemoration at some point in return. A will preserved from sixth-century Egypt shows the relation between a monastery's annual receipt of *prosphorai* in the form of grain and wine and its performance of commemorative liturgies (also called *prosphorai*). It states that if the testator's heirs should neglect to give a monastery the annual *prosphorai* of grain and wine that the testator specified in his will, then the monastery itself must demand these from his heirs to ensure that his 'holy *prosphora*' (i.e., his annual commemorative liturgy) might be performed 'forever' (*P.Cair.Masp.* III 67324.2–8). Thus, a monastery's performance of a donor's *prosphora* commemorative services depended on its prior receipt of that donor's material *prosphorai*.[21]

An inscription affixed to a seventh-century altar in a Nessana church below the acropolis attests an analogous expectation. Calling on God to 'remember those who provided the *karpophoriai*' (Μνήσθετι Κύριε ... τῶν κα]ρποφορο[ύντων ... κ]αί),[22] it not only suggests that donors who contributed to the building of the altar at Nessana would later receive remembrance, but also presents such remembrance as both the ultimate motivation and the ultimate reward behind their contributions. The *prosphorai* recorded in *P.Ness.* III 79 probably had a similar dual motive: though explicitly given to fund the construction of the monastery's women's quarters and atrium, they almost certainly would have also been given with an expectation of receiving later remembrance in a liturgy.

---

[20] This assumes that it is correct to interpret *oikos* in its standard meaning of house or household. Kraemer suggests instead that these were regional anchoretic communities founded by the named individuals, which seems an unnecessary speculation.

[21] Unfortunately, the portions of this document explaining the circumstances of this commemorative endowment are lost. For distinctions between *donationes inter vivos* and *mortis causa* (the latter attested in papyri only from late sixth century onward), see Thomas, *Private Religious Foundations*, pp. 79–80.

[22] Figuras, 'Greek Inscriptions from Nessana', p. 233. *Prosphorai* were sometimes equated with such *karpophoriai*, or contributions: *Codex Iustiniaus* I.3.38, 2–4, Cyril of Scythopolis, *Vita Euthymii* 50.

Furthermore, given the apparent correspondence between the presumed date of the *prosphora* register and the presumed date of the building of the Sergius monastery itself, we may speculate that *P.Ness*. III 79 recorded lay offerings given to build those parts of the monastery at the time of its foundation. Giovanni Ruffini has explored the role played by a prominent Nessana family, the Patricius-Sergius family, both in building the church of Sts Sergius and Bacchus and in supplying the abbots of its monastery, emphasising the family's ambition to make the church-monastic complex one of the most elegant in the region.[23] But *P.Ness*. III 79 (which Ruffini does not discuss) suggests that this monastery was not considered a private or exclusive institution. Almost all the offerings it received for the women's quarters and atrium came from locals, who may have felt inclined to fund structures that they, as Nessanites, might regularly use as guests.[24]

To summarise, I disagree with Trombley that the *eulogiai* given at Nessana represented an ecclesiastical tax, and agree with Kraemer that they represented genuine religious gifts; I agree with Kraemer that *prosphorai* donations were usually given with an expectation that they would eventually receive commemoration in return. However, I do not agree with him that they were always given just for that specific purpose (hence it is incorrect to translate *prosphorai* as commemorative 'masses', as Kraemer did in his translation: see Appendix). The question remains how blessings differed from offerings at a conceptual level and why the writer of *P.Ness*. III 79 distinguished so carefully between the two. I propose that this effort reflected an ethical and practical need to separate donations that imposed obligations on the monks of St Sergius from those that did not.

Within the document itself, this interpretation is supported in the case of *prosphorai* not only by the inclusion of prepositional phrases recording the purposes for which donors expected monks to use these offerings, but also by the multiple stroke marks that the monastic steward or scribe made beside those *prosphorai* entries. Kraemer proposed that these marks recorded the monastery's initial receipt of an offering and the steps it followed to fulfil the obligation(s) that came with it: 'One portion of the account [ll. 25–43, i.e., the register of *prosphorai*] has been thoroughly checked by other hands, or at later times ... [these] probably indicate the

---

[23] Ruffini, 'Village Life', pp. 209–17.

[24] Both the atrium and the women's quarters (*matronikia*) would have been open to lay visitors; the latter was probably a reception room for females like the one built outside the Seridos monastery near Gaza: Barsanuphius, *Questiones et responses* 595 (translation: Neyt and de Angelis-Noah, *Barsanuphe et Jean de Gaza*). Almost all donors of Nessana *prosphorai* are male, but in one case a couple, George and Nona (i.e., 'nun', l. 63), give for the *matronikia*.

various steps in carrying out the obligation ... such as assignment to a priest and fulfilment of the obligation.'[25] Eight of the entries have three stroke marks, one has four; virtually all are connected to donations 'earmarked' for some specific purpose (ll. 27, 31, 35, 37, 39). Indeed, Egyptian papyri similarly use double stroke marks to record the receipt or dispatch of an item and performance of some act related to it.[26] Accordingly, while we do not know what the marks in this papyrus signified, it is hard not to surmise that they acknowledged first the initial receipt of the offering, then its use in some task related to the women's quarters or atrium (e.g., the purchase of construction materials), then (perhaps) the completion of some commemorative task, such as the inclusion of a donor's name in an inscription or liturgy. In other words, they recorded the fulfilment of an obligation, while also reflecting a concern to make sure that that fulfilment was carefully recorded.

What is striking about *P.Ness.* III 79, however, is not only how many of these marks are placed beside the entries for offerings, but also how few (only one, l. 46) are placed beside the entries for blessings. Whatever their purpose, the relative number of strokes for one type of gift in contrast to the other indicates that offerings and blessings differed in the levels of obligations and accountability they imposed on the monastery. Indeed, the fact that none of the blessings entries include prepositional phrases 'earmarking' them for specific purposes, beyond their destination, as the headings state, 'for the monastery of St Sergius' or 'for the festival of St Sergius', implies that such donations imposed fewer obligations on the monks towards their donors. So again, what accounts for these categorical distinctions and differences in recordkeeping in this document?

Offerings and Blessings in Early Byzantine Hagiography

Since no other papyrus treats *prosphorai* and *eulogiai* together, at this point we must go outside the papyrological record and turn to literary sources. For comparanda, it is perhaps worth noting that, when the Carolingian cleric Amalar of Metz wrote a treatise on church liturgical practices 250 years later, he distinguished between two types of Christian religious gifts, classifying one as *munera* and the other as *dona*. According to Amalar, *munera* given to a church or monastery were 'offered for some certain

---

[25] *P.Ness.* III p. 229.
[26] For example, *SB* XXII 15598, published originally in Papaconstantinou, 'Conversions monétaires byzantines'. I thank Arietta Papaconstantinou for this example.

service or reward, just as we offer to God to obtain release from sins'. This made them different from *dona* given to a church or monastery, to which he does not assign any specific purpose.[27] Thus, Amalar seems to have recognised a distinction in the ninth-century West between donations to a church or monastery that entailed the fulfilment of certain obligations to their donors ('some certain service or reward'), and those that did not.[28]

No similar statement survives from early Byzantium, but Greek hagiography shows that contemporaries did in fact recognise differences between Christian gifts called *prosphorai* and Christian gifts called *eulogiai*. While the concept of an offering is familiar to scholars,[29] that of a blessing is far less so, except in connection to items called *eulogiai* obtained at pilgrimage sites and healing shrines, often packaged in clay or lead ampullae stamped *EULOGIA*.[30] As I have explained extensively elsewhere,[31] however, such items represent just one manifestation of this particular donative category. Indeed, *eulogiai* are the type of material gift most frequently attested in hagiography from the fifth century onward, when references to blessings in hagiography begin to outnumber references to offerings by a ratio of two to one, and references to alms – ἐλεημοσύνη/*eleemosyne* – by more than three to one.[32] Usually attested in the form of food or cash, they are depicted as being given either by lay people to holy people (i.e., to monks or clerics), or the other way around. Conceptually, the basic ideas defining this category of gift are found in 2 Cor. 9:5–12. Here, Paul explains to his Corinthian

---

[27] Amalar of Metz, *Expositio missae: Dominus vobiscum*, can. 27 (Hannsens, *Amalarii episcopi*, 1. 306): 'Dona sunt quae voluntarie donantur; munera sunt quae pro aliquo munere vel mercede offeruntur, sicut nos offerimus Deo, ut peccata nostra dimitantur.'

[28] Jussen, 'Religious Discourses of the Gift', p. 191 calls Amalar's testimony a 'lone voice among the everyday semantics of authors and preachers in whose texts *munus* precisely did not have the meaning that Amalar invoked'. Unfamiliar though I am with the material and context, I suspect Jussen dismisses Amalar's observation too quickly. Jussen observes that language of repayment rarely appears in connection to *munera* (which he translates as 'offerings') because they were thought to repay God for benefits already bestowed, and so did not expect further repayment. But that does not mean these were given without hope of future salvation; and, even if God would consider not the gift but the giver, it was the giving of the *munus* that made God consider the relative merits of a giver in the first place. Jussen is also unclear on the distinction between *munus* and *donum*; though admitting them to be conceptually different (p. 177), he otherwise treats them as conceptually equivalent. This seems to be the basis for Chris Wickham's statement, 'We have found ... no serious distinction at all between *donum* and *munus*' (Wickham, 'Conclusion', p. 242).

[29] See above, n. 4, with Zeisel, 'An Economic Survey of the Early Byzantine Church', pp. 67–86 and Daly and Nesserath, 'Opfer'.

[30] For example, see Vikan, 'Art, Medicine, and Magic', and Déroche, 'Quelques interrogations à propos de la Vie de Syméon'.

[31] Most comprehensively in Caner, *The Rich and the Pure*, pp. 127–59.

[32] Caner, 'Alms, Blessings, Offerings', pp. 31–3.

community what kind of gift he wants them to provide for their leaders ('the holy ones', he calls them) at Jerusalem:

> I thought it necessary to ask the brothers to ... arrange in advance this blessing [*eulogia*] that you promised, so that it may be ready as a blessing [*eulogia*] and not an extortion [*pleonexia*]. [6] The point is this: he who sows sparingly will reap sparingly, but he who sows in blessings [*ep' eulogiais*] will reap in blessings [*ep' eulogiais*]. [7] So let each give as his heart intended, not with grief or compulsion, for God loves a cheerful giver. [8] And God can make every grace be in surplus for you, so that having enough of everything, you may have a surplus for every good work, [9] as it is written,
>   He scatters abroad, He gives to the poor,
>   His righteousness endures forever [Ps 112.9].
> [10] Indeed, He who supplies seeds to the sower and bread for food will ... multiply your seed for sowing and make the harvest of your righteousness increase. [11] In every way you will be enriched for every generosity, which will produce thanksgiving to God through us; [12] for this ministration not only relieves the wants of the holy ones, but also generates surplus through many thanksgivings to God.[33]

No other gift is described at such length and detail in the Christian New Testament. For our purposes, Paul's passage is important because it establishes as *eulogiai* the gifts that Christians should give to supply the wants of their 'holy ones', and because it defines such blessings as things not to be given out of any sense of extortion, force or grief – in other words, not to reflect (or impose) any sense of involuntary obligation on its giver or recipient.

It is clear that early Byzantine hagiographers were mindful of, and concerned to convey, the facets of the *eulogia* gift ideal sketched out by Paul. Before the fifth century, most references to material blessings pertain to items (usually leftover bread from a Eucharist) sent between church

---

[33] 2 Cor. 9:5–12: τὴν προεπηγγελμένην εὐλογίαν ὑμῶν, ταύτην ἑτοίμην εἶναι οὕτως ὡς εὐλογίαν καὶ μὴ ὡς πλεονεξίαν. Τοῦτο δέ, ὁ σπείρων φειδομένως καὶ θερίσει, καὶ ὁ σπείρων ἐπ' εὐλογίαις ἐπ' εὐλογίαις καὶ θερίσει. ἕκαστος καθὼς προῄρηται τῇ καρδίᾳ, μὴ ἐκ λύπης ἢ ἐξ ἀνάγκης· ἱλαρὸν γὰρ δότην ἀγαπᾷ ὁ θεός. δυνατεῖ δὲ ὁ θεὸς πᾶσαν χάριν περισσεῦσαι εἰς ὑμᾶς, ἵνα ἐν παντὶ πάντοτε πᾶσαν αὐτάρκειαν ἔχοντες περισσεύητε εἰς πᾶν ἔργον ἀγαθόν, καθὼς γέγραπται, Ἐσκόρπισεν, ἔδωκεν τοῖς πένησιν, ἡ δικαιοσύνη αὐτοῦ μένει εἰς τὸν αἰῶνα. ὁ δὲ ἐπιχορηγῶν σπόρον τῷ σπείροντι καὶ ἄρτον εἰς βρῶσιν χορηγήσει καὶ πληθυνεῖ τὸν σπόρον ὑμῶν καὶ αὐξήσει τὰ γενήατα τῆς δικαιοσύνης ὑμῶν· ἐν παντὶ πλουτιζόμενοι εἰς πᾶσαν ἁπλότητα, ἥτις κατεργάζεται δι' ἡμῶν εὐχαριστίαν τῷ θεῷ. ὅτι ἡ διακονία τῆς λειτουργίας ταύτης οὐ μόνον ἐστὶν προσαναπληροῦσα τὰ ὑστερήματα τῶν ἁγίων, ἀλλὰ καὶ περισσεύουσα διὰ πολλῶν εὐχαριστιῶν τῷ θεῷ.

leaders or communities on Sundays or festival occasions.[34] This custom is also attested in *P.Ness.* III 79 and *P.Ness.* III 50; as noted above, the latter records a bishop's request that a *eulogia* be provided on his behalf at Nessana on the occasion of the festival of St Sergius (see also *P.Ness.* III 51 and 52). Starting in the fourth century, however, we also find many references to monasteries providing blessings of food or drink as hospitality to lay visitors, or to lay people providing *eulogiai* of cash, grain or wine to monks and monasteries. The latter are depicted as being given either annually or on a one-time basis, sometimes as coins handed out to hermits or abbots lined up in Jerusalem or a nearby desert (Theodore of Petra, *Vita Theodosii* 27.10–21, 28.9;[35] John Moschus, *Pratum spirituale* 157;[36] Sophronius of Jerusalem, *Vita Syncleticae Jordanis* 7–8).[37] Such depictions date to the sixth and early seventh centuries, making them contemporaneous with *P. Ness.* III 79 and the Nessana donations in question.

It is clear that such blessings were not simply considered a gift of alms.[38] On the other hand, it is tempting to equate them to gifts of 'first fruits' (ἀπαρχαί/*aparchai*) or 'fruitbearings' (καρποφορίαι/*karpophoriai*) that churches and monasteries expected lay people to donate from the proceeds of their harvests or commerce annually at Pentecost,[39] and which we know some Egyptian monasteries systematically collected from local villagers.[40] To the extent that such lay donations or contributions were given voluntarily with good will, they could indeed be treated as equivalent to a blessing: in one instance, a hagiographer refers to the donation a bishop received from a widow first as a 'fruit-bearing' and then as a 'blessing' (Leontius of Neapolis, *Vita Iohannis Eleemosynarii* 9).[41] This indicates that, if given with the right spirit, a *karphoria* was tantamount to a *eulogia*.

Nonetheless, fruit-bearings are overwhelmingly depicted as gifts given to God or to his holy people as expressions of gratitude for the receipt of God-given wealth or health, stemming from a bounteous harvest or

---

[34] See especially Stuiber, 'Eulogia'. Kuchenbuch, '*Porcus donativus*', pp. 209–18 observes that, in the medieval West, *eulogiae* became a form of 'servile ... *munuscula*' imposed by lords and priests on peasants; he notes, however (p. 218), that this was considered an abuse.
[35] Edition in Usener, *Der heilige Theodosios*.
[36] Translation in Wortley, *The Spiritual Meadow*.
[37] See Flusin and Paramelle, 'De Syncletica in Deserto Jordanis'.
[38] Caner, *The Rich and the Pure*, p. 133.
[39] See *Constitutiones apostolorum* 2.25, 34–5, 7.29.3, 8.30 (translation: Metzger, *Les Constitutions apostoliques*); Bradshaw, 'The Offering of the Firstfruits of Creation'; Caner, *The Rich and the Pure*, pp. 160–2.
[40] See above, n. 16.
[41] Edition and translation in Festugière and Rydén, *Léontios de Néapolis*, pp. 343–409.

charismatic healing or prayer.[42] Blessings, in contrast, are never identified as gifts of gratitude, and are depicted frequently as gifts given by holy people to lay people as by the laity to holy people. In either case, they are presented as divinely inspired expressions of kindness, most often given either as hospitality or in the form of resources that enabled recipients to provide something kindly, cheerfully, and hospitably for others.

This gratuitous and, in effect, 'disinterested' aspect of a *eulogia* is especially emphasised. For example, when describing Empress Verina's receipt of *eulogiai* while visiting a fifth-century abbess in Constantinople named Matrona, Matrona's hagiographer comments, '[Matrona] asked for nothing at all whatsoever in return, even though the empress very much expected that she would petition her for something, seeing that the blessed one ... was in no way affluent.' The empress, he adds, 'was exceedingly impressed by [Matrona's] not asking for anything' (*Vita Matronae Pergensis* 32).[43] Matrona's hagiographer thus emphatically depicted a *eulogia* as a gift that imposed no obligation on its receiver to do or give back anything in return. We find this likewise emphasised in the case of a layperson giving a *eulogia* to a holy person. An anecdote attributed to John Moschus depicts a donor giving a blessing of gold coins to the abbot of a Palestinian monastery while simultaneously telling him to use it in any way he pleased: 'Please accept this *eulogia* and administer it as you wish, father', says the donor. 'Take these and, whether for the poor or for something else, administer them as you want and as you know how' (John Moschus, *Pratum spirituale* 231).[44] Like Matrona's hagiographer, Moschus explicitly associates a *eulogia* here with a lack of obligation – or rather, with a freedom to use the *eulogia* in whatever way its monastic recipient wished.

This emphasis in hagiographical literature may have been meant both to clarify what was expected of lay readers should they ever give such *eulogiai* donations, and to remind them that *eulogiai* receivers should be left free from any obligation to use the gift in a certain way or to provide something in return. To explain how a blessing might represent both a disinterested gift and one that promised profit for its giver (2 Cor. 9:10–11), hagiographers developed Paul's assertion that such gifts ultimately derived from

---

[42] Caner, *The Rich and the Pure*, pp. 187–91.
[43] Edition in *Acta Sanctorum (Novembris)* 3: 805B: οὐδὲν ᾐτήσατο παρ' αὐτῆς τὸ σύνολον, καὶ μάλιστα προσδοκώσης τῆς βασιλίσσης ἐξαιτηθῆναί τι παρ' αὐτῆς, καίτοι ... τῆς μακαρίας καὶ μηδὲν εὐπορούσης. ὠφεληθεῖσα οὖν ... ἡ Ἀγούστα ὑπερεκπερισσοῦ ἐκ τοῦ μήτε αἰτηθῆναί τι παρ' αὐτῆς. Translation in Featherstone and Mango, 'Life of St. Matrona of Perge'.
[44] Edition in Nissen, 'Unbekannte Erzählungen aus dem Pratum Spirituale', p. 369: λάβε τὴν εὐλογίαν ταύτην καὶ διοίκησον αὐτήν, ὅσα ἂν κελεύσῃς ... λάβε αὐτά ... καὶ ὡς κελεύεις θέλεις πτωχοῖς, θέλεις ἄλλως, διοίκησον αὐτά, ὡς οἶδας.

whatever surplus God had given a Christian (2 Cor. 9:8). According to this conceit, human donors merely served as vectors through which God disseminated His bounties, so that any reward or compensation owed for giving a blessing was the responsibility of God, not its recipient. Whether or not the rationale behind such gifts was widely understood outside of church or monastic circles, it was crucial for explaining why gifts of *eulogiai* did not oblige clerics or monks to give or do anything in return for their donors, as well as for identifying *eulogiai* as a source of sacred wealth in early Byzantine hagiography.[45]

By contrast, early Byzantine hagiographers depict gifts of *prosphorai* far less often and with far less complexity. Following the Septuagint and New Testament (for example, Wis. 34:19, 50:13–14; Ps. 39:7; Acts 21:26; Rom. 15:16; Heb. 10:5, 8, 10, 18; Eph. 5:2), they almost uniformly depict offerings simply as gifts of gratitude given by humans to God. Once received by a church or monastery, *prosphorai* were identified as God's property, and could not be used to advance the personal interests of any individual member of the church or monastic institution (Cyril of Scythopolis, *Vita Sabae* 50).[46] They were especially connected with liturgical sacrifices (i.e., Eucharists, known as 'the holy *prosphora*' itself), with supporting other spiritual services of priests or monks, or with the construction or procurement of long-term assets that might advance a church's or monastery's long-term liturgical mission. Thus, Melania the Younger is depicted as receiving 200 *solidi* from a layperson as a *prosphora* to buy the stones to build a monastery in which to perform perpetual psalmodies on the Mount of Olives in Jerusalem (Gerontius, *Vita Melaniae iunioris* 49), and John the Almsgiver was reportedly offered half a pound of gold coins so that he might perform prayers for the donor's son; we are told that John put the coins under an altar, then performed liturgical prayers according to his donor's request (Leontius of Neapolis, *Vita Ioannis Eleemosynarii* 25).

A Modern Analogy for Offerings and Blessings: Restricted and Unrestricted Gifts

Hagiography thus attests that offerings and blessings differed by the level of obligation they imposed. Indeed, institutional administration was associated with handling *prosphorai* to a degree not found in relation to *eulogiai*.

---

[45] Caner, *The Rich and the Pure*, pp. 156–9.
[46] For a comprehensive discussion of laws against alienating offerings or using them for personal ends, see Farag, *What Makes a Church Sacred?*

When writing his will in 695, Jacob, abbot of the monastery of Apa Phoibammon in seventh-century Egypt (Deir el-Bahri), mentioned that managing the *prosphorai* his monastery had received had been one of his chief responsibilities as abbot.[47] Hagiography attests the presence at a sixth-century Palestinian monastery of a monk called a *prosphorarios* – i.e., a monastic officer whose duty was to look after the *prosphorai* a monastery received (Cyril of Scythopolis, *Vita Sabae* 58). No such official is attested for handling *eulogiai*, suggesting again that *prosphorai* entailed more accountability than *eulogiai* gifts.

To appreciate this distinction in modern terms, we may consider a practice commonly found in modern non-profit institutions. Fundraisers for schools, hospitals and philanthropic organisations have long made it a practice, when soliciting donations, to distinguish between 'restricted' and 'unrestricted' gifts.[48] Restricted gifts are earmarked to support projects of personal interest to donors (like a scholarship or a sports complex) and come with an expectation that they will not be used for any other purpose. Such gifts account for the majority of donations that non-profits receive.[49] In contrast, unrestricted gifts are not tied to specified uses or obligations, based on the donors' trust that their recipients will properly administer them to advance the interests and goals of the institution. Just as the sums given as *prosphorai* in early Byzantine sources tend to be more lavish than those of *eulogiai* – and just as *prosphorai* in early Byzantine sources tend to be associated with more permanent institutional activities or structures – restricted gifts tend to be more important for creating long-term structures and endowments than unrestricted gifts. Yet, by all accounts, modern institutions especially desire to receive unrestricted gifts. That is because these give administrators far greater latitude and flexibility to cope with unglamorous but necessary financial demands, like expenditures on bills, salaries, or broken equipment, which non-profit institutions continually face while seeking to advance the ideals of their programmes.

Though it is impossible to generalise about the administrative needs or preferences of an early Byzantine church or monastery with comparable

---

[47] *P.KRU* 65 (re-edited as text 4 in Garel, *Héritage et transmission*, pp. 249–76); Thomas, *Private Religious Foundations*, p. 80.
[48] Bryce, 'The Public's Trust in Nonprofit Organizations', pp. 118–22.
[49] An estimated 98 per cent of gifts to Indiana University are restricted, being directed to build up particular schools, departments, or programs. My thanks to the IU Foundation for this information. See also www.nolo.com/legal-encyclopedia/nonprofit-gifts-when-strings-attached-32421.html.

certainty, the restricted/unrestricted model provides a usefully illuminating basis for comparison. We know that churches and monasteries similarly used the *eulogiai* they received to address routine or unexpected needs, ranging from the provision of weekly rations to internal members of a church or monastic institution, to the less predictable but potentially onerous need to provide hospitality or alms for visitors at its gate. Indeed, hagiographers frequently depict monasteries being given *eulogiai* of cash, wheat, or wine for exactly such ad hoc institutional purposes, emphasising that their proper allocation depended solely on the scruples of the cleric or abbot who received them (see, for example, John Moschus, *Pratum spirituale* 231: 'Take these and, whether for the poor or for something else, administer them as you want and as you know how'). No *prosphora* is depicted as being similarly used to fund such discretionary activities. Indeed, this discretionary, 'unrestricted' aspect of *eulogiai* in church and monastic institutions may explain why such gifts have left fewer traces than *prosphorai* in the papyrological record. Blessings imposed no obligation on monasteries for a particular use, and so did not require careful recordkeeping, unlike offerings, which required careful recordkeeping precisely because they did impose such obligations.[50]

Ethics and the Stewardship Procedures in *P.Ness.* III 79

In the preceding discussion, I have sought to establish conceptual rationales to explain the distinctions and stewardship practices attested in *P.Ness.* III 79. I conclude by focusing on ethical considerations. Hagiographical representations notwithstanding, it is clear that *prosphorai* counted more than *eulogiai* for securing the long-term prosperity of most church and monastic institutions, and that the stewards of these institutions often took whatever blessings they needed for their ad hoc purposes, from whatever offerings they had been given, to present to God. An analogous practice is explicitly condoned in the fourth-century *Apostolic Constitutions*, a church manual that permits clerics to take for themselves, as *eulogiai*, whatever

---

[50] Schmelz, *Kirchliche Amtsträger im spätantiken Ägypten*, pp. 205–6 notes that *P.Vindob.Worp* 14 refers to *eulogiai* sent from a steward via a priest to a lector, an entirely internal chain of transmission and use that suggests it was a matter of a church ration. For other examples from Egyptian papyri, see Caner, *The Rich and the Pure*, p. 156.

bread *prosphorai* (bread brought by lay people as offerings for the Eucharist) remained after a church liturgy.[51] This is consistent with Paul's explanation that *eulogiai* ultimately derive from whatever remained leftover from God's goods. Indeed, the latitude given to decide how best to use lay offerings is indicated by Cyril of Scythopolis' portrait of Sabas, the leader of a Palestinian *laura* whose ascetic reputation prompted many to bring him *prosphorai*: 'the blessed one preferred to spend most of what was offered on buildings and the maintenance of the place. Whatever he thought was pleasing to God, this he did, and none of his subjects dared oppose him in anything' (Cyril of Scythopolis, *Vita Sabae* 18).[52] Whether Sabas enjoyed such latitude because his donors had not specified the purpose of their *prosphorai*, Cyril does not say. But he does emphasise that Sabas applied 'most of what was offered' to the long-term structural needs of his institution, and that all else he did with them was 'pleasing to God'.

It is pointless to speculate how such a saint might have used lay offerings in a way that was not pleasing to God. But we know that early Byzantine donors occasionally suspected that their offerings might not, in fact, be used properly. This seems to have been one reason why some monasteries had administrative committees whose responsibility was to authenticate bequests to their institutions.[53] This would have helped assure donors that several people in the institution would be aware of their bequests and their intended purpose, rather than just one or two who might be tempted to use the donations as they wished. It may also explain why Nessana's Sergius monastery was so diligent in separating and keeping track of the offerings it received. Keeping careful, transparent records of the fulfilment of obligations to donors would not only build trust and goodwill, but would also encourage those donors to continue to give. Indeed, *P.Ness.* III 79 shows the Sergius monastery managed to persuade at least one donor, Theodore son of Stephan, to give an offering 'for the atrium' two years in a row.

But another ethical problem may also explain the care taken at Nessana. One challenge confronting church and monastic leaders was how to accept any gift without becoming beholden to their donors. In

---

[51] *Constitutiones apostolorum* 8.31; the (probably genuine) title states that the *eulogiai* refer to leftover *prosphorai*. See also Mosch., *prat.* 42, and Caner, 'Alms, Blessings, Offerings', pp. 34–5.

[52] Edition in Schwartz, *Kyrillos von Skythopolis*, p. 102, l. 26–p. 103, l. 5: ὁ δὲ μακαρίτης τὰ πλεῖστα τῶν προσφερομένων εἰς οἰκοδομὰς μᾶλλον καὶ εἰς σύστασιν τοῦ τόπου ἀνήλισκεν. καὶ ὅπερ εὐάρεστον ἐνόμιζεν εἶναι τῶι θεῶι, τοῦτο ἐποίει καὶ οὐδεὶς τῶν ὑπ' αὐτὸν ἐτόλμα ἔν τινι ἐναντιωθῆναι αὐτῶι.

[53] Wipszycka, *Moines et communautés monastiques*, p. 549.

early Byzantium this was especially associated with lay offerings. According to the late sixth-century historian Barhadbeshabba Arbaya, Bishop Nestorius of Constantinople defended himself against charges of corruption in the 430s by claiming he had never touched the things offered to him as bishop: 'how can anyone say I cared for offerings and favours [*b-qurbane wa b-taybute*] ... ? Never did I let myself get misled by such things. For I know that they oblige whomever they snare to act like a slave and do what they're told, whatever it might be.'[54]

Hagiography indicates that one of the 'best practices' for holy people faced with this ethical challenge was to convert any suspect patronal offering into a blessing by giving it away as a gift from God to someone in need.[55] That would have depended, however, on having a saint's ability to detect the motives behind such gifts and give away any that seemed to advance a patron's interests rather than God's. A much more mundane, but transparent, practice is illustrated by *P. Ness.* III 79: first, identify the obligation that attended each gift, then carefully separate any that were expressly tied to a patron's interest from any that were not.

To conclude, *P.Ness.* III 79 demonstrates that early Byzantine monasteries carefully differentiated between offerings and blessings, between gifts that imposed patronal obligations and those that did not. While it does not prove that such monasteries conceptualised offerings and blessings in terms of restricted and unrestricted gifts, the modern analogy reminds us of the potential difficulties that non-profits of any era might face when relying on a donor's goodwill for significant material resources. Perhaps most important is that *P. Ness.* III 79 shows that the Sergius monastery was concerned to keep track of its own resources and the wishes of its patrons at once. Presumably this helped ensure integrity within the monastery, while maintaining the goodwill of donors outside it. And these two immaterial assets, integrity and goodwill, would have been crucial for securing the long-term prosperity of any early Byzantine monastery.

---

[54] Barhadbeshabba Arbaya, *Historia Ecclesiastica* 21: Nau, *Le seconde partie de l'Histoire de Barhadbeshabba 'Arbaïa*, §526.

[55] Caner, *The Rich and the Poor*, pp. 146–9.

Appendix: Transliteration and Translation of *P.Ness.* III 79

Text[56]

```
        + γν(ῶσις) εἰσωδιασμος κρα( ) πρo( ) [
        / παρ(ὰ) Γωμασερου [

        / παρ(ὰ) τοῦ πρεσβ(υτέρου) Σωβετώ[ης
        / παρ(ὰ) Γεωργίου πρεσβ(υτέρου) . . . [
  5     / παρ(ὰ) γυνēκες γ' [
        / γυνὲ ἀπὸ Σωβ[άτων
        / παρ(ὰ) Θεωδόρου . . [
        / παρ(ὰ) Γεωργίου . . [
        / παρ(ὰ) τινος Νεωτερου . . [
 10     / παρ(ὰ) τινος Σωβετι[νοῦ
        / παρ(ὰ) υἱὸς Θεμου Σωβετινοῦ [
        / παρ(ὰ) . . . ε θερου Ἀμμονίο[υ
        / παρ(ὰ) ἀδελφοῦ Κ . αε . . [
        / παρ(ὰ) τινος Ἐλ[ουζ(ηνοῦ) ?
 15     / παρ(ὰ) Στεφάνο[υ Ἐ]λ[ουζ(ηνοῦ) ?
        / παρ(ὰ) Μαρκέου ἀπὸ Σωβ[άτων ?
        / παρ(ὰ) τον Φακειδινον . [
        / παρ(ὰ) Ζενοβίου Πυργεωτου σ [
        / παρ(ὰ) γυνι ἀπὸ Βετομολαχον [
 20     / παρ(ὰ) ἀνθρόπου ειυς . . . [
        / παρ(ὰ) Γεωργίου πρεσβ(υτέρου) [
        / παρ(ὰ) τινος ἀπὸ Ἀρ[
        / παρ(ὰ) Σωεδον - - [
        παρ(ὰ) Αβδαλγου οἰκοδόμ(ου) [
 25     + λ(ό)γ(ος) εἰσωδίον προσφορᾶς εἰς τὴν μον(ὴν) εἰς τὰ μ[
        Χ παρ(ὰ) Αρμαλα Σαλιου ——— [
            Χ\ παρ(ὰ) Θεωδόρου Στεφάνου [εἰ]ς τὴν αὐλήν [
        Χ παρ(ὰ) Θεωδόρου Βετομολαχον εἰς τὸν οἶκο(ν) Γομα[σερ(ου)
        / παρ(ὰ) τινος Σωβετινοῦ εἰς τὰ ματρον[ίκι]α [
 30     Χ\ παρ(ὰ) Μαλχονος ἀπὸ Βηρθειβας [
        # παρ(ὰ) Σεργίου εἰς τὰ ματρονίκια . [
        Χ\ παρ(ὰ) Ζοναινου Σαμονα ——— [
        Χ παρ(ὰ) Καειουμου Σαμονα ——— [
        Χ παρ(ὰ) τῆς γυνεκὸς Ζεριζας [
```

[56] The following reproduces the *editio princeps* in *P.Ness.* III pp. 229–31; I have boldened the lines with register headings.

35 Χ\ παρ(ὰ) Μενᾶς ἀπὸ Βοτεους εἰς τὸν οἶκο(ν) Γομασ[ερ(ου)
    Χ\ παρ(ὰ) Ζοναινου Ἀβρααμί[ου] . . . . [
    Χ\ παρ(ὰ) Σεργίου ἀπὸ Βοτεους εἰς τὸν οἶκο(ν) Γομασερ(ου) [
    / παρ(ὰ) τῆς πενθερᾶς τοῦ ἀββᾶ Ἠλίου . . . [
    Χ\ παρ(ὰ) Ἰωάνου ἀπὸ Βετωμολαχον εἰς τὴν α[ὐλήν
40 Χ\ παρ(ὰ) Ωσεδου Σωβετινοῦ ——— [
    Χ παρ(ὰ) Ἰωάννου Στεφάνου Ἐλουζ(ηνοῦ) [
    Χ παρ(ὰ) Ἀμονίου χροισοχόος [
    Χ παρ(ὰ) Ἰωάννου Ροκεος Ἐλουζ(ηνοῦ) εἰς τὸν οἶ[κο(ν) Γομασερ(ου)
        + λ(ό)γ(ος) εἰσωδίον εὐλογία[ς εἰς τ]ὴν μ(ονὴ)ν τοῦ ἁγί(ου) Σεργίο[υ]
45 / παρ(ὰ) Ἀβρααμίου Αεδου [
    Χ παρ(ὰ) τοῦ αδελφ(οῦ) Αλγομεου Αρακενου [
    / παρ(ὰ) τοῦ υἱοῦ Αλχεφρι ἀπ(ὸ) Σουδανον [
    / παρ(ὰ) Κυριακοῦ ἀπ(ὸ) Βεδοροθης [
    / παρ(ὰ) τῆς ἀδελφῆς αὐτοῦ Ταμαλγα [
50 / παρ(ὰ) τοισουρθον [
    / παρ(ὰ) Ζαχαρίου Αλθουεθηλ Σωβετώης [
    παρ(ὰ) ἀβᾶ Βίκτορος πρεσβ(υ)τ(έρου) Σωβετώης [
    παρ(ὰ) τῆς γυνκ(ὸς) Γεωργί(ου) Δαρεβου Ἐλουσ(ηνοῦ) [
    / παρ(ὰ) Ζοναινου Ἀβρααμίου——— [
55 παρ(ὰ) Ἰωάννης Ἀβρααμίου Ἐλουσ(ηνοῦ) [
    +λ(ό)γ(ος) εἰσωδίον εὐλογίας εἰ[ς] τὴν ἑορτὶν τοῦ ἁγί(ου) Σεργίου .[
    παρ(ὰ) τινος Βεροσαβῆς [
    +/ ιδ / δ πα(ρὰ) Θεοδόρῳ Στεφάνου εἰς τὴν αὐλή[ν
    / πα(ρὰ) κυρ(ί)ῳ Ἰωάννῃ ὀπτίονι Πακιδιν[ω
60 / πα(ρὰ) κυρ(ί)ῳ Μάριον Πικιδινω [
    πα(ρὰ) Σιλουανοῦ Θαβαθας [
    / πα(ρὰ) Γεωργίου (καὶ) Νόνα εἰς τὰ ματρονίκια [
    / πα(ρὰ) Γεωργίου Αρσαφου [
    / πα(ρὰ) τινος Φακιδινω εἰς τὸν οἶκον Ζονα[ινου
65 / πα(ρὰ) Στεφάνου Ἀγαθειμέρου [
    / οἴνου κ(υά)θ(ος) εἰς τὸν οἶκ(ον) Αβδελα . . . [
    / (καὶ) εἰς τὸν οἶκ(ον) Ἰωάνου Κοτεμου [

Translation[57]

I

+ Register of receipts ...

from Juhāmir ..., the priest from Sobata ..., George, priest ..., three women ..., woman from Sobata ..., Theodore ..., George ..., a certain inhabitant of Neoteros ..., a certain inhabitant of Sobata ..., a son of Taim, inhabitant of Sobata ..., ... theros son of Ammonios, a brother of ..., a certain inhabitant of Elusa ..., Stephan, inhabitant of Elusa ..., Marcius from Sobata ..., the inhabitants of Phakida (?) ..., Zenobios son of Pyrgeotos (?) ..., a woman from Betomolacha ..., a man from ..., George, priest ..., a certain man from Ar ......, Suwaid, ditto ..., 'Abd al-Gā builder ...

II

+ Account of receipts for masses, to the monastery for the (women's quarters?)

from Ḥarmala son of Ṣāliḥ, ditto ..., Theodore son of Stephan, for the atrium ..., Theodore, inhabitant of Betomolaca, for the house of Juhāmir ..., a certain inhabitant of Sobata for the women's quarters ..., Malchon, from Berthiba ..., Sergius for the women's quarters ..., Zunayn, son of Samonas, ditto ..., Qayyūm son of Samonas, ditto ..., the wife of Zerizas ..., Menas, inhabitant of Boteos, for the house of Juhāmir ..., Zunayn son of Abraham ..., Sergius, inhabitant of Boteos, for the house of Juhāmir ..., the mother-in-law of Father Elias ..., John, from Betomolacha, for the atrium ..., Usaid, inhabitant of Sobata, ditto ..., John son of Stephan, inhabitant of Elusa ..., Amonios, goldsmith (?) ..., John son of Raqī', inhabitant of Elusa, for the house of Juhāmir (?) ...

III

+ Account of receipts of donations to the monastery of St Sergius

from Abraham son of 'Ā'idh ..., the brother of al-Jumā'a son of Arakenos ..., the son of al-Khafri, from Sudanon ..., Cyriacus from Bedorotha ..., his sister, Taim al-Gā ..., (?) ..., Zacharias son of ath-Thuwaitil, inhabitant of Sobata ..., father Victor, priest, inhabitant of Sobata ..., the wife of George son of Ḍārib, inhabitant of Elusa ..., Zunayn son of Abraham, ditto ..., John son of Abraham, inhabitant of Elusa ...

---

[57] The following translation is Kraemer's, except that I have substituted 'atrium' for his 'court'.

IV
+ Account of receipts of donations for the feast of St Sergius from a certain inhabitant of Berosaba ...

V
+ 14/4 (? 4th indiction ?) from Theodore son of Stephan, for the atrium ..., John, Esq., quartermaster (?), inhabitant of Pacidino ..., Marius, Esq. inhabitant of Picidino ..., Silvanus son of Thābit ..., George and Nona, for the women's quarters ..., George son of Ruṣafi ..., a certain inhabitant of Phacidino, for the house of Zunayn ..., Stephan son of Agathemeros ..., jigger of wine for the house of 'Abd Allāh ... also for the house of John son of Quthaim ...

Bibliography

Batiffol, P. *Études de liturgie et d'archéologie chrétienne* (Paris: Picard, 1911).

Bradshaw, P. 'The Offering of the Firstfruits of Creation: An Historical Study' in R. McMichael Jr. (ed.), *Creation and Liturgy: Studies in Honor of H. Boone Porter* (Washington, DC: Pastoral Press, 1993), pp. 29–41.

Bryce, H. J. 'The Public's Trust in Nonprofit Organizations: The Role of Relationship Marketing and Management', *California Management Review*, 49 (2007), 112–31.

Caner, D. 'Alms, Blessings, Offerings: The Repertoire of Christian Gifts in Early Byzantine Hagiography' in M. Satlow (ed.), *The Gift in Antiquity* (Oxford: Oxford University Press, 2018), pp. 25–44.

Caner, D. *The Rich and the Pure: Philanthropy and the Making of Christian Society in Early Byzantium* (Berkeley: University of California Press, 2021).

Clark, E. *Life of Melania the Younger: Introduction, Translation, and Commentary* (New York and Toronto: Edwin Mellen Press, 1984).

Colt, D. *Excavations at Nessana (Auja Hafir, Palestine)*, vol. 1 (London: British School of Archaeology, 1962).

Daly, R. J. and Nesserath, T. 'Opfer', *Reallexicon für Antike und Christentum*, 26 (2014), 143–206.

Davies, W. and Fouracre, P. (eds.) *The Languages of Gift in the Early Middle Ages* (Cambridge: Cambridge University Press, 2010).

Déroche, V. 'Quelques interrogations à propos de la *Vie de Syméon Stylite de Jeune*', *Eranos*, 94 (1996), 65–83.

Farag, M. *What Makes a Church Sacred? Legal and Ritual Perspectives from Late Antiquity* (Berkeley: University of California Press, 2021).

Featherstone, J. and Mango, C. 'Life of St. Matrona of Perge' in A.-M. Talbot (ed.), *Holy Women of Byzantium* (Washington, DC: Dumbarton Oaks, 1996), pp. 13–64.

Festugière, A.-J. and Rydén, L. *Léontios de Néapolis: Vie de Syméon le Fou et Vie de Jean de Chypre* (Paris: Geuthner, 1974).

Figueras, P. 'Greek Inscriptions from Nessana' in D. Urman (ed.), *Nessana: Excavations and Studies I* (Beer-Sheva: Ben Gurion University in the Negev Press, 2004), pp. 222–42.

Finley, M. *Ancient History: Evidence and Models* (New York: Penguin, 1985).

Flusin, B. and Paramelle, J. 'De Syncletica in Deserto Jordanis (BHG 1318 w)', *Analecta Bollandiana*, 100 (1982), 291–317.

Garel, E. *Héritage et transmission dans le monachisme égyptien* (Cairo: Institut français d'institut orientale, 2020).

Gascou, J. 'Monasteries, Economic Activities of' in A. S. Atiya (ed.), *The Coptic Encyclopedia*, vol. 5 (New York: Macmillan Press, 1999), pp. 1639–45.

Gutwein, K. C. *Third Palestine: A Regional Study in Urbanization* (Washington, DC: University Press of America, 1981).

Hannsens, J.-M. *Amalarii episcopi. Opera liturgica omnia* (Vatican City: Biblioteca apostolica vaticana, 1948).

Jussen, B. 'Religious Discourses of the Gift in the Middle Ages: Semantic Evidence (Second to Twelfth Centuries)' in G. Algazi, V. Groebner, and B. Jussen (eds.), *Negotiating the Gift: Pre-Modern Figurations of Exchange* (Göttingen: Vandenhoeck und Ruprecht, 2003), pp. 173–92.

Kaplan, M. 'The Economy of Byzantine Monasteries' in A. I. Beach and I. Cochelin (eds.), *The Cambridge History of Medieval Monasticism in the Latin West*, vol. 1 (Cambridge: Cambridge University Press, 2020), pp. 340–62.

Klein, K. 'Von Hesychie zu Ökonomie: Zur Finanzierung der Wüstenklöster Palästinas (5.-6. Jh.)', *Millennium: Jahrbuch zu Kultur und Geschichte des ersten Jahrtausends n.Chr. / Yearbook on the Culture and History of the First Millennium C.E.*, 15 (2018), 37–68.

Kuchenbuch, L. (2003) '*Porcus donativus*: Language Uses and Gifting in Seigneurial Records between the Eighth and the Twelfth Centuries' in G. Algazi, V. Groebner, and B. Jussen (eds.), *Negotiating the Gift: Pre-Modern Figurations of Exchange* (Göttingen: Vandenhoeck und Ruprecht, 2003), pp. 193–246.

López, A. *Shenoute of Atripe and the Uses of Poverty: Rural Patronage, Religious Conflict and Monasticism in Late Antique Egypt* (Berkeley: University of California Press, 2013).

Metzger, M. *Les constitutions apostoliques*, 3 vols (Paris: Éditions du Cerf, 1985–7).

Nau, F. *Le seconde partie de l'Histoire de Barhadbeshabba 'Arbaïa* (Paris: Firmin Didot, 1913).

Neyt, F. and de Angelis-Noah, P. *Barsanuphe et Jean de Gaza: Correspondance*, vol. 2.2: *Aux Cénobites, Lettres 399-616* (Paris: Éditions du Cerf, 2001).

Nissen, T. 'Unbekannte Erzählungen aus dem Pratum Spirituale', *Byzantinische Zeitschrift*, 38 (1938), 354–72.

Papaconstantinou, A. 'Conversions monétaires byzantines. P.Vindob.G. 1265', *Tyche*, 9 (1994), 93–8.

Papaconstantinou, A. 'Donation and Negotiation: Formal Gifts to Religious Institutions in Late Antiquity' in J.-M. Spieser and É. Yota (eds.), *Donations et donateurs dans la société et l'art byzantins* (Paris: Desclée de Brouwer, 2012), pp. 75–93.

Patlagean, É. *Pauvreté économique et pauvreté sociale à Byzance, 4e-7e siècles* (Paris: Mouton, 1977).

Price, R. M. *Cyril of Scythopolis: The Lives of the Monks of Palestine* (Kalamazoo: Cistercian Publications, 1991).

Ruffini, G. 'Village Life and Family Power in Late Antique Nessana', *Transactions of the American Philological Association*, 141 (2011), 201–25.

Schenke, G. 'Monastic Control over Agriculture and Farming: New Evidence from the Egyptian Monastery of Bawit Concerning the Payment of *APARCHE*' in A. Delattre, M. Legendre, and P. M. Sijpesteijn (eds.), *Authority and Control in the Countryside: From Antiquity to Islam and the Middle East (6th–10th Century)* (Leiden: Brill, 2019), pp. 420–31.

Schmelz, G. *Kirchliche Amtsträger im spätantiken Ägypten nach den Aussagen der griechischen und koptischen Papyri und Ostraka* (Munich: K. G. Saur, 2002).

Schwartz, E. *Kyrillos von Skythopolis* (Leipzig: Hinrichs, 1939).

Silber, I. F. 'Echoes of Sacrifice? Repertoires of Giving in the Great Religions' in A. I. Baumgarten (ed.), *Sacrifice in Religious Experience* (Leiden: Brill, 2002), pp. 291–312.

Stuiber, A. 'Eulogia', *Reallexikon für Antike und Christentum*, 6 (1966), 900–28.

Thomas, J. P. *Private Religious Foundations in the Byzantine Empire* (Washington, DC: Dumbarton Oaks, 1987).

Trombley, F. 'From *Kastron* to *Qaṣr*: Nessana between Byzantium and the Umayyad Caliphate *ca.* 602–689' in E. B. Aitken and J. M. Fossey (eds.), *The Levant: Crossroads of Late Antiquity. History, Religions and Archaeology* (Leiden: Brill, 2014), pp. 180–223.

Urman, D. 'Nessana Excavations 1987–1995' in D. Urman (ed.), *Nessana: Excavations and Studies I* (Beer-Sheva: Ben Gurion University in the Negev Press, 2004), pp. 1*–118*.

Usener, H. *Der heilige Theodosios. Schriften des Theodoros und Kyrillos* (Leipzig: Teubner, 1890).

Vikan, G. 'Art, Medicine, and Magic in Early Byzantium', *Dumbarton Oaks Papers*, 38 (1984), 65–86.

Wickham, C. 'Conclusion' in W. Davies and P. Fouracre (eds.) *The Languages of Gift in the Early Middle Ages* (Cambridge: Cambridge University Press, 2010), pp. 238–61.

Wipszycka, E. *Les ressources et les activités économiques des églises en Égypte du Ve au VIIIe siècle* (Brussels: Fondation égyptologique Reine Élisabeth, 1972).

Wipszycka, E. *Moines et communautés monastiques en Egypte, IVe–VIIIe siecles* (Warsaw: The Raphael Taubenschlag Foundation, 2009).
Wipszycka, E. 'Resources and Economic Activities of the Egyptian Monastic Communities (4th–8th Century)', *Journal of Juristic Papyrology*, 41 (2011), 159–263.
Wortley, J. *The Spiritual Meadow (Pratum spirituale) by John Moschus* (Kalamazoo: Cistercian Publications, 1992).
Zeisel, W. 'An Economic Survey of the Early Byzantine Church', unpublished PhD thesis, Rutgers University, 1975.

11 | Staple for Body and Soul: Working at and Visiting the Upper Egyptian Monastery Deir Anba Hadra

LENA SOPHIE KRASTEL, SEBASTIAN OLSCHOK, AND TONIO SEBASTIAN RICHTER

Introduction

This contribution provides a short overview of recently explored evidence from the Upper Egyptian monastery Deir Anba Hadra and its relevance for the issue of monastic economy. Since documents such as letters and accounts are not available to date, the physical remains and the epigraphic record are the only testimonies for Deir Anba Hadra that reveal information about the economic activities of this monastery. While the archaeological remains shed light on the material economy – the production, consumption and to some extent possibly the regional and supra-regional exchange of goods – the focus of the Coptic inscriptions is mainly on the spiritual economy – the visitation of the monastery for religious purposes and the economic aspects involved.

In what follows, we begin by briefly discussing the monastery of Anba Hadra with a focus on its embeddedness in the Christian community of the First Cataract region. We then turn to the primary focus of this chapter, the economic background of the monastery that is traceable in the archaeological remains of the economic complex and the epigraphic evidence found throughout the monastery.

The Monastery of Anba Hadra

Deir Anba Hadra, formerly known as the monastery of St Simeon,[1] is located on the west bank of Aswan, the ancient town of Syene, across from Elephantine Island, about a kilometre inland on the gebel overlooking

---

[1] Having heard that name from locals, Urbain Bouriant was the first to designate the monastery as Deir Amba-Samaan in 1893 (Bouriant, 'Notes de voyage', p. 179). Although Pére Michel Jullien (Jullien, 'Quelques anciens couvents', p. 284) had already found out in 1903 that the monastery was dedicated to Anba Hadra, the name introduced by Bouriant was and still is often used by travellers and researchers (for example, 'Le couvent de Saint Siméon' in De Morgan *et al.*, *Catalogue des monuments*, pp. 129–40 or Monneret de Villard, *Il monastero di S. Simeone*). Coptic inscriptions from Deir Anba Hadra confirm that the monastery was dedicated to Anba Hadra, a saintly hermit and bishop of Aswan in the fourth century; see the *dipinto* of the monk Petro (published in Dijkstra and van der Vliet, 'King Zachari'; republished in Krastel, 'Words for

a desert valley. Its ruin, dominated by the monumental *qasr*, belongs to the best-preserved specimens of monastic architecture from late antique and early Islamic Egypt.

After occasional surveys in the later nineteenth and early twentieth centuries,[2] the monastery was excavated from 1924 to 1926 by Ugo Monneret de Villard. The architectural and archaeological results were released in various preliminary reports and in a final publication in 1927.[3] Although the edition of the finds[4] was intended in a second volume, only a portion of the textual evidence from Deir Anba Hadra has been published so far.[5] In 2013, the German Archaeological Institute resumed investigation, starting with an epigraphic survey. In 2014, a larger project was initiated under the title 'Deir Anba Hadra – Epigraphy, Art and Architecture of the Monastery on the West Bank of Aswan'.[6] The archaeological and epigraphic work from which this paper emerged forms part of the research unit 'Deir Anba Hadra. Socio-Cultural and Economic Significance of a Holy Place in Upper Egypt from Late Antiquity up to the Early Mamluk Period'[7] run by the authors in the framework of the Berlin cluster of excellency TOPOI under the umbrella of the larger

---

the Living', pp. 181–3) written on the south wall of the northern aisle of the monastic church and a funerary stela found by Ugo Monneret de Villard in the monastery in 1925 (published in Munier, 'Les stèles coptes', no. 176). See also van Loon, 'Le Deir Anba Hadra', p. 137 n. 1.

[2] For example, Pellegrino Matteucci in 1877 (Matteucci, 'Lettere'), Gaston Maspero in the 1880s (Maspero, 'Rapport à l'Institut égyptien', pp. 223–6), Jacques de Morgan and Urbain Bouriant in 1893 (De Morgan et al., *Catalogue des monuments*, pp. 129–40) and Jean Clédat in 1903 (Clédat, 'Notes d'archéologie copte' and Clédat, 'Les inscriptions'); for a brief overview, see van Loon, 'Le Deir Anba Hadra', pp. 140–7.

[3] Monneret de Villard, 'Rapporto preliminare'; Monneret de Villard, 'Descrizione generale'; Monneret de Villard, *Description générale*; and, the final publication, Monneret de Villard, *Il monastero di S. Simeone*.

[4] In a short article describing the Italian excavations in Egypt, Monneret de Villard mentioned that he found several fragments of Coptic funerary stelae, ca. 200 Coptic and 30 Arabic ostraca and many fragments of papyrus, parchment, and paper (see Monneret de Villard, 'La missione archeologica', pp. 272–3). Aside from the Coptic funerary stelae, the whereabouts of these finds are still unknown. However, it cannot be excluded that at least some of the Coptic and Arabic fragments kept in the Biblioteca dell'Accademia Nazionale dei Lincei e Corsiniana (signature Or. 280, 1–3) originate from Deir Anba Hadra (Valentina Sagaria Rossi, personal communication in November 2017). See also Soldati, 'Una lettera copta'; Soldati, 'A New Bifolium'.

[5] Some Arabic manuscripts were published by David Margoliouth and Eric Holmyard in 1931 (Margoliouth and Holmyard, 'Arabic Documents'), the Coptic funerary stelae by Henri Munier in 1930/1 (Munier, 'Les stèles coptes'), two Coptic fragments of the Pachomian Vita and a parchment fragment with sections of the Apocalypse by Louis Lefort between 1941 and 1943 (Lefort, 'Glanures Pachômiennes', pp. 135–8; Lefort, *Les vies coptes*; Lefort, 'Prologue de l'Apocalypse'), a tenth-/eleventh-century Coptic letter and a parchment *bifolium* by Agostino Soldati in 2018 and 2020, respectively (Soldati, 'Una lettera copta'; Soldati, 'A New Bifolium').

[6] See www.dainst.org/projekt/-/project-display/63443 (accessed 19 March 2018).

[7] See www.topoi.org/project/b-4-6 (accessed 19 March 2018).

project.⁸ The overall objectives of this project, for the most part beyond the scope of this paper, are: the study and comparison of Coptic, Christian Arabic and Muslim epigraphic practice in synchronic and diachronic perspectives; the development and functionality of Deir Anba Hadra at a local, regional and supra-regional scale; the typology of local ecclesiastic architecture, decoration programmes, and epigraphic phraseology; the encounter and interaction between Christians and Muslims in Fatimid, Ayyubid and Mamluk Aswan; and the economy and trade in the First Cataract region.⁹

The large complex of Deir Anba Hadra extends over two terraces of sandstone (Fig. 11.1), the upper one undercut by a row of little quarries from the Pharaonic period. One of these man-made caves may indeed have been the starting point of the development of the spot into a holy place. The entire complex is enclosed by a wall, up to 6 m in height, which gives the place the appearance of a fortress, though its effective functionality for military defence might have been rather limited, and its purpose might have partly been the symbolic segregation of the outside world from the monastic sphere. The main entrance via the eastern gate leads to the lower terrace with its main building, the church. It is a representative of a so-called *Achtstützenbau*, which is characterised by a roof construction with a brick dome resting on eight support elements. The *Achtstützenbau* is a particular kind of the Upper Egyptian type of church with the central nave roofed by more than one dome (Grossmann's *Langhaus-Kuppelkirche*).¹⁰ The western wall with a rare specimen of a western apse stands immediately in front of the

---

[8] The research agenda of the recent 'update' of Monneret de Villard's achievements encompasses Coptic epigraphy (stelae and secondary inscriptions) done by Lena Krastel, who provided the epigraphic data underlying this paper (see below, section entitled 'The Coptic Epigraphic Evidence and its Economic Aspects'), Arabic inscriptions dealt with by Ralph Bodenstein, Christopher Braun, Anna Chrysostomides, and Sara Hassan, painted decoration studied by Gertrud van Loon, analysis and conservation of plasters and mortars done by Alexandra Winkels, the building history of the church studied and reconstructed by Heike Lehmann and Max Dzembritzki, Sebastian Olschok's study of the architectural and usage history of the economic wing (see below, section entitled 'The Workshop Complex of Deir Anba Hadra'), the study of watering devices by Asmaa el-Sayegh, and last, but not least, Mennat-Allah El Dorry's research on archaeobotanical samples from the monastery.

[9] For an overview of the project, see Bodenstein, 'Epigraphik'; Krastel, 'Die koptischen Stelen'; Krastel, 'Words for the Living'; Krastel, 'Deir Anba Hadra'; Krastel and Richter, 'Eine koptische historische Inschrift'; Lehmann, 'Deir Anba Hadra'; Lehmann, 'Geometrie und Augenmaß'; Lehmann, 'Geometry by Eye'; Olschok, 'Deir Anba Hadra'; Richter, 'Das Kloster Deir Anba Hadra'; Richter, 'Koptische und arabische Inschriften'; Richter, 'Epigraphie, Bau- und Nutzungsgeschichte'; van Loon, 'Le Deir Anba Hadra'; van Loon, 'Le cimetière'; and van Loon, 'An Unusual Representation'. A final publication of the Deir Anba Hadra Project is in preparation.

[10] See Grossmann, *Mittelalterliche Langhaus-Kuppelkirchen*, pp. 7–13; and for the recent state of research, Lehmann, 'Deir Anba Hadra'; Lehmann, 'Geometrie und Augenmaß'; Lehmann, 'Geometry by Eye'.

Fig. 11.1. The upper and the lower terrace of Deir Anba Hadra (after Monneret de Villard, *Il monastero di S. Simeone*, vol. 1, figs. 39 and 87).

rock cliff separating the lower and upper terraces. Through the erection of this wall, one of the caves formed by quarrying work was partly cut off, while its major part was left intact and thus integrated into the spatial concept of the extended church. The walls and the roof of this cave are coated with high-quality figurative and ornamental painted decoration. The cave predates the architectural development of the church, or at least its western part.[11]

---

[11] Recent research conducted by Heike Lehmann and Max Dzembritzki has clearly shown that there was a time before the erection of the domed nave of the church, when an open place paved with limestone slabs extended between the decorated cave in the west and the triconch sanctuary, the nucleus of the later church, in the east.

Stylistic comparison[12] dates the embellishment of the cave to the seventh or eighth century,[13] which provides a hypothetical *terminus post quem* for the building history of the church and consequently for the foundation of the monastery. We do not yet understand the original liturgical purpose of the decorated cave,[14] but it is likely that it was at some time identified as the hermitage of Saint Hatre. This can be assumed on the basis of a *dipinto* (K_19_002) written on the south wall of the northern aisle of the church. *Dipinto* K_19_002, dated to Diocletian year 672 (=956)[15] and to regnal year 1 of a king Zacharia (one of the Christian kings of Makuria who sporadically took control over Aswan in the last years before the establishment of the Fatimid state), is a commemorative inscription for a deceased monk about whom it says: ⲉϥϩⲛⲡⲙⲁ ⲛϣⲱ(ⲡⲉ) ⲛⲁⲡⲁ ϩⲁⲧⲣⲉ ⲛⲥⲟⲩⲁⲛ 'while he was in the dwelling place of Apa Hatre of Aswan'. This designation implies, as Dijkstra and van der Vliet suggest,[16] that Deir Anba Hadra was at that time called the 'monastery of Apa Hatre'; more specifically it would mean that Deir Anba Hadra was by that time identified as the very spot where Hatre's dwelling place in his lifetime as a hermit had been located.[17]

Two narrow stairs in and besides the church lead from the lower terrace, the part of the monastery generally accessible to lay worshippers and visitors,

---

[12] See Bénazeth, 'Coptic Monastery', pp. 84–5, no. 52 A–B for monastic paintings on wood from Bawit.

[13] This date can already be found in earlier scholarly literature and was *grosso modo* validated by Gertrud van Loon.

[14] Indeed, the earliest testimony for Hatre on the spot of Deir Anba Hadra is his image in the cave at the north-western corner of the church. Only Hatre's halo and his right hand are still visible, but his identity can be inferred from an accompanying inscription. It is striking that the figure of Hatre is not highlighted or even in a prominent position. He is just standing in a row of thirty-seven saints together with persons from the Old Testament, such as King David, apostles, such as Peter and Paul, holy monks of supra-regional fame, such as Shenoute of Atripe, as well as local hermits from the First Cataract region, such as Banouphiel and Zebulon, with whom Hatre seems to be grouped if there is any discernible grouping at all. The painted decoration of the cave is being studied by Gertrud van Loon, who kindly shared her preliminary results with us. She apostrophised the decoration programme of the cave as 'a paradise of saints': no single saint is given particular prominence; the viewer is surrounded by a 'cloud of witnesses'. It is therefore possible but not proven that the decoration of the cave in the seventh/eighth century was already related to some cult of Saint Hatre. See van Loon, 'An Unusual Representation'. See also Dijkstra and van der Vliet, *Coptic Life of Aaron*, pp. 153 and 172.

[15] For the date, see Krastel, 'Words for the living', pp. 181–3, no. 1.

[16] Dijkstra and van der Vliet, 'King Zachari'.

[17] Although the usage of 'place of NN' as the equivalent for saying 'monastery of Saint NN' is normally restricted to ⲡⲙⲁ, the Coptic word for 'place', of Saint *NN* (or alternatively the Greek word ⲧⲟⲡⲟⲥ 'place') alone, a close parallel, also highlighted by Dijkstra and van der Vliet, is the Theban monastery of Epiphanius, which is likewise called ⲡⲙⲁ ⲛϣⲱⲡⲉ 'the dwelling place' of Epiphanius. Since this Theban monastery indeed contains the former dwelling place of its historical founding father, this is of particular interest in our instance.

to the upper terrace, the part of the monastery reserved for its inhabitants and staff. The entire northern area of the upper terrace is occupied by the monumental keep, with rising walls still extant up to the second floor. The ground floor of the *qasr* contained monks' cells, with their characteristic brick loungers, the refectory, dining hall, with likewise well-paralleled circular seats,[18] and the kitchen. The first floor contained a row of well-paved rooms of unknown function. The southern area of the upper terrace displays substantial architectural remains of workshops and economic appliances which we will discuss later in the article.

Before turning to the economic evidence of Deir Anba Hadra, it is important to briefly discuss the embeddedness of the monastery in the Christian community of the First Cataract region.

Christianity and Monasticism in the First Cataract Region

Since Syene, as well as Philae, were bishoprics from the fourth century onwards,[19] the monastery of Anba Hadra is only one – even though one of the best investigated and best recorded – religious institution in the First Cataract region. Due to the modern development of the ancient city of Syene and the poor documentation of excavations on Elephantine Island at the beginning of the twentieth century,[20] relatively little is known about the Christian settlements and their religious institutions in the surroundings of Aswan.[21] Nevertheless, the archaeological and textual evidence provides information on several churches and monasteries situated on the east and west banks of the Nile and on Elephantine Island. The archaeological remains of a church in the Temple of Isis,[22] the now demolished church

---

[18] For parallels at Deir el-Bachit (western Thebes), see Burkard and Eichner, 'Zwischen pharaonischen Gräbern und Ruinen'; Burkard *et al.*, 'Die spätantike/koptische Klosteranlage'; Eichner and Fauerbach, 'Die spätantike/koptische Klosteranlage'.

[19] See Dijkstra, *Philae*, pp. 51–63. For a list of the bishops from Syene, see Dijkstra, *Philae*, p. 359 (Appendix 4); Dekker, 'Memorial Stone', pp. 22–3. For a new study regarding three bishops of Syene, see Schmidt, 'Drei Bischöfe von Syene'. For a hitherto unknown bishop, see also Dijkstra, 'Of Fish and Vendors', pp. 67–8.

[20] For the excavations of the German and the French teams on Elephantine Island, see Honroth, Rubensohn, and Zucker, 'Ausgrabungen auf Elephantine' and Delange, *Les fouilles françaises*. The excavations were focused on the discovery of papyri. Generally, nineteenth- and early twentieth-century archaeologists in Egypt were easily ready to sacrifice presumed 'Coptic' structures – usually the uppermost strata of long-lasting settlements – without much concern for documentation, in order to more quickly reach pharaonic strata.

[21] For a brief overview of Aswan and Elephantine Island in Late Antiquity and early Islamic times, see Dijkstra, *Philae*, pp. 51–122 as well as F. Arnold, *Elephantine XXX*, pp. 17–28.

[22] For a brief overview, see Bresciani and Pernigotti, *Assuan*, pp. 38–41; Dijkstra, 'Reuse of the Temple of Isis'; Dijkstra, 'Fate of the Temples', pp. 414–16; Dijkstra, *Syene I*, pp. 11–18; Dijkstra

of Psote,[23] and a baptistry with a martyr's tomb nearby which possibly belong to a main church[24] were found in Syene while recent excavations uncovered the remains of three different churches – the church in the *pronaos* of the Temple of Khnum,[25] a church on a platform above a quay wall,[26] and the so-called 'Christian basilica'[27] – on Elephantine Island. Textual evidence, such as the medieval manuscript known as the 'History of the churches and monasteries of Egypt'[28] compiled at the end of the twelfth or the beginning of the thirteenth century, as well as papyri and ostraca found in the First Cataract region, contain information on several churches and monasteries in the neighbourhood of Syene, which are no longer preserved and partly not even traceable.[29] Of particular interest for the research on Deir Anba Hadra is the mention of a church of Hatre which was once located on Elephantine Island. According to the previously mentioned medieval manuscript, the mortal remains of Bishop Hadra were buried in this church and a large monastery was erected close-by.[30] Moreover, on the west bank of the Nile, some kilometres north of Deir Anba Hadra, lie the ruins of another monastery, Deir Qubbet el-Hawa, which is situated on a hill overlooking the Nile Valley. Although most parts of this monastery are still covered with sand and only the monastic church and some structures on the upper terrace have been excavated so far, it is obvious that both monasteries – Deir Anba Hadra and Deir Qubbet el-Hawa – share some architectural features[31] and might have been connected in one way or another. Such a connection is apparent, for example, in a letter found at Qubbet el-Hawa which dates to the seventh century AD

---

and van Loon, 'A Church Dedicated to the Virgin Mary'; Dijkstra and van Loon, 'Christian Wall Paintings'.

[23] Jaritz, 'Die Kirche des heiligen Psōti'.

[24] See von Pilgrim *et al.*, 'The Town of Syene', pp. 253–4; Dijkstra, *Philae*, pp. 109–10; Dijkstra, 'Fate of the Temples', pp. 416–17; Martin-Kilcher, 'Areal 6'.

[25] See Grossmann, *Elephantine II*, pp. 75–111; Delange, *Les fouilles françaises*, pp. 272–3; Dijkstra, *Philae*, p. 112.

[26] Dijkstra, *Philae*, p. 118.   [27] Dijkstra, *Philae*, pp. 118–19.

[28] Edited by Basil Evetts in 1895 (Evetts, *Churches and Monasteries*, pp. 274–7, fols 100b–102a). Although often attributed to Abu Salih or Abu el-Makarim, this manuscript was written by several authors. See Zanetti, 'Abū l-Makārim'; den Heijer, 'Coptic Historiography', pp. 77–81.

[29] See Timm, *Das christlich-koptische Ägypten*, vol. 1, pp. 222–35 and vol. 3, pp. 1044–9.

[30] Evetts, *Churches and Monasteries*, p. 276, fol. 101b.

[31] Although Grossmann's study on the architecture of the Upper Egyptian churches of Deir Anba Hadra, Deir Qubbet el-Hawa, and Deir el-Qubania is now partly outdated, the churches are still similar in architecture. Moreover, both Deir Anba Hadra and Deir Qubbet el-Hawa are built on two terraces with the church on the lower level and the *qasr* on the upper level. See Grossmann, 'Ein neuer Achtstützenbau'; Dekker, '"New" Discoveries at Dayr Qubbet el-Hawâ'; Dekker, 'An Updated Plan'; Abdin, 'Monastery of Qubbat al-Hawa'; Barba Colmenero and Torallas Tovar, 'Archaeological and Epigraphic Survey'.

and mentions the monastery of Anba Hadra.[32] Since the Coptic funerary stelae found at Deir Anba Hadra and at Qubbet el-Hawa[33] show striking similarities in their formularies as well as in their processing techniques, one may assume that some or perhaps most of these monumental inscriptions were produced in the same workshop, which might have been located in the vicinity. Moreover, Deir Anba Hadra also had relations with the bishop's sees in Syene and on Philae. A few funerary stelae presumably found in Deir Anba Hadra suggest that some monks were not only members of the monastic community of Deir Anba Hadra but also bishops of Syene or Philae.[34]

The monastery of Anba Hadra was not only connected with Christian institutions in and around Aswan but also with other churches and monasteries in Egypt. This becomes apparent, for example, from funerary stelae produced for monastics and ecclesiastics from other parts of Egypt who were buried at the cemetery of Deir Anba Hadra.[35] Another example is the case of the painter Merkourios. Merkourios, a monk from the Apa Shenoute monastery near Sohag, worked in the first quarter of the fourteenth century as a painter in various monasteries in Upper Egypt and left inscriptions in several of them, including two inscriptions in Deir Anba Hadra.[36] Therefore, the monastery of Anba Hadra may have been involved in an exchange of artisans of whatever kind with other monasteries in Egypt.

---

[32] See Torallas Tovar and Zomeño, 'Notas'; Barba Colmenero and Torallas Tovar, 'Archaeological and Epigraphic Survey', p. 156, O.QH Jaen 1. For further information on Deir Qubbet el-Hawa, see also Dekker, 'Memorial Stone'; Torallas Tovar, 'Cristianismo en Asuán', as well as Torallas Tovar and Zomeño, 'De nuevo en la orilla oeste'.

[33] In December 2012, some Coptic funerary stelae were found at Qubbet el-Hawa. Apart from the memorial stone of Bishop Joseph III (published by Dekker, 'Memorial Stone'), these stelae are still unpublished. Nevertheless, the formulary of the stelae is similar to the formulary known from Deir Anba Hadra but differs in the first and the last lines of text. We warmly thank Magdy Abdin (SCA Aswan) for the information on these stelae.

[34] One of the best examples is the funerary stela of Pousi, bishop of Philae and 'the first father of this monastery', which can presumably be linked with the monastery of Anba Hadra. For the text of the stela, see Bouriant, 'Notice des monuments coptes', pp. 69–70, no. 22; for the provenance see Maspero, *Guide du visiteur*, pp. 368–9, no. 5415; for a tentative dating see Dijkstra, *Philae*, pp. 325–6, n. 93 and Dekker, 'Memorial Stone', pp. 15–16.

[35] See the funerary stela of the deacon Pesynthios (Munier, 'Les stèles coptes', no. 104) who was a monk from the (monastery of) Saint John at Tkleopatra in the Hermopolite nome (Drew-Bear, *Le nome Hermopolite*, pp. 141–3).

[36] For Merkourios and his inscriptions, see Crum, 'Inscriptions', pp. 554–5 (A1); Clédat, 'Les inscriptions', pp. 55, room no. IV, and 56; Coquin, 'Les inscriptions pariétales', pp. 277–8 (Inscr. P); Dilley, 'Appendix I', pp. 292 (T.e.I.8.i-1), 296 (NLR.n.i-1), and 299 (N.w.i-1 and N.w.i-6); Delattre, Dijkstra, and van der Vliet, 'Christian Inscriptions', pp. 270, 274 (no. 31), and 275 (no. 40).

While the monastery of Anba Hadra was thus embedded in a regional and supra-regional structure of Christian institutions, it was also a self-sufficient community running its own production of foodstuff and commodities. These activities were located in a separated area on the upper terrace of the monastery.

The Workshop Complex of Deir Anba Hadra: Archaeological Evidence for the Monastic Economy

In this section, we will discuss the spatial development of the monastery's economic area, the facilities that are found there *in situ*, and the kind of production for which they were used, in order to answer the question of the nature and scale of the monastic production in this area. Was it just about its inhabitants' consumption, or can we assume that the monastery's produce was also intended for a local or supra-regional market?

The economic area of Deir Anba Hadra (Fig. 11.2) consists of twenty-one spatial units forming a complex of 37 by 22 m. Most rooms are elongated in a north–south direction (tilted to the west by about 17 degrees).

The whole complex grew and developed gradually from a single oblong (approximately 18 by 4 m), vault-covered building (the, still undivided, rooms OT_83 and 84), which stands out by its elaborate equipment: lime-plastered flooring and plastered benches running along the walls are very much like those found in the church of the monastery. This nucleus building displays overall similarities to a type of building usually identified as an oratory, that is to say, a place used for the liturgy of the hours, as known from several Upper Egyptian monasteries.[37] These similarities include a north–south orientation, an entrance in the south and a niche in the central part of the eastern wall.[38] It is not entirely clear whether the building OT_83/84 originally – before it was to become the nucleus of the economic complex – served as an oratory and was only at a later point transformed and reused for economic purposes, or whether it was planned as a storage room from the beginning. In any case, its south-eastern part was at some point dismantled and equipped with a dome-shaped large oven (diameter: 1.6 m; height: 0.9 m) and two installations which might have been smaller ovens or hearths (*kanun*). The large oven was embedded in

---

[37] See, for example, rooms 5 and 6 at Bawit: Grossmann, *Christliche Architektur*, pp. 280–1.
[38] Grossmann, *Christliche Architektur*, pp. 279–82.

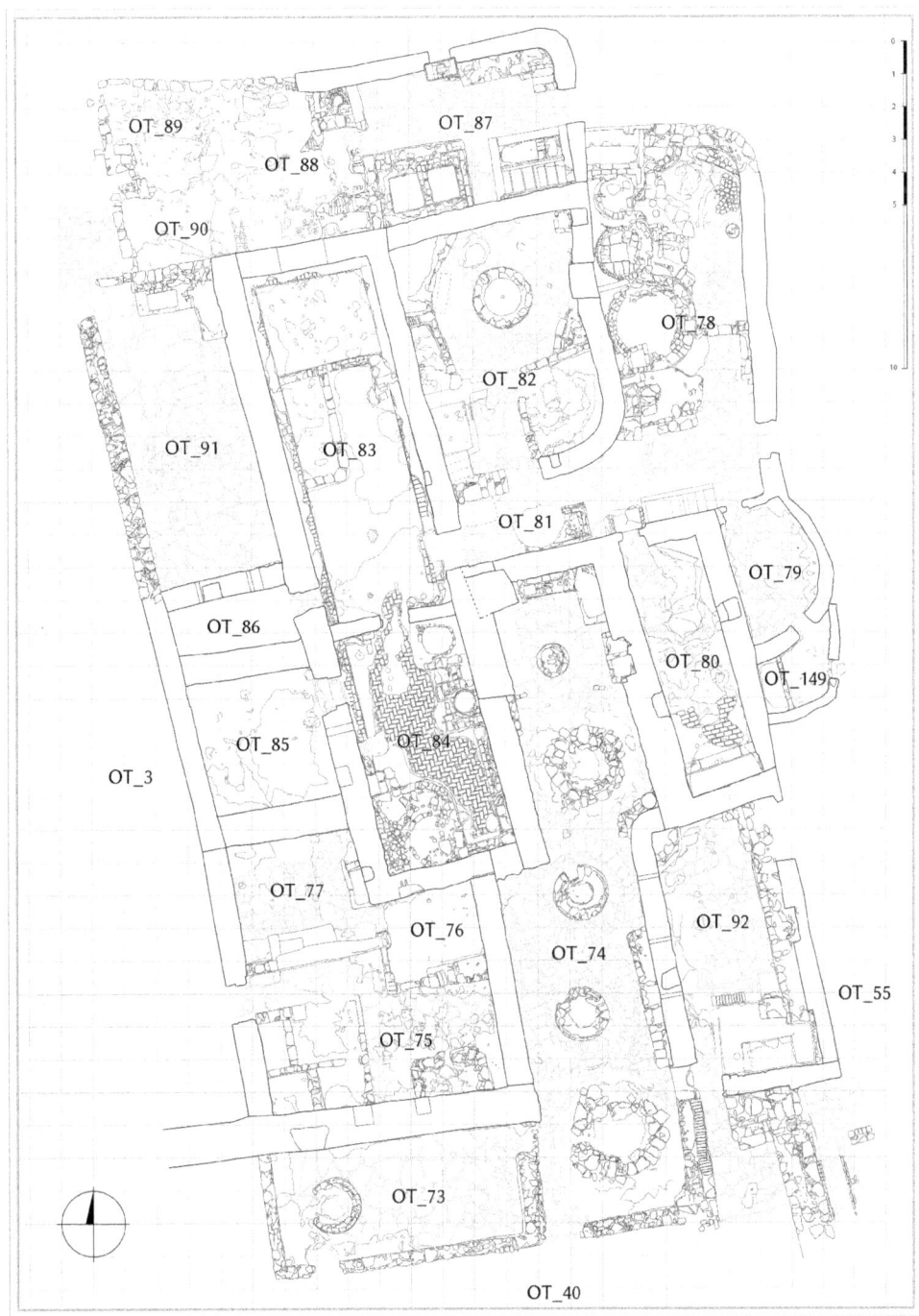

Fig. 11.2. Schematic floor plan of the economic area (drawing: Sebastian Olschok).

a platform with steps leading upwards. It is possible that another oven or a second part of the large oven was situated here, in which case this facility would have been a two-chambered oven. Examples of this type are found in kitchens in Kellia, interestingly always in combination with hearths.[39] The entrance in the south was at some point blocked and the wall behind the eastern niche was opened, to become a new entrance.

In the course of time other rooms and courtyards were added to this building. The first annex was a clay-paved courtyard to the west. Parts of the western wall of the nucleus were broken through in order to construct a door connecting the nucleus with the courtyard. The courtyard was later divided into two vaulted rooms (OT_85 and 86) and a smaller stone-paved yard (OT_91). This stone-paved yard was equipped with two mudbrick beds and was connected by one of the vaulted rooms to the nucleus (OT_83) of the complex in the east. A second door leads northwards to the western entrance gate of the monastery. The yard and its adjacent room probably served as a passage area for goods coming into or being brought out of the complex.

Another elongated courtyard (OT_74) is situated at the eastern side of the nucleus. Traces of three mill platforms constructed of mudbrick and plastered with clay, each of them of 1.7 m in diameter, can still be seen here (Fig. 11.3). The paving stones around these platforms are thoroughly

Fig. 11.3. Mill platforms in OT_74 (photo: Sebastian Olschok).

[39] For example, Eremitage 195, see Henein and Wuttmann, *Kellia II*, pp. 209–12.

smoothed, thus indicating heavy walking around the platforms. The appearance of this area closely resembles the milling area of the bakeries excavated in Pompeii Region I, insula XII. The flour mills of Pompeii display a distinctive hourglass-shaped millstone (*catillus*) running on a conical stone (*meta*) and resting on a platform, to be driven by animals.[40] Since hourglass shaped *catilli* are also known from Roman Egypt[41] it seems plausible to reconstruct four flour mills of this type in OT_74. This yard was later extended to the south and equipped with a fourth mill of similar type. A crushing basin with sunken socket with its fitting round-edge runner is located in the northern part of the building (OT_82). Both basin and runner are made of granite. Installations of this type were typically used for oil production. Monneret de Villard mentioned substantial amounts of residue found in this area, which he called 'sesame'.[42] This, however, seems to be a misinterpretation, since a more recent analysis of such vegetable remains revealed them to be residues of castor oil plant.[43] It is thus a viable assumption to identify this room as a place for castor oil production, although a press, as is essential for castor oil production, has not yet been found. Since lever presses or larger screw presses would leave archaeological traces, one may assume that a portable wooden screw press was in use.[44]

Four rooms (OT_87–90) in the north are later additions to the economic complex. Two large basins (each of them with an estimated volume of approximately 600 litres) constructed of mudbricks and connected through a window stand next to a rectangular installation made of sandstone and burned bricks (Fig. 11.4). This installation consists of a treading floor with small channels leading into a rectangular basin. Monneret de Villard found substantial residues of salt here and concluded that this facility must have been used for salt production.[45] Installations for salt production are, however, well known and exhibit almost no similarities with the installations found here. It is more likely that they were used for *garum* production and wine production (treading floor and settling vats), or something else, such that the whole installation formed part of a fullery (rinsing basins and press). It is also possible that both installations served different, unconnected purposes.

---

[40] Mayeske, 'A Pompeian Bakery', pp. 151–2.   [41] Meeks, 'Les meules rotatives', p. 26.
[42] Monneret de Villard, *Il monastero di S. Simeone*, p. 93.
[43] Hönigsberg, 'Römische Ölmühlen', p. 78.
[44] Frankel, *Wine and Oil Production*, p. 126. Examples are found, for example, in the monasteries of St Antony and St Paul on the Red Sea shore (personal observation Sebastian Olschok, 15 February 2017).
[45] Monneret de Villard, *Il monastero di S. Simeone*, p. 95.

Fig. 11.4. Rectangular installation in OT_87 (photo: Sebastian Olschok).

The building history of the south-eastern area (OT_92) of the complex is too complicated to be dealt with in detail here; more than six building phases can be distinguished. The southern part of the room is taken in by a rectangular basin with a pedestal at the southern wall (Fig. 11.5). Two steps lead down to the bottom of the basin resting on the bedrock. This basin was not dug into the floor; rather its sidewalls were erected with stones, and its rearside, later being filled with rubble, was covered with a paving slab and a plaster layer. The basin resembles structures excavated in Qasr Ibrim and identified as storage crypts. However, the question remains what purpose the later addition of the pedestal served.[46]

The eastern part (OT_78) was the latest addition to the complex. The north of this room is still covered in ash layers. Three ovens were found here, two were placed there originally, and a third was dug into already accumulated layers of ash at a later time. It is possible that other ovens are hidden here as well. The two original ovens are circular constructions, 1.47 m in diameter, with a dome constructed from fired bricks resting 0.8 m above ground level on pedestals. A large circular structure (diameter 2.8 m) is located in the southern part of the room. Its 0.6 m thick wall of sandstone and fired bricks was constructed up to a height of 0.9 m and had a step at

[46] Plumley and Adams, 'Qasr Ibrîm, 1972', p. 222.

Fig. 11.5. Rectangular basin in OT_92 (photo: Sebastian Olschok).

the south. Seven layers of fired bricks form a rectangular shaft (0.45 by 0.56 m) in the south-western corner of the ring. Layers of fired bricks constructed at the top of this ring structure indicate the former existence of a superstructure. Excavations in its central area have shown that this structure was roughly plastered with clay inside and filled with rubble. The lack of any traces of firing disproved the first assumptions that this installation could have been another oven. Comparison with similar installations in Egypt and Sudan, however, provides further hints. Round beehive shaped grain silos were common in Egypt and Nubia since the Middle Kingdom, usually equipped with a sunken floor.[47] 'Silo-like affairs' resting on stone foundations have been excavated in Dorginarti.[48] However, the shafts leading into the substructure are without comparison, though they could have served to extract grain from the silo, since it has an opening to the room.

[47] D. Arnold, *Lexikon*, p. 136. [48] Knudstad, 'Serra east and Dorginarti', p. 183.

To summarise and briefly conclude: seven ovens and hearths, four mills, a crushing basin and four installations for storage have been identified so far. The building stratigraphy allows certain practices to be connected with certain building phases. After the nucleus building (OT_83/84) was no longer used for the liturgy of the hours, it was divided into two rooms. While the northern room OT_83 remained vaulted, the vault and a part of the eastern wall of the southern room OT_84 were dismantled, and the room was equipped with an oven platform and two hearths. The yard OT_74 with its flour mills and the storage areas OT_85, 86 and 91 formed a kitchen or bakery. Storage rooms (OT_73–77, OT_80, OT_92) were constructed in the south and east of the kitchen/bakery. The castor bean crushing basin was constructed in a later phase. Room OT_82 was constructed afterwards around the crushing basin, leaving space for the path of the draught animals, the edge roller, and a second room, probably for the portable screw press. In the northern part of the workshop complex, four rooms (OT_87–90) were successively added and equipped with basins which could have served different purposes (fullery, winery, oil press, *garum* production). The ovens and silo in the latest addition (OT_78) seem to indicate that the ovens in the nucleus at that time either were not in use any more or served different purposes.

A large part of the workshop complex was thus destined for the storage and production of bread and its ingredients. The simultaneous existence of three – at a later time four – flour mills as well as the size of the oven platform in OT_84 suggests a large-scale production. Since bread was a main component of monastic (as of any) diet, and about eighty monks (according to the number of bedsteads in the *qasr*) plus visitors needed to be fed, it must be assumed that the outcome of this staple production was consumed inside the monastery. The same might be true for castor oil production. Castor oil was mainly used to run oil lamps,[49] for which purpose significant demand must have existed in a monastery the size of Deir Anba Hadra.[50] The kind of production in the northern part of the complex could only be inferred (most likely *garum* production), but it seems at any rate that it likewise provided a staple at the subsistence level of the monastic community. Although both wine and *garum* are typical commercial goods, and the sherds of large Late Roman amphorae are scattered all over the site, the extant basin's maximum capacity of approximately 1,200 litres would – for a monastery the size of Deir Anba Hadra – rather indicate monastic consumption than even small-scale trade.

---

[49] Sandy, *Production and Use of Vegetable Oils*, pp. 39–40.
[50] Sandy, *Production and Use of Vegetable Oils*, pp. 49–52.

In conclusion, the economic activities conducted in the monastery's central workshop area helped the monastery more-or-less to keep its economic autonomy as far as staple food is concerned. However, unlike our expectations and initial hypothesis, they did not provide the monastery a channel to feed into the local or even supra-regional trade and consequently to raise income for the monastery.

If the monastery entered trade at a larger scale, such business might be connected with a kiln and its associated facilities in the south-western corner of the upper terrace of the monastery, outside our workshop area (and thus outside the scope of the archaeological work so far conducted by the current project). The ascertainable manufacturing capacity of this kiln extends far beyond any plausible need of the monastery. Therefore, it has been suggested that the monastery was a likely production site of the so-called 'pink ware' that characterises the ceramic industry of Aswan in Late Antiquity and had a wide distribution throughout Upper Egypt.[51]

Apart from the archaeological evidence that provides insight into the material economy of the monastery – the production and storage of staple goods and ceramics – the monastery of Anba Hadra provides evidence for another sector of the economy, based on spiritual goods. The epigraphic record, comprising large numbers of Coptic and Arabic inscriptions, not only grants us valuable information on issues such as the building history of the monastery, the lasting use of the Copic language in the Middle Ages, and its eventual replacement by Arabic, it also offers a possible scenario of a spiritual economy run by the monastery. In the next section, the Coptic share of epigraphic activities will first be introduced, and then questioned in terms of what it tells us about the local monastic economy.

The Coptic Epigraphic Evidence and its Economic Aspects

Two Main Corpora of Epigraphic Evidence from Deir Anba Hadra

The Coptic epigraphic record from Deir Anba Hadra comprises two large corpora: a corpus of 146 extant funerary stelae,[52] for the most part made for monastics (usually men but interestingly also a few women), and a corpus

---

[51] Adams, *Ceramic Industries*, p. 24.

[52] In 1930/1, Henri Munier published 178 funerary stelae or fragments thereof (Munier, 'Les stèles coptes'), which he thought belonged to the monastery of Anba Hadra. Since only 146 stelae were found during excavations, the provenance of the other stelae is still unknown. Nevertheless, since their formulary is quite similar to the formulary of the stelae found at Deir Anba Hadra, these stelae could also derive from the monastery.

of some 300 Coptic secondary inscriptions[53] left in the monastery by worshippers – visitors as well as inhabitants. In the characteristic formulas of both corpora, the concept of ⲣⲡⲙⲉⲉⲩⲉ *r-p-meeue* 'to remember someone' is prominent. Moreover, one exceptional epigraphic item, a sandstone plate engraved with an inscription commemorating a pious endowment, completes the epigraphic record from Deir Anba Hadra.

In what follows, the corpus of funerary stelae from Deir Anba Hadra is introduced, including formularies and ways of referring to the deceased, to provide a point of comparison for the secondary inscriptions and their formulary and their ways of referring to their beneficiaries. After this, an institutional and economic background of the practice of leaving secondary inscriptions at Deir Anba Hadra is addressed. In our last point, we briefly discuss the socio-economic aspects of the inscription commemorating a pious endowment.

Funerary Stelae, Their Formulary, and How It Refers to the Deceased

The 146 funerary stelae from Deir Anba Hadra date from the late seventh up to the ninth centuries.[54] Their standard formulary generally records two sets of data forming part of the concept of ⲡⲉϩⲟⲟⲩ ⲙⲡⲣⲡⲙⲉⲉⲩⲉ ⲛ- (*pehoou mprpmeeue n-*) 'someone's day of remembrance': the identification of the deceased by name and epithets, and the date of his or her death according to day, month, and indiction year, plus, from the eighth century onwards, also according to a Diocletian year.[55] Only the youngest of three diachronically subsequent varieties or recensions of this standard formulary, its so-called third recension, concludes with a prayer for the salvation of the deceased's soul.[56]

---

[53] The term 'secondary inscriptions' refers to (generally more private, less official) inscriptions which were not part of the original, or to any overall regular decoration programme, but which were applied as later additions (which does not exclude the possibility that their making would be somehow restricted and regulated by official authorities). A similar functional distinction established in epigraphy uses the terms 'inscription' vs. 'graffito', but we reserve 'graffito' as a technical term to *scratched* secondary inscriptions (as opposed to '*dipinti*' referring to *ink-written* secondary inscriptions). This distinction is regularly applied in classical studies. A detailed explanation of the term graffito – also in contrast to *dipinto* – can be found in Lohmann, *Graffiti*, pp. 3–37.

[54] Munier, 'Les stèles coptes', pp. 258–9; Krause, 'Die Formulare der christlichen Grabsteine Nubiens', p. 79.

[55] For further information on the Diocletian era, see Bagnall and Worp, *Chronological Systems*, pp. 63–87; Ochała, *Chronological Systems*, pp. 31–97.

[56] For the recensions of this standard formulary, see Munier, 'Les stèles coptes', pp. 258–9; Krause, 'Die Formulare der christlichen Grabsteine Nubiens', p. 79.

Table 11.1. *Reference to the deceased in the funerary stelae (standard formulary) of Deir Anba Hadra (seventh–ninth centuries).*

I) General attributes
ⲡ(ⲉⲛ)ⲙⲁⲕⲁⲣⲓⲟⲥ (ⲛ-ⲥⲟⲛ / ⲉⲓⲱⲧ) (ⲁⲡⲁ)
'The (our) blessed (brother / father) (Apa)'

II) Identification
Name (given name mostly *without* indication of filiation and/or place of origin)

III) Individual attributes
ⲡⲉ(ⲡⲣⲉⲥⲃⲩⲧⲉⲣⲟⲥ / ⲇⲓⲁⲕⲟⲛⲟⲥ ⲁⲩⲱ ⲡ)ⲙⲟⲛⲟⲭⲟⲥ / ⲡⲡⲓⲥⲧⲟⲥ / ⲡⲁⲛⲟⲃⲁⲥ
'the (priest / deacon and) monk / novice(?) / Nubian(?)'

The reference to the deceased is consistent in what it says and what it does not say (Table 11.1). It starts with (I) **general attributes**, among which the most general one, ⲡ(ⲉⲛ)ⲙⲁⲕⲁⲣⲓⲟⲥ (*p(en)makarios*) 'the/our blessed one', occurs always, while ⲥⲟⲛ (*son*) 'brother', ⲉⲓⲱⲧ (*iôt*) 'father', and ⲁⲡⲁ (*apa*) 'Apa', indicating particular ranks, appear occasionally. The **identification of the deceased** (II) is delimited to one single element, his or her given name. This rule holds with a few exceptions,[57] in which the filiation or the place of origin are recorded. Among the **individual attributes** (III), the most regularly occuring is ⲡⲙⲟⲛⲁⲭⲟⲥ (*pmonakʰos*) 'the monk' which is also the only one associated with ecclesiastic titles such as ⲡⲉⲡⲣⲉⲥⲃⲩⲧⲉⲣⲟⲥ (*pepresbyteros*) / ⲡⲇⲓⲁⲕⲟⲛⲟⲥ (*pdiakonos*) 'the priest' or 'the deacon'. The attribute ⲡⲡⲓⲥⲧⲟⲥ (*ppistos*) 'the faithful' is borne by people who are neither *monakʰos* 'monk' nor *panobas* 'Nubian' (for which see below), some of whom, however, bear the general attribute ⲥⲟⲛ (*son*) 'brother'. Therefore, we would like to interpret this term as a designation of novices, as Walter Till and Ewa Wipszycka have already done.[58] The third attested individual attribute, ⲡⲁⲛⲟⲃⲁⲥ (*panobas*), is usually translated as 'the Nubian'.[59] No other ethnic attribute, however, is

---

[57] We counted nine exceptions out of 146 items (dates in brackets): the filiation is given in Munier, 'Les stèles coptes', no. 103 (786), no. 106 (805), no. 112 (857/866), no. 114 (872), and no. 117 (990), while the place of origin is mentioned in Munier, 'Les stèles coptes', no. 53 (716), no. 104 (796), nos. 116+120 (884/888/895) and no. 176 (undatable).

[58] See *P.KRU* 65.45–54; Till, *Erbrechtliche Untersuchungen*, p. 155; Wipszycka, *Moines et communautés monastiques*, pp. 381–3. See also Förster, *Wörterbuch*, pp. 647–8. This term has also been interpreted as a designation of postulants (see *P.Mon.Epiph.* 125* [n. 5 to the translation on p. 345, and n. 1 to the transcription on p. 184] and MacCoull, *Coptic Legal Documents*, p. 31 n. 11) or for lay brothers (Monneret de Villard, *Il monastero di S. Simeone*, p. 139). See also Garel, 'Vouloir ou ne pas vouloir', pp. 250–3.

[59] See Munier, 'Les stèles coptes', no. 26, no. 28, no. 39*bis*, no. 49, no. 50 and no. 127. For the name 'Anouba', see Dijkstra, *Philae*, pp. 152–3, n. 95; Dijkstra and van der Vliet, *Coptic Life of Aaron*, p. 200.

attested in the corpus, and this one, whenever occurring, is always used in a paradigmatic opposition to functional titles such as 'monk' and 'novice'. Even though etymologically an ethnonym, it seems possible that its actual meaning in the local monastic terminology was that of a functional title of some kind, instead of merely a reference to the ethnic identity of its bearer.

The sandstone stela of Mena (DAH_M073; *SB Kopt.* I 571; Fig. 11.6) is a good example of the funerary stelae of Deir Anba Hadra. It was found by Monneret de Villard in the monastic church in 1926 and measures 52 cm in height, 32.5 cm in width, and 6 cm in thickness.[60]

> J(esu)s Ch(rist). The day of the remembrance of our blessed brother Mena, priest, on which he went to rest. Written on the first of the month Thot, of the fifth indiction, in the year 468 (since Diocletian) (= 30 August 751).[61]

Fig. 11.6. Funerary stela of the priest Mena (photo: Kathryn E. Piquette; drawing: Isa Böhme; © Coptic Museum, Cairo/German Archaeological Institute, Cairo).

---

[60] The stela, now kept in the Coptic Museum in Cairo (inv. no. 9700), was originally published by Munier, 'Les stèles coptes', no. 73.

[61] † ιc † χc † | πεϩοου м̄|π̄ρ̄π̄μεευε | м̄πενμακα|ριος ν̄coν | мнna πεπρε/ | ντaчмτοn | м̄моч n̄ϩнτч | εγραφ/ м̄ᴴ θωθ | ᾱ // ιnᴅ/ ε | ετους υξη.

After the typical invocation 'Jesus Christ' and the introductory formula 'the day of remembrance', the designation of the deceased starts with a general attribute, 'our blessed brother', followed by the identification of the deceased, Mena. The designation closes with his ecclesiastic title. The inscription ends with the death formula and the date of death.

The Making of Memory: Secondary Inscriptions at Deir Anba Hadra and How They Refer to Their Beneficiaries

The second Coptic epigraphic corpus from Deir Anba Hadra, and the one that interests us here, comprises about 300 secondary inscriptions, graffiti and *dipinti* left in the monastery mostly by visitors, sometimes by inhabitants of the monastery. The distribution of these inscriptions in the monastery is clearly ruled by spatial hierarchies. The church yields the major share of inscriptions, some 170 items, although large parts of its wall surfaces, once presumably covered with inscriptions,[62] are now deprived of plaster. Some thirty Coptic secondary inscriptions (ca. 10 per cent) provide absolute dates,[63] mostly according to the Era of the Martyrs, only in a few cases named after Diocletian, and in one case according to the Hejira year. The earliest ones date to the second half of the tenth century, some to the twelfth, the thirteenth, the fourteenth and one even to the early fifteenth century. In terms of chronology, the corpus of Coptic secondary inscriptions barely overlaps with the Coptic funerary stelae which do not date beyond the ninth century, except one single outlier dating to the year 990.[64] The overall chronological separation between funerary and secondary inscriptions is one of the historical riddles we still have to tackle, and it is a caveat when dealing with differences in the formulary in functional terms.

The standard formulary (Table 11.2) of the visitors' inscriptions consists of, first, a **self-designation** (I): 'I (this poor / humble / miserable / sinner / your servant) *NN*, son of *NN*, (the deacon / priest) (from the town of ...)', and second, depending on the intended addressee of the inscription – God or other visitors –, a **prayer or request** (II), such as, 'God, have mercy on me / him! / Forgive me! / Remember me, Lord, when you come in your kingship! /

---

[62] While the eastern part of the monastic church at Deir Anba Hadra is in a better shape than the western one, it is the other way round at Deir Qubbet el-Hawa, where the western part is full of (Coptic and Arabic) inscriptions. Therefore, one may assume that also the western walls of the church of Deir Anba Hadra were originally filled with inscriptions.

[63] There are some more inscriptions with a dating formulary where the actual date is lost or illegible.

[64] Munier, 'Les stèles coptes', no. 117.

Table 11.2. *Standard formulary of visitors' inscriptions (tenth–fourteenth centuries).*

Self-designation
'I (this poor / humble / miserable / sinner / your servant) *NN*, son of *NN*, (the deacon / priest) (from the town of ...)'
Prayer / request
'God, have mercy on me! / him! / Forgive me! / Remember me, Lord, when you come in your kingship! / Remember me in love! / Whoever will be reading this text, say " ... ". / Pray for me / him / in love!'
(Date of day and / or year)
(Concluding formula) Amen! / May it happen!

Remember me in love! / Whoever will be reading this text, say " ... ". / Pray for me / him / in love!'. A **date of day and / or year** (III) and a **concluding formula** (IV) such as 'Amen! / May it happen!' are optional.

Examining closely how the beneficiaries' self-identification is phrased (Table 11.3), we find that it almost always starts with a **topicalising pronominal** (I) ⲁⲛⲟⲕ / ⲉⲅⲱ (*anok* / *ego*) 'I, (as for) me', followed by a phrase of **self-humiliation** (II), such as ⲡⲓϩⲏⲕⲉ / ⲉⲗⲁⲭⲓⲥⲧⲟⲥ / ⲧⲁⲗⲉⲡⲟⲣⲟⲥ (ⲛ)ⲣⲉϥⲣⲛⲟⲃⲉ / ⲡⲉⲕϩⲙϩⲁⲗ (*pihêke / elak^histos / taleporos (n)refrnobe / pekhmhal*) 'this poor / humble / miserable one / sinner / your servant'. The indication of the **beneficiary's identity** (III) is usually composed of several elements: first, his (exclusively male persons are attested) given name; second, his father's name; third, in some cases, his grandfather's name; and fourth, additional **individual attributes** such as the beneficiary's title of profession or his place of origin. The attested places, including Armant, Esna, Edfu and Aswan, evoke an idea of the hinterland of the monastery's attraction to visitors to the north of Aswan.[65]

---

[65] Names of cities: Babylon (ⲃⲁⲃⲩⲗⲱⲛ: K_50*, K_78_001); el-Balyana (ⲧⲡⲟⲩⲣⲓⲁⲛⲏ: K_71_004), Edfu (ⲉⲧⲃⲟⲩ: K_33_002*); Armant (ⲣⲙⲟⲛⲑ: K_76_001, OT_120_N_005); Esna (ⲥⲛⲏ: K_31_004*, K_68_007; ⲗⲁⲧⲱⲛ ⲡⲟⲗⲓⲥ: K_21; K_31_004*, K_96_002); Aswan (ⲥⲟⲩⲁⲛ: K_39*); names of monasteries: ⲡⲙⲁ ⲛϣⲱ(ⲡⲉ) ⲛⲁⲡⲁ ϩⲁⲧⲣⲉ ⲛⲥⲟⲩⲁⲛ K_19_002 'the dwelling place of Apa Hatre of Aswan'; ⲡⲙⲟⲛⲁⲥⲧⲏⲣⲓⲟⲛ ⲁⲡⲁ ⲃⲓⲕⲧⲱⲣ K_31_003*, K_32_003*, OT_116_W_001 'the monastery of Apa Victor'; ⲡⲙⲱⲛⲱⲥⲧⲉⲣⲓⲱⲛ ⲁⲡⲁ [ⲙ]ⲁⲑⲑⲉⲟⲥ K_31_002 'the monastery of Apa Mathew'; ⲡⲙⲟⲛⲁⲥⲧⲏⲣⲓⲟⲛ ⲡⲙⲁ[ⲣ]ⲧⲏⲣⲓⲟⲥ ⲙⲉⲣⲕⲟⲩⲣⲓⲁⲥ ϩⲛⲧⲡⲟⲗⲓⲥ ⲉⲧⲃⲟⲩ K_33_002* 'the monastery of the martyr Merkourios in the town of Edfu'. A funerary stela (Munier, 'Les stèles coptes', no. 104) belongs to a man from the monastery of Saint John at Tkleopatra (Κλεοπάρτρας κώμη in the Hermopolite nome; see Drew-Bear, *Le nome Hermopolite*, pp. 141–3) and another one (Munier, 'Les stèles coptes', no. 53) to a monk and *oikonomos* from a church (or monastery) of the Holy Virgin, possibly in the vicinity of Aswan. An inscription on a massive sandstone block (Munier, 'Les stèles coptes', no. 121) commemorates a man from the city of Pemdje, the Coptic name of Oxyrhynchus (modern el-Bahnasa).

Table 11.3. *Self-identification of the beneficiary in secondary inscriptions (eleventh–fourteenth centuries).*

I) Topicalisation
ⲁⲛⲟⲕ / ⲉⲅⲱ
'I,'

II) Self-humiliation
(ⲡⲓϩⲏⲕⲉ / ⲉⲗⲁⲭⲓⲥⲧⲟⲥ / ⲧⲁⲗⲉⲡⲟⲣⲟⲥ (ⲛ)ⲣⲉϥⲣⲛⲟⲃⲉ / ⲡⲉⲕϩⲙϩⲁⲗ)
'(this poor / humble / miserable / sinner / your servant)'

III) Name
... ⲡϣⲏⲣⲉ ⲛ- / ⲩⲩ / ⲩⲓⲩ ... (ⲡϣⲏⲣⲉ ⲛ- / ⲩⲩ / ⲩⲓⲩ)
'[*Name*] son of [*father's name*] (son of [*grand father's name*])'

IV) Individual attributes
(title / profession, place of origin)

Some secondary inscriptions written in Greek display certain Old Nubian tendencies, thereby testifying to visitors coming from the Christian kingdom of Makuria.[66]

The *dipinto* of Petros[67] (OT_120_S_018; Fig. 11.7) is a good example for the formulary used in the secondary inscriptions of Deir Anba Hadra. It is located on the south wall of room 120 on the first floor of the *qasr*. The inscription, covering an area of 9 cm in height and 12.5 cm in width, is written in black ink on the lower part of the wall. The language is Sahidic Coptic:

> I, this humble Petros, son of the priest Archelaos. God, have mercy on him. Amen. May it happen. May it happen.[68]

This *dipinto* offers a typical self-designation comprising 'I', the self-humiliating apposition 'this humble' normally chosen by clerics, thus also indicating profession, followed by the beneficiary's identity which is composed of his proper name, Petros, and his father's title and name. Thereafter, the *dipinto* contains a prayer directed to God with the beneficiary mentioned in the third person. Although the self-designation is written in the first person, it is common to refer to the beneficiary of the prayer either in the first or in the third person. The inscription closes with a confirmation.

---

[66] K_32_002, K_50* and K_62_001*. For the first one, the so-called Koudanbes inscription, a new publication by Adam Łajtar is in preparation (Łajtar, 'The So-Called Kudanbes Inscription').

[67] See Krastel, 'Words for the Living', pp. 179–80.

[68] ⲁⲛⲟⲕ ⲡⲓⲉⲗⲁⲭⲓⲥⲧⲟⲥ | ⲡⲉⲧⲣⲟⲥ ⲡϣⲏⲣⲉ ⲡⲣⲥ | ⲁⲗⲭⲁⲗⲁⲟⲥ ⲧⲛⲉ | ⲛⲁ ⲛⲁϥ ⲁⲙⲏⲛ | ⲉϥⲉϣⲱⲡⲉ | ⲉϥⲉϣⲱⲡⲉ.

Fig. 11.7. *Dipinto* of Petros, processed with DStretch (photo: Kathryn E. Piquette, © DAH Project).

The Content of Secondary Inscriptions at Deir Anba Hadra

As mentioned before, commemoration is most prominent in the secondary inscriptions of Deir Anba Hadra and elsewhere; in some way, this is what the practice of leaving visitors' inscriptions is all about. The key term to render the notion of commemoration is ⲙⲉⲉⲩⲉ (*meeue*) 'remembrance'. The owner, or *ego* of the inscription, wants to become the beneficiary of remembrance, therefore making statements such as: ⲁⲣⲓⲡⲁⲙⲉⲉⲩⲉ (ⲛⲁⲅⲁⲡⲏ) (*ari-pameeue* (*nagape*)) 'Remember me (in love)!'. The agentive role of commemoration can be assigned to different instances. In some cases, the request for remembrance is addressed to other worshippers, when it reads ⲁⲣⲓⲡⲁⲙⲉⲉⲩⲉ ⲛⲁⲅⲁⲡⲏ ⲟⲩⲟⲛ ⲛⲓⲙ ⲉⲧⲛⲁⲱϣ ⲛⲛⲓⲥϩⲁⲓ (*ari-pameeue nagapê ouon nim etna'ôsh nnishai*) 'Remember me in love, everybody who will be reading this text!'. Passing fellow-visitors are thereby asked to say a prayer for the *ego*'s soul.

In other cases, the addressee of the request for commemoration is God, when it reads ⲁⲣⲓⲡⲙⲉⲉⲩⲉ ⲡϭⲥ ⲙⲡⲉⲕϩⲙϩⲁⲗ (*ari-pameeue pč(oi)s mpekhmhal*) 'Remember, Lord, your servant NN!'. A prominent way to phrase such a prayer for God's remembrance is to quote from the Gospel of Luke 23:42: ⲁⲣⲓⲡⲁⲙⲉⲉⲩⲉ ⲡϫⲟⲉⲓⲥ ⲉⲕϣⲁⲛⲉⲓ ϩⲛⲧⲉⲕⲙⲛⲧⲉⲣⲟ (*ari-pameeue pčoeis ekšan-ei hn-tekmntero*) 'Remember me, Lord, when you come in your kingship!'. These words are spoken by the 'repentant' thief crucified at the right hand of Jesus, who then replies: 'Verily, I say to you, today shall you be with me in paradise', which is a variant of the formula provided in the newest edition of Nestle and Aland's Greek New Testament: Ἰησοῦ, μνήσθητί μου ὅταν ἔλθῃς εἰς τὴν βασιλείαν σου (*Iêsou, mnêstheti mou hotan eltês eis tên basileían sou*) 'Jesus, remember me, when you come into your kingdom!'[69] Detached from the New Testament, this Coptic variant is only occasionally recorded in graffiti and *dipinti*, as well as colophons. While this formula is frequently attested in the epigraphic evidence of Deir Anba Hadra[70] and Deir Qubbet el-Hawa,[71] it is scarcely attested otherwise in the Coptic epigraphic or documentary record in Egypt.[72] Whether this distribution has an objective reason or is just emerging from the state of preservation or the publication status of secondary inscriptions is difficult to determine at present.

Secondary Inscriptions as a Spiritual Commodity?

Moving on from this overview of the inscriptional material, the present issue is whether and how secondary inscriptions and their placement on the monastery's walls were embedded in a professional, institutional, and economic framework and interaction. Were these inscriptions written secretly on private initiative, or were they carried out by permission or even technical support from the monastic administration?

Looking at the apparently informal and, indeed, secondary character of the majority, they may at a first glance give the impression of a private

---

[69] Nestle and Aland, *Novum Testamentum Graece*.
[70] Attested in K_4_003, K_19_001, K_77_008, K_77_009, K_77_011, K_77_013, OT_94_W_002*, OT_95_O_002, OT_95_O_003, OT_95_W_003 and OT_95_W_006. A similar version is also attested in the Christian-Arabic inscription A_K_31_003; see Lagaron-Khalifa, 'Les graffiti arabo-chrétiens', 95–7, no. 7, DAH_06.
[71] See Dekker, 'An Updated Plan', p. 132, no. 1.
[72] It may be hinted at in a Coptic inscription from the monastery of Qubania (it just says 'Remember me, Lord': Junker, *Das Kloster am Isisberg*, p. 48, no. 2); see also a colophon from Esna in van Lantschoot, *Recueil des colophons*, no. CXIV. Greek variants are also attested in Nubia (in the church of Abd el-Gadir and the cathedral of Faras); see Łajtar, 'Varia Nubica', pp. 103–6. In graffiti from 'Gebel Maktub' near Qasr Ibrim, the formula is attested several times; see Łajtar and van der Vliet, 'A View from a Hill', especially p. 161. It seems that the epigraphic reference to Luke 23:42 is one of the features of Christian decorum shared between the south of Egypt and Lower Nubia.

activity, based on private decisions. However, this risks looking at religious testimonies of a religious practice through the eyes of modern travellers, and placing a medieval pious practice on a level with touristic habits evidenced by inscriptions left not just at Deir Anba Hadra but all over Egypt by European visitors during the last 200 years. An ancient pilgrim or traveller, visiting the holy place, could have waited for an unwatched moment to scratch his name in the wall, but is this what we have to envisage as the regular procedure?

It seems that our inscriptions point to another scenario. Certain features lead to the interpretation that their production resulted from an organised service, perhaps offered by the administration of the monastery to visitors. Many inscriptions are written in red or black ink, not a mandatory travelling untensil. Moreover, some of them are written in the characteristic cursive writing style that we first know from seventh- and eighth-century professional scribes of documentary writings. In the latest phase of Coptic written culture, this style, a token of professionalism from its beginnings, changed its functional domain from day-to-day documents to the sphere of commemorative texts, especially colophons, a palaeographic development thus indicating a change of this style in terms of prestige. The application of this writing style to the graphemic design of commemorative inscriptions could mean that professional instances were involved therein: professional in terms of writing proficiency, but also in terms of access to sacred space.

It is striking to find cases of intentionally cursive writing styles even applied to scratched inscriptions, i.e., to a writing technology which in merely practical terms does not invite cursive and ligatured forms. Fig. 11.8

Fig. 11.8. Cursive graffito on the north wall of the northern aisle of the church (K_4_003) (photo: Lena S. Krastel, © DAH Project).

presents an example of this enterprise, showing the frequently attested formula ⲁⲣⲓⲡⲁⲙⲉⲉⲩⲉ ⲛⲁⲅⲁⲡⲏ ⲉⲕϣⲁⲛⲉⲓ ϩⲛⲧⲉⲕⲙⲛⲧⲉⲣⲟ (*ari pameeue nagapê ekšanei hn tekmntero*) 'Remember me when you come in your kingship!'.

The evidence of palaeographic features, the sophisticated choice of certain text sections, the recurrent use of fixed formularies, the educated way of playing with variables – put succinctly, the overall decorum of how to inscribe the more and less accessible parts of a holy space – may be seen as tokens of some kind of control executed by the authorities of the monastery over the epigraphic activities of its visitors. Leaving an inscription of several lines at a prominent place in the church was not something that could be done in a moment, and it could hardly happen secretly, the less so since the content of the inscriptions was in a regular way the full self-identification of its beneficiary. Moreover, unwanted or unpermitted inscriptions could easily be removed. This leads us to understand the context of the epigraphic practice of secondary inscriptions as being framed in the model of 'exchange of religious and economic capital'. The extant inscriptions may thus not be the remains of some visitors' boldness but could rather point to a more regular and more complex kind of communication between the visitors and the authorities of the monastery.

Having discussed the two large corpora of Coptic inscriptions found in Deir Anba Hadra and having suggested economic implications for one of them – the corpus of secondary inscriptions – we cannot stop without touching upon one extraordinary inscription that gives unique insight into a socio-economic strategy.

An Inscription Commemorating a Pious Endowment and Its Economic Implications

In 1893, Jacques de Morgan found a fragment of an inscribed sandstone slab in the church of Deir Anba Hadra and published the Coptic text in 1894.[73] The text was catalogued by Crum in 1902 and dealt with by Dekker in 2006.[74] Recently two further fragments[75] of the slab have been identified. Although the inscription is still incomplete and parts of it are scarcely legible, it is now overall comprehensible as the epigraphic commemoration

---

[73] De Morgan et al., *Catalogue des monuments*, p. 139 n. 1. This fragment is kept in the Coptic Museum in Cairo, inv. no. 9741 (formerly Egyptian Museum, Cairo, CG 8322, JE 30430).

[74] See Crum, *Catalogue général*, p. 77, no. 8322; Dekker, 'Monasticism', pp. 44–5.

[75] Both fragments are stored in the Coptic Museum in Cairo. One fragment is kept under the inv. no. 10975 (formerly Egyptian Museum, Cairo, JE 68422); the current inventory number of the other fragment (formerly Egyptian Museum, Cairo, JE 68449) is still unknown.

of a pious endowment in favour of the poor of Syene and Elephantine, based on agricultural yields from a founded plot of arable land.[76] The text is shaped along the lines of Coptic donation and foundation inscriptions, as mainly known from building inscriptions and the colophons of donated books.[77] A preliminary translation is provided here:

> By the holy power of the Trinity and the solicitude for the poor of the pious father Apa [A]braha[m], bishop of [S]yene and Elephantine, [who] has been bearing great efforts and considerable expenses for a long time [un]til he established this estate [... for] the [fee]ding of the widows and [for the ... of the orph]ans. He who is appointed [as its manager] at any time, he shall administer its yi[eld] like a tenant: half (of the yield) for (the payment) of the peasants, the cattle, and the working expenses, the other half belongs to the poor of Syene and Elephantine. Whoever will disregard this order of [...] of God will aban[don him in the hour of] his (mortal) agony [...] the ste[ward].

The inscription commemorates an endowment initiated by a Bishop Abraham of Syene who is known solely from this inscription and may have been alive when it was written. It can be tentatively dated to the eighth century.[78] The monastery of Anba Hadra, not mentioned in the inscription, is the place where the inscription was found and where it was probably publicised. It is therefore not unlikely that the monastery was involved in or even directly responsible for the administration of the landed property and accordingly for the feeding of the poor. Care for the poor is a well-attested occupation of Coptic monasteries. Legal documents and monastic correspondences from the Theban area in the sixth to eighth centuries, for example, show a whole range of legal transactions and economic strategies with the purpose, or secondary aim, of addressing the need of the poor, as well as the role, often initiative, taken by the monasteries therein.[79] In *P.KRU* 13, for example, Kyriakos, abbot of the monastery of Apa Phoibammon (Deir el-Bahri), sells parts of two houses and declares that he will put the proceeds into the feeding of the poor and monastic needs.[80]

---

[76] The publication of this inscription by Lena S. Krastel is in preparation.

[77] See Schaten, 'Griechische und koptische Bauinschriften'; van Lantschoot, *Recueil des colophons*.

[78] Since the inscription bears no absolute date, this date is merely a suggestion based on palaeographical and internal features of the inscription: formulae known from seventh-/eighth-century Coptic lease contracts are applied; the verb προεϲτα (the Greek *prohistêmi*) and the related formula 'he who will be appointed as manager, etc.' is so far attested in Coptic child donation documents from the later eighth century. Since the institution attested here is so close to the *waqf*, the 8th century may be the *terminus non ante*.

[79] See Schmelz, *Kirchliche Amtsträger*, p. 170.

[80] For a translation, see Till, *Die koptischen Rechtsurkunden*, pp. 108–10 and MacCoull, *Coptic Legal Documents*, pp. 147–50.

Such documents provide a context for the endowment inscription from Deir Anba Hadra, a unique specimen of its genre and testimony for the charitable activities conducted by the monastery of Anba Hadra in providing staple for the body (of the poor) and the soul (of the pious founder).

Conclusion

Although economic documents such as letters, accounts, and legal deeds from Deir Anba Hadra are still missing, archaeological and epigraphic evidence illuminates various kinds and aspects of the monastery's economic activity. Physical remains of workshops and their facilities allow us to reconstruct the intramural production of staple food and other subsistence produce, such as lamp oil. In terms of quantities, this production might have met the demand of what the monastery needed for consumption. The scale of economic activities emerging from our investigation of the monastery's central workshop area does not provide evidence of monastic production for trade. It has been argued, however, that the kiln of Deir Anba Hadra could have fed the local and supra-regional market with Aswan 'pink ware'.

Again, lacking documentary evidence, we do not know whether the monastic economy was self-sustaining also in terms of self-grown arable crops such as grain, oil seed, or wine, to be processed in its workshops. We do, however, have one testimony granting us glimpses of ecclesiastic landed property: the unique eighth-century(?) inscription commemorating a pious foundation shows the monastery endowing a share of the annual crops to be spent for the sake of the poor of Aswan. This inscription gives an account of charitable aspects of the monastic economy of Deir Anba Hadra, as we find them in documents, for example, from Theban monasteries. Another aspect which we call spiritual economy is accessible through the corpus of secondary inscriptions written on the walls of the monastery. Based on our observation that many inscriptions are written carefully and professionally in black or red ink by experienced hands at prominent positions in the monastery, we conclude that the pious practice of leaving inscriptions on the monastery's walls was not merely tolerated but probably encouraged and supported by monastic authorities. We further argue that these authorities may have capitalised on the benefits of commemoration at the holy place and of the forgiveness of sins, as on valuable spiritual commodities, thus providing a very concrete example of what Bourdieu would have called the exchange of religious and economic capital.

Bibliography

Abdin, M. A. 'The Monastery of Qubbat al-Hawa' in D. Raue, S. J. Seidlmayer, and P. Speiser (eds.), *The First Cataract of the Nile. One Region – Diverse Perspectives* (Berlin and Boston, MA: De Gruyter, 2013), pp. 1–3.

Adams, W. Y. *Ceramic Industries of Medieval Nubia* (Lexington, KY: University Press of Kentucky, 1986).

Arnold, D. *Lexikon der ägyptischen Baukunst*, 2nd edition (Munich: Artemis & Winkler, 1997).

Arnold, F. *Elephantine XXX. Die Nachnutzung des Chnumtempelbezirks. Wohnbebauung der Spätantike und des Frühmittelalters* (Mainz: Philipp von Zabern, 2003).

Bagnall, R. S. and Worp, K. A. *Chronological Systems of Byzantine Egypt*, 2nd edition (Leiden and Boston, MA: Brill, 2004).

Barba Colmenero, V. and Torallas Tovar, S. 'Archaeological and Epigraphic Survey of the Coptic Monastery at Qubbat el-Hawa (Aswan)' in P. Buzi (ed.), *Coptic Literature in Context (4th–13th c.): Cultural Landscape, Literary Production, and Manuscript Archaeology* (Rome: Edizioni Quasar, 2020), pp. 149–60.

Bénazeth, D. 'The Coptic Monastery of Bawit' in H. C. Evans and B. Ratcliff (eds.), *Byzantium and Islam. Age of Transition, 7th–9th Century* (New York: Metropolitan Museum of Art, 2012), pp. 81–6.

Bodenstein, R. 'Epigraphik, Bau- und Nutzungsgeschichte des Klosters Deir Anba Hadra: Die Arbeiten des Jahres 2018 bis Juni 2019', *e-Forschungsberichte des Deutschen Archäologischen Instituts*, 2/2019 (2019), 21–7.

Bouriant, U. 'Notice des monuments coptes du Musée de Boulaq', *Recueil de travaux relatifs à la philologie et à archéologie égyptienne et assyrienne*, 5 (1884), 60–70.

Bouriant, U. 'Notes de voyage', *Recueil de travaux relatifs à la philologie et à archéologie égyptienne et assyrienne*, 15 (1893), 176–89.

Bresciani, E. and Pernigotti, S. *Assuan* (Pisa: Giardini, 1978).

Burkard, G. and Eichner, I. 'Zwischen pharaonischen Gräbern und Ruinen: Das Kloster Deir el-Bachit in Theben-West' in G. Dreyer and D. Polz (eds.), *Begegnung mit der Vergangenheit: 100 Jahre in Ägypten: Deutsches Archäologisches Institut Kairo 1907–2007* (Mainz: Philipp von Zabern, 2007), pp. 270–4.

Burkard, G., Mackensen, M., and Polz, D. 'Die spätantike/koptische Klosteranlage Deir el-Bachit in Dra' Abu el-Naga (Oberägypten): Erster Vorbericht', *Mitteilungen des Deutschen Archäologischen Instituts, Abteilung Kairo*, 59 (2003), 41–65.

Clédat, J. 'Notes d'archéologie copte', *Annales de Service des Antiquités de l'Égypte*, 9 (1908), 213–30.

Clédat, J. 'Les inscriptions de Saint-Siméon', *Recueil de travaux relatifs à la philologie et à archéologie égyptienne et assyrienne*, 37 (1915), 41–57.

Coquin, R.-G. 'Les inscriptions pariétales des monastères d'Esna: Dayr al-Šuhadā' – Dayr al-Faḫūrī', *Bulletin de l'Institut français d'archéologie orientale*, 75 (1975), 241–84.

Crum, W. E. *Catalogue général des antiquités égyptiennes du Musée du Caire, nos. 8001-8741. Coptic Monuments* (Cairo: Institut français d'archéologie orientale, 1902).

Crum, W. E. 'Inscriptions from Shenoute's Monastery', *Journal of Theological Studies*, 5 (1904), 552–69.

de Morgan, J., Bouriant, U., Legrain, G., Jéquier, G. and Barsanti, A. *Catalogue des monuments et inscriptions de l'Égypte antique, Première série: Haute Égypte, tome I: De la frontière de Nubie a Kom Ombos* (Vienna: Adolphe Holzhausen, 1894).

Dekker, R. 'Monasticism in the First Cataract Region. Dayr Anbā Hadrā, Dayr Qubbat al-Hawā and Dayr al-Kubāniyya and Their Relations with the World outside the Walls', unpublished Master's dissertation, University of Leiden, 2006.

Dekker, R. '"New" Discoveries at Dayr Qubbat al-Hawâ, Aswān. Architecture, Wall Paintings and Dates', *Eastern Christian Art*, 5 (2008), 19–36.

Dekker, R. 'An Updated Plan of the Church at Dayr Qubbat al-Hawa' in G. Gabra and H. Takla (eds.), *Christianity and Monasticism in Aswān and Nubia* (Cairo and New York: American University in Cairo Press, 2013), pp. 117–35.

Dekker, R. 'The Memorial Stone of Bishop Joseph III of Aswan' in A. Łajtar, G. Ochała, and J. van der Vliet (eds.), *Nubian Voices II. New Texts and Studies on Christian Nubian Culture* (Warsaw: Taubenschlag Press, 2015), pp. 5–25.

Delange, É. (ed.) *Les fouilles françaises d'Éléphantine (Assouan) 1906–1911. Les archives Clermont-Ganneau et Clédat*, 2 vols (Paris: Academie des inscriptions et belles-lettres, 2012).

Delattre, A., Dijkstra, J. H. F., and van der Vliet, J. 'Christian Inscriptions from Egypt and Nubia 4', *Bulletin of the American Society of Papyrologists*, 54 (2017), 261–86.

den Heijer, J. 'Coptic Historiography in the Fāṭimid, Ayyūbid and Early Mamlūk Periods', *Medieval Encounters*, 2 (1996), 67–98.

Dijkstra, J. H. F. *Philae and the End of Ancient Egyptian Religion. A Regional Study of Religious Transformation (298–642 CE)* (Leuven, Paris, and Dudley, MA: Peeters, 2008).

Dijkstra, J. H. F. 'The Reuse of the Temple of Isis at Aswan as a Church in Late Antiquity', *Journal of the Canadian Society for Coptic Studies*, 1 (2010), 33–45.

Dijkstra, J. H. F. 'The Fate of the Temples in Late Antique Egypt' in L. Lavan and M. Mulryan (eds.), *The Archaeology of Late Antique 'Paganism'* (Leiden and Boston, MA: Brill, 2011), pp. 389–436.

Dijkstra, J. H. F. *Syene I. The Figural and Textual Graffiti from the Temple of Isis at Aswan* (Mainz: Philipp von Zabern, 2012).

Dijkstra, J. H. F. 'Of Fish and Vendors. The Khnum Temple Graffiti Project' in S. C. Dirksen and L. S. Krastel (eds.), *Epigraphy through Five Millennia: Texts and Images in Context* (Wiesbaden: Harrassowitz, 2020), pp. 61–71.

Dijkstra, J. H. F. and van der Vliet, J. '"In Year One of King Zachari". Evidence of a New Nubian King from the Monastery of St. Simeon at Aswān', *Beiträge zur Sudanforschung*, 8 (2003), 31–9.

Dijkstra, J. H. F. and van der Vliet, J. *The Coptic Life of Aaron. Critical Edition, Translation and Commentary* (Leiden and Boston, MA: Brill, 2020).

Dijkstra, J. H. F. and van Loon, G. J. M. 'A Church Dedicated to the Virgin Mary in the Temple of Isis at Aswan?', *Eastern Christian Art*, 7 (2010), 1–16.

Dijkstra, J. H. F. and van Loon, G. J. M. 'The Christian Wall Paintings from the Temple of Isis at Aswan Revisited' in G. Gabra and H. N. Takla (eds.), *Christianity and Monasticism in Aswān and Nubia* (Cairo and New York: AUC Press, 2013), pp. 137–56.

Dilley, P. C. 'Appendix I: The Greek and Coptic Inscriptions in the Red Monastery Church', in E. S. Bolman (ed.), *The Red Monastery Church. Beauty and Asceticism in Upper Egypt* (New Haven and London: Yale University Press, 2016), pp. 288–300.

Drew-Bear, M. *Le nome Hermopolite. Toponymes et sites* (Missoula, MT: Scholars Press, 1979).

Eichner, I. and Fauerbach, U. 'Die spätantike/koptische Klosteranlage Deir el-Bachit in Dra' Abu el-Naga (Oberägypten): Zweiter Vorbericht', *Mitteilungen des Deutschen Archäologischen Instituts, Abteilung Kairo*, 61 (2005), 139–52.

Evetts, B. T. A. *The Churches and Monasteries of Egypt. Attributed to Abû Ṣâliḥ, the Armenian* (Oxford: Clarendon Press, 1895).

Förster, H. *Wörterbuch der griechischen Wörter in den koptischen dokumentarischen Texten* (Berlin and New York: De Gruyter, 2002).

Frankel, R. *Wine and Oil Production in Antiquity in Israel and Other Mediterranean Countries* (Sheffield: Sheffield Academic Press, 1999).

Garel, E. 'Vouloir ou ne pas vouloir: devenir moine à Thebes au VIIe–VIIIe siècle d'apres les texts documentaires' in A. Boud'hors and C. Louis (eds.), *Études coptes XV. Dix-septième journée d'études (Lisbonne, 18–20 juin 2015)* (Paris: Boccard, 2018), pp. 245–54.

Grossmann, P. *Elephantine II. Kirche und spätantike Hausanlagen im Chnumtempelhof. Beschreibung und typologische Untersuchung* (Mainz: Philipp von Zabern, 1980).

Grossmann, P. *Mittelalterliche Langhaus-Kuppelkirchen und verwandte Typen in Oberägypten. Eine Studie zum mittelalterlichen Kirchenbau in Ägypten* (Glückstadt: Verlag J. J. Augustin GmbH, 1982).

Grossmann, P. 'Ein neuer Achtstützenbau im Raum von Aswān in Oberägypten', *Bibliothèque d'étude*, 97.1 (1985), 339–48.

Grossmann, P. *Christliche Architektur in Ägypten* (Leiden, Boston, MA, and Cologne: Brill, 2002).

Henein, N. H. and Wuttmann, M. *Kellia II. L'ermitage copte QR195 1,1. Archéologie et architecture* (Cairo: Institut français d'archéologie orientale, 2000).

Hönigsberg, P. 'Römische Ölmühlen mahlen noch in Oberägypten', *Mitteilungen des Deutschen Archäologischen Instituts, Abteilung Kairo*, 18 (1962), 70–9.

Honroth, W., Rubensohn, O., and Zucker, F. 'Bericht über die Ausgrabungen auf Elephantine in den Jahren 1906–1908', *Zeitschrift für ägyptische Sprache und Altertumskunde*, 46 (1910), 14–61.

Jaritz, H. 'Die Kirche des heiligen Psōti vor der Stadtmauer von Assuan', *Bibliothèque d'étude*, 97.2 (1985), 1–19.

Jullien, M. 'Quelques anciens couvents de l'Égypte', *Les Missions catholique. Bulletin hebdomadaire de l'oeuvre de la propagation de la foi*, 35 (1903), 283–7.

Junker, H. *Das Kloster am Isisberg. Bericht über die Grabungen der Akademie der Wissenschaften in Wien bei El-Kubanieh. Winter 1910-1911, Dritter Teil* (Vienna and Leipzig: Hölder-Pichler-Tempsky AG, 1922).

Knudstad, J. 'Serra East and Dorginarti. A Preliminary Report on the 1963–64 Excavations of the University of Chicago Oriental Institute Sudan Expedition', *Kush*, 14 (1966), 165–86.

Krastel, L. S. 'Die koptischen Stelen des Deir Anba Hadra im Koptischen Museum. Die Arbeiten des Jahres 2017', *e-Forschungsberichte des Deutschen Archäologischen Instituts*, 2/2017 (2017), 35–8.

Krastel, L. S. 'Words for the Living and the Dead. Coptic Inscriptions of Deir Anba Hadra' in S. C. Dirksen and L. S. Krastel (eds.), *Epigraphy through Five Millennia: Texts and Images in Context* (Wiesbaden: Harrassowitz, 2020), pp. 169–93.

Krastel, L. S. 'Deir Anba Hadra, Funerary Stelae of' in *Claremont Coptic Encyclopedia*, 2021, available at https://ccdl.claremont.edu/digital/collection/cce/id/2177 (accessed 30 November 2022).

Krastel, L. S. and Richter, T. S. 'Eine koptische historische Inschrift im Deir Anba Hadra bei Assuan' in R. Bußmann, I. Hafemann, R. Schiestl, and D. A. Werning (eds.), *Spuren der altägyptischen Gesellschaft. Festschrift für Stephan J. Seidlmayer* (Berlin: de Gruyter, 2022), pp. 483–502.

Krause, M. 'Die Formulare der christlichen Grabsteine Nubiens' in K. Michałowski (ed.), *Nubia. Récentes recherches. Actes du colloque nubiologique international au Musée national de Varsovie, 19–22 juin 1972* (Warsaw: Musée National, 1975), pp. 76–82.

Lagaron-Khalifa, A. 'Les graffiti arabo-chrétiens d'Égypte et de Palestine à l'époque médiévale (VII–XIVe siècle). Présentation et contextualisation d'un corpus d'étude', unpublished PhD dissertation, Université Aix Marseille, 2020.

Łajtar, A. 'Varia Nubica XII–XIX', *Journal of Juristic Papyrology*, 39 (2009), 83–119.

Łajtar, A. 'The So-Called Kudanbes Inscription in Deir Anba Hadra (St. Simeon Monastery) near Aswan: an Attempt at a New Reading and Interpretation' in A. Łajtar (ed.), *Nubica. Studies in History and Epigraphy of the Middle Nile Region in Christian Times* (Leiden: Peeters, in preparation).

Łajtar, A. and van der Vliet, J. 'A View from a Hill: A First Presentation of the Rock Graffiti of "Gebel Maktub"' in J. van der Vliet and J. L. Hagen (eds.), *Qasr Ibrim, between Egypt and Africa. Studies in Cultural Exchange (Nino Symposium, Leiden, 11–12 December 2009)* (Leuven: Peeters, 2013), pp. 157–66.

Lefort, L. T. 'Le prologue de l'Apocalypse en sahidique', *Le Muséon*, 54 (1941), 107–10.

Lefort, L. T. 'Glanures Pachômiennes', *Le Muséon*, 54 (1941), 111–38.

Lefort, L. T. *Les vies coptes de Saint Pachôme et de ses premiers successeurs* (Leuven: Bureaux de Muséon, 1943).

Lehmann, H. 'Deir Anba Hadra. Neue Untersuchungen eines koptischen Klosters bei Aswan (Ägypten)', *INSITU. Zeitschrift für Architekturgeschichte*, 1/2016 (2016), 7–26.

Lehmann, H. 'Geometrie und Augenmaß. Überlegungen zur Anwendung historischen Bauwissens in der Gewölbekonstruktion der Klosterkirche des Deir Anba Hadra bei Aswan (Ägypten)', *INSITU. Zeitschrift für Architekturgeschichte*, 2/2018 (2018), 175–86.

Lehmann, H. 'Geometry by Eye: Medieval Vaulting of the Anba Hadra Church (Egypt)' in J. Mascarenhas-Mateus and A. P. Pires, *History of Construction Cultures*, vol. 2 (Leiden: CRC Press, 2021), pp. 325–32.

Lohmann, P. *Graffiti als Interaktionsform. Geritzte Inschriften in den Wohnhäusern Pompejis* (Berlin and Boston, MA: De Gruyter, 2018).

MacCoull, L. S. B. *Coptic Legal Documents. Law as Vernacular Text and Experience in Late Antique Egypt* (Tempe, AZ: ACMRS; Turnhout: Brepols, 2009).

Margoliouth, D. S. and Holmyard, E. J. 'Arabic Documents from the Monneret Collection', *Islamica*, 4 (1929–31), 249–71.

Martin-Kilcher, S. 'Areal 6: Teile eines spätantiken christlichen Sakralkonplexes mit Grabkammer und Baptisterium sowie weitere Strukturen' in S. Martin-Kilcher and J. Wininger (eds.), *Syene III. Untersuchungen zur römischen Keramik und weiteren Funden aus Syene/Assuan (1.–7. Jahrhundert AD). Grabungen 2001–2004* (Gladbeck: PeWe-Verlag, 2017), pp. 197–238.

Maspero, G. *Guide du visiteur au Musée de Boulaq* (Boulaq: Musée de Boulaq, 1883).

Maspero, G. 'Rapport à l'Institut égyptien sur les fouilles et travaux executes en Égypte pendant l'hiver de 1885–1886', *Bulletin de l'Institut Égyptien*, 7, série 2 (1887), 196–251.

Matteucci, P. 'Lettere del dott. Matteucci', *Bollettino della Socièta geografica italiana*, 14 (1877), 459–62.

Mayeske, B. J. 'A Pompeian Bakery on the Via Dell'Abbondanza' in R. I. Curtis (ed.), *Studia Pompeiana et Classica in Honor of Wilhelmina F. Jashemski*, 2 vols (New Rochelle: A. D. Caratzas, 1988), vol. 1, pp. 149–66.

Meeks, D. 'Les meules rotatives en Égypte. Datation et usages' in D. Garcia and D. Meeks (eds.), *Techniques et économie antiques et médiévales: le temps de l'innovation. Colloque international (C.N.R.S.) Aix-en-Provence 21–23 Mai 1996* (Paris: Errance, 1997), pp. 20–8.

Monneret de Villard, U. 'Rapporto preliminare sugli scavi al Monastero di S. Simeone presso Aswan', *Rendiconti della R. Accademia Nazionale dei Lincei. Classe di scienze morali, storiche e filologiche*, ser. 6, vol. I, fasc. 6 (1925), 289–303.

Monneret de Villard, U. 'Descrizione generale de Monastero di San Simeon presso Aswân', *Annales de Service des Antiquités de l'Égypte*, 26 (1926), 211–45.

Monneret de Villard, U. *Description générale du Monastère de Snt. Siméon à Aswân* (Milan: Comité de conservation des monuments de l'art arabe, 1927).

Monneret de Villard, U. *Il monastero di S. Simeone presso Aswân*, vol. I: *Descrizione archeologica* (Milan: Tipografia e liberia pontificia arcivescovile S. Giuseppe, 1927).

Monneret de Villard, U. 'La missione archeologica italiana in Egitto, 1921–28', *Oriente moderno*, 8 (1928), 268–77.

Munier, H. 'Les stèles coptes du Monastère de Saint-Siméon à Assouan', *Aegyptus*, 11 (1930/1), 257–300, 433–84.

Nestle, E. and Aland, B. *Novum Testamentum Graece*, 28th revised edition (Stuttgart: Deutsche Bibelgesellschaft and Katholische Bibelanstalt, 2017).

Ochała, G. *Chronological Systems of Christian Nubia* (Warsaw: Taubenschlag Press, 2011).

Olschok, S. 'Deir Anba Hadra – Ein Kloster im Fokus', *Blickpunkt Archäologie*, 3 (2016), 223–9.

Plumley, J. M. and Adams, W. Y. 'Qasr Ibrîm, 1972', *Journal of Egyptian Archaeology*, 60 (1974), 212–38.

Richter, T. S. 'Das Kloster Deir Anba Hadra. Epigraphie, Kunst- und Bauforschung auf dem Westufer von Assuan', *Archäologie in Ägypten*, 3 (2015), 20–5.

Richter, T. S. 'Koptische und arabische Inschriften sowie archäologisch-bauforscherische Untersuchungen im Simeonskloster bei Assuan', *e-Forschungsberichte des Deutschen Archäologischen Instituts*, 1/2015 (2015), 8–10.

Richter, T. S. 'Epigraphie, Bau- und Nutzungsgeschichte des Klosters Deir Anba Hadra', *e-Forschungsberichte des Deutschen Archäologischen Instituts*, 2/2017 (2017), 1–6.

Sandy, D. B. *The Production and Use of Vegetable Oils in Ptolemaic Egypt* (Atlanta, GA: Schlars Press, 1989).

Schaten, S. 'Griechische und koptische Bauinschriften' in S. Emmel, M. Krause, S. G. Richter, and S. Schaten (eds.), *Ägypten und Nubien in spätantiker und christlicher Zeit. Akten des 6. Internationalen Koptologenkongresses Münster, 20.-26. Juli 1996*, vol. 2. *Schrifttum, Sprache und Gedankenwelt* (Wiesbaden: Reichert, 1999), pp. 305-14.

Schmelz, G. *Kirchliche Amtsträger im spätantiken Ägypten nach den Aussagen der griechischen und koptischen Papyri und Ostraka* (Leipzig: de Gruyter, 2002).

Schmidt, S. 'Drei Bischöfe von Syene namens Joseph. Inschriften, Tonlämpchen und ein Ostrakon mit einem Beitrag von R. Duttenhöfer', *Journal of Juristic Papyrology*, 48 (2018), 185-205.

Soldati, A. 'Una lettera copta dal monastero di Anbā Hadrà presso Aswān', *Aeygptus*, 98 (2018), 189-96.

Soldati, A. 'A New Bifolium from the Monastery of Anbā Hadrà (Ms. Rome, Biblioteca Corsiniana, 280.C1) as Historical Source for the Coptic Episcopal See of Aswān' in P. Buzi (ed.), *Coptic Literature in Context (4th-13th c.). Cultural Landscape, Literary Production, and Manuscript Archaeology* (Rome: Edizioni Quasar, 2020), pp. 169-82.

Till, W. C. *Erbrechtliche Untersuchungen auf Grund der koptischen Urkunden* (Vienna: Rudolf M. Rohrer, 1954).

Till, W. C. *Die koptischen Rechtsurkunden aus Theben* (Vienna: Hermann Böhlaus Nachfolger, 1964).

Timm, S. *Das christlich-koptische Ägypten in arabischer Zeit*, 7 vols. (Wiesbaden: Dr. Ludwig Reichert Verlag, 1984-2007).

Torallas Tovar, S. 'Cristianismo en Asuán: nuevos y viejos hallazgos epigráficos en la orilla oeste del Nilo', *Collectanea Christiana Orientalia*, 7 (2010), 297-9.

Torallas Tovar, S. and Zomeño, A. 'De nuevo en la orilla oeste del Nilo: tercera campaña en los restos arqueológicos cristianos de Qubbet el-Hawa (Asuán)', *Collectanea Christiana Orientalia*, 8 (2011), 305-8.

Torallas Tovar, S. and Zomeño, A. 'Notas sobre la ocupación Cristiana de la orilla oeste de Asuán: a propósito de una campaña arqueológica española a orillas del Nilo' in L. A. García Moreno and E. Sánchez Medina (eds.), *Del Nilo al Guadalquivir: il estudios sobre las fuentes de la conquista islámica: homenaje al professor Yves Modéran* (Madrid: Real Academia de la Historia, 2013), pp. 393-404.

van Lantschoot, A. *Recueil des colophons des manuscrits chrétiens d'Égypte*, 2 vols. (Leuven: Istas, 1929).

van Loon, G. J. M. 'Le Deir Anba Hadra à Assouan. Un nouveau depart des recherches' in A. Boud'hors and C. Louis (eds.), *Études Coptes XV. Dix-septième journée d'études (Lisbonne, 18-20 juin 2015)* (Paris: Boccard, 2018), pp. 137-55.

van Loon, G. J. M. 'Le cimetière du Deir Anba Hadra et les fouilles de Jean Clédat' in A. Boud'hors, E. Garel, C. Louis, and N. Vanthieghem (eds.), *Études Coptes XVI. Dix-huitième journée d'études (Bruxelles, 22-24 juin 2017)* (Paris: de Boccard, 2020), pp. 105-26.

van Loon, G. J. M. 'An Unusual Representation of King David in the So-Called "Cave of Anba Hadra" in Dayr Anba Hadra near Aswan' in H. N. Takla (ed.), *Acts of the Eleventh International Congress of Coptic Studies (Claremont, CA, July 25–30, 2016)* (Leuven: Peeters, forthcoming).

von Pilgrim, C., Bruhn, K.-C., Dijkstra, J. H. F., and Wininger, J. 'The Town of Syene. Report on the 3rd and 4th Season in Aswan', *Mitteilungen des Deutschen Archäologischen Instituts, Abteilung Kairo*, 62 (2006), 215–77.

Wipszycka, E. *Moines et communautés monastiques en Égypte (IVe–VIIIe siècles)* (Warsaw: Taubenschlag Press, 2009).

Zanetti, U. 'Abū l-Makārim and Abū Ṣāliḥ', *Bulletin de la Société d'Archéologie Copte*, 34 (1995), 85–138.

12 | The Monastic Landscape of Mount Nebo: An Economic Pattern in the Province of *Arabia*

DAVIDE BIANCHI

Introduction

The monastery of the Memorial of Moses on Mt Nebo in Jordan is organised around the cult of one of the most venerable figures of the Old Testament. The current study examines the development of this monastery through the Byzantine and early Islamic periods, focusing on its economic components. After a geographical and historical introduction of the Nebo monastic landscape, with attention paid to the latest archaeological discoveries, two aspects of the sanctuary of Moses will be investigated: first, the agricultural production of the region and the connections between the *coenobium* and the colonies of monks that dwelt in the surrounding valleys; second, religious and lay patronage.[1]

Mt Nebo rises on the Transjordanian plateau 7 km west of the city of Madaba (Fig. 12.1).[2] The site is surrounded by several *wadis*: from east to west, Wadi en-Naml, Uyun Mousa, Mehterjeh or Methterkeh, and Tarafa; in the south, el-Afrit, el-Judeideh, el-Kanisah, el-Heri, and el-Adeimeh.[3] The western slope descends towards the Jordan Valley. Mt Nebo reaches an altitude of 800 m.a.s.l. on the top of the Balqa plateau, while the two most western peaks are respectively 790 m.a.s.l. (Mukhayyat) and 710 m.a.s.l. (Siyagha).[4] In this area, two archaeological sites – 5 km apart – have been identified.[5]

Khirbet el-Mukhayyat is the Arabic name of the remains of the ancient town of Nebo.[6] The excavation of the oldest phases of the town's necropolis

---

[1] For a general overview of the monasteries in Palestine and Arabia, see Bianchi, *A Shrine to Moses*, pp. 19–23; Patrich, 'Recent Archaeological Research'; and Hamarneh in Chapter 2.

[2] On the Nebo region, see Saller, *Memorial of Moses*, pp. 1–5; Bianchi, *A Shrine to Moses*, pp. 24–31.

[3] Saller, Memorial of Moses, p. 2.

[4] The altitudes are those reported in Saller, *Memorial of Moses*, p. 2 and Piccirillo, *La montagna del Nebo*, p. 17.

[5] For the archaeological surveys in the Nebo region, see Glueck, 'Explorations in Eastern Palestine'; Graham and Harrison, 'The 2000 Mukhayyat Topographic Survey'; Mortensen *et al.*, *Mount Nebo*.

[6] The excavation on the site of Khirbet el-Mukhayyat mainly concerned the churches and the necropolises. Wilfrid Laurier University (Ontario, Canada) has begun a new research project

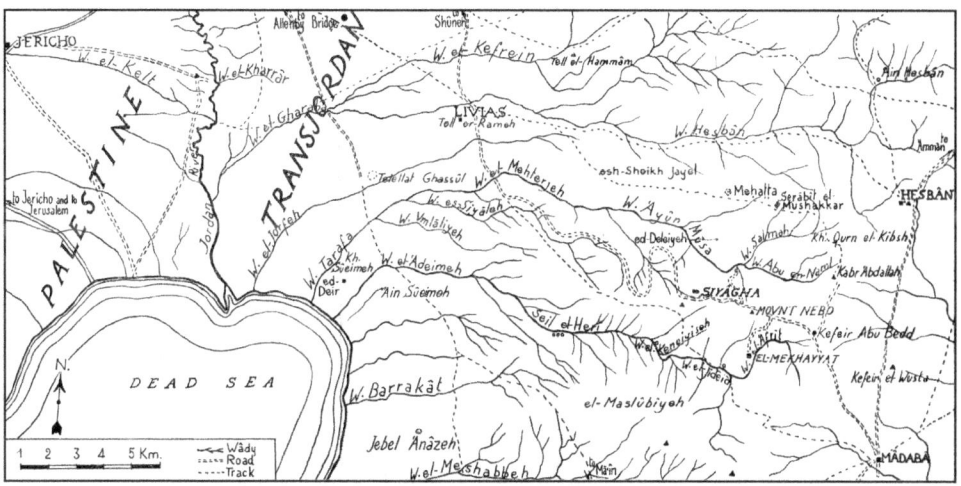

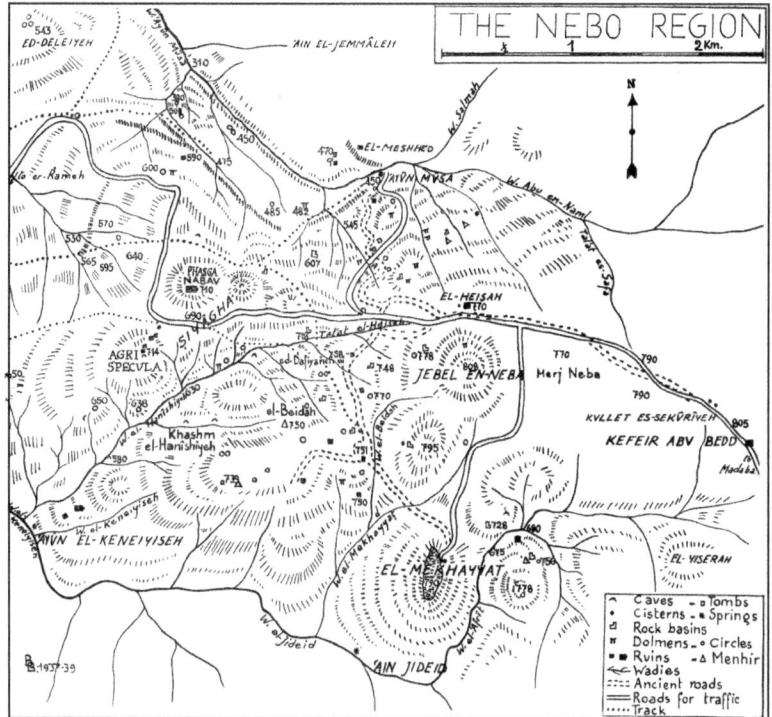

Fig. 12.1. Topographic map of the Nebo region (after Saller, Memorial of Moses, figs 1–2).

aimed at understanding the entire inhabited area; see Foran *et al.*, 'The Second Season of Excavation'.

have presented votive statuettes and grave goods that date to the Iron Age.[7] The site is known from the Bible (Is. 15:1–9, Jer. 48:1–9) and from the stela of King Mesha of Moab (ninth century BC) discovered in Dhiban, which mentions the conquest of the city of Nebo and its destruction.[8] The excavations of Sylvester Saller and Michele Piccirillo were centred on the Christian buildings attested on the Tell. The church of St George and that of Sts Lot and Procopius on the Acropolis, the church of Amos and Casiseos with the chapel of the Priest John, and the monastery of Ain el-Kanisah in Wadi Afrit were brought to light.[9]

Ras Siyagha is a name of ancient Aramaic origin, meaning 'monastery, community of monks'.[10] Here, a group of Christian monks built a church to commemorate Moses' vision of the Promised Land and the place where he died (Deut. 34:1–7). In addition to the monastery of Siyagha, other ecclesiastical buildings have been identified in the valleys: the Kayanos church and the church of the Deacon Thomas in the Uyun Mousa, and the chapel of the Theotokos in the Wadi Ain el-Kanisah.[11]

The Monastic Complex of Siyagha

The *coenobium* of Siyagha takes up 6,640 m² and consists of several monastic cells arranged around a three-aisled basilica (Fig. 12.2). Between 1933 and 1935, Saller, on behalf of the Studium Biblicum Franciscanum in Jerusalem, led the first systematic excavation of the monastic complex.[12] In 1963 archaeological research continued under the direction of Virgilio Corbo, and in 1976 Michele Piccirillo became the director of the archaeological mission.[13] The latter carried out surveys in the valleys around Mt Nebo and identified several small monasteries and rock caves adapted for

---

[7] For a detailed analysis on this topic, see Benedettucci, 'The Iron Age', pp. 121–5, and Benedettucci, *Il paese di Moab*.

[8] Mt Nebo is indicated in the Hebrew Bible by three terms: Nebo, Pisgah, and Abarim. These three designations are also found, interchangeably, in the texts of the pilgrims and in some mosaic inscriptions. On Nebo in the Biblical tradition, see Cortese and Niccacci, 'Nebo in Biblical Tradition', pp. 53–7.

[9] Piccirillo, 'Churches of Nebo', pp. 221–44.

[10] On the etymological study of the name Siyagha, see Saller, *Memorial of Moses*, pp. 115–17.

[11] For a summary study of these complexes, see Piccirillo, 'The Monastic Presence', pp. 215–17 and Piccirillo, *L'Arabia Cristiana*, pp. 100–6. On the mosaic floors, see Piccirillo, *Mosaics of Jordan*, pp. 186–93.

[12] For the history of the exploration and of the archaeological research of Mt Nebo, see Saller, *Memorial of Moses*, pp. 11–22, Piccirillo, 'The Exploration', and Bianchi, *A Shrine to Moses*, pp. 24–31.

[13] Corbo, 'Scavi archeologici', pp. 273–81, and Piccirillo, 'Campagna archeologica nella Basilica'.

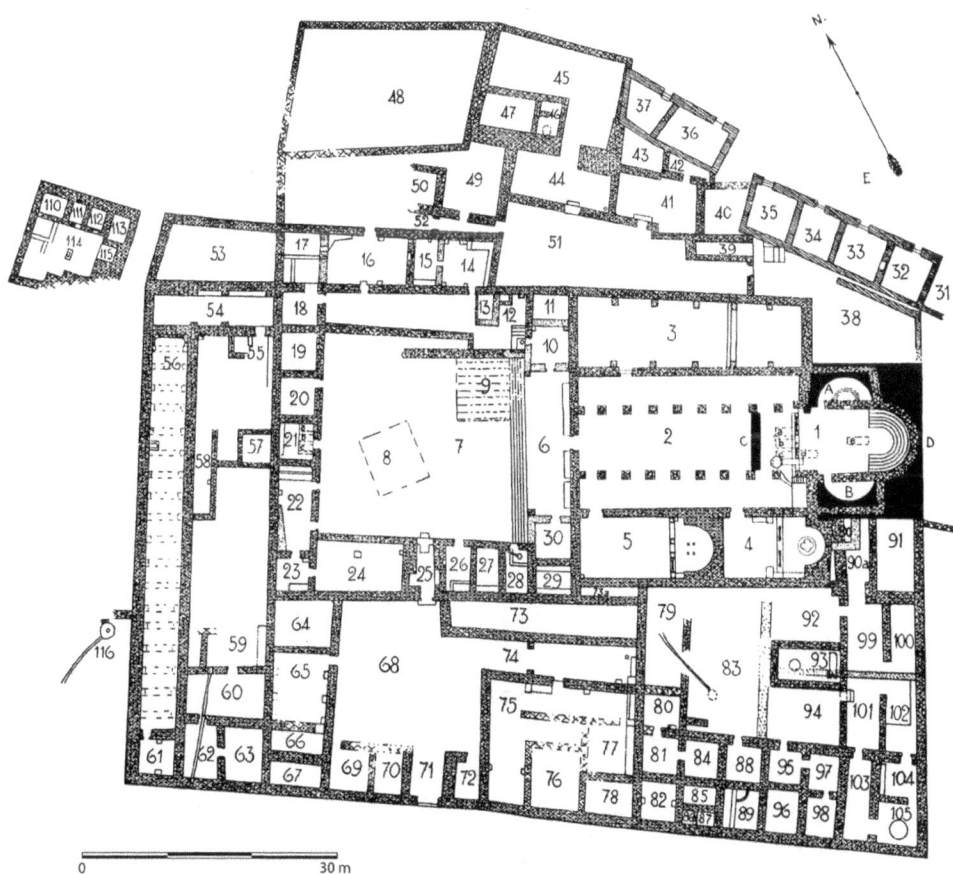

Fig. 12.2. General map of the monastic complex of Siyagha (after Saller, *Memorial of Moses*, pl. 161).

eremitical purposes. Between 1980 and 2000, the team led by Piccirillo excavated large sections of the monastery of Siyagha, and Eugenio Alliata uncovered the eastern sector of the complex.[14] Alliata, assisted by the author, also directed the excavation that took place from 2012 to 2014.[15]

The written sources provide information about the development of monasticism in the Nebo region. The *Itinerarium Egeriae*, a travelogue related to the famous pilgrim Egeria, recalls the presence of a group of hermits who dwelled close to the so-called 'Springs of Moses' in the Uyun Mousa valley at the foot of Mt Nebo at the end of the fourth century.[16] The

---

[14] Alliata, 'Nuovo settore del monastero'. [15] Bianchi, *A Shrine to Moses*, pp. 35–115.
[16] *Itinerarium Egeriae* 10.9; 11.1–3; edition and translation: McGowan and Bradsaw, *Pilgrimage of Egeria*, p. 124. Several textual sources attest to many hermits dwelling in natural caves in the valley of the River Jordan; see Piccirillo, 'Monks and Monasteries', p. 18; Hamarneh, 'Il fenomeno rupestre', pp. 361–5.

availability of water resources, fertile land and proximity to the road systems encouraged the establishment of the first monks. Although they lived in the valleys, they accompanied pilgrims to the sanctuary on the top of Mt Nebo, as mentioned by the pilgrim Egeria.[17] This connection between the mountain and the valleys continued with the network of monasteries that developed in the following centuries.

The biography of Peter the Iberian, bishop of Gaza, mentions two trips that the bishop made to the Memorial of Moses in 430 and 477.[18] The text recalls a coenobitic community dwelling on Mt Nebo and the meeting between the bishop and an Egyptian monk, who escaped from the attacks of the Mazices at the monasteries of Scetis.[19] The meeting took place in a room in the monastery: 'a cell, approximately five cubits in length and breadth and not very well illuminated'.[20] The monastic community grew to such an extent that, one century later, the Pilgrim from Piacenza (in 570) saw many hermitages in the valleys around the Memorial of Moses.[21]

The material data collected during the archaeological excavation has allowed us to establish a chronology for the monastery's architectural development.[22] The first building of the monastic complex is a rectangular basilica divided internally into three aisles dated to the second half of the fifth century (Fig. 12.3). In the centre of the chancel (*presbytery*), located to the east, there was an empty burial (which has been identified as a memorial structure – *memoria* – probably remembering Moses' death), the focal point for the Christian devotees.[23] The northern and southern walls of the chancel divided two lateral spaces perhaps used as sacristies (*pastophoria*). Beyond the eastern wall, there were three rooms, of which the central one had a burial function.[24]

---

[17] Egeria recalls the geomorphologic characteristics of Mt Nebo: the slope was very steep and only a small group of monks could reach the summit of the mountain; see *Itinerarium Egeriae* 11.4; edition and translation: McGowan and Bradsaw, *Pilgrimage of Egeria*, p. 124.

[18] On the visits of Peter the Iberian to Mt Nebo, see Saller, *Memorial of Moses*, p. 110; Piccirillo, 'The Monastic Presence', pp. 193–4; Piccirillo, *Arabia Cristiana*, pp. 100–2.

[19] John Rufus, *Vita Petri Iberi*, 83–5; edition and translation: Horn and Phenix Jr.

[20] John Rufus, *Vita Petri Iberi*, 85; edition and translation: Horn and Phenix Jr.

[21] The Pilgrim from Piacenza does not mention the *coenobium* on top of the mountain, but does mention the presence of numerous hermitages and the salutary properties of the Baths of Moses; see Wilkinson, *Jerusalem Pilgrims*, pp. 81–2.

[22] For the updated architectural phases of the church, see Bianchi, *A Shrine to Moses*, pp. 70–80.

[23] Bianchi, 'Le sepolture nei contesti ecclesiastici'; Bianchi, *A Shrine to Moses*, pp. 61–7 and 70–6. For a comparative study of the burials in the ecclesiastical contexts of Jordan, see Eger, 'The Rock Chamber Necropolis'; Schick, 'Types of Burials in Churches'.

[24] In this room are three burials, of which the central one (identified as an *ad sanctos* burial) is arranged following the same axis of the nave. In fact, the presence of only one skeleton confirms the privileged character of this tomb, which is perhaps suitable for the burial of a high-ranking monastic figure. The other tombs may have provided burial space to other monks and presbyters who were deemed worthy of being buried in the immediate vicinity of the burial

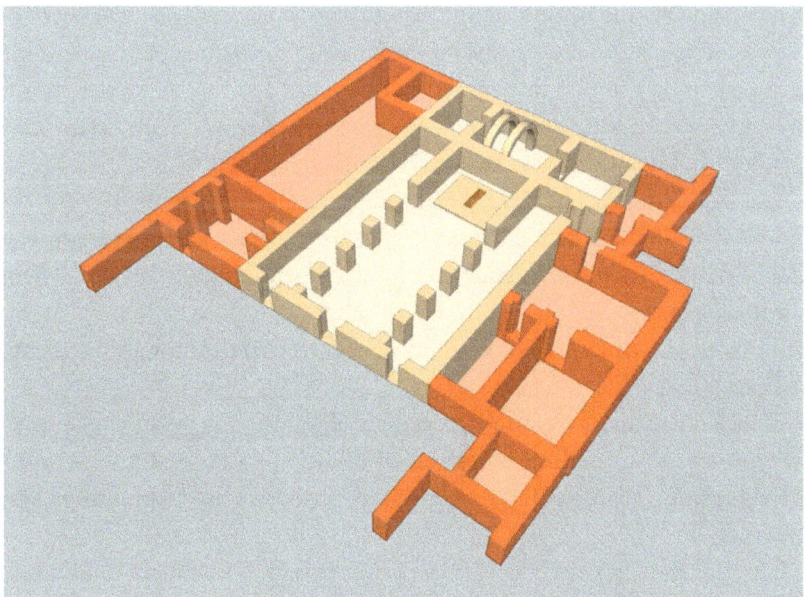

Fig. 12.3. First architectural phase of the basilica of the Memorial of Moses according to the new hypothesis, second half of fifth century AD (digital drawing by the author).

The first monastic cells date to this same period. They were located around the basilica and the square (*atrium*) in front of the church.[25] Among them, some were paved with mosaics, comprising white cubes (*tesserae*) or simple geometric patterns. Worthy of attention are rooms 17 and 22, in which two drainage channels that conveyed the wastewater outside the complex were identified.[26] Moreover, room 21, at the centre of the western wing and directly in front of the door to the basilica, contained three tombs full of skeletal remains belonging to more than a hundred bodies.[27]

According to Saller, the cells around the basilica are contemporary with rooms 31–37 located on the terraces on the mountain's northern slope. He suggests that the latter could represent a transition from the independent hermitage (*monasteria*) to the large monastic complex enclosed by a wall.[28] In this regard, the excavations brought to light natural and artificial caves created by stone quarrying and adapted as

---

structure linked to the memory of Moses. For a description of the tombs, see Sanmorì, 'Funerary Practices'.

[25] Saller, *Memorial of Moses*, pp. 117–31; Piccirillo, 'The Monastic Presence', p. 204. The ancient northern entrance to the atrium in front of the basilica façade was discovered in August 2016.

[26] For a study of the water system of the monastery of Nebo, see Bianchi, 'Restore the Body' (especially p. 33) and Saller, *Memorial of Moses*, pp. 130 and 145–6.

[27] Sanmorì, 'Funerary Practices', p. 414.   [28] Saller, *Memorial of Moses*, pp. 132–40.

hermitages (rooms 107 and 108).[29] Another example is the so-called hermitage of Procapis (a name given on the basis of the name contained within a medallion in the mosaic pavement of the northern room), located on the western slope of Mt Nebo.[30] This two-storey dwelling was completely independent and equipped with two cisterns for water supply.

At the Wadi Ain el-Kanisah, the mosaic inscription mentioning the monk George the Recluse (Γεωργίου ἐγκλιστοῦ) provides important evidence on the existence of a monk who lived in solitude in his cell.[31] This particular form of monastic life requires that the recluse be granted assistance from other monks, who may have belonged to the monastic communities of the Mt Nebo region.[32]

These cases demonstrate that on Mt Nebo monks practised both an eremitic and a coenobitic lifestyle. In addition to the main *coenobium* surrounding the basilica, there are also isolated buildings for hermits.[33]

During the first decades of the sixth century, the church underwent a radical transformation.[34] The three rooms behind the chancel were demolished to lengthen the aisles and add a new chancel. A special chamber for liturgical purposes (*diakonikon*) with a baptismal font was built on the north terrace, one metre beneath the nave.[35] On the floor, a mosaic funded by three wealthy donors (*skolastikoi*) was laid.[36] Towards the end of the sixth century, a new mosaic floor replaced the previous one in the *diakonikon*, and the financial patronage of the bishop Sergius of Madaba and the hegumenos Martyrios allowed the construction of a new chapel with

---

[29] These two hermitages consist of two grottoes and two smaller rooms that opened onto a central hall with mosaics; see Piccirillo, 'The Monastic Presence', p. 199.

[30] Piccirillo, 'The Monastic Presence', pp. 199–203. For the mosaic inscription, see Di Segni, 'Greek Inscriptions', pp. 438–9, n. 35.

[31] Di Segni, 'Greek Inscriptions', pp. 449–50, n. 56.

[32] Numerous recluses' towers are attested in southern Syria, while inscriptions and literary sources shows the presence of this phenomenon also in Scythopolis and in the Great Laura. On this topic, see Peña et al., *Les reclus syriens*, pp. 93–122.

[33] A parallel of the coexistence of the two monastic forms is found in Ainon-Sapsaphas; see Waheeb, *Betania oltre il Giordano*, pp. 62–70.

[34] For the list of hegumenoi at the Memorial of Moses, see Piccirillo, 'The Monastic Presence', pp. 194–6. On the episcopal sees in the province of *Arabia*, see Piccirillo, 'Gruppi episcopali nelle tre Palestine', pp. 484–501.

[35] Piccirillo, *Chiese e Mosaici di Madaba*, pp. 155–7; Alliata and Bianchi, 'Architectural Phasing', pp. 168–71.

[36] On the iconography of the mosaic, see Piccirillo, 'The Mosaics', pp. 274–87; Hamarneh, 'Evergetismo ecclesiastico e laico'. For the linguistic and epigraphic analysis of the Greek inscription, see Di Segni, 'Greek Inscriptions', pp. 429–30.

a baptismal font on the southern side of the basilica (597–8).[37] The last addition occurred in the first decade of the seventh century, when the bishop Leontius of Madaba and the hegumenoi Martyrios and Theodoros promoted the construction of a chapel in honour of the 'God-bearer' (Theotokos).[38]

According to Saller and Piccirillo, a perimeter wall surrounded most of the monastic structures, except the south-east wing in the late sixth century, in the same period as the basilica renovation.[39] This dating, however, deserves a careful review in light of recent ceramic studies. Indeed, ceramic sherds of Umayyad date were recovered from a layer in room 103, which was located below Saller's excavation and was cut by the perimeter wall.[40] The ceramic record suggests that some renovation works may have occurred in the south wing of the monastery at the beginning of the Abbasid era, perhaps after the earthquake of 749, which also involved the restoration of the basilica's apse.[41]

Agricultural Production

In order to access the management of cultivated lands and the production of wine, bread, and other products it is necessary to investigate the monastery's rural landscape. The study of the agricultural territory is not an easy task, as previous research has focused mainly on individual structures without considering the interrelations between the monasteries and their rural environment. Moreover, recent building activity and the creation of modern roads have prevented a complete understanding of agricultural activities. In order to obtain a proper understanding, three aspects must be taken into consideration: the physical environment and water management resources, production facilities, and palaeobotanical finds.

---

[37] This renovation of the complex did not substantially change the plan of the Basilica; see Alliata and Bianchi, 'Architectural Phasing', pp. 176–7.
[38] Alliata and Bianchi, 'Architectural Phasing', p. 178.
[39] Saller, *Memorial of Moses*, pp. 164–71; Piccirillo, 'The Monastic Presence', pp. 204–5.
[40] Bianchi, *A Shrine to Moses*, pp. 100–8. For the report on Saller's excavation of room 103, see Saller, *Memorial of Moses*, p. 181.
[41] Bianchi, *A Shrine to Moses*, p. 80. Archaeological records showing a continuity of life up to the ninth century are preserved in other Jordanian monastic complexes. For example, restorations dated to the eighth century took place in the monasteries of Mar Liyas near Tishbe, in the complex of Deir Ain Abata and in the monastery of Jebel Harun; see Di Segni, 'Varia Arabica', pp. 579–80; Politis, *Sanctuary of Lot*, pp. 115–58; and Rajala and Fiema, 'The Baptismal Fonts', pp. 240–1. On the issues related to the transition between the Umayyad and Abbasid periods, see Hamarneh, *Topografia cristiana*, pp. 223–9, Walmsley, 'The Village Ascendant'; Haldon, 'Social Transformation'; and Hamarneh, 'Monasteries in Rural Context'.

Physical Environment and Water Management Resources

Focusing on the orography of Mt Nebo, an irregular slope characterises the spur of Siyagha. The northern, western, and southern slopes are very steep, while the eastern area is flatter. Saller's photographical and written documentation enables a reconstruction of the ancient landscape. On the south of the monastery, Saller mentions the presence of ruins of regular masonry that were probably used as a support for terracing works related to agricultural tillage.[42] He also describes other walls located on the southern slope of the mountain, built for the protection of the cisterns and the water supply systems of the complex (Fig. 12.4).[43] The soil composition of this area, partially protected by the strong winds coming from the northern and western sides of the mountain, is the most suitable for agricultural activities. Furthermore, the presence of several cisterns and walls in this area, outside of the monastic complex, supports the hypothesis of an agricultural use of these lands.[44] Altogether, the archaeological evidence suggests an agricultural model common to other monasteries in the region. Research on agricultural terracing at other Jordanian monastic complexes provides comparisons for the agrarian landscape of Mt Nebo. The closest comparanda are found at the sanctuary of Lot at Deir Ain Abata, Ain Qattara, and possibly Jebel Harun near Petra.[45] The collection of rainwater that flowed through the *wadis* and was channelled into the large cisterns at these sites permitted the irrigation of the soil, which could become particularly dry during the summer.

Rainwater also flowed down to the valleys through numerous other *wadis*.[46] At Uyun Mousa there are two springs that flow from the northern side of Siyagha; today, the water is used to irrigate gardens, as it most likely would have been in Late Antiquity. The presence of the springs, the greater fertility of the soil, and the mild temperatures of the valley even in winter, due to a lower altitude, contributed to the development of the agricultural

---

[42] Saller, *Memorial of Moses*, pp. 197–9.

[43] Saller, *Memorial of Moses*, pp. 199–207. For an updated study of the water system of the Nebo with references to irrigation structures and specific parallels to Jordanian monasteries, see Bianchi, 'Restore the Body'.

[44] In the southern sector of the monastery the following cisterns have been found: cistern 116 (7.80 m deep with a 7.30–7.50 round bottom diameter); cistern 118 (6 x 12.5 m and 8.5 m deep) at the centre area enclosed by walls 119, 120, 121 and 117, equipped with two sedimentation vats and trenches for collecting water which flowed from a local small *wadi*; cistern 122 (6.5 m deep with 6.5 m diameter) which collected the water of the hill's south-eastern slope. Bianchi, 'Restore the Body', pp. 30–4. For the analytical description of water structures, see Saller, *Memorial of Moses*, pp. 196–205.

[45] On this topic, see Politis, *Sanctuary of Lot*, p. 115; Piccirillo, *Chiese e mosaici di Madaba*, pp. 248–9.

[46] See above and note 3.

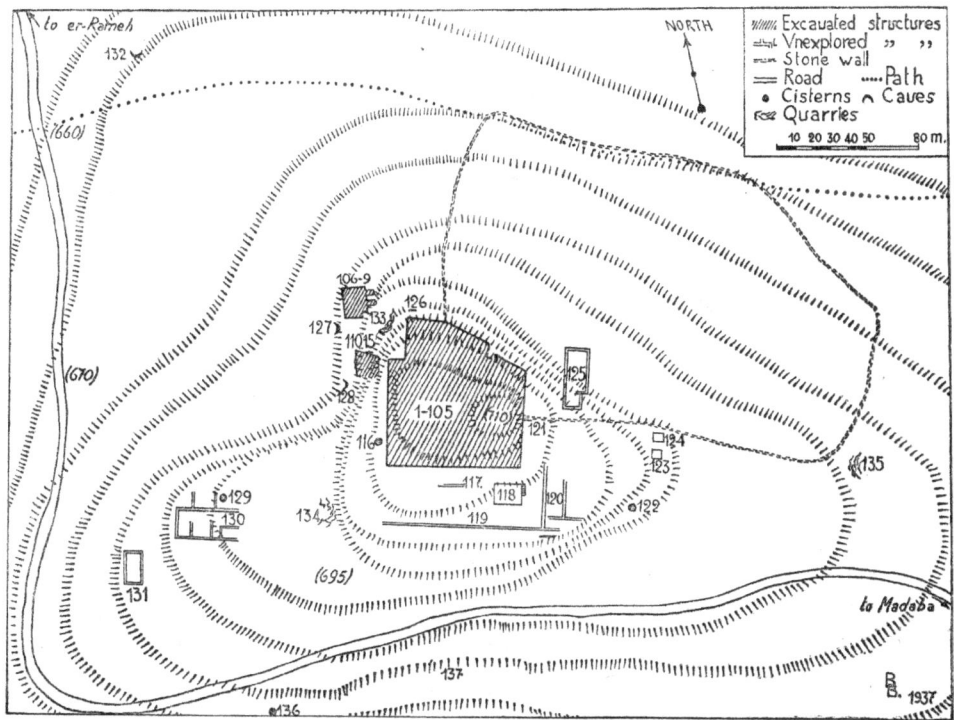

Fig. 12.4. Map of the north-western spur of Siyagha (after Saller, *Memorial of Moses*, fig. 3).

landscape. For these reasons, it is possible to suggest that the *coenobium* of Siyagha benefited from agricultural products from the valleys. In support of this hypothesis, it is important to point out the short distances between the monastery of Siyagha, the village of Khirbet el-Mukkayat, and the monasteries in the valleys: the main *coenobium* holds a central position, from which the other localities are about 4–5 km.

Regarding the division of the agricultural territory, it is not possible to determine which lands belonged to the monastic community and which to the villages due to the absence of written documents, specific boundary markers, and epigraphic references.[47] The villages in the provinces of *Arabia* and *Palaestina Tertia* were included in the territorial jurisdiction of diocesan centres, and the local clergy was involved in the management of the agricultural lands.[48] Indeed, the clergy not only acted with

---

[47] On this topic, see Dagron, 'Entre village et cité'; Walmsley, 'The Village Ascendant'.

[48] Dagron, 'Entre village et cité', pp. 44–7; Meimaris, *Sacred Names*, pp. 214–17; Feissel, 'L'évêque, titres et fonctions', pp. 814–18; Hamarneh, *Topografia cristiana*, pp. 225–6. See also Hamarneh in Chapter 2.

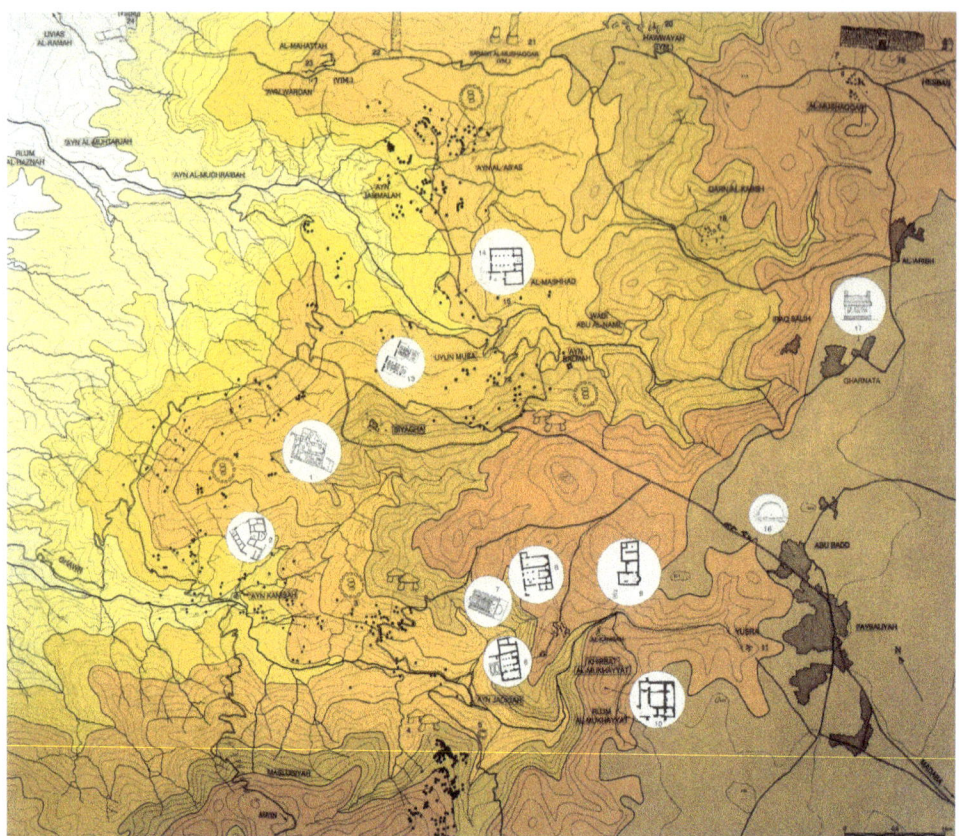

Fig. 12.5. Map of the ecclesiastical building in the Nebo region (after Piccirillo and Alliata, *Mount Nebo*, pl. 1).

ecclesiastical patronage, but was also in charge of regulating sale and purchase contracts, wills, and territorial disputes among the peasants.[49]

Mosaic inscriptions also suggest a relationship between the Siyagha monastery and the monasteries in the valleys (Fig. 12.5). A mosaic inscription found in the monastic complex of Kayanos at Uyun Mousa suggests this connection. The four-line dedicatory inscription set in the mosaic floor of the lower church mentions the father Rabebos, who also occurs in the Rabebos funerary room on Siyagha.[50] According to Leah Di Segni, this name could refer to the hegumenos

---

[49] Hamarneh, *Topografia cristiana*, p. 237.
[50] On the Kayanos church in the valley of 'Uyun Mousa, see Piccirillo and Alliata, 'La chiesa del monastero di Kaianos'. For the Greek inscription in the Rabebos funerary room, see Di Segni, 'Greek Inscriptions', pp. 437–8, n. 34.

Robebos, with the typical vocalic exchange common in the epigraphic texts of the province *Arabia*.⁵¹

However, in other cases, the monasteries of the valleys could be governed or used by their own hegumenoi. The inscription in the chapel of the Theotokos monastery in Wadi Ain el-Kanisah mentions Abraham, hegumenos and archimandrite of the whole desert (τῷ ἡγουμένῳ καὶ ἀρχιμανδρίτῃ πάσης τῆς ἐρήμου).⁵² Although the epithet suggests that Abraham could be the abbot of the monastery of Theodosius, in the desert of Jerusalem near Bethlehem (who held the office of archimandrite of all the *coenobia*), or the abbot of the Laura of San Saba (who was responsible for the laurites and hermits), Di Segni suggests that it is possible that the monasteries of the Madaba region had a leader of their own.⁵³ In this way, the hermitage of Ain el-Kanisah could be used occasionally by the archimandrite, maybe for Lent spiritual retreats.⁵⁴

Production Facilities

The discovery of numerous production facilities confirms that vines and wheat were cultivated in the Mt Nebo region. On the top of Mt Nebo, a winepress was found beyond the west wall of the monastery (rooms 110–115 in Fig. 12.2; Fig. 12.6). The winepress was located in the central mosaic room, off which there were three smaller rooms and two drain basins for gathering the must.⁵⁵ The winepress installation of Mt Nebo is one-third smaller than the well-known press in Khirbet Yajuz, 11 km north-west of Amman, which produced 69 litres of must per hectare.⁵⁶ The medium size of the Nebo structure suggests a limited production, only for the monastic community, but Saller mentions a second winepress near the road between Siyagha and Khirbet el-Mukhayyat, which shows that there may well have been a larger production.⁵⁷ In the monastery of el-Kanisah in Wadi 'Afrit, one

---

[51] Di Segni, 'Greek Inscriptions', p. 438; Piccirillo, 'Monastic Presence', p. 196; see Hamarneh, Chapter 2.

[52] Di Segni, 'Greek Inscriptions', pp. 448–9, n. 55. More generally on the monastery of the Theotokos in Wadi Ain el-Kanisah, see Saller, 'Hellenistic to Arabic Remains at Nebo', pp. 48–62; Piccirillo, 'Le due iscrizioni della cappella della Theotokos'; and Piccirillo, 'La chapelle de la Theotokos'.

[53] Di Segni, 'Greek Inscriptions', pp. 448–9.   [54] Di Segni, 'Greek Inscriptions', p. 449.

[55] Rooms 113–115; see Saller, *Memorial of Moses*, pp. 194–5; Piccirillo, 'The Monastic Presence', p. 205; Hamarneh, *Topografia cristiana*, p. 207.

[56] On the winepress installation of Khirbet Yajuz, see Khalil and al-Nammari, 'Two Large Wine Presses'.

[57] Saller, *Memorial of Moses*, p. 195, n. 2. For parallels of the winepresses in Israel and the method for calculating wine production, see Ashkenazi and Aviam, 'Monasteries, Monks, and Villages

Fig. 12.6. Wine press from the Siyagha monastic complex (photo by M. Piccirillo © SBF Archive, Jerusalem).

winepress placed on two interconnected levels and a kitchen with a small millstone for grain were identified.[58] In the provinces of *Arabia* and *Palaestina Tertia*, winepresses were documented in twenty-three monasteries; and in the diocese of Madaba, they are attested in the monasteries of Ain Qattara, Deir er-Riyashi, Khirbet el-Kursi, and the Stylite tower complex as well as the monastery at Umm er-Rasas.[59]

Regarding the baking of bread, the Siyagha complex had three ovens in rooms 93, 105, and 103 (Fig. 12.7).[60] Two additional ovens were located a little further to the south of the monastery, near the modern Franciscan

---

in Western Galilee', pp. 276–81. More generally on this topic, see Frankel, 'Presses for Oil and Wine'; Hirschfeld, 'The Expansion of Rural Settlements'; and Taxel, 'Rural Monasticism'.

[58] Piccirillo, 'The Monastic Presence', pp. 205–9.

[59] For a survey of the wineries, see Hamarneh, 'Monasteries in Rural Context', pp. 289–91; for more detail on the individual production facilities, see Piccirillo and Alliata, *Umm er-Rasas*, pp. 249–50, 260, and 301–2.

[60] Saller, *Memorial of Moses*, pp. 170–4 and 181–2.

Fig. 12.7. The oven found in room 103 (photo by M. Piccirillo © SBF Archive, Jerusalem).

monastery.[61] A large quantity of bread was necessary for liturgical purposes and for the sustenance of monks and pilgrims visiting the sanctuary of Moses.[62] Although no grain crusher has been identified in the monastic complexes of Nebo, local processing cannot be excluded.[63]

The pottery found at Nebo reveals the same ceramic assemblage as the pottery sherds from Umm er-Rasas, Jerash, and even Pella.[64] We can therefore exclude a local ceramic production, although the discovery of a lamp with its mould may indicate the proximity of pottery kilns.[65]

Palaeobotanical Remains

During the excavation of the monastery of Siyagha, vegetal remains were recovered, specifically olive and date pits, pistachio shells, and wheat and barley grains.[66] Animal bones with butcher marks were also found. This palaeobotanical record is also well reflected in the written sources. In the *Life of St Mary of Egypt*, Sophronius recalls the supplies taken by Palestinian

---

[61] On the ovens identified in the monastery of Siyagha see, Bianchi, *A Shrine to Moses*, pp. 178–84.

[62] On the bakery activity of the monastic communities, see Corbo, 'L'ambiente materiale della vita dei monaci'.

[63] For a list of grain mills discovered in the monastic complexes of Jordan, see Hamarneh, *Topografia cristiana*, pp. 304–8.

[64] On the pottery from Pella, see Walmsley, 'The Umayyad Period'; Walmsley, 'The Umayyad Pottery and Its Antecedents'. On the pottery from Umm er-Rasas, see Sanmorì and Pappalardo, 'Ceramica dalla chiesa di San Paolo'; Pappalardo, 'Il cortile a sud della chiesa di S. Paolo'; Pappalardo, 'Ceramica e piccoli oggetti'. On the pottery from Jerash, see Watson, 'Jerash Bowls'.

[65] The lamp was found in room 56; see Piccirillo, 'Ricerca storico-archeologica in Giordania'; Bianchi, *A Shrine to Moses*, pp. 197–200.

[66] Cereals, particularly barley, were also recovered in the monastery of St Lot in Deir Ain Abata and at Jebel Harun; see Hoppé, 'The Macroscopic Plant Remains', pp. 518 and 521.

monks during their wanderings in the desert.[67] He mentions figs, palm dates, and various legumes. The later Arab geographers Ya'qubi, Baladhuri, and al-Maqdisi[68] also report that the Balqa region was used for the cultivation of cereals, almonds, and fruits, and also for raising sheep.[69]

Religious and Lay Patronage

The buildings in the monasteries of Mt Nebo required considerable wealth for their construction and maintenance. Indeed, currency flow in the monastic coffers was essential for architectural works and for the monks' day-to-day needs. Among the coins found in the monastery of Siyagha,[70] archaeologists discovered a hoard of 230 copper coins, mainly *folles*, hidden in the wall of a cell and dated to the sixth century, together with hundreds of smaller denominations among the scattered finds, with a total value of two gold tremisses.[71] Although there is no written evidence for such coin reserves, this amount could either be a small reserve for the payment of workers or an accumulation of votive offerings.[72]

Archaeological and epigraphic records indicate from which forms of patronage the monasteries of Mt Nebo benefited. Three categories of people contributed to the economy of the monastery through their donations: pilgrims, lay people from nearby villages, and the bishops of Madaba. Since the beginning of the fifth century, the area had several Christian settlements[73] and became an important landmark for both monks and pilgrims.[74] Pilgrims enjoyed the religious hospitality offered by the monasteries, including meals, water, shelter, liturgical practices, and guides to the

---

[67] Kouli, 'Life of St. Mary of Egypt', p. 74.
[68] al-Ya'qubi 327.20 (ed. Houtsma); Baladhuri 116.20 (ed. De Goeje); al-Maqdisi 162.4–6 (ed. De Goeje). See Hamarneh, *Topografia cristiana*, p. 230.
[69] On this issue, see Walmsley, 'Land, Resources and Industry'.
[70] On other coins found in the monastery, see Gitler, 'The Coins'; and Callegher, 'Monte Nebo-Siyâgha'.
[71] Callegher suggests that this sum would correspond to two months' wages counted in gold currency, but paid in bronze; see Callegher, 'Un "tesoro" dal Monte Nebo-Siyagha', p. 325.
[72] Callegher, 'Un "tesoro" dal Monte Nebo-Siyagha', p. 327. Useful parallels for the price of daily subsistence in Egypt between the fourth and seventh centuries are provided in the Life of John the Almsgiver by Leontius of Neapolis; see Cavallero *et al.*, *Leoncio de Neàpolis*, pp. 138–40 and Hamarneh, 'Denaro', p. 134, n. 22.
[73] Saller and Bagatti, *The Town of Nebo*.
[74] A very interesting parallel with the monasteries of Samaria is pointed out in the study of Taxel, 'Rural Monasticism', p. 67. On the same topic, see Patrich, 'Monastic Landscapes'; Di Segni, 'Monk and Society', p. 36; and Limor, 'Holy Journey', pp. 332–3. For the Egyptian area, see Bagnall, 'Monks and Property'.

sacred sites.⁷⁵ In return, pilgrims donated to the monasteries, a good parallel for which is the legacy of a devotee to the monastery of St Aaron on Jebel Harun near Petra.⁷⁶

The sanctuary of Moses was part of the wider Jordanian network of monasteries linked with biblical figures of the Old and New Testaments.⁷⁷ In addition to the aforementioned monastery dedicated to the high priest Aaron, brother of the prophet Moses,⁷⁸ pilgrims used to visit the monastery of Lot near the city of Zoara-Ghor es-Safi,⁷⁹ the monastic complex of Mar Liyas-St Elijah near Thisbe,⁸⁰ and the monastery of Ainon-Sapsaphas in the Wadi el-Kharrar, connected to the memory of Christ's baptism site.⁸¹ Of these institutions, the latter is the only one to have received funds from the imperial treasury for its endowment (five *solidi*).⁸²

The mosaic inscriptions found in the basilica of Mt Nebo mention wealthy donors. Among them, in the mosaic inscription of the *diakonikon*-baptistery dated to 530/1, are the names of three lawyers (σχολαστικόι): Muselius with his wife Sergius, Philadelphus, and Gothus (Fig. 12.8).⁸³ Additionally, the inscriptions of Stephen and Elias, sons of Comitissa, in the church of Saints Lot and Procopius and in the church of St George at Khirbet el-Mukhayyat reflects the patronage of the local rural community.⁸⁴ Evidence of donors also occurs in the inscriptions of the monasteries in the valleys. Here, names and portraits refer to the local Greek or Semitic population and even to the soldiers of the Arab tribes.⁸⁵

Furthermore, the mosaic inscriptions of the monastery of Nebo show the euergetism of the bishopric of Madaba.⁸⁶ Almost all bishops from the fifth to the sixth century supported building activity in the monasteries of the Nebo region, particularly Elijah (531–6) and the northern *diakonikon*, Sergios I (576–98) and the southern baptistery, and Leontius (603–8) and

---

[75] Taxel, 'Rural Monasticism', p. 67; Limor, 'Holy Journey', pp. 332–3; Voltaggio, '*Perambulatio per monasteria*', pp. 321–2; Whiting, 'Monastery Hostels'.
[76] Frösén and Miettunen, 'Aaron in Religious Literature', p. 12.
[77] More on this topic in Bianchi, *A Shrine to Moses*, pp. 125–32.
[78] Fiema et al., *Petra: The Mountain of Aaron II*.   [79] Politis, *Sanctuary of Lot*.
[80] Piccirillo, *Chiese e mosaici della Giordania settentrionale*, p. 17; Michel, *Les églises d'époque byzantine*, p. 420; Piccirillo, 'Dall'archeologia alla storia', pp. 99–100.
[81] Hamarneh and Roncalli, 'Wadi al-Kharrar', p. 199; Waheeb, *Betania oltre il Giordano*.
[82] Hamarneh, 'Monasteries in Rural Context', p. 280, n. 39.
[83] Di Segni, 'Greek Inscriptions', pp. 429–30, n. 6.
[84] Di Segni, 'Greek Inscriptions', pp. 439–40, n. 36.
[85] Hamarneh, 'Ritratti e immagini di donatori'; Habas, 'Donations and Donors'.
[86] On the investment of Church funds for construction works in the monastery, see Feissel, 'L'évêque, titres et fonctions'; Rapp, 'The Elite Status of Bishops'; and Rapp, *Holy Bishops in Late Antiquity*.

Fig. 12.8. The mosaic of the northern *diakonikon*-baptistery (photo by M. Piccirillo © SBF Archive, Jerusalem).

the chapel of Theotokos. Other inscriptions mention the involvement of the diocesan clergy, as in the monastery of Kayanos at ʿUyun Mousa. The epigraphic text mentions the deacon Salaman, the steward (*oikonomos*) of the diocese of Madaba, who provided financial help to build the church on the behalf of the bishopric.[87] The active involvement of the bishop was also common practice in rural areas, because the diocesan bishops were often chosen from among the monks. However, in the case of Madada, there is

---

[87] Di Segni, 'Greek Inscriptions', p. 453, n. 61.

no evidence of this situation. Furthermore, the task of the bishop also included the collection of tithes from urban and rural communities and their transfer to estates located in the countryside.[88]

Conclusion

The various factors analysed above outline the economic reality in the monastic region of Mt Nebo. As a result of the sanctuary of Moses in the monastery of Siyagha, this complex was part of the Transjordanian network of *coenobia* related to the devotion to biblical figures. Pilgrimage to this devotional place contributed to its richness and fame. Furthermore, lay donors and the diocesan bishops financed many construction projects in the monastic church, as well as high quality mosaics.

The winepresses and the terracing found in the monasteries of Mt Nebo indicate that the agricultural production in this land was widespread. The hegumenoi of the Siyagha complex may also have had jurisdiction over the smaller monasteries in the surrounding valleys: the mosaic inscriptions and the presence of winepresses and water resources in the valley suggest a system of networks between the main *coenobium* and other monasteries. In order to obtain a more detailed understanding of the economy of the monastery, further investigation is required on agricultural structures, in particular the production capacity of winepresses in order to determine the quantities produced. Most peripheral hermitages could also be intended for local ascetics or monks coming from other regions of the Middle East, especially from Palestine.

Bibliography

al-Baladhuri, *Kitab Futuh al-Buldun*, edited by M. De Goeje (Leiden: Brill, 1866).
al-Maqdisi, *Kitab Ahsan al-Taqasim fi Ma'rifat al-Aqalim*, edited by M. De Goeje (Leiden: Brill, 1906).
al-Ya'qubi, Ahmad b. Abi Ya'qub, *Ta 'rīkh*, edited by M. T. Houtsma, 2 vols (Leiden: Brill, 1883).
Alliata, E. 'Nuovo settore del monastero al Monte Nebo-Siyagha' in C. Bottini, L. Di Segni, and E. Alliata (eds.), *Christian Archaeology in the Holy Land. New Discoveries. Essays in Honour of Virgilio C. Corbo, OFM* (Jerusalem: Franciscan Printing Press, 1990), pp. 427–66.

---

[88] Kaplan, *Les hommes et la terre à Byzance*, pp. 152–5; Hamarneh, *Topografia cristiana*, pp. 225–6, n. 797.

Alliata, E. and Bianchi, S. 'The Architectural Phasing of the Memorial of Moses' in M. Piccirillo and E. Alliata (eds.), *Mount Nebo: New Archaeological Excavations 1967-1997* (Jerusalem: Franciscan Printing Press, 1998), pp. 115-91.

Ashkenazi, J. and Aviam, M. 'Monasteries, Monks, and Villages in Western Galilee in Late Antiquity', *Journal of Late Antiquity*, 5.2 (2013), 269-97.

Bagnall, R. S. 'Monks and Property: Rhetoric, Law and Patronage in the *Apophthegmata Patrum* and the Papyri', *Greek, Roman and Byzantine Studies*, 42 (2001), 7-24.

Benedettucci, F. M. 'The Iron Age' in M. Piccirillo and E. Alliata (eds.), *Mount Nebo: New Archaeological Excavations 1967-1997* (Jerusalem: Franciscan Printing Press, 1998), pp. 110-27.

Benedettucci, F. M. *Il paese di Moab nell'età del ferro* (Rome: Edizione Artemide, 2017).

Bianchi, D. 'Restore the Body, Soothe the Soul: The Water Systems of the Jordanian Monasteries' in L. Nigro, M. Nucciotti, and E. Gallo (eds.), *Precious Water. Paths of Jordanian Civilizations as Seen in the Italian Archaeological Excavations. Proceedings of an International Conference Held in Amman, October 18th 2016* (Rome: Università degli Studi La Sapienza, 2017), pp. 29-41.

Bianchi, D. 'Le sepolture nei contesti ecclesiastici transgiordani: alcuni casi per un'indagine preliminare', *Mitteilungen zur Christlichen Archäologie*, 24 (2018), 37-56.

Bianchi, D. *A Shrine to Moses. A Reappraisal of the Mount Nebo Monastic Complex between Byzantium and Islam* (Vienna: Verlag der Österreichischen Akademie der Wissenschaften, 2021).

Callegher, B. 'Monte Nebo-Siyâgha: nota numismatica all'intervento nei Loci 802/803 (2009)', *Liber Annuus*, 60 (2010), 416-18.

Callegher, B. 'Un "tesoro" dal Monte Nebo-Siyagha: folles bizantini del VI secolo per un controvalore di due tremissi' in L. D. Chrupcała (ed.), *Christ Is Here! Studies in Biblical and Christian Archaeology in Memory of Fr Michele Piccirillo OFM* (Milan: Edizioni Terra Santa 2012), pp. 319-39.

Cavallero, P. A., Ubierna, P., Capboscq, A., Lastra Sheridan, J., Sapere, A., Fernández, T., Bohdziewicz, S., and Santos, D. (eds.) *Leoncio de Neápolis, Vida de Juan el limosnero* (Buenos Aires: Universidad de Buenos Aires, 2011).

Corbo, V. 'L'ambiente materiale della vita dei monaci di Palestina nel periodo bizantino', *Il monachesimo orientale. Orientalia christiana analecta*, 153 (1958), 235-57.

Corbo, V. 'Scavi archeologici sotto i mosaici della basilica del Monte Nebo (Siyagha)', *Liber Annuus*, 20 (1970), 273-98.

Cortese, E. and Niccacci, A. 'Nebo in Biblical Tradition' in M. Piccirillo and E. Alliata (eds.), *Mount Nebo: New Archaeological Excavations 1967-1997* (Jerusalem: Franciscan Printing Press, 1998), pp. 53-64.

Dagron, G. 'Entre village et cité: la bourgade rurale des IVe-VIIe siècles en Orient', *ΚΟΙΝΩΝΙΑ*, 3 (1979), 29–52.

Di Segni, L. 'The Greek Inscriptions' in M. Piccirillo and E. Alliata (eds.), *Mount Nebo: New Archaeological Excavations 1967–1997* (Jerusalem: Franciscan Printing Press 1998), pp. 425–67.

Di Segni, L. 'Monk and Society: The Case of Palestine' in J. Patrich (ed.), *The Sabaite Heritage in the Orthodox Church from the Fifth Century to the Present* (Leuven: Peeters, 2001), pp. 31–6.

Di Segni, L. 'Varia Arabica. Greek Inscriptions from Jordan' in M. Piccirillo (ed.), *Ricerca storico-archeologica in Giordania XXVI-2006*, special edition of *Liber Annuus*, 56 (2006), 578–92.

Eger, C. 'The Rock Chamber Necropolis of Khirbat Yajuz and Church Burials in the Province of *Arabia*' in C. Eger and M. Mackensen (eds.), *Death and Burial in the Near East from Roman to Islamic Times. Research in Syria, Lebanon, Jordan and Egypt* (Wiesbaden: Reichert Verlag, 2018), pp. 149–70.

Feissel, D. 'L'évêque, titres et fonctions d'après les inscriptions grecques jusqu'au VIIe siècle' in N. Duval, F. Baritel, and P. Pergola (eds.), *Actes du XIe Congrès International d'Archéologie Chrétienne Lyon, Vienne, Grenoble, Genève, Aoste (21-28 septembre 1986)*, vol. II (Rome: École française de Rome and Vatican City: Pontificio Instituto di Archeologia Cristiana 1989), pp. 801–28.

Fiema, Z. T., Frösén, J., and Holappa, M. (eds.) *Petra: The Mountain of Aaron II. The Nabataean Sanctuary and the Byzantine Monastery* (Helsinki: Societas Scientiarum Fennica, 2016).

Foran, D., Dolan, A., and Edwards, S. 'The Second Season of Excavation of the Khirbat al-Mukhayyat Archaeological Project', *Liber Annuus*, 66 (2016), 301–19.

Frankel, R. 'Presses for Oil and Wine in the Southern Levant in the Byzantine Period', *Dumbarton Oaks Papers*, 51 (1997), 73–84.

Frösén, J. and Miettunen, P. 'Aaron in Religious Literature, Myth and Legend' in Z. T. Fiema and J. Frösén (eds.), *Petra: The Mountain of Aaron I. The Church and the Chapel* (Helsinki: Societas Scientiarum Fennica, 2008), pp. 5–25.

Gitler, H. 'The Coins' in M. Piccirillo and E. Alliata (eds.), *Mount Nebo: New Archaeological Excavations 1967–1997* (Jerusalem: Franciscan Printing Press 1998), pp. 550–67.

Glueck, N. 'Explorations in Eastern Palestine: II', *Annual of the American Schools of Oriental Research*, 15.9 (1935), 1–149, 151–61, 163–202.

Graham, A. J. and Harrison, T. P. 'The 2000 Mukhayyat Topographic Survey', *Liber Annuus*, 51 (2001), 476–8.

Habas, L. 'Donations and Donors as Reflected in the Mosaic Pavements of Transjordan's Churches in the Byzantine and Umayyad Periods' in K. Kogman-Appel and M. Meyer (eds.), *Between Judaism and Christianity. Art Historical Essays in Honor of Elisheva (Elisabeth) Revel-Neher* (Leiden and Boston, MA: Brill, 2009), pp. 73–90.

Haldon, J. 'Social Transformation in the 6th–9th c. East' in W. Bowden, A. Gotteridge, and C. Machado (eds.), *Social and Political Life in Late Antiquity* (Leiden and Boston, MA: Brill, 2006), pp. 603–47.

Hamarneh, B. 'Evergetismo ecclesiastico e laico nella Giordania bizantina ed omayyade nel V–VIII secolo. Testimonianze epigrafiche', *Vetera Christianorum*, 33 (1996), 57–75.

Hamarneh, B. 'Ritratti e immagini di donatori nei mosaici della Giordania' in N. Cambi and E. Marin (eds.), *Radovi XIII. Međunarodnog kongresa za starokršćansku arheologiju. Acta XIII Congressus Internationalis Archaeologiae Christianae. Split – Poreč (25.9. – 1.10.1994)*, Split – Poreč: Arheološki Muzej, vol. II (Vatican City: Pontificio Istituto di Archeologia Cristiana, 1998), pp. 411–22.

Hamarneh, B. *Topografia cristiana ed insediamenti rurali nel territorio dell'odierna Giordania nelle epoche bizantina ed islamica: V–VIII sec.* (Vatican City: Pontificio Istituto di Archeologia Cristiana, 2003).

Hamarneh, B. 'Monasteries in Rural Context in Byzantine Arabia and Palaestina Tertia: A Reassessment' in L. D. Chrupcała (ed.), *Christ Is Here! Studies in Biblical and Christian Archaeology in Memory of Fr Michele Piccirillo OFM* (Milan: Edizioni Terra Santa, 2012), pp. 275–96.

Hamarneh, B. 'Il fenomeno rupestre nell'Oriente Bizantino: il caso delle province di Arabia e di Palaestina Tertia', in J. Lopéz-Quiroga and A. Tejera (eds.), *In concavis petrarum habitaverunt. El fenómeno rupestre en el Mediterráneo Medieval: de la investigación a la puesta en valor* (Oxford: Archeopress, 2014), pp. 361–74.

Hamarneh, B. 'Denaro' in P. Cesaretti and B. Hamarneh (eds.), *Testo agiografico e orizzonte visivo. Riconstestualizzare le vite dei saloi Simeone e Andrea (BHG 1677, 115z)* (Rome: Edizioni Nuova Cultura, 2016), pp. 131–5.

Hamarneh, B. and Roncalli, A. 'Wadi al-Kharrar – Sapsaphas. Gli scavi archeologici nel luogo del Battesimo' in V. Sonzogni (ed.), *Giordania: Terrasanta di meditazione. Progetto del Parco del Battesimo* (Bergamo: Corponove, 2009), pp. 194–212.

Hirschfeld, Y. 'The Expansion of Rural Settlements during the Fourth–Fifth Centuries C.E. in Palestine' in J. Lefort, C. Morrisson, and J.-P. Sodini (eds.), *Les villages dans l'Empire byzantin (IVe–XVe siècle)* (Paris: Lethielleux, 2005), pp. 523–37.

Hoppé, C. 'The Macroscopic Plant Remains' in K. D. Politis (ed.), *Sanctuary of Lot at Deir 'Ain 'Abata in Jordan* (Amman: Jordan Distribution Agency, 2012), pp. 518–22.

Horn, C. B. and Phenix Jr., R. R. *John Rufus: The Lives of Peter the Iberian, Theodosius of Jerusalem, and the Monk Romanus* (Atlanta: Society of Biblical Literature, 2008).

Kaplan, M. *Les hommes et la terre à Byzance du VIe au XIe siècle. Propriété et exploitation du sol* (Paris: Publications de la Sorbonne, 1992).

Khalil, L. A. and al-Nammari, F. M. 'Two Large Wine Presses at Khirbet Yajuz, Jordan', *Bulletin of the American Schools of Oriental Research*, 318 (2000), 41–57.

Kouli, M. 'Life of St. Mary of Egypt' in A. M. Talbot (ed.), *Holy Women of Byzantium: Ten Saints' Lives in Translation* (Washington, DC: Dumbarton Oaks, 1996), pp. 65–93.

Limor, O. '"Holy Journey": Pilgrimage and Christian Sacred Landscape' in O. Limor and G. G. Stroumsa (eds.), *Christians and Christianity in the Holy Land: From the Origins to the Latin Kingdom* (Turnhout: Brepols, 2006), pp. 321–53.

McGowan, A. and Bradshaw, P. F. *The Pilgrimage of Egeria. A New Translation of the Itinerarium Egeriae with Introduction and Commentary* (Collegeville, MN: Liturgical Press Academic: 2018).

Meimaris, Y. E. *Sacred Names, Saints, Martyrs and Church Officials in the Greek Inscriptions and Papyri Pertaining to the Christian Church of Palestine* (Athens: National Hellenic Research Foundation, Centre for Greek and Roman Antiquity, 1986).

Michel, A. *Les églises d'époque byzantine et umayyade de la Jordanie: Ve–VIIIe siècle. Typologie architectural et aménagements liturgiques* (Turnhout: Brepols 2001).

Mortensen, P., Thuesen, I., and Demant Mortensen, I. *Mount Nebo, an Archaeological Survey of the Region. I: The Palaeolithic and the Neolithic Periods* (Aarhus: Aarhus University Press, 2013).

Pappalardo, C. 'Il cortile a Sud della chiesa di S. Paolo ad Umm al-Rasas / Kastron Mefa'a in Giordania', *Liber Annuus*, 52 (2002), 385–440.

Pappalardo, C. 'Ceramica e piccoli oggetti dallo scavo della chiesa del Reliquiario ad Umm al-Rasas', *Liber Annuus*, 56 (2006), 389–98.

Patrich, J. 'Monastic Landscapes' in W. Bowden, L. Lavan, and C. Machado (eds.), *Recent Research on the Late Antique Countryside* (Leiden and Boston, MA: Brill, 2004), pp. 413–45.

Patrich, J. 'Recent Archaeological Research on Monasteries in Palæstina Byzantina. An Update on Distribution' in O. Delouis and M. Mossakowska-Gaubert (eds.), *La vie quotidienne des moines en Orient et en Occident (IVe–Xe siècle)*, vol. 2: *Questions transversales* (Cairo: Ifao, 2019), pp. 77–106.

Peña, I., Castellana, P. and Fernandez, R. *Les reclus syriens: recherches sur les anciennes formes de vie solitaire en Syrie* (Jerusalem: Franciscan Printing Press 1980).

Piccirillo, M. 'Campagna archeologica nella Basilica di Mosè Profeta sul Monte Nebo Siyagha', *Liber Annuus*, 26 (1976), 281–318.

Piccirillo, M. *Chiese e mosaici della Giordania settentrionale* (Jerusalem: Franciscan Printing Press, 1981).

Piccirillo, M. *Chiese e mosaici di Madaba* (Cinisello Balsamo: Edizioni Paoline, 1989).

Piccirillo, M. 'Gruppi episcopali nelle tre Palestine e in Arabia?' in N. Duval, F. Baritel, and P. Pergola (eds.), *Actes du XIe Congrès International d'Archéologie Chrétienne: Lyon, Vienne, Grenoble, Genève et Aoste (21-28 septembre 1986)*, vol. I (Rome: École française de Rome and Vatican City: Pontificio Instituto di Archeologia Cristiana, 1989), pp. 459-501.

Piccirillo, M. 'Monks and Monasteries in Jordan from the Byzantine to the Abbasid Period', *Al-Liqa' Journal*, 1 (1992), 17-30.

Piccirillo, M. *Mosaics of Jordan* (Amman: American Centre of Oriental Research, 1993).

Piccirillo, M. 'Le due iscrizioni della cappella della Theotokos nel wadi Ayn al-Kanisah – Monte Nebo', *Liber Annuus*, 44 (1994), 521-38.

Piccirillo, M. 'Ricerca storico-archeologica in Giordania', *Liber Annuus*, 44 (1994), 638-40.

Piccirillo, M. 'La chapelle de la Theotokos dans le Wadi Ayn al-Kanisah au Mont Nébo en Jordanie', *Annual of the Department of Antiquities of Jordan*, 39 (1995), 409-20.

Piccirillo, M. *La montagna del Nebo* (Jerusalem: Franciscan Printing Press, 1997).

Piccirillo, M. 'The Exploration' in M. Piccirillo and E. Alliata (eds.), *Mount Nebo: New Archaeological Excavations 1967-1997* (Jerusalem: Franciscan Printing Press 1998), pp. 13-52.

Piccirillo, M. 'The Monastic Presence' in M. Piccirillo and E. Alliata, (eds.), *Mount Nebo: New Archaeological Excavations 1967-1997* (Jerusalem: Franciscan Printing Press, 1998), pp. 193-219.

Piccirillo, M. 'The Churches of Nebo. New Discoveries' in M. Piccirillo and E. Alliata (eds.), *Mount Nebo: New Archaeological Excavations 1967-1997* (Jerusalem: Franciscan Printing Press, 1998), pp. 221-64.

Piccirillo, M. 'The Mosaics' in M. Piccirillo and E. Alliata (eds.) *Mount Nebo: New Archaeological Excavations 1967-1997* (Jerusalem: Franciscan Printing Press, 1998), pp. 265-371.

Piccirillo, M. *L'Arabia Cristiana. Dalla Provincia imperiale al primo periodo islamico* (Milan: Jaca Book, 2002).

Piccirillo, M. 'Dall'archeologia alla storia. Nuove evidenze per una rettifica di luoghi comuni riguardanti le province di Palestina e di Arabia nei secoli IV-VIII d.C.' in A. C. Quintavalle (ed.), *Medioevo Mediterraneo: l'Occidente, Bisanzio e l'Islam dal Tardoantico al secolo XII. VII Convegno Internazionale di Studi (Parma – Palazzo Sanvitale, 21-25 settembre 2004)* (Milan: Electa, 2007), pp. 95-111.

Piccirillo, M. and Alliata, E. 'La chiesa del monastero di Kaianos alle Ayoun Mousa sul Monte Nebo' in P. Pergola (ed.), *Quaeritur inventus colitur. Miscellanea in onore di Padre Umberto Maria Fasola, B* (Vatican City: Pontificio Istituto di Archeologia Cristiana, 1989), pp. 563-86.

Piccirillo, M. and Alliata, E. (eds.) *Umm er-Rasas Mayfa'ah I. Gli scavi del complesso di Santo Stefano* (Jerusalem: Franciscan Printing Press, 1994).

Piccirillo, M. and Alliata, E. (eds.) *Mount Nebo: New Archaeological Excavations 1967–1997* (Jerusalem: Franciscan Printing Press, 1998).

Politis, K. D. *Sanctuary of Lot at Deir 'Ain 'Abata in Jordan* (Amman: Jordan Distribution Agency, 2012).

Rajala, A. and Fiema, Z. T. 'The Baptismal Fonts' in Z. T. Fiema and J. Frösén (eds.), *Petra: The Mountain of Aaron I. The Church and the Chapel* (Helsinki: Societas Scientiarum Fennica, 2008), pp. 235–45.

Rapp, C. 'The Elite Status of Bishops in Late Antiquity in Ecclesiastical, Spiritual, and Social Contexts', *Arethusa*, 33.3 (2000), 379–99.

Rapp, C. *Holy Bishops in Late Antiquity: The Nature of Christian Leadership in an Age of Transition* (Berkeley: University of California Press, 2005).

Saller, S. J. *The Memorial of Moses on Mount Nebo*, 2 vols (Jerusalem: Franciscan Printing Press, 1941).

Saller, S. J. 'Hellenistic to Arabic Remains at Nebo, Jordan', *Liber Annuus*, 17 (1967), 5–64.

Saller, S. J. and Bagatti, B. *The Town of Nebo, with a Brief Survey of Other Ancient Christian Monuments in Transjordan* (Jerusalem: Franciscan Printing Press, 1949).

Sanmorì, C. 'The Funerary Practices' in M. Piccirillo and E. Alliata (eds.), *Mount Nebo: New Archaeological Excavations 1967–1997* (Jerusalem: Franciscan Printing Press 1998), pp. 413–24.

Sanmorì, C. and Pappalardo, C. 'Ceramica dalla chiesa di San Paolo e dalla cappella dei Pavoni – Umm al-Rasas', *Liber Annuus*, 47 (1997), 395–428.

Schick, R. 'Types of Burials in Churches in Jordan in the Byzantine and Early Islamic Periods' in C. Eger and M. Mackensen (eds.), *Death and Burial in the Near East from Roman to Islamic Times. Research in Syria, Lebanon, Jordan and Egypt* (Wiesbaden: Reichert Verlag, 2018), pp. 171–80.

Taxel, I. 'Rural Monasticism at the Foothills of Southern Samaria and Judaea in the Byzantine Period: Asceticism, Agriculture and Pilgrimage', *Bulletin of the Anglo-Israel Archaeological Society*, 26 (2008), 57–73.

Voltaggio, M. '*Perambulatio per monasteria*. Accoglienza monastica lungo le vie di pellegrinaggio in Terra Santa' in L. Ermini Pani (ed.), *Teoria e pratica del lavoro nel monachesimo altomedievale: atti del Convegno internazionale di studio (Roma–Subiaco, 7–9 giugno 2013)* (Spoleto: Fondazione Centro italiano di studi sull'Alto Medioevo, 2015), pp. 321–46.

Waheeb, M. *Betania oltre il Giordano: la scoperta del luogo dove fu battezzato Gesù* (Milan: Edizioni Terra Santa, 2016).

Walmsley, A. G. 'The Umayyad Period' in A. McNicoll, R. H. Smith, and B. Henness (eds.), *Pella in Jordan 1. An Interim Report on the Joint University of Sydney and the College of Wooster Excavations at Pella 1979–1981* (Canberra: Australian National Gallery, 1986), pp. 123–42.

Walmsley, A. G. 'The Umayyad Pottery and its Antecedents' in A. McNicoll, R. H. Smith, and B. Henness (eds.), *Pella in Jordan 1. An Interim Report on the Joint University of Sydney and the College of Wooster Excavations at Pella 1979-1981* (Canberra: Australian National Gallery, 1986), pp. 143–72.

Walmsley, A. G. 'Land, Resources and Industry in Early Islamic Jordan (7th–11th Century). Current Research and Future Directions in Studies', *The History and Archaeology of Jordan*, 6 (1997), 345–51.

Walmsley, A. G. 'The Village Ascendant in Byzantine and Early Islamic Jordan: Socio-Economic Forces and Cultural Responses' in J. Lefort, C. Morrisson, and J.-P. Sodini (eds.), *Les villages dans l'Empire byzantin (IVe–XVe siècle)* (Paris: Lethielleux, 2005), pp. 511–22.

Watson, P. 'Jerash Bowls: Study of a Provincial Group of Byzantine Decorated Fine Ware', *Syria. Reveu d'Art Oriental et d'Archéologie*, 66.1 (1989), 223–61.

Whiting, M. 'Monastery Hostels in Late Antique Syria, Palestine and Transjordan' in Z. T. Fiema, J. Frösén, and M. Holappa (eds.), *Petra: The Mountain of Aaron II. The Nabataean Sanctuary and the Byzantine Monastery* (Helsinki: Societas Scientiarum Fennica, 2016), pp. 108–13.

Wilkinson, J. *Jerusalem Pilgrims before the Crusades* (Warminster: Aris & Phillips, 1977).

13 | Travel in the Texts: Monastic Journeys in Late Antique Egypt

PAULA TUTTY

In the hagiographical literature that describes the lives of fourth- and fifth-century Egyptian monks, travel is a common theme. Novices make trips to speak with their elders, monks make journeys to the nearest village in order to sell their wares, and hermits are described travelling far away from civilisation into the wilderness.¹ One of the most famous portrayals of such early monks, *The Life of St Antony*, describes how, when pursued by bothersome disciples, Antony retreats to a mountain and learns to grow his own produce in order to be self-sufficient in his solitude.² Despite the fact that travel is such a common topic, the documented journeys of early monks, and the many circumstances that led to such travel, is a theme that is seldom explored by scholars.³ In part, this may be due to the misconception – one that still continues to be held by some – which holds that Egyptian monks were isolated within the confines of the desert, a point of view that owes much to the writings of the eminent historian Peter Brown. In 1971, Brown suggested that Egyptian monks did not interact with local society in the way that monks from Syria, Asia Minor, and Palestine did. His rationale was that life in the desert, and the immense effort needed to survive in such inhospitable conditions, effectively isolated monks from the outside world.⁴ Brown returned to this theme in 1988, evoking a vivid description of Egyptian ascetics surviving on a meagre diet provided through manual labour, as hired hands in local villages.⁵ Brown,

---

¹ See the references to Egypt in Dietz, *Wandering Monks* and Caner, *Wandering, Begging Monks*. The question of monks selling handicrafts, particularly baskets, is discussed in Wipszycka, 'Resources and Economic Activities', pp. 172–3.
² *Vita Antonii* §49–50; translation in Vivian and Athanassakis, *The Life of Antony*, pp. 162–7. Also discussed by Caner, *Wandering, Begging Monks*, pp. 19–24.
³ For evidence of travel in general, including several references to monastic travel, see Kotsifou, 'Papyrological Evidence of Travelling'.
⁴ For example, in Brown, 'The Rise and Function of the Holy Man', p. 83, he states that 'The links between the holy man and society constantly yielded to the pressure of this great fact. To survive at all in the hostile environment of such a desert, the Egyptian had to transplant into it the tenacious and all-absorbing routines of the villages of the οἰκουμένη. To live at all, a man had to remain in one place, earning his living from manual labour, from pottery and reed-weaving.'
⁵ Brown, *The Body and Society*, pp. 218–20. Brown later revised his views on the attitude of Egyptian monks toward organised and communal labour in Brown, *Treasure in Heaven*, pp. 71–107.

in common with other historians of the period, had based much of his description of Egyptian monks on his reading of the *Apophthegmata Patrum*. Since then, the historicity of this particular group of texts, and their claim to an Egyptian origin, has been called into question.[6] The *Apophthegmata Patrum* is now valued more by modern historians of monasticism as guidebooks for the practice of *imitatio partum* rather than as historical works based on treasured memories.[7] Fourth- and fifth-century monasticism is now considered to be a phenomenon that expressed itself as vigorously within the towns and villages of Egypt as it did in the barren regions that bordered the fertile lands that lie alongside the length of the River Nile.[8] Monks may have ideologically renounced the world, but they also had familial, economic, and social ties that required their attention.

In this study, I will show how the theme of travel is a prominent one in the surviving documentation and acts as a witness for the economic activities of fourth- and fifth-century monks in Egypt and their roles as participants in the social and economic activities of the period. It needs to be acknowledged that the surviving documentation for fourth-century monasticism is somewhat sparse, the provenance of the vast majority of it is not known, and it cannot be assumed that what survives is in any way representative of the overall monastic experience. Nevertheless, this body of evidence remains an invaluable resource for the information it contains concerning the daily lives of monks and their preoccupations.

In total, five collections of monastic letters survive from fourth- and fifth-century Egypt, as well as several isolated examples of monastic epistles.[9] Not all of these individual collections explicitly mention travel, even if the activities of the monks seem to imply it.[10] Two letter collections are particularly useful for the study of travel: the archive of Nepheros, a priest from the monastery of Hathor, and the monastic letters found in

---

[6] Particularly as a result of the project led by Samuel Rubenson at the University of Lund, *Early Monasticism and Classical Paideia* (MOPAI). Their database of sayings texts, 'Monastica', is accessible at http://monastica.ht.lu.se/ (accessed 16/02/2022). See also, Rubenson, 'Textual Fluidity' and Rubenson, 'Formation and Re-formations'.

[7] A point made by Goehring, 'Monastic Diversity', p. 61; see also Larsen, 'Re-drawing the Interpretive Map' and Larsen, 'The Apophthegmata Patrum'.

[8] Wipszycka, 'Le monachisme égyptien', pp. 1–10; Goehring, 'The World Engaged'.

[9] For an overview of surviving letter collections and individual letters from this period see, Choat, 'Monastic Letters'.

[10] Such as the various activities evidenced in Vivian, 'Holy Men and Businessmen', pp. 253–63; see also, Tutty, 'The Political and Philanthropic Role'.

the cartonnage of the Nag Hammadi Codices.[11] Christian literature, in particular late antique travelogues, also add detail on the topic of monastic tourism.[12] Within these hagiographical materials, we are provided with vivid snapshots of monastic life as seen through the eyes of the visiting pilgrims and their Christian audiences. The idealised picture that emerges in such literature provides a cultural backdrop against which the documents of monks can then be read and discussed with reference to the corresponding late antique literary and religious frameworks.

Travel for economic reasons is a familiar theme in the wider study of monasticism, even if it is underrepresented in studies of fourth- and fifth-century monks. Yet, as I shall demonstrate, travels undertaken for economic purposes certainly dominate the surviving record for the fourth and fifth centuries in Egypt. Journeys were also undertaken for a variety of other reasons: monks made active interventions in the many religious disputes of the fourth and fifth centuries in ways that sometimes required them to journey far beyond the borders of Egypt. Certain monks appear to have travelled to enhance their spiritual practices, while others were forced to travel due to the turbulence of world events. Many questions remain to be answered regarding these journeys. Further research needs to be undertaken into the lives and writings of early monks in order to understand more fully their participation in economic activities, their movements, and their influence on the development of early Christianity, and many documents still lie untranslated in museum vaults. Only partial answers can be given here to questions raised on issues such as the frequency of monastic travel, the type of transport used, and the ways in which travel enhanced the economic development of monastic communities. However, by beginning with the available sources, it is possible to gain some insight into the travels of early Egyptian monks, the way in which their journeys supported their economic endeavours, and the contribution travel made to the development of monasticism.

Business and Travel in the Letters of Nepheros

The correspondence of Nepheros of the monastery of Hathor in the Herakleopolite nome contains by far the most detailed information regarding monastic travel for the reasons of trade and exchange in fourth-century

---

[11] For the Nepheros archive, see Kramer and Shelton, *Das Archiv des Nepheros*. The letters of the cartonnage of the Nag Hammadi Codices are edited in Barns et al., *Nag Hammadi Codices*.

[12] In particular, Rufinus' *Historia Monachorum* and Palladius' *Historia Lausiaca*.

Egypt.[13] There are sixteen letters addressed to Nepheros, which, based on the evidence of the prices given for goods, date to the second half of the fourth century.[14] If Kramer and Shelton are correct, the monastery of Hathor in which Nepheros dwelt may have belonged to the Melitian Church.[15] If this is the case, the surviving correspondence gives no hint that the arrangements there were significantly different from the organisation of any other of the well-known and relatively contemporaneous monastic communities such as those of Pachomius, and that of Shenoute, which was founded a few decades later.[16] There is no reason, therefore, why evidence from such a setting should not be of use in illuminating organisational practices that would have been common in many other religious communities of the period.[17]

There are various indications that the monastic community at Hathor was well organised in a way that enabled it to provide for many of its daily needs. From the Nepheros letters, it is clear that the monastery owned its own forge, had a pottery workshop and a mill, and contained granaries for the storage of wheat.[18] Despite this relative self-sufficiency, there are a number of replies in the letters to requests from Nepheros for the purchase of goods in Alexandria. Whilst the precise location of the monastery of Hathor is unknown, the letters sent from there mention several towns and villages that lay close by, including Ankyropolis (modern El Hibeh). The distance from Ankyropolis to Alexandria is approximately 400 km, and in fourth-century Egypt, at a time when journeys of any reasonable distance would typically have been undertaken by boat, it would have taken just under four days to journey to Alexandria, with a slightly lengthier return journey of four-and-a-half days.[19]

Many of the surviving letters that discuss the Alexandrian sales and purchases are written to a man, presumably a layperson, named Paul, who

---

[13] The precise location of this monastery, assuming there was only one monastery in the vicinity called Hathor, is disputed. It appears to have been located in the Cynopolite or Heracleopolite nome, or on the border of both; see Kramer and Shelton, *Das Archiv des Nepheros*, pp. 11–14; Choat, 'Fourth-Century Monasticism', p. 96; Lundhaug and Jenott, *Monastic Origins*, p. 45.

[14] The editors suggest a date later than 344, based on the high prices and the lack of overlap with the early fourth-century archive of Paieous from the same monastery; see, Kramer and Shelton, *Das Archiv des Nepheros*, pp. 3–5. Bagnall, 'Fourth-Century Prices', pp. 74–5, suggests a date in or after 352, based on letter 8.

[15] Kramer and Shelton, *Das Archiv des Nepheros*, pp. 11–14.

[16] Evidence for the living arrangements of the Melitian monasteries is discussed in Goehring, 'Melitian Monastic Organization'.

[17] Choat, 'Review of Hans Hauben'. [18] Kramer and Shelton, *Das Archiv des Nepheros*, p. 14.

[19] To calculate travel distance and time, I have used ORBIS, the Stanford Geospacial Network of the Roman World, http://orbis.stanford.edu (accessed 16/02/2022).

acts on behalf of the monastery.[20] Paul and his wife Tapiam appear to know the members of the community well, for they send greetings to a number of brothers there and discuss business transactions that involve monks known to Nepheros. Paul speaks in terms of exile, but whether this is enforced or merely a reference to their temporary state is not made clear.[21] Paul organises the sale of unnamed 'bundles', the proceeds from which seem to have partly funded the purchase of oil in *P.Neph.* 4. He writes, 'You have thought me worthy to order me to take the three bundles and supervise their sale and send you oil. So they have been sold for fourteen myriads and the barrel of oil has been purchased for sixty myriads.'[22] What was sold is not clarified, but it is likely that this is a reference to some of the produce of the monastery; tow is suggested by the editors, hay by Bagnall.[23] A myriad was worth 10,000 denarii, or eighty talents, the price of a modius (approximately 9 l.) of wheat in 338. It would therefore seem that these are not large quantities.[24] In *P.Neph.* 8, a further purchase is made of five sextarii (= 132.5 l.) of oil for 60 myriads, while three minas (approximately 1.5 kg) of iron is said to cost twenty myriads.[25] As revealed by the letters, it is not always easy to procure the oil, a problem that necessitates an apology from Paul in *P.Neph.* 3 for his inability to obtain it. The continued preoccupation with oil continues in *P.Neph.* 5, which also indicates that iron was difficult to obtain. It is understandable that the monastery would need to send off for iron, which would not necessarily have been obtainable locally, but it is less clear why such relatively small quantities of oil were needed from Alexandria, particularly as oil was a product that would have been easily procurable locally. One suggestion is that this is a reference to special consecrated oil for use in liturgical ceremonies.[26]

How these goods were transported to and from the monastery is not discussed in the letters. The use of camels appears frequently within later monastic texts, but, as noted earlier, a boat would be the easiest and most logical form of transportation in view of the distances involved.[27] *P.Neph.* 1

---

[20] Nine letters are written by Paul, *P.Neph.* 1–9.
[21] Vivian, 'Holy Men and Businessmen', p. 257.
[22] κατηξίωσας δὲ κελεῦσαί μοι τὰ τρία δε[σ]μίδι\α/ λαβόντα διοικῆσαι καὶ εἰς χρίαν σου ἔλαιον ἀποστεῖλαι. ἐπράθησαν οὖν ἐκ μυριάδων δεκατεσσάρων. ἠγοράσθη δὲ τὸ ἀγγῖον τοῦ ἐλαίου μυριάδων ἑξήκοντα. Bagnall, *Egypt in Late Antiquity*, p. 30, considers the oil in question to refer probably to some form of vegetable oil.
[23] Bagnall, 'Fourth-Century Prices', pp. 75–6.
[24] Tainter, *Collapse of Complex Societies*, p. 143.   [25] Bagnall, 'Fourth-Century Prices', p. 75.
[26] Vivian, 'Holy Men and Businessmen', p. 258.
[27] For the use of the camel as a means of transport, see Bacot, 'The Camel, the Wagon, and the Donkey'. For transport by boat, see Bacot, 'La circulation du vin dans les monastères d'Égypte', pp. 274–6.

confirms that this is probably the case, when Paul states that he wishes to bring his children to see Nepheros 'in the boat'. Whether the boat in question belonged to the community or was leased for this particular journey is not possible to ascertain, and no other references to the boat are to be found within this letter collection.[28] Paul sometimes asks other people to carry his purchases back to him; in *P.Neph.* 5 he mentions that he has sent back oil through his sister Taese, who was placed at Nepheros' 'service' (εἰς σὴν ὑπηρεσίαν). What is meant by 'service' is unclear in this instance. Taese may have been a member of the monastic community. However, the letter collection is absent of any further possible allusions to a twinned female community and, indeed, fails to mention nuns in any other context. If Taese worked in some lay capacity for the monks, this is significant as it raises the possibility that lay women might have been permitted to work alongside the monks in this community. How much contact there was between monks and women, whether laywomen or nuns, is hard to judge. The Pachomian federation's rules, for example – in the form that has come down to us – had strictures prohibiting women from entering the monastery. However, within the Pachomian literature itself, we find women coming into direct contact with male monks on several occasions.[29] Further evidence that fourth-century monks had some measure of contact with women, or at least performed transactions with them, can be found in the letter of Proteria to Sansnos, discussed below.[30]

Goods and letters transported between the monastery of Hathor and Alexandria sometimes seem to have involved travelling monks, if we assume that the references to brothers in these cases are references to monks.[31] In *P.Neph.* 5, 'our brothers' Aspidas and Paul are mentioned as having previously delivered letters from Paul to Nepheros. In *P.Neph.* 6, 'my honoured brother Theodosius' plans to take ten sextarii of oil back to the monastery. Other journeys also involve monks who write directly to Nepheros on the course of their journeys. In *P.Neph.* 12, a monk named Serapion arrives at a place named Omboi (Ὄμβων), plausibly a reference to Kom Ombo nearly 700 km away from the presumed locality of Hathor,

---

[28] The ownership of boats in the Pachomian federation is discussed by Goehring in 'The Ship of the Pachomian Federation'.

[29] For example, in the Bohairic *Life of Pachomius* (SBo) 27, we learn that the Pachomian nuns were overseen by a senior monk named Peter. Compare SBo 37, 41; the first Greek recension (G^1) 132, 134; and Precepts (the set of Pachomian rules generally assumed to have been authored by Pachomius) 53, 119; translations in Veilleux, *Pachomian Koinonia I–III*.

[30] *P.Nag.Hamm.* 72.

[31] Caution in this matter is advised by Choat, 'Monastic Letters on Papyrus', pp. 47–8, who notes the popular use of the term 'brother' in lay and religious contexts.

a journey that would have taken at least one week to complete by boat.³² The reason for this journey is not made clear, and it is difficult to determine why a monk from Heracleopolis would need to travel such a distance. Serapion shows concern regarding the coming harvest in a certain small field. It is possible that this field is his responsibility and even, perhaps, his property, for if the field belonged to the monastery it would seem odd, as Kramer and Shelton point out, that no-one in the monastery was able to oversee it and make the harvest arrangements in his absence.³³ Serapion calls on Nepheros to search out a certain Paul, who is a sailor from (or in) Toeto (modern Tahta) near Antaiopolis (modern Qaw el-Kebir) and obtain scythes from him. The implication is that the sailor, along with his sons, is to use the scythes to harvest the grain mentioned in the letter. Much of the context is missing in this instance, but the involvement of the monk Serapion with the harvest, with the added complexity of his absence on a long journey, demonstrates that monastic life in the fourth century was reliant on a multitude of social and economic ties.

In *P.Neph.* 11, a monk named Kapiton writes from a trip he was making to Pselemachis in the Heracleopolite nome and Tampeti in the Oxyrhynchite nome. Lacunae in this letter render it somewhat obscure, but what is clear is that Kapiton had his clothes stolen in Pselemachis and there was perhaps some involvement by the inhabitants of Tampeti. Of further significance is the mention that Nepheros himself will also be journeying to Tampeti to visit a certain father Pamoun. In another letter, *P.Neph.* 15, Nepheros is invited to 'come south' to visit an unknown location, or perhaps person, called Pmeshout. The suggestion that leading monastic figures commonly ventured out on such journeys is also confirmed by a letter, *P.Lond.* VI 1922, from the archive of Apa Paieous, a monk who most likely lived in the same monastery of Hathor a generation earlier.³⁴ This letter reminds the recipient that he had said that he would 'come north', and the author states that they are all impatient to see him. It would seem that senior figures from monastic communities were obliged, or perhaps desired, to spend at least part of their time visiting others, whether it be the monks under their charge or other religious

---

³² γράφω σοι, ἄπα Νεφερῶς καθὼς ἐξῆλθα ἀπὸ σοῦ, χάρις τ[ῷ] θεῷ, ἦλθα εἰς Ὄμβων (*P.Neph.* 12, 12–13), 'I am writing to you, Apa Nepheros, that when I left you, I came, thank God, to Omboi (Kom Ombos?).'

³³ Kramer and Shelton, *Das Archiv des Nepheros*, p. 74.

³⁴ During circa the 330s. For the connection of the Apa Paieous archive to the monastery of Hathor and the archive of Nepheros, see Choat, 'Monastic Letters on Papyrus', pp. 25–9. *P. Lond.* VI 22, although included in the Paieous archive, appears, according to the name traces, to be addressed to another monk, for which see Choat, 'Monastic Letters on Papyrus', p. 25, n. 44.

figures and organisations. This situation is also underlined by the Pachomian *Lives*, in which numerous references can be found to Pachomius' travels around his monasteries in order to keep a watchful eye on them and their inhabitants.[35]

Transporting Goods at Nag Hammadi

Journeys and transport are also a focal point of the Nag Hammadi letters, in which they are made on land and by boat in order to secure the necessities of life. In *P.Nag.Hamm.* 72, the aforementioned woman named Proteria calls upon two monks, Sansnos and Psatos (or Psas), to locate chaff for her animals. She asks them, 'Can you, where you are, possibly look for a little chaff for my animals? For they are short of it and I cannot buy any here. When you can, write to me about the price, how much for the wagon (load) and where the boat comes.'[36] In this case, the boat might belong to Proteria herself, but the ownership of boats by monastic communities was not unusual, even in this early period, as was seen earlier in the letters of Nepheros. It is mentioned frequently in the Pachomian literature where boats are used for the transport of people and goods. So, for example, in the Bohairic *Life of Pachomius* (SBo), we are told that a boat carrying flax for the making of clothes had sunk (SBo 183). A boat full of wheat was donated to the monastery of Tse (SBo 53), and the bishop of Smin also donated a boat (SBo 54). When the monastery founded by Petronios at Tbew joined the federation, Petronius' father donated, 'all he had: sheep, goats, cattle, camels, donkeys, carts, and all he possessed, including boats' (SBo 56).[37] A document that attests to this early ownership of boats by the federation is *SB* XXII 15311, dated 367/8.[38] This text, a register of grain supply, also notes that part of the grain was loaded aboard 'a monastery boat at Tabennesi'.

As Chrysi Kotsifou points out, it is unlikely that the majority of Egypt's population would have had recourse to a boat in the fourth century.[39] Not owning a boat caused many difficulties for occasional travellers, as they were not always easy to procure for hire, and even then, the leasing of a boat

---

[35] SBo 50–53, 59, 60, 72, 108; G¹ 30, 54, 60.

[36] Σανσνῶτι καὶ Ψάτος μοναχοῖς Προτηρ[ία] χέρ(ειν) εἰ δυνατὸν παρ' ὑμῖν ἐστιν τὸ ἐραυνῆσαι ὀλίγον ἄχυρον πρὸς τὴν ὑπηρεσίαν τῶν ἐμῶν κῶν διότι ὑστεροῦσι, καὶ οὐχ εὑρίσκω ἐνταῦθα ἀγοράσαι. ἐπὴν δὲ εὕρητε, πέμψατέ με ὑπὲρ τὴν τιμην ὅτι πόσον τὴν ἄμαξαν ἀχύρου, καὶ ἵνα ἔρχεται τὸ πλοῖον.

[37] Translation from Veilleux, *Pachomian Koinonia I*, p. 77.

[38] Worp, 'SB XIV 11972 Fr.A'; Choat, 'Property Ownership'.

[39] Kotsifou, 'Papyrological Evidence of Travelling', pp. 60–1.

was highly expensive. The purchase of a boat would have required the prospective buyer to save several years of income, unless they were very wealthy.[40] Therefore, whether they leased or owned a boat, the monks of Nag Hammadi must have been reasonably well endowed as they, like their correspondent Proteria, were able to make use of boats to transport agricultural produce. In *P.Nag.Hamm* 67, instructions are given involving the movement of grain to a monastery or monastic cell (τὸ μονάχιον): 'put the small quantity of grain on the boat; make him transport it to the monastery with your asses and put it in the storage bin (*or* vessel)'.[41] The amount of grain may only be small (although what 'small' signifies as an actual measure is unknowable), but some measure of organisation is implied, as this task involves not only the shipping of grain, but the management of animals for its transport and afterwards overseeing the storage of grain.

P.Nag.Hamm. 68, as in the letter of Proteria, discusses the procurement of a large quantity of chaff, this time ten loads, from the same monk Sansnos, but this time for a man named Harpocration. Other people are involved in these efforts, including the man who comes for the wheat mentioned in *P.Nag.Hamm.* 75. Moving a large amount of chaff such as that mentioned in *P.Nag.Hamm.* 68 would have required the use of a cart and donkeys, mules, or even oxen. A cart would have been an expensive item in Late Antiquity, as it involved not only having enough money to commission and pay for such a large item, but the ownership of the animals needed to pull it. As Bagnall points out, the cost of a single donkey was the equivalent of five to ten months of an average person's income. The animals would also need feeding, care, and maintenance, all of which would be a considerable expense.[42] It is not necessary to assume that the monks themselves owned the cart, but they did have access to it, even if this was only temporarily through a leasing agreement. While Egypt was heavily reliant on the Nile for most of its transport needs, animals and carts – although far more expensive – were useful for delivering goods over short inland distances.[43] All of this seemingly demonstrates that in the area

---

[40] Bagnall, *Egypt in Late Antiquity*, pp. 34–8. As Bagnall notes, evidence for the cost of boats is scarce, but a long lease for a *hellenikon* boat capable of carrying 400 artaba of wheat cost the equivalent of sixteen to twenty-seven years' wages based on various occupations (*P.Lond.* III 1164h, AD 212).

[41] δέδωκ( ) εἰς τὸ πλοῖον [τὸ]ν ὀλίγον σῖτον. ποιήσῃς αὐτὸν μετακ[ομί]ζεσθαι εἰς τὸ μονάχιον διὰ τῶν ὑμετέρω[ν] κτηνῶν καὶ θεῖναι αὐτὰ εἰς σιρόν (lines 6–10).

[42] Bagnall, *Egypt in Late Antiquity*, p. 38.

[43] The oft-quoted analysis by Jones, *The Later Roman Empire*, pp. 841–2, notes that, using Diocletian's *Edict of Maximum Prices* and the cost of transporting wheat, transporting a wagonload of wheat by donkey would double the price of the wheat after a 300 mile journey. By camel, it would double after 375 miles. The price quoted for maritime transport

near Nag Hammadi there was a community of monks who were able to pay for such transport, with money that was perhaps recouped through economic activity or personal wealth. How far the monks themselves partook in these tasks is unclear, but, even if they used middlemen, such journeys are evidence for economic engagement with the local society.

Pachomian Travels to Alexandria

Alexandria, the seat of the Patriarch and the commercial hub of the eastern Mediterranean, might be expected to loom large in any description of late antique travel in Egypt.[44] As discussed earlier, delegates from the monastery of Hathor were frequent visitors there. Within the Pachomian literature, there are several mentions of monks, and would-be monks, travelling between the Pachomian monasteries in Upper Egypt and Alexandria, a journey of approximately six days' length according to one Pachomian source.[45] One significant character who is said to have made this journey is Theodore the Alexandrian, who, according to the Bohairic *Life of Pachomius*, travelled to the monastery at Pbow by boat, having been a lector in a church in Alexandria. The arrival of large numbers of Greek-speaking men to join the Pachomian federation resulted in Theodore's employment as housemaster to novices who needed to learn Egyptian.[46] In the *Letter of Ammon*, Ammon recounts how, as a young man living in Alexandria, he took the opportunity to journey back to the Thebaid with visiting Pachomian monks in Alexandria.[47] The origin of the *Letter of Ammon* may be obscure, but the theme of a young man journeying to begin a new life in the highly esteemed Pachomian monasteries is a plausible one, and one that is echoed elsewhere in the literature.[48]

With the building of each new Pachomian monastery, with the exception of the monastery of Phnoum at Latopolis, the federation drew

---

demonstrates that it would be cheaper to ship grain from one end of the Mediterranean to the other rather than to cart it 75 miles. These extremes in scale have, however, been challenged in Adams, *Land Transport in Roman Egypt*, pp. 4–8, who suggests that land transport was more well-used and cost efficient than often presumed, so that we should be looking, rather, at the integration of different types of transport.

[44] For an introduction to late antique Alexandria, see Haas, *Alexandria in Late Antiquity*.

[45] The *Historia Horsiesi*; see, Crum, *Der Papyruscodex saec. VI-VII der Philippsbibliothek in Cheltenham*, pp. 12–21.

[46] SBo 89–91; see Veilleux, *Pachomian Koinonia I*, pp. 17–23.

[47] Goehring, *The Letter of Ammon*, p. 190.

[48] For example, SBo 107; see Veilleux, *Pachomian Koinonia I*, pp. 150–1. See also the examples given by Goehring, 'The Pachomian Federation and Lower Egypt', pp. 50–1.

geographically closer to the capital.[49] In 391, Pachomian monks, at the behest of Bishop Theophilos, took up residence at Canopus, a mere twelve kilometres away from Alexandria, at the monastery of Metanoia. As James Goehring notes, the attitude of the Pachomians in this respect was different from that of the later Shenoutean monks; no record survives of an attempt to expand the latter community, and there are no references in the Shenoutean literature of groups of non-Egyptian-speaking monks at the monasteries.[50] There is, as far as I am aware, a single reference in the Bohairic *Life of Shenoute* to the existence of a refectory for foreigners.[51] Whether this refers to foreign monks within the monastery or foreign visitors is not clear, but, in any case, its inclusion in the *Life* does not necessarily reflect any sanction of such a place by Shenoute himself or his immediate successors.[52] Not all monasteries may have been as focused on expansion as the Pachomians, but this does not preclude the fact that both Shenoutean and other groups of monks would have had opportunities to travel outside of their communities. In the Shenoutean canons, rules controlling the movement of monks outside of the monastery make this apparent.[53] For example, when monks are travelling far from the monastery, they are permitted to pull out a thorn from another's foot without seeking permission.[54] While it is plausible that travellers from Shenoute's White Monastery may have visited Alexandria, it is not possible to ascertain this from the surviving literature.

Despite the relative ease of travel along the Nile, effective communications and demands of obedience to a centralised command structure would have been difficult to maintain for the Pachomians. Goehring notes how the monastery of Metanoia, located close to Alexandria, remained loyal to the Patriarch, to the extent of producing three Chalcedonian Patriarchs from among its ranks during a period when the monks of Upper Egypt were noted for their anti-Chalcedonian sentiments.[55] According to the hagiography of Abraham of Farshut, non-Chalcedonian monks were purged from the Pachomian monasteries in the sixth century, and

---

[49] Goehring, 'The Pachomian Federation and Lower Egypt', pp. 51–2.
[50] Goehring, 'The Pachomian Federation and Lower Egypt', pp. 52–3.
[51] Leipoldt, *Sinuthii Archimandritae*, vol. 1, p. 73.
[52] Shore, 'Extracts from Besa's "Life of Shenoute"', p. 142.
[53] Movement outside of the monastery and the rules pertaining to it are discussed in Layton, *Canons of Our Fathers*, p. 60 n.18.
[54] Located in Canon 8, Codex YA 314–15 = IT-NB IB17 (70)v–(71)r; designation according to Emmel, *Shenoute's Literary Corpus*. Text and translations in Layton, *Canons of Our Fathers*, pp. 124–5; Leipoldt, *Sinuthii Archimandritae*, vol. 4, p. 123.
[55] Goehring, 'The Pachomian Federation and Lower Egypt', p. 55.

Abraham himself was removed as abbot.[56] While the expansion into the north by the Pachomian federation may initially have been seen as a positive move, as Goehring suggests, it later led to the development of 'dual centres of gravity', which came into conflict in a manner that helped to foster the eventual downfall of the Pachomian federation.[57]

Religious Turmoil and Monastic Journeys

The schism that developed in the early fourth century between the Melitians (or, as they styled themselves, the 'Church of the Martyrs') and the officially recognised Church hierarchy had repercussions for monks who became involved.[58] The dispute in Alexandria had its origin during the time of the Diocletian persecution when the Patriarch, Peter of Alexandria, fled from the city, and in his absence, Bishop Melitius of Lycopolis ordained priests and other bishops who were located outside of his own diocese – a move highly resented by the returning Patriarch. Peter died in 311, but the power struggle between Melitius and his followers with the Patriarchs of Alexandria continued.[59] The ensuing arguments were the cause of several lengthy journeys made by monastic figures, particularly those who had fallen out with the authorities in Alexandria. Evidence presented by Bishop Athanasius of Alexandria (a man who himself suffered exile five times) includes a quoted letter written by Pinnes the presbyter of the monastery of Ptemenykurkeos in the Antaiopolite nome to John Archaph the Melitian bishop of Memphis. This letter, dating from circa 334, was, he purports, written on behalf of Pinnes by a fellow monk, Papnoute. In it, Pinnes discusses the secretion within the monastery of the Melitian bishop Arsenius, whom Athanasius has been accused of murdering. It is quoted here at some length as it conveys well the drama of the situation as it unfolded in the monastery.

> I wish you to know that Athanasius sent his deacon to search everywhere for Arsenius and Pekusius the Presbyter and Silvanus the brother of Elijah and Tapenacerameus, and Paul the monk from Hypsele, the one whom he first fell in with, confessed that Arsenius was with us. Upon learning this

---

[56] Goehring, 'Community Disaster'. For the text with translation, see Goehring, *Politics, Monasticism and Miracles*.
[57] Goehring, 'The Pachomian Federation and Lower Egypt', p. 57.
[58] Harmless, *Desert Christians*, p. 14.
[59] The schism and its dynamic are not well understood; see the comments of Van Nuffelen, 'The Melitian Schism'.

we had him put on board a vessel to sail southwards with Elijah the monk. Afterwards the deacon returned again suddenly with some others and entered our monastery in search of the same Arsenius but they did not find him because, as I said before, we had sent him southwards. But they sent me and Elijah the monk, who took him out of the way, to Alexandria and brought us before the Duke.[60]

In this case, the unfortunate monk Elijah, along with the presbyter Pinnes, found himself taken forcibly to Alexandria in order to face a round of hostile questioning. In that same year, an even longer journey was required of Apa Paieous from the monastery of Hathor near Hipponon (modern Qararah), who describes how he had been summoned to Caesarea Maritima in Palestine by the Emperor Constantine in order to attend a synod to discuss the conflict between Athanasius and the Melitians.[61] This journey would have taken Apa Paieous a minimum of eight days, travelling perhaps by boat from the monastery in the Upper Cynopolite nome, down the Nile, and then by boat along the Mediterranean sea coast (although he may have preferred the well-trodden road built through the Sinai).[62] Paieous, aware that this could be a lengthy trip, was forced to make preparations for his prolonged absence and appointed his brother Gerontios to act in his stead over the coming months.

It was not only Melitian monks who were forced to undertake travels because of Church disputes. An epic account is recorded in the Bohairic *Life of Shenoute* of his journey to Ephesus in 431 to support Bishop Cyril,[63] something to which Shenoute himself alludes in several of his sermons.[64] Such travels by elite monks need not have been undertaken frequently, but

---

[60] *Defence against the Arians* 67; translation in Robertson, *Athanasius*, p. 136.
[61] P.Lond. VI 1913; discussed in Choat, 'Monastic Letters on Papyrus', pp. 25–6.
[62] Calculations made using the ORBIS website (see n. 19).
[63] Besa's *Life of Shenoute*, 128–30; Leipoldt, *Sinuthii Archimandritae*, vol. 1, pp. 57–9 and translation in Bell, *Besa*, p. 47. The *Life* also describes Shenoute's speedy visit to Emperor Theodosius at Constantinople, travelling on a cloud (*Life of Shenoute*, 53–67; Leipoldt, *Sinuthii Archimandritae*, vol. 1, pp. 29–35; translation in Bell, *Besa*, pp. 57–61).
[64] For example, Shenoute comments on his visit to Ephesus in *I Have Been Reading the Holy Gospels*, stating, 'And this saying having become clear to me, I understood it right then in this very year after we returned from Ephesus'; translation by Moussa, '*I Have Been Reading the Holy Gospels*', p. 117. It is also mentioned in *Blessed Are They Who Observe Justice* (*Discourses* 4, Work 9 = XH 295–6; see Emmel, *Shenoute's Literary Corpus*, p. 625); *Since It Is Necessary to Pursue the Devil* (*Discourses* 4, Work 2 = *Discourses* 8, Work 29 = DU 97; see Emmel, *Shenoute's Literary Corpus*, pp. 619–20); and *I Have Said Many Times* in *Canons* 8 (Emmel, *Shenoute's Literary Corpus*, pp. 594 and 596–7). See also the comments of Emmel, *Shenoute's Literary Corpus*, p. 8. Shenoute mentions his rejection of Nestorius in *I Am Amazed* (Emmel, *Shenoute's Literary Corpus*, p. 464; discussed in Lundhaug, 'Shenoute's Heresiological Polemics').

it is a point of some significance that Egyptian monks were at times expected to travel to participate in Church councils, in order to comment on theological disputes and provide support for various factions.

Religious Tourism and Monastic Wanderings

Monastic sites at Nitria and Scetis benefited from what might be described as 'religious tourism', and some of these trips are recounted in fourth-century travelogues such as Rufinus' *Historia Monachorum* and Palladius' *Historia Lausiaca*.[65] Locations such as Nitria and Scetis profited well from the donations of enthusiastic and wealthy tourists from Rome and beyond. They were, however, not just monastic showcases populated by Egyptians, but monastic settlements that proved highly attractive to men and women who were either already monks or nuns or were eager to become so. Several cases are cited in the hagiographical literature of religious travellers who made the decision to travel to Egypt in order to benefit from an ascetic experience. One example is that of Porphyrios from Thessalonica. The *Vita Porphyrii* claims that he spent time as a monk in Egypt before eventually becoming the bishop of Gaza.[66] Similarly, the Syrian Adelphius was, it is claimed, a disciple of Antony before setting off for Edessa.[67] The claim that an eminent person had once been a monk in Scetis had a certain cultural cache, and it is not necessary to conclude that all these monastic figures had actually lived in the deserts of Egypt. Nevertheless, it seems reasonable to suggest that a considerable number of foreign monks would have visited Egypt in their youth. Here, they could expect some form of ascetic apprenticeship about which they had read or heard in accounts such as Palladius' *Historia Lausiaca*.

Egyptian monks are also reputed to have travelled across the border to Palestine, a fact that is hardly surprising, as the Gaza region acted as a conduit between Egypt and the rest of the eastern Mediterranean world. The city of Gaza was a key commercial centre and famous not only for its market, but for its school of rhetoric, which counted among its members such eminent figures as the fifth-century Procopius of Gaza.[68]

---

[65] The history of this practice is discussed in Hunt, 'Travel, Tourism and Piety' and Frank, 'The Historia Monachorum'. Cassian, a fourth-century native of Scythia Minor, also wrote about his experiences in Kellia in his *Conferences*; translation in Stewart, *Cassian the Monk*.
[66] Greek edition, with translation, in Grégoire and Kugener, *Marc le diacre*.
[67] Rubenson, 'The Egyptian Relations of Early Palestinian Monasticism', pp. 40–2.
[68] Glucker, *The City of Gaza*, pp. 51–3.

From this region, caravan routes travelled to Syria, Egypt, and Arabia. At the port of Maiumas (Constantia), sea traders came from cities dotted throughout the Mediterranean.[69] According to literary sources, several monasteries were based in the region, some of which may have attracted visitors from Egypt.[70] The documentary evidence is silent on this point, but the monastic literature lays claim to several notable Egyptians residing here. The fourth-century Silvanus, it is said, brought his community of twelve monks to live here following attacks by marauders on Scetis in 380.[71] In *The Life of Peter the Iberian* (who, we are told, was an Iberian prince), Peter claims to have met an Egyptian hermit in the Jordan Valley in 429.[72] Whether this meeting actually took place or not, there are literary clues to suggest that there was a close connection between the monks of Egypt and those of Palestine. The *Ascetic Discourses*, for example, attributed to an Isaiah of Scetis (assumed to be from Gaza originally), is an early monastic work.[73] With its multitude of influences from around the Graeco-Roman world, it is a vivid testament to an international multilingual and literate monastic culture that existed throughout the wider region.[74] Further attestations to the movement of monks from Egypt into Palestine and beyond are found in the sixth-century *Spiritual Meadow* of John Moscos and the *Lives* of Euthymius and Sabas.[75] Although these accounts are literary, they do reflect the geographical reality that Gaza was accessible for Egyptian monks, who were either passing through on their way to other destinations or settling there.

The Cares of this World: Involuntary Travels

Independent monks who wandered from place to place at will were in particular considered problematic by state and Church authorities. They did not fit into any institutional structure and were essentially self-willed and without recognised leadership, and thus were not restricted by the

---

[69] Van Dam, 'Gaza'.
[70] Discussed in Hirschfeld, 'The Monasteries of Gaza'; see also Bitton-Ashkelony and Kofsky, 'Gazan Monasticism'.
[71] The wanderings of Silvanus and his monks are discussed in Chitty, *The Desert a City*, pp. 71–4.
[72] Rubenson, 'The Egyptian Relations of Early Palestinian Monasticism', pp. 42–3.
[73] The earliest surviving fragments of this work certainly date from the late fifth or early sixth century, which goes some way to supporting an early date; see Chryssavgis and Penkett, *Abba Isaiah of Scetis*, p. 32.
[74] Unattested borrowings from the works of Athanasius, Evagrius Ponticus, John Cassian, and Macarius the Great among others are discernible in this work.
[75] See references in Chryssavgis and Penkett, *Abba Isaiah of Scetis*, p. 15

physical and regulatory boundaries found in other monastic contexts.[76] Between 370 and 371, Emperor Valens established several laws regarding the behaviour of such monks, including, according to Jerome, an order that monks should be forced to serve as soldiers. Jerome, in his *Chronicum*, states that 'Valens made a law that monks must do military service, and ordered that any who did not want to should be beaten to death with their own staves.'[77] Jerome further tells us that, in the same year, 'Many of the monks at Nitria were slaughtered by the tribunes and the soldiers.'[78] In support of this claim, Cassian states that Abbot Piamun wrote to him, saying that he had travelled with monks from Egypt and the Thebaid who had been exiled to the mines of Pontus and Armenia under Valens in the 370s.[79] Palladius, too, claims that Nitrian monks were imprisoned or exiled under Valens.[80]

Valens' jaundiced view on the matter of wandering monks was shared, to some extent, by Cassian and Jerome, who, while in many ways enthusiastic supporters of monasticism, uttered harsh condemnations against wandering and free-living monks, people whom they considered to be frauds and idlers.[81] The monks who were allegedly persecuted by Valens may well have been perceived by a large section of society as freeloaders, calling themselves monks merely to avoid being drafted. While it is possible that some young monks were indeed taken away and drafted into the army, as Jerome suggests, there is no known documentary evidence to support this. It is significant, perhaps, that the claimed punishment for refusal – being beaten with staves – was at the time the traditional punishment for desertion.[82]

Certain travelling monks were famously involved in outbreaks of violence and unrest throughout the empire and were subsequently viewed

---

[76] A point developed in Choat, 'Development and Usage of Terms for "Monk"', pp. 17–21. These wandering and free-spirited monks are also the main theme of Caner, *Wandering, Begging Monks*.

[77] 'Valens lege data ut monachi militarent, nolentes fustibus iussit interfici', Jerome's *Chronicle* for the year 375; see Helm and Treu, *Die Chronik des Hieronymus*, p. 248. It should be noted, however, that Jerome is the only witness for this allegation.

[78] 'Multi monachorum Nitriae per tribunos et milites caesi'; Helm and Treu, *Die Chronik des Hieronymus*, p. 248.

[79] Casian, *Conferences* 18.7 'Temporibus siquidem Luci, qui Arrianae perfidiae episcopus fuit, sub Valentis imperio, dum diaconiam nostris fratribus deferimus, his videlicet qui de Aegypto et Thebaida fuerant ob catholicae fidei perseverantiam metallis Ponti atque Armeniae relegati'; text in Cassien and Pichery, *Conferences*, vol. 2, p. 21; translation in Lenski, 'Valens and the Monks', p. 98 n. 26.

[80] Lenski, 'Valens and the Monks', p. 98.   [81] Sterk, *Renouncing the World*, p. 165.

[82] As evidenced in the third-century legal compilation, the *Digest*; see, Lee, 'Morale and the Roman Experience of Battle', p. 204.

suspiciously by the secular and religious authorities.[83] In Syria in the 380s, monks were prominent in anti-pagan and anti-Jewish activities, which included damage to several notable shrines and synagogues. As a result, the emperors Theodosius I, Valentinian, and Arcadius drafted a constitution on 2 September 390 in Verona to Tatianus, the Praetorian Prefect, noting that '[i]f any persons should be found in the profession of monks, they shall be ordered to seek out and to inhabit desert places and desolate solitudes'.[84] This act was repealed two years later, but the movements of monks were still viewed with suspicion. In 439, and again in 472, monks were barred from entering Constantinople without written permission from their bishop.[85] The Fourth Ecumenical Council in 451 also censured monks who wandered the cities: canon 18 forbade the joining of secret societies and canon 23 dealt with the organisation of lawless and heretical monks. Their involvement in temporal affairs was also forbidden.[86]

How far this issue of wandering monks was a problem in Egypt is not easy to ascertain. One infamous case of unrest is recorded for 414/15, when, according to the fifth-century historian Socrates, a group of 500 monks, who had travelled to the capital from Nitria in support of the Patriarch Cyril, attacked the prefect Orestes in the streets of Alexandria with such violence that even his guards fled in fear.[87] The actual number of monks given in this case may be questioned, but they were apparently of sufficient numbers to form an intimidating mob. To what degree bishops, even those as strong-minded as the Patriarch Cyril, were able to control such monks is debatable. Marcian, in response to later anti-Chalcedonian riots, wrote a letter in circa 454 telling Alexandrian monks to 'keep your own selves also from unspeakable canons and contrary assemblies, lest in addition to the loss of your souls you should be subjected to legal punishments'.[88] It is apparent why the travels of some monks, whether wandering monks or even monks from established monasteries such as those located at Nitria, were not always desirable to the state authorities, and it could require strong measures to control them.

---

[83] As discussed in Caner, *Wandering, Begging Monks*.
[84] *Codex Theodosianus* 16.4.1. on *De Monachis*; translated by Pharr et al., *The Theodosian Code*, p. 449.
[85] Sterk, *Renouncing the World*, p. 166.
[86] Percival, *The Seven Ecumenical Councils*, pp. 281–4.
[87] Socrates, *Historia Ecclesiastica* 7.14. Orestes was only saved through the intervention of the Alexandrian populace.
[88] Translation in Haas, *Alexandria in Late Antiquity*, p. 266. For the letter of Marcian to the Alexandrians, see Mansi, *Sacrorum conciliorum*, vol. vii, pp. 481–4.

Monastic Travels and International Literature

At the monastery at Naqlun in the Fayum, material has been unearthed showing that, despite the popular depiction of the majority of Egyptian monks as illiterate peasants, certain early monks seem to have possessed sophisticated reading materials.[89] A fifth-century fragment of Book 11 of Livy's *History of Rome* was discovered in hermitage 1 in 1986.[90] This Latin fragment deals with the military actions that took place during the third consulship of Postumius Megellus in 291 BC, a historical event that has seemingly little connection to the world of the Christian monk in Egypt.[91] The fragment was found among the contents of the cartonnage material in which it ended its days, and at some point this book may well have been in the personal possession of someone in the monastic community before it was reused in this practical manner.

Documentation from non-Egyptian sources also made its way into other Christian communities, as evidenced by the find at Kellis (Dakhla Oasis) of a Christian invocation, *P.Kellis* VII 126, which was written on the back of an official Latin document. Monks living in communities that had few resources would have made the most of any materials that came to hand. At hermitage 25 at Naqlun, for example, documents such as a tax receipt and a list of grain deliveries were found with copies of psalms written on the verso.[92] Monks wishing to obtain books for their own use would have found it convenient, as well as economically prudent, to borrow and copy books belonging to their associates. Evidence for such a practice includes a colophon in Codex VI of the Nag Hammadi Codices, which states 'I have copied this one text of his. Indeed, very many of his (texts) have come to me. I have not copied them, thinking that they have (already) come to you ... For the texts of that one which have come to me are numerous.'[93] If we accept that the Nag Hammadi Codices originated in a monastic context, then, as Lundhaug and Jenott point out, this colophon demonstrates the existence of an early monastic network of book exchange, something that

---

[89] This trope continues to be popular, despite the work of many commentators, including Rubenson, *The Letters of St. Antony*; Bagnall, *Egypt in Late Antiquity*, pp. 258–60; Wipszycka, 'Le monachisme égyptien', pp. 40–3; Sheridan, 'The Spiritual and Intellectual World', pp. 54–9.

[90] P.Naqlun Inv.15/86, edited by Bravo and Griffin, 'Un frammento del libro XI di Tito Livio?'; see also Gabrielli, 'Lucius Postumius Megellus'.

[91] Palmer, 'A New Fragment of Livy'.   [92] Derda, 'Polish Excavations at Deir el-Naqlun', p. 126.

[93] Nag Hammadi Codex VI 65.8–14; Coptic text in Parrott, 'The Scribal Note VI,7a: 65,8–14', p. 392; discussed and translated in Lundhaug and Jenott, *Monastic Origins*, pp. 197–206.

could have been further facilitated by monastic journeys throughout and beyond Egypt.[94]

The discovery of the Livy fragment *in situ* is a reminder that the provenance of so many late antique works in Egypt is unknown to us. How many of the important and unique Christian codices that are considered to date from the fourth and fifth centuries were produced within a monastic milieu? Egyptian monasteries are known to have had large libraries in later centuries, although the contents of these libraries have long since been dissipated and destroyed.[95] It is not inconceivable that works from many parts of the empire may have found their way up the Nile and into the monasteries of Upper Egypt and beyond due, at least in some part, to the journeys of monks. Questions regarding the size and range in content of early monastic libraries have been raised in connection with one important find known as 'The Dishna Papers'. This collection of fourth- to sixth-century materials, found near Dishna in Upper Egypt, includes Biblical works, hymns, word lists, a story concerning Hadrian written in Latin, Melito's *Peri Pascha*, plays by Menander and, it is suggested, copies of letters written by Pachomius.[96] James Robinson contended that these are the remains of the library of one of the Pachomian monasteries that lay very close to the site of the discovery.[97] Plausibly, elements of the Dishna Papers, along with the Nag Hammadi Codices, form a group of materials that originated in a monastic setting, the surviving remnants of one or more monastic libraries, whose contents reflect the wide range of backgrounds and origins of the monks who comprised communities such as the Pachomian federation.[98] The fact that Pachomian monks, for example, are known to have travelled frequently, and regularly made their way to that most important cultural centre, Alexandria, would aid our understanding of how such collections may have been formed.

---

[94] Lundhaug and Jenott, *Monastic Origins*, p. 206.

[95] Most notably, the library of the White Monastery of Apa Shenoute, for which see Emmel, *Shenoute's Literary Corpus*, pp. 15–31. On the later St Michael library from the Fayum, see Achi in Chapter 9.

[96] Also known as the 'Bodmer Papyri', because the largest group of these materials were bought by Martin Bodmer. Other materials considered to be part of the Dishna Papers were dispersed around various museums and private buyers so that the total content of the library is a matter of dispute. For the discovery and a possible list of contents, see Robinson, *The Story of the Bodmer Papyri*, pp. 151–72. A more conservative list, omitting the Pachomian letter rolls, has been drawn up by Kasser, 'Bodmer Library'. The issue of the dating of the materials is discussed by Nongbri, 'The Limits of Palaeographic Dating of Literary Papyri'; see also, Nongbri, 'Reconsidering the Place of Papyrus Bodmer XIV–XV (P75)'.

[97] Robinson, 'The Discovering and Marketing of Coptic Manuscripts'.

[98] Lundhaug, 'Dishna Papers and the Nag Hammadi Codices'.

Conclusion

An examination of the documentary evidence for the journeys and travel arrangements of fourth- and fifth-century Egyptian monastics and their associates provides invaluable information on the social and economic activities of early monks. It also gives insight into some of the ways in which monastic communities were able to develop into highly influential and economically industrious organisations in later centuries. Despite the large gaps that exist in the data that survives from this period, some indications are available that can inform us about the highly significant role played by travel in the lives of a sizeable number of monks. In particular, the letter collections associated with the monastery of Hathor demonstrate how monks and their representatives were called upon to travel throughout the local region and to Alexandria in order to conduct their business. The unnamed bundles sold by Paul on behalf of the monastery (*P.Neph.* 4), for example, are indicative of the fact that a surplus of goods was produced at this particular monastery and traded to buy other provisions. The allusions to land ownership by the monk Serapion at the monastery of Nepheros also raise questions regarding the extent to which monks had private ownership of land and goods in this early period and needed to make provisions for the cultivation of such lands, even while absent, at the behest of the community. As demonstrated by the Pachomian literature, donations to monastic communities were not uncommon and included land and boats, such as those allegedly donated by the parents of Petronius, who additionally gave the monastery resources that were useful for the transport of goods, i.e., camels, donkeys, and carts. The popularity of such donations, perhaps perceived as a pious act, would have been a major factor in the successful establishment and growth of monastic communities. It is unfortunate, then, that little other evidence survives to attest to the acquisition of land and goods by monasteries in this period, although this is perhaps not surprising when we consider that the monastic movement was in its infancy. What does survive, however, indicates that monastic communities were able to grow rapidly through the beneficence of wealthy donors and the economic and commercial activities of the monks themselves.

The logistics of travel to cater for the needs of members of the monastic community are evident in the Nag Hammadi letters. The monks make provision for their basic necessities using a variety of modes of transportation, including boats and carts. It is not necessarily the case that the monks owned these means of transport, nor need it be the case that they themselves loaded and unloaded their provisions. However, the fact that they had control over this movement indicates a certain authority in the matter, which may point to ownership in this particular instance. As the letter of Proteria (*P.Nag.Hamm.* 72) makes evident, the monks were also involved in the procurement of goods for their neighbours. This suggests that the monks were well connected and able to source goods and services in the locality. It is unfortunate that the provenance of these letters, pasted scraps found among the cartonnage material that made up the Nag Hammadi Codices, means that only a small selection of letters survives from this group of monks. Nevertheless, enough survives to show that this was a reasonably affluent and well-organised community that was part of a social network.

Monastic travels that took place due to social and religious upheavals have their own significance for what they can tell us of the wider roles and responsibilities of monks in fourth- and fifth-century Egyptian society. That monks were at times considered to be a disruptive and even dangerous influence provides an idea of the size and fluidity of this vigorous new movement, not only in Egypt, but across the Roman Empire. The difficulties faced in asserting control over what was in effect a rather disparate and volatile movement are made apparent by the body of legislation drawn up by rulers who attempted to curtail the wanderings of monks and place them under the subordination of their monastic superiors. The curtailment of travel witnessed in the rules of the Shenoutean monasteries, for example, draws attention to the perceived need for monastic leaders to manage movement. How successful such attempts were in reality is difficult to know, but it is plausible to imagine that not all monks and nuns obeyed the rules. Monks might have been encouraged, as in the examples given in the Pachomian literature, to travel in order to join their monastic communities, but independent wanderings were less welcome, unless, perhaps, in instances where these journeys were a path to even greater solitude, as described in hagiographical literature, such as the *Life of St Antony*. Despite the disapproval of the state and Church hierarchy, examples of independently minded wandering monks continue to be found in the records of the sixth century and beyond, highlighting the continued multifaceted nature of the monastic movement.

Descriptions of monastic tourism to places such as Nitria are important for the insight given into a particular section of the monastic community – one that based its economic survival on the expectation of donations by wealthy sponsors. To what extent monks living in such places were financed by wealthy foreigners is difficult to determine, but monks must have relied for their survival on regular and generous handouts, unless, that is, they were in possession of considerable quantities of personal wealth. The disappearance of the communities based at Scetis and Nitria have traditionally been accounted for by the depredations of marauding tribesmen. A simpler solution may be that these communities simply became unsustainable due to rising numbers and a fall in donations as a result of political upheavals occurring beyond the borders of Egypt. The exact reason is a matter for conjecture, but the lack of a regular supply of generous visitors cannot have been helpful in securing the long-term maintenance of such monastic communities.

Travel as a factor in the exchange of ideas and the import and export of literature is difficult to quantify, particularly as the provenance of the vast majority of late antique codices is unknown. However, as can be seen in the evidence found in the colophons of the Nag Hammadi Codices, some form of exchange was taking place between people who used Coptic as a preferred language for the copying, translation, and production of literature. A hypothesised link between local monasteries, the Nag Hammadi Codices, and the so-called Dishna Papers supports the suggestion that some monks were involved in literary networks that produced and exchanged books that had been originally written in a range of languages and that covered a variety of subject matters. These are works, including some that were deemed 'unorthodox' by Church authorities, that could plausibly have been acquired during travels abroad or had been donated by visitors to the monasteries.

As new documentation is uncovered, whether through excavation or during ongoing work on the many untranslated Coptic and Greek materials that lie within museums and university collections worldwide, more will surely be revealed of early monastic communities in Egypt and the economic and social activities of monks and nuns. It is hardly possible, given the scarcity of readily available evidence, to make confident pronouncements regarding the overarching picture of early monastic life in Egypt, except to acknowledge that monks lived in a variety of social and geographic settings. However, as has been shown here, an exploration of the documentation that is available clearly demonstrates that Egyptian monks were economically active from the early fourth century onward and, consequently, that frequent travels for trade and exchange, as well as for purposes more traditionally associated with religious activities, were a regular feature of monastic life.

Bibliography

Adams, C. *Land Transport in Roman Egypt: A Study of Economics and Administration in a Roman Province* (Oxford: Oxford University Press, 2007).

Bacot, S. 'The Camel, the Wagon, and the Donkey in Later Roman Egypt', *Bulletin of the American Society of Papyrologists*, 22 (1985), 1–6.

Bacot, S. 'La circulation du vin dans les monastères d'Égypte à l'époque copte' in N. Grimal and B. Menu (eds.), *Le commerce en Égypte ancienne* (Cairo: Institut Français d'Archéologie Orientale, 1998), pp. 269–88.

Bagnall, R. S. 'Fourth-Century Prices: New Evidence and Further Thoughts', *Zeitschrift für Papyrologie und Epigraphik*, 76 (1989), 69–76.

Bagnall, R. S. *Egypt in Late Antiquity* (Princeton: Princeton University Press, 1993).

Barns, J. W. B., Browne, G. M., and Shelton, J. C. *Nag Hammadi Codices: Greek and Coptic Papyri from the Cartonnage of the Covers* (Leiden: Brill, 1981).

Bell, D. N. *Besa: The Life of Shenoute* (Kalamazoo: Cistercian Publications, 1983).

Bitton-Ashkelony, B. and Kofsky, A. 'Gazan Monasticism in the Fourth–Sixth Centuries: From Anchoritic to Cenobitic', *Proche-Orient Chrétien*, 50.1–2 (2000), 14–62.

Bravo, B. and Griffin, M. T. 'Un frammento del libro XI di Tito Livio?', *Athenaeum. Studi periodici di letteratura e storia dell'antichità, Università di Pavia*, 66 (1988), 447–521.

Brown, P. 'The Rise and Function of the Holy Man in Late Antiquity', *The Journal of Roman Studies*, 61 (1971), 80–101.

Brown, P. *The Body and Society: Men, Women, and Sexual Renunciation in Early Christianity* (New York: Columbia University Press, 1988).

Brown, P. *Treasure in Heaven: The Holy Poor in Early Christianity* (Charlottesville: University of Virginia Press, 2016).

Caner, D. *Wandering, Begging Monks: Spiritual Authority and the Promotion of Monasticism in Late Antiquity* (Berkeley: University of California Press, 2002).

Cassien, J. and Pichery, E. *Conferences*, 3 vols (Paris: Éditions du Cerf, 1955–9).

Chitty, D. J. *The Desert a City: An Introduction to the Study of Egyptian and Palestinian Monasticism under the Christian Empire* (Crestwood, NY: St. Vladimir's Seminary Press, 1999).

Choat, M. 'The Development and Usage of Terms for "Monk" in Late Antique Egypt', *Jahrbuch für Antike und Christentum*, 45 (2002), 5–23.

Choat, M. 'Fourth-Century Monasticism in the Papyri' in B. Palme (ed.), *Akten des 23. Internationalen Papyrologenkongresses: Wien, 22.–28. Juli 2001* (Vienna: Verlag der Osterreichischen Akademie der Wissenschaften, 2007), pp. 94–101.

Choat, M. 'Property Ownership and Tax Payment' in A. Boud'hors, J. Clackson, C. Louis, and P. Sijpesteijn (eds.), *Monastic Estates in Late Antique and Early Islamic Egypt: Ostraca, Papyri, and Essays in Memory of Sarah Clackson* (Cincinnati: American Society of Papyrologists, 2009), pp. 129–40.

Choat, M. 'Review of Hans Hauben, *Studies on the Melitian Schism in Egypt (AD 306–335)*. Edited by Peter van Nuffelen', *Bryn Mawr Classical Review* (2013), available at www.bmcreview.org/2013/12/20131228.html.

Choat, M. 'Monastic Letters on Papyrus from Late Antique Egypt' in M. Choat and M.-C. Giorda (eds.), *Writing and Communication in Early Egyptian Monasticism* (Leiden: Brill, 2017), pp. 17–72.

Chryssavgis, J. and Penkett, R. *Abba Isaiah of Scetis. Ascetic Discources* (Kalamazoo: Cistercian Publications, 2002).

Crum, W. E. *Der Papyruscodex saec. VI–VII der Philippsbibliothek in Cheltenham: Koptische theologische Schriften* (Strasbourg: Karl J. Trübner, 1915).

Derda, T. 'Polish Excavations at Deir el-Naqlun 1986–1991: Interdependence of Archaeology and Papyrology' in A. Bülow-Jacobsen (ed.), *Proceedings of the 20th International Congress of Papyrologists, Copenhagen 23–29 August, 1992* (Copenhagen: Museum Tusculanum Press, 1994), pp. 124–30.

Dietz, M. *Wandering Monks, Virgins, and Pilgrims: Ascetic Travel in the Mediterranean World, A.D. 300–800* (University Park, PA: Pennsylvania State University Press, 2005).

Emmel, S. *Shenoute's Literary Corpus*, 2 vols (Leuven: Peters, 2004).

Frank, G. 'The Historia Monachorum in Aegypto and Ancient Travel Writing', in E. A. Livingstone (ed.) *Studia Patristica, Vol. XXX: Biblica et Apocrypha, Ascetica, Liturgica* (Leuven: Peeters, 1999), pp. 191–5.

Gabrielli, C. 'Lucius Postumius Megellus at Gabi: A New Fragment of Livy', *Classical Quarterly*, 53.1 (2003), 247–59.

Glucker, C. A. M. *The City of Gaza in the Roman and Byzantine Periods* (Oxford: Archaeopress, 1987).

Goehring, J. E. *The Letter of Ammon and Pachomian Monasticism* (Berlin: De Gruyter, 1985).

Goehring, J. E. 'The World Engaged: The Social and Economic World of Early Egyptian Monasticism' in J. E. Goehring, C. W. Hedrick, J. T. Sanders, and H. D. Betz (eds.), *Gnosticism and the Early Christian World: Essays in Honor of James M. Robinson* (Sonoma, CA: Polebridge Press, 1990), pp. 134–44.

Goehring, J. E. 'Melitian Monastic Organization: A Challenge to Pachomian Originality' in E. A. Livingstone (ed.), *Studia Patristica XXV. Papers Presented at the Eleventh International Conference on Patristic Studies Held in Oxford 1991: Biblica Et Apocrypha, Orientalia, Ascetica* (Leuven: Peeters, 1993), pp. 388–95.

Goehring, J. E. 'Monastic Diversity and Ideological Boundaries in Fourth-Century Christian Egypt', *Journal of Early Christian Studies*, 5.1 (1997), 61–84.

Goehring, J. E. 'Community Disaster and the Making of a Saint' in G. Gabra and H. N. Takla (eds.), *Christianity and Monasticism in Upper Egypt: Nag Hammadi–Esna* (Cairo: The American University in Cairo Press, 2010), pp. 49–61.

Goehring, J. E. 'The Ship of the Pachomian Federation: Metaphor and Meaning in a Late Account of Pachomian Monasticism' in P. Buzi and A. Camplani (eds.), *Literary Production and Intellectual Trends: Studies in Honor of Tito Orlandi* (Rome: Institutum Patristicum Augustinianum, 2011), pp. 289–303.

Goehring, J. E. *Politics, Monasticism and Miracles in Sixth Century Upper Egypt: A Critical Edition and Translation of the Coptic Texts on Abraham of Farshut* (Tübingen: Mohr Siebeck, 2012).

Goehring, J. E. 'The Pachomian Federation and Lower Egypt: The Ties that Bind' in G. Gabra and H. N. Takla (eds.), *Christianity and Monasticism in Northern Egypt: Beni Suef, Giza, Cairo, and the Nile Delta* (Cairo: The American University in Cairo Press, 2017), pp. 49–60.

Grégoire, H. and Kugener, M. A. *Marc le diacre, vie de Porphyre, évêque de Gaza* (Paris: Les Belles Lettres, 1930).

Haas, C. *Alexandria in Late Antiquity: Topography and Social Conflict* (Baltimore: Johns Hopkins University Press, 1997).

Harmless, W. *Desert Christians: An Introduction to the Literature of Early Monasticism* (Oxford: Oxford University Press, 2004).

Helm, R. and Treu, U. *Band 7. Die Chronik des Hieronymus. Hieronymi Chronicon* (Berlin: Akademie-Verlag, 1984).

Hirschfeld, Y. 'The Monasteries of Gaza: An Archaeological Review' in B. B. Askhelony and A. Kofsky (eds.), *Christian Gaza in Late Antiquity* (Leiden: Brill, 2004), pp. 61–88.

Hunt, E. D. 'Travel, Tourism and Piety in the Roman Empire', *Echos du monde classique*, 25.3 (1984), 391–417.

Jones, A. H. M. *The Later Roman Empire, 284–602: A Social Economic and Administrative Survey*, 3 vols (Oxford: Blackwell, 1964).

Kasser, R. 'Bodmer Library' in A. S. Atiya (ed.), *The Coptic Encyclopedia* (New York: Macmillan, 1991), pp. 48–53.

Kotsifou, C. 'Papyrological Evidence of Travelling in Byzantine Egypt' in C. Riggs and A. McDonald (eds.), *Current Research in Egyptology 2000* (Oxford: Archaeopress, 2000), pp. 57–64.

Kramer, B. and Shelton, J. C. *Das Archiv des Nepheros und verwandte Texte* (Mainz am Rhein: v. Zabern, 1987).

Larsen, L. I. 'The Apophthegmata Patrum: Rustic Rumination or Rhetorical Recitation', *Patristica Nordica Annuaria*, 23 (2008), 21–31.

Larsen, L. I. 'Re-drawing the Interpretive Map: Monastic Education as Civic Formation in the Apophthegmata Patrum', *Coptica*, 22 (2014), 1 34.

Layton, B. *The Canons of Our Fathers: Monastic Rules of Shenoute* (Oxford: Oxford University Press, 2014).

Lee, A. D. 'Morale and the Roman Experience of Battle' in A. B. Lloyd and C. Gilliver (eds.), *Battle in Antiquity* (Swansea: Classical Press of Wales, 2009), pp. 199–218.

Leipoldt, J. *Sinuthii Archimandritae: Vita et Opera Omnia*, 4 vols (Paris: Imprimérie national, 1906–8).

Lenski, N. 'Valens and the Monks: Cudgeling and Conscription as a Means of Social Control', *Dumbarton Oaks Papers*, 58 (2004), 93–117.

Lundhaug, H. 'Shenoute's Heresiological Polemics and its Context(s)' in D. Brakke, J. Ulrich, and A.-C. Jacobsen (eds.), *Invention, Rewriting, Usurpation: Discursive Fights over Religious Traditions in Antiquity* (Frankfurt: Peter Lang, 2012), pp. 239–61.

Lundhaug, H. 'The Dishna Papers and the Nag Hammadi Codices: The Remains of a Single Monastic Library?' in L. Jenott and H. Lundhaug (eds.), *The Nag Hammadi Codices and Late Antique Egypt* (Tübingen: Mohr Siebeck, 2018), pp. 329–86.

Lundhaug, H. and Jenott, L. (eds.) *The Monastic Origins of the Nag Hammadi Codices* (Tübingen: Mohr Siebeck, 2015).

Mansi, G. D. *Sacrorum conciliorum nova et amplissima collectio*, 31 vols (Paris: H. Welter, 1692–9).

Moussa, M. *'I Have Been Reading the Holy Gospels* by Shenoute of Atripe (Discourses 8, Work 1): Coptic Text, Translation, and Commentary', unpublished PhD thesis, Catholic University of America, 2010.

Nongbri, B. 'The Limits of Palaeographic Dating of Literary Papyri: Some Observations on the Date and Provenance of P. Bodmer II (P66)', *Museum Helveticum*, 71 (2014), 1–35.

Nongbri, B. 'Reconsidering the Place of Papyrus Bodmer XIV–XV (P75) in the Textual Criticism of the New Testament', *Journal of Biblical Literature*, 135.2 (2016), 405–37.

Palmer, R. E. A. 'A New Fragment of Livy Throws Light on the Roman Postumii and Latin Gabii', *Athenaeum. Studi periodici di letteratura e storia dell'antichità, Università di Pavia*, 68 (1990), 5–18.

Parrott, D. M. 'The Scribal Note VI,7a: 65,8-14' in D. M. Parrott (ed.), *Nag Hammadi Codices V,2-5 and VI, with Papyrus Berolinensis 8502, 1 and 4* (Leiden: Brill, 1979), pp. 389–93.

Percival, H. R. *The Seven Ecumenical Councils of the Undivided Church: Their Canons and Dogmatic Decrees* (Oxford: Parker, 1900).

Pharr, C., Davidson, T. S., and Pharr, M. B. (eds.) *The Theodosian Code and Novels, and the Sirmondian Constitutions* (Princeton: Princeton University Press, 1952).

Robertson, A. *Athanasius: Select Works and Letters* (Oxford: Parker, 1891).

Robinson, J. M. 'The Discovering and Marketing of Coptic Manuscripts: The Nag Hammadi Codices and the Bodmer Papyri' in B. A. Pearson and J. E. Goehring (eds.), *The Roots of Egyptian Christianity* (Philadelphia: Fortress Press, 1986), pp. 2-25.

Robinson, J. M. *The Story of the Bodmer Papyri: From the First Monastery's Library in Upper Egypt to Geneva and Dublin* (Eugene, OR: Cascade Books, 2011).

Rubenson, S. *The Letters of St. Antony: Monasticism and the Making of a Saint* (Minneapolis: Fortress Press, 1995).

Rubenson, S. 'The Egyptian Relations of Early Palestinian Monasticism' in A. O'Mahony, G. Gunner, and K. Hintlian (eds.), *The Christian Heritage in the Holy Land* (London: Scorpion Cavendish, 1995), pp. 35-54.

Rubenson, S. 'The Formation and Re-formations of the Sayings of the Desert Fathers' in M. Vinzent and S. Rubenson (ed.), *Studia Patristica Vol. LV: Papers Presented at the Sixteenth International Conference of Patristic Studies held in Oxford 2011: 3. Early Monasticism and Classical Paideia* (Leuven: Peters, 2013), pp. 5-22.

Rubenson, S. 'Textual Fluidity in Early Monasticism: Sayings, Sermons and Stories' in L. I. Lied and H. Lundhaug (eds.), *Snapshots of Evolving Traditions: Jewish and Christian Manuscript Culture, Textual Fluidity, and New Philology* (Berlin: De Gruyter, 2017), pp. 178-200.

Sheridan, M. 'The Spiritual and Intellectual World of Early Monasticism' in M. Sheridan (ed.), *From the Nile to the Rhone and Beyond: Studies in Early Monastic Literature* (Rome: Pontificio Ateneo S. Anselmo, 2012), pp. 47-88.

Shore, A. F. 'Extracts from Besa's "Life of Shenoute"', *The Journal of Egyptian Archaeology*, 65 (1979), 134-43.

Sterk, A. *Renouncing the World Yet Leading the Church: The Monk-Bishop in Late Antiquity* (Cambridge, MA: Harvard University Press, 2004).

Stewart, C. *Cassian the Monk* (Oxford: Oxford University Press, 1998).

Tainter, J. *The Collapse of Complex Societies* (Cambridge: Cambridge University Press, 1988).

Tutty, P. 'The Political and Philanthropic Role of Monastic Figures and Monasteries as Revealed in Fourth-Century Coptic and Greek Correspondence' in M. Vinzent (ed.), *Studia Patristica XCI, Volume 17: Biblica; Philosophica, Theologica, Ethica; Hagiographica; Ascetica* (Leuven: Peeters, 2017), pp. 353-63.

Van Dam, R. 'Gaza', in G. W. Bowersock, P. Brown, and O. Grabar (eds.), *Late Antiquity: A Guide to the Postclassical World* (Cambridge, MA: Harvard University Press, 1999), p. 463.

Van Nuffelen, P. 'The Melitian Schism: Development, Sources and Interpretation' in P. Van Nuffelen (ed.), *Studies on the Melitian Schism in Egypt (AD 306-335)* (Farnham: Ashgate Variorum, 2012), pp. xi-xxxvi.

Veilleux, A. *Pachomian Koinonia I: The Life of Saint Pachomius* (Kalamazoo: Cistercian Publications, 1980).

Veilleux, A. *Pachomian Koinonia II: Pachomian Chronicles and Rules* (Kalamazoo: Cistercian Publications, 1981).

Veilleux, A. *Pachomian Koinonia III: Instructions, Letters, and Other Writings of Saint Pachomius and His Disciples* (Kalamazoo: Cistercian Publications, 1982).

Vivian, T. 'Holy Men and Businessmen: Monks as Intercessors in Fourth-Century Egypt as Illustrated by the Papyri and Ostraca', *Cistercian Studies Quarterly*, 39 (2004), 235–69.

Vivian, T. and Athanassakis, A. N. *The Life of Antony by Athanasius of Alexandria: The Greek Life of Antony, the Coptic Life of Antony and an Encomium on Saint Antony by John Shmūn and a Letter to the Disciples of Antony by Serapion of Thmuis* (Kalamazoo: Cistercian Publications, 2003).

Wipszycka, E. 'Le monachisme égyptien et les villes', *Travaux et mémoires*, 12 (1994), 1–44.

Wipszycka, E. 'Resources and Economic Activities of the Egyptian Monastic Communities (4th–8th Century)', *The Journal of Juristic Papyrology* 41 (2011), 159–263.

Worp, K. A. 'SB XIV 11972 Fr.A: Eine Neuedition', *Archiv für Papyrusforschung und verwandte Gebiete*, 39 (1993), 29–34.

Glossary

Aggeia	Greek name of a vessel and measure.
Anchoritic	A solitary eremitic monastic lifestyle.
Archimandrite	A superior abbot in charge of more than one monastery.
Artaba	Egyptian dry measure for wheat, barley, beans, etc.; capacity is variable.
Aroura	Standard unit of area for land in Egypt, approximately 2/3 acre, 0.275 hectare.
Astika	A type of tax.
Coenobitic	A communal and commensal type of monasticism.
Comes	Title of a senior official (borrowed from Latin).
Diakonikon	A chamber within a church for liturgical purposes.
Dinar	Gold coin of the Arab period.
Denarius/denarii	Currency unit (equivalent of four drachmas).
Dipinto	A painted inscription.
Drachma	Basic currency unit of Ptolemaic and Roman Egypt, specific as silver or bronze depending on circumstances.
Epimeletes	A financial officer in Egypt.
Follis/folles	Bronze coin(s); the value of this unit varied over time.
Gebel	Mountain, Egyptian dialect.
Grammateus	Administrative title; without further modification, typically translated as 'secretary'.

Hegumenos/hegumenoi	The leader of a monastery; similar to the title of Abbot.
Indiction	Term for the cycle of taxation, fixed at fifteen years in AD 312.
Jebel	Mountain, Syrian dialect.
Kanun	Open-topped stove-like oven.
Keration/keratia	Fraction (sometimes 1/24) of a *solidus*.
Kome	Village.
Kometika	A type of tax.
Kouri	Liquid measure, typically of wine.
Kyra (f) / Kyrios (m) / Kyrioi (pl.)	Respectful form of address; literally 'lord, lady, master'.
Laura	A type of monastic settlement comprising cells for hermits with a communal church and sometimes also a refectory.
Miaphysite	Adherent of a theological position about the nature of Christ, asserting the union of human and divine in a single nature.
Mina	Unit of weight and currency worth 100 drachmas.
Myriad	Unit of weight and currency worth 10,000 denarii.
Nome	Regional administrative unit in Egypt.
Oikonomos	Economic overseer of a monastery.
Presbyter	'Elder'; term used both for village elders and Christian priests.
Presbyterium	The sanctuary within a church.
Qasr	Castle or fortress.
Semi-anchoritic	A solitary eremitic monastic lifestyle but organised around a communal centre in which the Eucharist and communal meals took place.
Sextarius/sextarii	A liquid measure, literally a 'sixth' part, approximately a pint.

Solidus/solidi	Standard gold coin following Diocletian's reform at the end of the third century AD.
Talent	Unit of weight, but also a unit of (bronze) currency especially in the Byzantine period.
Tannur	Open-topped clay oven for baking flat breads.
Tesserae	Small block, of various materials, used in mosaics.
Theotokos	God-bearer.
Tremis	One-third of a solidus.
Wadi	Valley.
Xeneion	Hostel.
Xenodochium	Guesthouse.

Index

Aaron, 43, 46, 349
Abbasid, 53, 234, 341
abbot, 46, 47, 49, 50, 54, 55, 56, 58, 63, 131, 194, 278, 280, 284, 285, 287, 288, 324, 345, 370, 374
Abraham of Farshut, 369
Abraham, bishop of Syene and Elephantine, 324
Abu Mena, 23
Adaima, 166, 167, 168
administration
    Arab, 138
    monastic, 43, 54, 55, 133, 286, 321, 322, 324
    village, 92
Aela, 278
agriculture, 22, 45, 49, 52, 59, 64, 227, 274
    fields, 49, 53, 55, 57, 59, 64, 85, 92, 139, 203, 204, 365
Ainun-Saphsaphas, 42, 43
Ajlun, 43
Akhmim, *see* Panopolis
Akoris, 137
al-Isfahani, Abu al-Faraj, 53
al-Maqdisi, 348
al-Waqidi, 53
Aleppo, 53
Alexandria, 110, 111, 134, 362–4, 368–71, 375, 377, 378
Amarna, 17, 218, *see also* Kom el-Nana
Amman, 54, 56
Ammon, letter of, 368
Ammonios, Count, 85, 89
ampelourgoi, 139
amphora, 86, 115, 130, 132, 133, 135–7, 202, 204, 312
animal
    stall, 223
Antaiopolis, 79, 365
Anthony of Choziba, 49
Antinoe, 134
Antony, Saint, 1–3, 152, 359, 372
Apa Paieous, 365, 371
aparchai, 278, 284

aparche, 139
Aphrodito, 15, 27, 76–95, 134–5, 140, 141, 243
Apion estate, 8, 139, 141, 145
Apophthegmata Patrum, 3, 158, 239, 360
Arab conquest, 77
Arabia, 15, 41–64, 343, 345, 346, 373
Arabic, 63, 76, 101, 235, 274, 300, 313, 334
archaeobotany, 163, 221–2
archaeozoology, 163
archimandrite, 54, 141, 345
Armant, 318
Assiut, 76, 130
Assumption, feast of, 47
astika tax, 79, 80, 82, 83, 87, 95, 135
Aswan, 17, 26, 130, 135, 196, 222, 298–306, 313, 318, 324, 325
asylum, 47
Athanasius, 242
Athanasius, Saint, 1, 3, 152, 370, 371
Athribis, *see* Atripe
Atripe, 19, 196
Ayyubid period, 300

Bahariya Oasis, 28
bakehouses, *see* bakeries
bakeries, 46, 153, 155, 157, 164, 169, 312
Baladhuri, 348
baptism, 14, 25, 43, 340, 341, 349
Barsauma, monk, 42
basilica, 278, 304, 336, 338, 339, 340, 341, 349
Basilius, 116–18
basins, 17, 140, 155, 156, 309, 310, 312, 345
baskets, 4, 104, 240, 241, 257
Bawit, 11, 17, 18, 20, 92, 100, 107, 108, 122, 130–4, 137–47, 163, 172, 220
beans, 152
bequests, 13, 146, 289
Bethlehem, 57, 345
Bishop Nicholas, 116–18
boats, 26, 133, 362–8, 371, 378
body, 158, 248, 325
bones

animal, 19, 347
fish, 19
human, 23
books
  cost of, 21, 234, 236, 237, 238–41, 255, 257
  donation of, 324
  exchange of, 233, 376, 380
  possession of, 376
  production of, 8, 21, 27, 28, 100, 233–63, 376
bread, 21, 43, 152, 153, 158, 176, 201, 216, 226, 283, 289, 312, 341, 347
  flour, 154, 309, 312
  mill, 153, 222, 223, 308–9, 312, 346, 362
  oven, 163, 164, 165–7, 171, 175, 200
  production of, 152, 156, 157, 158, 159, 164, 169, 176, 200, 312, 346
British Museum, 10
brother, 47, 120, 159, 219, 263, 283, 315, 316, 317, 349, 363, 364, 370, 371
buffalo, 216, 217
burials, 25, 105, 183, 185, 186, 205, 338

cadastre, 79, 80, 82–4, 85, 86, 89, 92, 93, 135
calefactorium, 192
caliph, 53, 234
Callinicum, 185, 205
calves, 18
camels, 60, 107, 133, 218, 224, 363, 366, 378
carts, 366, 367, 378
cattle, 213, 215, 216, 219, 220, 225, 226, 324, 366
cells, monastic, 1, 28, 46, 54, 106, 132, 183, 184, 238, 303, 336, 338, 339, 340, 348, 367
cemeteries, 185, 305
ceramics, *see* pottery
cereals, 60, 64, 147, 218, 348
  barley, 60, 61, 62, 131, 347
  straw, 212, 223
  wheat, 140, 158, 243, 277, 288, 345, 347, 362
chorion/choria (fiscal units), 89, 90, 92, 93, 117
Choziba, 49, 54
church of Hatre, 304
church of Psote, 304
church of Sts Sergius and Bacchus, 274, 280
coenobitic lifestyle, 203, 340
coenobitic monastery, 7, 15, 43, 45, 54, 99, 100, 131, 182, 183, 186, 203, 338
Constantine, Emperor, 22, 371
Coptic, 9, 10, 11, 21, 28, 76, 84, 101, 130, 137, 212, 213, 219, 227, 233, 234, 235, 236, 247, 248, 251, 256, 298, 300, 305, 313, 314, 317, 319, 321, 322, 323, 324, 380
  Sahidic, 236, 319
Coptic Museum, 247, 262

courtyard, 119, 153, 155, 156, 164, 165, 166, 166, 168, 184, 217, 308
cows, 214, 216, 217, 224
credit, 110–13, 120
creditors, 12, 100, 112
cultivation, 19, 57, 59, 61, 62, 129, 139, 147, 348, 378
Cyril of Alexandria, bishop, 371, 375
Cyril of Scythopolis, 3, 41, 45, 46, 49, 57, 60, 278, 286, 287, 289

date palms, 62
Dead Sea, 42, 54, 57, 61
deeds, 48, 325
Deir Ain Abata, 55, 57, 61, 342
Deir Anba Hadra, 24, 130, 135, 196, 198, 222, 223, 298–325
Deir el-Bachit, 167, 168, 172, 198, 202
Deir el-Bala'izah, 24, 100, 107, 108, 130, 132
demosion (tax), 139
Dhiban, 336
diet, monastic, 18, 43, 62, 64, 132, 152, 153, 158, 162, 163, 174, 176, 207, 221, 312, 359
diocese, 55, 56, 346, 350, 370
Diocletianic Edict, 244
Dioscorus of Aphrodito, 76–8, 84, 86, 88, 89, 92
donations, 4, 10, 13, 20, 22, 45, 46, 47, 50, 51, 55, 57, 64, 88, 203, 205, 207, 244, 247, 257, 260, 271–90, 324, 348, 372, 378, 379
donkeys, 216, 218, 366, 367, 378
donors, 23, 47, 51, 55, 140, 174, 205, 241, 248, 254, 257–63, 273–90, 340, 349, 351, 378
Dorginarti, 311
drink, 158, 160, 284
drought, 49, 56, 61
dung, 153, 212–27
dye, 108

Ed-Deir, 184
Edfu, 244, 318
Egeria, 337, 338
Elephantine Island, 298, 303, 304
elite, 22, 23, 55, 160, 215, 371
Elusa, 41, 47, 63
Emesa, 51
Emmaus–Nicopolis, 50
endowments, 4, 62, 63, 64, 287, 314, 323–5, 349
Ephraim, Saint, 183
epitropos, 55
Era of the Martyrs, 317
Esna, 166, 167, 168, 224, 318
Eudokia, Empress, 22
euergetism, 51, 349

Euphratensis, 183
Euphrates, River, 53, 186
Evagrius of Pontus, 161, 162
ez-Zantur, 61, 62

fasting, 153, 158, 207
Fatimid period, 234, 302
Fayum Oasis, 15, 17, 21, 101, 106, 109, 130, 133, 136, 139, 166, 233–63, 376
fertiliser, 225
fig trees, 62
First Cataract, 298, 300, 303, 304
first fruit, 278, 284
fish, 19, 111, 158
fish sauce, *see garum*
Flavius Phoibammon, 134
flax, 19, 366
fodder, 61, 131, 217–24
follis/folles, 348
food
    consumption, 18–21, 61, 62, 152, 159, 205, 243, 255, 298, 312, 325
    preparation, 8, 152, 153, 156, 158–76, 190, 199, 200, 201, 213, 217, 223
Frange, resident monk of Theban Tomb 29, 28, 100
fruit/fruit trees, 53, 62, 204, 348
fuel, 62, 135, 159, 167, 175, 176, 212–27
fullery, 309, 312

Gadara, 52
Galilee, Western, 14, 23, 52, 61
gardens, 46, 49, 53, 57, 59, 62, 152, 158, 187, 201, 202, 203, 204, 342
garum, 153, 309, 312
Gaza, 3, 48, 115, 274, 338, 372, 373
George, Saint, 47
Ghazali, 196
Ghor, 61
Ghor es-Safi, 61, 349
gifts, 13, 20, 22, 25, 238, 271–90
    dona, 281, 282
    eulogiai (blessings), 43, 272, 273, 275–89
    munera, 281
    prosphorai (offerings), 271–90
goats, 217, 242, 243, 255, 366
goldsmith, 108, 293
governors, 53, 88
graffiti, 317, 321
grain, 60, 61, 147, 152, 158, 204, 241, 257, 279, 284, 311, 325, 346, 347, 365, 366, 367, 376
    silos, 202, 204, 311, 312
Gregory the Great, Pope, 48

guesthouses, 47, 48

Hamamat Ma'in, 58
Hejira, 317
Helena, Empress, 22
hermitages, 15, 24, 54, 99–122, 166, 224, 302, 338, 339, 340, 345, 351, 376
hermits, 3, 46, 47, 54, 100, 183, 186, 284, 302, 337, 340, 345, 359, 373
Hermopolite nome, 11, 82, 130, 134, 139, 145
Hesban, 55
Hilarion, Saint, 3, 41
hirta, 183, 186
Historia Lausiaca, 372
Historia Monachorum, 372
Holy Land, xii, 7, 15, 43
horses, 216
Horsiesios, Regulations of, 152
hospices, 47, 78
hospitals, 19, 20, 47, 287
hostels, 47, 48, 204
household archaeology, 153, 154–7, 173, 190

Ibion Sesembythis, 134
illnesses, 50, 158
infirmaries, 169, 175
ink, 250, 257, 319, 322, 325
Isaiah of Scetis, 373
Islamic period, 54, 61, 62, 170, 174, 299, 334

Jebel Harun, 59–62, 342, 349
Jerash, 347
Jericho, 46, 47
Jerome, Saint, 3, 41, 162, 374
Jerusalem, 7, 22, 46, 48, 50, 187, 274, 283, 284, 286, 336, 345
John Cassian, 158
John Moschus, 49, 285
John the Almsgiver, 286
Jordan Valley, 334, 373
Jordan, River, 50–64
Judean Desert, 13, 24, 45, 57, 60, 278
Justinian, Emperor, 22
Justinianic legislation, 54

karpophoriai (fruitbearings), 279, 284
Kellia, 7, 24, 161, 163, 166, 169, 172, 175, 224, 308
Khan el-Ahmar, 57
Khirbet adh-Dharih, 62
Khirbet Daria, 51
Khirbet ed-Deir, 50, 57, 200, 201
Khirbet el-Mukhayyat, 334, 345, 349

Khirbet el-Murassas, *see* monastery of Martyrius
Khirbet es-Samra, 51
Khirbet Siyar al-Ghanam, 57
kitchens, 119, 120, 152–76, 181–207, 218, 303, 308, 312, 346
Kom el-Nana, 17, 19, 174, 222–26, 227, *see also* Amarna
kometika tax, 79, 82, 83, 95

lamps, 137, 250, 312, 347
Laura of Euthymius, 46, 47, 49
Laura of San Saba, 50, 345
lay people, 79, 282, 284, 285, 289, 348
lay people (in monasteries)
  servants, 121
leather, 21, 104, 236, 239, 256, 257
legal documents, 165, 324
legumes, *see* pulses
Leontius of Damascus, 54, 61
Limestone Massif, 14
liturgical calendar, 173
liturgical services, 278
liturgy, 169, 279, 281, 289, 306, 312
livestock, 10, 21, 226, 227, 236, 255
Livias, 42
loans, 100, 111–3, 138, 141, 142, 147
locusts, 49
luxury, 160, 161, 174

Ma'ale Adummim, 187
Madaba, 51, 60, 62, 334, 340, 341, 345, 346, 348, 349, 350
Makuria, 302, 319
Mamluk period, 299, 300
markets, 22, 63, 130, 248, 306, 325, 372
Matrona, 285
Melania the Elder, 22
Melania the Younger, 22, 286
Melitian, 370, 371
Melitian Church, 362
Memorial of Moses, *see* Mount Nebo
Merkourios, 305
Mesopotamia, 183, 185
metanoia, 258, 259, 263
Middle Kingdom, 311
monastery of Apa Apollo, 11, 17, 20, 92, 122, 130, 131, 137, 141, 143, 145, 163, *see also* Bawit
monastery of Apa Jeremias, 17, 130, 131, 134, 136, 137, 169, 172, 195, 196, 219, 220, 222, 223, *see also* Saqqara

monastery of Apa Paul, Western Thebes, *see* Deir el-Bachit
monastery of Apa Phoibammon, 10, 12, 147, 167, 168, 287, 324
monastery of Apa Shenoute, *see* White Monastery
monastery of Apa Sourous, 15, 80, 92, 95, 135, 140
monastery of Apa Thomas, 17, 130, 131, 133, 138, 169, 172, *see also* Wadi Sarga
monastery of Hathor, 360, 361, 362, 364, 365, 368, 371, 378
monastery of Hipponon, 141
monastery of John the Little, 163, 166, 172, 174, 222–27, *see also* Wadi Natrun
monastery of Kalamon, 110, 236, 249, 250
monastery of Kayanos, 51, 56, 58, 336, 344, 350
monastery of Mar Elijas, 62
monastery of Mar Zakkai, 186, *see* Tell Bi'a
monastery of Martyrius, 187, 191
monastery of Metanoia, 369
monastery of Smin, 86, 135
monastery of St Aaron, *see* Jebel Harun
monastery of St Antony, 154, 155
monastery of St Catherine, 48
monastery of St Hilarion, 47
monastery of St Paul, 154
monastery of St Sergius, 51, 275, 276, 278, 280, 281, 289, 290
monastery of St Simeon, *see* Deir Anba Hadra
monastery of the Holy Virgin, 252, 255
monastery of the Theotokos, 54, 55, 62, 336, 341, 345, 350
monastery of Theodosius, 46, 345
money, 13, 16, 21, 48, 100, 108, 111, 112, 113, 121, 134, 236, 240, 241, 248, 367, 368
Moses, resident of Theban Tomb 29, 131
Mount Hor, 43
Mount Nebo, 26, 43, 51, 54, 55, 56, 58, 62, 334–51
Mount of Olives, 286
mud stoppers, 132
Muslim, 300

Nag Hammadi, 361–80
Naqlun, 99–122, 166–9, 172, 249, 376
Nebo, *see* Mount Nebo
necropolis, 167, 334
Negev, 13, 25, 41, 45, 52, 274
Nepheros, archive of, 26, 361, 362, 364, 365, 378
Nessana, 13, 50–52, 61, 64, 271–90
New Kingdom, 10, 218, 225

New Testament, 26, 236, 240, 247, 283, 286, 321, 349
Nikephorion, *see* Callinicum
Nile Delta, 218, 225
Nile Valley, xiii, 9, 29, 99, 130, 133, 137, 278, 304
Nile, River, 19, 26, 28, 115, 136, 147, 222, 225, 303, 304, 360, 367, 369, 371, 377
Nitria, 372, 374, 375, 379, 380
novices, 156, 203, 315, 316, 359, 368
Nubia/Nubian, 19, 28, 195, 196, 311, 315, 319

oikonomos, 54, 55, 56, 89, 122, 152, 258, 350
oil, 13, 14, 28, 63, 115, 158, 202, 325, 363, 364
  castor, 18, 309, 312
  for lamps, 18, 325
  olive, 18, 213
  press, 18, 62, 82, 136, 184, 212, 312
  production of, 92, 137, 309, 312
  sesame, 18
Old Kingdom, 218
Old Testament, 26, 236, 247, 334, 349
oratory, 46, 89, 306
orchards, 79, 203, 204
Osrhoene, 183
ostracon/ ostraca, 10, 16, 28, 100, 137, 138, 144, 145, 146, 158, 218, 219, 238, 239, 304
oven, 153, 159–76, 200, 201, 213–24, 306, 308, 310, 311, 312, 346
  hearth, 164, 169, 170, 171, 174, 175, 306, 308, 312
  kanun, 159, 166, 171, 174, 223, 224, 306
  stove, 159–75, 223
  tannur, 200, 201
Oxyrhyncha, village of, 106, 109
Oxyrhynchite nome, 141, 144, 242, 365
Oxyrhynchus, 9

Pachomian federation, 130, 364, 368, 370, 377
Pachomius, Saint, 152, 162, 199, 247, 362, 366, 368, 377
painters, 21, 233, 236, 248, 251–3, 256–7, 259, 263, 305
Palm Sunday, feast of, 47
palm trees, 10
Panopolis, 15, 135
paramonarius, 56
patronage, 22, 23, 27, 43, 45, 54, 64, 334, 340, 344, 348–51
patrons, 22, 137, 234, 237, 257, 259, 260, 261, 290
Pella, 347
Peter the Iberian, 338, 373

Petra, 13, 42, 43, 46–9, 59, 61, 62, 342, 349
  papyri, 46, 48, 57, 62, 64
Pharan, 50
Pharaonic period, 10, 21, 300
Philae, 303, 305
Piacenza pilgrim, 26, 46, 47, 338
pilgrimage, 3, 7, 22–4, 27, 43, 54, 274, 282, 351
pilgrims, 23, 24, 41, 43, 47, 122, 171, 175, 184, 203, 322, 337, 338, 347–9, 361
  flasks, 23
  souvenirs, 16, 23, 115, 116, 214
  tokens, 23
pistachios, 347
plague, 49
plantations, 203
Pompeii, 309
poor, 26, 46, 47, 49, 203, 215, 240, 283, 285, 288, 303, 317, 318, 324, 325
Porphyry of Gaza, 50
potters, 115, 135
pottery, 16, 17, 23, 104, 116, 135, 136, 137, 140, 153, 156, 163, 164, 169, 171, 186, 196, 201, 204, 213, 214, 238, 313, 341, 347
  cooking pots, 115, 168
  kiln, 130, 140, 347
  miniature vessels, 16, 113, 115
  production, 17, 21, 28, 135
  storage, 130
  workshop, 17, 85, 86, 115, 135, 136, 137, 362
poultry, 18
prayers, 1, 3, 24, 25, 258, 285, 286, 314, 317, 319, 320, 321
niche, 119
Procopius of Gaza, 372
Ptepouhar, 236, 249, 251, 258
pulses, 60, 62, 348
  beans, 158
  broad beans, 62
  chickpeas, 62
  lentils, 62, 159
  lupin, 62

Qal'at Sim'an, 23
Qasr el-Banat, 184, 204
Qasr el-Wizz, 196, 198
Qasr Ibrim, 310
quarries/ quarrying, 301, 339
Qubbet el-Hawa, 304, 305, 321

Rabbula, Canons of, 184, 203
rainwater, 59, 204, 342
refectory, 24, 163, 167, 168, 169, 172, 181–207, 303, 369

remembrance, 279, 314, 317, 320, 321
renunciation, 99, 239
Rihab, 51, 56
rope, 4
rules, monastic, 18, 20, 152, 153, 158, 162, 183, 199, 205, 237, 241, 364, 369, 379

Sabas, Saint, 46, 49, 60, 62, 289, 373
salt/salted food, 19, 111, 131, 152, 158, 309
Samuel of Kalamon, 106, 110, 249
Saqqara, 130, 131, 136, 137, 172, 195, 196, 219, 220, 223
Saracen, 45, 49, 60
Sayings of the Desert Fathers, see Apophthegmata Patrum
Scetis, 338, 372, 373, 380
scribes, 21, 93, 107, 108, 139, 233–63, 276, 280, 322
sebakh, 219, 220
Sergius, Saint, 50, 51, 56, 274–81, 284
sharecropping, 139, 145
sheep, 18, 216, 217, 218, 242, 243, 244, 255, 348, 366
Shelomi, 52, 61
shelter, 53, 348
Shenoute of Atripe, Saint, 12, 23, 132, 135, 162, 163, 199, 241, 247, 369, 371
Shivta, 47
silos, 311
Sir, 53
Siyagha, 334–51
skolastikoi, 340
slaves, 46, 290
smells, 152, 173, 175
Sobaita, 47
Sohag, 76, 81, 130, 172, 176, 196, 247, 252, 305
solidus/solidi, 48, 83, 90, 111, 112, 239, 240, 243, 244, 245, 278, 286, 349
Sophronius, 46, 284, 347
soul, 257, 314, 320, 325, 375
Sozomen, 42
stelae, funerary, 305, 313–16, 317
Stephan the Sabaite, Saint, 54
steward, 56, 122, 141, 152, 273, 276, 280, 288, 350
storage, 16, 21, 111, 113, 119, 120, 137, 146, 166, 167, 169, 175, 176, 195, 204, 218, 306, 310, 312, 313, 362, 367
stylites, 7, 54, 56, 57, 183, 346
Sudan, 311
Syene, see Aswan

tables (in monasteries), 162, 172, 193, 197

taste, 172, 173, 175, 199, 206
tax/taxation, 15, 48, 51, 63, 79–94, 112, 134, 138, 142, 144, 242, 275, 277–8, 280, 376
tax register, 83, 86, 90
Tebetny, 106, 109, 121, 122
Tell Bi'a, 181–207
Tell Tuneinir, 185, 195
temple, 42, 59, 99, 130, 137
Temple of Hatshepsut, 10
Temple of Isis, 303
Temple of Khnum, 304
Temseu Skordon, 83, 84
textile, 19, 156, 160, 241
    dye shop, 19
    loom installation, 19
    production, 19, 28
Theban region, 147, 167, 324, 325
Thebes, 10, 28, 131, 172, 215, 237, 242, 255
Tigris, River, 53
tithe, 278, 351
tombs, 24, 28, 100, 130, 131, 167, 304, 339
Touton, 236, 249, 251, 252, 254, 258, 259
trade, 17, 20, 22, 25, 26, 27, 61, 108, 204, 225, 226, 274, 278, 300, 312, 313, 325, 361, 373, 378, 380
transportation, 17, 18, 363, 378
travel/travellers, 366–80
tremis/tremisses, 245, 348
Tur Abdin, 182, 188
Turmanin, 184
Tuttul, 181, 186

Umayyad period, 54, 76, 77, 341
Umm er-Rasas, 51, 56, 57, 346, 347
Uyun Mousa, 42, 51, 56, 58, 334, 336, 337, 342, 344, 350

Valens, Emperor, 374
vegetables, 49, 59, 64, 152, 158, 204, 226
Verina, Empress, 285
vinegar, 141
vineyards, 20, 47, 53, 55, 79, 85, 129–47

Wadi el-Kharrar, 349
Wadi el-Natrun, 163, 166
Wadi Musa, 63
Wadi Natrun, 197
Wadi Sarga, 17, 107, 108, 130–3, 138, 146, 147, 169
water, 45, 59, 132, 141, 152, 153, 163, 167, 186, 199, 204, 338, 348, 351
    cisterns, 46, 52, 58, 59, 167, 184, 201, 204, 340, 342

water (Cont.)
   irrigation, 85, 134, 139, 140, 202, 204, 342
   management, 201, 341, 342
   qaddus pots, 17
   saqiyya, 17, 215, 217
   wastewater, 339
White Monastery, 12, 18, 19, 23, 80, 81, 87, 88, 93, 94, 135, 158, 162, 176, 196, 240, 241, 247, 252, 257, 305, 362, 369, 379
wills, 47, 159, 279, 287, 344
wine, 53, 86, 108, 112, 117, 147, 158, 202, 213, 241, 274, 275, 279, 284, 288, 294, 312, 325, 341
   as food ration, 131
   as payment, 131
   boiled, 138, 144
   consumption, 20, 132, 133, 141
   distribution of, 112, 113, 118
   donation of, 118
   for use in liturgy, 131
   list from Saqqara, 131
   production, 8, 16, 63, 135, 136, 138, 146, 309, 312
   used in liturgy, 63
   winepress, 14, 18, 52, 58, 63, 64, 135, 345, 346, 351
wine jars, 131
   angeia, 140
   delivery in Thoth, 138, 139, 140
   empty (*koupha*), 132, 137, 139
   LRA 1, 136
   LRA 7, 137
wool, 18, 48, 154, 242, 243, 257
worship, 1, 20, 23, 24, 77, 130, 302, 314, 320
writing, cursive, 322

xenodochium, *see* guesthouses

Zeno, Emperor, 22

For EU product safety concerns, contact us at Calle de José Abascal, 56–1°, 28003 Madrid, Spain or eugpsr@cambridge.org.